D1117086

The Works of William James

Editors
Frederick H. Burkhardt, General Editor
Fredson Bowers, Textual Editor
Ignas K. Skrupskelis, Associate Editor

Advisory Board

Max H. Fisch
John J. McDermott
Maurice Mandelbaum

Eugene T. Long
Edward H. Madden
H. S. Thayer

*This edition of the Works of William James
is sponsored by the American Council of
Learned Societies*

This volume is edited by
Frederick H. Burkhardt
Fredson Bowers
Ignas K. Skrupskelis

Introduction by
Peter H. Hare

William James in 1907

courtesy Houghton Library, Harvard University

Some Problems of Philosophy

William James

HARVARD UNIVERSITY PRESS
Cambridge, Massachusetts
and London, England
1979

Copyright © 1979 by the President and Fellows of Harvard College

All rights reserved

Printed in the United States of America

CENTER FOR
SCHOLARLY EDITIONS

AN APPROVED EDITION

MODERN LANGUAGE
ASSOCIATION OF AMERICA

Library of Congress Cataloging in Publication Data
James, William, 1842–1910.
Some problems of philosophy.
(The works of William James)
Includes bibliographical references and index.
1. Philosophy—Addresses, essays, lectures.
I. Burkhardt, Frederick Henry, 1912– II. Bowers,
Fredson Thayer. III. Skrupskelis, Ignas K., 1938–
IV. Title.
B945.J23S6   1979   110   78-20804
ISBN 0-674-82035-5

833567

LIBRARY
ALMA COLLEGE
ALMA, MICHIGAN

Foreword

Some Problems of Philosophy, William James's last and most metaphysical book, is the seventh volume to be published in The Works of William James. The text has been prepared in accordance with the editorial policy established for the edition as a whole in its inaugural volume, *Pragmatism*. Briefly stated, that policy has as its object to provide the reader with an authoritative text based on the principles of modern textual criticism. These principles, and the techniques involved in the preparation of such a text, are set forth in the Note on the Editorial Method.

The edition seeks to present James's writings in the form that represents as closely as possible his final intentions, with such additional material as will make his text understandable in terms of its background and references, and by relating it to pertinent manuscript material in the substantial collection of James papers in the Houghton Library at Harvard University. While no attempt is made to provide any interpretation of James's philosophy, the editors have sought to provide a dependable foundation for scholarly work of the future.

In producing the present volume, the Textual Editor has been presented with problems of extraordinary complexity. As is well known, James was at work on it when he died in 1910. He left behind a manuscript, of which a considerable part has been preserved, some of it in draft and some in final form. We also have a ribbon and a carbon copy of the first typescript, made by James's daughter Peggy. James worked over both of these independently, and at different times, so that each represents a different state of re-

v

vision. The two typescripts sometimes contain different revisions of the original manuscript and, occasionally, represent conflicting intentions. Comparison with the original manuscript also reveals that James overlooked some of his daughter's typing errors.

When Horace M. Kallen, James's student and friend, undertook to prepare the work for publication in 1911, he used as his printer's copy still another typescript which Peggy had made from one of the earlier copies, a typescript which in its turn departed from copy.

Kallen was apparently unaware of the existence of the manuscript and never utilized it in his editing, but he did incorporate some of the revisions James had made in the earlier ribbon and carbon copies. His collation was not, however, thorough, and his choice of James's differing revisions depended on his personal taste rather than any rational editorial procedure or any attempt to establish James's final intent. In addition, he occasionally made his own textual interventions to clarify or complete James's expressions. Because the typescripts he worked with had incomplete chapter divisions and headings, he reorganized and added to them, with the advice of Ralph Barton Perry. The difference this made in the chapter divisions and headings as they appear in the present edition, which restores the intention of James's manuscript, can be seen in the following table:

ACLS edition			*The edition of 1911*	
Chapter I	Philosophy and Its Critics			Same
Chapter II	The Problems of Metaphysics			Same
Chapter III	The Problem of Being			Same
Chapter IV	Percept and Concept		Chapter IV	Percept and Concept— The Import of Concepts
			Chapter V	Percept and Concept— The Abuse of Concepts
			Chapter VI	Percept and Concept— Some Corollaries
Chapter V	The One and the Many		Chapter VII	The One and the Many
			Chapter VIII	The One and the Many (*continued*)—Values and Defects
Chapter VI	The Problem of Novelty		Chapter IX	The Problem of Novelty

Thus, *Some Problems of Philosophy* as it was published in 1911 was both an altered and an incomplete text, mainly because it was produced without reference to the original manuscript. The present edition for the first time makes available a text that is as authoritative as the documents permit, in the absence of James's own final approval and supervision of publication.

This text has been established by Fredson Bowers, Linden Kent Professor of English, Emeritus, at the University of Virginia, the Textual Editor of the Works. Professor Bowers has also provided, in the textual introduction and the apparatus, a record of the long and complicated history of the text and the basis of the editorial decisions made in its preparation. The textual apparatus is organized in a way that will enable scholars to reconstruct the documents used in the editing.

The Associate Editor, Professor Ignas K. Skrupskelis of the University of South Carolina, is responsible for the section of reference Notes to the text and for the Index.

The Introduction, by Professor Peter H. Hare of the State University of New York at Buffalo, provides the reader with the biographical and historical context of the work, together with an analysis of its philosophical content and significance.

The Key to the Pagination of Editions at the end of the volume correlates the pages of the present text with those of the original 1911 Longmans, Green edition and its subsequent reprintings.

The Advisory Board of scholars listed in the front matter gave general policy guidance and many specific suggestions to the editors. It was appointed by the American Council of Learned Societies, which sponsors this edition of the Works.

It remains for the editors to acknowledge their indebtedness to the individuals and institutions that have helped make this volume possible.

The National Endowment for the Humanities has generously provided funds for the editorial work and also for the preparation of camera-ready copy for the apparatus and other end matter. Dr. George F. Farr, Jr., of the Division of Research Grants, deserves special thanks for his patient and sympathetic support and encouragement of the entire project.

Mr. Alexander James and Dr. William Bond of the Houghton Library have granted permission to use and reproduce both printed and manuscript texts in the James Collection at Harvard University. Miss Marte-Eliza Shaw and the members of the staff of the Houghton Reading Room have been unfailingly helpful and patient in making the James Papers available to the editors.

The Reference Room staff of the Alderman Library at the University of Virginia have provided assistance with foreign-language quotations and with locating materials pertinent to the textual work.

The University of South Carolina, which cooperated in the planning of the edition as a whole, has continued to provide research assistance and working space to the Associate Editor.

The Department of Special Collections of the Stanford University Libraries provided the letters of William James to F. C. S. Schiller and permission to reproduce them. The Stanford University Archives made available the letter of January 14, 1905, to President David Starr Jordan of Stanford.

The letter to Elizabeth Glendower Evans of August 25, 1902, is printed by courtesy of the Schlesinger Library of Radcliffe College; the letter of May 21, 1906, and the postcard of April 24, 1906, both to Giovanni Papini, are reproduced by courtesy of Signora Anna Casini.

Professor David Nordloh of Indiana University examined the volume for the seal of the Center for Scholarly Editions.

Mrs. Audrone Skrupskelis helped the Associate Editor with indexing and proofreading.

Mr. H. R. Hillman, Jr., of the Pangloss Bookshop, Cambridge, Massachusetts, permitted the Associate Editor to examine books from James's library.

Finally, Anne Quigley, Chief Research Assistant to the Textual Editor, and her staff, Richard Rainville, Elizabeth M. Berkeley,

Foreword

Mary Mikalson, Ann Tuley, Wilma Bradbeer, Janice Cauwels, and Judith Nelson, prepared the manuscript for publication, work which for this volume in particular required great skill and meticulous attention to detail. Especial thanks are due to Mr. Rainville for identifying William James's own typing in one section and for his careful checking through all of the complex evidence of the documents.

Frederick H. Burkhardt

Contents

Introduction
by
Peter H. Hare

Until a few weeks before his death William James continued work on *Some Problems of Philosophy*. In a memorandum dated July 26, 1910, he directed publication of the manuscript and gave a brief account of his intentions in writing it—one that raises as many questions as it answers: "Say it is fragmentary and unrevised. Call it 'A beginning of an introduction to philosophy.' Say that I hoped by it to round out my system, which now is too much like an arch built only on one side."[1] Although his modest description of the manuscript as "fragmentary and unrevised" and as a "beginning of an introduction" is clear enough, the expression of hope that follows is puzzling. How could James (or any philosopher) reasonably hope to "round out" a philosophical system by writing an introductory textbook? Surely the presentation of a philosophical system is an enterprise different from that of introducing undergraduates to some basic problems of philosophy. Systematic treatises in metaphysics are hardly appropriate reading for beginners, and sophisticated philosophers with a taste for technical metaphysics cannot be expected to take seriously an introductory text. How could a philosopher of such consummate literary skill and sensitivity to the needs of an audience make the mistake of trying to address such different audiences simultaneously? How could he

[1] *Some Problems of Philosophy*, p. 5. References to *Some Problems of Philosophy*, designated in these pages as *SPP*, are to the present volume. References to *Pragmatism, The Meaning of Truth, A Pluralistic Universe, Essays in Radical Empiricism*, and "The Sentiment of Rationality" (in *Essays in Philosophy*) are to this edition of THE WORKS OF WILLIAM JAMES. All other references to James's work are to first printings.

xiii

think it reasonable to combine in one book discussions as technical as any he ever published in the professional journals with discussions as lucid—if not so colorful and provocative—as any in his popular lectures?

James's account of his intentions is puzzling in another respect. If *Some Problems of Philosophy* was intended to "round out [his] system, which now is too much like an arch built only on one side," what missing side is presented here? The book appears, as far as it is completed, to be a comprehensive restatement or outline of his metaphysics, not a development of a side of his philosophy neglected in earlier publications. In any event, if the book were a development of a neglected aspect of his philosophy, surely the one-sidedness of such a book would have made it even less appropriate as an introductory text than a technical presentation of his entire metaphysical system.

A review of relevant parts of James's biography will, I believe, provide at least tentative answers to these questions. We need to attend not only to his expressions in the last few years of his life of an intention to write an introductory textbook but also to his numerous expressions over a much longer period of an intention to put in one book a metaphysical system for advanced students and professional philosophers. It will also be crucial to note how James thought philosophy was *best* written.

In rough outline, James's central interests in the last decades of his life developed from psychology in the 1880s, to ethics and religion in the 1890s, finally to systematic philosophy between 1900 and 1910.[2] Although systematic philosophy did not become his chief preoccupation until later, it is illuminating to trace this interest from the early nineties. In 1891, while preparing the condensed edition of his *Principles of Psychology*, James mentioned to George Howison the possibility of getting out "another and a more 'metaphysical' book."[3] But two years later, when Howison recalled his intention of writing a book of metaphysics, James responded:

[2] Cf. Ralph Barton Perry, *The Thought and Character of William James* (Boston: Little, Brown, 1935), II, 363. Hereafter citations in the text will be made by the abbreviation *TC*. Ethics and religion, of course, were among James's fundamental interests from his earliest thinking in the 1860s.

[3] *The Letters of William James* (Boston: Atlantic Monthly Press, 1920), I, 305. Hereafter citations in the text will be made by *Letters*.

Introduction

I am unutterably amused, or rather amused and saddened, by your extraordinary reference to my book on metaphysic. I have never even attained to the dream of the possibility of such a thing, much less to the execution, and I now foresee that I never shall. A curious sense of incapacity, a sere-and-yellow-leafiness, has come over me in the past year, which makes all psychologizing and philosophizing seem a nullity, and the cultivation of the soil to be a man's only honest pursuit. At any rate my intellectual higgledy-piggledyism can never lead to a system of metaphysics (*TC*, I, 773–774).

James's disclaimer to Howison is unconvincing. It is apparent that he was feeling one of the periodic revulsions against serious intellectual work of any kind that were so characteristic of him. In the grip of this mood, "psychologizing" seemed to him as much a "nullity" as "philosophizing." James continued to harbor a desire to write a book of metaphysics, though he saw that his "intellectual higgledy-piggledyism" made the task especially difficult. Thanks partly to this trait of character, it had taken him twelve years of frustrating labor to finish the *Principles of Psychology*, but he *had* finished that monumental two-volume work. No one knew better than James what temperamental difficulties he had in writing a systematic treatise, yet the publication of the *Principles* was standing proof for him that he could somehow summon the resources to do the job if he thought it important enough. "The joke of it," he wrote his wife, "is that I, who have always considered myself a thing of glimpses, of discontinuity, of *aperçus*, with no power of doing a big job, suddenly realize at the *end* of this task that it is the biggest book on psychology in any language except Wundt's, Rosmini's and Daniel Greenleaf Thompson's!" (*Letters*, I, 295).

Even in the early 1890s James had definite views on the shape that books of metaphysical synthesis should ideally take—views made clear in comments on the work of others. "Paulsen's *Einleitung*," he said in 1893, "is the greatest treat I have enjoyed of late. His synthesis is to my mind almost lamentably unsatisfactory, but the book makes a station, an *étape*, in the expression of things" (*Letters*, I, 346). Two years later in a preface to the American edition of this introductory text he said that philosophy for Paulsen "is nothing if it do not connect itself with active human ideals. . . . He writes a style of which even English readers must feel the euphony as well as admire the clearness, and which (unconsciously, no doubt, to the author) reveals his heart as much as it displays his technical mastery. . . . The one immense merit of his work . . . is its perfect candor and frank abandonment of dogmatic pretence."[4]

Plainly James's admiration for the book was not limited to its usefulness as an introductory text. He considered it a *stylistic* "treat" as a book of philosophical synthesis. Though James was "personally doubtful of many propositions" in the book and inclined to propose a different sort of synthesis, Paulsen's book remained for him a model of the style in which philosophical synthesis should, if possible, be presented. In the last ten years of his life he often found himself embroiled in technical controversy on special problems in metaphysics and epistemology and frustrated in his desire to achieve metaphysical synthesis, yet he never entirely lost the conviction that any philosophical synthesis, including his own, could somehow be made technically sound and still as readable as Paulsen's book. James may have been guilty of wishful thinking in regard to his own temperament and in regard to the limitations of synthesis in twentieth-century philosophy; nonetheless, his work at the end of his life on *Some Problems of Philosophy* was an effort, and a remarkably successful effort, to make that synthesis, that stylistic treat, at long last come true. But before about 1905 such a treat was a remote ideal.

Although, as we have seen, James planned to write a book of metaphysics as early as 1891, it was not until about 1901 that he began to feel an urgent need to write a technically sophisticated and systematic treatise on the subject. Between 1891 and 1901 he had in his higgledy-piggledy way developed metaphysical ideas—in popular lectures, in his courses at Harvard, and in *The Will to Believe and Other Essays in Popular Philosophy*. In correspondence he repeatedly pledged to write a book that would satisfy readers who wanted a book of systematic metaphysics and also satisfy what he perceived as a pressing need for a new philosophical synthesis. Although by any standard he was enormously productive in the last few years of his life, his college duties, popular lectures, and poor health drained off enough energy so that, instead of writing a book of systematic metaphysics, he continued to work out his metaphysical ideas in lectures and articles. The articles originally

---

[4] Friedrich Paulsen, *Introduction to Philosophy*, trans. Frank Thilly (New York: Henry Holt, 1895), pp. iii, vi [*Essays in Philosophy*, WORKS, pp. 90, 92–93].

published in 1904–5 that appeared posthumously in *Essays in Radical Empiricism* and the articles collected in *The Meaning of Truth* contain philosophy as technical as any James ever wrote. The lectures published as *Pragmatism* in 1907 and those published as *A Pluralistic Universe* in 1909 were largely untechnical and unsystematic but contained most of the elements of his metaphysical system.

It is usually thought that James's mercurial genius, disinclination to be rigorous, popularity as a lecturer, poor health, and the intrinsic difficulty of the intellectual problems are sufficient to explain his failure to write a book of systematic metaphysics. There was another, equally serious, impediment. A technical and unreadable metaphysical treatise was offensive to James *morally* as well as aesthetically. "I am interested," he wrote in 1905, "in a metaphysical system ('Radical Empiricism') which has been forming itself within me, more interested, in fact, than I have ever been in anything else; but it is very difficult to get it into shape for any connected exposition: and, though it contains very practical elements, I find it almost impossible to put it into popular form. *Technical* writing on *philosophical* subjects, meanwhile, is certainly a crime against the human race!" (*TC*, II, 387). Even though James joked about it, this was not just the repugnance commonly felt by the well-educated toward unreadable prose. It was one of James's most profound convictions that a metaphysical treatise, unlike a scientific treatise, should be something its readers can *live by*; and they cannot be expected to live by something they can grasp only confusedly through a screen of minute distinctions. No matter how impressive the technical achievement of a metaphysical system, such a system is ultimately pointless, James felt, if it does not express a *Weltanschauung*, an attitude toward life, a picture of the universe, whose practical implications can be emotionally as well as intellectually grasped by readers. " 'The best philosopher,' " he insisted, " 'is the man who can think most *simply*.' "[5]

In 1904 James found that he could write the introductory material to his treatise, where there was no problem with technical terms, but as soon as he confronted special problems he became bogged down in technicality. Able to fill many notebooks and manila envelopes with disconnected notes, many of which he put

---

[5] A quotation from John Grote used in *A Pluralistic Universe*, WORKS, p. 12.

to good use in advanced courses and in articles published in professional journals during this period, he was frustrated in his attempts to shape the material into the readable expression of a *Weltanschauung* that he felt a metaphysical system should be.

With such feelings of frustration, it is not surprising that the next year he concluded: "Important things are being published; but all of them too technical. The thing will never clear up satisfactorily till someone writes out its resultant in decent English" (*Letters*, II, 235). He gave lectures at Wellesley, Chicago, and Glenmore that ranged widely and untechnically over his philosophy and contained much material that later appeared in *Pragmatism, A Pluralistic Universe*, and *Essays in Radical Empiricism* as well as in *Some Problems of Philosophy*.[6] At Harvard during the fall of this same year he gave a general introduction to philosophy using as a textbook Paulsen's *Introduction*, a book that he had used at least once before, in 1895.[7] He accepted an invitation from Stanford University to give a course during the spring term of 1906 and planned the course as a repetition of his general introduction at Harvard. This course and its sequels at Harvard in 1906-7 were partly the basis for *Some Problems of Philosophy*. While lecturing at Stanford, he still spoke of his project of a systematic and technical metaphysics on a grand scale, his "everlastingly postponed book" (*Letters*, II, 240); it seems, however, that the project was more and more displaced not only by the writing and delivery of the lectures published in 1907 as *Pragmatism* but also by what now appeared to him as a more promising way of outlining his metaphysics and presenting his *Weltanschauung* to the world—an introductory textbook. What, then, could be more natural than for James to attempt to follow Paulsen's example? At this time he seems also to have been inspired by the readable way that Giovanni Papini and Henri Bergson sketched metaphysical systems akin to his own. Although distinct from the project of the everlastingly postponed book, the introductory textbook grew naturally out of the frustrations he had experienced with his earlier plan. The re-

---

6 For James's notes for these lectures, see *Pragmatism*, Works, Appendix III.

7 Paulsen, *Introduction*, p. vii. James remarks in the Preface that "I have been using advance sheets of the first three quarters of the translation as a text-book in one of my courses . . . in a long experience as a teacher, it is one of the very few textbooks about which I have heard no grumbling" [*Essays in Philosophy*, Works, p. 93].

strictions of the format of an introductory text would, he must have hoped, allow him to refuse—with a clear intellectual conscience—to grapple unreadably with certain technical difficulties and permit him to present his philosophical system with the clarity he had so long sought.

We can now provide at least tentative answers to the questions raised by the account James gave of his intentions in writing the book. James could, I suggest, intend both to present his philosophical system and to introduce beginners to philosophy in the same book because he had the conviction (perhaps an outrageous one!) that a systematic metaphysical treatise can and should be intelligible to the uninitiated.

The question of what neglected side of the arch of his philosophy he intended to present is more difficult to answer. The metaphor is one he had used a few years earlier in 1906: "I hate to leave the volumes I have already published without their logical complement. It is an esthetic tragedy to have a bridge begun, and stopped in the middle of an arch" (*Letters*, II, 259). This earlier use of the metaphor came *before* the publication of *Pragmatism*, *The Meaning of Truth*, and *A Pluralistic Universe*. The only book that had not been published in 1906 and still had not been published on his death was the posthumously published collection of articles for which James projected the title *Essays in Radical Empiricism*. Since "radical empiricism" was a label he frequently used for his entire metaphysical system, it cannot be that radical empiricism was the neglected side he had in mind. As we shall see, the topic discussed in most depth in *Some Problems of Philosophy* is novelty or growth, so that topic might seem to be the neglected part of his philosophy to which he refers. However, novelty and growth are discussed significantly, if briefly, in *A Pluralistic Universe*. The most plausible interpretation of his use of the metaphor in both 1906 and 1910 is that he was using it somewhat loosely and simply felt that he had not yet in a book effectively presented as a coherent whole his metaphysical system and was convinced that nothing was more crucial to the comprehension of his radical empiricism than an understanding of the relation between concepts and percepts and of novelty. Consequently, James was in no danger of presenting as an introductory text a one-sided account of his metaphysical system. The emphasis given to the discussion of novelty, like the emphasis given to the relation between concepts and percepts, seems to have been intended simply as an aid in giving readers ready access to the center of his metaphysical vision.[8]

The sober and restrained tone of the entire book is set in the first chapter where James discusses the nature of philosophy. Exuberance and even playfulness were characteristic of much of his earlier writing. His inclination was toward the use of striking metaphors. While no one could be more emphatic than he on the importance of philosophical ideas for human life, he poked fun at the pedantry of other philosophers by translating their elaborate formulas into earthy language that shocked some of his readers but delighted others. Whether because he thought he had already sufficiently exposed the absurdities of philosophical language in earlier writings or because he thought his customary levity and colorful language would distract his readers from understanding the philosophical system he had been so long working to outline, he chose in this book to restrain his sense of humor and to present his views as simply and straightforwardly as possible with relatively few witticisms and striking metaphors.

His discussion of the nature of philosophy in particular was restrained in another important respect. Though the nature of philosophical thinking was a topic he had often written about, his emphasis had usually been on the *temperaments* of different philosophers and on the *motives* of philosophizing. The notion of philosophy as an expression of temperament was one he got at the beginning of his career from Charles Renouvier, and one of his most important early articles, "The Sentiment of Rationality" (1879), was a discussion of the motives of philosophical thinking.[9] Near the end of his career he still stressed the role of temperament and motive in philosophy in *Pragmatism* (1907) and in *A Pluralistic Universe* (1909) and suggested that philosophy is to be judged on the basis of its success in satisfying important psychological

[8] It is probably significant that in a letter to James of November 25, 1902, C. S. Peirce said that his doctrine of "synechism" was "the keystone of the arch" of his system. Since James regarded his own views on novelty as closely related to Peirce's synechism, it was perhaps natural for James to suppose that his doctrine of novelty could fit into his arch in much the same way that synechism fitted into Peirce's arch. See Charles Sanders Peirce, *Collected Papers* (Cambridge, Mass.: Harvard University Press, 1931–58), VIII, ¶ 257.

[9] *Mind*, 4 (July 1879), 317–346 [*Essays in Philosophy*, WORKS, pp. 32–64].

needs. Why he avoided his characteristic psychology of philosophy here is not clear. Perhaps he believed that it would be a pedagogical mistake. Such an account of philosophical thinking, although true enough, might tend to discredit the entire philosophical enterprise. James had always understood scientific inquiry to be governed as much by temperament and motive as philosophy, but he chose here to avoid such evenhanded psychologizing, in which philosophy seemed inevitably to lose more credit than science, and instead, relying on the widespread credibility of science, explained science as specialized philosophy. In short, he seems to have restrained both his psychologizing and his sense of humor for pedagogical reasons.

James chose to present a miscellany of views on the uses and nature of philosophy and to defend the philosophical enterprise against some popular objections. He speaks first of the educational value of philosophy in much the same way he had spoken of it more than thirty years before. In 1876 he had described philosophy as a "habit of always seeing an alternative, of not taking the usual for granted, of making conventionalities fluid again . . . it means the possession of mental perspective" (*Letters*, I, 190). Now he says philosophy is an attitude that "sees the familiar as if it were strange . . . . It rouses us from our native 'dogmatic slumber' and breaks up our caked prejudices" (*SPP*, p. 11).

Having indicated its educational value, James goes on to present a conception of philosophy that corresponds in important respects to the conception that appears in the Paulsen book he had used as a text in his introductory course. Paulsen says that "philosophy is simply the continually-repeated attempt to arrive at a comprehensive and systematic knowledge of the form and connection, the meaning and import of all things. . . . [Philosophy is distinguished from the sciences] neither by a special method nor by a special subject matter."[10] After citing Paulsen, James says: "Philosophy in the full sense is only *man thinking*, thinking about generalities rather than about particulars. But whether about generalities or particulars, man thinks always by the same methods. . . . Philosophy, taken as something distinct from science or from practical affairs, follows no method peculiar to itself" (*SPP*, p. 14).

To the objection that, unlike science, philosophy makes no progress, James replies by giving historical examples of how, when the

10 Paulsen, *Introduction*, pp. 2–3, 18.

solution of a particular philosophical problem is found, that part of philosophy is considered a science and philosophy consequently is "the residuum of unanswered problems" (*SPP*, p. 17). Moreover, philosophy's progress in becoming less dogmatic and more interested in verification has made possible the development of the sciences. To a second objection that philosophy is dogmatic, James responds that, although philosophers have often in the past been dogmatic, they need not be any less hypothetical in their methods than scientists. He concedes the historical validity of the charge that philosophy is aloof but sees no reason why philosophy cannot ultimately get "into as close contact as realistic novelists with the facts of life" (*SPP*, p. 19).

James does not, however, propose to discuss the entire range of philosophical problems—only the problems of metaphysics, and only some of them.

As he explains in the next chapter, James favors a broad understanding of what metaphysics is and believes there is no point in formulating more than a rough definition of the subject. We can best get an idea of the nature of metaphysics, he suggests, by looking at examples of metaphysical problems. Although he had read widely and carefully in the history of metaphysics and particularly in Continental and British metaphysics in the late nineteenth century, the contrast between his approach to the subject and the approach prevalent among his predecessors is apparent. While James wished to be a systematic metaphysician, he hoped to be more open, flexible, concrete, and less restricted by abstract formulas and definitions than his predecessors; at the same time, unlike his skeptical contemporaries, he was convinced that most metaphysical problems are genuine puzzles—not puzzles created by abuse of language or failure to use the methods of science. Use of the philosophical method he had developed in earlier writings, "the pragmatic method," would make possible, he believed, the *clarification* and not the dismissal of metaphysical problems, hypotheses, arguments, and concepts, and such clarification would naturally lead, he hoped, to the new metaphysical synthesis of radical empiricism.

The problem of why anything exists at all is the first problem he takes up, and his treatment illustrates well his way of approaching any metaphysical problem. He starts by describing vividly how the problem can arise concretely: "One need only shut oneself in a closet and begin to think of the fact of one's being there" (*SPP*,

p. 27). He next shows that philosophers are unsuccessful in their attempts to avoid the need to solve the problem by dismissing it as the product of misuse of language and logic and goes on to describe briefly the chief types of solution of the problem—those of rationalism and empiricism—and concludes that in an important sense no solution can be found: "Existence has in the end to be assumed and begged" (*SPP*, p. 29). Early in his career he had said, "The bottom of Being is left logically opaque to us, a *datum* in the strict sense of the word, something which we simply come upon and find,"[11] a view that did not change in the intervening years. The problem of being, he thought, cannot be solved if 'solution' means rational explanation; the problem can be 'solved' only by the practical acceptance of being as a gift. More humility in the face of experience, he suggests, is called for in metaphysics. "No one school can," he chides his colleagues, "give itself superior airs. For all of us alike, Fact forms a datum" (*SPP*, p. 30). The acceptance of an ultimate given, James felt, put him squarely in the empirical tradition.

In addition to illustrating his approach to metaphysical problems and exhibiting his commitment to empiricism, James's brief discussion of the problem of being in this early chapter allows him to mention the central datum on which his metaphysical system is based—the datum of novelty and growth. "*Within experience*," he writes, "phenomena come and go. There are novelties; there are losses. The world seems, on the concrete and proximate level at least, really to grow" (*SPP*, p. 29).

Much of the remainder of the book depends on James's account of the relations between concepts and percepts. To understand the significance of this account requires some understanding of the distinctive character of his empiricism and its relation to the history of philosophy.

From his earliest philosophizing James opposed the rationalists' insistence that all order, truth, and reality are to be found beyond sense experience. On various occasions he attacked different historical proponents of this disparagement of experience. Such otherwise diverse figures as Plato, Kant, and Hegel he took to task. Among his contemporaries, Bradley and Royce were the chief villains. Decade after decade James devoted painstaking analysis to the job of showing that none of the ingenious stratagems proposed

---

11 "The Sentiment of Rationality," p. 342 [*Essays in Philosophy*, WORKS, p. 59].

to find reality by transcending experience were successful. While he believed that all attempts to transcend experience were dismal failures, he was unsatisfied by the historical figures who claimed to base their philosophies on experience—the empiricists. Again, different historical figures were attacked on different occasions. Hume and Mill came in for much criticism, and his old friend Chauncey Wright was the contemporary empiricist whose views he took most seriously. As James saw it, the basic problem with traditional empiricism was that, in its own way, it departed from common sense almost as much as did rationalism. After empiricists finished analyzing the world in terms of atomic sensations, there was not much left, he felt, that was recognizable by common sense. Such common-sense realities as the self, material objects, causation, and freedom of the will turned out, in the empiricist analysis, to be fictions.

Although he never felt any inclination to abandon empiricism, whose reliance on fact he applauded, he sought some way to revise empiricism to bring it into accord with common-sense beliefs. It took him many years of intellectual struggle to work out a more satisfactory empiricism. The key idea in his new or "radical" empiricism was that empiricists had been using an artificial and impoverished notion of experience. If we recognize, James argued, that experience is much richer than empiricists have supposed hitherto and includes such common-sense realities as relatedness, tendency, and continuous transition, we will be able, as empiricists, to vindicate common-sense beliefs and will not in desperation seek the realities needed for practical activity in worlds transcending experience. The notion of experience as a continuous flux is, in short, the key to James's empiricist defense of a common-sense realism.

James devotes a chapter to giving as straightforward an introduction as he can to the relations between this primal unstructured flux of perception and structured thinking in terms of discrete concepts. Whereas rationalists like to exalt conceptual knowledge as more noble and as independent of perception, empiricists recognize, he says, that concepts originate in perception. Even more important than recognition of the origin of concepts is recognition of their function and significance. Empiricists rightly insist that the significance of concepts lies primarily in their making it possible for us to handle better the perceptual order. Here he introduces the teleological view of concepts he had held since as early as the 1870s. "[A conception] is a *telelogical instrument*. It is," he had written in 1879, "a partial aspect of a thing which *for our purpose* we regard as its essential aspect." [12] Or, as he says here: "We *harness* perceptual reality in concepts in order to drive it better to our ends" (*SPP*, p. 39). His account of the function of concepts also leads him to the pragmatic theory of meaning he had first publicly adopted in 1898 and had discussed in detail in *Pragmatism*. The meaning of a concept, according to what he here calls *"the Pragmatic Rule,"* lies in the difference its truth makes in perceptual experience. In short, James hopes in this chapter to have convinced his readers that the conceptual order is primarily a means of practical adaptation to the perceptual flux.

The radical empiricist account of the relation between concepts and percepts is defended in more detail in another chapter. The villain in this tale of the abuse of concepts appears as "intellectualism" and the hero as "empiricism." "Intellectualism" is used as a synonym of "rationalism," a usage that may confuse the reader. As becomes clear when several specific puzzles are described, *traditional* empiricism is as much a species of intellectualism as is rationalism. Intellectualism is, for James, the misguided attempt to understand solely in terms of discrete and static concepts the continuity of change in the perceptually given; such an attempt is made by old-fashioned empiricists as well as by rationalists. Hume, usually considered the most thoroughgoing of empiricists, James mentions by name as one of the philosophers guilty of introducing the first intellectualist puzzle he lists—causation. Other puzzles are also found in traditional empiricism and rationalism alike. It would have been helpful if, here and in others of his writings, James had more often made it plain that he is attacking *two* species of intellectualism—rationalism and old-fashioned empiricism—and that the empiricism he says is "confirmed" is his *radical* empiricism, since only radical empiricism takes a continuous flux as the perceptually given.

Having dealt some devastating blows to the intellectualist use of concepts, James in the spirit of fair-mindedness and restraint makes important concessions to his opponents. Concepts, he says, are "just as 'real' in their eternal way as percepts are in their temporal way . . . [for the pragmatic reason that] we cannot live a mo-

[12] Ibid., p. 319 [WORKS, p. 34].

ment without taking account of them" (*SPP*, pp. 55–56). Nevertheless this "eternal" reality is inferior because it lacks many of the characteristics of temporal reality, which "contains all these ideal systems" of eternal concepts (*SPP*, p. 56). He emphasizes that his attack on intellectualism is compatible with a kind of logical realism. He sees no need to accept the nominalist doctrine that the only thing that snow and paper have in common when we call them "white" is a name. When we say that two things have the same quality, we mean (according to the pragmatic rule) "either *a*) that no difference can be found between them when compared, or *b*) that we can substitute the one for the other in certain operations without changing the result" (*SPP*, p. 57). Surprisingly, he concludes that this amounts to affirming "the platonic doctrine that concepts are singulars, that concept-stuff is inalterable, and that physical realities are constituted by the various concept-stuffs of which they 'partake' " (*SPP*, p. 58). But in the preceding paragraph he had drastically qualified such a conclusion by remarking that, although "the nominalist doctrine is false of things of that conceptual sort . . . [it is true] of things in the perpetual flux." He seems to allow the intellectualists their logical realism in the conceptual realm provided it does not interfere with a nominalist account of the perceptual flux.

This concession would surely fail to satisfy the platonists, who wish to make the conceptual realm primary and the perceptual derivative, and it is misleading for James to describe himself as affirming the platonic doctrine. It would be more accurate to say that he is supporting the *positive* assertion of the platonists that concepts have an eternal reality while rejecting their *negative* assertion that things in the perceptual realm do not have reality except as derived from concepts. As in the discussion of so many other metaphysical issues, James is inclined to accept the affirmations of different theories while rejecting their negations. He is a logical realist only in the sense that he insists that we must take account of the eternal and independent reality of concepts without permitting that reality to displace or obscure the perceptual flux that is primary for practical purposes.

Having presented his radical empiricism through a discussion of concepts and percepts, James moves on to pluralism, another fundamental doctrine in his metaphysics, presented through an account of pragmatically distinguished meanings of "unity."

As he indicates in his dedication of *Some Problems of Philosophy* to Renouvier, James had been a pluralist from the time of his first contact with Renouvier's pluralism in the late 1860s. A pluralist by conviction from that time on, he was ruefully unable to marshal the arguments needed to *demonstrate* the truth of pluralism until the 1890s. The monism of absolute idealism was the reigning metaphysics of the end of the nineteenth century, and one of his colleagues and close friends in the Harvard department, Josiah Royce, was a leading champion of such a monism. During much of his career James was engaged in a pitched battle with the absolute.

The discussion of pluralism specifically in terms of the pragmatic meanings of "unity," which can be traced back to his first statement of the pragmatic theory of meaning in 1898,[13] was ground he covered again and again in the last few years of his life after he had satisfied himself that the arguments for the absolute were fallacious. In 1903–4 he gave a Metaphysical Seminary in which he distinguished different meanings of oneness; variations on the same theme appear in lectures he gave at Wellesley, Chicago, and Glenmore in 1905 and in lectures given in 1906–7 and published as *Pragmatism*. The list of kinds of unity varies; on one occasion he omits or mentions only briefly some meanings discussed in detail on other occasions; but the treatment in *Some Problems of Philosophy* is substantially the same as what had appeared in *Pragmatism*. The topic was one he considered so central to his metaphysical system that the title he planned at one time to give to the abandoned magnum opus was *The Many and the One*. Thus, the points he had made in print not long before when expounding pragmatism as a philosophical method and as an epistemology bore repeating in condensed form in the book in which he was attempting to outline his metaphysical system.

Before he describes the different meanings of "unity," James makes the general and fundamental point that he does not intend to defend pluralism to the exclusion of all unities. Once again he accepts the affirmations of rival theories while rejecting their negations. He accepts monism's claim that there are genuine connections in the world and rejects only the claim that there is *nothing but* unity. By the same token, he accepts pluralism's claim that re-

---

[13] "Philosophical Conceptions and Practical Results," University of California, *University Chronicle*, 1 (September 1898), 305 ff., reprinted in *Pragmatism*, WORKS, Appendix I, pp. 267 ff.

ality exists distributively but rejects any pluralistic denial of the reality of specific kinds of unity.

After giving historical examples of "ineffable or unintelligible ways of accounting for the world's oneness" (*SPP*, p. 66), he distinguishes several meanings of "unity" pragmatically, distinguishing the consequences of each, and he summarizes by saying that "the world is 'one' in some respects, and 'many' in others" (*SPP*, p. 70). This, for James, is much more than an exercise in the pragmatic theory of meaning; it *matters* whether one believes that reality is completely unified. Monistic belief, James writes, is beneficial in that it provides "religious stability and peace" (*SPP*, p. 71), but otherwise it wreaks havoc in our practical and theoretical dealings with the world. Monism entails, for example, fatalism and the impossibility of free will. Pluralism, on the other hand, avoids such problems and has the advantage of being in accord with both scientific experience and "the moral and dramatic expressiveness of life" (*SPP*, p. 74).

As I indicated earlier, James regarded the concept of novelty as central to his *Weltanschauung*, so it is not surprising that, once he has acquainted readers with his radical empiricism, with pragmatism, and with pluralism, he expounds his ideas on that topic in the remaining chapters of the manuscript as he left it at his death. In describing both his plans for the technical magnum opus he abandoned and his plans for the introductory text, he had often mentioned "tychism" as one of the main elements of his system and understood tychism to be a doctrine "which represents order as being gradually won and always in the making" (*Letters*, II, 204). He had borrowed C. S. Peirce's term for the theory that the ultimate origins of things are plural and spontaneous.

To suppose, however, that in these final chapters he is presenting the tychism he had so long endorsed is to overlook an important change in James's views during the period in which he was working on the book and many other projects. In 1907, at least partly as a result of reading Henri Bergson's *Creative Evolution*, he decided that tychism, at least as he had formerly defended it, was a mistake. He enthusiastically wrote to Bergson:

I feel that at bottom we are fighting the same fight, you a commander, I in the ranks. The position we are rescuing is "tychism" and a really growing world. But whereas I have hitherto found no better way of defending tychism than by affirming the spontaneous addition of *discrete* elements of being (or their subtraction), thereby playing the game with intellectualist weapons, you set things straight at a single stroke by your fundamental conception of the continuously creative nature of reality (Harvard, bMS Am 1092.9 [743]).

Two years later in the lecture on Bergson published in *A Pluralistic Universe* he explained in some detail, without mentioning tychism by name, why he endorsed Bergson's account of continuous growth; in an Appendix to the same book he suggested that Peirce's tychism was "practically synonymous with Bergson's 'devenir réel' "[14] and that Bergson, like Peirce, had wisely combined tychism with a theory of continuity ("synechism" in Peirce) so that "novelty . . . doesn't arrive by jumps and jolts."[15]

James seems to have been struggling to find a way to combine his long-held view that growth occurs in novel "jumps" with a recognition of continuity. Originally he had argued for novel jumps that made room for free will and moral endeavor primarily as an alternative to determinism. Reading Bergson had convinced him that such a theory of discrete units of growth was playing into the hands of the intellectualists, whose habit of substituting discreteness for the real continuity of the perceptual flux he had been more and more severely criticizing. Later that year, after *A Pluralistic Universe* was published, he was inclined to abandon tychism altogether in favor of synechism.

So long as I was held by the intellectualist logic of identity, the only form I could give to novelty was tychistic, *i.e.*, I thought that a world in which discrete elements were annihilated, and others created in their place, was the best descriptive account we could give of things . . . . This sticks in the human crop—none of my students became good tychists! Nor am I one any longer, since Bergson's *synechism* has shown me another way of saving novelty . . . . Not tychism then, but synechism (if we must talk Greek) is the solution! (*TC*, II, 656).

[14] *A Pluralistic Universe*, WORKS, p. 153.

[15] Ibid. But as early as March 13, 1897, Peirce had written James: "I am much encouraged at your thinking well of 'tychism.' But tychism is only a part and corollary of the general principle of Synechism. That is what I have been studying these last fifteen years, and I become more and more encouraged and delighted with the way it seems to fit all the wards of your lock" (Peirce, *Collected Papers*, VIII, ¶ 252). When he was sent proof sheets of this Appendix to *A Pluralistic Universe* in 1909, however, Peirce objected strenuously—and with good reason—to being assimilated to Bergson (*TC*, II, 438).

But we should not draw the mistaken conclusion that in *Some Problems*, because he avoids using the term tychism, his theory of continuity has simply displaced his theory of novel jumps. Rather, what has happened is that he has abandoned a term he associates with *completely* discrete change and tried to work out a theory that recognizes both discreteness and continuity in growth.

In an important sense he never abandoned tychism as a central part of his metaphysics; earlier, when he had spoken of tychism as essential to his system, all he had really meant was that the view that novelty is real—however novelty comes about—was one of his basic tenets. He retained tychism in that broad sense while abandoning tychism as a claim that discrete change is the whole story of novelty. To throw over completely the idea that change is discrete would be to contradict his psychological insights into the "buds" of experience and views on the infinite he had, as we shall see, held since the 1870s. The task he assigns himself in the discussion of novelty and growth in *Some Problems* is somehow to bring all his views on novelty and growth together into one coherent doctrine.

After briefly explaining that conceptualism has as much difficulty explaining novelty as other aspects of the perceptual flux, James plunges into an account of how conceptualism fails in its attempts to understand change by means of mathematical concepts, the concept of the infinite in particular. After reviewing Zeno's paradoxes of motion and Kant's antinomies, he introduces Renouvier's solution of the problem.

In the late 1870s he had studied Renouvier's articles on the infinite and had written him a largely sympathetic letter (*TC*, I, 659n). Again in 1893 he studied Renouvier carefully, wrote thirty pages of notes in preparation for his lectures in Philosophy 3, and reached rather different conclusions—conclusions close to those presented in *Some Problems* (*TC*, I, 491). James was looking for a way to rescue novelty from the problem of the infinite without banning the infinite from actuality altogether and suggested that such a rescue could be managed by distinguishing between a "standing" and a "growing" infinite. Standing things such as space, past time, and existing things can be accepted as infinite if we pragmatically grasp "the standing infinite" as referring distributively to "each" or "any" member of a series no one of which is absent, rather than referring collectively to a bounded total. But conceiving of a *growing* infinite presents more serious difficulties. A continuous process of change cannot be conceived of as an infinite succession of steps because "what is continuous must be divisible *ad infinitum*" (*SPP*, p. 87), and one can never get from one point to another by successively traversing or counting out an infinite number of points between. Conceiving of change or growth as discontinuous for that reason seemed unavoidable to James.

After giving this view of the infinite, essentially unchanged from 1893, James critically reviews alternative views, giving special attention to views published since he had last worked on the problem. He had spent much time, as entries in his diary indicate, struggling to make sense of such recent and abstruse works as Bertrand Russell's *Principles of Mathematics*. He meets these technically formidable opponents on their own ground and restrains himself from dismissing them as incorrigible intellectualists. Consequently, the discussion here is as technical as any he ever wrote, and one wonders how he could hope that a beginning student could understand it!

Having finished what he apologetically calls "this disagreeable polemic" (*SPP*, p. 93), he finds himself confirmed in his view that growth occurs by "finite and perceptible units of approach" (*SPP*, p. 93), though the process once completed can be understood conceptually and distributively as a standing infinite. This still leaves him, as he recognizes, with the problem of how to make the discreteness of the growing infinite square with the continuity of the perceptual flux, and he ends the discussion with a promise (regrettably a promise he did not live to fulfill) to work this out after he has dealt with the problem of causality (*SPP*, p. 95).

He is concerned to defend a common-sense view of causality that steers a middle course between the completely loose universe of the positivist and the block universe of the determinist. There must, he thinks, be enough causal continuity in the world to account for lawfulness and the real potentialities of things and not so much causal continuity in the world that novelty and free will are impossible. Such a middle, commonsensical course he had advocated since the early 1870s, when he wrote "Against Nihilism," a criticism of the positivism (that is, nihilism) of Chauncey Wright and a remarkable adumbration of the metaphysical views he developed in detail at the end of his life (*TC*, I, 525–528).

In the first part of his discussion of causality James reviews various ways philosophers historically have discredited common sense, giving examples both of philosophers who have steered toward excessive looseness and of those who have gone too far in the direction of a block universe. He then goes on to defend the common-sense view by appeal to his radical empiricist doctrine that we directly perceive relations, including causal relations. This defense he had given in some detail in "The Experience of Activity" in 1905. What activity means, he wrote, "is clear to anyone who has lived through the experience, but to no one else; just as 'loud,' 'red,' 'sweet,' mean something only to beings with ears, eyes and tongues. The *percipi* in these originals of experience is the *esse*; the curtain is the picture. If there is anything hiding in the background, it ought not to be called activity, but should get itself another name."[16] This statement is repeated verbatim in the present text except that "causal agency" is substituted for "activity" (*SPP*, p. 107). But he reminds us that the reality of causation does not entail determinism. There is room for novelty because "the end is defined beforehand in most cases only as a general direction" (*SPP*, p. 107).

James recognizes that his account seems to entail a universe composed solely of minds, since he describes causal activity in terms of the inward experiencing of minds, and presumably causation among physical objects outside our bodies would have to be inwardly experienced by those objects—something only minds could do. Feeling for many years much sympathy for panpsychism, he had often been on the brink of accepting such a metaphysics, but it seemed to him to be a major topic calling for separate treatment. Almost certainly a place for such a discussion would have been planned had he lived to finish his book. The unfinished manuscript follows closely much of the printed syllabus for Philosophy 1a that includes a lengthy discussion of idealism—including panpsychism (*TC*, II, 445–446).

Except for the fideism that is the subject of the Appendix to be discussed shortly, the doctrine of pure experience seems the only essential aspect of his metaphysics omitted entirely from the present manuscript. Very likely he planned to include a discussion of it as either an important part of what he had to say about idealism or as a separate chapter.

16 *Psychological Review*, 12 (January 1905), 7 [*Essays in Radical Empiricism*, WORKS, p. 85].

James found no aspect of his philosophy more widely misunderstood than his views on the subject of the Appendix to this volume, "Faith and the Right to Believe." This was part of a syllabus for his introductory course that he asked to have published as part of the introductory text. His views on these matters were formed early in his career and changed little in their essentials thereafter. In a period of severe depression he read Renouvier and on April 30, 1870, wrote in his diary:

I think that yesterday was a crisis in my life. I finished the first part of Renouvier's second *Essais* and see no reason why his definition of free will—"the sustaining of a thought *because I choose to* when I might have other thoughts"—need be the definition of an illusion. At any rate, I will assume for the present—until next year—that it is no illusion. My first act of free will shall be to believe in free will (*TC*, I, 323).

A few years later, when he published a review in which he spoke of a "duty to believe," he was chastized by Chauncey Wright and conceded that he did not mean to affirm more than the right to believe, a right that Wright agreed was legitimate. Although "The Sentiment of Rationality," an important earlier statement of the doctrine in the context of a discussion of the motives of philosophizing, did not get him into much trouble, his publications in the 1890s were misunderstood and condemned by a host of philosophers. Again he concluded that he would have been less misunderstood if he had spoken only of the Right to Believe. In the controversy that followed the publication of "The Will to Believe" both as a separate article and as the title essay of *The Will to Believe and Other Essays in Popular Philosophy*, he wrote letters to J. Mark Baldwin that adumbrate the statement of the doctrine in the Appendix to *Some Problems*:

This is essentially a will of complacence, assent, encouragement, towards a belief already there,—not, of course, an *absolute* belief, but such beliefs as any of us have, strong inclinations to believe, but threatened. The inner process is a succession of "synthetic judgments." What is so good, *may* be, *ought* to be, *must* be, *shall* be,—so far as I am concerned, I won't admit the opposite. . . . The only discussion which is of practical importance is discussion of *probable* things; and if any general laws of value can be laid down as binding individuals in their relations to such, I have yet to learn them. "Don't guess" would abolish

three-quarters of life at a stroke; and probably condemn us in advance
to lose the truth in most cases.

What I meant by the title [he wrote in a second letter] was the state of
mind of the man who finds an impulse in him toward a believing attitude, and who resolves not to quench it simply because doubts of its
truth are possible. Its opposite would be the maxim: Believe in nothing
which you can possibly doubt (*TC*, II, 243–245).

In an address given to the Pacific Coast Unitarian Club in San
Francisco in 1906 (about the time the material in the Appendix
was written) the "inner process" mentioned in the first of these
letters was elaborated into "faith's form of argument" very close
in wording to the "faith-ladder" of the Appendix.[17] As in other
parts of his philosophy, James considered himself to be defending
common sense and was understandably upset by the charge repeatedly made that he was encouraging self-indulgent license and
dogmatic make-believe. Replacement of talk about the Will to
Believe by talk about the Right to Believe and his discussion of the
inner faith-ladder he hoped would make his views *seem* as well as
be commonsensical. He expected that greater emphasis on what it
means to act on probabilities and on the *social* role of faith in contributing to a pluralistic and melioristic world (as opposed to *personal* salvation or therapy) would be helpful in that respect, too,
but he saw no reason to change his basic account of the dictates of
common sense.

The reception of *Some Problems of Philosophy* was friendly in
large part. Though the book was "enhanced in value by a sense of
momentous loss,"[18] the admiration expressed by reviewers was
more than the expression of affection for a universally beloved
figure. There was genuine recognition of the value of James's determination and power to make philosophy human and meaningful to general readers and professional philosophers alike. Those
who had come to expect stylistic delights in James's writing were
not disappointed by this posthumous publication. He was com-
mended for "making the reader feel as he reads that he is himself

[17] "Reason and Faith," *Journal of Philosophy*, XXIV (April 14, 1927), 198.
[18] Joseph Jastrow, "The Legacy of William James," *The Dial*, LII (January 1,
1912), 12.

participating in the creative thinking of the author,"[19] for the "vivifying touch of his style,"[20] and for expounding his views "with even more than his usual clearness and force."[21] Also common were comments that in this work, as compared to his earlier works, he was inclined to state the other side of the case more fairly and thoroughly: "In the treatment of contending views . . . there is somewhat more of a judicial procedure, including a respectful unfolding of the enemy's thought."[22] But he was praised for more than his expository powers. Even those who took exception to some of his views recognized that parts of the book were "as good philosophical discussion as James ever wrote," and "the chapters on the Infinite . . . are probably not surpassed by anything in his philosophical works."[23] Dickinson S. Miller, an early American practitioner of philosophical analysis who often was critical of him for not being analytic enough, thought James had not written as acute analyses since *The Principles of Psychology*, his first book: "We see here, not chiefly the impressionist, but that intent analyst who was not infrequently to the fore in the 'Principles of Psychology.' "[24]

The degree to which the book is a systematic restatement of views developed in earlier publications was commonly noted, and a French reviewer could find nothing essentially new except precision of statement.[25] Yet new elements were noted: William Pepperell Montague and George H. Sabine were particularly impressed by James's discussion of infinity; Miller found new "the discussions of infinity and of cause, the elaborate argument to prove the breakdown of intellectualism, and the telling defence of philosophy against the assailants who would brand it as unprogressive and unpractical. . . . On the whole, the interest of the book centres in the asserted breakdown of intellectualism, or rationalism."[26] The Oxford philosopher A. D. Lindsay considered James's attempt "to

19 W. P. Montague, review of *Some Problems of Philosophy*, *Journal of Philosophy, Psychology, and Scientific Methods*, IX (January 4, 1912), 25.

20 Dickinson S. Miller (unsigned), review of *Some Problems of Philosophy*, *The Nation*, XCIII (September 14, 1911), 240.

21 Montague, review of *SPP*, p. 22.

22 Miller, review of *SPP*, p. 241.

23 George H. Sabine, review of *Some Problems of Philosophy*, *International Journal of Ethics*, XXII (1912), 217–218.

24 Miller, review of *SPP*, p. 241.

25 *Revue des Sciences Philosophiques et Théologiques*, VII (1913), 282.

26 Miller, review of *SPP*, p. 241.

describe a philosophy which shall be scientific . . . the great interest of the book."[27]

Most criticism focused on his attack on concepts, which he was thought to have carried too far; but before considering these criticisms, something must be said about a different sort of criticism offered by Lindsay, who was puzzled by James's comments on the nature of philosophy.

Lindsay finds three conceptions of philosophy presented in James's first chapter: 1) philosophy as a collective name for questions that have not been answered satisfactorily enough for the answers to become special sciences, 2) philosophy as the coordination of all the sciences, and 3) philosophy as man thinking about generalities instead of particulars. What James does in discussing problems of metaphysics appears to be philosophy in the third sense, but how, Lindsay asks, does that square with his other suggestions about the nature of philosophy. "The nature of philosophy," Lindsay complains, has been left "singularly indefinite. . . . There is no warrant for thinking that the general problems enumerated in the second chapter are to be studied in the same way as the problems within a single science; or, if we take the wider meaning of philosophy, the co-ordination of the sciences with one another is not necessarily achieved by the same methods as the building up of any one of the sciences."[28] At some length he asks a number of penetrating questions about the relations between these conceptions of philosophy, and his points seem well taken. James rather casually combined some comments on the subject matter and method of philosophy by Paulsen with some views of James Ward on the relative progress of philosophy and science, and he does not appear to have given much thought to the sorts of questions Lindsay raises. Unlike the rest of the book, the views presented on the nature of philosophy were not a mature formulation of ideas painstakingly developed in earlier writings over many years. As we have noted, James may have had good reason to avoid reformulating his account of the motives of philosophizing in an introductory text, but in breaking new ground he ran the risk of presenting the "singularly indefinite" conception of philosophy with which Lindsay finds fault. It should be noted, however, that

[27] A. D. Lindsay, review of *Some Problems of Philosophy*, *Hibbert Journal*, X (January 1912), 490.

[28] Ibid.

no less discerning a critic than Dickinson Miller devoted considerable space in his review to two very long quotations from James's discussion of the nature of philosophy and indicated his approval. Perhaps Miller found the general approach to philosophy as being progressive, practical, and closely related to science so inspiring that he did not worry about whether it was altogether coherent.

Among the critics of James's attack on concepts let us first discuss Dickinson Miller. Miller was a friend, a former student, and a fellow empiricist whom James acknowledged as having played a crucial role in the early development of his pragmatist theory of knowledge. Miller wrote:

For our own part we regret that he has stated the matter as though a prevailing habit of short-sighted analysis were a vice inherent in concepts themselves. Continuity, activity, happening—not to mention biting and crowing—are all concepts. If there is in them something not capable of analysis, then we have only to remind ourselves that this is true of all concepts whatever. It is expected to be true of them. The author holds further that reality, when stated with the aid of concepts and of logic, turns out to be self-contradictory and thus discredits the aid we have employed. But may it not prove that, wherever this is the case, there has been some needless ineptitude in the concepts or some needless assumption in the logic? With certain concepts and certain assumptions, no doubt, his thesis is made good.[29]

Miller put his finger on an important feature of the way James defended radical empiricism at the end of his life in *A Pluralistic Universe* as well as in *Some Problems.* His earlier radical empiricism had been an insistence that we directly experience much more than philosophers have traditionally supposed. Most importantly, we experience relations, and once we explore the implications of the fact that we experience relations, we find that many epistemological and metaphysical problems can be solved. Although James never abandoned this doctrine, in his last work, written under the influence of Bergson, he went beyond radical empiricism as a defense of the perception of relations to a radical empiricism that launched an attack on the use of concepts many of which in no way threatened relations as given in the perceptual flux. He came to argue (intermittently) that concepts, any concepts, unavoidably falsify and make self-contradictory the perceptual flux

[29] Miller, review of *SPP*, p. 241.

because they are inherently static and discrete. This newly aggressive radical empiricism is what Miller challenged. He pointed out that James, after all, used with notable success the concepts of continuity, activity, and the like in describing the perceptual flux and thereby showed that it is only *specific* concepts that misrepresent the flux. Miller seems to have been quite fair in his suggestion that James should have confined his protest to those concepts that imply that there is more discreteness and lack of movement in the perceptually given than is actually to be found there.[30]

Another interesting, though less judicious, criticism of James's attack on concepts was made by Arthur O. Lovejoy, whom James had once praised, on the basis of two articles entitled "The Thirteen Pragmatisms," for his "genius for distinguishing." Lovejoy discussed James as a metaphysician in the "apostolic succession of French temporalism."

The agency by which real time is 'denatured' is, for him . . . "conceptual thought" in general; the fundamental antithesis which gives rise to his anti-intellectualism is that of "the perceptual flux" *vs.* the "static concept." The critique of mere intellect thus engendered, it ought to be said, proves when analyzed to be of a somewhat indeterminate and ambiguous sort. James seems to have treated as virtually equivalent three quite different charges against conceptual thought: first, that concepts can not "completely cover," and do not themselves possess, all the attributes of the perceptual flux they represent; second, that conceptual thought introduces into the representation of the flux certain positive attributes which the flux can be known not to possess; third, that the perceptual flux is inherently self-contradictory, from the 'conceptual' point of view. The first of these charges, as I have intimated earlier in these studies, seems to me to be a truism which by no means compels one to accept extremely despondent views of 'the intellect.' . . . James's position in his latest-written books was instructively equivocal and uncertain. That conceptual thinking gives a positively false picture of the flux he maintains, in some sense, throughout, but he can be shown to give three different and incompatible accounts of the properties of this flux as actually experienced, and at least two different accounts of the nature of the falsification of it wrought by the intellect.[31]

[30] George Sabine (review of *SPP*, pp. 218–221) makes the same point in a somewhat different way.

[31] "The Problem of Time in Recent French Philosophy, III, Time and Continuity: Pillon and James," *Philosophical Review*, XXI (1912), 538 ff.

Because he thought it was free from the anti-intellectualist influence of Bergson, Lovejoy favored what he distinguished as James's third account of the temporal flux, an account to be found in his discussion of the infinite: "This third doctrine is that the sequence of changes in consciousness which constitutes the perceptual flux and grounds our idea of time, is a discreet sequence."[32]

What Lovejoy failed to understand was that James had a problem in giving an account of the flux that was independent of the influence of Bergson. As we have noted, James was aware that he needed somehow to make his account of the growing infinite in terms of discrete drops of experience compatible with his view that we perceive continuities in novel growth, a view essential to his commonsensical understanding of causation, potentialities of material objects, the self, and so on. Although Bergson's anti-intellectualism doubtless led James to an overzealous attack on the discrete and the static, James's recognition of the reality of continuity in the perceptual flux was a fundamental insight that antedated by decades his contact with Bergson. His problem, which he did not live to solve,[33] was to invent *concepts* that would fairly capture, without self-contradiction, both the continuity and the discreteness of the perceptual flux.

Not all those who commented on James's contrast between conception and perception were as put off by his occasional anti-intellectualism as were Miller, Sabine, and Lovejoy. F. C. S. Schiller, a fellow pragmatist at Oxford, charitably suggested that the restrictions of an introductory text were responsible for the difficulties.

[32] Ibid., p. 543.

[33] Perry (*TC*, II, 666) speculates plausibly that James would have solved the problem along the following lines: "He would have described a sequence of happenings in which events occur like strokes or pulses, with a thrust of their own; but in which they would at the same time be continuous—in the sense of conjunction or nextness, rather than in the sense of connection. Their continuity would not consist in the link between them, but in the *absence* of any such intermediary. Being thus in direct contact, they would be subject to 'osmosis.' Event *a* would look forward to, and in some measure anticipate, *b*; *b*, when it came, would in some measure fulfill this anticipation, and look back upon *a*. The prospect of *a*, and the retrospect of *b*, would overlap; *a* would be qualified by *b*-about-to-come, and *b* by *a*-just-past. This would not contradict the discrete order of dynamic beats or initiatives: they would begin apart, and run together. Nor would the progressive character of the change contradict the requirements of freedom. Each event would come as an unfolding, as something 'called-for' or 'looked-for', but would also have in it an element of surprise."

He knew that it is equally untrue that 'concepts' are fixed and that 'percepts' are mere particulars; but he did not think it possible in an introductory book completely to set aside the traditional phraseology and to start from the fully concrete, immediately experienced, meaning-attitude, and to show how 'percepts' and 'concepts' both grow out of this. As he wrote to me as lately as 4th May, 1910, "I have caught the meaning of the fluidity of concepts long since: also I have always known that percepts (in the plural) are just as much artefacts as any concept is". But he realised also that, to state the facts adequately, there would be needed a new logic . . . . To what now passes as 'logic' James felt so strong a repugnance that he did not shrink from describing himself as "almost blind logically."[34]

In the letter from which Schiller quoted, James had referred to the Appendix to *A Pluralistic Universe*, "On the Notion of Reality as Changing," as a statement of the fluidity of concepts (*TC*, II, 512). In that Appendix James does not so much say that concepts falsify the present perceptual flux as that changing reality must be constantly reconceptualized to capture novelties. This suggests that fundamentally James did not wish to discredit all conceptual thinking but only to encourage the development of more flexible thinking.

Schiller was writing a book on logic from a pragmatist perspective during the last year of James's life, and they exchanged chapter drafts. The two philosophers seem to have taken it for granted that they were both forging new concepts to solve old philosophical problems; consequently Schiller would naturally read the more extremely anti-intellectualist passages in *Some Problems* as either pedagogical conveniences or harmless expressions of James's temperamental repugnance toward formal logic.

A somewhat less charitable but probably more accurate interpretation of those passages is that James's excessive anti-intellectualism in later life coexisted with a more fundamental and long-standing interest in using his powers of imaginative analysis and his sensitivity to nuances of feeling to forge new philosophical concepts that would capture the concreteness of experience. There had always been a romantic side to James's temperament, but it had never prevented him from doing the most exacting kind of thinking in psychology and philosophy. The romantic side of

[34] F. C. S. Schiller, review of *Some Problems of Philosophy*, *Mind*, n.s. XX (October 1911), 573.

Some Problems should be kept in perspective and not allowed to obscure the fundamental features of the metaphysics James outlined so lucidly and persuasively. For much of his career it was James's fondest wish to construct a metaphysical system. After many frustrations, distractions, and false starts he largely completed an outline of such a system in *Some Problems of Philosophy*.

Some Problems of Philosophy

A Beginning of an Introduction
to Philosophy

'. . . he [Charles Renouvier] was one of the greatest of philosophic *characters*, and but for the decisive impression made on me in the 'seventies by his masterly advocacy of pluralism, I might never have got free from the monistic superstition under which I had grown up. The present volume, in short, might never have been written. This is why, feeling endlessly thankful as I do, I dedicate this text-book to the great Renouvier's memory.' [85]

Prefatory Note

For several years before his death Professor William James cherished the purpose of stating his views on certain problems of metaphysics in a book addressed particularly to readers of philosophy. He began the actual writing of this 'introductory text-book for students in metaphysics,' as he once called it, in March, 1909, and to complete it was at last his dearest ambition. But illness, and other demands on his diminished strength, continued to interfere, and what is now published is all that he had succeeded in writing when he died in August, 1910.

Two typewritten copies of his unfinished manuscript were found. They had been corrected separately. A comparison of the independent alterations in the two copies showed few and slight differences of phrase and detail, and indicated no formed intention to make substantial changes; yet the author perhaps expected to make some further alterations in a final revision if he could finish the book, for in a memorandum dated July 26, 1910, in which he directed the publication of the manuscript, he wrote: '*Say it is fragmentary and unrevised.*'

This memorandum continues, '*Call it "A beginning of an introduction to philosophy." Say that I hoped by it to round out my system, which now is too much like an arch built only on one side.*'

In compliance with the author's request left in the same memorandum, his pupil and friend, Dr. H. M. Kallen, has compared

5

the two versions of the manuscript and largely prepared the book for the press. The divisions and headings in the manuscript were incomplete, and for helpful suggestions as to these grateful acknowledgments are also due to Professor R. B. Perry.

HENRY JAMES, JR.

CAMBRIDGE, March 25, 1911.

Contents

7

Contents

Chapter I

Philosophy and Its Critics

The progress of society is due to the fact that individuals vary from the human average in all sorts of directions, and that the originality which they show is often so attractive or useful, that they are recognized by their tribe as leaders, and become setters of new ideals and objects of envy or imitation.

Among the variations, every generation of men produces some individuals exceptionally preoccupied with theory. Such men find matter for puzzle and astonishment where no one else does. Their imagination invents explanations and combines them. They store up the learning of their time, utter prophecies and warnings, and are regarded as sages. Philosophy, etymologically meaning the love of wisdom, is the work of this class of minds, regarded with an indulgent relish, if not with admiration, even by those who do not understand them or believe much in the truth which they proclaim.

Philosophy, thus become a race heritage, forms in its totality a monstrously unwieldy mass of learning. So taken, there is no reason why any special science like chemistry, or astronomy, should be excluded from it. By common consent, however, and for reasons presently to be explained, special sciences are to-day excluded, and what remains is manageable enough to be taught under the name of philosophy by one man if his interests be broad enough.

If this were a german text-book I should first give my abstract definition of the topic, thus limited by usage, then proceed to display its *begriff und eintheilung,* and its *aufgabe und methode.* But as such displays are usually unintelligible to beginners, and unnecessary after reading the book, it will conduce to brevity to omit that chapter altogether, useful tho it might possibly be to more advanced readers as a summary of what is to follow.

I will tarry a moment, however, over the matter of definition. Limited by the omission of the special sciences, the name philosophy has come more and more to denote ideas of universal scope exclusively. The principles of explanation that underlie all things without exception, the elements common to gods and men and animals and stones, the first *whence* and the last *whither* of the cosmic procession, the conditions of all knowing, and the most general rules of human action—these furnish the problems generally deemed philosophic *par excellence*; and the 'philosopher' is the man who finds the most to say about them. Philosophy is defined in the usual scholastic text-books as 'the knowledge of things in general by their ultimate causes, so far as natural reason can attain to such knowledge.' This means that explanation of the universe at large, not description of its details, is what philosophy must aim at; and so it happens that a view of anything is termed 'philosophic' just in proportion as it is broad and connected with other views, and as it uses principles not proximate or intermediate, but ultimate and all-embracing, to justify itself. Any very sweeping view of the world is a philosophy, in this sense, even tho it may be a vague one. It is a *weltanschauung,* an intellectualized attitude towards life. Professor Dewey well describes the constitution of all the philosophies that actually exist, when he says that "philosophy expresses a certain attitude, purpose, and temper of conjoined intellect and will rather than a discipline whose boundaries can be neatly marked off:"[1]

To know the chief rival attitudes towards life, as the history of human thinking has developed them, and to have heard some of the reasons they can give for themselves, ought surely to be considered an essential part of liberal education. Philosophy, indeed, in one sense of the term is only a compendious name for the spirit in education which the word 'college' stands for in America. Things can be taught in dry dogmatic ways or in a philosophic way. At a technical school a man may grow into a first-rate instrument for

[1] Compare the article 'Philosophy' in Baldwin's *Dictionary of Philosophy and Psychology,* ii, 291.

doing a certain job, but he may miss all the graciousness of mind suggested by the term 'liberal culture.' He may remain a cad, and not a gentleman, intellectually pinned down to his one narrow subject, literal, unable to suppose anything different from what he has seen, without imagination, atmosphere or mental perspective.

Philosophy, beginning in wonder, as Plato and Aristotle said, is able to fancy everything different from what it is. It sees the familiar as if it were strange, and the strange as if it were familiar. It can take things up and lay them down again. Its mind is full of air that plays round every subject. It rouses us from our native 'dogmatic slumber' and breaks up our caked prejudices. Historically it has always been a sort of fecundation of four different human interests, science, poetry, religion, and logic, by one another. It has sought by hard reasoning for results emotionally valuable. To have some contact with it, to catch its influence, is thus good for both literary and scientific students. By its poetry it appeals to literary minds; but its logic stiffens them up and remedies their softness. By its logic it speaks to the scientific; but softens them by its other aspects, and saves them from too dry a technicality.

Both types of student ought to get from philosophy a liberal spirit, ought to get more air, more mental background. "Hast any philosophy in thee, Shepherd?"—this question of Touchstone's is the one with which men should always meet one another. A man with *no* philosophy in him is the most inauspicious and unprofitable of all possible social mates.

I say nothing in all this of what may be called the gymnastic use of philosophic study, the purely intellectual power gained by defining such high and abstract concepts and discriminating between them.

In spite of the advantages thus enumerated, the study of philosophy has systematic enemies, and they were never as numerous as at the present day. The definite conquests of science and the apparent indefiniteness of philosophy's results partly account for this; to say nothing of man's native rudeness of mind, which maliciously enjoys deriding long words and abstractions. 'Scholastic jargon,' 'mediaeval dialectics,' are for many people synonyms of the word philosophy. With his 'obscure and uncertain speculations as to the intimate nature and causes of things' the philosopher is likened to 'a blind man in a dark room looking for a black cat that isn't there.' His occupation is described as 'the art of endlessly

disputing without coming to any conclusion,' or more contemptu-
ously still as the "systematische Missbrauch einer eben zu diesem
Zwecke erfundenen Terminologie."

Only to a very limited degree is this sort of hostility reasonable.
I will take up some of the current objections in successive order,
since to reply to them will be a convenient way of entering into
the interior of our subject.

Objection 1.

Whereas the 'sciences' make steady progress, and yield applications of matchless utility, philosophy makes no theoretic progress,
and shows no practical applications.

Reply. The opposition is unjustly founded, for the sciences are
themselves branches of the tree of philosophy. As fast as questions
got accurately answered, the answers were called 'scientific,' and
what men call 'philosophy' to-day is but the residuum of questions
still unanswered. At this very moment we are seeing two sciences,
psychology and general biology, drop off from the parent trunk
and take independent root as specialties. The more general philosophy cannot as a rule follow the voluminous details of any
special science.

A backward glance at the evolution of philosophy will reward
us here. The earliest philosophers in every land were encyclopaedic
sages, lovers of wisdom, sometimes with, and sometimes without a
dominantly ethical or religious interest. They were just men curious beyond immediate practical need, and no particular problem, but rather the problematic generally, was their specialty.
China, Persia, Egypt, India had such wise men, but those of Greece
are the only sages who until very recently have influenced the
course of western thinking. The earlier greek philosophy lasted,
roughly speaking, for about two hundred and fifty years, say from
6oo B.C. onwards. Such men as Thales, Heraclitus, Pythagoras,
Parmenides, Anaxagoras, Empedocles, Democritus, were mathematicians, theologians, politicians, astronomers, and physicists. All
the learning of their time, such as it was, was at their disposal. Plato
and Aristotle continued their tradition, and the great mediaeval
philosophers only enlarged its field of application. If we turn to
Saint Thomas Aquinas's great *Summa*, written in the thirteenth
century, we find opinions expressed about literally everything,

from God down to matter, with angels, men, and demons taken in on the way. The relations of almost everything with everything else, of the creator with his creatures, of knower with known, of substances with forms, of mind with body, of sin with salvation, come successively up for treatment. A theology, a psychology, a system of duties and morals are given in fullest detail, while physics and logic are established in their universal principles. The impression made on the reader is of almost superhuman intellectual resources.

It is true that Saint Thomas's method of handling the mass of fact, or supposed fact, which he treated, was different from that to which we are accustomed. He deduced and proved everything, either from fixed principles of reason, or from holy scripture. The properties and changes of bodies, for example, were explained by the two principles of matter and form, as Aristotle had taught. Matter was the quantitative, determinable, passive element; form the qualitative, unifying, determining and active principle. All activity was for an end. Things could act on each other only when in contact. The number of species of things was determinate, and their differences discrete, etc., etc.[2]

By the beginning of the seventeenth century men were tired of the elaborate *a priori* methods of scholasticism. Suárez's treatises availed not to keep them in the fashion. But the 'new philosophy' of Descartes, which displaced the scholastic teaching, sweeping over Europe like wildfire, preserved the same encyclopaedic character. We think of Descartes now a days as the metaphysician who said *Cogito, ergo sum*, separated mind from matter as two contrasted 'substances,' and gave a renovated proof of God's existence. But his contemporaries thought of him much more as we think of Herbert Spencer in our day, as a great cosmic evolutionist, who explained by 'the redistribution of matter and motion' and the laws of impact, the rotations of the heavens, the circulation of the blood, the refraction of light, the apparatus of vision and of nervous action, the passions of the soul and the connexion of the mind and body.

Descartes died in 1650. With Locke's *Essay Concerning Human Understanding*, published in 1690, philosophy for the first time

---

[2] J. Rickaby's *General Metaphysics* (Longmans, Green, and Co.) gives a popular account of the essentials of St. Thomas's philosophy of Nature. Thomas M. Harper's *Metaphysics of the School* (Macmillan) goes into minute detail.

turned more exclusively to the problem of knowledge, and became 'critical.' This subjective tendency developed; and altho the school of Leibnitz, who was the pattern of a universal sage, still kept up the more universal tradition—Leibnitz's follower Wolff published systematic treatises on *everything*, physical as well as moral—Hume, who succeeded Locke, woke Kant 'from his dogmatic slumber,' and since Kant's time the word 'philosophy' has come to stand for mental and moral speculations far more than for physical theories. Until a comparatively recent time, philosophy was taught in our colleges under the name of 'mental and moral philosophy,' or 'philosophy of the human mind,' exclusively, to distinguish it from 'natural philosophy.'

But the older tradition is the better as well as the completer one. To know the actual peculiarities of the world we are born into is surely as important as to know what makes worlds anyhow abstractly possible. Yet this latter knowledge has been treated by many since Kant's time as the only knowledge worthy of being called philosophical. Common men feel the question 'what is Nature like?' to be as momentous as the kantian question 'how is Nature possible?', so philosophy, in order not to lose human respect, must take some notice of the actual constitution of reality. There are signs to-day of a return to the more objective tradition. For an excellent defence of it I refer my readers to Paulsen's *Introduction to Philosophy*.[3]

Philosophy in the full sense is only *man thinking*, thinking about generalities rather than about particulars. But whether about generalities or particulars, man thinks always by the same methods. He observes, discriminates, generalizes, classifies, looks for causes, traces analogies, and makes hypotheses. Philosophy, taken as something distinct from science or from practical affairs, follows no method peculiar to itself. All our thinking to-day has evolved gradually out of primitive human thought, and the only really important changes that have come over its manner (as distinguished from the matters in which it believes) are a greater hesitancy in asserting its convictions, and the habit of seeking verification[4] for them whenever it can. It will be instructive to trace very briefly the origins of our present habits of thought.

Auguste Comte, the founder of a philosophy which he called

[3] Translated by Thilly (1895), pp. 19–44.
[4] Compare G. H. Lewes: *Aristotle* (1864), chap. iv.

'positive,'[5] said that human theory on any subject always took three forms in succession. In the 'theological' stage of theorizing phenomena are explained by spirits producing them; in the 'metaphysical' stage their essential feature is made into an abstract idea, and this is placed behind them as if it were an explanation; in the 'positive' stage phenomena are simply described as to their coexistences and successions. Their 'laws' are formulated, but no explanation of their nature or existence is sought after. Thus a 'Spiritus rector' would be a theological, a 'principle of attraction' would be a metaphysical, and a 'law of the squares' would be a positive, theory of the planetary movements.

Comte's account is too sharp and definite. Anthropology shows that the earliest attempts at human theorizing mixed the theological and metaphysical together. Common things needed no special explanation, remarkable things alone, odd things, especially deaths, calamities, diseases, called for it. What made things act was the mysterious energy in them, and the more *awful* they were, the more of this *mana* they possessed. The great thing was to acquire *mana* oneself. 'Sympathetic magic' is the collective name for what seems to have been the primitive philosophy here. You could act on anything by controlling anything else that either was associated with it or resembled it. If you wished to injure an enemy you should either make an image of him, or get some of his hair or other belongings, or get his name written. Injuring the substitute, you then made him suffer correspondingly. If you wished the rain to come, you sprinkled the ground, if the wind, you whistled, etc. If you would have yams grow well in your garden, put a stone there that looks like a yam. Would you cure jaundice, give turmeric, that makes things look yellow; or give poppies for troubles of the head, because their seed vessels form a 'head.' This 'doctrine of signatures' played a great part in early medicine. The various 'mancies and 'mantics come in here, in which witchcraft and incipient science are indistinguishably intermixed. 'Sympathetic' theorizing persists to the present day. 'Thoughts are things' for a contemporary school—and on the whole a good school—of practical philosophy. Cultivate the thought of what you desire, affirm it, and it will bring all similar thoughts from elsewhere to reinforce it, so that finally your wish will be fulfilled.[6]

5 *Cours de philosophie positive*, six volumes, Paris (1830–1842).
6 Compare Prentice Mulford's works and others of the 'new thought' type.—For

Little by little more 'positive' ways of considering things began to prevail. Common elements in phenomena began to be singled out and to form the basis of generalizations. But these elements at first had necessarily to be the more dramatic or humanly interesting ones. The cold, the hot, the wet, the dry in things explained their behavior. Some bodies were naturally warm, others cold. Motions were 'natural' or 'violent.' The heavens moved in circles because circular motion was the most 'perfect.' The lever was explained by the greater quantity of perfection embodied in the movement of its longer arm. The sun went south in winter to escape the cold. Precious or beautiful things had exceptional properties. Peacock's flesh resisted putrefaction. The loadstone would drop the iron which it held if the superiorly powerful diamond was brought near, etc.[7]

Such ideas sound to us grotesque, but imagine no tracks made for us by scientific ancestors, and what aspects would *we* single out from nature to understand things by? Not till the beginning of the seventeenth century did the more insipid kinds of regularity in things attract men's attention away from the properties originally picked out. Few of us realize how short the career of what we know as 'science' has been. Three hundred and fifty years ago hardly anyone believed in the Copernican planetary theory. Optical combinations were not discovered. The circulation of the blood, the weight of the air, the conduction of heat, the laws of motion were unknown; the common pump was inexplicable; there were no clocks; no thermometers; no general gravitation; the world was five thousand years old; spirits moved the planets; alchemy, magic, astrology imposed on everyone. Modern science began only after 1600, with Kepler, Galileo, Descartes, Torricelli, Pascal, Harvey, Newton, Huyghens, and Boyle. Five men telling one another in succession the discoveries which their lives had witnessed could deliver the whole of it into our hands: Harvey might have told Newton, who might have told Voltaire; Voltaire might have told Dalton,

---

primitive sympathetic magic consult the chapter on Analogy in J. Jastrow: *Fact and Fable*, etc.; F. B. Jevons: *Introduction to the History of Religion*, chap. iv; J. G. Frazer: *The Golden Bough*, chap. i, § 2; R. R. Marett: *The Threshold of Religion*, *passim*; A. O. Lovejoy, in *The Monist*, vol. xvi, p. 357.

[7] On greek science, see W. Whewell's *History of the Inductive Sciences*, vol. i, Book I; G. H. Lewes, *Aristotle*, *passim*.

who might have told Huxley, who might have told readers of this book.

The men who began this work of emancipation were philosophers in the original sense of the word, universal sages. Galileo said that he had spent more years on philosophy than months on mathematics. Descartes was a universal philosopher in the fullest sense of the term. But the fertility of the newer conceptions made special departments of truth grow at such a rate that they became too unwieldy with details for the more universal minds to carry them, so the special sciences of mechanics, astronomy and physics began to drop off from the parent stem.

No one could have forseen in advance the extraordinary fertility of the more insipid mathematical aspects which these geniuses ferretted out. No one could have dreamed of the control over nature which the search for their concomitant variations would give. 'Laws' describe these variations; and all our present laws of nature have as their model the proportionality of v to t, and of s to t^2 which Galileo first laid bare. Pascal's discovery of the proportionality of altitude to barometric height, Newton's of acceleration to distance, Boyle's of air-volume to pressure, Descartes' of sine to sine in the refracted ray were the first fruits of Galileo's discovery. There was no question of agencies, nothing animistic or sympathetic in this new way of taking nature. It was description only of concomitant variations, after the particular quantities that varied had been successfully abstracted out. The result soon showed itself in a differentiation of human knowledge into two spheres, one called 'science,' within which the more definite laws apply, the other 'general philosophy,' in which they do not.

The state of mind called positivistic is the result. Down with philosophy! is the cry of innumerable scientific minds. Give us measurable facts only, phenomena, without the mind's additions, without entities or principles that pretend to explain. It is largely from this kind of mind that the objection that philosophy has made no progress, proceeds.

It is obvious enough that if every step forward which philosophy makes, every question to which an accurate answer is found, gets credited to 'science,' the residuum of unanswered problems will alone remain to constitute the domain of philosophy, and will alone bear her name. In point of fact this is just what is happening.

Philosophy has become a collective name for questions that have not yet been answered to the satisfaction of all by whom they have been asked. It does not follow that because some of these questions have waited two thousand years for an answer no answer will ever be forthcoming. Two thousand years probably measure but one paragraph in that great romance of adventure called the history of the intellect of man. The extraordinary progress of the last three hundred years is due to a rather sudden finding of the way in which a certain order of questions ought to be attacked, questions admitting of mathematical treatment. But to assume therefore that the only possible philosophy must be mechanical and mathematical, and to disparage all inquiry into the other sorts of question, is to forget the extreme diversity of aspects under which reality undoubtedly exists. To the spiritual questions the proper avenues of philosophic approach will also undoubtedly be found. They have to some extent been found already. In some respects, indeed, 'science' has made less progress than 'philosophy'—its most general conceptions would astonish neither Aristotle nor Descartes could they revisit our earth. The composition of things from elements, their evolution, the conservation of energy, the idea of a universal determinism, would seem to them commonplace enough—the little things, the microscopes, electric lights, telephones, and details of the sciences, would be to them the awe-inspiring things. But if they opened our books on metaphysics or visited a philosophic lecture-room, everything would sound strange. The whole idealistic or 'critical' attitude of our time would be novel, and it would be long before they took it in.[8]

Objection 2.

Philosophy is dogmatic, and pretends to settle things by pure reason, whereas the only fruitful mode of getting at truth is to appeal to concrete experience. Science collects, classes and analyzes facts, and thereby far outstrips philosophy.

Reply. This objection is historically valid. Too many philosophers have aimed at closed systems, established *a priori*, claiming infallibility, and to be accepted or rejected only as totals. The sciences on the other hand, using hypotheses only, but always seeking to verify them by experiment or observation, open a way for

---

[8] The reader will find all that I have said, and much more, set forth in an excellent article by James Ward in *Mind*, vol. xv (1890), p. 213.

indefinite self-correction and increase. At the present day, it is getting more and more difficult for dogmatists claiming finality for their systems, to get a hearing in educated circles. Hypothesis and verification, the watchwords of science, have set the fashion too strongly in academic minds.

Since philosophers are only man thinking about things in the most comprehensive possible way, they can use any method whatever freely. Philosophy must, in any case, complete the sciences, and must incorporate their methods. One cannot see why, if such a policy should appear advisable, philosophy might not end by forswearing all dogmatism whatever, and become as hypothetical in her manners as the most empirical science of them all.

Objection 3.

Philosophy is out of touch with real life, for which it substitutes abstractions. The real world is various, tangled, painful. Philosophers almost without exception have treated it as noble, simple, and perfect, ignoring the complexity of fact, and indulging in a sort of optimism that exposes their systems to the contempt of common men, and to the satire of such writers as Voltaire and Schopenhauer. The great popular success of Schopenhauer is due to the fact that, first among philosophers, he spoke the concrete truth about the ills of life.

Reply. This objection also is historically valid, but no reason appears why philosophy should keep aloof from reality permanently. Her manners may change as she successfully developes. The thin and noble abstractions may give way to more solid and real constructions, when the materials and methods for making such constructions shall be more and more securely ascertained. In the end philosophers may get into as close contact as realistic novelists with the facts of life.

Conclusion.

In its original acception, meaning the completest knowledge of the universe, philosophy must include the results of all the sciences, and cannot be contrasted with the latter. It simply aims at making of science what Herbert Spencer calls a system of *'completely-unified* knowledge.'[9] In the more modern sense, of some-

[9] See the excellent chapter in Spencer's *First Principles* entitled 'Philosophy Defined.'

thing contrasted with the sciences, philosophy means 'metaphysics.' The older sense is the more worthy sense, and as the results of the sciences get more available for co-ordination, and the conditions for finding truth in different kinds of question get more methodically defined, we may hope that the term will revert to its original meaning. Science, metaphysics and religion may then again form a single body of wisdom, and lend each other mutual support.

At present this hope is far from its fulfilment. I propose in this book to take philosophy in the narrow sense of metaphysics, and to let both religion and the results of the sciences alone.

Chapter II

The Problems of Metaphysics

No exact definition of the term metaphysics is possible, and to name some of the problems it treats of is the best way of getting at the meaning of the word. It means the discussion of various obscure, abstract, and universal questions which the sciences and life in general suggest but do not solve; questions left over, as it were; questions, all of them very broad and deep, and relating to the whole of things, or to the ultimate elements thereof. Instead of a definition let me cite a few examples in a random order, of such questions:—

What are 'thoughts' and what are 'things'? and how are they connected?

What do we mean when we say 'truth'?

Is there a common stuff out of which all facts are made?

How comes there to be a world at all? and might it as well not have been?

Which is the most real kind of reality?

What binds all things into one universe?

Is unity or diversity more fundamental?

Have all things one origin? or many?

Is everything predestined, or are some things (our wills for example) free?

Is the world infinite or finite in amount?

Are its parts continuous, or are there vacua?

What is God?—or the gods?

How are mind and body joined? Do they act upon each other?

How does anything act on anything else?

How can one thing change into or grow out of another thing?

Are space and time beings?—or what?

In knowledge how does the object get into the mind?—or the mind get *at* the object?

We know by means of universal notions—are these also real? Or are only particular things real?

What is meant by a 'thing'?

'Principles of reason'—are they inborn or derived?

Are 'beauty' and 'good' matters of opinion only? Or have they objective validity? And if so, what does the phrase mean?

Such are specimens of the kind of question termed metaphysical. Kant said that the three essential metaphysical questions were:—

What can I know?

What should I do?

What may I hope?

A glance at all such questions suffices to rule out such a definition of metaphysics as that of Christian Wolff, who called it 'the science of what is possible,' as distinguished from that of what is actual, for most of the questions relate to actual fact. One may say that metaphysics inquires into the cause, the substance, the meaning and the outcome, of all things. Or one may call it the science of the most universal principles of reality (whether experienced by us or not), in their connexion with one another and with our powers of knowledge. 'Principles' here may mean either *entities*, like 'atoms,' 'souls'; or logical laws, like 'A thing must either exist or not exist'; or generalized facts, like 'things can act only after they exist.' But the principles are so numerous, and the 'science' of them is so far from completion, that such definitions have only a decorative value. *The serious work of metaphysics is done over the separate single questions.* If these should get severally cleared up, talk of metaphysics as a unified science might rightfully begin. This book proposes to handle only a few separate problems, leaving others untouched.

These problems are for the most part real; that is, but few of them result from a misuse of terms in stating them. 'Things,' for example, either are or are not composed of one stuff; they either

have or have not a single origin; they either are or are not completely predetermined, etc. Such alternatives may indeed be impossible of decision; but until this is conclusively proved of them,
they confront us legitimately, and someone must take charge of
them and keep account of the solutions that are proposed, even if
he do not himself add new ones. The opinions of the learned regarding them must, in short, be classified and responsibly discussed. For instance, how many opinions are possible as to the
origin of the world? Spencer says that the world must have been
either eternal, or self-created, or created by an outside power—so
for him there are only three. Is this correct? If so, which of the
three views seems the most reasonable?—and why? In a moment
we are in the thick of metaphysics. We have to be metaphysicians
even to decide with Spencer that neither mode of origin is think-
able and that the whole problem is unreal.

Some hypotheses may be absurd on their face, because they are
self-contradictory. If, for example, infinity means 'what can never
be completed by successive synthesis,' the notion of anything made
by the successive addition of infinitely numerous parts, and yet
completed, is absurd. Other hypotheses, for example that everything in nature contributes to a single supreme purpose, may be
insusceptible either of proof or of disproof. Other hypotheses
again, for instance that *vacua* exist, may be susceptible of probable solution. The classing of the hypotheses is thus as necessary
as the classing of the problems, and both must be recognized as
constituting a serious branch of learning.[1] There must in short be
metaphysicians. Let us for a while become metaphysicians ourselves.

As we survey the history of metaphysics we soon realize that two
pretty distinct types of mind have filled it with their warfare. Let
us call them the rationalist and the empiricist types of mind. A
saying of Coleridge's is often quoted, to the effect that everyone
is born either a platonist or an aristotelian. By aristotelian he meant
empiricist, and by platonist he meant rationalist; but altho the
contrast between the two greek philosophers exists in the sense in
which Coleridge meant it, both of them were rationalists as compared with the kind of empiricism which Democritus and Protagoras developed; and Coleridge had better have taken either of
those names instead of Aristotle as his empiricist example.

[1] Consult here Paul Janet: *Principes de métaphysique*, etc., 1897, Leçons i, ii.

Rationalists are the men of principles, empiricists the men of facts; but, since principles are universals, and facts are particulars, perhaps the best way of characterizing the two tendencies is to say that rationalist thinking proceeds most willingly by going from wholes to parts, while empiricist thinking goes from parts to wholes. Plato, the archrationalist, explained the details of nature by their participation in 'ideas,' which all depended on the supreme idea of 'the good.' Democritus and Protagoras were empiricists. The former explained the whole cosmos, including gods as well as men, and thoughts as well as things, by their composition out of atomic elements; Protagoras explained truth, which for Plato was the absolute system of the ideas, as a collective name for men's opinions.

Rationalists prefer to deduce facts from principles. Empiricists to explain principles as inductions from facts. Is thought for the sake of life? or is life for the sake of thought? Empiricism inclines to the former, rationalism to the latter branch of the alternative. God's life, according to Aristotle and Hegel, is pure theory. The mood of admiration is natural to rationalism. Its theories are usually optimistic, supplementing the experienced world by clean and pure ideal constructions. Aristotle and Plato, the Scholastics, Descartes, Spinosa, Leibnitz, Kant, and Hegel are examples of this. They claimed absolute finality for their systems, in the noble architecture of which, as their authors believed, truth was eternally embalmed. This temper of finality is foreign to empiricist minds. They may be dogmatic about their method of building on 'hard facts,' but they are willing to be sceptical about any conclusions reached by the method at a given time. They aim at accuracy of detail rather than at completeness; are contented to be fragmentary; are less inspiring than the rationalists, often treating the high as a case of 'nothing but' the low (virtue 'nothing but' self-interest well understood, etc.); but they usually keep more in touch with actual life, are less subjective, and their spirit is obviously more 'scientific' in the hackneyed sense of that term. Socrates, Locke, Berkeley, Hume, the Mills, F. A. Lange, Dewey, F. C. S. Schiller, Bergson, and other contemporaries are specimens of this type. Of course we find mixed minds in abundance, and few philosophers are typical in either class. Kant may fairly be called mixed. Lotze and Royce are mixed. The author of the present volume is weakly endowed on the rationalist side, and his book will show a strong leaning towards empiricism. The clash of the two ways of looking at things will be emphasized throughout the volume.[2]

I will now enter the interior of the subject by discussing special problems as examples of metaphysical inquiry; and in order not to conceal any of the skeletons in the philosophic closet, I will start with the worst problem possible, the so-called 'ontological' problem, or question of how there comes to be anything at all.

[2] Compare W. James: 'The Sentiment of Rationality,' in *The Will to Believe* (Longmans, Green, and Co., 1897), p. 63 f. [*ed.*, p. 57f.]; *Pragmatism* (*ibid.*), chap. i; *A Pluralistic Universe* (*ibid.*), chap. i.

Chapter III

The Problem of Being

How comes the world to be here at all instead of the nonentity which might be imagined in its place? Schopenhauer's remarks on this question may be considered classical. "Apart from man," he says, "no being wonders at its own existence. When man first becomes conscious he takes himself for granted, as something needing no explanation. But not for long; for, with the rise of the first reflexion, that *wonder* begins which is the mother of metaphysics, and which made Aristotle say that men now and always seek to philosophize because of wonder.—The lower a man stands in intellectual respects the less of a riddle does existence seem to him . . . but, the clearer his consciousness becomes the more the problem grasps him in its greatness. In fact the unrest which keeps the never stopping clock of metaphysics going is the thought that the non-existence of this world is just as possible as its existence. Nay more, we soon conceive the world as something the non-existence of which not only is conceivable but would indeed be preferable to its existence; so that our wonder passes easily into a brooding over that fatality which nevertheless could call such a world into being, and mislead the immense force that could produce and preserve it into an activity so hostile to its own interests. The philosophic wonder thus becomes a sad astonishment, and like the overture to Don Giovanni, philosophy begins with a minor chord."[1]

[1] *The World as Will and Representation*: Appendix 17, 'On the metaphysical need of man,' abridged.

26

One need only shut oneself in a closet and begin to think of the fact of one's being there, of one's queer bodily shape in the darkness (a thing to make children scream at, as Stevenson says), of one's fantastic character and all, to have the wonder steal over the detail as much as over the general fact of being, and to see that it is only familiarity that blunts it. Not only that *anything* should be, but that *this* very thing should be, is mysterious! Philosophy stares, but brings no reasoned solution, for from nothing to being there is no logical bridge.

Attempts are sometimes made to banish the question rather than to give it an answer. Those who ask it, we are told, extend illegitimately to the whole of being the contrast to a supposed alternative non-being which only particular beings possess. These indeed were not, and now are. But being in general, or in some shape, always was, and you cannot rightly bring the whole of it into relation with a primordial nonentity. Whether as God or as material atoms, it is itself primal and eternal.

But if you call any being whatever eternal, some philosophers have always been ready to taunt you with the paradox inherent in the assumption. Is past eternity completed? they ask: If so, they go on, it must have had a beginning; for whether your imagination traverses it forwards or backwards, it offers an identical content or stuff to be measured; and if the amount comes to an end in one way, it ought to come to an end in the other. In other words, since we now witness its end, some past moment must have witnessed its beginning. If, however, it had a beginning, when was that, and why? You are up again against the previous nothing, and don't see how it ever passed into being. This dilemma, of having to choose between a regress which, altho called infinite, has nevertheless come to a termination, and an absolute first, has played a great part in philosophy's history.

Other attempts still are made at exorcising the question. Non-being is not, said Parmenides and Zeno, only being is, so what is is necessarily being—being in short is necessary. Others, calling the idea of nonentity no real idea, have said that on the absence of an idea no genuine problem can be founded. More curtly still, the whole ontological wonder has been called diseased, a case of *grübelsucht* like asking "why am I myself?" or "why is a triangle a triangle?"

Rationalistic minds here and there have however sought to reduce the mystery. Some forms of Being have been deemed more natural, so to say, or more inevitable and necessary than others. Empiricists of the evolutionary type—Herbert Spencer seems a good example—have assumed that whatever had the least of reality, was weakest, faintest, most imperceptible, most nascent, might come easiest first, and be the earliest successor to nonentity. Little by little the fuller grades of being might have added themselves in the same gradual way until the whole universe grew up.

To others not the minimum, but the maximum of being has seemed the easiest *first* for the intellect to accept. "The perfection of a thing doesn't keep it from existing," Spinosa said, "on the contrary it founds its existence."[2] It is mere prejudice to assume that it is harder for the great than for the little to be, and that easiest of all it is to be nothing. What makes things difficult in any line is the alien obstructions that are met with, and the smaller and weaker the thing the more power over it these have. Some things are so great and inclusive that to be is implied in their very nature. The anselmian or ontological proof of God's existence, sometimes called the cartesian proof, criticized by Saint Thomas, rejected by Kant, re-defended by Hegel, follows this line of thought. What is conceived as imperfect may lack being among its other lacks, but if God, who is expressly defined as *Ens perfectissimum*, lacked anything whatever he would contradict his own definition. He cannot lack being therefore: He is *Ens necessarium*, *Ens realissimum*, as well as *Ens perfectissimum*.[3] Hegel, in his lordly way, says "it would be strange if . . . God were not rich enough to embrace so poor a category as Being, the very poorest and most abstract of all." This is somewhat in line with Kant's saying that a real dollar does not contain one cent more than an imaginary dollar. At the beginning of his *Logic* Hegel seeks in another way to mediate nonentity with being. Since 'being' in the abstract, *mere* being, means nothing in particular, it is indistinguishable from 'nothing'; and he seems dimly to think that this constitutes an identity between the two notions, of which some use may be made in getting from one to the other. Other still queerer attempts show well the ratio-

[2] *Ethics*, Part i, Prop. 11, scholium.

[3] St. Anselm: *Proslogium*, etc., tr. by Deane, Chicago, 1903; Descartes: *Meditations*, V; Kant: *Critique of Pure Reason, Transcendental Dialectic*, 'On the impossibility of an ontological proof,' etc.

nalist temper. Mathematically you can deduce 1 from 0 by the following process: $\frac{0}{0}=\frac{1-1}{1-1}=1$. Or physically if all being has (as it seems to have) a 'polar' construction, so that every positive part of it has its negative, we get the simple equation: $+1-1=0$, *plus* and *minus* being the signs of polarity in physics.

It is not probable that the reader will be satisfied with any of these solutions, and contemporary philosophers, even rationalistically minded ones, have on the whole agreed that no one has intelligibly banished the mystery of *fact*. Whether the original Nothing burst into God and vanished, as night vanishes in day, while God thereupon became the creative principle of all lesser beings, or whether all things have foisted or shaped themselves imperceptibly into existence, the same amount of existence has in the end to be assumed and begged by the philosopher. To comminute the difficulty is not to quench it. If you are a rationalist you beg a kilogram of being at once, we will say; if you are an empiricist you beg a thousand successive grams; but you beg the same amount in each case, and you are the same beggar whatever you may pretend. You leave the logical riddle untouched, of how the coming of whatever is, came it all at once, or came it piecemeal, can be intellectually understood.[4]

If being gradually *grew*, its quantity was of course not always the same, and may not be the same hereafter. To most philosophers this view has seemed absurd, neither God, nor primordial matter, nor energy being supposed to admit of increase or decrease. The orthodox opinion is that the quantity of reality must at all costs be 'conserved,' and the waxing and waning of our phenomenal experiences must be treated as surface appearances which leave the deeps untouched.

Nevertheless, *within experience*, phenomena come and go. There are novelties; there are losses. The world seems, on the concrete and proximate level at least, really to grow. So the question recurs: how do our finite experiences come into being from moment to moment? By inertia? By perpetual creation? Do the new ones come at the *call* of the old ones? Why don't they all go out like a candle?

---

[4] In more technical language, one may say that fact or being is 'contingent,' or matter of 'chance,' so far as our intellect is concerned. The conditions of its appearance are uncertain, unforeseeable when future, and when past, elusive.

Who can tell off-hand? The question of Being is the darkest in all philosophy. All of us are beggars here, and no one school can speak disdainfully of another or give itself superior airs. For all of us alike, Fact forms a datum, gift, or *vorgefundenes*, which we cannot burrow under, explain, or get behind. It makes itself somehow, and our business is far more with its *what* than with its *whence* or *why*.

Chapter IV

Percept and Concept

Their difference.

The problem convenient to take up next in order will be that of the difference between thoughts and things. 'Things' are known to us by our senses, and are called 'presentations' by some authors, to distinguish them from the ideas or 'representations' which we may have when our senses are closed. I myself have grown accustomed to use the words 'percept' and 'concept' in treating of the contrast, but concepts flow out of percepts and into them again, they are so interlaced, and our life rests on them so interchangeably and undiscriminatingly, that it is often difficult to impart quickly to beginners a clear notion of the difference meant. Sensation and thought in man are mingled, but they vary independently. In our quadrupedal relatives thought proper is at a minimum, but we have no reason to suppose that their immediate life of feeling is either less or more copious than ours. Feeling must have been originally self-sufficing; and thought appears as a superadded function, adapting us to a wider environment than that of which brutes take account. Some parts of the stream of feeling must be more intense, emphatic, and exciting than others in animals as well as in ourselves; but whereas lower animals simply react upon these more salient sensations by appropriate movements, higher animals remember them, and men react on them intellectually, by using nouns, adjectives, and verbs to identify them when they meet them elsewhere.

The great difference between percepts and concepts[1] is that percepts are continuous and concepts are discrete. Not discrete in their *being*, for conception as an *act* is part of the flux of feeling, but discrete from each other in their several *meanings*. Each concept means just what it singly means, and nothing else; and if the conceiver doesn't know whether he means this or means that, it shows that his concept is imperfectly formed. The perceptual flux as such, on the contrary, *means* nothing, and is but what it immediately is; and no matter how small a tract of it be taken, it is always a much-at-once, and contains innumerable aspects and characters which conception can pick out and isolate, and thereafter always intend. It shows duration, intensity, complexity or simplicity, interestingness, excitingness, pleasantness or their opposites. Data from all our senses enter into it, merged in a general extensiveness of which each occupies a big or little share. Yet all these parts leave its unity unbroken. Its boundaries are no more distinct than are those of the field of vision. Boundaries are things that intervene; but here nothing intervenes save parts of the perceptual flux itself, and these are overflowed by what they separate, so that whatever we distinguish and isolate conceptually is found perceptually to telescope and compenetrate and diffuse into its neighbors. The cuts we make are purely ideal. If my reader can succeed in abstracting from all conceptual interpretation and lapse back into his immediate sensible life at this very moment, he will find it to be what someone has called a big blooming buzzing confusion, as free from contradiction in its 'much-at-onceness' as it is all alive and evidently there.[2]

The conceptual order.

Out of this aboriginal sensible muchness attention carves out objects, which conception then names and identifies forever—in the

---

[1] In what follows I shall freely use synonyms for these two terms. 'Idea,' 'thought,' and 'intellection' are synonymous with 'concept.' Instead of 'percept' I shall often speak of 'sensation,' 'feeling,' 'intuition,' and sometimes of 'sensible experience' or of the 'immediate flow' of conscious life. Since Hegel's time what is simply perceived has been called the 'immediate,' while the 'mediated' is synonymous with what is conceived.

[2] Compare W. James: *A Pluralistic Universe*, pp. 282–288 [*ed.*, pp. 127–130]. Also *Psychology, Briefer Course*, pp. 157–166.

sky 'constellations,' on the earth 'beach,' 'sea,' 'cliff,' 'bushes,' 'grass.' Out of time we cut 'days' and 'nights,' 'summers' and 'winters.' We say *what* each part of the sensible continuum is, and all these abstracted *whats* are *concepts*.[3] *The intellectual life of man consists almost wholly in his substituting a conceptual order for the perceptual order in which his experience originally comes.* But before tracing the consequences of the substitution, I must say something about the conceptual order itself.[4]

Trains of concepts unmixed with percepts grow frequent in the adult mind; and parts of these conceptual trains arrest our attention just as parts of the perceptual flow did, giving rise to concepts of a higher order of abstractness. So subtle is the discernment of man, and so great the power of some men to single out the most fugitive elements of what passes before them, that these new formations have no limit. Aspect within aspect, quality after quality, relation upon relation, absences and negations as well as present features, end by being noted and their names added to the store of nouns, verbs, adjectives, conjunctions, and prepositions by which the human mind interprets life. Every new book verbalizes some new concept, which becomes important in proportion to the use that can be made of it. Different universes of thought thus arise, with specific sorts of relation among their ingredients. The world of common-sense 'things'; the world of material tasks to be done;

[3] On the function of conception consult Sir William Hamilton's *Lectures on Logic*, ix, x; H. L. Mansel: *Prolegomena Logica*, chap. i; A. Schopenhauer: *The World as Will*, etc., Supplements vi and vii to Book I; W. James: *Principles of Psychology*, chap. xii; *Briefer Course*, chap. xiv. Also G. J. Romanes: *Mental Evolution in Man*, chaps. iii and iv; Th. Ribot: *L'Évolution des idées générales*, chap. vi; Th. Ruyssen: *Essai sur l'évolution psychologique du jugement*, chap. vii; Laromiguière: *Leçons de philosophie*, 2me. Partie, 12me. Leçon. The account I give directly contradicts that which Kant gave and which has prevailed since Kant's time. Kant always speaks of the aboriginal sensible flux as a 'manifold' of which he considers the essential character to be its *disconnectedness*. To get any togetherness at all into it requires, he thinks, the agency of the 'transcendental ego of apperception'; and to get any definite connexions requires that of the understanding, with its synthetizing concepts or 'categories.' "Die Verbindung (*conjunctio*) eines Mannigfaltigen überhaupt kann niemals durch Sinne in uns kommen, und kann also auch nicht in der reinen Form der sinnlichen Anschauung zugleich mit enthalten sein; denn sie ist ein Aktus der Spontaneität der Vorstellungskraft, und, da man diese, zum Unterschiede von der Sinnlichkeit, Verstand nennen muss, so ist alle Verbindung . . . eine Verstandeshandlung." *Krit. d. reinen Vernunft*, 2te Aufg., pp. 129–130.—The reader must decide which account agrees best with his own actual experience.

[4] The substitution was first described in these terms by S. H. Hodgson in his *Philosophy of Reflection*, vol. i, pp. 288–310.

the mathematical world of pure forms; the world of ethical propositions; the worlds of logic, of music, etc.—all abstracted and
generalized from long-forgotten perceptual instances from which
they have as it were flowered out—return and merge themselves
again in the particulars of our present and future perception. By
those *whats* we apperceive all our *thises*. Percepts and concepts interpenetrate and melt together, impregnate and fertilize each other.
Neither, taken alone, knows reality in its completeness. We need
them both, as we need both our legs to walk with.

From Aristotle downwards philosophers have frankly admitted
the indispensability, for complete knowledge of fact, of both the
sensational and the intellectual contribution.[5] For complete knowledge of fact, I say; but facts are particulars and connect themselves
with practical necessities and the arts; and greek philosophers soon
formed the notion that a knowledge of so-called 'universals,' consisting of concepts of abstract forms, qualities, numbers, and relations, was the only knowledge worthy of the truly philosophic mind.
Particular facts decay and our perceptions of them vary. A concept
never varies; and between such unvarying terms the relations must
be constant and express eternal verities. Hence there arose a tendency, which has lasted all through philosophy, to contrast the
knowledge of universals and intelligibles, as godlike, dignified,
and honorable to the knower, with that of particulars and sensibles
as something relatively base which more allies us with the beasts.[6]

[5] See, for example, Book I, chap. ii, of Aristotle's *Metaphysics*.

[6] Plato in numerous places, but chiefly in Books VI and VII of the *Republic*, contrasts perceptual knowledge as 'opinion' with real knowledge, to the latter's glory.
For an excellent historic sketch of this platonistic view see the first part of E. Laas's
Idealismus und Positivismus, 1879.—For other expressions of the ultra-intellectualistic
view read Plotinus on the Intellect in C. M. Bakewell's *Source Book in Ancient Philosophy*, N. Y. 1907, pp. 353 f.; Bossuet: *Traité de la connaissance de Dieu*, chap. iv,
§§ v, vi; R. Cudworth: *A Treatise Concerning Eternal and Immutable Morality*,
Books III and IV.—"Plato," writes Prof. Santayana, "thought that all the truth and
meaning of earthly things was the reference they contained to a heavenly original.
This heavenly original we remember and recognize even among the distortions, disappearances, and multiplications of its ephemeral copies. . . . The impressions themselves have no permanence, no intelligible essence, but, as Plato said, they never
really exist, but are always either arising or ceasing to be. There must be, he tells us,
an eternal and clearly definable object of which the visible appearances to us are
the multiform semblance; now by one trait now by another the phantom before us
reminds us of that half-forgotten celestial reality and makes us utter its name . . . .
We, and the whole universe, exist only in the attempt to return to our perfection,
to lose ourselves again in God. That ineffable good is our natural possession; all we
honour in this life is but the partial recovery of our birthright; every delightful thing

Percept and Concept

Two views of conceptual knowledge.

For rationalistic writers conceptual knowledge was not only the more noble knowledge, but it originated independently of all perceptual particulars. Such concepts as God, perfection, eternity, infinity, immutability, identity, absolute beauty, truth, justice, necessity, freedom, duty, worth, etc., and the part they play in our mind, are, it was supposed, impossible to explain as results of practical experience. The empiricist view, and probably the true view, is that they do result from practical experience.[7] But a more important question than that as to the origin of our concepts is that as to their functional use and value:—is *that* tied down to perceptual experience, or out of all relation to it? Is conceptual knowledge self-sufficing and a revelation all by itself, quite apart from its uses in helping to a better understanding of the world of sense?

We shall see in later places (pages 40, 55) that the various conceptual universes referred to on page 33 can be considered in complete abstraction from perceptual reality, and, that when they are so considered, all sorts of fixed relations can be discovered among their parts. The *a priori* sciences of logic, mathematics, ethics and aesthetics (so far as the last two can be called sciences at all) result. Conceptual knowledge must thus be called a self-sufficing revelation; and by rationalistic writers it has always been treated as admitting us to a diviner world, the world of universal rather than that of perishing facts, of essential qualities, immutable relations, eternal principles of truth and right. Emerson writes: "Generalization is

---

is like a rift in the clouds through which we catch a glimpse of our native heaven. If that heaven seems so far away and the idea of it so dim and unreal, it is because we are so far from perfect, so much immersed in what is alien and destructive to the soul." (G. Santayana: 'Platonic Love in Some Italian Poets,' in *Interpretations of Poetry and Religion*, 1900.) This is the interpretation of Plato which has been current since Aristotle. It should be said that its profundity has been challenged by Prof. A. J. Stewart. (*Plato's Doctrine of Ideas*, Oxford, 1909.)

Aristotle found great fault with Plato's treatment of ideas as heavenly originals, but he agreed with him fully as to the superior excellence of the conceptual or theoretic life. In chapters 7 and 8 of Book X of the *Nicomachean Ethics* he extols contemplation of universal relations as alone yielding pure happiness. "The life of God, in all its exceeding blessedness, will consist in the exercise of philosophic thought; and of all human activities, that will be the happiest which is most akin to the divine."

[7] John Locke, in his *Essay Concerning Human Understanding*, Books I and II, was the great popularizer of this doctrine. Condillac's *Traité des sensations*, Helvétius's work *De l'homme*, and James Mill's *Analysis of the Human Mind* were more radical successors of Locke's great book.

always a new influx of the divinity into the mind. Hence the thrill that attends it." And a disciple of Hegel, after exalting the knowledge of "the General, Unchangeable, and alone Valuable" above that of "the Particular, Sensible, and Transient," adds that if you reproach philosophy with being unable to make a single grass-blade grow, or even to know how it does grow, the reply is that since such a particular 'how' stands not above but below knowledge, strictly so called, such an ignorance argues no defect.[8]

The empiricist view.

To this ultra-rationalistic opinion the empiricist contention that *the significance of concepts consists always in their relation to perceptual particulars* has been opposed. Made of percepts, or distilled from parts of percepts, their essential office, it has been said, is to coalesce with percepts again, bringing the mind back into the perceptual world with a better command of the situation there. Certainly whenever we *can* do this with our concepts, we do *more* with them than when we leave them flocking with their abstract and motionless companions. It is possible therefore to join the rationalists in allowing conceptual knowledge to be self-sufficing, while at the same time one joins the empiricists in maintaining that the full *value* of such knowledge is got only by combining it with perceptual reality again. This mediating attitude is that which this book must adopt. But to understand the nature of concepts better we must now go on to distinguish their *function* from their *content*.

The concept 'man,' to take an example, is three things: 1. the word itself; 2. a vague picture of the human form which has its own value in the way of beauty or not; and 3. an instrument for symbolizing certain objects from which we may expect human treatment when occasion arrives. Similarly of 'triangle,' 'cosine'— they have their substantive value both as words and as images suggested, but they also have a functional value whenever they lead us elsewhere in discourse.

There are concepts, however, the image-part of which is so faint that their whole value seems to be functional. 'God,' 'cause,' 'num-

---

[8] Michelet: Hegel's *Werke*, vii, p. 15, quoted by A. Gratry: *De la connaissance de l'âme*, i, p. 231. Compare the similar claim for philosophy in W. Wallace's *Prolegomena to Hegel*, 2nd ed., 1894, pp. 28–29, and the long and radical statement of the same view in Book IV of Ralph Cudworth's *Treatise Concerning Eternal and Immutable Morality*.

ber,' 'substance,' 'soul,' for example, suggest no definite picture; and their significance seems to consist entirely in their *tendency*, in the further turn which they may give to our action or our thought.[9] We cannot rest in the contemplation of their form, as we can in that of a 'circle' or a 'man'; we must pass beyond.

Now however beautiful or otherwise worthy of stationary contemplation the substantive part of a concept may be, the more important part of its significance may naturally be held to be the consequences to which it leads. These may lie either in the way of making us think, or in the way of making us act. Whoever has a clear idea of these knows effectively what the concept practically signifies, whether its substantive content be interesting in its own right or not.

This consideration has led to a method of interpreting concepts to which I shall give the name of

The pragmatic rule.[10]

The pragmatic rule is that the meaning of a concept may always be found, if not in some sensible particular which it directly designates, then in some particular difference in the course of human experience which its being true will make. Test every concept by the question "What sensible difference to anybody will its truth make?" and you are in the best possible position for understanding what it means and for discussing its importance. If, questioning whether a certain concept be true or false, you can think of absolutely nothing that would practically differ in the two cases, you may assume that the alternative is meaningless and that your concept is no distinct idea. If two concepts lead you to infer the same particular consequence, then you may assume that they embody the same meaning under different names.

This rule applies to concepts of every order of complexity, from simple terms to propositions uniting many terms.

So many disputes in philosophy hinge upon ill-defined words and ideas, each side claiming its own word or idea to be true, that any accepted method of making meanings clear must be of great utility. No method can be handier of application than our prag-

[9] On this functional tendency compare H. Taine: *On Intelligence*, Book I, chap. ii (1870).

[10] Compare W. James: *Pragmatism*, chap. ii and *passim*; also Baldwin's *Dictionary of Philosophy*, article 'Pragmatism,' by C. S. Peirce.

matic rule. If you claim that any idea is true, assign at the same time some difference that its being true will make in some possible person's history, and we shall know, not only just what you are really claiming, but also how important an issue it is, and how to go to work to verify the claim. In obeying this rule we neglect the substantive content of the concept, and follow its function only. This neglect might seem at first sight to need excuse, for the content often has a value of its own which might conceivably add lustre to reality, if it existed, apart from any modification wrought by it in the other parts of reality. Thus it is often supposed that 'Idealism' is a theory precious in itself, even tho no definite change in the details of our experience can be deduced from it. Later discussion will show that this is a superficial view, and that particular consequences are the only criterion of a concept's meaning, and the only test of its truth.

Instances are hardly called for, they are so obvious. That A and B are 'equal,' for example, means either that 'you will find no difference' when you pass from one to the other, or that in substituting one for the other in certain operations 'you will get the same result both times.' 'Substance' means that 'a definite group of sensations will recur.' 'Incommensurable' means that 'you are always confronted with a remainder.' 'Infinite' means either that, or that 'you can count as many units in a part as you can in the whole.' 'More' and 'less' mean certain sensations, varying according to the matter. 'Freedom' means 'no feeling of sensible restraint.' 'Necessity' means that 'your way is blocked in all directions save one.' 'God' means that 'you can dismiss certain kinds of fear,' 'cause' that 'you may expect certain sequences,' etc., etc. We shall find plenty of examples in the rest of this book; so I go back now to the more general question of whether the whole import of the world of concepts lies in its relation to perceptual experience, or whether it be also an independent revelation of truth. Great ambiguity is possible in answering this question, so we must mind our Ps and Qs.

The origin of concepts lies in their utility.

The first thing to notice is that in the earliest stages of human intelligence, so far as we can guess at them, thought proper must have had an exclusively practical use. Men classed their sensations, substituting concepts for them, in order to 'work them for what they were worth,' and to prepare for what might lie ahead. Class-names suggest consequences that have attached themselves on other occasions to other members of the class—consequences which the present percept will also probably or certainly show.[11] The present percept in its immediacy may thus often sink to the status of a bare sign of the consequences which the substituted concept suggests.

The substitution of concepts and their connexions, of a whole conceptual order, in short, for the immediate perceptual flow, thus widens enormously our mental panorama. Had we no concepts we should live simply 'getting' each successive moment of experience, as the sessile sea-anemone on its rock receives whatever nourishment the wash of the waves may bring. With concepts, we go in quest of the absent, meet the remote, actively turn this way or that, bend our experience, and make it tell us whither it is bound. We change its order, run it backwards, bring far bits together and separate near bits, jump about over its surface instead of plowing through its continuity, string its items on as many ideal diagrams as our mind can frame. All these are ways of handling the perceptual flux and meeting distant parts of it; and as far as this primary function of conception goes, we can only conclude it to be what I began by calling it, a faculty superadded to our barely perceptual consciousness for its use in practically adapting us to a larger environment than that of which brutes take account.[12] We *harness* perceptual reality in concepts in order to drive it better to our ends.

The theoretic use of concepts.

Does our conceptual translation of the perceptual flux enable us also to *understand* the latter better? What do we mean by making us 'understand'? Applying our pragmatic rule to the interpretation of the word, we see that the better we understand anything the more we are able to *tell about it*. Judged by this test, concepts do make us understand our percepts better: knowing *what* these are, we can tell all sorts of farther truths about them, based on the

[11] For the practical uses of conception compare W. James: *Principles of Psychology*, chap. xxii; I. E. Miller: *The Psychology of Thinking*, 1909, *passim*, but especially chaps. xv, xvi, xvii.

[12] Herbert Spencer in his *Psychology*, Parts iii and iv, has at great length tried to show that such adaptation is the sole meaning of our intellect.

relation of those whats to other whats. The whole system of relations, spatial, temporal, and logical, of our fact, gets plotted out.
An ancient philosophical opinion, inherited from Aristotle, is that
we do not understand a thing until we know it by its causes. When
the maid-servant says that 'the cat' broke the tea-cup, she would
have us conceive the fracture in a causally explanatory way. No
otherwise when Clerk Maxwell asks us to conceive of gas-elasticity
as due to molecular bombardment. An imaginary agent out of
sight becomes in each case a part of the cosmic context in which
we now place the percept to be explained; and the explanation is
valid in so far as the new causal *that* is itself conceived in a context
that makes its existence probable, and with a nature agreeable to
the effects it is imagined to produce. All our scientific explanations
would seem to conform to this simple type, of the 'necessary cat.'
The conceived order of nature, built round the perceived order
and explaining it theoretically, as we say, is only a system of hypothetically imagined *thats*, the *whats* of which harmoniously connect themselves with the *what* of any *that* which we immediately
perceive.

The system is essentially a topographic system, a system of the
distribution of things. It tells us what's what, and where's where.
In so far forth it merely prolongs that opening up of the perspective of practical consequences which we found to be the primordial
utility of the conceiving faculty: it adapts us to an immense environment. Working by the causes of things, we gain advantages
which we never should have compassed had we worked by the
things alone.

The a priori sciences.

But in order to reach such results the concepts in the explanatory
system must, I said, 'harmoniously connect.' What does that mean?
Is this also only a practical advantage, or is it something more? It
seems something more, for it points to the fact that when concepts
of various sorts are once constructed, new relations are then found
between them, connecting them in peculiarly intimate, 'rational,'
and unchangeable ways. In another book[13] I have tried to show
that these rational relations are all products of our faculty of comparison and of our sense of 'more.' The sciences which exhibit
these relations are the so-called *a priori* sciences of mathematic and

[13] *Principles of Psychology,* 1890, chap. xxviii.

logic.[14] But these sciences express relations of comparison and identification exclusively. Geometry and algebra, for example, first define certain conceptual objects, and then establish equations between them, substituting equals for equals. Logic has been defined
as 'the substitution of similars'; and in general one may say that the
perception of likeness and unlikeness generates the whole of 'rational' or 'necessary' truth. Nothing *happens* in the worlds of logic,
mathematics or moral and aesthetic preference. The static nature
of the relations in these worlds is what gives to the propositions
that express them their 'eternal' character: The binomial theorem,
e.g., expresses the value of any power of any sum of two terms, to
the end of time.

These vast unmoving systems of universals form the new worlds
of thought of which I spoke upon page 33. The terms are elements (or are framed of elements) abstracted from the perceptual
flux; but in their abstract shape we note relations between them
(and again between these relations) which enable us to set up various schemes of fixed serial orders or of 'more and more.' The terms
are indeed man-made, but the order, being established solely by
comparison, is fixed by the nature of the terms on the one hand,
and by our power of perceiving relations on the other. Thus two
abstract twos are always the same as an abstract four; what contains
the container contains the contained, of whatever material either
be made; equals added to equals always give equal results, in the
world in which abstract equality is the only property the terms are
supposed to possess; the more than the more is more than the less,
no matter in what direction of more-ness we advance; if you dot off
a term in one series every time you dot off one in another, the two
series will either never end, or will come to an end together, or
one will be exhausted first; etc., etc.; the result being those skeletons of 'rational' or 'necessary' truth in which our logic- and mathe-
matic-books (sometimes our philosophy-books) arrange their universal terms.

What explanation means in physics.

The 'rationalization' of any mass of perceptual fact consists in
first assimilating its concrete terms, one by one, to so many terms

[14] The 'necessary' character of the abstract truths which these sciences exhibit is
well explained by G. H. Lewes: *Problems of Life and Mind*, Problem I, chaps. iv, xiii,
especially p. 405 f. of the english edition (1874).

of the conceptual series, and then in assuming that the relations intuitively found among the latter are what connect the former too. Thus we rationalize gas-pressure by identifying it with the blows of hypothetic molecules; then we see that the more closely the molecules are crowded the more frequent the blows upon the containing walls will become; then we discern the exact proportionality of the crowding with the number of blows; so that finally Mariotte's empirical law gets rationally explained. All our transformations of the sense-order into a more rational equivalent are similar to this one. We interrogate the beautiful apparition, as Emerson calls it, which our senses ceaselessly raise upon our path, and the items there refer us to their interpretants in the shape of concepts in some static arrangement which our mind has already made out of its concepts alone. The interpretants are then substituted for the sensations, which thus get rationally conceived. To 'explain' means to co-ordinate, one to one, the *thises* of the perceptual flow with the *whats* of the ideal manifold, whichever it be.[15]

We may well call this a theoretic conquest over the order in which nature originally comes. The conceptual order into which we translate our experience seems not only a means of practical adaptation, but the revelation of a deeper level of reality in things. Being more constant, it is *truer*, less illusory, than the perceptual order, and ought to command our attention more.

Concepts bring new values.

There is still another reason why conception appears as an exalted function. Concepts not only guide us over the map of life, but we *revalue* life by their use. Their relation to percepts is like that of sight to touch. Sight indeed helps us by preparing us for contacts while they are yet far off, but it endows us in addition with a new world of optical splendor interesting enough all by itself to occupy a busy life. Just so do concepts bring their proper splendor. The mere possession of such vast and simple pictures is an inspiring good: they arouse new feelings of sublimity, power, and admiration, new interests and motivations.

Ideality often clings to things only when they are taken thus abstractly. 'Causes,' as anti-slavery, democracy, etc., dwindle when realized in their sordid particulars. Abstractions will touch us when we are callous to the concrete instances in which they lie embodied.

[15] Compare W. Ostwald: *Vorlesungen über Naturphilosophie*, Sechste Vorlesung.

Loyal in our measure to particular ideals, we soon set up abstract Loyalty as something of a superior order to be infinitely loyal to; and Truth at large becomes a 'momentous issue,' compared with which truths in detail are poor scraps, 'mere crumbling successes.'[16] So strongly do objects that come as universal and eternal arouse our sensibilities, so greatly do life's values deepen when we translate percepts into ideas! The translation appears as far more than the original's equivalent.

Concepts thus play three distinct parts in human life:

1. They steer us practically every day, and provide an immense map of relations among the elements of things, which map, tho not now yet on some possible future occasion, may help to steer us practically.

2. They bring new values into our perceptual life, they reanimate our wills, and make our action turn upon new points of emphasis.

3. The map which the mind frames out of them is an object which possesses, when once it has been framed, an independent existence. It suffices all by itself for purposes of study. The 'eternal' truths it contains would have to be acknowledged even were the world of sense annihilated.

We thus see clearly what is gained and what is lost when percepts are translated into concepts. Perception is solely of the here and now; conception is of the like and unlike, of the future, of the past, and of the far away. But this map of what surrounds the present, like all maps, is only a surface; its features are but abstract signs and symbols of things that in themselves are concrete bits of sensible experience. We have but to weigh extent against content, thickness against spread, and we see that for some purposes the one, for other purposes the other, has the higher value. Who can

[16] J. Royce: *The Philosophy of Loyalty*, 1908, particularly lecture seven, section five.—Emerson writes: "Each man sees over his own experience a certain stain of error, whilst that of other men looks fair and ideal. Let any man go back to those delicious relations which make the beauty of his life, which have given him sincerest instruction and nourishment, he will shrink and moan. Alas! I know not why, but infinite compunctions embitter in mature life the remembrances of budding joy, and cover every beloved name. Every thing is beautiful seen from the point of view of the intellect, or as truth. But all is sour, if seen as experience. Details are melancholy; the plan is seemly and noble. In the actual world—the painful kingdom of time and place—dwell care, and canker, and fear. With thought, with the ideal, is immortal hilarity, the rose of joy. Round it all the Muses sing. But grief cleaves to names, and persons, and the partial interests of to-day and yesterday." (Essay on 'Love.')

decide off-hand which is absolutely better, to live or to understand life? We must do both alternately, and a man can no more limit himself to either than a pair of scissors can cut with a single one of its blades.

The intellectualist creed.

In spite of this obvious need of holding our percepts fast if our conceptual powers are to mean anything distinct, there has always been a tendency among philosophers to treat conception as the more essential thing in knowledge.[17] The platonizing persuasion has ever been that the intelligible order ought to supersede the senses rather than interpret them. The senses, according to this opinion, are organs of wavering illusion that stand in the way of knowledge in the inalterable sense of the term. They are an unfortunate complication on which philosophers may safely turn their backs.

"Your sensational modalities," writes one of these, "are but darkness, remember that. Mount higher, up to reason, and you will see light. Impose silence on your senses, your imagination, and your passions, and you will then hear the pure voice of interior truth, the clear and evident replies of our common mistress [reason]. Never confound that evidence which results from the comparison of ideas with the vivacity of those feelings which touch and move you. . . . We must follow reason despite the caresses, the threats and the insults of the body to which we are conjoined, despite the action of the objects that surround us. . . . I exhort you to recognize the difference there is between knowing and feeling, between our clear ideas, and our sensations always obscure and confused."[18]

This is the traditional intellectualist creed. When Plato, its originator, first thought of concepts as forming an entirely separate world and treated this as the only object fit for the study of immortal minds, he lit up an entirely new sort of enthusiasm in the human breast. These objects were precious objects, concrete things were dross. Introduced by Dion, who had studied at Athens, to

---

[17] The traditional rationalist view would have it that to understand life, without entering its turmoil, is the absolutely better part. Philosophy's "special work," writes William Wallace, "is to comprehend the world, not try to make it better" (*Prolegomena to the Study of Hegel's Philosophy*, 2nd. ed., Oxford, 1894, p. 29).

[18] Malebranche: *Entretiens sur la métaphysique*, 3me. Entretien, viii, ix.

the corrupt and worldly court of the tyrant of Syracuse, Plato, as Plutarch tells us, "was received with wonderful kindness and respect. . . . The citizens began to entertain marvellous hopes of a speedy reformation, when they observed the modesty which now ruled in the banquets, and the general decorum which prevailed in all the court, their tyrant himself also behaving with gentleness and humanity . . . . There was a general passion for reasoning and philosophy, insomuch that the very palace, it is reported, was filled with dust by the concourse of the students in mathematics who were working their problems there [in the sand]. . . . Some professed to be indignant that the Athenians, who formerly had come to Syracuse with a great fleet and numerous army, and perished miserably without being able to take the city, should now, by means of one sophister, overturn the sovereignty of Dionysius; inveigling him to cashier his guard of 10,000 lances, dismiss a navy of 400 galleys, disband an army of 10,000 horse and many times over that number of foot, and go seek in the schools an unknown and imaginary bliss, and learn by the mathematics how to be happy."

Defects of the conceptual translation.

Having now set forth the merits of the conceptual translation, I must next proceed to show its shortcomings. We extend our view when we insert our percepts into our conceptual map: We learn *about* them, and of some of them we transfigure the value. But the map remains superficial through the abstractness, and false through the discreteness of its terms; and the whole operation, so far from making things appear more rational, becomes the source of quite gratuitous unintelligibilities. Conceptual knowledge is forever inadequate to the fulness of the reality to be known. Reality consists of existential particulars as well as of essences and universals and class-names, and of existential particulars we become aware only in the perceptual flux. The flux can never be superseded, we must carry it with us to the bitter end of our cognitive business, keeping it in the midst of the translation even when the latter proves illuminating, and falling back on it alone when the translation gives out. 'The insuperability of sensation' would be a short expression of my thesis.

To prove it, I must show: 1. That concepts are secondary formations, inadequate, and only ministerial; and 2. That they falsify as well as omit, and make the flux impossible to understand.

45

1. Conception is a secondary process, not indispensable to life. It presupposes perception, which is self-sufficing, as all lower creatures in whom conscious life goes on by reflex adaptations show.

To understand a concept you must know what it *means*. It means always some *this*, or some abstract portion of a *this*, with which we first made acquaintance in the perceptual world, or else some grouping of such abstract portions. All conceptual content is borrowed: to know what the concept 'colour' means you must have *seen* red, or blue, or green. To know what 'resistance' means, you must have made some effort; to know what 'motion' means, you must have had some experience, active or passive, thereof. This applies as much to concepts of the most rarefied order as to qualities like 'bright' and 'loud.' To know what the word 'illation' means one must once have sweated through some particular argument. To know what a 'proportion' means one must have compared ratios in some sensible case. You can create new concepts out of old elements, but the elements must have been perceptually given; and the famous world of universals would disappear like a soap-bubble, if the definite contents of feeling, the *thises* and *thats*, which its terms severally denote, could be at once withdrawn. Whether our concepts live by returning to the perceptual world or not, they live by having come from it. It is the nourishing ground from which their sap is drawn.

2. Conceptual treatment of perceptual reality makes it seem paradoxical and incomprehensible; and when radically and consistently carried out, it leads to the opinion that perceptual experience is not reality at all, but an appearance or illusion.

Why concepts are inadequate.

Briefly, this is a consequence of two facts: First, that when we substitute concepts for percepts, we substitute their relations too. But since the relations of concepts are of static comparison only, it is impossible to substitute them for the dynamic relations with which the perceptual flux is filled. Secondly, the conceptual scheme, consisting as it does of discontinuous terms, can only cover the perceptual flux in spots and incompletely. The one is no full measure of the other, essential features of the flux escaping whenever we put concepts in its place.

This needs considerable explanation, for we have concepts not only of qualities and relations, but of happenings and actions; and it might seem as if these could make the conceptual order active.[19] But this would be a false interpretation. The concepts themselves are fixed, even tho they designate parts that move in the flux; they act not, even tho they designate activities; and when we substitute them and their order, we substitute a scheme the intrinsically stationary nature of which is not altered by the fact that some of its terms symbolize changing originals. The concept of 'change,' for example, is always that fixed concept. If it changed, its original self would have to stay to mark what it had changed from; and even then the change would be a perceived continuous process, of which the translation into concepts could only consist in the judgment that later and earlier parts of it *differed*—such 'differences' being conceived as absolutely static relations.

Origin of intellectualism.

Whenever we conceive a thing we '*define*' it; and if we still don't understand, we define our definition. Thus I define a certain percept by saying 'this is motion,' or 'I am moving'; and then I define motion by calling it the 'being in new positions at new moments of time.' This habit of telling what everything is becomes inveterate. The farther we push it, the more we learn *about* our subject of discourse, and we end by thinking that knowing the latter al-

---

19 Prof. Hibben, in an article in the *Philosophical Review*, vol. xix, pp. 125 ff. (1910), seeks to defend the conceptual order against attacks similar to those in the text, which, he thinks, come from misapprehensions of the true function of logic. "The peculiar function of thought is to represent the continuous," he says, and he proves it by the example of the calculus. I reply that the calculus, in substituting for certain perceptual continuities its peculiar symbols, lets us follow changes point by point, and is thus their *practical*, but not their *sensible* equivalent. It can't *reveal* any change to one who never felt it, but it can lead him to where the change would lead him. It may practically replace the change, but it cannot *reproduce* it. What I am contending for is that the non-reproducible part of reality is an essential part of the content of philosophy, whilst Hibben and the logicists seem to believe that conception, if only adequately attained to, might be all-sufficient. "It is the peculiar duty and privilege of philosophy," Mr. Hibben writes, "to exalt the prerogatives of intellect." He claims that universals are able to deal adequately with particulars, and that concepts do not so exclude each other, as my text has accused them of doing. Of course 'synthetic' concepts abound, with subconcepts included in them, and the *a priori* world is full of them. But they are all designative; and I think that no careful reader of my text will accuse me of identifying 'knowledge' with either perception or conception absolutely or exclusively. Perception gives 'intension,' conception gives 'extension' to our knowledge.

ways consists in getting farther and farther away from the mere perceptual datum. This uncriticized habit, added to the intrinsic charm of the conceptual form, is the source of 'intellectualism' in philosophy.

Inadequacy of intellectualism.

But intellectualism quickly breaks down. When we try to exhaust motion by conceiving it as a summation of parts, *ad infinitum*, we find only insufficiency. Altho, when you have a continuum given, you can make cuts and dots in it *ad libitum*, enumerating the dots and cuts won't give you your continuum back. The rationalist mind admits this; but instead of seeing that the fault is with the concepts, it blames the perceptual flux. This, Kant contends, has no reality in itself, being a mere apparitional birthplace for concepts, to be substituted indefinitely. When these themselves are seen never to attain to a completed sum, reality is sought by such thinkers outside both of the perceptual flow and of the conceptual scheme. Kant lodges it before the flow, in the shape of so-called 'things in themselves';[20] others place it beyond perception, as an 'Absolute' (Bradley), or represent it as a Mind whose ways of thinking transcend ours (Green, the Cairds, Royce). In either case, both our percepts and our concepts are held by such philosophers to falsify reality; but the concepts less than the percepts, for they are static, and by all rationalistic authors the ultimate reality is supposed to be static also, while perceptual life fairly boils over with activity and change.

Examples of the puzzles introduced by the conceptual translation.

If we take a few examples, we can see how great a number of the troubles of philosophy come from assuming that to be understood (or 'known' in the only worthy sense of the word) our flowing life must be cut into discrete bits and pinned upon a fixed relational scheme.

Example 1. *Activity and causation are incomprehensible,* for the conceptual scheme yields nothing like them. Nothing *happens* therein: the concept 'dog' doesn't bite; the concept 'cock' doesn't

[20] We must suppose Noumena, says Kant, "in order to set bounds to the objective validity of sense-knowledge" (*Krit. d. reinen Vernunft*, 2nd ed., p. 310). The old moral need of somehow rebuking 'sinnlichkeit'!

48

crow. Concepts are 'timeless,' and can only be juxtaposed and compared. So Hume and Kant translate the fact of causation into the crude juxtaposition of two phenomena; and later authors, wishing to mitigate the crudeness, resolve the adjacency, whenever they can, into identity: cause and effect must be the same reality in disguise, and our perception of difference in these successions thus becomes an illusion. Lotze elaborately establishes that the 'influencing' of one thing by another is inconceivable. 'Influence' is a concept; and, as such, a distinct third thing, to be identified neither with the agent nor the patient. What becomes of it on its way from the former to the latter? And when it finds the latter, how does it act upon it? By a second influence which it puts forth in turn?—But then again how? etc., etc.—till our whole intuition of activity gets branded as illusory because you can't possibly reproduce its flowing substance by juxtaposing the discrete. Intellectualism draws the dynamic continuity out of nature as you draw the thread out of a string of beads.

Example 2. *Knowledge is impossible*; for knower is one concept, and known is another. Discrete, separated by a chasm, they are mutually 'transcendent' things, so that how an object can ever get into a subject, or a subject ever get at an object, has become the most unanswerable of philosophic riddles. An insincere riddle, too, for the most hardened 'epistemologist' never really doubts that knowledge somehow does come off.

Example 3. *Personal identity is conceptually impossible.* 'Ideas' and 'states of mind' are discrete concepts, and a series of them in time means a plurality of disconnected terms. To such an atomistic plurality the associationists reduce our mental life. Shocked at the discontinuous character of their scheme, the spiritualists assume a 'soul' or 'ego' to melt the separate ideas into one collective consciousness. But this ego itself is but another discrete concept; and the only way not to pile up more puzzles is to endow it with an incomprehensible power of producing that very character of manyness-in-oneness of which rationalists refuse the gift when offered in its immediate perceptual form.

Example 4. *Motion and change are impossible.* Perception changes pulsewise, but the pulses continue each other and melt their bounds. In conceptual translation, however, a continuum can only stand for elements with other elements between them *ad infinitum,* all separately conceived; and such an infinite series can never be exhausted by successive addition. From the time of Zeno the Eleatic this intrinsic contradictoriness of continuous change has been one of the worst skulls at intellectualism's banquet.

Example 5. *Resemblance, in the way in which we naively perceive it, is an illusion.* Resemblance must be *defined;* and when defined it reduces to a mixture of identity with otherness. To know a likeness understandingly we must be able to abstract the identical point distinctly. If we fail of this, we remain in our perceptual limbo of 'confusion.'

Example 6. *Our immediate life is full of the sense of direction, but no concept of the direction of a process is possible until the process is completed.* Defined as it is by a beginning and an ending, a direction can never be prospectively but only retrospectively known. Our perceptual discernment beforehand of the way we are going, and all our dim foretastes of the future, have therefore to be treated as inexplicable or illusory features of experience.

Example 7. *No real thing can be in two relations at once;* the same moon, for example, can't be seen both by you and by me. For the concept 'seen by you' is not the concept 'seen by me'; and if, taking the moon as a grammatical subject and predicating one of these concepts of it, you then predicate the other also, you become guilty of the logical sin of saying that a thing can both be A and be not-A at once. Learned trifling again; for clear tho the conceptual contradictions be, nobody sincerely disbelieves that two men see the same thing.

Example 8. *No relation can be comprehended or held to be real in the form in which we innocently assume it.* A relation is a distinct concept; and when you try to make two other concepts continuous by putting a relation between them, you only increase the discontinuity. You have now conceived three things instead of two, and have two gaps instead of one to bridge over. Continuity is impossible in the conceptual world.

Example 9. *The very relation of subject to predicate in our judgments, the backbone of conceptual thinking itself, is unintelligible and self-contradictory.* Predicates are ready-made universal ideas by which we qualify perceptual singulars or other ideas. Sugar, for example, we say 'is' sweet. But if the sugar was *already* sweet, you have made no step in knowledge; whilst if not so already, you are identifying it with a concept with which, in its universality, the particular sugar cannot be identical. Thus neither the sugar as described, nor your description, is comprehensible.[21]

Relation of philosophers to the 'dialectic' difficulties.

These profundities of inconceivability, and many others like them, arise from the vain attempt to reconvert the manifold into which our conception has resolved things, back into the continuum out of which it came. The concept 'many' is not the concept 'one'; therefore the manyness-in-oneness which perception offers is impossible to construe intellectually. Youthful readers will find such difficulties too whimsical to be taken seriously; but since the days of the greek sophists these dialectic puzzles have lain beneath the surface of all our thinking like the shoals and snags in the Mississippi river; and the more intellectually conscientious the thinkers have been, the less have they allowed themselves to disregard them. But most philosophers have noticed this or that puzzle only, and ignored the others. The pyrrhonian Sceptics first, then Hegel,[22] then in our day Bradley and Bergson, are the only writers I know who have faced them collectively, and proposed a solution applicable to them all.

The Sceptics gave up the whole notion of truth light-heartedly, and advised their pupils not to care about it.[23] Hegel wrote so abominably that I cannot understand him, and will say nothing about him here.[24] Bradley and Bergson write with beautiful clearness and their arguments continue all that I have said.

[21] I have cited in the text only such conceptual puzzles as have become classic in philosophy, but the concepts current in physical science have also developed mutual oppugnancies which (altho not yet classic commonplaces in philosophy) are beginning to make physicists doubt whether such notions develope unconditional 'truth.' Many physicists now think that the concepts of 'matter,' 'mass,' 'atom,' 'ether,' 'inertia,' 'force,' etc. are not so much duplicates of hidden realities in nature as mental instruments to handle nature by after-substitution of their scheme. They are considered 'artefacts,' not revelations, like the kilogram or the imperial yard. The literature here is copious: J. B. Stallo's *Concepts and Theories of Modern Physics* (1882) especially pp. 136–140 is fundamental. Mach, Ostwald, Pearson, Duhem, Milhaud, Le Roy, Wilbois, H. Poincaré, are other critics of a similar sort.

[22] I omit Herbart, perhaps wrongly.

[23] See any history of philosophy, *sub voce* Pyrrho.

[24] Hegel connects immediate perception with ideal truth by a ladder of intermediary concepts—at least I suppose they are concepts. The best opinion among his interpreters seems to be that ideal truth does not abolish immediate perception, but preserves it as an indispensable 'moment.' Compare, e.g., H. W. Dresser: *The Philosophy of the Spirit*, 1908, Supplementary Essay, 'The Element of Irrationality

Bradley on percept and concept.

Mr. Bradley agrees that immediate feeling possesses a native wholeness which conceptual treatment analyzes into a many, but can't unite again. In every 'this' as merely felt, Bradley says, we 'encounter' reality, but we encounter it only as a fragment, see it, as it were, only 'through a hole.'[25] Our sole practicable way of extending and completing this fragment is by using our intellect with its universal ideas. But with ideas, that harmonious compenetration of manyness-in-oneness which feeling originally gave is no longer possible. Concepts indeed extend our *this*, but lose the inner secret of its wholeness; so when ideal 'truth' is substituted for 'reality' the very nature of 'reality' disappears.

The fault being due entirely to the conceptual form in which we have to think things, one might naturally expect that one who recognizes its inferiority to the perceptual form as clearly as Mr. Bradley does, would try to save both forms for philosophy, delimiting their scopes, and showing how, as our experience works, they supplement each other. This is M. Bergson's procedure; but Bradley, tho a traitor to orthodox intellectualism in holding fast to feeling as a revealer of the inner oneness of reality, has yet remained orthodox enough to refuse to admit feeling into 'philosophy' at all. "For worse or for better," he writes, "the man who stands on particular feeling must remain outside of philosophy." The philosopher's business, according to Mr. Bradley, is to qualify the real 'ideally' (i.e. by concepts) and never to look back. The 'ideas' meanwhile yield nothing but a patchwork, and show no unity like that which living perception gave. What shall one do in these perplexing circumstances? Unwilling to go back, Bradley only goes more desperately forward. He makes a flying leap ahead, and assumes, beyond the vanishing point of the whole conceptual perspective, an 'absolute' reality, in which the coherency of feeling and the completeness of the intellectual ideal shall unite in some indescribable way. Such an absolute totality-in-unity *can* be, it *must* be, it *shall* be, it *is*, he says. Upon this incomprehensible metaphysical object the Bradleyan metaphysic establishes its domain.[26]

---

in the Hegelian Dialectic.' In other words Hegel doesn't pull up the ladder after him when he gets to the top, and may therefore be counted as a non-intellectualist, in spite of his desperately intellectualist *tone*.

[25] F. H. Bradley: *The Principles of Logic*, Book I, chap. ii, 29–32.

[26] Mr. Bradley has expressed himself most pregnantly in an article in vol. xviii,

Criticism of Bradley.

The sincerity of Bradley's criticisms has cleared the air of metaphysics and made havoc with old party lines. But, critical as he is, Mr. Bradley preserves one prejudice uncriticized—perception 'untransmuted' must not, cannot, shall not, enter into final 'truth.' Such loyalty to a blank direction in thought, no matter where it leads you, is pathetic: concepts disintegrate—no matter, their way must be pursued; percepts are integral—no matter, they must be left behind. When anti-sensationalism has become an obstinacy like this, one feels that it draws near its end.

Since it is only the conceptual form which forces the dialectic contradictions upon the innocent sensible reality, the remedy would seem to be simple. Use concepts when they help, and drop them when they hinder, understanding; and take reality bodily and integrally up into philosophy in exactly the perceptual shape in which it comes. The aboriginal flow of feeling sins only by a quantitative defect. There is always much-at-once of it, but there is never enough, and we desiderate the rest. The only way to get the rest without wading through all future time in the person of numberless perceivers, is to substitute our various conceptual systems which, monstrous abridgments tho they be, are nevertheless each an equivalent, for some partial purpose, of some partial aspect of the full perceptual reality which we can never grasp.

This, essentially, is Bergson's view of the matter, and with it I think that we should rest content.[27]

Summary.

I will now sum up compendiously the result of what precedes. If the aim of philosophy were the taking full possession of all reality by the mind, then nothing short of the whole of immediate perceptual experience could be the subject-matter of philosophy, for only in such experience is reality intimately and concretely found. But the philosopher, altho he is unable as a finite being to compass more than a few passing moments of such experience, is yet

---

n.s., of *Mind*, p. 489. See also his *Appearance and Reality, passim,* especially the Appendix to the second edition.

[27] Bergson's most compendious statement of his doctrine is the 'Introduction à la métaphysique,' in the *Revue de métaphysique et de morale,* 1903, p. 1.—For a brief comparison between him and Bradley, see an essay by W. James, in the *Journal of Philosophy,* vol. vii, no. 2 [See *Essays in Philosophy,* WORKS, pp. 151–156].

able to extend his knowledge beyond such moments by ideal symbols of the other moments.[28] He thus commands vicariously innumerable perceptions that are out of range. But the concepts by which he does this, being thin extracts from perception, are always insufficient representatives thereof; and, altho they yield wide information, must never be treated after the rationalistic fashion, as if they gave a deeper quality of truth. The deeper features of reality are found only in perceptual experience. Here alone do we acquaint ourselves with continuity, or the immersion of one thing in another, here alone with self, with substance, with qualities, with activity in its various modes, with time, with cause, with change, with novelty, with tendency, with freedom. Against all such features of reality the method of conceptual translation, when candidly and critically followed out, can only raise its *non possumus*, and brand them as unreal or absurd.

Some corollaries.

I. The first corollary of this conclusion is that *the tendency known in philosophy as empiricism, becomes confirmed.* Empiricism proceeds from parts to wholes, treating the parts as fundamental both in the order of being and in the order of our knowledge.[29] In human experience the parts are percepts, built out into wholes by our conceptual additions. The percepts are singulars that change incessantly and never return exactly as they were before. This brings an element of concrete novelty into our experience. This novelty finds no representation in the conceptual method, for concepts are abstracted from experiences already seen or given, and he who uses them to divine the new can never do so but in ready-made and ancient terms. Whatever actual novelty the future may contain (and the singularity and individuality of each moment makes it novel) escapes conceptual treatment altogether. Properly speaking, con-

---

[28] It would seem that in 'mystical' ways, he may extend his vision to even a wider perceptual panorama than that usually open to the scientific mind. I understand Bergson to favor some such idea as this. See W. James: *Journal of Philosophy*, vii, 4 [See *Essays in Philosophy*, WORKS, pp. 157–165]. The subject of mystical knowledge, as yet very imperfectly understood, has been neglected both by philosophers and scientific men.

[29] Naturally this applies in the present place only to the greater whole which philosophy considers, the universe namely, and its parts, for there are plenty of minor wholes (animal and social organisms, for example) in which both the being of the parts and our understanding of the parts are founded.

cepts are post-mortem preparations, sufficient only for retrospective understanding; and when we use them to define the universe prospectively we ought to realize that they can give only a bare abstract outline or approximate sketch, in the filling out of which perception must be invoked.

Rationalistic philosophy has always aspired to a rounded-in view of the whole of things, a closed system of kinds, from which the notion of any essential novelty being possible, is ruled-out in advance. For empiricism, on the other hand, reality cannot be thus confined by a conceptual ring-fence. It overflows, exceeds, and alters; and what novelties it may turn into can be known adequately only by following its singularities from moment to moment as our experience grows. Empiricist philosophy thus renounces the pretension to an all-inclusive vision. It ekes out the narrowness of personal experience by concepts which it finds useful but not sovereign; but it stays inside the flux of life expectantly, recording facts, not fulminating laws, and never pretending that man's relation to the totality of things as a philosopher is essentially different from his relation to the parts of things as a daily patient or agent in the practical current of events. Philosophy, like life, must keep the doors and windows open.

In the remainder of this book we shall hold fast to this empiricist view. We shall insist that, as reality is created temporally day by day, concepts, altho a magnificent sketch-map for showing us our bearings, can never fitly supersede perception, and that the 'eternal' systems which they form should least of all be regarded as realms of being to know which is a kind of knowing that casts the knowledge of particulars altogether into the shade. That rationalist assumption is quite beside the mark. Thus does philosophy prove again that essential identity with science which we argued for in our first chapter.[30]

II. The conceptual systems are distinct realms of reality. The last paragraph does not mean that concepts and the relations between them are not just as 'real' in their eternal way as percepts

---

[30] One way of stating the empiricist contention is to say that the 'alogical' enters into philosophy on an equal footing with the 'logical.' Mr. Belfort Bax, in his book *The Roots of Reality* (1907), formulates his empiricism (such as it is) in this way. (See particularly chap. iii.) Compare also E. D. Fawcett: *The Individual and Reality*, *passim*, but especially Part ii, chaps. iv and v.

are in their temporal way. What is it to be 'real'? The best definition I know is that which the pragmatist rule gives: 'anything is real of which we find ourselves obliged to take account in any way.'[31] Concepts are thus as real as percepts, for we cannot live a moment without taking account of them. But the 'eternal' kind of being which they enjoy is inferior to the temporal kind, because it is so static and schematic and lacks so many characters which temporal reality possesses. Philosophy must thus recognize many realms of reality which mutually interpenetrate. The conceptual systems of our mathematics, logic, aesthetics, ethics, are such realms, each strung upon some peculiar form of relation, and each differing from perceptual reality in that in no one of them is history or happening displayed. Perceptual reality involves and contains all these ideal systems, and vastly more besides.

III. The self-sameness of ideal objects. A concept, it was said above, means always the same thing: Change means always change, white always white, a circle always a circle. On this self-sameness of conceptual objects the static and eternal character of our systems of ideal truth is based; for a relation, once perceived to obtain, must obtain always, between terms that do not alter. But many persons find difficulty in admitting that a concept used in different contexts *can* be intrinsically the same. When we call both snow and paper 'white' it is supposed by these thinkers that there must be two predicates in the field. As James Mill says:[32] "Every colour is an individual colour, every size is an individual size, every shape is an individual shape. But things have no individual colour in common, no individual shape in common, no individual size in common; that is to say, they have neither shape, colour, nor size in common. What, then, is it which they have in common, which the mind can take into view? Those who affirmed that it was something, could by no means tell. They substituted words for things; using vague and mystical phrases, which, when examined, meant nothing." The truth, according to this nominalist author, is that the only thing that can be possessed in common by two objects is the same *name*. Black in the coat and black in the shoe are the

---

[31] Prof. A. E. Taylor gives this pragmatist definition in his *Elements of Metaphysics* (1903), p. 51. On the nature of 'logical' reality, cf. B. Russell: *Principles of Mathematics.*

[32] *Analysis of the Human Mind* (1869), vol. i, p. 249.

same only in so far forth as both shoe and coat are *called* black—the fact that on this view the *name* can never twice be the 'same' being quite overlooked. What now does the concept 'same' signify? Applying, as usual, the pragmatic rule, we find that when we call two objects the same we mean either *a*) that no difference can be found between them when compared, or *b*) that we can substitute the one for the other in certain operations without changing the result. If we are to discuss sameness profitably we must bear these pragmatic meanings in mind.

Do then the snow and the paper show no difference in colour? And can we use them indifferently in operations? They may certainly replace each other for reflecting light, or be used indifferently as backgrounds to set off anything dark, or serve as equally good samples of what the word 'white' signifies. But the snow may be dirty and the paper pinkish or yellowish without ceasing to be called 'white'; or both snow and paper in one light may differ from their own selves in another, and still be 'white,'—so the no-difference criterion seems to be at fault. This physical difficulty (which all house painters know) of matching two tints so exactly as to show no difference seems to be the sort of fact that nominalists have in mind when they say that our ideal meanings are never twice the same. Must we therefore admit that such a concept as 'white' can never keep exactly the same meaning?

It would be absurd to say so, for we know that under all the modifications wrought by changing light, dirt, impurity in pigment, etc., there is an element of colour-quality, different from other colour-qualities, which we mean that our word *shall* inalterably signify. The impossibility of isolating and fixing this quality physically is irrelevant, so long as we can isolate and fix it mentally, and decide that whenever we say 'white,' that identical quality, whether applied rightly or wrongly, is what we shall be held to *mean*. Our *meanings* can be the same as often as we intend to have them so, quite irrespective of whether what is meant be a physical possibility or not. Half the ideas we make use of are of impossible or problematic things—zeros, infinites, fourth dimensions, limits of ideal perfection, forces, relations sundered from their terms, or terms defined only conceptually, by their relations to other terms which may be equally fictitious. 'White' means a colour-quality which the mind creates (following no matter what cue) and which it can decree to be there under all physical disguises. *That* white is always the same white. What sense can there be in insisting that altho we ourselves have fixed it as the same, it cannot *be* the same twice over? It works perfectly for us on the supposition that it is there self-identically; so the nominalist doctrine is false of things of that conceptual sort, and true only of things in the perceptual flux.

What I am affirming here is the platonic doctrine that concepts are singulars, that concept-stuff is inalterable, and that physical realities are constituted by the various concept-stuffs of which they 'partake.' It is known as 'logical realism' in the history of philosophy; and has usually been more favored by rationalistic than by empiricist minds. For rationalism, concept-stuff is primordial and perceptual things are secondary in nature. The present book, which treats concrete percepts as primordial and concepts as of secondary origin, may be regarded as somewhat excentric in its attempt to combine logical realism with an otherwise empiricist mode of thought.[33]

IV. Concepts and percepts are consubstantial. I mean by this that they are made of the same kind of stuff, and melt into each other when we handle them together. How could it be otherwise when the concepts are like evaporations out of the bosom of perception, into which they condense again whenever practical service summons them? No one can tell, of the thing he now holds in his hand and reads, how much comes in through his eyes and fingers, and how much, from his apperceiving intellect, unites with that and makes of it this particular 'book.' The universal and the particular parts of the experience are literally immersed in each other, and both are indispensable. Conception is not like a painted hook, on which no real chain can be hung; for we hang concepts upon percepts, and percepts upon concepts interchangeably and indefinitely; and the relation of the two is much more like what we find in those cylindrical 'panoramas' in which a painted background continues a real foreground so cunningly that one fails to detect the joint. The world we practically live in is one in which it is impossible (except by theoretic retrospection) to disentangle the

---

[33] For additional remarks in favor of the sameness of conceptual objects, see W. James in *Mind*, vol. iv, 1879, pp. 331–335 [See *Essays in Philosophy*, WORKS, pp. 49–51]; F. H. Bradley: *Ethical Studies* (1876), pp. 151–154, and *Principles of Logic* (1883), pp. 260 ff., 282 ff.—The nominalistic view is presented by James Mill, as above, and by John Stuart Mill in his *System of Logic*, 8th ed. (1872), vol. i, p. 77.

contributions of intellect from those of sense. They are wrapt and rolled together as a gunshot in the mountains is wrapt and rolled in fold on fold of echo and reverberative clamor. Even so do intellectual reverberations enlarge and prolong the perceptual experience which they envelope, associating it with remoter parts of existence. And the ideas of these in turn work like those resonators that pick out partial tones in complex sounds. They help us to decompose our percept into parts and to abstract and isolate its elements.

The two mental functions thus play into each other's hands. Perception awakens thought, and thought in turn enriches perception. The more we see, the more we think; while the more we think, the more we see in our immediate experiences, and the greater grows the detail, and the more significant the articulateness of our perception.[34]

Later, when we come to treat of causal activity, we shall see how practically momentous is this enlargement of the span of our knowledge through the wrapping of our percepts in ideas. It is the whole coil and compound of both by which effects are determined, and they may then be different effects from those to which the perceptual nucleus would by itself give rise. But the point is a difficult one, and at the present stage of our argument this brief mention of it must suffice.

V. An objection replied to. Readers who by this time agree that, however important our conceptual systems may practically be, they are secondary and ministerial forms of being, will now feel able to return and embrace the flux of their hourly experience with a hearty feeling that, however little of it at a time may be given, what is given is absolutely real. Rationalistic thought, with its exclusive interest in the unchanging and the general, has always derealized the passing pulses of our life. It is no small service on empiricism's part to have exorcised rationalism's veto, and reflectively justified our instinctive feeling about immediate experience.

[34] Compare F. C. S. Schiller: 'Thought and Immediacy,' in the *Journal of Philosophy,* vol. iii, p. 234.—The interpenetration goes so deep that we may even act as if experience consisted of nothing but the different kinds of concept-stuff into which we are enabled to analyze it. Such concept-stuff may often be treated, for purposes of action and even of discussion, as if it were a full equivalent for reality. But it is needless to repeat, after what precedes, that no amount of it can be a *full* equivalent, and that in point of genesis it remains a secondary formation.

"Other world!" says Emerson, "there is no other world,"—than this one, namely, in which our several biographies are founded. "Natur hat weder Kern noch Schale," writes Goethe, "Alles ist sie mit einem Male. Dich prüfe du nur allermeist, Ob du Kern oder Schale seist." The belief in the genuineness of each particular moment in which we sensibly feel the squeeze of this world's life, as we actually do work here, or work is done upon us, is an Eden from which rationalists seek in vain to expel us, now that we have criticized their state of mind.

But they still make one last attempt, and charge us with self-stultification.

'Your own belief in the particular moments,' they insist, 'so far as it is based on reflective argument (and is not a mere omission to doubt, like that of cows and horses) is grounded in abstraction and conception. Only by using concepts have you established percepts in reality. The concepts are the vital things, then, and the percepts are dependent on them for the character of "reality" with which your reasoning has now endowed them. You stand self-contradicted: concepts appear as the sole triumphant instruments of truth, for you have to employ their proper authority, even when seeking to instal perception in authority above them.'

The objection is specious; but it disappears the moment one recollects that in the last resort a concept can only be *designative*; and that the concept 'reality,' which we restore to immediate perception, is no new conceptual creation, but only a kind of practical relation to our Will, *perceptively experienced*,[35] which reasoning had temporarily interfered with, but which, when the reasoning was neutralized by still farther reasoning, reverted to its original seat as if nothing had happened. That concepts can neutralize other concepts is one of their great practical functions. This answers also the charge that it is self-contradictory to use concepts to undermine the credit of conception in general. The best way to show that a knife won't cut is to try to cut with it. Rationalism itself it is that has so fatally undermined conception, by finding that, when worked beyond a certain point, it only piles up dialectic contradictions.[36]

[35] Compare W. James: *Principles of Psychology*, chap. xxi, 'The Perception of Reality.'

[36] Compare farther, as to this objection, a note in W. James: *A Pluralistic Universe*, pp. 339–343 [*ed.*, pp. 122–124].

Chapter V

The One and the Many

The full nature, as distinguished from the full amount, of reality, we now believe to be given only in the perceptual flux. But tho the flux is continuous from next to next, non-adjacent portions of it are separated by parts that intervene, and such separation seems in a variety of cases to work a positive disconnection. The latter part, e.g., may contain no element surviving from the earlier part, may be unlike it, may forget it, may be shut-off from it by physical barriers, or what not. Thus when we use our intellect for cutting up the flux and individualizing its members, we have (provisionally and practically at any rate) to treat an enormous number of these as if they were unrelated, or related only remotely, to one another. We handle them piecemeal or distributively, and look at the entire flux as if it were their sum or collection. This encourages the empiricist notion that the parts are distinct and that the whole is a resultant.

This doctrine rationalism opposes, contending that the whole is fundamental, that the parts derive from it and all belong with one another, that the separations we uncritically accept are illusory, and that the entire universe, instead of being a sum, is the only genuine unit in existence, constituting (in the words often quoted from d'Alembert) 'un seul fait et une grande vérité.'

The alternative here is known as that between pluralism and monism. It is the most pregnant of all the dilemmas of philosophy, altho it is only in our time that it has been articulated distinctly. Does reality exist distributively? or collectively?—in the shape of *eaches, everys, anys, eithers*? or only in the shape of an *all* or *whole*? An identical *content* is compatible with either form obtaining, the latin *omnes* or *cuncti*, or the german *alle* or *sämmtliche*, expressing the alternative familiarly. Pluralism stands for the distributive, monism for the collective form of being.

Please note that pluralism need not be supposed at the outset to stand for any particular kind or amount of disconnection between the many beings which it assumes. It only has the negative significance of contradicting monism's thesis that there is absolutely *no* disconnection. The irreducible *outness* of *any*thing, however infinitesimal, from *any*thing else, in *any* respect, would be enough, if it were solidly established, to ruin the monistic doctrine.

I hope that the reader begins to be pained here by the extreme vagueness of the terms I am using. To say that there is 'no disconnection,' is on the face of it simply silly, for we find practical disconnections without number. My pocket is disconnected with Mr. Morgan's bank-account, and King Edward the VIIth's mind is disconnected with this book. Monism must mean that all such apparent disconnections are bridged over by some deeper absolute union in which it believes, and this union must in some way be more *real* than the practical separations that appear upon the surface.

In point of historical fact monism has generally kept itself vague and mystical as regards the ultimate principle of unity. To be One is more wonderful than to be many, so the principle of things *must* be One, but of that One no exact account is given. Plotinus simply calls it the One. "The One is all things and yet no one of them. . . . For the very reason that none of them was in the One, are all of them derived from it. Furthermore, in order that they may be real existences, the One is not an existence, but the father of existences. And the generation of existence is as it were the first act of generation. Being perfect by reason of neither seeking nor possessing nor needing anything, the One overflows as it were, and what overflows forms another hypostasis. . . . How should the most perfect and primal good stay shut up in itself as if it were envious or impotent? . . . Necessarily, then, something comes from it."[1] This is like the

---

[1] Compare the passages in C. M. Bakewell's *Source Book in Ancient Philosophy,*

hindoo doctrine of the *Brahman,* or of the *Âtman.* In the *Bhagavad-gita* the holy Krishna, speaking for the One, says: "I am the immolation. I am the whole sacrificial rite. I am the libation offered to ancestors. I am the drug. I am the incantation. I am the sacrificial butter also. I am the fire. I am the incense. I am the father, the mother, the sustainer, the grandfather of this universe,—the mystic doctrine, the purification, the syllable 'Om!'. . . the path, the supporter, the master, the witness, the habitation, the refuge, the friend, the origin, the dissolution, the place, the receptacle, the inexhaustible seed. I heat (the world). I withhold and pour out the rain. I am ambrosia and death, the existing and the non-existing. . . . I am the same to all beings. I have neither foe nor friend. . . . Place thy heart on me, worshiping me, sacrificing to me, saluting me."[2]

I call this sort of monism mystical, for it not only revels in formulas that defy understanding,[3] but it often accredits itself by appealing to states of illumination not vouchsafed to common men. Thus Porphyry, in his life of Plotinus, after saying that he himself once had such an insight, when 68 years old, adds that whilst he lived with Plotinus, the latter four times had the happiness of approaching the supreme God and consciously uniting with him in a real and ineffable act. The regular mystical way of attaining the vision of the One is by ascetic training, fundamentally the same in all religious systems. But this ineffable kind of Oneness is not strictly philosophical, for philosophy is essentially talkative and explicit, so I must pass it by.

The usual philosophic way of reaching deeper oneness has been by the conception of *substance.* First used by the Greeks, this notion

---

pp. 363–370, or the first four books of the 5th Ennead generally, in M. N. Bouillier's translation.

[2] J. C. Thomson's translation, chap. ix.

[3] Al-Ghazzali, the Mohammedan philosopher and mystic, gives a more theistic version of essentially the same idea: "Allah is the guider aright and the leader astray; he does what he wills, and decides what he wishes; there is no opposer of his decision and no repeller of his decree. He created the Garden, and created for it a people, then used them in obedience, and he created the Fire and created for it a people, then used them in rebellion. . . . Then he said, as has been handed down from the Prophet, 'These are in the Garden and I care not; and these are in the Fire and I care not.' So he is Allah Most High, the King, the Reality; 'He is not asked concerning what he does; but they are asked.'" (D. B. Macdonald's translation, in *Hartford Seminary Record,* January 1910.)—Compare for other quotations, W. James: *The Varieties of Religious Experience,* pp. 415–422.

was elaborated with great care during the middle ages. Defined as any being that exists *per se*, so that it needs no further subject in which to inhere (*Ens ita per se existens, ut non indigeat alio tamquam subjecto, cui inhaereat, ad existendum*) a 'substance' was first distinguished from all 'accidents' (which do require such a subject of inhesion—*cujus esse est inesse*). It was then identified with the 'principle of individuality' in things, and with their 'essence,' and divided into various types, for example into first and second, simple and compound, complete and incomplete, specific and individual, material and spiritual substances. God on this view is a substance, for he exists *per se*, as well as *a se*; but of secondary beings, he is the creator, not the substance, for once created, they also exist *per se* tho not *a se*. Thus, for scholasticism, the notion of substance is only a partial unifier, and in its totality the universe forms a pluralism from the substance-point-of-view.[4]

Spinosa broke away from the scholastic doctrine. He began his *Ethics* by demonstrating that only one substance is possible, and that that substance can only be the infinite and necessary God.[5]

---

[4] Consult the word 'substance' in the index of any scholastic manual such as J. Rickaby: *General Metaphysics*, A. Stöckl: *Lehrbuch d. Phil.*, or P. M. Liberatore: *Compendium Logicae et Metaphysicae.*

[5] Spinosa has expressed his doctrine briefly in the Appendix to Part I of his *Ethics*: "I have now explained," he says, "the nature of God, and his properties; such as that he exists necessarily; that he is unique; that what he is and does flows from the sole necessity of his nature; that he is the free cause of all things whatever; that all things are in God and depend on him in such wise that they can neither be nor be conceived without him; and finally, that all things have been predetermined by God, not indeed by the freedom of his will, or according to his good pleasure, but in virtue of his absolute nature or his infinite potentiality."—Spinosa goes on to refute the vulgar notion of *final causes*. God pursues no ends—if he did he would lack something. He acts out of the logical necessity of the fulness of his nature.—I find another good monistic statement in a book of the spinosistic type:—"The existence of every compound object in manifestation does not lie in the object itself, but lies in the universal existence which is an absolute unit, containing in itself all that is manifested. All the particularized beings, therefore, . . . are incessantly changing one into the other, coming and going, forming and dissolving through the one universal cause of the *potential universe*, which is the absolute unity of universal existence, depending on the one general law, the one mathematical bond, which is the absolute being, and it changes not in all eternity. Thus, . . . it is the universe as a whole, *in its potential being*, from which the physical universe is individualized; and its being is a mathematical inference from a mathematical or an intellectual universe which was and ever is previously formed by an intellect standing and existing by itself. This mathematical or intellectual universe I call Absolute Intellectuality, the God of the Universe." (Solomon J. Silberstein: *The Disclosures of the Universal Mysteries*, New York, 1896, pp. 12–13.)

This heresy brought reprobation on Spinosa, but it has been favored by philosophers and poets ever since. The pantheistic spinosistic unity was too sublime a prospect not to captivate the mind. It was not till Locke, Berkeley and Hume began to put in their 'critical' work that the suspicion began to gain currency that the notion of substance might be only a word masquerading in the shape of an idea.[6]

Locke believed in substances, yet confessed that "we have no such clear idea at all . . . but only an uncertain *supposition of we know not what* . . . which we take to be the substratum, or support, of those ideas we do know."[7] He criticized the notion of personal substances as the principles of self-sameness in our different minds. *Experientially*, our personal identity consists, he said, in nothing more than the functional and perceptible fact that our later states of mind continue and remember our earlier ones.[8] Berkeley applied the same sort of criticism to the notion of bodily substance. When I consider, he says, the two parts ('*being*,' in general, and '*supporting accidents*') "which make the signification of the words *material substance*, I am convinced there is no distinct meaning annexed to them. . . . Suppose an intelligence without the help of external bodies, to be affected with the same train of sensations or ideas that you are, imprinted in the same order and with like vividness in his mind. I ask whether that intelligence hath not all the reason to believe the existence of corporeal substances, represented by his ideas, and exciting them in his mind, that you can possibly have for believing the same thing?"[9] Certain *grouped sensations*, in short, are all that corporeal substances are *known-as*, therefore the only meaning which the word 'matter' can claim is that it denotes such sensations and their groupings. They are the only verifiable aspect of the word.

[6] No one believes that such words as 'winter,' 'army,' 'house,' denote substances. They designate collective facts, of which the parts are held together by means that can be experientially traced. Even when we can't define what groups the effects together, as in 'poison,' 'sickness,' 'strength,' we don't assume a substance, but are willing that the word should designate some phenomenal agency yet to be found out. Nominalists treat all substances after this analogy, and consider 'matter,' 'gold,' 'soul' as but the names of so many grouped properties, of which the bond of union must be, not some unknowable substance corresponding to the name, but rather some hidden portion of the whole phenomenal fact.

[7] *Essay Concerning Human Understanding*, Book I, chap. iv, § 18.

[8] *Ibid.*, Book II, chap. xxvii, §§ 9–27.

[9] *Principles of Human Knowledge*, Part i, §§ 17, 20.

The reader will recognize that in these criticisms our own pragmatic rule is used. What difference in practical experience is it supposed to make that we have each a personal substantial principle? This difference, that we can remember and appropriate our past, calling it 'mine.' What difference that in this book there is a substantial principle? This, that certain optical and tactile sensations cling permanently together in a cluster. The fact that *certain perceptual experiences do seem to belong together* is thus all that the word substance means. Hume carries the criticism to the last degree of clearness:—"We have no idea of substance," he says, "distinct from that of a collection of particular qualities, nor have we any other meaning when we either talk or reason concerning it. The idea of a substance ... is nothing but a collection of simple ideas, that are united by the imagination, and have a particular name assigned them, by which we are able to recal that collection."[10] Kant's treatment of substance agrees with Hume's in denying all positive content to the notion. It differs in insisting that, by attaching shifting percepts to the permanent name, the category of substance unites them *necessarily* together, and thus makes nature intelligible. It is impossible to assent to this. The grouping of qualities becomes no more intelligible when you call substance a 'category' than when you call it a bare word.[11]

Let us now turn our backs upon ineffable or unintelligible ways of accounting for the world's oneness, and inquire whether, instead of being a *principle*, the 'oneness' affirmed may not merely be a name like 'substance,' descriptive of the fact that certain *specific and verifiable connexions* are found among the parts of the experiential flux. This brings us back to our pragmatic rule: Suppose there is a oneness in things, what may it be known-as? What differences to you and me will it make?

Our question thus turns upside down, and sets us on a much more promising inquiry. We can easily conceive of things that shall have no connexion whatever with each other. We may assume them to inhabit different times and spaces, as the dreams of

---

[10] *Treatise of Human Nature*, Part i, § 6.

[11] *Critique of Pure Reason*: First Analogy of Experience. For further criticism of the Substance-concept see J. S. Mill: *A System of Logic*, Book I, chap. iii, §§ 6–9; B. P. Bowne: *Metaphysics*, Part i, chap. i. Bowne uses the words *being* and *substance* as synonymous.

different persons do even now. They may be so unlike and incommensurable, and so inert towards one another, as never to jostle or interfere. Even now there may actually be whole universes so disparate from ours that we who know ours have no means of perceiving that they exist. We *conceive* their diversity, however; and by that fact the whole lot of them form what is known in logic as one 'universe of discourse.' To form a universe of discourse argues, as this example shows, no further kind of connexion. The importance attached by certain monistic writers to the fact that any chaos may become a 'universe' by being merely named, is to me incomprehensible. We must seek something better in the way of oneness than this abstract susceptibility of being mentally considered together and named by a collective noun.

What connexions may be perceived, concretely or in point of fact, among the parts of the collection abstractly designated as our 'world'?

There are innumerable modes of union among its parts, some obtaining on a larger, some on a smaller scale. Not all the parts of our world are united *mechanically*, for some can move without the others moving. They all seem united by *gravitation*, however, so far as they are material things. Some again of these are united *chemically*, while others are not; and the like is true of thermic, optical, electrical and other *physical* connexions. These connexions are specifications of what we *mean by the word oneness* when we apply it to our world. We should not call it one unless its parts were connected in these and other ways. But then it is clear that by the same logic we ought to call it 'many,' so far as its parts are *dis*connected in these same ways, chemically inert towards one another, or non-conductors to electricity, light and heat. In all these modes of union, some parts of the world prove to be conjoined with other parts, so that if you choose your line of influence and your items rightly, you may travel from pole to pole without an interruption. If, however, you choose them wrongly, you meet with obstacles and non-conductors from the outset, and cannot travel at all. There is thus neither absolute oneness nor absolute manyness from the physical point of view, but a mixture of well-definable modes of both. Moreover, neither the oneness nor the manyness seems the more essential attribute, they are co-ordinate features of the natural world.

There are plenty of other practical differences meant by calling a thing One. Our world, being strung along in time and space, has *temporal and spatial unity*. But time and space relate things by *determinately sundering* them, so it is hard to say whether the world ought more to be called 'one' or 'many' in this spatial or temporal regard.

The like is true of the *generic oneness* which comes from so many of the world's parts being similar. When two things are similar you can make inferences from the one which will hold good of the other, so that this kind of union among things, so far as it obtains, is inexpressibly precious from the logical point of view. But an infinite heterogeneity among things exists alongside of whatever likeness of kind we discover; and our world appears no more distinctly or essentially as a One than as a Many, from this generic point of view.

We have touched on the *noetic unity* predicable of the world in consequence of our being able to mean the whole of it at once. Widely different from such unification by an abstract designation, would be the concrete noetic union wrought by an all-knower of perceptual type who should be acquainted at one stroke with every part of what exists. In such an absolute all-knower post-kantian idealists believe. Kant, they say, virtually replaced the notion of Substance by the more intelligible notion of Subject. The 'I am conscious of it' which on some witness's part must accompany every possible experience, means in the last resort, we are told, one individual witness of the total frame of things, world without end, amen. You may call his undivided act of omniscience instantaneous or eternal, whichever you like, for time is its *object* just as everything else is, and itself is not in time.

We shall find reasons later for treating noetic monism as an unverified hypothesis. Over against it there stands the noetic pluralism which we verify every moment when we seek information from our friends. According to this, everything in the world might be known by somebody, yet not everything by the same knower, or in one single cognitive act—much as all mankind is knit in one network of acquaintance, A knowing B, B knowing C . . . Y knowing Z, and Z possibly knowing A again, without the possibility of anyone knowing everybody at once. This concatenated knowing, going from next to next, is altogether different from the consolidated knowing supposed to be exercised by the absolute mind. It makes a coherent type of universe, yet a universe in which the widest knower that exists may yet remain ignorant of much that is known to others.

There are other systems of concatenation besides the noetic concatenation. We ourselves are constantly adding to the connexions of things, organizing labor-unions, establishing postal, consular, mercantile, railroad, telegraph, colonial, and other systems that bind us and things together in ever wider reticulations. Some of these systems involve others, some do not. You can't have a telephone system without air and copper connexions but you can have air and copper connexions without telephones. You can't have love without acquaintance, but you can have acquaintance without love, etc. The same thing, moreover, can belong to many systems, as when a man is connected with other objects by heat, by gravitation, by love, and by knowledge.

From the point of view of these partial systems, the world hangs together from next to next in a variety of ways, so that when you are off of one thing you can always be on to something else, without ever dropping out of your world. Gravitation is the only positively known sort of connexion among things that reminds us of the consolidated or monistic form of union. If a *mass* should change anywhere, the mutual gravitation of all things would instantaneously alter.

Teleological and aesthetic unions are other forms of systematic union. The world is full of partial purposes, of partial stories. That they all form chapters of one supreme purpose and inclusive story is the monistic conjecture. They *seem*, meanwhile, simply to run alongside of each other—either irrelevantly, or, where they interfere, leading to mutual frustrations—so the appearance of things is invincibly pluralistic from this purposive point of view.

It is a common belief that all particular beings have one origin and source, either in God, or in atoms all equally old. There is no real novelty, it is believed, in the Universe, the new things that appear having either been eternally prefigured in the absolute, or being results of the same *primordia rerum*, atoms or monads, getting into new mixtures. But the question of Being is so obscure anyhow, that whether realities have burst into existence all at once, by a single 'bang,' as it were; or whether they come piecemeal, and have different ages (so that real novelties may be leaking into our universe all the time), may here be left an open question, tho it is undoubtedly intellectually *economical* to suppose that all things are equally old, and that no novelties leak in.

These results are what the Oneness of the Universe is *known-as*. They *are* the oneness, pragmatically considered. A world coherent in any of these ways would be no chaos but a universe of such or such a grade. (The grades might differ, however. The parts, e.g., might have space-relations, but nothing more; or they might also gravitate; or exchange heat; or know, or love one another, etc.)

Such is the *cash-value* of the world's unity, empirically realized. Its total unity is the sum of all the partial unities. It consists of them and follows upon them. Such an idea, however, outrages rationalistic minds, which habitually despise all this practical small-change. Such minds insist on a deeper, more through-and-through union of all things in the absolute, 'each in all and all in each,' as the *prior condition* of these empirically ascertained connexions. But this may be only a case of the usual worship of abstractions, like calling 'bad weather' the cause of to-day's rain, etc., or accounting for a man's features by his 'face,' when really the rain *is* the bad weather, is what you *mean by* 'bad weather,' just as the features are what you mean by the face.

To sum up, the world is 'one' in some respects, and 'many' in others. But the respects must be distinctly specified, if either statement is to be more than the emptiest abstraction. Once we are committed to this soberer view, the question of the One or the Many may well cease to appear important. The amount either of unity or plurality is in short only a matter for observation to ascertain and write down, in statements which will have to be complicated, in spite of every effort to be concise.

The monistic theory.

We might dismiss the subject with these words,[12] were it not for the fact that further consequences follow from the rival hypotheses, and make of the alternative of monism or pluralism what I called it on page 61, the most 'pregnant' of all the dilemmas of metaphysics.

[12] For an amplification of what precedes, the lecture on 'The One and the Many' in W. James: *Pragmatism* (1907), may be referred to.

The One and the Many

To begin with, the attribute 'One' seems for many persons to confer a *value*, an ineffable illustriousness and dignity upon the world, with which the conception of it as an irreducible 'many' is believed to clash.

Secondly, a through-and-through noetic connexion of everything with absolutely everything else is in some quarters held to be indispensable to the world's *rationality*. Only then might we believe that all things really do *belong* together, instead of being connected by the bare conjunctions 'with' or 'and.' The notion that this latter pluralistic arrangement may obtain is deemed 'irrational'; and of course it does make the world partly alogical, or non-rational, from a purely intellectual point of view.

Monism thus holds the oneness to be the more vital and essential element. The entire cosmos must be a consolidated unit, within which each member is determined by the whole to be just *that*, and from which the slightest incipiency of independence anywhere is ruled out. With Spinosa, monism likes to believe that all things follow from the essence of God as necessarily as from the nature of a triangle it follows that the angles are equal to two right angles. The whole is what yields the parts, not the parts the whole. The universe is *tight*, monism claims, not *loose*; and you must take the irreducible whole of it just as it is offered, or have no part or lot in it at all. The only alternative allowed by monistic writers is to confess the world's non-rationality—and no philosopher can permit himself to do that. The form of monism regnant at the present day in philosophic circles is *absolute idealism*. For this way of thinking, the world exists no otherwise than as the object of one infinitely knowing mind. The analogy that suggests the hypothesis here is that of our own finite fields of consciousness, which at every moment envisage a much-at-once composed of parts related variously, and in which both the conjunctions and the disjunctions that appear are there only in so far as we are there as their witnesses, so that they are both 'noetically' and monistically based.

We may well admit the sublimity of this noetic monism and of its vague vision of an underlying connexion among all phenomena without exception.[13] It shows itself also able to confer religious stability and peace, and it invokes the authority of mysticism in its

[13] In its essential features, Spinosa was its first prophet, Fichte and Hegel its middle exponents, and Josiah Royce its best contemporary representative.

favor. Yet, on the other hand, like many another concept unconditionally carried out, it introduces into philosophy puzzles peculiar to itself, as follows:—

1. *It doesn't account for our finite Consciousness.* If nothing exists but as the Absolute Mind knows it, how can anything exist *otherwise than* as that Mind knows it? That Mind knows each thing in one act of knowledge, along with every other thing. Finite minds know things *without* other things, and this ignorance is the source of most of their woes. We are thus not simply objects to an all-knowing Subject: we are subjects on our own account and know *differently* from its knowing.

2. *It creates a problem of Evil.* Evil, for pluralism, presents only the *practical* problem of how to get rid of it. For monism the puzzle is *theoretical*:—how, if Perfection be the source, should there be Imperfection? If the world as known to the Absolute be perfect, why should it be known otherwise, in myriads of inferior finite editions *also*? The perfect edition surely was enough. How do the breakage and dispersion and ignorance get in?

3. *It contradicts the character of reality as perceptually experienced.* Of our world, change seems an essential ingredient. There is history. There are novelties, struggles, losses, gains. But the world of the Absolute is represented as unchanging, eternal, or 'out of time,' and is foreign to our powers either of apprehension or of appreciation. Monism usually treats the sense-world as a *mirage* or illusion.

4. *It is fatalistic.* Possibility, as distinguished from necessity on the one hand and from impossibility on the other, is an essential category of human thinking. For monism, it is a pure illusion; for whatever *is* is necessary, and aught else is impossible, if the world be such a Unit of fact as monists pretend.

Our sense of 'freedom' supposes that some things at least are decided here and now, that the passing moment may contain some novelty, be an original starting-point of events, and not merely transmit a push from elsewhere. We imagine that in some respects at least the future may not be co-implicated with the past, but may be really *addable* to it, and indeed addable in one shape *or* another, so that the next turn in events can at any given moment genuinely be ambiguous, i.e., possibly this, but also possibly that.

Monism rules out this whole conception of possibles, so native to our common sense. The future and the past are linked, she is obliged to say; there can be no genuine novelty anywhere, for to suppose that the universe has a constitution simply additive, with nothing to link things together save what the words 'plus,' 'with' or 'and' stand for, is repugnant to our reason.

Pluralism, on the other hand, taking perceptual experience at its face-value, is free from all these difficulties. It protests against working our ideas in a vacuum made of conceptual abstractions. Some parts of our world, it admits, cannot exist out of their wholes; but others, it says, can. To some extent the world *seems* genuinely additive: it may really be so. We can't *explain* conceptually *how* genuine novelties can come; but if one did come we could experience *that* it came. We do in fact experience perceptual novelties all the while. Our perceptual experience overlaps our conceptual reason: the *that* transcends the *why*. So the common-sense view of life, as something really dramatic, with work done, and things decided here and now, is acceptable to pluralism. 'Free-will' means nothing but real novelty; so pluralism accepts the notion of free-will.

But pluralism, accepting a universe unfinished, with doors and windows open to possibilities uncontrollable in advance, gives us less religious certainty than monism, with its absolutely closed-in world. It is true that monism's religious certainty is not *rationally* based, but is only a faith that "sees the All-Good in the All-Real." In point of fact, however, monism is usually willing to exert this optimistic faith: its world is certain to be saved, yes, is saved already, unconditionally and from eternity, in spite of all the phenomenal appearances of risk.[14] A world working out an uncertain destiny, as the phenomenal world appears to be doing, is an intolerable idea to the rationalistic mind.

Pluralism, on the other hand, is neither optimistic nor pessimistic, but *melioristic* rather. The world, it thinks, *may* be saved, *on condition that its parts shall do their best*. But shipwreck in detail, or even on the whole, is among the open possibilities.

There is thus a practical lack of balance about pluralism, which contrasts with monism's *peace of mind*. The one is a more *moral*, the other a more *religious* view; and different men usually let this sort of consideration determine their belief.[15]

[14] For an eloquent expression of the monistic position, from the religious point of view, read J. Royce: *The World and the Individual*, vol. ii, lectures viii, ix, x.

[15] See, as to this religious difference, the closing Lecture in W. James's *Pragmatism*.

So far I have sought only to show the respective implications of the rival doctrines without dogmatically deciding which is the more true. It is obvious that pluralism has three great advantages:—

1. It is more 'scientific,' in that it insists that when oneness is predicated, it shall mean definitely ascertainable conjunctive forms. With these the disjunctions ascertainable among things are exactly on a par. The two are co-ordinate aspects of reality. To make the conjunctions more vital and primordial than the separations, monism has to abandon verifiable experience and proclaim a unity that is indescribable.

2. It agrees more with the moral and dramatic expressiveness of life.

3. It is not obliged to stand for any particular amount of plurality, for it triumphs over monism if the least morsel of disconnectedness is once found undeniably to exist. 'Ever not *quite*' is all it says to monism; while monism is obliged to prove that what pluralism asserts can in no amount whatever possibly be true—an infinitely harder task.

The advantages of monism, in turn, are its natural affinity with a certain kind of religious faith, and the peculiar emotional value of the conception that the world is a unitary fact.

So far has our use of the pragmatic rule brought us towards understanding this dilemma. The reader will by this time feel for himself the essential practical difference which it involves. The word 'absence' seems to indicate it. The monistic principle implies that nothing that is can in any way whatever be absent from anything else that is. The pluralistic principle, on the other hand, is quite compatible with some things being absent from operations in which other things find themselves singly or collectively engaged. *Which* things are absent, from which other things, and *when*—these of course are questions which a pluralistic philosophy can settle only by an exact study of details. The past, the present, and the future in perception, for example, are absent from one another, while in imagination they are present or absent as the case may be. If the time-content of the world be not one monistic block of being, if some part at least of the future, is added to the past without being virtually one therewith, or implicitly contained therein, then it is absent really as well as phenomenally and may be called an absolute *novelty* in the world's history in so far forth.

Towards this issue, of the reality or unreality of the novelty that appears, the pragmatic difference between monism and pluralism seems to converge. That we ourselves may be authors of genuine novelty is the thesis of the doctrine of free-will. That genuine novelties can occur means that from the point of view of what is already given, what comes may have to be treated as a matter of *chance*. We are led thus to ask the question: In what manner does new being come?—Is it through and through the consequence of older being? Or is it matter of chance so far as older being goes?— which is the same thing as asking: Is it original, in the strict sense of the word?

We connect again here with what was said at the end of Chapter III. We there agreed that being is a datum or gift and has to be begged by the philosopher; but we left the question open as to whether he must beg it all at once or beg it bit by bit or in instalments? The latter is the more consistently empiricist view, and I shall begin to defend it in the chapter that follows.

Chapter VI

The Problem of Novelty

The impotence to explain being which we have attributed to all philosophers is, it will be recollected, a conceptual impotence. It is when thinking abstractly of the whole of being at once, as it confronts us ready-made, that we feel our powerlessness so acutely. Possibly, if we followed the empiricist method, considering the parts rather than the whole, and imagining ourselves inside of them perceptually, the subject might defy us less provokingly. We are thus brought back to the problem with which Chapter III left off. When perceptible amounts of new phenomenal being come to birth, must we hold them to be in all points predetermined and necessary outgrowths of the Being already there, or shall we rather admit the possibility that originality may thus instil itself into reality?

If we take concrete perceptual experience, the question can be answered in only one way. 'The same returns not, save to bring the different.' Time keeps budding into new moments, every one of which presents a content which in its individuality never was before and will never be again. Of no concrete bit of experience was an exact duplicate ever framed. "My youth," writes Delbœuf, "has it not taken flight, carrying away with it love, illusion, poetry, and freedom from care, and leaving with me instead science, austere always, often sad and morose, which sometimes I would willingly forget, which repeats to me hour by hour its graver lessons, or chills me by its threats? Will Time, which untiringly piles deaths on births and births on deaths, ever remake an Aristotle or an Archimedes, a Newton or a Descartes? Can our earth ever cover itself again with those gigantic ferns, those immense equisetaceans, in the midst of which the same antediluvian monsters will crawl and wallow as they did of yore? . . . No, what has been will not, cannot, be again. Time moves on with an unfaltering tread, and never strikes twice an identical hour. The instants of which the existence of the world is composed are all dissimilar, . . . and whatever may be done, something remains that can never be reversed."[1]

The everlasting coming of concrete novelty into being is so obvious that the rationalizing intellect, bent ever on explaining what is by what was, and having no logical principle but identity to explain by, treats the perceptual flux as a phenomenal illusion, resulting from the unceasing re-combination in new forms of mixture, of inalterable elements, coeval with the world. These elements are supposed to be the only real beings; and, for the intellect once grasped by the vision of them, there can be nothing genuinely new under the sun. The world's history, according to molecular science, signifies only the 'redistribution' of the unchanged atoms of the primal firemist, parting and meeting so as to appear to us spectators in the infinitely diversified configurations which we name as processes and things.[2]

---

[1] J. Delbœuf: *Revue philosophique*, vol. ix, p. 138 (1880).—On the infinite variety of reality, compare also W. T. Marvin: *An Introduction to Systematic Philosophy*, N. Y., 1903, pp. 22–30.

[2] The atomistic philosophy, which has proved so potent a scientific instrument of explanation, was first formulated by Democritus who died 370 B.C. His life overlapped that of Aristotle, who took what on the whole may be called a biological view of the world, and for whom 'forms' were as real as elements. The conflict of the two modes of explanation has lasted to our day, for some chemists still defend the Aristotelian tradition which the authority of Descartes had interrupted for so long, and deny our right to say that 'water' is not a simple entity, or that oxygen and hydrogen atoms persist in it unchanged. Compare W. Ostwald: *Die Überwindung des wissenschaftlichen Materialismus* (1895), p. 12: "The atomistic view assumes that when in iron-oxide, for example, all the sensible properties both of iron and of oxygen have vanished, iron and oxygen are nevertheless there but now manifest other properties. We are so used to this assumption that it is hard for us to feel its oddity, nay, even its absurdity. When, however, we reflect that all that we know of a given kind of matter is its properties, we realize that the assertion that the matter is still there, but without any of those properties, is not far removed from nonsense." Compare the same author's *Principles of Inorganic Chemistry*, english translation, 2nd ed. (1904), p. 149 f.—Also P. Duhem: 'La Notion de mixte,' in the *Revue de philosophie*, vol. i, p. 452 ff. (1901).—The whole notion of the eternal fixity of elements is melting away

So far as physical Nature goes few of us experience any temptation to postulate real novelty. The notion of eternal elements and their mixture serves us in so many ways, that we adopt unhesitatingly the theory that primordial being is inalterable in its attributes as well as in its quantity, and that the laws by which we describe its habits are uniform in the strictest mathematical sense. These are the absolute conceptual foundations, we think, spread beneath the surface of perceptual variety. It is when we come to human lives, that our point of view changes. It is hard to imagine that our own subjective experiences are 'really' only molecular arrangements, even tho the molecules be conceived as beings of a psychic kind. A material fact may indeed be different from what we feel it to be, but what sense is there in saying that a feeling, which has no other nature than to be felt, is not *as* it is felt? Psychologically considered, our experiences resist conceptual reduction, and our fields of consciousness, taken simply *as such*, remain just what they appear, even tho facts of a molecular order should prove to be the signals of the appearance. Biography is the concrete form in which all that is is immediately given; the perceptual flux is the authentic stuff of each of our biographies, and yields a perfect effervescence of novelty all the time. New men and women, books, accidents, events, inventions, enterprises, burst unceasingly upon the world. It is vain to resolve these into ancient elements, or to say that they belong to ancient kinds, so long as no one of them in its full individuality ever was here before or will ever come again. Men of science and philosophy, the moment they forget their theoretic abstractions, live in their biographies as much as anyone else, and believe as naively that fact even now is making, and that they themselves, by doing 'original work,' help to determine what the future shall become.

I have already compared the *live* or perceptual order with the conceptual order from this point of view. Conception knows no way of explaining save by deducing the identical from the identical, so if the world is to be conceptually rationalized no novelty can really come. This is one of the traits in that general bankruptcy of conceptualism which I enumerated in Chapter IV—conceptualism can *name* change and growth, but can translate them into no

---

before the new discoveries about radiant matter.—See for radical statements G. Le Bon: *L'Évolution de la matière.*

terms of its own, and is forced to contradict the indestructible sense of life within us by denying that reality grows.

It may seem to the youthful student a rather 'far cry' from this question of the possibility of novelty to the 'problem of the infinite,' but in the history of speculation, the two problems have been connected. Novelty seems to violate continuity; continuity seems to involve 'infinitely' shaded gradation; infinity connects with number; and number with fact in general—for facts have to be numbered. It has thus come to pass that the non-existence of an infinite number has been held to necessitate the finite character of the constitution of fact; and along with this its discontinuous genesis, or, in other words, its coming into being by discrete increments of novelty, however small.

Thus we find the problem of the infinite already lying across our path. It will be better to interrupt at this point our discussion of the more enveloping question of novelty at large, and to get the minor problem out of our way first. I turn then to the problem of the Infinite.

Chapter VII

First Sub-Problem
The Continuum and the Infinite

The problem is as to which is the more rational supposition, that of continuous or that of discontinuous additions to whatever amount or kind of reality already exists.

On the theory of discontinuity, time, change, etc., would grow by finite buds or drops, either nothing coming at all, or certain units of amount bursting into being 'at a stroke.' Every feature of the universe would on this view have a finite numerical constitution. Just as atoms, not half- or quarter-atoms, are the minimum of matter that can be, and every finite amount of matter contains a finite number of atoms, so any amounts of time, space, change, etc., which we might assume would be composed of a finite number of minimal amounts of time, space and change.

Such a discrete composition is what actually obtains in our perceptual experience. We either perceive nothing, or something already there in sensible amount. This fact is what in psychology is known as the law of the 'threshold.' Either your experience is of no content, of no change, or it is of a perceptible amount of content or change. Your acquaintance with reality grows literally by buds or drops of perception. Intellectually and on reflection you can divide these into components, but as immediately given, they come totally or not at all.

If, however, we take time and space as concepts, not as perceptual data, we don't well see how they *can* have this atomistic constitution. For if the drops or atoms are themselves without duration or extension it is inconceivable that by adding any number of them together times or spaces should accrue. If, on the other hand, they are minute durations or extensions, it is impossible to treat them as real minima. Each temporal drop must have a later and an earlier half, each spatial unit a right and a left half, and these halves must themselves have halves, and so on *ad infinitum*, so that with the notion that the constitution of things is continuous and not discrete, that of a divisibility *ad infinitum* is inseparably bound up. This infinite divisibility of some facts, coupled with the infinite expansibility of others (space, time, number) has given rise to one of the most obstinate of philosophy's dialectic problems. Let me take up, in as simple a way as I am able to, the *problem of the Infinite*.

There is a pseudo-problem 'How can the finite know the infinite?' which has troubled some english heads.[1] But one might as well make a problem of 'How can the fat know the lean?' When we come to treat of knowledge, such problems will vanish. The real problem of the infinite began with the famous arguments against motion, of Zeno the Eleatic. The school of Pythagoras was pluralistic. 'Things are numbers,' the master had said, meaning apparently that reality was made of points which one might number.[2] Zeno's arguments were meant to show, not that motion couldn't really take place, but that it couldn't truly be conceived as taking place by the successive occupancy of points. If a flying arrow occupies at each point of time a determinate point of space, its motion becomes nothing but a sum of rests, for it exists not out of any point, and *in* the point it doesn't move. Motion cannot truly occur as thus discretely constituted.

Still better known than the 'arrow' is the 'Achilles' paradox. Suppose Achilles to race with a tortoise, and to move twice as fast as his rival, to whom he gives an inch of head-start. By the time he has completed that inch, or in other words advanced to the tortoise's starting-point, the tortoise is half an inch ahead of him. While Achilles is traversing that half inch, the tortoise is travers-

[1] In H. Calderwood's *Philosophy of the Infinite* one will find the subordinate difficulties discussed, with almost no consciousness shown of the important ones.
[2] I follow here J. Burnet: *Early Greek Philosophers* (the chapter on the Pythagoreans), and Paul Tannery: 'Le Concept scientifique du continu' in the *Revue philosophique*, xx, 385.

ing a quarter of an inch, etc., so that the successive points occupied by the runners simultaneously form a convergent series of distances from the starting-point of Achilles. Measured in inches, these distances would run as follows:—

$$1+\tfrac{1}{2}+\tfrac{1}{4}+\tfrac{1}{8}+\tfrac{1}{16} \cdot \cdot \cdot \cdot +\tfrac{1}{n} \cdot \cdot \cdot \cdot \tfrac{1}{\infty}$$

Zeno now assumes that space must be infinitely divisible. But if so, then the number of points to be occupied cannot all be enumerated in succession, for the series begun above is interminable. Each time that Achilles gets to the tortoise's last point it is but to find that the tortoise has already moved to a further point; and altho the interval between the points quickly grows infinitesimal, it is mathematically impossible that the two racers should reach any one point at the same moment. If Achilles *could* overtake the tortoise, it would be at the end of two inches; and if his speed were two inches a second, it would be at the end of the first second;[3] but the argument shows that he simply cannot overtake the animal. To do so would oblige him to exhaust, by traversing one by one, the whole of them, a series of points which the law of their formation obliges to come never to an end.

Zeno's various arguments were meant to establish the 'Eleatic' doctrine of real being, which was monistic. The *minima sensibilia* of which space, time, motion, and change consist for our perception are not real 'beings,' for they subdivide themselves *ad infinitum*. The nature of real being is to be entire or continuous. Our perception, being of a hopeless 'many,' thus is false.

Our own mathematicians have meanwhile constructed what they regard as an adequate continuum, composed of points or numbers. When I speak again of that I shall have occasion to return to the Achilles-fallacy, so called. At present I will pass without transition to the next great historic attack upon the problem of the infinite, which is the section on the 'Antinomies' in Kant's *Critique of Pure Reason*.

Kant's views need a few points of preparation, as follows:—

1. That real or objective existence must be *determinate* existence may be regarded as an axiom in ontology. We may be dim

---

[3] This shows how shallow is that common 'exposure' of Zeno's 'sophism,' which charges it with trying to prove that to overtake the tortoise, Achilles would require an *infinitely long* time.

as to just how many stars we see in the Pleiades, or doubtful whose count to believe regarding them; but seeing and belief are subjective affections, and the stars by themselves, we are sure, exist in definite number. 'Even the hairs of our head are numbered,' we feel certain, tho no man shall ever count them.[4] Any existent reality, taken in itself, must therefore be *countable*, and to any group of such realities some definite number must be applicable.

2. Kant defines infinity as 'that which can never be completely measured by the successive addition of units'—in other words as that which defies complete enumeration.

3. Kant lays it down as axiomatic that if anything is 'given' as an existent reality, the whole sum of the 'conditions' required to account for it must similarly be given, or have been given. Thus if a cubic yard of space be 'given,' all the 'parts' which are its conditions must equally be given. If a certain date in past time be real, then the previous dates must also have been real. If an effect be given, the whole series of its causes must have been given, etc., etc.

But the 'conditions' in these cases defy enumeration: the parts of space grow less and less, *ad infinitum*, times and causes form series that are infinitely regressive for our counting, and of no such infinite series can a 'whole' be formed. Any such series has a variable value, for the number of its terms is indefinite; whereas the conditions under consideration ought, if the 'whole sum of them' be really given, to exist (by the principle 1 above) in fixed numerical amount.[5]

---

[4] Of the origin in our experience of this singularly solid postulate, I will say nothing here.

[5] The contradiction between the infinity in the *form* of the conditions, and the numerical determinateness implied in the *fact* of them, was ascribed by Kant to the 'antinomic' form of our experience. His solution of the puzzle was by the way of 'idealism,' and is one of the prettiest strokes in his philosophy. Since the conditions can't exist in the shape of a totalized amount, it must be, he says, that they don't exist independently, or *an sich*, but only as 'phenomena,' or *for us*. Indefiniteness of amount is not incompatible with merely phenomenal existence, for *actual* phenomena, whether conditioned or conditioning, are there for us only in finite amount, as given to perception at any moment; and the infinite form of them means only that we can go on perceiving, conceiving or imagining more and more about them, world without end. It doesn't mean that what we go on thus to represent shall have been already there by itself, apart from our acts of representation. 'Experience,' for idealism, thus falls into two parts, a phenomenal given part which is finite, and a conditioning infinite part which is not given, but only possible to experience hereafter. Kant distinguishes this second part, as only *aufgegeben* (or set to us as a task), from the first part as *gegeben* (or already extant).

Such was the form of the puzzle of the infinite, as Kant propounded it. The reader will observe a bad ambiguity in the statement. When he speaks of the 'absolute totality of the synthesis' of the conditions, the words suggest that a completed collection of them must exist or have existed. When we hear that 'the whole sum of them must be given' we interpret it to mean that they must be given *in the form of a whole sum*, whereas all that the logical situation requires is that *no one of them should be lacking*, an entirely different demand, and one that can be gratified as well in an infinitely growing as in a terminated series. The same things can always be taken either collectively or distributively, talked of either as 'all,' or as 'each' or 'any.' Either treatment can be applied equally well to what exists in finite number; and 'all that is there' will be covered both times. But things which appear under the form of endless series can be talked of only distributively, if we wish to leave none out. When we say that 'any,' 'each,' or 'every' one of Kant's conditions must be fulfilled, we are therefore on impeccable ground, even tho the conditions should form a series as endless as that of the whole numbers, to which we are forever able to add one. But if we say that 'all' must be fulfilled, and imagine 'all' to signify a sum harvested and gathered-in, and represented by a number, we not only make a requirement utterly uncalled for by the logic of the situation, but we create puzzles and incomprehensibilities that otherwise would not exist, and that may require, to get rid of them again, hypotheses as violent as Kant's idealism.

In the works of Charles Renouvier, the strongest philosopher of France during the second half of the XIXth Century, the problem of the infinite again played a pivotal part. Starting from the principle of the numerical determinateness of reality (*supra*, page 82) —the 'principe du nombre,' as he called it—and recognizing that the series of numbers 1, 2, 3, 4, . . . etc., leads to no final 'infinith' number, he concluded that such realities as present beings, past events and causes, steps of change and parts of matter, must needs exist in limited amount. This made of him a radical pluralist. Better, he said, admit that being gives itself to us abruptly, that there are first beginnings, absolute numbers, and definite cessations, however intellectually opaque to us they may seem, than try to rationalize all this arbitrariness of fact by working-in explanatory conditions which would involve in every case the self-contradiction of things being paid-in and completed, altho they are infinite in formal composition.

With these principles, Renouvier could believe in absolute novelties, unmediated beginnings, gifts, chance, freedom, and acts of faith. Fact, for him, overlapped; conceptual explanation fell short; reality must in the end be begged piecemeal, not everlastingly deduced from other reality. This, the empiricist, as distinguished from the rationalist view, is the hypothesis set forth at the end of our last chapter. I think that Renouvier made mistakes, and I find his whole philosophic manner and apparatus too scholastic. But he was one of the greatest of philosophic *characters*, and but for the decisive impression made on me in the 'seventies by his masterly advocacy of pluralism, I might never have got free from the monistic superstition under which I had grown up. The present volume, in short, might never have been written. This is why, feeling endlessly thankful as I do, I dedicate this text-book to the great Renouvier's memory.[6]

Kant's and Renouvier's dealings with the infinite are fine examples of the way in which philosophers have always been wont to infer matters of fact from conceptual considerations. Real novelty would be a matter of fact; and so would be the idealistic constitution of experience; but Kant and Renouvier deduce these facts from the purely logical impossibility of an infinite number of conditions getting completed. It seems a very short cut to truth; but if the logic holds firm, it may be a fair cut,[7] and the possibility obliges us to scrutinize the situation with increasing care.

Proceeding so to do, we immediately find that in the class of in-

---

[6] Renouvier's works make a very long list. The fundamental one is the *Essais de critique générale* (1st ed., 1854–1864, in four, 2nd ed., 1875, in six volumes). Of his latest opinions *Le Personnalisme* (1903) gives perhaps the most manageable account; while the last chapter of his *Esquisse d'une classification systématique des doctrines philosophiques* (entitled 'Comment je suis arrivé à cette conclusion') is an autobiographic sketch of his dealings with the problem of the infinite. His *Derniers entretiens*, dictated while dying, at the age of eighty-eight, is a most impressive document, coming as if from a man out of Plutarch.

[7] Let me say now that we shall ourselves conclude that change completed by steps infinite in number is inadmissible. This is hardly *inferring* fact from conceptual considerations, it is only concluding that a certain conceptual hypothesis regarding the fact of change won't work satisfactorily. The field is thus open for any other hypothesis; and the one which we shall adopt is simply that which the face of perceptual experience suggests.

finitely conditioned things, we must distinguish two sub-classes, as follows:—

1. Things conceived as *standing*, like space, past time, existing beings.

2. Things conceived as *growing*, like motion, change, activity.

In the standing class there seems to be no valid objection to admitting both real existence, and a numerical copiousness demanding infinity for its description. If, for instance, we consider the stars, and assume the number of them to be infinite, we need only suppose that to each several term of the endless series 1, 2, 3, 4, . . . *n* . . . , there corresponds one star. The numbers, growing endlessly as you count, would then never exceed the stars standing there to receive them. Each number would find its own star waiting from eternity to be numbered, and this *in infinitum*, some star that ever was, matching each number that shall be used. As there is no 'all' to the numbers, so there need be none to the stars. One cannot well see how the existence of *each* star should oblige the whole *class* 'star' to be of one number rather than of another, or require it to be of any determinate number. What I say here of stars applies to the component parts of space and matter, and to those of past time.[8]

So long as we keep taking such facts piecemeal, and talk of them distributively as 'any' or 'each,' the existence of them in infinite form offers no logical difficulty. But there is a psychological tendency to slip from the distributive to the collective way of talking, and this produces a sort of mental flicker and dazzle out of which the dialectic difficulties emerge. 'If each condition be there,' we say, 'then *all* are there, for there cannot be eaches that do not make an all.' Rightly taken, the phrase 'all are there' means only that 'not one is absent.' But in the mouths of most people, it surreptitiously foists in the wholly irrelevant notion of a bounded total.

There are other similar confusions. How, it may be asked in

[8] Past time may offer difficulty to the student as it has to better men! It has terminated in the present moment, paid itself out and made an 'amount.' But this amount can be counted in both directions; and in both, one may think, it ought to give the same result. If, when counted forward, it came to an end in the present, then when counted backward, it must, we are told, come to a like end in the past. It must have had a beginning, therefore, and its amount must be finite.—The sophism here is gross, and amounts to saying that what has one bound must have two. The 'end' of the forward counting *is* the 'beginning' of the backward counting, and is the only beginning logically implied. The ending of a series in no way prejudices the question whether it were beginningless or not; and this applies as well to tracts of time as to the abstract regression which 'negative' numbers form.

Locke's words, can a 'growing measure' fail to overtake a 'standing bulk'? Any standing existence must some time be overtaken by a growing number-series, must be finished or finited in its numerical determination. But this again foists in the notion of a bound. What is given as 'standing' in the cases under review is not a 'bulk,' but *each* star, atom, past date, or what not; and to call these eaches a 'bulk' is to beg the very point at issue.

But probably the real reason why we object to a standing infinity is the reason that made Hegel speak of it as the 'false' infinite. It is that the vertiginous chase after ever more space, ever more past time, ever more subdivision, seems endlessly *stupid*. What need is there, what use is there, for *so much*? Not that any amount of anything is absolutely too big to *be*; but that some amounts are too big for our imagination to wish to caress them. So we fall back with a feeling of relief on some form or other of the finitist hypothesis.[9]

If now we turn from static to growing forms of being, we find ourselves confronted by much more serious difficulties. Zeno's and Kant's dialectic holds good wherever, *before* an end can be reached, a succession of terms, endless by definition, must needs be totally counted out. This is the case with every process of change, however small; with every event which we conceive as unrolling itself continuously. What is continuous must be divisible *ad infinitum*; and from division to division here you can't proceed by addition (or by what Kant calls the successive synthesis of units) and touch a farther limit. You can indeed define what the limit ought to be, but you can't reach it *by this process*. That Achilles should occupy *in succession* 'all' the points in a single continuous inch of space, is as inadmissible a conception as that he should count the series of whole numbers, 1, 2, 3, 4, etc., to 'infinite,' and reach an end. The terms are not 'enumerable' in that order; and the order it is that makes the whole difficulty. An infinite 'regression' like the rearward perspective of time offers no such contradiction, for it comes not in that order. Its 'end' is what we start with;

[9] The reader will note how emphatically in all this discussion, I am insisting on the distributive or piecemeal point of view. The distributive is identical with the pluralistic, as the collective is with the monistic conception. We shall, I think, perceive more and more clearly as this book proceeds, that *piecemeal existence is independent of complete collectibility*, and that some facts, at any rate, exist only distributively, or in the form of a set of eaches which (even if in finite number) need not in any intelligible sense either experience themselves, or get experienced by anything else, as members of an all.

and each successive 'more' which our imagination has to add, *ad infinitum,* is thought of as already having been paid-in, and not as having yet to be paid before the end can be attained. Starting with our end, we have to wait for nothing. The infinity here is of the 'standing' variety. It is, in the words of Kant's pun, *gegeben*, not *aufgegeben*. In the other case, of a continuous process to be traversed, it is, on the contrary, *aufgegeben*: it is a *task*—not only for our philosophic imagination, but for any real agent who might try physically to compass the entire performance. Such an agent is bound by logic to find always a remainder, something ever yet to be paid, like the balance due on a debt, with even the interest of which we don't catcn up.

Infinitum in actu pertransiri nequit, said scholasticism; and every continuous quantum to be gradually traversed is conceived as such an infinite. The quickest way to avoid the contradiction would seem to be to give up that conception, and to treat real processes of change no longer as being continuous, but as taking place by finite, not infinitesimal steps, like the successive drops by which a cask of water is filled, when whole drops fall into it at once or nothing. This is the radically pluralist, empiricist, or perceptualist position, which I characterized in speaking of Renouvier (above, pages 84–85). We shall have to end by adopting it in principle ourselves, qaalifying it so as to fit it closely to perceptual experience.

Meanwhile we are challenged by a certain school of critics who think that what in mathematics is called 'the new infinite' has quashed the old antinomies, and who treat anyone whom the notion of a completed infinite in any form still bothers as a very *naif* person. *Naif* tho I am in mathematics, I must, notwithstanding the dryness of the subject, add a word in rebuttal of these criticisms, some of which, as repeated by novices, tend decidedly towards mystification.

The 'new infinite' and the 'number-continuum' are outgrowths of a general attempt to accomplish what has been called the 'arithmetization' ($\dot{\alpha}\rho\iota\theta\mu\dot{o}\varsigma$ meaning number) of all quantity. Certain *quanta* (grades of intensity or other difference, amounts of space) have until recently been supposed to be immediate data of perceptive sensibility or 'intuition'; but philosophical mathematicians have now succeeded in getting a conceptual equivalent for them in the shape of collections of numbers created by interpolation between one another indefinitely. We can halve any line in space, and halve its halves, and so on. But between the cuts thus made and numbered, room is left for infinite others created by using 3 as a divisor, for infinite others still made by using 5, 7, etc., until all possible 'rational' divisions of the line shall have been made. Between these it is now shown that interpolation of cuts numbered 'irrationally' is still possible *ad infinitum,* and that with these the line gets at last filled *full,* its continuity now being wholly translated into these numbered cuts, and their number being infinite. "Of the celebrated formula that continuity means 'unity in multiplicity,' the multiplicity alone subsists, the unity disappears,"[10]— as indeed it does in all conceptual translations—and the original sensible intuition of the line's extent gets treated, from the mathematical point of view, as a "mass of unanalyzed prejudice" by Russell, or sneered at by Cantor as "a kind of religious dogma."[11]

So much for the number-continuum. As for the 'new infinite,' that means only a new definition of infinity. If we compare the indefinitely growing number-series, 1, 2, 3, 4, ... n, ... in its entirety, with any component part of it, like 'even' numbers, 'prime' numbers, or 'square' numbers, we are confronted with a paradox. No one of the parts, thus named, of the number-series, is 'equal' to the whole, collectively taken; yet any one of them is 'similar' to the whole, in the sense that you can set up a one-to-one relation between its several elements and each and every element of the whole, so that the part and the whole prove to be of what logicians call the same 'class,' numerically. Thus, in spite of the fact that even numbers, prime numbers, and square numbers are much fewer and rarer than numbers in general, and only form a part of numbers *überhaupt,* they appear to be equally copious for purposes of counting. The terms of each such partial series can be numbered by using the natural integers in succession. There is, for instance, a first prime, a second prime, etc., *ad infinitum;* and, queerer-sounding still, since *every* integer, odd or even, can be doubled, it would seem that the even numbers alone cannot in the nature of things be less multitudinous than that series of both odd and even numbers of which the whole natural series consists.

These paradoxical consequences result, as one sees immediately, from the fact that the infinity of the number-series is of the 'growing' variety (above, page 87). They were long treated as a *reductio*

[10] H. Poincaré: *La Science et l'hypothèse,* p. 30.
[11] B. Russell: *The Principles of Mathematics,* i, 260, 287.

ad absurdum of the notion that such a variable series spells infinity *in act,* or can ever be translated into standing or collective form.[12] But contemporary mathematicians have taken the bull by the horns. Instead of treating such paradoxical properties of indefinitely growing series as *reductiones ad absurdum,* they have turned them into the proper definition of infinite classes of things. Any class is now called infinite if its parts are numerically similar to itself. If its parts are numerically dissimilar, it is finite. This definition now separates the conception of the class of finite from that of infinite objects.

Next, certain concepts called 'transfinite numbers' are now *created by definition.* They are decreed to belong to the infinite class, and yet not to be formed by adding one to one *ad infinitum,* but rather to be postulated outright as coming *after each and all of the numbers formed by such addition.*[13] Cantor gives the name of 'Omega' to the lowest of these possible transfinite numbers. It would, for instance, be the number of the point at which Achilles overtakes the tortoise—if he does overtake him?—by exhausting all the intervening points successively. Or it would be the number of the stars, in case their counting couldn't terminate. Or again it would be the number of miles away at which parallel lines meet—if they do meet. It is in short a 'limit' to the whole class of numbers that grow one by one; and like other limits, it proves a useful conceptual bridge for passing us from one range of facts to another.

The first sort of fact we pass to with its help is the number of the number-continuum or point-continuum described above (page 89) as generated by infinitely repeated subdivision. The making of the subdivisions is an infinitely growing process; but the number

---

[12] The fact that, taken distributively, or paired each to each, the terms in one endlessly growing series should be a match for those in another (or 'similar' to them) is quite compatible with the two series being collectively of vastly unequal amounts. You need only make the steps of difference, or distances, between the terms much longer in one series than in the other, to get numerically similar multitudes, with greatly unequal magnitudes, of content. Moreover, the moment either series should stop growing, the 'similarity' would cease to exist.

[13] The class of 'all numbers that come before the first transfinite' is a definitely limited conception, provided we take the numbers as *eaches* or *anys,* for then any and every one of them will have by definition to come *before* the transfinite number comes—even tho they form no whole, and there be no last one of them, and tho the transfinite have no immediate predecessor. The transfinite is, in a word, not an ordinal conception, at least it does not continue the order of entire numbers.

of subdivisions that can be made has for its limit the transfinite number Omega just imagined and defined. Thus is a growing assimilated to a standing multitude; thus is a number that is variable practically equated (by the process of passing to the limit) with one that is fixed; thus do we circumvent the law of indefinite addition or division, which previously was the only way in which infinity was constructable, and reach a constant infinite at a bound. This infinite number may now be substituted for any continuous finite quantum, however small the latter may perceptually appear to be.

When I spoke of 'mystification,' just now, I had partly in mind the contemptuous way in which some enthusiasts for the 'new infinite' treat those who still cling to the superstition that 'the whole is greater than the part.' Because any point whatever in an imaginary inch is now conceivable as being matched by some point in a quarter-inch or half-inch, this numerical 'similarity' of the different quanta, taken point-wise, is treated as if it signified that half-inches, quarter-inches, and inches are mathematically identical things anyhow, and that their differences are facts which we may scientifically neglect. I may misunderstand the newest expounders of Zeno's famous 'sophism' but what they say seems to me virtually to be equivalent to this.

Mr. Bertrand Russell (whom I don't accuse of mystification, for Heaven knows he tries to make things clear!) treats the Achilles-puzzle as if the difficulty lay only in seeing how the paths traversed by the two runners (measured after the race is run, and assumed then to consist of nothing but points of position coincident with points upon a common scale of time) should have the same time-measure if they be not themselves of the same length. But they are of different lengths; for owing to the tortoise's head-start, the tortoise's path is only a part of the path of Achilles. How then, if time-points are to be the medium of measurement, can the longer path not take the longer time?

The remedy, for Mr. Russell (if I rightly understand him), lies in noting that the points in question are conceived as being infinitely numerous in both paths, and that where infinite multitudes are in question, to say that the whole is greater than the part is false. For each and every point traversed by the tortoise there is one point traversed by Achilles at a corresponding point of time;

and the exact correspondence, point by point, of either one of these three sets of points with both the others, makes of them similar and equally copious sets from the numerical point of view. There is thus no recurrent 'remainder' of the tortoise's head-start with which Achilles can't catch up—which he can reduce indefinitely, but can't annul. The books balance perfectly. The last point in Achilles' path, the last point in the tortoise's, and the last time-instant of the race are terms which mathematically coincide. With this, which seems to me Mr. Russell's way of analyzing the situation, the puzzle is supposed to disappear.[14]

It seems to me, however, that Mr. Russell's statements dodge the real difficulty, which concerns the 'growing' variety of infinity exclusively, and not the 'standing' variety which is all that he envisages when he assumes the race already to have been run, and thinks that the only problem that remains is that of numerically equating the paths. The real difficulty may almost be called physical, for it attends the *process of formation* of the paths. Moreover, *two* paths are not needed—that of either runner alone, or even the lapse of empty time, involves the difficulty, which is that of touching a goal when an interval needing to be traversed first keeps permanently reproducing itself and getting in your way. Of course the same quantum can be produced in various manners. This page which I am now painfully writing, letter after letter, will be *printed* at one single stroke. God, as the orthodox believe, produced the space-continuum, with its infinite parts already standing in it, by an instantaneous *fiat*. Past time now stands in infinite perspective, and may conceivably have been created so, as Kant imagined, for our retrospection only, and all at once. 'Omega' was created by a single decree, a single act of definition in Prof. Cantor's mind. But whoso actually *traverses* a continuum can do so by no instantaneous act. Be it short or long, each point must be occupied in its due order of succession; and if the points are necessarily infinite, their end cannot be reached, for the 'remainder,' in this kind of process, is just what one cannot neglect. 'Enumeration' is in short the sole possible method of occupation of the series of positions implied in the famous race; and when Mr. Russell solves the puzzle by saying,

---

14 Mr. Russell's own statements of the puzzle as well as of the remedy are too technical to be followed verbatim in a book like this. As he finds it necessary to paraphrase the puzzle, so I find it convenient to paraphrase him, sincerely hoping that no injustice has been done.

as he does, that "the definition of whole and part *without enumera-tion* is the key to the whole mystery,"[15] he seems to me deliberately to throw away his case.[16]

After this disagreeable polemic, I conclude that the new infinite need no longer block the way to the empiricist opinion which we reached provisionally on page 88. Irrelevant tho they be to facts the 'conditions' of which are of the 'standing' sort, the criticisms of Leibnitz, Kant, Cauchy, Renouvier, Evellin and others, apply legitimately to all cases of supposedly continuous growth or change. The 'conditions' here have to be fulfilled *seriatim*; and if the series which they form were endless, its limit, if 'successive synthesis' were the only way of reaching it, could simply not be reached. Either we must stomach logical contradiction, therefore, or we must admit that the limit is reached in these successive cases by finite and perceptible units of approach—drops, buds, steps, or whatever we please to term them, of change, coming wholly when

[15] *The Principles of Mathematics*, i, 361.—Mr. Russell gives a *Tristram Shandy* paradox as a counterpart to the Achilles. Since it took T. S. (according to Sterne) two years to write the history of the first two days of his life, common sense would con-clude that at that rate the life never could be written. But Mr. Russell proves the contrary; for, as days and years have no last term, and the nth day may be written in the nth year, any assigned day will be written about, and no part of the life remain unwritten. But Mr. Russell's proof cannot be applied to the real world without the hypothesis of a physically growing infinity which he expresses by saying: *"if T. S. lives for ever, and doesn't weary of his task."* In all real cases of continuous change a simi-larly absurd hypothesis must be made. The agent of the change must 'live for ever,' in the sense of outliving an endless set of points of time, and 'not wearying' of his impossible task.

[16] Being almost blind mathematically and logically, I feel considerable shyness in differing from such superior minds, yet what can one do but follow one's own dim light?—The literature of the new infinite is so technical that it is impossible to cite details of it in a non-mathematical work like this. Students who are interested should consult Baldwin's *Dictionary of Philosophy*, article 'continuity'; the tables of con-tents of B. Russell's *Principles of Mathematics*, of L. Couturat's *Infini mathématique*, or of his *Principes des mathématiques*. A still more rigorous exposition may be found in E. V. Huntington: 'The Continuum as a Type of Order,' in the *Annals of Mathe-matics*, vols. vi and vii (reprint for sale at publication-office, Harvard University). Compare also C. S. Peirce's paper in the *Monist*, ii, 537–546, as well as the presidential address of E. W. Hobson, in the *Proceedings of the London Mathematical Society*, vol. xxxv.—For more popular discussions see J. Royce: *The World and the Individual*, vol. i, Supplementary Essay; Keyser: *Journal of Philosophy*, etc., vol. i, 29, and *Hibbert Journal*, vol. vii, 380–390; S. Waterlow in *Aristotelian Soc. Proceedings*, 1910; J. Leighton: *Philosophical Review*, vol. xiii, 497; and finally the tables of contents of H. Poincaré's three recent little books with the word 'Science' in their titles.—The liveliest short attack which I know upon infinites completed by successive synthesis is that in G. S. Fullerton's *System of Metaphysics*, chap. xi.

they do come, or coming not at all. Such seems to be the nature of concrete experience, which changes always by sensible amounts or stays unchanged. The infinite character we find in it is woven into it by our later conception indefinitely repeating the act of subdividing any given amount supposed. The facts do not resist the subsequent conceptual treatment; but we need not believe that it necessarily reproduces the operation by which they were originally brought into existence.

The antinomy of mathematically continuous growth is thus but one more of those many ways in which our conceptual transformation of perceptual experience makes it less comprehensible than ever. That being should immediately and by finite quantities add itself to being, may indeed be something which an onlooking intellect fails to understand; but that being should be identified with the consummation of an endless chain of units (such as 'points') no one of which contains any amount whatever of the being (such as 'space') expected to result, this is something which our intellect not only fails to understand, but which it finds absurd. The substitution of 'arithmetization' for intuition (p. 88) thus seems, if taken as a description of reality, to be only a partial success. Better accept, as Renouvier says, the opaquely given data of perception than concepts inwardly absurd.[17]

So much for the 'problem of the infinite,' and for the interpretation of continuous change by the new definition of infinity. We

[17] The point-continuum illustrates beautifully my complaint that the intellectualistic method turns the flowing into the static and discrete (above, p. 46). The buds or steps of process which perception accepts as primal gifts of being, correspond logically to the 'infinitesimals' (minutest quanta of motion, change, or what not) of which the latest mathematic is supposed to have got rid. Mr. Russell accordingly finds himself obliged, just like Zeno, to treat motion as an unreality: "Weierstrass," he says, "by strictly banishing all infinitesimals, has at last shown that we live in an unchanging world, and that the arrow, at every moment of its flight, is truly at rest" (*op. cit.*, p. 347). "We must entirely reject the notion of a *state* of motion," he says elsewhere. "Motion consists *merely* in the occupation of different places at different times . . . . There is no transition from place to place, no consecutive moment or consecutive position, no such thing as velocity except in the sense of a real number which is the limit of a certain set of quotients" (p. 473).—The mathematical 'continuum,' so called, becomes thus an absolute *dis*continuum in any physical or experiential sense. Extremes meet; and altho Russell and Zeno agree in denying perceptual motion, for the one a pure unity, for the other a pure multiplicity takes its place.—It is probable that Russell's denial of change, etc., is meant to apply only to the mathematical world. It would be unfair to charge him with writing metaphysics in these passages, altho he gives no warning that this may not be the case.

find that the picture of a reality changing by steps finite in number and discrete remains quite as acceptable to our understanding and as congenial to our imagination as before; so, after this dry and barren chapter, we take up our main topic of inquiry just where we laid it down. Does reality grow by abrupt increments of novelty, or not? The contrast between discontinuity and continuity now confronts us in another form. The mathematical definition of continuous quantity as 'that between any two elements or terms of which there is another term,' is directly opposed to the more empirical or perceptual notion that anything is continuous when its parts appear as immediate next neighbors, with absolutely nothing between. Our business lies hereafter with the perceptual account, but before we settle definitively to its discussion, another classic problem of philosophy 'the problem of causality' had better be got out of the way.

Chapter VIII

Second Sub-Problem
Cause and Effect: The Conceptual View

If reality changes by finite sensible steps, the question whether the bits of it that come are radically new, remains unsettled still. Remember our situation at the end of Chapter III. Being *überhaupt* or at large, we there found to be undeduceable. For our *intellect* it remains a casual and contingent quantum that is simply found or begged. May it be begged bit by bit, as it adds itself? Or must we beg it only once, by assuming it either to be eternal, or to have come in an instant that co-implicated all the rest of time? Did or did not 'the first morning of creation write what the last day of reckoning shall read'? With these questions Monism and Pluralism stand face to face again. The classic obstacle to pluralism has always been what is known as the 'principle of causality.' This principle has been taken to mean that the effect in some way already exists in the cause. If this be so, the effect cannot be absolutely novel, and in no radical sense can pluralism be true.

We must therefore review the facts of causation. I take them in conceptual translation before considering them in perceptual form.

The first definite inquiry into causes was made by Aristotle.[1] The 'why' of anything, he said, is furnished by four principles: the material cause of it (as when brass makes a statue); the formal cause (as when the ratio of two to one makes an octave); the efficient

[1] Book II, chapter iii of his *Physics*, or Book V, chapter ii of his *Metaphysics*, gives what is essential in his views.

cause (as when a father makes a child); and the final cause (as when one 'exercises' for the sake of health). Christian philosophy adopted the four causes; but what one generally means by the cause of anything is its 'efficient' cause, and in what immediately follows I shall speak of that alone.

An efficient cause is scholastically defined as that which *produces something else by a real activity proceeding from itself.* This is unquestionably the view of common sense; and scholasticism is only common sense grown quite articulate. Passing over the many classes of efficient cause which scholastic philosophy specifies, I will enumerate three important sub-principles it supposes to follow from the above definition. Thus:

1. No effect can come into being without a cause. This may be verbally taken; but if, avoiding the word effect, it be taken in the sense that *nothing can happen* without a cause, it is the famous 'principle of causality' which, when combined with the next two principles, is supposed to establish the block-universe, and to render the pluralistic hypothesis absurd.

2. The effect is always proportionate to the cause, and the cause to the effect.

3. Whatever is in the effect must in some way, whether formally, virtually, or eminently, have been also in the cause. ['Formally' here means that the cause resembles the effect, as when one motion causes another motion; virtually means that the cause somehow involves that effect, without resembling it, as when an artist causes a statue but possesses not himself its beauty; 'eminently' means that the cause, tho unlike the effect, is superior to it in perfection, as when a man overcomes a lion's strength by greater cunning.]

Nemo dat quod non habet is the real principle from which the causal philosophy flows; and the proposition *Causa aequat effectum* practically sums the whole of it up.[2] It is plain that each moment of the universe must contain all the causes of which the next moment contains effects, or to put it with extreme concision, it is plain that each moment in its totality causes the next moment.[3]

[2] Read for a concise statement of the School-doctrine of causation the account in J. Rickaby: *General Metaphysics*, Book II, chap. iii. I omit from my text various subordinate maxims which have played a great part in causal philosophy, as 'the cause of a cause is the cause of its effects'; 'the same causes produce the same effects'; 'causes act only when present'; 'a cause must exist before it can act,' etc.

[3] This notion follows also from the consideration of conditioning circumstances being at bottom as indispensable as causes for producing effects. "The cause, phi-

But if the maxim holds firm that *Quidquid est in effectu debet esse prius aliquo modo in causa*, it follows that the next moment can contain nothing genuinely original, and that the novelty that appears to leak into our lives so unremittingly must be an illusion ascribable to the shallowness of the perceptual point of view.

Scholasticism always respected common sense, and in this case escaped the frank denial of all genuine novelty by the vague qualification 'aliquo modo.' This allowed the effect also to *differ, aliquo modo,* from its cause. But conceptual necessities have ruled the situation, and have ended, as usual, by driving nature and perception to the wall. A cause and its effect are two numerically discrete concepts, and yet in some inscrutable way the former must 'produce' the latter. How can it intelligibly do so, save by already hiding the latter in itself? Numerically two, cause and effect must be generically one, in spite of the perceptual appearances; and causation changes thus from a concretely experienced relation between differents into one between similars abstractly thought of as more real.[4] The cause becomes a reason, the effect a consequence; and since logical consequence follows only from the same to the same, the older vaguer causation-philosophy develops into the sharp rationalistic dogma that cause and effect are two names for one persistent being and that if the successive moments of the universe be causally connected, no genuine novelty leaks in.

The overthrow of perception by conception took a long time to complete itself in this field. The first step was the theory of 'occasionalism,' to which Descartes led the way by his doctrine that mental and physical substance, the one consisting purely of thought, the other purely of extension, were absolutely dissimilar. If this were so, any such causal intercourse as we instinctively perceive

---

losophically speaking, is the sum total of the conditions positive and negative," says J. S. Mill (*Logic*, 8th ed., i, 383). This is equivalent to the entire state of the universe at the moment that precedes the effect. But neither is the 'effect' in that case the one fragmentary event which our attention first abstracted under that name. It is that fragment, but along with all its concomitants—or in other words it is the entire state of the universe at the second moment considered.

4 Sir William Hamilton expresses this very compactly: "What is the law of Causality? Simply this,—that when an object is presented phænomenally as commencing, we cannot but suppose that the complement [i.e. the amount] of existence, which it now contains, has previously been;—in other words, that all that we at present know as an effect must previously have existed in its causes; though what these causes are we may perhaps be altogether unable even to surmise." (End of Lecture xxxix of the *Metaphysics*.)

between body and mind ceased to be 'rational.' For thinkers of that age, 'God' was the great solvent of absurdities—he could get over every contradiction. Consequently Descartes' disciples Régis and Cordemoy, and especially Geulincx, denied the fact of psycho-physical interaction altogether. God, according to them, immediately caused the changes in our mind of which events in our body, and those in our body of which events in our mind appear to be the causes, but of which they are in reality only the signals or occasions. Leibnitz took the next step forward in quenching the claim to truth of our perceptions. He freed God from the duty of lending all this hourly assistance, by supposing him to have decreed on the day of creation that the changes in our several minds should coincide with those in our several bodies, after the manner in which clocks, wound up on the same day, thereafter keep time with one another. With this 'pre-established harmony' so called, the conceptual translation of the immediately given, with its never failing result of negating both activity and continuity, is complete. Instead of the dramatic flux of personal life, a bare 'one to one correspondence' between the terms of two causally unconnected series is set up. God is the sole cause of anything, and the cause of everything at once. The theory is as monistic as the rationalist heart can desire, and of course novelty would be impossible if it were true.

David Hume made the next step in discrediting common-sense causation. In the chapters on 'the idea of necessary connexion' both in his *Treatise of Human Nature* and in his *Essays,* he sought for a positive picture of the 'efficacy' of the 'power' which causes are assumed to exert, and failed to find it. He shows that neither in the physical nor in the mental world can we abstract or isolate any 'energy' trans-sent from causes to effects. This is as true of perception as it is of imagination. "All ideas are deriv'd from, and represent impressions. We never have any impression, that contains any power or efficacy. We never therefore have any idea of power." "We never can, by our utmost scrutiny, discover any thing but one event following another; without being able to comprehend any force or power, by which the cause operates, or any connexion between it and its supposed effect. . . . The necessary conclusion *seems* to be, that we have no idea of connexion or power at all, and that these words are absolutely without any meaning, when employed either in philosophical reasonings, or common life." "Nothing is more evident, than that the mind cannot form such an idea of two objects, as to conceive any connexion betwixt them, or comprehend distinctly that power or efficacy, by which they are united."

The pseudo-idea of a connexion, which we have, Hume then goes on to show, is nothing but the misinterpretation of a mental custom. When we have often experienced the same sequence of events, "we are carried by habit, upon the appearance of the first one, to expect its usual attendant, and to believe, that it will exist. . . . This customary transition of the imagination . . . is the sentiment or impression, from which we form the idea of power or necessary connexion. Nothing farther is in the case." "A cause is an object precedent and contiguous to another, and so united with it, that the idea of the one determines . . . the idea of the other."

Nothing could be more essentially pluralistic than the elements of Hume's philosophy. He made events rattle against their neighbors as drily as if they were dice in a box. He might with perfect consistency have believed in real novelties, and upheld free-will. But I said awhile ago that most empiricists had been half-hearted; and Hume was perhaps the most half-hearted of the lot. In his essay 'Of Liberty and Necessity' he insists that the sequences which we experience, tho between events absolutely disconnected, are yet absolutely uniform, and that nothing genuinely new can flower out of our lives.

The reader will recognize in Hume's famous pages a fresh example of the way in which conceptual translations always maltreat fact. Perceptually or concretely (as we shall notice in more detail later) causation names the manner in which some fields of consciousness introduce other fields. It is but one of the forms in which experience appears as a continuous flow. Our prepositions and conjunctions name other forms; and the variety of names show how successfully we can discriminate within the flow. But the conceptualist rule is to suppose that where there is a separate name there ought to be a fact as separate; and Hume, following this rule, and finding no such fact corresponding to the word 'power,' concludes that the word is meaningless. By this rule every conjunction and preposition in human speech is meaningless—*in, on, of, with, and, but, if,* are as meaningless as *for* and *because.* The truth is that neither the elements of fact nor the meanings of our words are separable as the words are. The original form in which fact comes is the perceptual *durcheinander,* holding terms as well as relations in solution, or interfused and cemented. Our reflective mind abstracts divers aspects in the muchness, as a man by looking through a tube may limit his attention to one part after another of a landscape. But abstraction is not insulation; and it no more breaks reality than the tube breaks the landscape. Concepts are notes, views taken on reality,[5] not pieces of it, as bricks are of a house. Causal activity, in short, may play its part in growing fact, even tho no substantive 'impression' of it should stand out by itself. Hume's assumption that any factor of reality must be separable, leads to his preposterous view that no relation can be real. "All events," he writes, "seem entirely loose and separate. One event follows another; but we never can observe any tye between them. They seem *conjoined*, but never *connected*." Nothing, in short, *belongs* with anything else.

Thus does the intellectualist method pulverize perception and triumph over life. Kant and his successors all espoused Hume's opinion that the immediately given is a disconnected 'manifold.' But unwilling simply to accept the manifold, as Hume did, they invoked a superior agent in the shape of what Kant called the 'transcendental ego of apperception' to patch its bits together by synthetic 'categories.' Among these categories Kant inscribes that of 'causality,' and in many quarters he passes for a repairer of the havoc that Hume made.

His chapter on cause[6] is the most confusedly written part of his famous *Critique*, and its meaning is often hard to catch. As I understand his text, he leaves things just where Hume did, save that where Hume says 'habit' he says 'rule.' They both cancel the notion that phenomena called causal ever exert 'power,' or that a single case would ever have suggested cause and effect. In other words Kant contradicts common sense as much as Hume does, and, like Hume, translates causation into mere time-succession; only whereas the order in time was essentially 'loose' for Hume, and only subjectively uniform, Kant calls its uniformity 'objective,' as obtaining in conformity to a law which our *Sinnlichkeit* receives from our *Verstand*. Non-causal sequences can be reversed; causal ones follow in conformity to *rule*.[7]

---

[5] These expressions are Bergson's.

[6] Entitled 'The Second Analogy of Experience,' it begins on page 232 of the second edition of his *Krit. d. reinen Vernunft*.

[7] Kant's whole notion of a 'rule' is inconstruable by me. What or whom does the

The word *Verstand* in Kant's account must not be taken as if the rule it is supposed to set to sensation made us *understand* things any better. It is a brute rule of sequence which reveals no 'tie.' The non-rationality of such a 'category' leaves it worthless for purposes of insight. It removes dynamic causation and substitutes no other explanation for the sequences found. It yields external descriptions only, and assimilates all cases to those where we discover no reason for the law ascertained.

Our 'laws of nature' do indeed in large part enumerate bare co-existences and successions. Yellowness and malleability coexist in gold; redness succeeds on boiling in lobsters, coagulation in eggs; and to him who asks for the *Why* of these uniformities, science only replies: 'not yet!' Meanwhile the laws are potent for prediction, and many writers on science tell us that this is all we can demand. To explain, according to the way of thinking called positivistic, is only to substitute wider or more familiar for narrower or less familiar laws, and the laws at their widest only express uniformities empiri-cally found. Why does the pump suck up the water? Because the air keeps pressing it into the tube. Why does the air press in? Because the earth attracts it. Why does the earth attract it? Because it attracts everything—such attraction being in the end only a more universal sort of fact. Laws, according to this view, only generalize facts, they don't in any intimate sense connect them.[8]

Against this purely inductive way of treating causal sequences, a more deductive interpretation has recently been urged. If the later member of a succession *could be deduced by logic* from the earlier member, the 'tie' in the particular sequence would be un-mistakeable. But logical ties carry us only from sames to sames;

---

rule bind? If it binds the *phenomenon* that follows (the 'effect'), we fall back into the popular dynamic view, and any single case would exhibit causal action, even were there no other cases in the world.—Or does it bind *the observer* of the case? But his own *sensations* of sequence are what bind him. Be a sequence causal or non-causal, if it is *sensible*, he cannot turn it backwards as he can his ideas.—Or does the rule bind *future sequences* and determine them to follow in the same order which the first se-quence observed? Since it obviously doesn't do this when the observer judges wrongly that the first sequence is causal, all we can say is that it is a rule whereby his *expec-tations of uniformity* follow his causal judgments, be these latter true or false. But wherein would this differ from the humian position? Kant in short *flounders*, and in no truthful sense can one keep repeating that he has 'refuted Hume.'

[8] For expressions of this view the student may consult J. S. Mill's *Logic*, Book III, chap. xii; W. S. Jevons's *Principles of Science*, Book VI; J. Venn's *Empirical Logic*, chap. xxi; K. Pearson's *Grammar of Science*, chap. iii.

so this last phase of scientific method is at bottom only the scholastic principle of *Causa aequat effectum* brought into sharper focus and illustrated more concretely. It is thoroughly monistic in its aims, and if it could be worked out in detail it would turn the real world into the procession of an eternal identity, with the appearances of which we are perceptually conscious occurring as a sort of by-product to which no 'scientific' importance should be attached.[9] In any case no *real* growth and no *real* novelty could effect an entrance into life.[10]

This negation of real novelty seems to be the upshot of the conceptualist philosophy of causation. This is why I called it on page 96 the classic obstacle to the acceptance of pluralism's additive world. The principle of causality begins as a hybrid between common sense and intellectualism:—what actively produces an effect, it says, must 'in some way' contain the 'power' of it already. But as nothing corresponding to the concept of power can be *insulated*, the activity-feature of the sequence erelong gets suppressed, and the vague latency, supposed to exist *aliquo modo* in the causal

---

9 "Consciousness," writes M. Couturat, to cite a handy expression of this mode of thought, "is properly speaking, the realm of the *unreal*. . . . What remains in our subjective consciousness, after all objective facts have been projected and located in space and time, is the rubbish and residuum of the construction of the universe, the formless mass of images that were unable to enter into the system of nature and put on the garment of reality" (*Revue de métaphysique*, etc., vol. v, p. 244).

10 I avoid amplifying this conception of cause and effect. An immense number of causal facts can indeed be explained satisfactorily by assuming that the effect is only a later position of the cause; and for the remainder we can fall back for comfort on the *aliquo modo* which gave such comfort in the past. Such an interpretation of nature, would of course relegate variety, activity and novelty to the limbo of illusions, as fast as it succeeded in making its static concepts cancel living facts. It is hard to be sincere, however, in following the conceptual method *ruthlessly*; and of the writers who think that in science causality must mean identity, some willingly allow that all such scientific explanation is more or less artificial, that identical 'molecules' and 'atoms' are like identical 'pounds' and 'yards,' only pegs in a conceptual arrangement for hanging percepts on in 'one to one relations,' so as to predict facts in 'elegant' or expeditious ways. This is the view of the conceptual universe which our own chapter iv has insisted on; and, taking scientific logic in this way, no harm is done. Almost no one is radical in using scientific logic metaphysically. Readers wishing for more discussion of the monistic view of cause, may consult G. H. Lewes: *Problems of Life and Mind*, Problem v, chap. iii; A. Riehl: *Der philosophische Kriticismus* (1879), 2ter Abschn., Kap. ii; G. Heymans: *Die Gesetze u. Elemente d. wissenschaftlichen Denkens*, §§ 83 to 88. Compare also B. P. Bowne: *Metaphysics*, revised edition, Part i, chap. iv. Perhaps the most instructive general discussion of causation is that in C. Sigwart: *Logic*, 2nd ed., § 73. Chapter v of Book III in J. S. Mill's *Logic* may be called classical.

phenomenon, of the effect about to be produced, is developed into a static relation of identity between two concepts which the mind substitutes for the percepts between which the causal tie originally was found.[11]

The resultant state of 'enlightened opinion' about cause is confused and unsatisfactory. Few philosophers hold radically to the identity-view. The view of the logicians of science is easier to believe but not easier to believe metaphysically, for it violates instinct almost as strongly. "Mathematicians make use, to connect the various interdependencies of quantities, of the general concept of 'function.' That a is a function of b ($a = f\,[b]$) means that with every alteration in the value of b, an alteration in that of a is always connected. If we generalize so as also to include qualitative dependences, we can conceive the universe as consisting of nothing but elements with functional relations between them; and science then has for its sole task the listing of the elements and the describing in the simplest possible terms the functional 'relations.' "[12] Changes, in short, occur, and ring throughout phenomena, but neither reasons, nor activities in the sense of agencies, have any place in this world of scientific logic, which, compared with the world of common sense, is so abstract as to be quite spectral, and merits the appellation (so often quoted from Mr. Bradley) of an "unearthly ballet of bloodless categories."

[11] I omit saying anything in my text about 'energetics.' Popular writers often appear to think that 'science' has demonstrated a monistic principle called 'energy,' which they connect with activity on the one hand and with quantity on the other. So far as I understand this difficult subject, 'energy' is not a *principle* at all, still less an active one. It is only a collective name for certain amounts of immediate perceptual reality, when such reality is measured in definite ways that allow its changes to be written so as to get constant sums. It is not an ontological theory at all, but a magnificently economic schematic device for keeping account of the functional variations of the surface of phenomena. It is eminently a case of 'non fingo hypotheses,' and since it tolerates perceptual reality, it ought to be regarded as neutral in our causal debate.

[12] W. Jerusalem: *Einleitung in die Philosophie*, 4te Aufl., p. 145.

Chapter IX

[Second Sub-Problem Continued]
Causation: The Perceptual View

Most persons remain quite incredulous when they are told that the rational principle of causality has exploded our native belief in activity as something real, and our naive assumption that genuinely new fact can be created by work done. "Le sens de la vie, qui s'indigne de tant de discours" awakens in them and snaps its fingers at the 'critical' view. The present writer also has just called the critical view an incomplete abstraction. But its 'functional laws' and schematisms are splendidly useful, and its negations are true oftener than is commonly supposed. We feel as if our 'will' immediately moved our members, and we ignore the brain-cells whose activity that will must first arouse; we think *we* cause the bell-ring, but we only close a contact and the battery in the cellar rings the bell; we think a certain star's light is the cause of our now seeing it, but ether-waves are the causes, and the star may have been extinguished long ago. We call the 'draft' the cause of our 'cold'; but without cooperant microbes the draft could do no harm. Mill says that causes must be *unconditional* antecedents, and Venn that they must be *close* ones. In nature's numerous successions so many links are hidden, that we seldom know exactly which antecedent is unconditional or which is close. Often the cause which we name only fits some other cause for producing the phenomenon; and things, as Mill says, are frequently then most active when we assume them to be acted upon.

This vast amount of error in our instinctive perceptions of causal activity encourages the conceptualist view. A step farther, and we begin to suspect that to suppose causal activity anywhere may be a blunder, and that only consecutions and juxtapositions can be real. Such sweeping scepticism is, however, quite uncalled for. Other parts of experience expose us to error, yet we do not say that in them is no truth. We see trains moving at stations, when they are really standing still, or we falsely feel ourselves to be moving, when we are giddy, without such errors leading us to deny that motion anywhere exists. It exists *elsewhere*; and the problem is to place it rightly. It is the same with all the other illusions of sense.

There is doubtless somewhere an original perceptual experience of the kind of thing that we mean by causation, and *that kind of thing* we locate in various other places, rightly or wrongly, as the case may be. Where now is the typical experience originally got?

Evidently it is got in our own personal activity-situations. In all of these what we feel is that a previous field of 'consciousness,' containing (in the midst of its complexity) the idea of a *result*, developes gradually into another field in which that result either appears as accomplished, or else is prevented by obstacles against which we still feel ourselves to press. As I now write, I am in one of these activity-situations. I 'strive' after words, which I only half prefigure, but which, when they shall have come, must satisfactorily complete the nascent sense I have of what they ought to be. The words are to run out of my pen, which I find that my hand actuates so obediently to desire, that I am hardly conscious either of resistance or of effort. Some of the words come wrong; and then I do feel a resistance, not muscular but mental, which instigates a new instalment of my activity, accompanied by more or less feeling of exertion. If the resistance were to my muscles, the exertion would contain an element of strain or squeeze which is less present where the resistance is only mental. If it proves considerable in either kind, I may leave off trying to overcome it; or, on the other hand, I may sustain my effort till I have succeeded in my aim.

It seems to me that in such a continuously developing experiential series our concrete perception of causality is found in operation. If the word have any meaning at all it must mean what there we live through. What 'efficacy' and 'activity' are *known-as* is what these appear.

The experiencer of such a situation feels the push, the obstacle, the will, the strain, the triumph, or the passive giving up, just as he feels the time, the space, the swiftness or intensity, the movement, the weight and colour, the pain and pleasure, the complexity, or whatever remaining characters the situation may involve. He goes through all that ever can be imagined where activity is supposed. The word 'activity' has no content save these experiences of process, obstruction, striving, strain, or release, ultimate *qualia* as they are of the life given us to be known.

No matter what 'efficacies' there may really be in this extraordinary universe, it is impossible to conceive of any one of them being either lived through or authentically known otherwise than in this dramatic shape of something sustaining a felt purpose against felt obstacles, and overcoming or being overcome. What 'sustaining' means here is clear to anyone who has lived through the experience, but to no one else; just as 'loud,' 'red,' 'sweet,' mean something only to beings with ears, eyes and tongues. The *percipi* in these originals of experience is the *esse*; the curtain is the picture. If there is anything hiding in the background, it ought not to be called causal agency, but should get itself another name.

The way in which we feel that our successive 'fields' continue each other in these cases is evidently what the orthodox doctrine means when it vaguely says that 'in some way' the cause 'contains' the effect. It contains it by proposing it as the end pursued. Since the desire of that end is the efficient cause, we see that in the total fact of personal activity final and efficient causes coalesce. Yet the effect is oftenest contained *aliquo modo* only, and seldom explicitly foreseen. The activity sets up more effects than it proposes literally. The end is defined beforehand in most cases only as a general direction, along which all sorts of novelties and surprises lie in wait. These words I write even now surprise me; yet I adopt them as effects of my scriptorial causality. Their being 'contained' means only their harmony and continuity with my general aim. They 'fill the bill' and I accept them, but the exact shape of them seems determined by something outside of my explicit will.

If we look at the general mass of things in the midst of which the life of men is passed, and ask 'how came they here?' the only broad answer is that man's desires preceded and produced them. If not all-sufficient causes, desire and will were at any rate what John Mill calls unconditional causes, indispensable causes namely, without which the effects could not have come at all. Human causal activity is the only known unconditional antecedent of the works of civilization; so we find, as Edward Carpenter says,[1] something like a law of nature, the law that a movement from feeling to thought and thence to action, from the world of dreams to the world of things, is everywhere going on. Since at each phase of this movement novelties turn up, we may fairly ask, with Carpenter, whether we are not here witnessing in our own personal experience what is really the essential process of creation. Isn't the world really growing in these activities of ours? and where we predicate activities elsewhere, have we a right to suppose aught different in kind from this?

To some such vague vision are we brought by taking our perceptual experience of action at its face-value, and following the analogies which it suggests.

I say vague vision, for even if our desires be an unconditional causal factor in the only part of the universe where we are intimately acquainted with the way creative work is done, desire is anything but a *close* factor, even there. The part of the world to which our desires lie closest is, by the consent of physiologists, the cortex of the brain. If they act causally, their first effect is there, and only through innumerable neural, muscular, and instrumental intermediaries is that last effect which they consciously aimed at brought to birth. Our trust in the face-value of perception was apparently misleading. There is no such continuity between cause-and-effect as in our activity-experiences was made to appear. There is disruption rather; and what we naively assume to be continuous is separated by causal successions of which perception is wholly unaware.

The logical conclusion would seem to be that even if the *kind* of thing that causation is were revealed to us in our own activity, we should be mistaken on the very threshold if we supposed that the *fact* of it is *there*. In other words, we seem in this line of experience to start with an illusion of place. It is as if a baby were born at a kinetoscope-show and his first experiences were of the illusions of movement that reigned in the place. The *nature* of movement would indeed be revealed to him, but the real *facts* of movement he would have to seek outside. Even so our will-acts may reveal the nature of causation, but just where the facts of causa-

[1] *The Art of Creation*, 1904, chap. i.

tion are located may be a farther problem.[2] With this farther problem, philosophy leaves off comparing conceptual with perceptual experience, and begins inquiring into physical and psychophysical facts. Perception has given us a positive idea of causal agency, but it remains to be ascertained whether what first appears as such is really such, whether aught else is really such, or finally whether nothing really such exists. Since with this we are led immediately into the mind-brain relation, and since that is such a complicated topic, we had better interrupt our study of causation provisionally at the present point, meaning to complete it when the problem of the mind's relation to the body comes up for review.

Our outcome so far seems therefore to be only this, that the attempt to treat 'cause' for conceptual purposes, as a separable link, has failed historically, and has led to the denial of efficient causation, and to the substitution for it of the bare descriptive notion of uniform sequence among events. Thus has intellectualist philosophy once more had to butcher our perceptual life in order to make it 'comprehensible.' Meanwhile the concrete perceptual flux, taken just as it comes, offers in our own activity-situations perfectly comprehensible instances of causal agency. The 'transitive' causation in them does not, it is true, stick out as a separate piece of fact for conception to fix upon. Rather does a whole subsequent field grow continuously out of a whole antecedent field because it seems to yield new being of the nature called for, while the feeling of causality-at-work flavors the entire concrete sequence as salt flavors the water in which it is dissolved.

If we took these experiences as the type of what actual causation is, we should have to ascribe to cases of causation outside of our own life, to physical cases also, an inwardly experiential nature. In other words we should have to espouse a so-called 'pan-psychic' philosophy. This complication, and the fact that hidden brain-events appear to be 'closer' effects than those which consciousness directly aims at, lead us to interrupt the subject here provisionally.

2 Cause-and-effect are in what is called a transitive relation: as 'more than more is more than less,' so 'cause of cause is cause of effect.' In a chain of causes, intermediaries can drop out and (logically at least) the relation still hold between the extreme terms, the wider causal span enveloping, without altering, the 'closer' one. This consideration may provisionally mitigate the impression of falsehood which psychophysical criticism finds in our consciousness of activity. The subject will come up later in more detail.

Our main result, up to this point, has been the contrast between the perceptual and the intellectualist treatment of it.[3]

[3] Almost no philosopher has admitted that perception can give us relations immediately. Relations have invariably been called the work of 'thought,' so cause must be a 'category.' The result is well shown in such a treatment of the subject as Mr. Shadworth Hodgson's, in his elaborate work the *Metaphysic of Experience*. "What we call conscious activity is not a consciousness of activity, in the sense of an immediate perception of it. Try to perceive activity or effort immediately, and you will fail; you will find *nothing* there to perceive" (vol. i, p. 180). As there is nothing there to conceive either, in the discrete manner which Mr. Hodgson desiderates, he has to conclude that "causality *per se* [why need it be *per se?*] . . . has no scientific or philosophical justification. . . . All cases of common-sense causality resolve themselves, on analysis, into cases of *post hoc, cum illo, evenit istud*. Hence we say, that the search for causes is given up in science and philosophy, and replaced by the search for real conditions [i.e., phenomenal antecedents merely] and the laws of real conditioning. . . . It must also be recognised, that realities answering to the terms cause and causality *per se* are impossible and non-existent" (vol. ii, 374–375). The author whose discussion most resembles my own (apart from Bergson's, of which more later) is Prof. James Ward in his *Naturalism and Agnosticism* (see the words 'activity' and 'causality' in the Index). Consult also the chapter on 'Mental Activity' in G. F. Stout's *Analytic Psychology*, vol. i. W. James's *Pluralistic Universe*, Appendix B, may also be consulted. Some authors seem to think that we do have an ideal conception of genuine activity which none of our experiences, least of all our personal ones, match. Hence, and not because activity is a spurious idea altogether, are all the activities we imagine, false. Mr. F. H. Bradley seems to occupy some such position, but I am not sure.

Appendix

Faith and the Right to Believe

'Intellectualism' is the belief that our mind comes upon a world complete in itself, and has the duty of ascertaining its contents; but has no power of re-determining its character, for that is already given.

Among Intellectualists two parties may be distinguished. Rationalizing intellectualists lay stress on deductive and 'dialectic' arguments, making large use of abstract concepts and pure logic (HEGEL, BRADLEY, TAYLOR, ROYCE). Empiricist intellectualists are more 'scientific,' and think that the character of the world must be sought in our sensible experiences, and found in hypotheses based exclusively thereon (CLIFFORD, PEARSON).

Both sides insist that in our conclusions personal preferences should play no part, and that no argument from what *ought to be* to what *is*, is valid. 'Faith,' being the greeting of our whole nature to a kind of world conceived as well adapted to that nature, is forbidden, until purely intellectual *evidence* that such *is* the actual world has come in. Even if evidence should eventually prove a faith true, the truth, says CLIFFORD, would have been 'stolen,' if assumed and acted on too soon.

Refusal to believe anything concerning which 'evidence' has not yet come in, would thus be the rule of intellectualism. Obviously it postulates certain conditions, which for aught we can see need not necessarily apply to all the dealings of our minds with the Universe to which they belong.

1. It postulates that *to escape error* is our paramount duty. Faith *may* grasp truth; but also it *may* not. By resisting it always, we are sure of escaping error; and if by the same act we renounce our chance at truth, that loss is the lesser evil, and should be incurred.

2. It postulates that in every respect the universe is finished in advance of our dealings with it;

That the knowledge of what it thus is, is best gained by a passively receptive mind, with no native sense of probability, or good-will towards any special result;

That 'evidence' not only needs no good-will for its reception; but is able, if patiently waited for, to neutralize ill-will;

Finally, that our beliefs and our acts based thereupon, although they are parts of the world, and although the world without them is unfinished, are yet such mere externalities as not to alter in any way the significance of the rest of the world when they are added to it.

In our dealings with many details of fact these postulates work well. Such details exist in advance of our opinion; truth concerning them is often of no pressing importance; and by believing nothing, we escape error while we wait. But even here we often *cannot* wait but must act, somehow; so we act on the most *probable* hypothesis, trusting that the event may prove us wise. Moreover, not to act on one belief, is often equivalent to acting as if the opposite belief were true, so inaction would not always be as 'passive' as the intellectualists assume. It is one attitude of will.

Again, Philosophy and Religion have to interpret the total character of the world, and it is by no means clear that here the intellectualist postulates obtain. It may be true all the while (even though the evidence be still imperfect) that, as PAULSEN says, "the natural order is at bottom a moral order." It may be true that work is still doing in the world-process, and that in that work we are called to bear our share. The character of the world's results may in part depend upon our acts. Our acts may depend on our religion,—on our not-resisting our faith-tendencies, or on our sustaining them in spite of 'evidence' being incomplete. These faith-tendencies in turn are but expressions of our good-will towards certain forms of result.

Such faith-tendencies are extremely active psychological forces, constantly outstripping evidence. The following steps may be called the 'faith-ladder':

1. There is nothing absurd in a certain view of the world being true, nothing self-contradictory;
2. It *might* have been true under certain conditions;
3. It *may* be true, even now;
4. It is *fit* to be true;
5. It *ought* to be true;
6. It *must* be true;
7. It *shall* be true, at any rate true for *me*.

Obviously this is no intellectual chain of inferences, like the *Sorites* of the logic-books. Yet it is a slope of good-will on which in the larger questions of life men habitually live.

Intellectualism's proclamation that our good-will, our 'will to believe,' is a pure disturber of truth, is itself an act of faith of the most arbitrary kind. It implies the will to insist on a universe of intellectualist constitution, and the willingness to stand in the way of a pluralistic universe's success, such success requiring the good-will and active faith, theoretical as well as practical, of all concerned, to make it 'come true.'

Intellectualism thus contradicts itself. It is a sufficient objection to it, that if a 'pluralistically' organized or 'co-operative' universe or the 'melioristic' universe above, were really here, the veto of Intellectualism on letting our good-will ever have any vote would debar us from ever admitting that universe to be true.

Faith thus remains as one of the inalienable birthrights of our mind. Of course it must remain a practical, and not a dogmatic attitude. It must go with toleration of other faiths, with the search for the most probable, and with the full consciousness of responsibilities and risks.

It may be regarded as a formative factor in the universe, if we be integral parts thereof, and co-determinants, by our behavior, of what its total character may be.

How we Act on Probabilities

In most emergencies we have to act on probability, and incur the risk of error.

'Probability' and 'possibility' are terms applied to things of the conditions of whose coming we are (to some degree at least) ignorant.

If we are entirely ignorant of the conditions that make a thing come, we call it a 'bare' possibility. If we know that some of the conditions already exist, it is for us in so far forth a 'grounded' possibility. It is in that case *probable* just in proportion as the said conditions are numerous, and few hindering conditions are in sight.

When the conditions are so numerous and confused that we can hardly follow them, we treat a thing as probable in proportion to the *frequency* with which things of that *kind* occur. Such frequency being a fraction, the probability is expressed by a fraction. Thus, if one death in 10,000 is by suicide, the antecedent probability of my death being a suicide is 1-10,000th. If one house in 5000 burns down annually, the probability that my house will burn is 1-5000th, etc.

Statistics show that in most kinds of thing the frequency is pretty regular. Insurance-companies bank on this regularity, undertaking to pay (say) 5000 dollars to each man whose house burns, provided he and the other houseowners each pay enough to give the company that sum, plus something more for profits and expenses.

The company, hedging on the large number of cases it deals with, and working by the long run, need run no risk of loss by the single fires.

The individual householder deals with his own single case exclusively. The probability of his house burning is only 1-5000, but if that lot befal he will lose everything. He has no 'long run' to go by, if his house takes fire, and he can't hedge as the company does, by taxing his more fortunate neighbors. But in this particular kind of risk, the company helps him out. It translates his one chance in 5000 of a big loss, into a certain loss 5000 times smaller, and the bargain is a fair one on both sides. It is clearly better for the man to lose *certainly*, but *fractionally*, than to trust to his 4999 chances of no loss, and then have the improbable chance befal.

But for most of our emergencies there is no insurance-company at hand, and fractional solutions are impossible. Seldom can we *act* fractionally. If the probability that a friend is waiting for you in Boston is 1-2, how should you act on that probability? By going as far as the bridge? Better stay at home! Or if the probability is 1-2 that your partner is a villain, how should you act on that probability? By treating him as a villain one day, and confiding your money and your secrets to him the next? That would be the worst of all solutions. In all such cases we must act wholly for one *or* the other horn of the dilemma. We must go in for the more probable alternative as if the other one did not exist, and suffer the full penalty if the event belie our faith.

Now the metaphysical and religious alternatives are largely of this kind. We have but this one life in which to take up our attitude towards them, no insurance-company is there to cover us, and if we are wrong, our error, even though it be not as great as the old hell-fire theology pretended, may yet be momentous. In such questions as that of the *character* of the world, of life being moral in its essential meaning, of our playing a vital part therein, etc., it would seem as if a certain *wholeness* in our faith were necessary. To calculate the probabilities and act fractionally, and treat life one day as a farce, and another day as a very serious business, would be to make the worst possible mess of it. Inaction also often counts as action. In many issues the inertia of one member will impede the success of the whole as much as his opposition will. To refuse, e.g., to testify against villainy, is practically to help it to prevail.[1]

THE PLURALISTIC OR MELIORISTIC UNIVERSE

Finally, if the 'melioristic' universe were *really* here, it would require the active good-will of all of us, in the way of belief as well as of our other activities, to bring it to a prosperous issue.

The melioristic universe is conceived after a *social* analogy, as a pluralism of independent powers. It will succeed just in proportion as more of these work for its success. If none work, it will fail. If each does his best, it will not fail. Its destiny thus hangs on an *if*, or on a lot of *ifs*—which amounts to saying (in the technical language of logic) that, the world being as yet unfinished, its total character can be expressed only by *hypothetical* and not by *categorical* propositions.

[Empiricism, believing in possibilities, is willing to formulate its universe in hypothetical propositions. Rationalism, believing only in impossibilities and necessities, insists on the contrary on their being categorical.]

As individual members of a pluralistic universe, we must recognize that even though we do *our* best, the other factors also will have a voice in the result. If they refuse to conspire, our good-will

[1] Cf. Wm. James: *The Will to Believe*, etc., pp. 1–31, and 90–110 [*ed.*, pp. 13–33, 76–89].

and labor may be thrown away. No insurance-company can here cover us or save us from the risks we run in being part of such a world.

We *must* take one of four attitudes in regard to the other powers: either

1. Follow intellectualist advice: wait for evidence; and while waiting, do nothing; or

2. *Mistrust* the other powers and, sure that the universe will fail, *let* it fail; or

3. *Trust* them; and at any rate do *our* best, in spite of the *if*; or, finally,

4. *Flounder*, spending one day in one attitude, another day in another.

This 4th way is no systematic solution. The 2nd way spells faith in failure. The 1st way may in practice be indistinguishable from the 2nd way. The 3rd way seems the only wise way.

"*If* we do *our* best, *and* the other powers do *their* best, the world will be perfected"—this proposition expresses no actual fact, but only the complexion of a fact thought of as eventually possible. As it stands, *no* conclusion can be positively deduced from it. A conclusion would require another premise of fact, which only we can supply. The original proposition *per se* has no pragmatic value whatsoever, apart from its *power to challenge our will to produce the premise of fact required*. Then indeed the perfected world emerges as a logical conclusion.

We can *create* the conclusion, then. We can and we may, as it were, jump with both feet off the ground into or towards a world of which we trust the other parts to meet our jump—and *only so* can the *making* of a perfected world of the pluralistic pattern ever take place. Only through our precursive trust in it can it come into being.

There is no inconsistency anywhere in this, and no 'vicious circle' unless a circle of poles holding themselves upright by leaning on one another, or a circle of dancers revolving by holding each other's hands, be 'vicious.'

The faith circle is so congruous with human nature that the only explanation of the veto that intellectualists pass upon it must be sought in the offensive character *to them* of the faiths of certain concrete persons.

Such possibilities of offense have, however, to be put up with on empiricist principles. The long run of experience may weed out the more foolish faiths. Those who held them will then have failed: but without the wiser faiths of the others the world could never be perfected.

(Compare G. LOWES DICKINSON: *Religion, a Criticism and a Forecast*, N. Y. 1905. Introduction; and chaps. iii, iv.)

Notes

Notes

The William James Collection is housed in the Houghton Library of Harvard University. It can be identified by the call number 'MS Am 1092', with, sometimes, either 'b' or 'f' as a prefix and a decimal following the numeral '2'. Many books from James's library are also preserved there; many of these are sufficiently identified by their call numbers, which begin either with 'WJ' or 'AC'. Other books from his library are in Harvard's Widener Library and elsewhere, and in such cases their location is stated. Still others were sold and have not been located. However, Ralph Barton Perry made a list, noting markings and annotations; this unpublished list can be consulted at Houghton.

Since work on this edition began, the Houghton Library has reclassified the manuscripts and many letters in the James Collection. A new and detailed guide was prepared in the spring of 1977. The new call numbers are used in the present notes. Apparently, in time, the 'WJ' class will be eliminated, but thus far only a few books have been affected. Some books have been transferred recently from Widener into Houghton, while others, reported by Perry as sold or not listed at all, have turned up in the Widener stacks. The concluding volumes of this edition will contain a complete account of James's library and will give the then current call numbers and locations. Since the same volumes will contain James's annotations, extensively indexed, only those annotations are noted in the present volume which appear to have a direct bearing upon the text at hand.

James was a very active reader who filled his books with annotations and markings. The term 'markings' refers to underlining, vertical lines in margins, exclamation points, question marks, the notation 'N.B.', and 'Qu' for 'quote'. James's style of marking is distinctive: the N.B.'s are such that the same vertical stroke serves for both the 'N' and the 'B', while his underlining often has a peculiar waver. Furthermore, James habitually filled the flyleaves of his books with indexes, in some cases simply jotting down a page number or two, in others, noting numerous subjects and marking passages for attention or quotation. Pages singled out in this fashion usually have markings. Thus, for books protected in Houghton, the risk of error in attributing a given marking to James is slight. The risk is greater for materials in open stacks such as those in Widener, where the only claim made is that the book was owned or used by James and that there are markings. Where the books have been sold, we are totally dependent upon Perry's reports.

All references to *Pragmatism*, *The Meaning of Truth*, *Essays in Radical Empiricism*, *A Pluralistic Universe*, the papers included in *Essays in Philosophy*, and *The Will to Believe* are to the volumes in the present edition (Cambridge, Mass.: Harvard University Press, 1975-), identified as WORKS, while others of James's works are cited in the original editions.

9.1 The] *Some Problems of Philosophy* grew out of James's teaching, especially Philosophy 1a given at Harvard in the fall of 1905, a course at Stanford in the first half of 1906, and Philosophy D at Harvard in the fall of the same year. Houghton preserves James's lecture notes for Philosophy 1a and the Stanford course (bMS Am 1092.9 [4516]), and two copies of the printed syllabus for use at Stanford, one annotated (bMS Am 1092.9 [4467]), the other, unannotated (bMS Am 1092.9 [4522]). The syllabus was revised for use in Philosophy D. Of this again, two copies are preserved, one annotated but incomplete (bMS Am 1092.9 [4466]), the other, complete but unannotated (bMS Am 1092.9 [4522]). This material will appear in full in the manuscript volumes of the WORKS.

10.16 scholastic] It has not been established whether this is a quotation or James's own formulation of a common view. Albert Stöckl (1823-1895), German scholastic philosopher, *Lehrbuch der Philosophie*, 4th ed., 2 vols. (Mainz: Franz Kirchheim, 1876), I, 5, defines philosophy as the "cognitio rerum per causas ultimas et altissimas naturali lumine comparata." Perry reports that an annotated copy of this work (1881) was sold from James's library.

10.26 Dewey] John Dewey (1859-1952), "Philosophy," in *Dictionary of Philosophy and Psychology*, ed. James Mark Baldwin, 3 vols. (New York: Macmillan, 1901-1905), II, 290-296. For James's view of Dewey see "The Chicago School," *Essays in Philosophy*, WORKS, pp. 102-106 and consult the indexes to *Pragmatism*, WORKS, and *The Meaning of Truth*, WORKS. The correspondence between James and Dewey is at Houghton (bMS Am 1092.9 [128-144] [885-889]).

10.36 'college'] James developed this view at greater length in "The Social Value of the College-Bred," *McClure's Magazine*, 30 (February 1908), 419-422, reprinted in *Memories and Studies* (New York: Longmans, Green, 1911).

11.6 Philosophy] Preserved at Houghton is James's set of *The Dialogues of Plato*, trans. B. Jowett, 4 vols. (Oxford: Clarendon, 1871) (WJ 835.70). The first three volumes are annotated, the fourth, containing the *Laws*, remains mostly uncut. That philosophy begins in wonder can be found in the *Theaetetus*, 155d (III, 377 in the Jowett translation). Aristotle expresses a similar view in the *Metaphysics*, 982b. According to Perry, annotated copies of Aristotle's *Metaphysics*, *Physics*, *Nicomachean Ethics*, *Politics*, and *On the Heavens*, all in the French translation of Jules Barthélemy-Saint-Hilaire, were sold from James's library. Preserved in Widener is James's copy of *Aristotle's Psychology*, ed. Edwin Wallace (Cambridge: University Press, 1882) (Ga 112. 160B), in both Greek and English. While the copy has been badly marked up by other users, several marginal entries are clearly by James. See also below, note to 35.33.

11.21 "Hast] One of James's favorite quotations from Shakespeare's *As You Like It*, act III, scene 2.

11.39 'a] The *Oxford Dictionary of Quotations*, 2nd ed. (London: Oxford University Press, 1953), p. 79, attributes this to Baron Charles Bowen (1835-1894), British jurist.

12.2 "systematische] Lothar Schmidt, *Das grosse Handbuch geflügelter Definitionen* (Munich: Moderne Verlags Gmbh, °1971), p. 345, gives "Was ist Philosophie? Die systematische Verdrehung einer eigens zu diesem Zweck erfundenen Terminologie" and attributes it to the *Fliegende Blätter*, a German humor magazine which began publication in 1846, but does not give a definite reference.

12.15 'philosophy'] Paul Janet (1823-1899), French philosopher, in *Principes de métaphysique et de psychologie: Leçons professées à la faculté des lettres de Paris, 1888-1894*, 2 vols. (Paris: Ch. Delagrave, 1897), I, 26, quotes the following passage from Théodore Simon Jouffroy (1796-1842), French philosopher: "Qu'est-ce donc que la philosophie? C'est la science de ce qui n'a pas encore pu devenir l'objet d'une science; c'est la science de toutes ces choses que l'intelligence n'a pas encore pu découvrir les moyens de connaître entièrement: c'est le reste de la science primitive totale." This text can be found in Jouffroy's *Nouveaux mélanges philosophiques*, 2nd ed. (Paris: Hachette, 1861), p. 122. I quote it as given by Janet. Perry reports that a marked copy of Janet's book was sold from James's library with "26, 30-31, 366-367" on the flyleaf of vol. I.

13.22 Suárez's] Francisco Suárez (1548-1617), Spanish scholastic philosopher and theologian.

13.24 Descartes] Houghton preserves the following works by Descartes from James's library: *Discours de la méthode* (together with *La Dioptrique* and *Les Météores*) (Paris, 1668) (*AC 85.J2376.Zz668d), annotated; *Les Principes de la philosophie* (Paris, 1681) (*AC 85.J2376.Zz681d), annotated; *Les Méditations métaphysiques* (Paris, 1673) (*AC 85.J2376.Zz673d), annotated; *Les Passions de l'âme* (Paris, 1650) (*FC 6.D4537.649pc), marked; *L'Homme de René Descartes et un traitté de la formation du foetus du mesme autheur* (Paris, 1664) (*AC 85.J2376.Zz664d), annotated. In Widener, from the library of Henry James, Sr., but given together with William James's books, are the *Lettres de Mr. Descartes*, 6 vols. (Paris, 1724-1725) (Phil 2520.76.55).

13.30 Spencer] Herbert Spencer (1820-1903), *First Principles of a New System of Philosophy* (London: Williams and Norgate, 1862; 2nd rev. ed., 1867). James's copy is of the revised edition (New York: D. Appleton, 1877) (WJ 582.24.4). It is very heavily annotated and marked. The *"redistribution of matter and motion"* occurs in sec. 92 (p. 277 in James's edition), where it is underlined and marked 'N. B.', and elsewhere.

13.35 Locke's] Houghton preserves James's annotated copy of the 31st edition of Locke's *Essay Concerning Human Understanding* (London: William Tegg, 1853) (WJ 551.13). It is dated by James, September 1876.

13.37 Rickaby's] John Rickaby (1847-1927), English Jesuit theologian and philosopher, *General Metaphysics* (New York: Benziger Brothers, 1890).

13.38 Harper's] Thomas Morton Harper (1821-1893), English Jesuit theologian and philosopher, *The Metaphysics of the School*, 3 vols. (London: Macmillan, 1879-1884).

14.3 Leibnitz] Houghton preserves James's annotated set of the *Œuvres philosophiques de Leibniz*, ed. Paul Janet, 2 vols. (Paris: Ladrange, 1866) (WJ 749.41).

14.4 Wolff] Christian Wolff (1679–1754), German philosopher. Widener preserves at least sixteen volumes from James's library of the writings of Christian Wolff, from several 18th century editions, with few markings or annotations. While these are listed among the books from James's library given to Harvard by the James family in 1923, they are further identified as coming from the library of Henry James, Sr.

14.5 Hume] Houghton preserves James's annotated copies of Hume's *Treatise of Human Nature*, ed. T. H. Green and T. H. Grose, 2 vols. (London: Longmans, Green, 1874) (WJ 540.54.2) and *An Enquiry Concerning Human Understanding*, vol. II of *Essays Moral, Political, and Literary*, ed. T. H. Green and T. H. Grose (London: Longmans, Green, 1875) (WJ 540.54). In both cases, the parts dealing with moral questions remain mostly uncut. Also at Houghton is vol. I of the *Essays*, in the edition by Green and Grose (London: Longmans, Green, 1875) (WJ 540.54), unmarked.

14.6 Kant] Houghton preserves the following works by Kant from James's library: *Prolegomena zu einer jeden künftigen Metaphysik* (Riga, 1783) (*AC 85.J2376.Zz783k), heavily marked, but only a few of the markings appear to be by James; *Anthropologie in pragmatischer Hinsicht abgefasst* (Königsberg, 1820) (*AC 85.J2376.Zz820k), dated by James, Berlin, January 1868, with some markings, but of uncertain origin; *Sämmtliche Werke*, ed. Karl Rosenkranz and F. W. Schubert, 14 vols. in 12 (Leipzig: Leopold Voss, 1838–1842) (*AC 85.J2376.Zz838k); *Kritik der reinen Vernunft*, ed. Erich Adickes (Berlin: Mayer & Müller, 1889) (*AC 85.J2376. Zz889k), interleaved (hence bound as two volumes) and heavily annotated; *Critique of Pure Reason*, trans. F. Max Müller, 2 vols. (London: Macmillan, 1881) (*AC 85.J2376.Zz881k), annotated; John P. Mahaffy, *Kant's Critical Philosophy for English Readers*, 3 vols. (London: Longmans, Green, 1872–1874) (*AC 85.J2376.Zz872k), only vols. 1 (in three fascicles) and 3 are preserved, annotated; *The Philosophy of Kant, as Contained in Extracts from His Own Writings*, trans. John Watson, new ed. (Glasgow: James Maclehose, 1894) (*AC 85.J2376.Zz894k2), annotated; *Kant's Critique of Practical Reason and Other Works on the Theory of Ethics*, trans. Thomas K. Abbott (London: Longmans, Green, Reader, & Dyer, 1879) (*AC 85.J2376.Zz879k); *Kant's Kritik of Judgment*, trans. J. H. Bernard (London: Macmillan, 1892) (*AC 85.J2376.Zz892k), annotated. Marginalia in the Adickes edition of the *Critique* are very extensive, less extensive in the Müller. Often they constitute a running criticism, with James developing an objection from page to page, alongside Kant's exposition. So as not to disturb this continuity, with a few exceptions, James's comments are not reproduced in the present volume. They will appear in full in the manuscript volumes of the edition.

14.6 'from] Introduction to the *Prolegomena* in *Sämmtliche Werke*, III, 9. Vol. III of Mahaffy's *Kant's Critical Philosophy* contains an English translation of the *Prolegomena* and is annotated by James.

14.10 colleges] Herbert W. Schneider, *A History of American Philosophy*, 2nd ed. (New York: Columbia University Press, 1963), pp. 208–220, sketches some of the terminological changes in philosophy in the 19th century. In 1839–1840, Harvard had a Department of Intellectual and Moral Philosophy,

Civil Polity, and Political Economy and a Department of Natural Philosophy. In the following year, the same departments appear with new names, the Department of Philosophy and the Department of Physics, respectively.

14.19 kantian] James could be referring to the *Critique of Pure Reason*, B160, and similar passages, or translating one of Kant's main transcendental questions, "Wie ist reine Naturwissenschaft möglich?" (*Critique of Pure Reason*, B20; *Prolegomena* [*Sämmtliche Werke*, III, 53]).

14.23 Paulsen's] Friedrich Paulsen (1846-1908), German philosopher. Paulsen's *Introduction to Philosophy*, trans. Frank Thilly (New York: Henry Holt, 1895) (WJ 350.68), appeared with an Introduction by James. For the relations between James and Paulsen see the notes to James's Introduction reprinted in *Essays in Philosophy*, WORKS, pp. 90-93. James is referring to part of the chapter on the "Nature and Import of Philosophy."

14.38 Comte] Auguste Comte (1798-1857). No works by Comte from James's library are known. James is referring to the law of the three stages discussed in Lesson I of the *Cours de philosophie positive*.

14.40 Lewes] George Henry Lewes (1817-1878), English philosopher, *Aristotle: A Chapter from the History of Science* (London: Smith, Elder, 1864): "It is not a difference in the problems so much as a difference in the Methods, which distinguishes ancient from modern investigation" (p. 67). Ch. IV is titled "The Metaphysical and Scientific Methods."

15.9 'Spiritus] In his *Inquiry into the Human Mind on the Principles of Common Sense*, ch. 2, sec. 1, Thomas Reid writes: "Whether, as some chemists conceive, every species of bodies hath a *spiritus rector*, a kind of soul, which causes the smell and all the specific virtues of that body, and which, being extremely volatile, flies about in the air in quest of a proper receptacle, I do not inquire. This, like most other theories, is perhaps rather the product of imagination than of just induction" (*The Works of Thomas Reid, D. D.*, ed. William Hamilton, 6th ed., 2 vols. [Edinburgh: MacLachlan and Stewart, 1863], I, 104). For James's copies of Reid's writings see *The Will to Believe*, WORKS, note to 23.5.

15.30 'doctrine] Joseph Jastrow (1863-1944), American psychologist, *Fact and Fable in Psychology* (Boston: Houghton, Mifflin, 1900), p. 263, discusses signatures in connection with his treatment of analogies. According to Jastrow, the doctrine is closely tied to a medical practice in which the curative agent is chosen because of its resemblance, in form or color, to the organ being treated. Perry reports that a copy of this book was given to Widener, but it has not been located.

15.34 'Thoughts] Prentice Mulford (1834-1891), American mind-cure advocate. In a volume of separately paged tracts titled *Selections from "Your Forces and How to Use Them"* (Groton, Mass., 1909), p. 11 of "The Accession of New Thought," Mulford writes: "Whatever the mind is set upon, or whatever it keeps most in view, that it is bringing to it, and the continual thought or imagining must at last take form and shape in the world of seen and tangible things." The slogan "Thoughts are things" is printed on the bottom of many pages throughout the volume.

16.29 Kepler] Johannes Kepler (1571-1630); Galileo Galilei (1564-1642); René Descartes (1596-1650); Evangelista Torricelli (1608-1647), Italian mathematician and physicist; Blaise Pascal (1623-1662); William Harvey (1578-1657); Isaac Newton (1642-1727); Christian Huygens (1629-1695),

Dutch physicist and astronomer; Robert Boyle (1627–1691), British chemist and physicist.

16.33 Voltaire] Voltaire (1694–1778); John Dalton (1766–1844), British chemist and physicist; Thomas Henry Huxley (1825–1895), British biologist and essayist. James used this device frequently.

16.34 Jastrow] *Fact and Fable in Psychology*, section titled "The Natural History of Analogy," pp. 236–274. Both syllabi (p. 1) in this context refer to Edward Burnett Tylor (1832–1917), British anthropologist, *Primitive Culture* (1871).

16.35 Jevons] Frank Byron Jevons (1858–1936), British historian of religion and philosopher, *An Introduction to the History of Religion* (London: Methuen, 1896). Ch. 4, pp. 28–40, is titled "Sympathetic Magic." Jevons argues that myths can be understood as explanatory hypotheses, attempts by primitive men to explain observed events. James's annotated copy of this work is preserved in Widener (R 118.96.9B), and contains the following index entry: "False causes 23, 28, 29." One letter from Jevons to James is at Houghton (bMS Am 1092, letter 452).

16.36 Frazer] James George Frazer (1854–1941), Scottish anthropologist, *The Golden Bough: A Study in Magic and Religion*, 2nd ed., revised, 3 vols. (London: Macmillan, 1900), I, 7–128. Ch. 1, sec. 2 is titled "Magic and Religion." Perry reports that a marked copy of this edition was sold from James's library, with the entry "magic and religion 129–30" on the flyleaf of vol. I. In the first edition, 2 vols. (London: Macmillan, 1890), ch. 1, sec. 2, while devoted to the same subject, is titled "Primitive Man and the Supernatural."

16.36 Marett] Robert Ranulph Marett (1866–1943), British anthropologist, *The Threshold of Religion* (London: Methuen, 1909). Perry reports that a marked copy of this work was sold from James's library from which unidentified letters were removed. In his diary for February 23, 1909 (bMS Am 1092.9 [4558]), James notes that he has finished reading this book.

16.37 Lovejoy] Arthur Oncken Lovejoy (1873–1962), American philosopher, "The Fundamental Concept of the Primitive Philosophy," *Monist*, 16 (July 1906), 357–382. At Houghton are Lovejoy's letters to James (bMS Am 1092, letters 512–517), and copies of two letters from James to Lovejoy (bMS Am 1092.1).

16.38 Whewell's] William Whewell (1794–1866), British philosopher and historian of science, *History of the Inductive Sciences, from the Earliest to the Present Time*, 3rd ed., 3 vols. (London: John W. Parker, 1857). Book I is titled "History of the Greek School Philosophy, with Reference to Physical Science."

17.18 Galileo] Whewell (II, 22–29), discusses Galileo's formulation of the laws of falling bodies that velocity is proportional to time and that "the spaces described from the beginning of the motion must be as the squares of the times" (II, 24).

17.18 Pascal's] Whewell (II, 52–53) describes Pascal's experiments with columns of mercury at different altitudes.

17.19 Newton's] Perhaps James has in mind the theory of universal gravitation for which, according to Whewell (II, 117), "the force by which the *different* planets are attracted to the sun is in the inverse proportion of the squares of their distances."

17.20 Boyle's] Whewell (II, 407) formulates the results of Boyle's experiments as follows: "when air is thus compressed, the density is *as* the pressure."

17.20 Descartes'] In his copy of Descartes' *Discours*, towards the end of the second discourse of *La Dioptrique*, on p. 113, James wrote: "Law of refraction discovered by Snell 1621, whose book Descartes had seen. Whewell II. 276." James's reference fits several editions of Whewell's *History*, including the three volume third edition, where on II, 276 Whewell discusses the relations between Willebrord Snell and Descartes. On p. 114 of the *Discours*, James wrote "sines."

18.39 Ward] James Ward (1843-1925), British philosopher and psychologist, "The Progress of Philosophy," *Mind*, 15 (April 1890), 213-233. For the relations between James and Ward see Ralph Barton Perry, *The Thought and Character of William James*, 2 vols. (Boston: Little, Brown, 1935), II, 644-657. At Houghton is James's presentation copy of Ward's *Naturalism and Agnosticism*, 2 vols. (London: Adam and Charles Black, 1899) (WJ 592.75), and a collection of pamphlets (WJ 592.75.2). The correspondence between James and Ward is also at Houghton (bMS Am 1092.9 [649-661] [3829-3854]). In the manuscript (fol. 31), in this note, James also refers to Paul Janet (see above, note to 12.15), leaving most of a line blank, perhaps in order to fill in later the title of some work, and to Wilhelm Jerusalem (1854-1923), German philosopher, *Einleitung in die Philosophie*, secs. 3, 4, 5. James's copy of this work, first published in 1899, has not been located. Jerusalem translated James's *Pragmatism* into German, *Pragmatismus* (Leipzig: W. Klinkhardt, 1908); his letters to James concerning the work of translation are preserved at Houghton (bMS Am 1092, letters 444-451). In Houghton is James's copy of *Die Urtheilsfunction* (Vienna: W. Braumüller, 1895) (WJ 742.25), while Perry reports that a marked copy of *Der kritische Idealismus und die reine Logik* (1905) was sold from James's library.

19.19 Voltaire] Perry reports that marked copies of vols. I and II of Voltaire's *Œuvres complètes* (1815) were sold from James's library, but this edition has not been identified.

19.20 Schopenhauer] Arthur Schopenhauer (1788-1860). Preserved at Houghton is James's copy of *Die Welt als Wille und Vorstellung*, 3rd ed., 2 vols. (Leipzig: F. A. Brockhaus, 1859) (*AC 85.J2376.Zz859s). The first volume is dated Paris, 1868. Perry reports that a marked copy of *Die beiden Grundprobleme der Ethik* (1881) was sold from James's library. The second edition of *The Letters of William James* (Boston: Little, Brown, 1926) contains a letter from James to Karl Hillebrand, August 10, 1883, in which James at some length explains his refusal to contribute for a monument to Schopenhauer (II, 362-364 [the edition is in one volume, but preserves the paging of the two volumes]).

19.35 Spencer] *First Principles* (1877), p. 134 (sec. 37): "Or to bring the definition to its simplest and clearest form: —Knowledge of the lowest kind is *un-unified* knowledge; Science is *partially-unified* knowledge; Philosophy is *completely-unified* knowledge." The phrase '*completely-unified*' is underlined in James's copy.

22.15 Kant] *Critique of Pure Reason*, A805=B833.

22.20 Wolff] Christian Wolff, *Logica* (Verona, 1735) (Phil 3910.1, copy in Widener from James's library), p. 9: "*Philosophia* est scientia possibilium, quatenus esse possunt." This discussion can be found in Wolff's *Preliminary Discourse on Philosophy in General*, trans. Richard J. Blackwell (Indianapolis: Bobbs-Merrill, 1963), p. 17.

23.9 Spencer] In *First Principles* Spencer writes: "Respecting the origin of the Universe three verbally intelligible suppositions may be made. We may assert that it is self-existent; or that it is self-created; or that it is created by an external agency. Which of these suppositions is most credible it is not needful here to inquire. The deeper question, into which this finally merges, is, whether any one of them is even conceivable in the true sense of the word" (p. 30 [sec. 11]). Spencer concludes: "So that in fact, impossible as it is to think of the actual universe as self-existing, we do but multiply impossibilities of thought by every attempt we make to explain its existence" (p. 36 [sec. 11]). On p. 36, James comments: "The three –isms then are absurd by leading each at last to the notion of *mere Being*, and this is absurd, as leading to an infinite regress."

23.17 'what] Kant, *Critique of Pure Reason*, A426=B454. In his copy of the Adickes edition, James commented at length upon this conception of infinity.

23.31 Coleridge's] From the *Specimens of the Table Talk of the Late Samuel Taylor Coleridge*, July 2, 1830: "Every man is born an Aristotelian or a Platonist. I do not think it possible that any one born an Aristotelian can become a Platonist; and I am sure no born Platonist can ever change into an Aristotelian. They are the two classes of men, beside which it is next to impossible to conceive a third. The one considers reason a quality, or attribute; the other considers it a power" (*The Complete Works of Samuel Taylor Coleridge*, ed. W. G. T. Shedd, VI [New York: Harper & Brothers, 1884], 336). Coleridge goes on to say that Aristotle is the "sovereign lord of the understanding; —the faculty judging by the senses" and that he is the "parent of science" (p. 336).

23.39 Janet] Lesson 1 is titled "La philosophie est-elle une science?", while lesson 2, "De quelques définitions récentes de la philosophie." Janet writes: "Ainsi la philosophie n'est pas seulement une science de problèmes, elle est quelque chose de plus; elle est *une science d'hypothèses*. . . . Ce qui fait l'incertitude, ce n'est pas l'absence de solution; c'est l'absence d'un *criterium* entre plusieurs solutions" (p. 8). On the following page, Janet refers to the same discussion in Spencer as does James at 23.9.

24.1 empiricists] In the syllabus for Philosophy D (p. 10), James claims that for empiricism "facts exist only in individual form. *Generals* are mental abstractions." In the margin, he comments on this text as follows: "my definition of empiricism."

24.6 Plato] James's index to vol. III of *The Dialogues of Plato* contains the entry "ideas 263ff," a reference to the *Parmenides*, 131 ff.

24.8 Protagoras] F. C. S. Schiller repeatedly argues that Plato misinterprets Protagoras, and that Protagoras is to be viewed as a major figure in the history of empiricism, especially important for the development of pragmatism. See Schiller's *Studies in Humanism* (London: Macmillan, 1907). For a note on Schiller, see below, note to 24.35.

24.17 Aristotle] See below, note to 35.33.

24.17 Hegel] For James's attitude towards Hegel see "On Some Hegelisms," *The Will to Believe*, WORKS, pp. 196–221; and "Hegel and His Method," *A Pluralistic Universe*, WORKS, pp. 43–62.

24.34 Berkeley] Preserved is James's annotated copy of *A Treatise Concerning the Principles of Human Knowledge*, ed. Charles P. Krauth (Philadelphia: J. B. Lippincott, 1874) (WJ 507.76). Perry reports that annotated copies of vols. I and II of *The Works of George Berkeley*, ed. A. C. Fraser (1871), were sold from James's library.

24.34 Mills] For a note on references in James's manuscripts to John Stuart Mill see *A Pluralistic Universe*, WORKS, note to 7.21; for James's copies of *An Examination of Sir William Hamilton's Philosophy* see *Essays in Philosophy*, WORKS, note to 17.40. Preserved is James's copy of *A System of Logic: Ratiocinative and Inductive*, 8th ed., 2 vols. (London: Longmans, Green, Reader, and Dyer, 1872) (WJ 555.51). Also at Houghton is James's copy of *Analysis of the Phenomena of the Human Mind* by James Mill (1773–1836), new ed., 2 vols. (London: Longmans, Green, Reader, and Dyer, 1869) (WJ 550.50).

24.34 Lange] Friedrich Albert Lange (1828–1875), German philosopher and sociologist. Perry reports that annotated copies of both volumes of Lange's *Geschichte des Materialismus* were sold from James's library and gives 1873 as the date of publication for vol. I.

24.35 Schiller] Ferdinand Canning Scott Schiller (1846–1937), British philosopher. The indexes to *Pragmatism*, WORKS, and *The Meaning of Truth*, WORKS, should be consulted for frequent references to Schiller. Perry reports that annotated copies of Schiller's *Riddles of the Sphinx* (1891) and *Humanism* (1903) were sold from James's library. James reviewed the latter work in the *Nation*, 78 (March 3, 1904), 175–176, reprinted in part in *Collected Essays and Reviews* (New York: Longmans, Green, 1920). Preserved is James's annotated copy of *Personal Idealism: Philosophical Essays by Eight Members of the University of Oxford*, ed. Henry Sturt (London: Macmillan, 1902) (WJ 583.89), containing Schiller's "Axioms as Postulates." James reviewed this work in *Mind*, n.s. 12 (1903), 93–97, reprinted in part in *Collected Essays* (1920). The extensive correspondence between James and Schiller is preserved at Houghton (bMS Am 1092.9 [3701-3704]; bMS Am 1092, letters 826–982) and in the Stanford University library.

24.35 Bergson] Henri Bergson (1859–1941). For the relations between James and Bergson see the notes to "Bergson and His Critique of Intellectualism," *A Pluralistic Universe*, WORKS, pp. 101–124 and "Bradley or Bergson?" *Essays in Philosophy*, WORKS, pp. 151–156.

24.38 Lotze] Rudolph Hermann Lotze (1817–1881), German philosopher. For references to some of Lotze's books from James's library see below, note to 49.7, and *A Pluralistic Universe*, WORKS, note to 8.5.

24.38 Royce] Josiah Royce (1855–1916), American philosopher, James's colleague at Harvard and one of his closer personal friends. For references to some of Royce's books preserved from James's library see below, note to 73.39, and *Pragmatism*, WORKS, note to 16.5.

26.2 Schopenhauer's] James did not use the available translation by R. B. Haldane and J. Kemp and treated Schopenhauer's text with freedom. The passages are taken from *Die Welt als Wille und Vorstellung*, II, 175–176, 189–190, from ch. 17, a supplement to bk. I. Both syllabi (p. 4) also refer to the English translation, "vol. II, p. 359." This reference fits various printings of the Haldane and Kemp translation, originally published as *The World as Will and Idea*, 3 vols. (London: Trübner, 1883–1886).

27.10 Attempts] Bruce W. Wilshire, *William James: The Essential Writings* (New York: Harper & Row, 1971), p. 7n, suggests that this is a criticism of a part of ch. 4 of *Creative Evolution*, on existence and the nothing. Wilshire cites James's letter to Bergson of June 13, 1907, written shortly after reading *Creative Evolution* (Perry, II, 620). Preserved is James's annotated copy of *L'Évolution créatrice* (Paris: Félix Alcan, 1907) (WJ 607.75.2), in which on pp. 299–322, in the section "L'Existence et le néant," there are markings but no annotations.

28.3 Spencer] James perhaps is referring to Spencer's law of evolution, according to which *"the matter passes from an indefinite, incoherent homogeneity to a definite, coherent heterogeneity"* (*First Principles*, p. 396 [sec. 145]). In James's copy, this passage is marked 'N. B.'

28.11 Spinosa] Houghton preserves James's annotated set of the *Œuvres de Spinoza*, ed. Émile Saisset, 3 vols. (Paris: Charpentier, 1861) (WJ 871.82). In this edition, the passage can be found on III, 14. Perry reports that vol. I of Spinoza's *Opera* (Jena, 1802), was sold from James's library.

28.20 Hegel] In an undated entry under "God" in his *Index Rerum* (bMS Am 1092.9 [4520]), James gives several references for the ontological argument, among them to *The Logic of Hegel Translated from the Encyclopaedia of the Philosophical Sciences*, trans. William Wallace (Oxford: Clarendon, 1874) (*AC 85.J2376.Zz874h), pp. 91 (sec. 51), 286–287 (sec. 193), and to Hegel's "Phil. d. Relig. II 210–218." Preserved from James's library are nine volumes of the second edition of Hegel's *Werke* (Berlin: Duncker und Humblot, 1840–1844) (WJ 737.32), in which vols. XI and XII contain the *Vorlesungen über die Philosophie der Religion*. The ontological argument is treated on pp. 210–218 of the second of the volumes.

28.25 Hegel] *The Logic of Hegel*, p. 92 (sec. 51). In James's copy, the passage is marked.

28.28 Kant's] *Critique of Pure Reason*, A599=B627. In James's copy, the passage is marked.

28.30 Hegel] *The Logic of Hegel*, pp. 135–144 (secs. 86–88). The identification of being with nothing does form a part of the opening triad of the *Wissenschaft der Logik*. There are few markings in James's copies of vols. 3–5 of the *Werke*, containing the *Wissenschaft der Logik*. On p. 139 of *The Logic of Hegel*, James comments: "Becoming = Being = 0, if all 3 are taken in Absolute abstraction. Either can equally well serve as the synthesis of the other two. If however you make Becoming diff! fm. the other 2 by making it a term of which *something* can be said, e. g. that it is a change in time, then it is certainly not given by the other two. Only when convertible with them by the common property of absolute emptiness of sense content, can they be said to evolve it."

28.37 Anselm] St. Anselm, *Proslogium; Monologium; An Appendix in Behalf of the Fool by Gaunilon; and Cur Deus Homo*, trans. Sidney Norton Deane (Chicago: The Open Court, 1903). In his *Index Rerum*, under "God," James cites chs. 2 and 3 of the *Proslogium*, in the translation by J. S. Maginnis, originally published in the *Bibliotheca Sacra*, 8 (1851), 529–553, 699–715. William Torrey Harris included extracts from Maginnis's translation in "Faith and Knowledge: Kant's Refutation of the Ontological Proof of the Being of

God," *Journal of Speculative Philosophy*, 15 (October 1881), 404–428. James separately cites Harris's article and the extracts from Maginnis included by Harris in an appendix to his article.

28.37 Descartes] James's index to the *Meditations* contains the entries "realite=entitè=perfection 188" and " 'Ontological argument' 128, 186, 282, 66." These page numbers correspond, in turn, to II, 56; II, 19; II, 55; II, 111; I, 181, in *The Philosophical Works of Descartes*, trans. Elizabeth S. Haldane and G. R. T. Ross, 2 vols. (1911; rpt. Cambridge, England: University Press, 1973). On p. 66 of his copy, James comments: "But just as the ideal triangle can only ['have' *del.*] = 2 ideal right angles—so the ideal god can only have ideal existence—painted hook + painted chain! *If* there is a mountain there is a valley: *if* there is a god he has existence."

28.38 Kant] *Critique of Pure Reason*, A592=B620–A602=B630. The marginalia are extensive in James's copy of Adickes at this point, among them, on p. 476, "But this goes back to the Wolffian definition of Nothwendig," and opposite p. 478, "Right back on Wolffian ground. Of what use then is his new def^{n} of nothwendig?"

29.1 Mathematically] In the syllabus for Philosophy D, p. 5, James writes: "I pass over pseudo-mathematical attempts to deduce Being, such as Oken's who, finding 'polarity' to be a character of reality, writes the equation +1−1=0." James is referring to Lorenz Oken (1779–1851), German naturalist and philosopher of nature. Oken's speculations can be found in his *Elements of Physiophilosophy*, trans. Alfred Tulk (London: Printed for the Ray Society, 1847). In the same syllabus, following the derivation of one from zero, James remarks: "Compare also KANT, R. & S. edition, pp. 148–152," a reference to Kant's *Versuch den Begriff der negativen Grössen in die Weltweisheit einzuführen*, in vol. I of the *Sämmtliche Werke*.

31.7 'percept'] In the Stanford syllabus, p. 5, James defines 'percept' as "what is present to the senses now and here," while in the syllabus for Philosophy D, a " 'percept' is an individual thing, present to the senses now and here" (p. 5).

33.7 substitution] In the Stanford syllabus, p. 6, James writes: "Thus we live mentally by *translating the perceptual order of our experience into a more intelligible order*. We conceive instead of perceiving, substituting generals for singulars, and names for things." James then remarks: "But note that the substitute is *emptier* than the original. Every concrete situation, or present piece of experience's flow, has a potential infinity of characters. In selecting any aspect of it as essential, we neglect the others."

33.24 Hamilton's] William Hamilton (1788–1856), Scottish philosopher. Perry reports that a copy of vol. I of Hamilton's *Lectures on Metaphysics and Logic* (1859) was sold from James's library. Vol. II of these *Lectures* contains the *Lectures on Logic*, ed. Henry L. Mansel and John Veitch. In the American edition (Boston: Gould and Lincoln, 1860), ch. 9 is called "Ennoematic.—B. Of Concepts in Special.—II. Their Subjective Relation—Quality," while ch. 10, "Ennoematic.—Imperfection of Concepts." In Widener is a copy of Hamilton's *Discussions on Philosophy and Literature, Education and University Reform*, 2nd ed. (London: Longman, Brown, Green and Longmans, 1853) (Phil 2035.30.1), from the library of Henry James, Sr., given together with James's books.

33.25 Mansel] Henry Longueville Mansel (1820–1871), English philosopher. Ch. 1 of Mansel's *Prolegomena Logica. An Inquiry into the Psychological Character of Logical Processes*, 2nd ed. (Oxford: H. Hammans, 1860), is titled "On Thought, as distinguished from other facts of Consciousness." Preserved from James's library is Mansel's *Philosophy of the Conditioned* (London: Alexander Strahan, 1866) (WJ 553.62.5) and *The Limits of Religious Thought* (Boston: Gould and Lincoln, 1859) (WJ 553.62). Widener has a copy of the *Prolegomena Logica*, in the edition cited, from the library of Henry James, Sr., with a few annotations by James (Phil 2130.35.2B).

33.25 Schopenhauer] Chs. 6–7 are supplements to bk. I of *Die Welt als Wille und Vorstellung*, II, 67–98.

33.26 James] *The Principles of Psychology*, 2 vols. (New York: Henry Holt, 1890), I, 459–482. Ch. 12 is titled "Conception."

33.27 *Briefer*] *Psychology* [Briefer Course] (New York: Henry Holt, 1892), 239–243. Ch. 14 is titled "Conception."

33.27 Romanes] George John Romanes (1848–1894), Canadian-born naturalist, *Mental Evolution in Man: Origin of Human Faculty* (New York: D. Appleton, 1889) (WJ 577.53.2). Ch. 3 (pp. 40–69) is titled "Logic of Recepts," while ch. 4 (pp. 70–84), "Logic of Concepts." On p. 80 of his copy, James comments: "The concept is simply more abstract and more definite."

33.28 Ribot] Théodule Armand Ribot (1839–1916), French psychologist, *L'Évolution des idées générales* (Paris: Félix Alcan, 1897). Ch. 6 is titled "Conclusion." In Widener are James's copies of Ribot's *Essai sur les passions* (Paris: Félix Alcan, 1907) (Phil 5400.18.15), *Les Maladies de la mémoire* (Paris: Baillière, 1881), and *Les Maladies de la volonté* (Paris: Baillière, 1883), the last two bound as a single volume (Phil 5400.22.2), with a letter to James from Ribot. Houghton preserves Ribot's letters to James (bMS Am 1092, letters 788–795) and copies of James's letters to Ribot (bMS Am 1092.1).

33.28 Ruyssen] Théodore Ruyssen (1868–1967), French philosopher, *Essai sur l'évolution psychologique du jugement* (Nimes: Imprimerie Coopérative "La Laborieuse," 1904). Perry reports that an annotated copy of this work was sold from James's library. In his diary for 1906, on an undated page headed "Memoranda," James lists Ruyssen among "Books to read" (MS Am 1092.9 [4555]).

33.29 Laromiguière] Pierre Laromiguière (1756–1837), French philosopher, *Leçons de philosophie, ou essai sur les facultés de l'âme*, II (Paris: Brunot-Labbe, 1818). Lesson 12 is titled "Réflexions sur ce qui précède. Indication des conséquences qui en résultent."

33.31 [2]Kant] *Critique of Pure Reason*, B129–B130. In his edition, Adickes gives the second edition text and in the margins, the original second edition page numbers. In James's copy of Adickes, there are extensive critical comments at this point.

33.43 Hodgson] Shadworth Hollway Hodgson (1832–1912), British philosopher. For the relations between James and Hodgson see Perry, I, 611–653. Preserved at Houghton are James's copies of Hodgson's *Time and Space: A Metaphysical Essay* (London: Longman, Green, Longman, Roberts, and Green, 1865) (WJ 539.18.6); *The Philosophy of Reflection*, 2 vols. (London: Longmans, Green, 1878) (WJ 539.18.4); *The Metaphysic of Experi-*

ence, 4 vols. (London: Longmans, Green, 1898) (WJ 539.18.2); and a collection of pamphlets (WJ 539.18). Perry reports that a copy of Hodgson's *Theory of Practice* (1870) was sold from James's library. The correspondence between James and Hodgson is preserved at Houghton (bMS Am 1092.9 [188-225] [969-998]). James is referring to the beginning of ch. 5 of *The Philosophy of Reflection*, on "Percept and Concept." James's index to the work contains the entry "Acquaintance vs. knowledge-about = percept vs. concept p. 295 NB." Elsewhere, James attributes the notion of substitution to Hippolyte Taine, see *Essays in Radical Empiricism*, WORKS, note to 31.26.

34.10 Aristotle] In the Stanford syllabus (p. 7), James writes: "So we have the paradox that while only singulars really *are*, what are *known* are only universals (ARISTOTLE)." While in the margin he adds: "Plato: 'The many are seen but not known, the ideas known, but not seen'," a reference to the *Republic*, 507b.

34.28 Laas's] Ernst Laas (1837-1885), German philosopher, *Idealismus und Positivismus. Eine kritische Auseinandersetzung*, I (Berlin: Weidmann, 1879). Perry reports that a marked copy of this work was sold from James's library. Houghton preserves James's copy of Laas's *Kants Analogien der Erfahrung* (Berlin: Weidmann, 1876) (WJ 748.5).

34.30 Bakewell's] Charles Montague Bakewell (1867-1957), American philosopher, *Source Book in Ancient Philosophy* (New York: Charles Scribner's Sons, 1907). Without identifying editions, Perry reports that a marked copy of this work was sold from James's library. Bakewell includes numerous short extracts from the *Enneads* of Plotinus, translated by B. A. G. Fuller.

34.31 Bossuet] Jacques Bénigne Bossuet (1627-1704), French bishop, *Traité de la connoissance de Dieu et de soi-même*. Sec. 5 of ch. 4 is titled "L'intelligence a pour objet des vérités éternelles, qui ne sont autre chose que Dieu même, où elles sont toujours subsistantes et toujours parfaitement entendues," while sec. 6, "L'âme connoît, par l'imperfection de son intelligence, qu'il y a ailleurs une intelligence parfaite." Preserved in Widener is an annotated copy of the unauthorized edition (1722), under the title *Introduction à la philosophie, ou de la connoissance de Dieu, et de soi-mesme* (38557.57.5), from the library of Henry James, Sr., given together with books from James's own library.

34.32 Cudworth] Ralph Cudworth (1617-1688), English philosopher, *A Treatise Concerning Eternal and Immutable Morality*. In the lecture notes for Philosophy 1a (p. 28 in James's numbering), James has "Cudworth p. 237+." In the edition of 1731 (London: James and John Knapton), p. 237 is the first page of bk. IV, where Cudworth writes: "No Individual Material Thing is always necessarily the same with it self, but Mutable and changeable. . . . But Intellection and Knowledge are the Active Comprehension of something, that is fixed and Immutable, and hath always a necessary Identity with it self."

34.33 Santayana] George Santayana (1863-1952), Spanish-born American philosopher, *Interpretations of Poetry and Religion* (New York: Charles Scribner's Sons, 1900), pp. 138-141. Perry reports that a marked copy of this work was sold from James's library. Preserved at Houghton is James's copy of "Platonic Love in Some Italian Poets," published as an unpaged pamphlet, *Platonism in the Italian Poets* (Buffalo: Pauls' Press, [1896]) (WJ 479.62.2). Preserved are vols. I, III, IV, V of *The Life of Reason or the*

Phases of Human Progress (New York: Charles Scribner's Sons, 1905–1906) (WJ 479.62). Houghton preserves the correspondence between James and Santayana (bMS Am 1092.9 [594–609] [3695–3700]).

35.25 Emerson] Ralph Waldo Emerson, *Essays*, 1st series (Boston: Fields, Osgood, 1869) (*AC 85.J2376.Zz869e), p. 280; in the Riverside Edition of *Emerson's Complete Works*, II (Boston: Houghton, Mifflin, 1884), 288. From the essay "Circles."

35.32 Stewart] John Alexander Stewart (1846–1933), Scottish philosopher, *Plato's Doctrine of Ideas* (Oxford: Clarendon, 1909). Perry reports that a copy of this work was sold from James's library, with markings on pp. 6–7 of the Introduction.

35.33 Aristotle] It has not been established whether James himself translated the passage from the *Nicomachean Ethics*, bk. 10, ch. 8. A more modern translation renders the same passage as follows: "Therefore the activity of God, which surpasses all others in blessedness, must be contemplative; and of human activities, therefore, that which is most akin to this must be most of the nature of happiness" (*The Works of Aristotle*, trans. W. D. Ross, IX [Oxford: Clarendon, 1925], 1178b). Numerous translations available to James were examined and none had "philosophic thought." The phrase seems to have no warrant in the Greek. In his translation, J. Barthélemy-Saint-Hilaire uses 'contemplatif' (*Morale d'Aristote*, II [Paris: A. Durand, 1856], 462). Alexander Grant translates a portion of this passage, but he too uses 'contemplation' (*The Ethics of Aristotle*, 2nd ed., 2 vols. [London: Longmans, Green, 1866], I, 234). Perry reports that both volumes of this edition were sold from James's library.

35.41 Condillac's] Étienne Bonnot, Abbé de Condillac (1715–1780), French philosopher. Widener preserves the *Œuvres philosophiques de Condillac*, 6 vols. in 2 (Paris, 1795) (Phil 2493.21) from the library of Henry James, Sr., given together with books from James's library. In *The Meaning of Truth*, WORKS, p. 14, James discusses Condillac's statue illustration.

35.41 Helvétius's] Claude Adrien Helvétius (1715–1771), French philosopher, *De l'homme, de ses facultés intellectuelles & de son éducation*. Perry reports that a copy of this work (1773) was sold from James's library, but the 1773 edition was in two volumes, while Perry's description suggests a one-volume edition.

36.35 Gratry] Auguste Joseph Alphonse Gratry (1805–1872), French philosopher, *Philosophie. De la connaissance de l'âme*, 5th edition, 2 vols. (Paris: Charles Douniol, 1898). Perry reports that a marked copy of vol. I in this edition was sold from James's library. Gratry is quoting from Carl Ludwig Michelet's Foreword to Hegel's *Vorlesungen über die Naturphilosophie als der Encyclopädie der philosophischen Wissenschaften im Grundrisse*, vol. VII of the *Werke*. Carl Ludwig Michelet (1801–1893), German philosopher.

36.36 Wallace's] William Wallace (1843–1897), British philosopher, *Prolegomena to the Study of Hegel's Philosophy and Especially of His Logic*, 2nd ed. (Oxford: Clarendon, 1894), the first edition being the Prolegomena to *The Logic of Hegel*. Perry reports that copies of the *Prolegomena*, Wallace's *Kant*, and his *Lectures and Essays on Natural Theology and Ethics* were sold from James's library.

37.36 Taine] Hippolyte Adolphe Taine (1828–1893), French psychologist and philosopher. Preserved is James's annotated copy of *De l'intelligence*,

2 vols. (Paris: Hachette, 1870) (WJ 684.41). The English translation did not appear until 1871, *On Intelligence*, trans. T. D. Haye (London: L. Reeve). Bk. I ch. 2 is titled "Des idées générales et de la substitution simple." Also preserved from James's library are copies of Taine's *Essais de critique et d'histoire* (Paris: Hachette, 1858) (*AC 85.J2376.Zz858t), signed Henry James, Paris, 1858, and *Le Positivisme anglais* (Paris: Baillière, 1864) (WJ 684.41.3).

37.39 Peirce] Charles Sanders Peirce (1839-1914), "Pragmatism," *Dictionary of Philosophy and Psychology*, II, 322. The correspondence between James and Peirce is at Houghton (bMS Am 1092, letters 657-759; bMS Am 1092.9 [3370-3427]). Numerous excerpts can be found in Perry. For another statement of the pragmatic rule see *The Meaning of Truth*, WORKS, pp. 37-38.

38.27 'God'] For a more detailed pragmatic treatment of 'God' see *Pragmatism*, WORKS, pp. 51-56, and *The Meaning of Truth*, WORKS, p. 103n.

39.35 James] "Reasoning," *The Principles of Psychology* (1890), II, 325-371.

39.36 Miller] Irving Elgar Miller (1869-1962), American educator, *The Psychology of Thinking* (New York: Macmillan, 1909). Perry reports that a marked copy of this work was sold from James's library. Chs. 15 and 16 are called "The Concept as an Element of Technique in Thinking," while ch. 17 is "The Concept and Instruction."

39.38 Spencer] James's very heavily annotated copy of Spencer's *The Principles of Psychology* was a reprint of the drastically altered second edition, 2 vols. (New York: D. Appleton, 1871-1873) (WJ 582.24.6). James criticizes Spencer's view of mind in "Remarks on Spencer's Definition of Mind as Correspondence," *Journal of Speculative Philosophy*, 12 (January 1878), 1-18, reprinted in *Essays in Philosophy*, WORKS.

40.7 Maxwell] James Clerk Maxwell (1831-1879), Scottish physicist.

40.39 *Principles*] "Necessary Truths and the Effects of Experience," *The Principles of Psychology* (1890), II, 617-689.

41.4 Logic] James perhaps is referring to William Stanley Jevons (1835-1882), English logician and economist, *The Substitution of Similars, the True Principle of Reasoning, Derived from a Modification of Aristotle's Dictum* (London: Macmillan, 1869). Preserved from James's library is Jevons's *Elementary Lessons in Logic* (London: Macmillan, 1870) (WJ 542.25), in which *The Substitution of Similars* is referred to.

41.38 Lewes] George Henry Lewes, *Problems of Life and Mind*, first series, 2 vols. (London: Trübner, 1874-1875). Problem I, ch. 4 (I, 275-284) is titled "The Reality of Abstractions," while ch. 13 (I, 390-414) is called "Necessary Truths." Perry reports that annotated copies of both volumes were sold from James's library, as well as two volumes of the three making up the second and third series.

42.8 Mariotte's] Edme Mariotte (1620-1684), French physicist.

42.39 Ostwald] Wilhelm Ostwald (1853-1932), German chemist. Ostwald taught at Harvard in 1905-1906 and was a frequent visitor in the James home. James's copy of Ostwald's *Vorlesungen über Naturphilosophie*, 2nd ed. (Leipzig: Veit, 1902) (WJ 767.88) is dated Chocorua, July 1902. Lecture 6 is titled "Die Mannigfaltigkeiten." Perry reports that a marked copy of

Ostwald's *Individuality and Immortality* was sold from James's library. Two letters from Ostwald to James are at Houghton (bMS Am 1092, letters 639–640).

43.31 Royce] Josiah Royce, *The Philosophy of Loyalty* (New York: Macmillan, 1908). While these phrases as such have not been found in Royce, the separate words can be found on pp. 338–340, the conclusion of sec. 5 of lecture 7, "Loyalty, Truth, and Reality," for the most part a criticism of James's pragmatism.

43.32 Emerson] *Essays* (1869), p. 155; (1884), p. 163.

44.39 Malebranche] Nicolas Malebranche (1638–1715). Preserved from James's library is vol. I of the *Œuvres de Malebranche*, ed. Jules Simon (Paris: Charpentier, 1871) (WJ 653.49), containing the *Entretiens sur la métaphysique*. James is quoting from pp. 47–49. James introduces 'sensational' into the sentence "vos modalités ne sont que ténèbres" and translates 'maître' as 'mistress'.

45.1 Plato] James is using John Dryden's translation of *Plutarch's Lives*, perhaps as revised by Arthur Hugh Clough since the revised version was more commonly available, although in the quoted passages there are no differences between Dryden's and Clough's versions. James appears to have made some changes deliberately and these have been allowed to stand. Of the many editions available, the one used by James has not been identified. The quotation was compared with Clough's revision, V (Boston: Little, Brown, 1859), 256–257. James is quoting from the life of Dion.

47.23 Hibben] John Grier Hibben (1861–1933), American philosopher, "The Philosophical Aspects of Evolution," *Philosophical Review*, 19 (March 1910), 113–136. Hibben is in part criticizing *A Pluralistic Universe*, especially "Bergson and His Critique of Intellectualism": "The charge is made against conceptual thinking that it cannot portray life because it cannot portray the continuous. On the contrary, it is the peculiar function of our thought to represent the continuous. Our perceptual intelligence sees things in detached fragments; our conceptual thought integrates them into a continuous whole. I may not be able to see a process but I can think it" (p. 128). Three letters from James to Hibben are in the Princeton University Library.

48.19 Bradley] Francis Herbert Bradley (1846–1924), English philosopher. For an account of the relations between James and Bradley see Perry, II, 485–493. James's letters to Bradley have been edited by J. C. Kenna, "Ten Unpublished Letters from William James, 1842–1910 to Francis Herbert Bradley, 1846–1924," *Mind*, n.s. 75 (1966), 309–331. Bradley's letters to James are in Houghton (bMS Am 1092.9 [85–114]). Criticism of Bradley can be found in most of James's works, see especially *Essays in Radical Empiricism*, WORKS, and "Bradley or Bergson?", *Essays in Philosophy*, WORKS.

48.20 Green] Thomas Hill Green (1836–1882), English philosopher. For Green's works in James's library see *A Pluralistic Universe*, WORKS, note to 8.37.

48.20 Cairds] John Caird (1820–1898), Scottish philosopher. Preserved in Widener is James's annotated copy of Caird's *Introduction to the Philosophy of Religion* (New York: Macmillan, 1880) (Phil 8582.1.2), signed by Henry James. Perry reports that an annotated copy of Caird's *Spinoza* was sold from James's library. Edward Caird (1835–1908), Scottish philosopher. For a note on Caird's works in James's library see *A Pluralistic Universe*,

WORKS, note to 7.4. One letter from Edward Caird to James is preserved at Houghton (bMS Am 1092, letter 62).

48.35 Kant] *Critique of Pure Reason*, A254=B310. In his interleaved copy of the *Critique*, Adickes's edition, opposite this passage James writes: "The Begriff of noumena necessary to prevent sensible knowledge from calling itself *all* knowledge. But why should n't it, if there be no noumena there? The arg^t then is: Noumena are necessary to *have* noumena by! Is this a vestige of the old moral need of somehow rebuking 'Sense'? See 413."

49.7 Lotze] James makes a similar claim about Lotze in *A Pluralistic Universe*, WORKS, pp. 30–31, and cites *Metaphysic*, sec. 69 ff. Preserved is James's copy of Lotze's *Metaphysic*, trans. B. Bosanquet (Oxford: Clarendon, 1884) (WJ 751.88.12). Lotze writes: "There cannot be a multiplicity of independent Things, but all elements, if reciprocal action is to be possible between them, must be regarded as parts of a single and real Being" (p. 125 [sec. 69]). In James's copy there are many markings in this section. Also preserved is a copy of the German, with marginalia in German, *Metaphysik* (Leipzig: S. Hirzel, 1879) (WJ 751.88.8).

49.18 *Knowledge*] For James's treatment of the knowledge relation see "The Function of Cognition" and "The Tigers in India" in *The Meaning of Truth*, WORKS, and "A World of Pure Experience," *Essays in Radical Empiricism*, especially WORKS, pp. 27–37.

49.25 *identity*] James's struggle with the problem of personal identity is reflected throughout *The Principles of Psychology*. His last view is stated in "Does 'Consciousness' Exist?," in *Essays in Radical Empiricism*, WORKS.

50.5 *Resemblance*] For James's controversy with Bradley on the notion of resemblance see "Mr. Bradley on Immediate Resemblance" and "Immediate Resemblance" reprinted in *Essays in Philosophy*, WORKS.

50.18 *two*] James discusses this question in "How Two Minds Can Know One Thing," *Essays in Radical Empiricism*, WORKS.

50.27 *relation*] James discusses this question in "The Thing and Its Relations," *Essays in Radical Empiricism*, WORKS.

51.33 Stallo's] John Bernard Stallo (1823–1900), German-born American philosopher of science, *The Concepts and Theories of Modern Physics* (New York: D. Appleton, 1882) (WJ 483.3). In James's copy, several passages on pp. 136–140 are marked.

51.34 Mach] Ernst Mach (1838–1916), Austrian physicist and philosopher. Mach's letters to James are preserved at Houghton (bMS Am 1092, letters 538–543). Also at Houghton are copies from James's library of *Die Analyse der Empfindungen*, 4th ed. (Jena: Fischer, 1903) (WJ 753.13); *Erkenntnis und Irrtum* (Leipzig: J. A. Barth, 1905) (WJ 753.13.2); *Grundlinien der Lehre von den Bewegungsempfindungen* (Leipzig: W. Engelmann, 1875) (WJ 753.13.4); *Die Mechanik in ihrer Entwickelung* (Leipzig: F. A. Brockhaus, 1883) (WJ 753.13.6); *Populär-wissenschaftliche Vorlesungen*, 3rd ed. (Leipzig: J. A. Barth, 1903) (WJ 753.13.8). Perry reports that a marked copy of Mach's *Popular Scientific Lectures*, trans. Thomas J. McCormack (1895), was sold from James's library.

51.34 Pearson] Karl Pearson (1857–1936), English scientist. Houghton preserves a copy of the second edition of *The Grammar of Science* (London: Adam and Charles Black, 1900) (*AC 85.J2376.Zz900p) from James's library, with some notes clearly not by James. James read *The Grammar of Science* in the 1890s (Perry, II, 463), and Perry lists a marked copy of the 1892 edition among books sold from James's library.

51.34 Duhem] Pierre Duhem (1861–1916), French physicist and historian of science. No works by Duhem from James's library are known.

51.34 Milhaud] Gaston Samuel Milhaud (1858–1918), French philosopher. For works by Milhaud from James's library see *Pragmatism*, WORKS, note to 6.6.

51.35 Le Roy] Edouard Le Roy (1870–1954), French philosopher. For James's reading of Le Roy's essays see *Pragmatism*, WORKS, note to 6.7.

51.35 Wilbois] Joseph Wilbois (b. 1874), French physicist and writer. For James's reading of Wilbois's essays see *Essays in Radical Empiricism*, WORKS, note to 132.36.

51.35 Poincaré] Henri Poincaré (1854–1912), French scientist. Perry lists Poincaré's *Science et méthode* (1908), *La Science et l'hypothèse* (1902), and *La Valeur de la science* (1905) among books sold from James's library. However, *La Valeur de la science* (Paris: Flammarion, [1905]) (WJ 671.41) was later given to Houghton by Perry.

51.35 critics] Mach, Ostwald, Pearson, Duhem, Milhaud, and Poincaré are listed in *Pragmatism*, WORKS, p. 34, as representatives of a tendency in which "human arbitrariness has driven divine necessity from scientific logic."

51.36 Herbart] Johann Friedrich Herbart (1776–1841), German philosopher and educator. Perry notes that Herbart's *Metaphysik*, ed. Hartenstein (1851), perhaps vol. II only, was sold from James's library, probably meaning thereby the *Schriften zur Metaphysik* from the *Sämmtliche Werke*, ed. G. Hartenstein.

51.41 Dresser] Horatio Willis Dresser (1866–1954), American lecturer and writer, received a doctorate in philosophy from Harvard in 1907. At least nine works by Dresser from James's library are preserved in Widener, *The Philosophy of the Spirit: A Study of the Spiritual Nature of Man and the Presence of God, with a Supplementary Essay on the Logic of Hegel* (New York: G. P. Putnam's Sons, 1908) is not among them. Dresser writes: "Our general thesis therefore is that *the study of the structural significance of immediacy in the Hegelian dialectic throws new light on that dialectic by revealing an element of irrationality; and hence supplies a central clue to the interpretation of the system as a whole, besides undermining the objections referred to above*" (p. 402). Dresser's work is in part a reply to James's "unappreciative comments on Hegel" (p. 397n).

52.33 *can*] This appears to be a case of the "faith-ladder," see below, p. 113.

52.39 Bradley] *The Principles of Logic* (London: Kegan Paul, Trench, 1883) (WJ 510.2.2), pp. 70–73. James's index contains the entry " 'Through a hole' 70."

52.40 Bradley] "Coherence and Contradiction," *Mind*, n.s. 18 (October 1909), pp. 489–508, reprinted in Bradley's *Essays on Truth and Reality* (Oxford: Clarendon, 1914). The quotation on 52.22–23 is from p. 501 in *Mind*. Houghton preserves James's very heavily annotated copy of *Appearance and Reality* (London: Swan Sonnenschein, 1893) (WJ 510.2). The second edition (1897) of this work contains an Appendix (pp. 553–597) with replies to criticisms.

53.13 concepts] On December 23, 1909, James wrote to Bradley: "I trust that you will not take offense, and that possibly the spirit may move you at some future time, when you feel very hearty, to say (in print) just why we *may* not use both perception and conception in philosophy as we use both blades of a pair of scissors" (Kenna, "Ten Unpublished Letters," p. 329).

53.36 Bergson's] "Introduction à la métaphysique," *Revue de Métaphysique et de Morale*, 11 (January 1903), 1–36. In James's set of the *Revue* (WJ 130.75), Bergson's essay is marked, but with only a few comments, among them "pragmatism" on p. 34.

54.33 James] "A Suggestion about Mysticism," *Journal of Philosophy, Psychology, and Scientific Methods*, 7 (February 17, 1910), 85–92. James treats mystical knowledge in *The Varieties of Religious Experience* (New York: Longmans, Green, 1902), pp. 422–423.

55.36 Bax] Ernest Belfort Bax (1854–1926), English socialist writer, *The Roots of Reality: Being Suggestions for a Philosophical Reconstruction* (London: E. Grant Richards, 1907). Perry reports that a marked copy was sold from James's library and that on a flyleaf, James had noted several pages, including p. 66. On p. 66, Bax has the following: "What we find, however, on analysis of the conditions of experience is, that this alogical element of particularity is as essential a principle in the completed synthesis as the universal itself in all its forms. (This is a point which the modern Platonists, the orthodox Hegelians, overlook.) But, on the other hand, it is no less true that the particular, the element over and above the universalising thought-form, has just as little meaning apart from this thought-form as the thought-form has apart from it." Ch. 3, from which the quoted passage comes, is titled "The Alogical and the Logical as Ultimate Elements."

55.38 Fawcett] Edward Douglas Fawcett (1866–1960), English writer and adventurer, *The Individual and Reality: An Essay Touching the First Principles of Metaphysics* (London: Longmans, Green, 1909). On the verso of the title-page, Fawcett prints an endorsement from James: "I hail your book as a great and powerful agency in the spreading of truth." Nine letters from Fawcett to James are preserved in Houghton (bMS Am 1092, letters 184–192). Ch. 4 of pt. II is titled "The Individual, the Organism, and Nature," while ch. 5, "The Unfolding in my Centre."

56.36 Taylor] Alfred Edward Taylor (1869–1945), British philosopher, *Elements of Metaphysics* (London: Methuen, 1903) (WJ 584.98). Taylor writes: "When we call the same object 'real' or a 'reality,' we lay the emphasis rather on the consideration that it is something of which we categorically *must* take account, whether we like it or not, if some purpose of our own is to get its fulfilment" (p. 51). Taylor is contrasting 'real' with 'is'. The latter indicates that something is an object for consciousness. Houghton preserves one letter from Taylor to James, dated May 20, 1904 (bMS Am 1092, letter 1134), in which he thanks James for appreciative comments about Taylor's metaphysics. On p. 51 of his copy, dated April 1904, James comments: "good pragmatic definition."

56.37 Russell] Bertrand Russell (1872–1970), *The Principles of Mathematics* (Cambridge, England: University Press, 1903) (*AC 85.J2376.Zz903r). For the controversy between James and Russell over pragmatism, including letters between them, see *The Meaning of Truth*, WORKS, especially Appendix IV.

58.33   joint]   The manuscript (fol. 95) at this point contains a deleted sentence with the note "Cf. E. B. Holt" attached to it. James is referring to Edwin Bissell Holt (1873–1946), American psychologist. Holt's letters to James are at Houghton (bMS Am 1092, letters 399–405).

58.36   James]   James is referring to "The Sentiment of Rationality."

58.37   Bradley]   *Ethical Studies* (London: Henry S. King, 1876), from the essay "My Station and Its Duties"; pp. 167–171 in the second edition (Oxford: Clarendon, 1927). James's index to *The Principles of Logic* contains the entries " 'Likeness', 261–2" and "Identity 264–8, 281–2, 284, 233—vs. difference 530, 133, 422–5."

58.39   *Logic*]   James is referring to bk. I, ch. 3, "Of the Things Denoted by Names," sec. 11, on "Resemblance." On I, 77, James has the following comments: "[But why can't the relation *in* one fact resemble that in the other, as well as the terms?]"; " $\overset{o}{\underset{o}{1}} = \overset{x}{\underset{x}{1}}$ "; "But germ, producing; + multitude are terms which connote relation"; "See exam. of Hamilton p. 315"; "Distinguish between this and sensation, emotion, thought *of* the same"; "Same *kind*."

59.34   Schiller]   "Thought and Immediacy," *Journal of Philosophy, Psychology, and Scientific Methods*, 3 (April 26, 1906), 234–237.

60.1   Emerson]   *Lectures and Biographical Sketches* (Boston: Houghton, Mifflin, 1884) (WJ 424.25.8), p. 192, vol. X of the Riverside Edition of *Emerson's Complete Works*. Impossible as that seems, James's copy is said to be a gift from his wife, June 1879.

60.3   Goethe]   From the poem "Allerdings," *Poetische Werke*, I (Berlin: Aufbau-Verlag, 1965), 556.

60.37   James]   *The Principles of Psychology* (1890), II, 283–324.

61.21   d'Alembert]   Jean le Rond d'Alembert (1717–1783), French philosopher and mathematician, *Discours préliminaire de l'Encyclopédie*, in *Œuvres philosophiques, historiques et littéraires*, I (Paris: Jean-François Bastien, 1805), 211.

62.19   Morgan's]   John Pierpont Morgan (1837–1913), American financier. In the manuscript (fol. 103), James originally had referred to John Davison Rockefeller (1839–1937), American industrialist.

62.39   Bakewell's]   James is quoting from Bakewell, pp. 371–372, excerpts from *Enneads*, V, bks. II and IV. Perry reports that marked copies of vols. I (1857) and III of *Les Ennéades*, trans. Marie Nicolas Bouillet, 3 vols. (Paris: Hachette, 1857–1861), were sold from James's library.

63.18   Porphyry]   Porphyry (about 232–305) arranged Plotinus's *Enneads* in their present form. His life of Plotinus is usually included in editions of Plotinus's works. In the manuscript (fol. 108), James cites *Les Ennéades*, trans. M. N. Bouillet, I, 27, as his source.

63.31   Thomson's]   *The Bhagavad-Gîtâ; A Discourse between Krishna and Arjuna on Divine Matters*, trans. J. Cockburn Thomson (Hertford: Stephen Austin, 1855), pp. 64–67. Perry reports that a marked copy of this work was sold from James's library with the note "66, The Monistic Idea 62+" on the flyleaf.

63.40   Macdonald's]   Duncan Black Macdonald (1863–1943), Scottish-born American Semiticist, "One Phase of the Doctrine of the Unity of God," *Hartford Seminary Record*, 20 (January 1910), 21–37. Macdonald is quoting an excerpt from al-Ghazzali, translated by Macdonald in his *Religious Attitude and Life in Islam* (1909; rpt. New York: AMS Press, 1970), 300-301. Macdonald acknowledges (p. 302) that his main thesis is borrowed from James.

64.3 *Ens*] Stöckl, II, 54. James wrote this sentence in the margin of his copy of Mill's *System of Logic*, I, 61.

64.6 *cujus*] Stöckl, II, 55, a quotation from St. Thomas.

64.20 Liberatore] Matteo Liberatore (1810-1892), Italian Roman Catholic theologian, *Compendium Logicae et Metaphysicae* (1868). In *The Principles of Psychology* (1890), II, 670n, James quotes from the third edition (Rome, 1880) of this work.

64.22 Spinosa] *Œuvres*, III, 39.

64.44 Silberstein] Solomon J. Silberstein (b. 1845), Lithuanian-born Jewish writer, *The Disclosures of the Universal Mysteries* (New York: Philip Cowen, 1896). The work is dedicated to James among others. James's copy, with a few markings possibly by him, is preserved in Widener (Phil 299.2). It was a gift to James from the author. In the prefatory "Concerning the Author's Writings," Silberstein quotes from James's letters to Edwin Robert Anderson Seligman and himself. On November 12, 1896, James wrote to Seligman that Silberstein's book has no "permanent value," that Silberstein had left out "the restrictions which followed the compliments in my letters," but that he likes "the old man" and is willing to be "immortalized" in Silberstein's Preface (original in the Columbia University Library).

65.27 *known-as*] For the origin of this phrase see *Pragmatism*, WORKS, note to 30.26.

65.40 *Essay*] The sections are numbered as in James's edition of Locke's *Essay* (p. 45). The same paragraph is sec. 19 in Alexander Campbell Fraser's edition, 2 vols. (Oxford: Clarendon, 1894), I, 107-108. In his index in the back of his copy, James has the entry "substance 45, 65, 103-5, 152, 188, 195, 202[,] 205, 271, 282, 383, 407."

65.41 *Ibid.*] *Essay* (1853), pp. 222-231. On p. 227, James writes: "What is the *practically* important principle of identity? soul[,] body or self?"

65.42 *Principles*] Berkeley, pp. 202-203, 204-205. On p. 202 of his copy James has written "meaninglessness of matter?—," on p. 204, "Suppose bodies—reason from them to ideas! uselessness of bodies," and p. 205, "Is existence per se self contradictory? The affirmation is," together with a comment on sec. 20, "Mill's argt. about substance." Most of these comments appear to have been intended for classroom use. James's index contains the entry "Best summary agst. matter to quote §20, p. 204."

66.35 *Treatise*] Hume, *Treatise*, I, 324. On I, 324, attached by a guideline to 'imagination', James has "ergo, not in reality."

66.36 *Critique*] *Critique of Pure Reason*, A182=B224-A189=B232. In his copy of Adickes, James makes numerous critical comments, including "What vile inconsistencies of language!" opposite p. 210.

66.37 Mill] *A System of Logic*, I, 60-72. James's index to vol. I contains the entry "Substance 63." There are many marginal comments on these pages, apparently made with teaching in mind.

66.38 Bowne] Borden Parker Bowne (1847-1910), American philosopher. Houghton preserves James's copy of Bowne's *Personalism* (Boston:

Notes

Houghton, Mifflin, 1908) (WJ 409.95). Perry reports that annotated copies of Bowne's *Introduction to Psychological Theory* (1887) and *Metaphysics* (1882), and a marked copy of *Theism* were sold from James's library. Several letters from James to Bowne are included in Francis John McConnell, *Borden Parker Bowne: His Life and His Philosophy* (New York: Abingdon Press, ᶜ1929), pp. 274–278. Copies of James's letters to Bowne, one not published by McConnell, are in Houghton (bMS Am 1092.1), as well as one original from Bowne to James (bMS Am 1092, letter 52). Pt. I, ch. 1 of Bowne's *Metaphysics: A Study in First Principles* (New York: Harper & Brothers, 1882), pp. 24–58, is titled "The Notion of Being."

70.37 amplification] For another discussion of unity see the Stanford syllabus, pp. 24–27, parts of which are reproduced in the present text.

71.38 Fichte] Johann Gottlieb Fichte (1762–1814). Houghton preserves from James's library Fichte's *Sämmtliche Werke*, ed. Immanuel Hermann Fichte (Berlin: Veit, 1845–1846) (WJ 728.13).

73.39 Royce] *The World and the Individual*, 2 vols. (New York: Macmillan, 1899–1901) (WJ 477.98.6). Vol. II, lectures 8–10 are titled respectively "The Moral Order," "The Struggle with Evil," "The Union of God and Man."

74.15 'Ever] Benjamin Paul Blood (1832–1919), American mystic, *The Flaw in Supremacy* (Amsterdam, N.Y.: B. P. Blood, 1893), p. 7. James quotes the passage which concludes with 'ever not quite' in *The Will to Believe*, WORKS, p. 6. For the relations between James and Blood see the notes to "A Pluralistic Mystic," in *Essays in Philosophy*, WORKS, pp. 172–190.

76.15 'The] Blood, *The Flaw in Supremacy*, p. 7.

76.19 Delbœuf] Joseph Remi Léopold Delbœuf (1831–1896), Belgian philosopher and psychologist. Preserved in Houghton is James's copy of Delbœuf's *Psychologie comme science naturelle* (Paris: Baillière, 1876) (WJ 617.48). Perry reports that marked copies of Delbœuf's *Prolégomènes philosophiques et la géométrie* (1860), *Essai de logique scientifique* (1863), and "Determinisme et liberté" from the *Bulletin de l'Academie Royale des Sciences, des Lettres et des Beaux-Arts de Belgique* (1882) were sold from James's library. Thirteen letters from Delbœuf to James are at Houghton (bMS Am 1092, letters 152–164). James is quoting from Delbœuf's "Le Sommeil et les rêves," *Revue Philosophique de la France et de l'Étranger*, 8 (1879), 329–356, 494–520; 9 (1880), 129–169, 413–437, 632–647.

77.25 Marvin] Walter T. Marvin (1872–1944), American philosopher, *An Introduction to Systematic Philosophy* (New York: Columbia University Press, 1903). Perry reports that an annotated copy of this work was sold from James's library.

77.34 Ostwald] Wilhelm Ostwald, *Die Überwindung des wissenschaftlichen Materialismus* (Leipzig: Veit, 1895), pp. 12–13.

77.42 *Principles*] Wilhelm Ostwald, *The Principles of Inorganic Chemistry*, trans. Alexander Findlay, 2nd ed., (London: Macmillan, 1904).

77.43 Duhem] Pierre Duhem, "La Notion de mixte," *Revue de Philosophie*, 1 (December 1900–December 1901), 69–99, 167–197, 331–357, 430–467, 730–745.

78.38–39 Le Bon] Gustave Le Bon (1841–1931), French social psychologist, *L'Évolution de la matière* (Paris: Flammarion, 1905). Perry reports that annotated copies of Le Bon's *Lois psychologiques de l'évolution des peuples* (1894) and *Psychologie des foules* (1895) were sold from James's library.

80.1 problem] For another treatment of the paradoxes of infinity see *A Pluralistic Universe*, WORKS, pp. 102–104. James's unpublished notes on the subject from the 1880s are at Houghton (bMS Am 1092.9 [4437] [4438]).

80.3 exists] James deleted in manuscript (fol. 160) the following sentence: "Discontinuous addition goes with what I shall call a *tychistic*, continuous addition with what I shall call a *synechistic* pattern of the universe." He also deleted the attached note (fol. 162) explaining that 'tychistic' is derived from a Greek word meaning "chance," and 'synechistic', from one meaning "connected." "I take these names from C. S. Peirce."

80.16 'threshold.'] For the term 'threshold' see James's *Human Immortality* (Boston: Houghton, Mifflin, 1898), pp. 23–24, 59–66.

81.36 Calderwood's] Henry Calderwood (1830–1897), British clergyman and philosopher, *Philosophy of the Infinite: A Treatise on Man's Knowledge of the Infinite Being, in Answer to Sir William Hamilton and Dr. Mansel*, 2nd ed. (Cambridge, Eng.: Macmillan, 1861). Preserved in Widener is James's annotated copy of Calderwood's *Relations of Mind and Brain* (London: Macmillan, 1879) (Phil 6112.1B).

81.38 Burnet] John Burnet (1863–1928), British historian of philosophy, *Early Greek Philosophy* (1892; 3rd ed., London: Adam & Charles Black, 1920). Ch. 7, pp. 276–309 is titled "The Pythagoreans." Perry reports that a copy of this work in an unidentified edition was sold from James's library, with markings especially in the section on Empedocles.

81.39 Tannery] Paul Tannery (1843–1904), French historian of science, "Le Concept scientifique du continu: Zénon d'Élée et Georg Cantor," *Revue Philosophique de la France et de l'Étranger*, 20 (1885), 385–410.

83.8 Kant] *Critique of Pure Reason*, A432=B460. James comments on this definition opposite p. 368 in Adickes.

83.11 Kant] *Critique of Pure Reason*, A497=B525. In his copy of Adickes, on pp. 414–415, James marks this passage, while on p. 351 (at A409=B436), he provides cross-references to pp. 415, 364, 469.

83.41 Kant] *Critique of Pure Reason*, A499=B527. There are comments opposite p. 416 and on p. 417 in Adickes.

84.26 Renouvier] Charles Renouvier (1815–1903), French philosopher. Perry reports that three volumes of the first edition of the *Essais de critique générale* were sold from James's library, with one volume dated by James March 19, 1870, another, December 1871. Preserved at Houghton are James's annotated copies of the second edition of the *Essais*: *Traité de logique générale* (Premier essai), 3 vols. (Paris: Bureau de la *Critique Philosophique*, 1875) (WJ 675.61.2); *Traité de psychologie rationnelle* (Deuxième essai), 3 vols. (Paris: Bureau de la *Critique Philosophique*, 1875) (WJ 675.61.4); *Les Principes de la nature* (Troisième essai), 2 vols. (Paris: Félix Alcan, 1892) (WJ 675.61.6). For a note on the letters between James and Renouvier and Renouvier's writings on James see *Essays in Philosophy*, WORKS, note to 23.1. Perry (I, 654–710), gives a detailed account of their relations. On June 12, 1904, to François Pillon, James writes: "I expected to have written at least 400 or 500 pp. of my magnum opus—a general treatise on philosophy which has been slowly maturing in my mind,—but I have written only 32 pages! ... My philosophy is what I call a radical empiricism, a pluralism, a 'tychism,' which represents order as being gradually won and always in the making. It is theistic, but not *essentially* so. . . . It is finitist; but it does not attribute to the question of the Infinite the great methodological importance which you and Renouvier attribute to it. . . . I have left unread his [Renouvier's] last publications, except for some parts of the Monodologie & the Personnalisme. He will remain a great figure in philosophic history" (bMS Am 1092.9 [3511]).

84.30 'principe] Roger Verneaux, *L'Idéalisme de Renouvier* (Paris: J. Vrin, 1945), p. 81, identifies the following formula as stating the "principe du nombre": "avec un tout donné, un nombre est toujours donné. Des choses qui sont, ou des parties quelconques de ces choses, formeront toujours des nombres, c'est-à-dire des nombres déterminés, différents de tous autres nombres. Sans cela, point de représentation, ni effective ni possible, d'un tout" (Renouvier, *Traité de logique générale*, I, 46–47).

85.22 Kant] Perry (I, 720) quotes the following from James's letter to Arthur O. Lovejoy, August 6, 1908: "But the only thing that ever seemed to me to have any permanent value in his [Kant's] system was his argument for idealism based on the antinomies."

85.30 *Personnalisme*] Renouvier, *Le Personnalisme suivi d'une étude sur la perception externe et sur la force* (Paris: Félix Alcan, 1903).

85.31 *Esquisse*] *Esquisse d'une classification systématique des doctrines philosophiques*, 2 vols. (Paris: Bureau de la *Critique Philosophique*, 1885–1886) (WJ 675.61). James's index to vol. II contains the entry "infinite 17."

85.33 *Derniers*] *Les Derniers entretiens*, ed. Louis Prat (Paris: Armand Colin, 1904).

86.32 men] James deleted in manuscript the following note: "E.g. Renouvier et Prat: la nouvelle monodologie" (fol. 70i^V), a reference to Renouvier and Louis Prat, *La Nouvelle monodologie* (Paris: Armand Colin, 1899).

87.1 Locke's] *Essay*, pp. 132–133 (bk. II, ch. 17, sec. 7). Locke, however, has "adjust a standing measure to a growing bulk."

87.9 Hegel] In his copy of *The Logic of Hegel*, on p. 149, in reference either to Hegel's treatment of limit in sec. 92 or of infinity in sec. 94, James comments: "This is mere drunkenness."

88.13 *Infinitum*] Stöckl, II, 48.

88.24 critics] A deleted portion of the manuscript (fol. 200) in this context mentions Bernard Bolzano (1781–1848), theologian and mathematician, and Richard Dedekind (1831–1916), German mathematician, besides those mentioned in the present text.

89.21 'similar'] In *The World and the Individual*, I, 510n, Royce indicates that he is using the term 'similar' to translate Dedekind's 'ähnlich'. Russell too uses 'similar' and defines it formally in *The Principles of Mathematics*, p. 361 (sec. 342).

89.39 Poincaré] *La Science et l'hypothèse* (Paris: Flammarion, [1902]): "De la célèbre formule, le continu est l'unité dans la multiplicité, la multiplicité seule subsiste, l'unité a disparu" (p. 30).

89.40 Russell] James's diary for 1910 (MS Am 1092.9 [4559]) shows that he spent much of February 1910 reading about infinity. For February 11, James writes "Spent a.m. in bed, reading B. Russell," while for the 12th, "Big gale during night. Read Russell." This series of entries ends with

one for March 2, "Coffee, & infinite, whose business I think I finisht up."
In James's copy of *The Principles of Mathematics*, part of the following
passage is marked: "We shall find it possible to give a general definition of
continuity, in which no appeal is made to the mass of unanalyzed prejudice
which Kantians call 'intuition'" (p. 260 [sec. 249]). On p. 287 (sec. 271),
James provided a cross-reference to p. 271 and marked most of the following:
"But that other kind of continuity, which was seen to belong to space, was
treated, as Cantor remarks, as a kind of religious dogma, and was exempted
from that conceptual analysis which is requisite to its comprehension. Indeed
it was often held to show, especially by philosophers, that any subject-matter
possessing it was not validly analyzable into elements." Both Russell and
Couturat (see below, note to 93.34) frequently refer to Georg Cantor (1845–
1918), Russian-born German mathematician and logician. Nothing by Cantor
from James's library is known.

91.34 Russell] Russell begins his discussion of Zeno's paradoxes on
p. 347 (sec. 327). On p. 348, opposite sec. 328, James writes: "Russells
handling of this seems to suppose that Z. is criticizing the intelligibility of the
idea of motion or denying the possibility of a logical definition of it. It seems
to me that Z. difficulty is not that at all but the practical difficulty of
exhausting it by *enumeration*." Russell states his solution formally on pp.
358–359 (sec. 340), and discusses it on subsequent pages. On p. 360 (sec.
341), opposite Russell's remark that common sense accepts the axiom that
"the whole cannot be similar to the part," James comments that "common
sense says 'equal,' not 'similar'." On the same page, opposite sec. 342, James
writes: "Classes are *postulates*, while things enumerated are *experienced*."
On p. 361, opposite sec. 343, James has: "It seems to revert to the legitimacy
of postulating ω as a limit to what has no limit—It is like calling a square the
limit of a line."

93.1 "the] The italics in the quotation are James's.

93.8 Leibnitz] In his indexes to the *Œuvres* of Leibniz, James has only
one entry on infinity, in the index to vol. II, "Infinity 86."

93.8 Cauchy] Augustin Louis Cauchy (1789–1857), French mathematician; François Jean Marie Auguste Evellin (1836–1910), French philosopher.
Zeno's Paradoxes, ed. Wesley C. Salmon (Indianapolis: Bobbs-Merrill, ^{c}1970),
discusses James's treatment of the paradoxes and also refers to the contributions of Cauchy and Evellin.

93.18 Sterne] Laurence Sterne (1713–1768), English novelist and hu-
morist, *The Life and Opinions of Tristram Shandy, Gentleman*. Russell states
the paradox on pp. 358–359 (sec. 340). On 93.24–25, in the quotation,
James is treating Russell's text freely.

93.33 Baldwin's] "Continuity," I, 224–225, by Henry Burchard Fine
(1858–1928), American mathematician.

93.34 Couturat's] Louis Couturat (1868–1914), French philosopher.
Preserved is James's annotated copy of Couturat's *De l'infini mathématique*
(Paris: Félix Alcan, 1896) (WJ 614.89). On a back flyleaf, James summarizes
Couturat as follows: "An infinite quantum is given in its totality when its law
of formation is given (e.g. 572). Cardinal number is primordial, and an infinite
number is not formed by addition of units. The same 'content' in units is
infinite or finite, according to the order in which they are taken together.
(450) Every quantum is anterior to its parts. Number, quantum & time are
independent conceptions." "Falsity of axiom whole $>$ part, 452" is one of

the entries in the index, while on p. 453, James comments: "This refutes the axiom by nominal technicalities." Also on p. 453, James writes: "where the whole + the part obey the same law of formation by which a certain ω is constructed, their limit is that ω, and to it they are both equivalent—is this the mystery?" Also preserved is Couturat's *Principes des mathématiques* (Paris: Félix Alcan, 1905) (WJ 614.89.2), with the following in James's index: "physical continuum denied, 90[;] infinite is an abstract concept, 63-4[;] 63 the number of numbers ambiguous phrase."

93.36 Huntington] Edward Vermilye Huntington (1874-1952), American mathematician. The Robbins Library at Harvard preserves James's marked offprint (H 18.12.1) of Huntington's "Continuum as a Type of Order: An Exposition of the Modern Theory. With an Appendix on Transfinite Numbers," *Annals of Mathematics*, 2nd series, 6 (July 1905), 151-184; 7 (October 1905), 15-43. It is inscribed to James.

93.38 Peirce's] "The Law of Mind," *Monist*, 2 (July 1892), 533-559. James is referring to a section titled "Infinity and Continuity in General" (pp. 537-546). The Robbins Library preserves vol. 2 of the *Monist* from James's library, with markings and a few marginal comments in the Peirce paper.

93.39 Hobson] Ernest William Hobson (1856-1933), English mathematician, "On the Infinite and the Infinitesimal in Mathematical Analysis," *Proceedings of the London Mathematical Society*, 35 (May 1902-January 1903), 117-139.

93.40 Royce] "Supplementary Essay: The One, the Many, and the Infinite," *The World and the Individual*, I, 473-588.

93.41 Keyser] Cassius Jackson Keyser (1862-1947), American mathematician, "Concerning the Concept and Existence-Proofs of the Infinite," *Journal of Philosophy, Psychology, and Scientific Methods*, 1 (January 21, 1904), 29-36, "The Message of Modern Mathematics to Theology," *Hibbert Journal*, 7 (1908-1909), 370-390. Preserved are vols. 1-5 of the *Journal of Philosophy* from James's library, with a few markings in the Keyser article (WJ 11.42).

93.42 Waterlow] Perhaps Sydney Philip Waterlow (1878-1944), British diplomat, "Some Philosophical Implications of Mr. Bertrand Russell's Logical Theory of Mathematics," *Proceedings of the Aristotelian Society*, n.s. X (1909-1910), 132-188. The article is signed simply "S. Waterlow."

93.43 Leighton] Joseph Alexander Leighton (1870-1954), American philosopher, "The Infinite New and Old," *Philosophical Review*, 13 (September 1904), 497-513.

93.44 Poincaré's] See above, note to 51.35.

93.46 Fullerton's] George Stuart Fullerton (1859-1925), American philosopher, *A System of Metaphysics* (New York: Macmillan, 1904). Ch. 11, pp. 172-183, is titled "Difficulties Connected with the Kantian Doctrine of Space." Houghton preserves James's copy of Fullerton's *Introduction to Philosophy* (New York: Macmillan, 1906) (WJ 430.50). Four letters from Fullerton to James are at Houghton (bMS Am 1092, letters 275-278) and a copy of one letter from James to Fullerton (bMS Am 1092.1).

94.30 "Weierstrass,"] Karl Weierstrass (1815-1897), German mathematician.

94.41 Russell's] "The only point where Zeno probably erred was in inferring (if he did infer) that, because there is no change, therefore the world must be in the same state at one time as at another" (p. 347).

96.9 'the] *Rubáiyát of Omar Khayyám*, trans. Edward FitzGerald, 3rd ed. (London: Bernard Quaritch, 1872) (*AC 85.J2376.Zz872), p. 19 (quatrain LXXIII).

97.6 *produces*] Stöckl, II, 90; Rickaby, p. 305.

97.19 The] Stöckl, II, 96.

97.21 Whatever] Stöckl, II, 96.

97.29 *Nemo*] Stöckl, II, 96.

97.37 maxims] Several of these maxims seem to be taken from Stöckl, II, 97. Rickaby's bk. II, ch. 3, pp. 298–351, is titled "Causality."

98.1 *Quidquid*] Stöckl, II, 96.

98.31 Mill] "The cause, then, philosophically speaking, is the sum total of the conditions, positive and negative taken together; the whole of the contingencies of every description, which being realized, the consequent invariably follows" (*A System of Logic*, I, 383).

98.36 Hamilton] *Lectures on Metaphysics*, ed. Henry L. Mansel and John Veitch (Boston: Gould and Lincoln, 1859), p. 549, vol. I of the *Lectures on Metaphysics and Logic*. See above, note to 33.24.

99.3 Régis] Pierre Sylvain Régis (1632–1707), French philosopher; Géraud de Cordemoy (1620–1684), French philosopher and historian; Arnold Geulincx (1624–1669), Flemish philosopher. No works by these writers from James's library are known.

99.9 Leibnitz] James's index to vol. I of Leibniz's *Œuvres* contains the entry "Pre-established harmony 465," a reference to bk. IV, sec. 11 of the *Nouveaux essais sur l'entendement humain*.

99.30 "All] *A Treatise of Human Nature*, I, 455 (bk. I, pt. III, sec. 14). In James's index to vol. I, two entries concerning causality refer to Green's "Introduction": "Cause 127-8" and "causal judgmt. depends on that of identity 265." One entry refers to Hume's text: "identity of cause & effect adumbrated 411."

99.33 "We] *An Enquiry Concerning Human Understanding* (sec. VII, pt. 2), *Essays Moral, Political, and Literary*, II, 61. James's index to this volume contains the entry " 'loose + separate' 61."

99.40 "Nothing] *Treatise*, I, 456.

100.7 "we] *Essays Moral*, II, 62.

100.11 "A] *Treatise*, I, 464.

100.20 'Of] Sec. 8 of the *Enquiry*, in *Essays Moral*, II, 65–84. On II, 76, James comments: "Does Hume say his doctrine is one of *necessity*? [Not in words; but in practical consequences it is identical]." On II, 79, where Hume writes that "liberty, when opposed to necessity, not to constraint, is the same thing with chance; which is universally allowed to have no existence," James with a guideline attaches the comment "i.e. with 'looseness and separateness' " to the word 'chance'.

101.10 "All] *Enquiry* (sec. VII, pt. 2), *Essays Moral*, II, 61.

101.38 'The] *Critique of Pure Reason*, A189–B232=A211–B256. In James's copy of Adickes, pp. 211–227, there are numerous critical comments.

101.40 Kant's] In a letter to Arthur O. Lovejoy, May 27, 1906, James offered much the same criticism similarly worded, while commenting on Lovejoy's "On Kant's Reply to Hume," *Archiv für Geschichte der Philosophie*, 19 (1906), 380–407 (Perry, I, 719). James used much the same wording in his copy of Adickes, between pp. 212–213.

102.40 Mill's] *A System of Logic*, I, 540–550, "Of the Explanation of Laws of Nature."

102.41 Jevons's] *The Principles of Science: A Treatise on Logic and Scientific Method*, 2 vols. (London: Macmillan, 1874). Perry records that Jevons's *Treatise on Logic* (1874) was sold from James's library. Bk. VI is titled "Reflections on the Results and Limits of Scientific Method."

102.41 Venn's] John Venn (1834–1923), British logician, *The Principles of Empirical or Inductive Logic* (London: Macmillan, 1889). Ch. 21 is titled "Explanation and Verification, as steps towards the methodization and establishment of our knowledge of Nature," pp. 492–506. Perry reports that a copy of this work as well as *The Logic of Chance* was sold from James's library.

102.42 Pearson's] Ch. 3 of *The Grammar of Science*, pp. 77–112, is titled "The Scientific Law." In his index, James lists the following page numbers under 'law': 82, 86, 90+, 103–4, 530, 107–8, 155, 174, 199, 205, and has "no reason extra mentem, 306" after his reference to pp. 107–8 and "alfabet image" after p. 155. In a passage marked by James, Pearson writes: "We are thus to understand by a law in science, *i.e.* by a 'law of nature,' a *résumé* in mental shorthand, which replaces for us a lengthy description of the sequences among out sense-impressions" (pp. 86–87). In *Pragmatism*, WORKS, p. 33, James uses 'conceptual shorthand' to express his own view of scientific law.

103.19 Couturat] "Essai critique sur *L'Hypothèse des atomes dans la science contemporaine*, par A. Hannequin," *Revue de Métaphysique et de Morale*, 4 (1896), 778–797; 5 (1897), 87–113, 221–247.

103.39 Lewes] First series, II, 404–442, "The Identity of Cause and Effect."

103.40 Riehl] Alois Riehl (1844–1924), Austrian philosopher, *Der philosophische Kriticismus und seine Bedeutung für die positive Wissenschaft*, 3 vols. (Leipzig: Engelmann, 1876–1887) (WJ 776.23). James is referring to vol. II, pt. I, *Die sinnlichen und logischen Grundlagen der Erkenntniss* (1879), pp. 236–270. Division 2, ch. 2 is titled "Der Satz vom Grunde und das Verhältniss der Causalität." On p. 236, James notes "Essentially the same doctrine as Sir Wm. Hamiltons, Metaph. vol. ii p. 239+." Vol. II, pt. II is a presentation copy from the author.

103.41 Heymans] Gerardus Heymans (1857–1930), Dutch philosopher, *Die Gesetze und Elemente des wissenschaftlichen Denkens*, 2nd ed. (Leipzig: J. A. Barth, 1905) (WJ 820.37.2), pp. 333–364. Also preserved is James's copy of Heymans' *Einführung in die Metaphysik auf Grundlage der Erfahrung* (Leipzig: J. A. Barth, 1905) (WJ 820.37).

103.42 Bowne] *Metaphysics*, 2nd ed. (New York: Harper & Brothers, 1898), pp. 68–93.

103.43 Sigwart] Christoph Sigwart (1830–1904), German philosopher, *Logic*, trans. Helen Dendy, 2 vols. (London: Swan Sonnenschein, 1895), II, 92–121, "The Concept of Efficient Action and Causality." Dendy translates the German second edition. For James's copies of the German original see *The Will to Believe*, WORKS, note to 20.14.

103.44 Mill's] *A System of Logic*, I, 373-426, "Of the Laws of Universal Causation." On I, 373, James comments: "Mill's *general* view of cause is literally post hoc = propter hoc."

104.22 Bradley] *The Principles of Logic*, p. 533: "That the glory of this world in the end is appearance leaves the world more glorious, if we feel it is a show of some fuller splendour; but the sensuous curtain is a deception and a cheat, if it hides some colourless movement of atoms, some spectral woof of impalpable abstractions, or unearthly ballet of bloodless categories."

104.24 'energetics.'] A conception of the physical universe associated primarily with Wilhelm Ostwald, as well as with Gustave Le Bon and others.

104.32 'non] From the conclusion of the General Scholium to Newton's *Mathematical Principles of Natural Philosophy*.

104.34 Jerusalem] *Einleitung in die Philosophie*, 4th ed. (Vienna: Wilhelm Braumüller, 1909), sec. 32.

105.16 Mill] "We may define, therefore, the cause of a phenomenon, to be the antecedent, or the concurrence of antecedents, on which it is invariably and *unconditionally* consequent" (*A System of Logic*, I, 392). In James's copy, part of this passage is marked.

105.17 Venn] *The Principles of Empirical or Inductive Logic*, p. 56.

105.22 Mill] In *A System of Logic*, Mill writes: "And things are never more active than in the production of those phenomena in which they are said to be acted upon. Thus, in the example of a stone falling to the earth, according to the theory of gravitation the stone is as much an agent as the earth, which not only attracts, but is itself attracted by, the stone" (I, 387).

107.8 known] James is inserting a page from "The Experience of Activity," *Essays in Radical Empiricism*, WORKS, pp. 84-85, but deleting a reference to Lotze's conception of entity, see *The Meaning of Truth*, WORKS, note to 64.17.

108.2 Carpenter] Edward Carpenter (1844-1929), English poet and essayist, *The Art of Creation: Essays on the Self and Its Powers* (London: George Allen, 1904): "So far, then, we seem to come upon something which we may call a Law of Nature, just as much as gravitation or any other law— the law, namely, that within ourselves there is a continual movement outwards from Feeling towards Thought, and then to Action; ... from the world of dreams to the world of actual things and what we call reality" (pp. 14-15). Perry reports that a marked copy of this work was sold from James's library. One letter from Carpenter to James is preserved at Houghton (bMS Am 1092, letter 68).

108.18 *close*] James deleted in manuscript (fol. 281) the comment "Mr. Venn's expression again."

109.34 transitive] James treats a similar question at greater length in *A Pluralistic Universe*, WORKS, pp. 151-152.

110.6 Hodgson's] *The Metaphysic of Experience*, I, 180-181. On I, 180, James comments: "But whence does he get this notion of an objective effort at all? It seems to me that effort 'means' the 'sense' of it, + [illegible] it." On an insert opposite I, 180, James has "vol. I, 180f effort differs from sense of effort, 447[;] vol II, 154, 374[;] III 71."

110.10 Hodgson] On II, 375, parts of the quoted passage are underlined and marked with an exclamation point.

110.18 Bergson's] In *Essays in Radical Empiricism*, WORKS, p. 83n, James cites Bergson's "Effort intellectuel," *Revue Philosophique de la France et de l'Étranger*, 53 (1902), 1–27.

110.19 Ward] In *Naturalism and Agnosticism*, II, 245, Ward writes: "If we ask for the conditions of this activity, we must transcend experience to get them. There would be little point in saying that the subject is a condition, for it only *is*, as it is active." James comments on this passage: "Yet it feels itself sometimes to be passive." On p. 246, James writes in the margin: "A thing must undergo something, must be alive, to be either active or passive."

110.20 Stout's] George Frederick Stout (1860–1944), English philosopher and psychologist. Houghton preserves James's copy of Stout's *Analytic Psychology*, 2 vols. (London: Swan Sonnenschein, 1896) (WJ 583.67), while in Widener is James's unannotated copy of *A Manual of Psychology*, 2nd ed. (London: University Tutorial Press, 1901) (Phil 5258.27.1). Two letters from Stout to James can be found in James's copy of the *Analytic Psychology*, several other letters are also at Houghton (bMS Am 1092, letters 1040–1042). James's notes, removed from the *Analytic Psychology*, are preserved (bMS Am 1092.9 [4407]). In his chapter on "The Concept of Mental Activity," I, 143–179 of *Analytic Psychology*, Stout criticizes James, to which James replies in "The Experience of Activity," *Essays in Radical Empiricism*, WORKS, p. 86n. In James's copy of *Analytic Psychology*, there are many marginal comments, some of them explaining what he meant in *The Principles of Psychology* (1890), I, 299–301, the text criticized by Stout.

110.21 Appendix] In the present edition, Appendix B, "The Experience of Activity," does not appear in *A Pluralistic Universe*, but is published as one of the *Essays in Radical Empiricism*.

110.25 Bradley] James discusses Bradley's view of activity and provides references in "The Experience of Activity," *Essays in Radical Empiricism*, WORKS, pp. 80–85.

111.18 CLIFFORD] William Kingdon Clifford (1845–1879), British mathematician and philosopher. James criticizes Clifford's view of faith in *The Will to Believe*, WORKS, pp. 17–18.

112.31 "the] Friedrich Paulsen, *Introduction to Philosophy*, p. 246.

113.2 'faith-ladder'] James discusses the faith-ladder in *A Pluralistic Universe*, WORKS, p. 148. In the Stanford notes, under the heading "Faith," James writes: "Its natural logic is the sorites: fit to be, ought to be, may be, must be, shall be, is, etc." (fol. 100).

115.19 'melioristic'] In *Pragmatism*, WORKS, pp. 137–138 and elsewhere, James claims that pragmatism favors meliorism. For some comments on the origin of this term see Jane Hume Clapperton, *Scientific Meliorism and the Evolution of Happiness* (London: Kegan Paul, Trench, 1885), viii–ix.

117.6 DICKINSON] Goldsworthy Lowes Dickinson (1862–1932), English writer, *Religion: A Criticism and a Forecast* (New York: McClure, Phillips, 1905) (WJ 518.13). In his copy, on p. 83, next to Dickinson's remark "once we begin to say 'I believe though truth testify against me'" (pp. 82–83), James writes: "who ever said this." Dickinson's letters to James are at Houghton (bMS Am 1092, letters 167–170).

I. K. S.

Appendixes

Appendix I

Draft Leaves and Fragment of a Rejected Section

a. Draft Leaves in bMS Am 1092.9 (4519)
(Box L, Notebook N^viii)

This draft for part of Chapter IV, "Percept and Concept," covers text found between 31.6 and 37.16. It is written in ink, with pencil alterations, on the rectos of leaves in a blue wove paper hardbound notebook, water-marked, from Partridge and Cooper, Chancery Lane, London. At the front of the notebook (as identified by the label on the inside front cover) are drafts for "Bradley or Bergson?" (McD 1910:1), "The Moral Equivalent of War" (McD 1910:3), and "A Suggestion about Mysticism" (McD 1910:2). However, the notebook had originally been turned end for end and reversed so that the earlier material of the draft for *Some Problems of Philosophy* was written forward in a normal manner (although appearing to be reversed on the versos when the notebook is held in the usual way). At the start of this reversed notebook there are two stubs of excised leaves and then a leaf written in pencil and foliated 2, beginning 'Perry's prima facie equality . . .'. This is followed by eighteen stubs and then the start of the *Some Problems* draft beginning with pencil numbered fols. 1 to 19. Each recto, except fols. 6, 14, and 16, is deleted by a vertical pencil stroke, and a stroke also deletes material when written on the versos, except for fol. 6^v. Beginning in mid-sentence and thus continuing text from one or more of the preceding eighteen excised leaves, pencil text is found on the versos of leaves 1–4. On fol. 2^v the pencil text does not fill the page, since an addition in ink to the recto *Problems* draft occupies the foot. This is the only evidence for the conjecture that the pencil writing was later than the ink, or *Problems* draft inscription, a hypothesis the more reasonable in that it accounts for the writing only on the versos. Between fols. 6 and 7 are eleven stubs so roughly cut that ink letters can be observed. After fol. 4^v the versos are usually blank although pencil jottings are found on fols. 6^v (an insert to fol. 7) and 9^v, and below the pencil material on 9^v appears an expansion of the footnote begun on fol. 9 and carried on to fol. 10. More pencil jottings occur on fol. 12^v. Between fols. 15 and 16 appear six rough-cut stubs. Folio 16 is blank except for a part-line of text at the head that links with nothing else. Expansions of recto text appear in pencil on the versos of fols. 16–18. After the end of the text on fol. 19 in mid-sentence, eighty-six stubs appear before the last leaf of "A Suggestion about Mysticism," or fol. 34 from the original start of the notebook. The verso of this leaf has a blank paste-over deleting pencil text written in the same reversed manner as the other *Some Problems* text and covering some of the matter taken up in final form in footnote 17 later in Chapter IV (44.35–38). It seems clear, thus, that the draft text of *Some Problems* continued for some eighty-six leaves beyond preserved fol. 19, and it seems probable that the last leaf of the text on the verso of the last leaf of "A Suggestion about Mysticism" was covered by the paste-over at the time these leaves were removed.

[*fol.* 1]
Concepts etc

It is important for the understanding of what follows that the reader should gain a clear idea of the difference between our merely sensitive experience, and the life of thought which is grafted on it. In our quadrupedal relatives thought proper is at a minimum, but we have no reason to suppose that their immediate life of feeling is less copious than ours. Sensitive life is originally & essentially self-sufficing; and thought appears as an added function, adapting us to a wider environment than that of which brutes take account.

Let me speak of the contrast as that between the perceptual order and the conceptual order of our [*fol.* 2] experience.ˣ [*in mrgn.* ˣsynonyms'] The intellectual life of man consists almost wholly in the substitution of a conceptual order for the perceptual order in which things originally come. This substitution is the work of several factors. Parts of the primary stream of feeling must be more intense, salient, and emphatic than others, [*fol.* 3] in animals as well as in ourselves, but whereas lower animals simply react upon these by movements, higher animals 'note' and remember them and men use nouns, adj[ec]tives & verbs to identify them by when they meet them elsewhere.

[*fol.* 4]

Our field of sense is at all times a continuum, within which we carve out objects. In the sky 'constellations,' on the earth 'beach' and 'sea,' 'cliff[,]' 'bushes,' 'grass.' We carve [*fol.* 5] [*begin clipping*] 'days' and 'nights,' 'summers' and 'winters' out of time. We say *what* each part of the immediately given continuum is; and all these *whats* are *concepts*. [*end clipping*] [*begin insertion from fol. 3*] A feature of experience thus abstracted, individualized, and generalized, is called a *concept*.ˣ

On the Concept Cf. S. H. Hodgson: The Philosophy of reflection, I, 288–310; G. J. Romanes: Mental Evolution in Man, Chaps. III & IV. W. James: Principles of Psych. Ch. XII. La romiguière: Lecons de Philosophie 2ᵐᵉ partie, 12ᵐᵉ Leçon. [*end insertion from fol. 3*]

Trains of concepts unmixed with percepts grow frequent in the adult mind, and parts of these conceptual trains arrest our attention just as parts of the perceptual flow did, giving rise to concepts of a higher order of abstractness. So subtle is the discernment of man, and so great the power of some men to single out the more fugitive elements of what passes before them, that these new formations have no limit. Aspect within aspect, quality after quality, relation upon relation, absences and negations as well as present features, end by being noted and their names added to the store of nouns, verbs, [*fol.* 6] adjectives, conjunctions, and prepositions by which the mind interprets life. Every new book verbalizes some new concept, which becomes important, according to the use that can be made of it. Different universes of thought thus arise, with specific sorts of relation among their ingredients. The 'real' world of common sense, the world of material things & tasks to be done; the mathematical world of pure forms; the world of ethical judgments[;] the worlds of logic, of music etc., abstracted and generalized from long-forgotten perceptual instances, return again [*fol.* 7] into the particulars of our present and future perception. [*fol.* 6ᵛ] By those whats we apperceive our thises[.] [*fol. 7 cont.*] Percepts & concepts coalesce & interpenetrate, seem to impregnate and fertilize each other. We need them both, as we need both our legs in walking[.] By sensation we are informed *that something particular is there*; *what the particular thing is* we know only by classing it in generalized form. Neither faculty, taken alone, knows reality in its completeness.

From Aristotleˣ downwards [*fol.* 8] philosophers have frankly

---

ˣ See, for example Book I, Chap II of his Metaphysics[.]

---

admitted the indispensability, for complete knowledge of of fact, both sensational and intellectual contribution.ˣ

Complete knowledge of *fact*! but facts are particulars, and connect themselves with practical necessities and the arts; and greek philosophers soon formed the notion that knowledge of so-called universals, meaning concepts of abstract forms, numbers, qualities, and relations, were the only knowledge worthy of the truly philosophic mind. Particular facts decay and our sense-perceptions of them vary. A concept never changes, meaning always that same idea, [*fol.* 9] and the relations between such unvarying terms are constant, and found eternal verities. Hence there arose a tendency, which has lasted all through philosophy, to contrast the knowledge of universals and intelligibles, as god-like, dignified, and honorable to the knower, with that of particulars & sensibles as something relatively base which we share with beasts.ˣ

ˣ Plato in numerous places, but chiefly in Books VI & VII of the Republic, contrasts perceptual knowledge as 'opinion,' (δόξα) with true knowledge (ἐπιστήμη), to the latter's glory. For other expressions of the ultra-rationalistic view, read the passage from Plotinus on the Intellect in [*fol.* 10] C. M. BAKEWELL'S Source book in ancient philosophy, N.Y. 1907, p. 353 f.; BOSSUET: Traité de la Connaissance de Dieu, Chap IV, §§ V, VI; R. CUDWORTH: a Treatise concerning eternal & immutable morality, Books III & IV. The *platonic* [*fol.* 9ᵛ] doctrine of 'ideas' so called, took its rise in that pursuit of something permanent in a world of change, of something absolute in a world of relativity, which is the essence of the rationalistic philosophy. "The whole natural world had come to seem to [Plato] like a world of dreams in which the illusive images succeed one another without other meaning than that which we derive from our strange power of recognition. . . . As resemblances to real things make up all the truth of our dream, and these recognitions all its meaning, so Plato tho't that all the truth and meaning of earthly things was the reference they contained to a heavenly original. This heavenly original we remember & recognize even among the distortions, disappearances & multiplications of its ephemeral copies. . . . The impressions themselves have no permanence, no intelligible essence, but, as [*fol.* 10 *cont.*] Plato said, they never really exist, but are always either arising or ceasing to be. There must be, he tells us, an eternal and clearly definable object of which the visible appearances to us are the multiform semblance; now by one trait, now by another, the phantom before us reminds us of that half-forgotten celestial reality & makes us utter its name. . . . We and the whole universe exist only in the attempt to return to our perfection, to lose ourselves again in God. That ineffable good is our natural possession; and all we honor in this life is but a partial recovery of our birthright; every delightful thing is like a rift in the clouds through which we catch a glimpse of our native heaven. And if that heaven seems so far away, and the idea of it so dim & unreal, it is because we are so far from perfect, so immersed in what is alien & destructive to the soul." G. Santayana: Platonism in the Italian Poets, 1896. For a sketch of platonism, see E. Laas: Idealismus u. positivismus. Theil I. 1879.

[*fol.* 11]

For rationalistic writers conceptual knowledge was not only the more noble knowledge, but it originated independently of all perceptual particulars. Such concepts as God, perfection, eternity, infinity, immutability; absolute beauty, truth, right, justice; necessity, freedom, duty, worth, etc.; and the part they play in our mind, are, it was supposed, impossible to explain as resulting from our practical experience. The empiricist view is that they do result from practical experience.[x]

---

[x] John Locke, in his Essay Concerning human Understanding Books i & ii was the great popularizer of this doctrine. Condillac's Traité des Sensations, Helvetius's work de l'Homme, & James Mill's Analysis of the Human Mind were his more radical successors. [*pencil insrtd.* 'Cite Laromiguière']

[————————————————————————————————]

[*fol.* 12]

But a more important question, than that as to the origin of our concepts is that of their *functional use and value*:—Is *that* out of all relation to perceptual experience, or not? Is conceptual knowledge [*fol.* 13] self-sufficing and a revelation all by its-|self, and apart from its uses in helping us to a better understanding of the world of sense-perception?

Rationalistic writers say: Yes, concepts, they think, admit us to a diviner world, and show us an altogether higher realm of being than sense-knowledge shows, the realm of universal rather than of perish-[*fol.* 14]ing facts, of essential qualities, immutable relations, eternal principles of truth & right. A disciple of Hegel, after exalting the knowledge of "the General, Unchangeable, and alone Valuable" above that of "the Particular, Sensible, and Transient," adds that if you reproach philosophy with being unable to make an individual grass-blade grow, or even to know how it does grow, the reply is that since such a "how" stands, not above, but below, *knowledge*, such an ignorance argues no limitation[.][x]

MICHELET: HEGEL'S works VII, 15. Quoted by GRATRY: de la Connaissance de l'Ame, I, 231.—It may be said that Hegel himself would doubtfully have subscribed to his disciple's view.

To this ultra rationalistic opinion I oppose the empiricist contention that *the significance of* [*fol.* 15] *concepts consists always in their relation to perceptual particulars*. Made of percepts or of parts of percepts, their office is to enable the mind to apply itself again to the world of percepts with a better command of the situation there.

[*fol.* 17]

To understand this empiricist contention better, let us begin by distinguishing in every concept the mental content of which it may intrinsically consist, from the function which it may exert in the whole system of other contents by which our experience is constituted. [*fol.* 16[v]] The word "man" for example is three things. 1. It is a verbal object by itself. 2. It carries with it a vague image of the human form, an image which may have its own intrinsic beauty and dignity. 3. It has also a representative [*fol.* 17 *cont.*] tative function in naming other objects from whom we may expect human treatment when occasion arrives. Similarly of 'triangle,' [*fol.* 17ᵛ] 'cosine.' They have their substantive value both as words and as images suggested, but they have a functional value whenever they lead [*fol.* 18] us elsewhere in discourse.

There are concepts, however, the 'image' part of whose content is so faint, that their whole value seems to be functional. 'God,' 'cause,' 'number[,]' 'substance,' 'soul,' for example suggest no definite sense-images, and their significance seems to consist entirely in the further turn which they may give to our action or our thought. We cannot rest in the contemplation of their substance as we can in that of a 'circle' or a 'man'; we must pass beyond.

Now, however beautiful or otherwise worthy of stationary contemplation [*fol.* 19] the substantive content of a concept may be, the more *important* part of its significance may very naturally be held to be the consequences to which it leads. These may lie either in the way of thought, or in the way of conduct. Whoever has a clear idea of these, knows effectively what the concept practically signifies, whether its substantive content have an independent interest of its own or not.

This consideration has led to a method of interpreting the significance of concepts, to which I shall give the name of

THE PRAGMATIC RULE.ˣ

[*fol.* 18ᵛ]

[————————————————————————]
ˣSee W. James: Pragmatism, Chap II, & passim; Baldwin's Dictionary of Philosophy, Article Pragmatism by C. S. Peirce.
[————————————————————————]
[*fol.* 19 *cont.*]
The pragmatic rule is that

[*in pencil under paste-over slip on front fol.* 34ᵛ]
be to make students who are beginners in filosofy get a clearer notion of what the distinction means.

Wallace says that we are here to know the world, not to make it better. This is the intellectualist position. Not to enter the world is the condition of loftiest being. But how does entering keep one from knowing? And may one not by entering learn something that to outsiders remains unknown. Passive onlooking loses part of the experience.

[preliminary fol. 2; pencil]
Perry's prima facie equality of all interests, due to his objective or realistic point of view, is a case in which the conceptual treatment *revalues. If* the concrete man has no sympathy beyond his present impulse, he will refuse to join the moral procession, and you can't make him do so, so long as he refuses intellectually to abstract from the present, and to treat his desire under the general concept. Most concrete men, however, are intellectual enough to join the procession. To such intellectuality as this, constituting moral "reasonableness," all that Bergson says applies. It is useful solely for *handling* life, not for explaining how it goes: It tells us how to act best. [In so far as moral action goes by this law it does explain how moral action goes, however[.]]

[fols. 1ᵛ–4ᵛ; pencil]
[fol. 1ᵛ] innumerable characters, such as size, duration,ˣ intensity; interest, complexity or simplicity, quality of sound, colour or smell, shape, interestingness, excitingness, pleasantness or their opposites. It is thus full of parts which nevertheless leave it its unbroken self. It has no more boundary than our field of vision has.ˣ It ran out of the past and runs into the future without *[fol.*

ˣ

2ᵛ] without our per[c]eiving how much is it & how much is its neighbor's. It is part of a continuum; and who says continuum in psychology means something free of bounds. Bounds *intervene*. Here nothing intervenes save parts of the perceptual flux itself

---
Th Ribot: l'Evolution des Idées generales, chap VI. Th. Ruyssen's Essai sur l'Evol. psych. du jugement, Chap VII
---

and these *[fol. 3ᵛ]* overflow into what they separate so that whatever we distinguish & isolate conceptually, is perceptually found to telescope, and diffuse into and compenetrate its neighbors. The cuts we make are purely ideal. If my reader can discard all conceptual interpretations and lapse back into his immediate sensible life at this moment, he will find it what someone has called a big buzzing blooming confusion [*mrgn. note:* Cf. P.U. pp. 282–289.] as unparadoxi[c]al in its much at onceness as it is alive and evidently there. *[fol. 4ᵛ]* [¶] Out of this aboriginal 'muchness' conception makes a 'many'; and out of the 'at once' it makes a 'one' and then it finds the union difficult of comprehension.

[*fol.* 12^v; *pencil*]
Self-sufficing, etc.
Good psychological justification for rationalist concept-worship in Santayana's lectures on Platonism in the Italian poets[.] Bring it in apropos of the new values.

Ratchet-simile in Wicksteed's letter[.] Also ratchet process in an article by Bush, J. of. P. October 09[.] [1]

[*fol.* 16; *ink*]
will in all cases let us compare

b. Fragment of a Rejected Section

In a separate folder within the collection of material for *Some Problems of Philosophy* are preserved fifteen sheets on L. L. Brown typewriter paper foliated 30, 34–35, 39–44, 55–60. The numbering of fol. 56 has been altered from 55; 35 is written over some other number that may be 15, a slip. Folios 56, 57, and 60 have written on their versos deleted text foliated, respectively, 27½, 28, and 29. Folios 58 and 59 were originally numbered 32 (over 31) and 33. The text on fol. 56 revises the lower part of fol. 29, fol. 30, and the upper part of fol. 31; fol. 57 continues the revision of original 31 (fol. 31 appears on the verso of present MS 52^V and is discussed below). Folio 60 looks like a revision, but its original has not been preserved. Folio 55 contains a large pasted-on slip which on its verso contains text from a fragment foliated 27. Folios 27½, 28, 29, 30, and 34 have been deleted by vertical ink strokes and manifestly represent leaves that have been revised as part of a transfer of early material to the later part of the sequence, as represented by the use of undeleted fols. 32–33 as renumbered fols. 58–59 after fols. 56–57 that revise text on fols. 29–31. Folios 55–60 (the rearranged and revised part of the sequence) follow a gap after fol. 44. Whereas the earlier sheets are numbered in the upper right corner, fols. 55–60 are numbered at the upper left, like the sheets on L. L. Brown paper in the final MS, ending with fol. 59.

Four leaves of the final MS are written on the backs of deleted text from this rejected sequence: fol. 50^V of MS is the sequence's fol. 38, 51^V is 37, 52^V is 31, and 57^V is 23, written over 22. This linking appears to establish that the rejected section, or chapter, represented by the sequence of leaves was written before or during the inscription of the early part of the MS on the L. L. Brown paper and before the start of the Chinese pagoda paper on what would have been fol. 49 of Chapter IV.

[1] Joseph H. Wicksteed reviewed *A Pluralistic Universe* in the *English Review*, 3 (1909), 357–368. Two letters to James are at Houghton (bMS Am 1092, letters 1168–1169).

Wendell T. Bush, "The Sources of Logic," *Journal of Philosophy, Psychology, and Scientific Methods*, 6 (October 14, 1909), 571–575. ED.]

In the transcript the four leaves of text from the versos of the final MS have been included. Although the lower part of fol. 29 and fols. 30–31 have been revised later as fols. 56–57, and though the inscription of fols. 56, 57, and 60 on the blank obverses of fols. 27½, 28, and 29 (and the slip on fol. 55 with fol. 27 on its verso) indicate that these leaves had been discarded from whatever form of the section that James thought of as final, they have been transcribed in order. This transcription means that rejected text begins the sequence; although the status of fol. 23 from 57ᵛ of the final MS is uncertain, the vertical ink line appears to be a deleting stroke as found on fols. 31 and 37–38 from the final MS sequence. However, fols. 32–33 have been removed from their original position and transcribed as 58–59 in the revised part.

[*fol. 23 over 22, deleted, on* MS *fol.* 57ᵛ] [cf. 30.3–5]
all philosophy stares at in the last resort, and stares at but does not answer; for between nothing and being there is no relation but mutual exclusion, nor any logical medium which could serve as a bridge for the intellect to pass from one to the other.

As regards the mystery that anything should be at all[,] all philosophers are thus equally helpless, and in this helplessness lies the confession of empiricism in all their systems. Being, as such, is for every system a *datum*, a *vorgefundenes*, a gift, something which we cannot intellectually burrow under, or 'get back of' or explain, but which we simply stand in front of, and accept, and submit to, and at best dissect and describe. It is there in point of fact, and there is an end of the

[*fragment of rejected fol.* 27 *on verso of paste-over text on fol.* 55]
particular respect, at least, no one can claim merit, superiority, or look down upon his rivals.

Concerning the second kind of superiority that might be claimed, namely that he begs most skilfully and economically who begs the kind of being that possesses most consequences and implications, there is much more to be said.

[*rejected fol.* 27½, *deleted, on fol.* 56ᵛ]
If in the world of positively related things, there are some which are grounds of possibility for others, it is clear that he who begs the deepest grounds will make his begging go the farthest:—the consequences will be given him in the bargain. Thus he who begged 'Space' would have the material of all geometry; he who begged 'music' would have that of all acoustics. He who begs any whole has already begged its elements by implication, whilst he who merely begs an element, must get the other elements by repetitions of the begging, before the whole comes into his possession.

Pregnancy in begging, or in more technical language, *economy of ontological assumption*, is thus one merit in philosophy.

[*rejected fol.* 28, *deleted, on fol.* 57ᵛ]
[*pencil note in upper left corner*: By supposing God you have his creation. By assuming a creation you dont have the god. They are contained "eminently."]

Spiritualistic philosophies in general claim this merit over materialisms. They beg immediately their highest, possible term, 'God' for example, or 'Mind,' and consider that all the lower things which God may create, or which Mind may represent among its objects, are already given in posse. In what is greater what is less can be involved, but out of the less you cannot evolve the greater save by repeated farther beggings. Mind, defined as a faculty of represen[ta]tion, may well have the representing of a material world among its virtualities, and whoso begs Mind thus [*rejected fol.* 29, *deleted, on fol.* 60ᵛ] begs 'Nature' also (provided you take Nature idealistically) as a transparent logical consequence. But whoso merely begs 'matter,' even though it were in the form of brain-matter, does not thereby beg 'mind' by any similarly transparent implication. Mind falls outside of matter's logical definition. If it be an outbirth of matter, we must either make a bald postulate to that effect, or learn the fact by crude experience; we cannot get it out of our original assumption.

It is not in the logical world only that certain things are grounds of other things. In the physical world also things are conditions of other things' existence. Parts of an animal, for instance, cannot live in detachment from one another. A hand cut off soon ceases to be a·hand. The whole organism is here the [*rejected fol.* 30, *deleted*] minimum that can be actual. If you wish to beg any part, you must beg the whole organism with its other parts included. Similarly you cannot have a portion of a soap bubble, the half of an apple, or a single drop of rain, except by going to a universe in which a whole bubble, apple or whole shower of rain, have already come into existence.

Now a natural and inevitable and very pretty and 'elegant' philosophic theory supposes that each portion of our actual universe of fact may lean for its existence upon the other portions, just as the parts of a living body lean upon one another. According to such a view this whole world just as it stands in all its details, is the minimum that can exist at all. The philosopher, if he assume anything, must assume that whole, and if he starts with any part by itself, supposing [*fol.* 31, *deleted, on* MS *fol.* 52ᵛ] it to be a smaller act of begging, this—only shows his ignorance:—when he comes to know his part more thoroughly, he will find all the other parts are presupposed in its existence.

This view is one of those ways of picturing the whole world after the pattern of some one part which interests us especially. Reflection shows us in many cases that things which we originally took to be unrelated are closely dependent on each other and form one system, and we universalize our observation. The books on natural theology show how the existence of the human race depends on the degree of saltness of the sea, or on the fact that at 40° Fahrenheit water begins to dilate again [*for fols.* 32–33, *see fols.* 58–59 *below*]

[*rejected fol.* 34, *deleted*]
different picture may be made. What these are we shall see in a moment. At present the begging of being is what directly concerns us.

So far as a believer in the thorough-going unity of the Universe thinks that the relations of interdepen[den]ce among its parts are not merely physical facts, but matters for eventual rational discernment, he belongs to the school of the philosophy of the Absolute, so-called, and is probably a transcendental Idealist. If so, his belief takes this form: he thinks that the meaning of the whole determines & neccessitates everything within it, and that no matter what part you begin by, if you only get acquainted with it intimately enough, it will lead you to the other parts, so that eventually [*fol.* 35 *over* 15] the whole will be re-instated. That whole is thus not only the minimum that can exist, it is the minimum that can be stably believed, or permanently imagined without contradiction; and it makes no difference how you formulate your ontological assumptions, whether you say the first thing was God,—or was Erebus and Night, or was a nebula, or was Abraham, or is yourself now thinking, or is the point of your pen writing,—it will make no difference; for in either case, all the rest, and indeed identically the same rest, will infallibly be begotten, as the one neccessary and only possible complement of the particular thing you start by begging. You can in fact only beg

[*fol.* 37, *deleted, on* MS *fol.* 51ᵛ]
is not, I believe, the only rational alternative to nothing. The philosopher who seeks to reconstruct it has always, as a matter of fact, to do so by reiterated separate acts of begging. Only the pitifullest fragments can be deduced by him from one another.

The elementary qualities of things are mutually disparate and external, there might be more of them, there might be fewer, so far as we can see[,] and the same is true of the numbers of things and of their quantities. [*mrgn. pencil note*: examples! | Quote Lotze] These determinations are *data*, facts that we simply find or assume, and could perfectly well imagine otherwise. The same is true of the positions and collocations of objects. Grant that the present collocations could be deduced, by using certain 'laws' of motion, from certain initial collocations. Each position in the initial collocation was an independent fact that now has to be separately [*fol.* 38, *deleted, on* MS *fol.* 50ᵛ] granted, and the only reason we can give for it is that the things appear to have 'come so.'

Of course it is easy to call this an effect of our ignorance. Doubtless if we were better instructed we should see more union than we do see. But whoever wrests this admission into a confession that there must be absolute union, and that if we possessed absolute intelligence the world would appear to us as a closed and completed unit, remains with the burden of proof upon his shoulders. No *Machtspruch* or *ipse dixit* can decide such a question; and although some degree of faith in one's intellectual ideals is in these metaphysical regions unavoidable[,] I think there are facts which ought to make those who indulge in this particular faith less unaware of their adventurousness.

[*fol.* 39ᵛ, *deleted*

The kind of fact that makes me doubt of thoroughgoing co-determination in things is the existence of different cycles of causation.]

[*fol.* 39]

After the irreducibly plural kinds and numbers and intensities and sizes and collocations and other individual determinations of things, what most makes *me* doubt of their absolute co-determination is what seems to be the prevalence in Nature of entirely disparate cycles of causation.

There are in fact systems of things in the world, within each of which the parts influence one another, but which, as systems, only influence each other by their totality. Mars and our earth, for instance, are such systems. They induce 'perturbations' in each other. But the perturbations in Mars are determined solely by the position of the earth's centres of gravity, and nothing that could happen on the [*fol.* 40] earth could make the slightest difference in Mars's orbit so long as it left the centres of gravity unaltered.

Well, nothing that originates upon this globe, nothing that men may do for example, can alter the globe's centre of gravity. Human history thus belongs to a cycle of causes irrelevant to planetary motion. The latter can be described without taking the least account of the former, and it is possible to imagine identical planetary perturbations taking place, in worlds where there should be an absolutely different human histories.

On a smaller scale we see the same sort of irrelevance in railway trains and steamships. All sorts of dramas and re-arrangements can occur among the passengers without making any difference what-ever in the speed or place of arrival, for the [*fol.* 41] time-schedule, engineer, and weather belong to an external cycle of causation. Similarly, the events that occur within a Moscow household need have no influence whatever on the occurrences in a household in New York; and even in the same street family histories can unroll themselves in absolute disconnection with one another.

In human cases like these, the fact of independent cycles is obvious, but it is no less obvious in the material world, wherever the statistical output of a process rather than the precise form of it is what makes the difference. The crops depend upon the total [*fol.* 42] amount of rain and sunshine, and the same crops would come, even though the sunny days were very differently distri-buted. [*pencil note*: Other examples]

[*fol.* 43]

Now it is of course easy to criticize all such examples. What *some* passengers might conceivably do on trains or steamers would make a difference in the arrival. What *some* men do inside of Moscow houses does make a difference in New York. If all the sunny days came bunched together in the first two thirds of the summer and all the rainy days in the last third, probably no crops would be gathered; and it may be that some day thanks to Science, men will get a leverage upon energy outside of the earth some-where, and perturb Mars in his orbit. In a more general and dogmatic way still, it may be said that all these cycles of operation which seem so independent of one another at a given time are collateral effects of common causes in the past, branches of a world-trunk to which they all point back, and which, necessitating them all just as they stand, binds them together into ontological [*fol.* 44ᵛ *pencil note*: Brouillon sheets] [*fol.* 44] unity. Effects of a common cause are just as much co-implicated, as if the one determined the other directly.

Such critical reflexions, I say, are easy; but the conclusion which they suggest, that "absolutely every event in the world is interlocked causally with every other"[x] is after all only an hy-

[x] W. T. Marvin: An Introduction to Systematic Philosophy, 1903, p. 269

pothesis. The truth of a notion does not neccessarily follow upon our ability to conceive it readily. In fact the besetting sin of the intellect is its tendency to let affirmation of truth follow immediately upon vivid conception, without waiting to weigh the possible alternatives. To this hastiness we are especially prone when

[*fol.* 55]
Problem 2:—Is primal being one or many?
[*begin paste-on*]
The only thing that philosophy can aspire to is to beg pregnantly and economically. Since in the world of fact some things are grounds of other things, he who begs the grounds will make his begging go the farthest, for the consequences will be given in the bargain. He who begs any whole has begged its parts by implication, while he who begs only a part, must beg the other parts successively before the whole comes into his possession. Thus he who begs 'God' has begged the whole creation 'eminently,' even if he hasn't begged it 'formally,'—to use an ancient philosophic distinction.
[*end paste-on*]
[*fol.* 56 *over* 55]
There are many wholes of which the parts cannot come into being unless the whole comes into being, nor persist unless the whole persists. Such are the organs of aminals that a hand ceases to be a hand if cut off from the body, is an old remark of Aristotle's. The entire body is here the minimum that can be actual. Similarly you can't have the half of a soap-bubble, the seed of an apple, or a single drop of rain, unless a whole bubble, apple, or shower have come into existence.

If the various particular facts which we find existing in the world were elements of the whole fact in this 'organic' sense of not being able to exist unless the whole existed, our obvious philosophic duty would be to beg the whole at a stroke, and get the parts by implication. We should be beggars, but elegant & economical, in other words truly philosophical beggars.

I have already defined rationalism to mean the reliance on wholes rather [*fol.* 57] than on parts as principles of explanation. Rationalistic minds have accordingly always favored a view of the world that made of its parts *organs*, organs incapable of existence by themselves, but *in* the whole, kept in being and supporting one another mutually. The whole universe, with all its details, is here conceived to be the minimum that can exist at all, and other than just that whole and outside of it there can, it is supposed, be nothing. A philosophy that thus imagines the world is a monism. Its principle is rationalistic; but it finds plenty of empiricist reasons making itself appear probable.

The books on natural theology show, for instance how the existence of the human race depends on the degree of saltness of the sea, or on the fact that at 40° Fahrenheit, water begins to dilate again in-[*fol.* 58(32)]instead of contracting. Or they show the climates and coast-lines of possible human habitation to result from the accidental direction of the spin which the parent nebula of the solar system once for all fell into. Floras and faunas are full of co-determinations so odd and unexpected that they seem almost humorous. Alter one creature, and the whole equilibrium changes fatally for entirely remote kinds of creature. Clover will depend on cats, ticks on the mongoose, for existence. This sort of interdependance may well have no limits; so it is supposed that if our mind were thoroughly enlightened we might perceive the whole world of actual fact to be an integral unit, of which no smallest [*fol.* 59(33)] fraction could be altered without alteration running through the entire system, and of which no element could be annihilated without the system falling into irremediable ruin like a piece of machinery from which the master-pin were withdrawn. This vision of the thoroughgoing implication of every member of the universe in every other member is the most beautiful of philosophic pictures. When a mind first frames it, it feels itself taking a distinct step forward and upward on the line of understanding, and it harbors a certain pity for other minds which have not reached the insight.

[*fol.* 60]

A round and radical and beautiful belief like this, tho it be but a conjecture, has undeniable authority. It maintains itself in spite of all objections. In point of fact, however, organic unities seem to be only partially realized achievements in the world of being. The elementary qualities of things, colours, warmth, sound, etc, for example are mutually disparate & external. We see no reason why, because we smell, we should also hear, or why there should be just so many atoms and no fewer, or why the positions of all things should be just what they are, or why there are just so many 'laws of nature.' All these things, qualities, numbers, collocations, laws, are so many *data*; and altho we can trace the present ones back to previous ones, and so to an initial state, the initial state itself takes the form of plural data rather than of a single datum, in spite of the fact that numerous organic unities may form part of it.

Appendix II

Alterations in:
Draft Leaves and Fragment of a Rejected Section
a. Draft Leaves in bMS Am 1092.9 (4519)
b. Fragment of a Rejected Section

a. Draft Leaves in bMS Am 1092.9 (4519)

154.4   gain a] *aft. del.* 'clear'; *bef. del.*
'somewhat'
154.4   difference] *ab. del.* 'relation['s'
del.]'
154.5   sensitive] *ab. del.* 'animal'
154.6   In our] 'In' *intrl.*; 'O' *unreduced*
in error
154.6–7   thought . . . a] *ab. del.*
'exert a'
154.7   minimum,] (*comma added*);
bef. del. 'of thought,'
154.7   we have] *ab. del.* 'there is'
154.7   their] 'ir' *added*
154.8   copious] *bef. del.* 'in them'
154.8   ours.] *ab. del.* 'it is in ourselves.'
154.8   Sensitive] ('S' *in pencil ov.* 's');
aft. pencil del. 'A [*ov.* 'The'] mere
[*ab. del.* 'purely']'
154.8–9 ^{2}is . . . essentially] *ab. del.*
'['is *the [ov. poss.* 'an']' *del.*] must
then be held to be *originally [*intrl.*]'
154.9   thought] *aft. del. insrtd.* 'human'
154.9   appears as an] ('appears' *bef. del.*
'thus [*ov.* 'as']'); *ab. del.* 'is *a [*undel.*
in error]'
154.10   added] *alt. fr.* 'supperadded'
154.10   adapting] (*alt. fr.* 'adaptation');
aft. del. '['useful in the first instance'
del.] ['an instrument' *del.*] *a means
[*insrtd.*] of'
154.10   us] *intrl.*
154.12   Let] *ov.* 'I[*poss. start of* 'f']'
154.12   speak['s' *del.*]] *aft. del.* 'contrast'
154.13   experience.^{x}] *fn. sign in pencil*
for mrgn. insrtd. '^{x}synonyms [*in*
pencil]' [*cf.* 32.33–38]
154.14   intellectual] *ab. del.* 'mental'
154.15   substitution] *aft. del. doubtful*
'tran'

154.15   conceptual] *aft. del.* 'secondary
[*intrl.*]'
154.15   perceptual] *aft. del.* 'perceptual order ['origin' *del.*]'
154.16   in which things] *intrl.*
154.16   come.] *ab. del.* 'experienced.'
154.16   This] *ov.* 'The'
154.17   work] *aft. del.* '[*del.* 'work of
*several ['human' *del.*] [*ab. del.* 'the
two'] faculties of *emphasis or [*ab.
del. 'selective'] attention, ['and'
del.] abstraction, and *naming.
[*period alt. fr. semicolon*] Some
salient ['emphasis' *del.*] feature of
the train of percepts arrests us, we
say what is that'] work of several
['distinctly human powers.' *del.*]
susceptibilities and powers. | 1. Em-
phasis in feeling | 2. Arrest of atten-
tion | *Feeling [*ov. illeg. word*]
emphatically | Attending'
154.17   primary] *intrl.*
154.17   feeling] *aft. del.* 'feel'
154.18   must be] *intrl. bef. del.* 'are
[*ab. del.* 'must be']'
154.19   lower] 'l' *ov. poss.* 's' *or* 'c'
154.19   simply] *aft. del.* 'react'
154.20   react] (*alt. fr.* 'reactions');
aft. del. 'make motor'
154.20   by movements,] ('by' *formed*
fr. orig. comma aft. 'these'); *insrtd.*
for del. 'the'
154.20   'note' and] *ab. del.* '[*del.* 'and
man *attend [*insrtd. for del. insrtd.*
'turn' *insrtd. for del.* 'turn' *ab. del.*
'attend'] to them in a ['more pr'
del.] more *mental [*ab. del.* 'sus-
tained'] way,'] attend mentally, *&
**retain, [*in pencil and pencil del.*]
[*intrl.*]'

169

154.21 ¹them] *ab. del.* '[', and identify, abstract, an' *del.*] retain [*intrl.
in pencil*] them, while'

154.21 and] *insrtd. for del. insrtd.*
'whilst' *ab. del. insrtd.* 'and'

154.21 use ['the names to' *del.*] . . .
to] *intrl. aft. del.* '*['not only attend
to them,' *del.*] **hold fast to [*pencil
del.*] ***them and [*undel. in error*]
[*ab. del.* '['abstract and' *del.*] *name
them, & [*pencil del.*]']'

154.22 by] *bef. del.* 'the same names'

154.22 elsewhere.] *ab. del.* 'upon
other occasions.'

154.24 is at all] *ab. del.* 'at any'

154.24 times] ('s' *added); bef. del.*
'['is' *del.*] comes as'

154.24 within which we] *ab. del.* 'but
our attention'

154.25 carve] *final* 's' *del.*

154.25 objects.] (*period added ov.
comma); aft. del.* 'things'; *bef. del.*
'within *it. [*period doubtful*]'

154.25 sky] *bef. del.* 'we *['remark'
del.] note [*ab. del.* 'see']'

154.25–26 'beach' . . . *'cliff‸' [*comma
omitted in error*] . . . 'grass.'] *alt. fr.*
'we part 'beach' from *'sea,' [*orig.
comma del., then comma added*]
and 'cliff' from 'beach,' 'bushes'
from 'cliff,' and 'grass' from 'bushes.' '

154.26 carve] *insrtd. for del.* 'break'

154.27 'days'] *aft. del. clipping* 'the
flow of time into'

154.27 out of time.] *ab. caret formed
fr. orig. period in clipping*

154.28–29 is; and ['we' *del.*]] *alt. fr.
clipping* 'is.'; *opp. mrgn. circled*
'*insert p 3 [*in pencil*]'

154.29 all] (*alt. fr. clipping* '[¶] All');
aft. del. clipping '[¶] A *what* is a
general head under which we class a
'*that.*' We class less general under
more general *whats* (*e.g.*, that is a
man, a biped, an animal, a living-
thing, a body, a substance, a being,
an object of our thought).'

154.29 *whats . . . concepts*] *underlines
added (words already ital. in clipping*)

154.30–31 A . . . concept.ˣ] *insrtd. fr.
fol.* 3 *for del. clipping* '*[Tradition-

ally, [*bkt. insrtd.*] a concept is said
to consist of the *essential character
or characters* of a thing, by which our
intellect knows it. [*opening paren
del. insrtd.*] A 'man' is a compound
of weight, shape, color, temperature,
strength, intelligence, *etc.] [*bkt. ov.
insrtd. closing paren*] etc., these being
concepts.'; *opp. mrgn.* '*Insert in
p. 5 [*in pencil*]'

154.30–31 individualized,] *aft. del.*
'['and' *del.*] identified, and'; *bef.
del.* 'identified'

154.31 *concept.ˣ*] *bef. ink and pencil
del.* '['Henceforwa ['H' *ov.* 'T[*poss.
start of* 'h']']' *del.*] Once *a [*undel.
in error ab. del.* 'the'] concept['s'
del.] is [*ov.* 'are'] formed we *'apperceive' **that [*ov.* 'their']
percept['s' *del.*] by ['them' *del.*]
it [*insrtd. for del.* 'think the perceptual experience ['through its' *del.*]
by its means'] ever *afterwards,
[*comma ov. period*] ['ˣ' *del.*] ['The'
del.] ['I' *del.*] ['Trains' *del.*] *and in
[*ab. del.* 'and through'] the adult
human mind, trains of concepts
*quite [*intrl.*] unmixed with *perceptual ingredients end by being
frequent. [*ab. del.* 'sensational
ingredients course through the
adult human mind.'] Parts of *these
[*ov.* 'them'] arrest our attention
*just as parts of the perceptual train
did, [*intrl.*] and give rise to concepts
of a higher order, and this process
*goes on without [*ab. del.* 'has no']
limit, *so that [*ab. del.* 'including']
every kind of relation, however subtle,
['with' *del. ab. del.* 'and'] absences
and negations, as well as positive elements, get ['fixed' *del.*] ['stamped'
del.] named and ['fixed' *del.*]
stamped and fixed, and added to the
storehouse of *named [*intrl.*] meanings by which the mind interprets
['its experiences.' *del.*] all the
experience it gains.'

154.32 On . . . Hodgson:] *del. then
reinstated by underdotting and mrgn.
circled* 'stet'; *bef. del.* 'Time & Space,'

154.34 IV.] (*period insrtd. for del.
semicolon*); *bef. del.* 'W. James,
Principles of Psychology, Chap. XII'

154.36 Trains] 'T' *ov.* 't'

154.36 concepts] *ab. del.* '['thought'
del.] concepts'

154.36 grow] *ab. del.* 'end by
becoming'

154.36–37 in the adult mind] ('I'
unreduced in error); *moved by
guideline from bef.* 'Trains' [154.36]

154.37 mind,] *comma ov. period*

154.37 and] *intrl.*

154.37 parts] 'p' *ov.* 'P'

154.37 conceptual trains] *intrl.*

154.38 did,] *comma ov. semicolon*

154.38–39 giving . . . abstractness.]
('of abstractness.' *in pencil aft. del.
period*); *intrl.*

154.39 So] 'S' *ov.* 's'; *aft. del.* 'and'

154.39 discernment] *ab. del.* 'analytic
attention'

154.40 some] *ab. del.* 'certain'

154.40 single [*ab. del.* 'dissect'] . . .
more] *insrtd. for del.* 'notice [*ab.
del.* 'abstract'] fugitive aspects
['and' *del.*] and discern and abstract'

154.41 elements] *ab. del.* 'aspects'

154.41 that] *bef. del.* 'concepts there
is no limit to'

155.1 have no limit.] *ab. caret formed
fr. orig. period*

155.1 Aspect] *aft. del.* 'Every aspect,
every relation, every'

155.1 within] *ab. del.* 'upon'

155.1 quality ['upon' *del.*] after
quality,] *intrl.*

155.3 noted] *ab. del.* 'stamped & fixed,'

155.3 their names] *insrtd. for del.
insrtd.* 'are'

155.3 added] *ab. del.* 'added'

155.4 nouns] *aft. del.* 'significant
[*intrl.*]'

155.5 mind] *bef. del.* 'reinterprets *its
[*intrl.*] old, experience and'

155.5 life.] *in pencil ab. del.* '['new'
del.] its [*pencil del.*] new *experiences. [*pencil del.*]'

155.5 verbalizes [*in pencil*] some] *ab.
del.* 'adds [*pencil del.*] its'

155.6 concept['s' *del.*],] *bef. del.*

'*some new word, [*intrl.*]'

155.6 becomes] *in pencil ab. pencil
del.* 'may or may not *be [*ab. ink
del.* 'prove']'

155.6 important,] *bef. del.* '['additions
to th' *del.*] helps to the interpretation,'

155.6 that] *ab. del.* 'which'

155.7 it.] *ab. del.* 'them or ['their'
del.] interpreting [*alt. fr.* 'interpretation'].'

155.8 sorts] *ab. del.* 'kinds'

155.8 ['so called' *del.*] 'real'] *ab. del.*
'physical [*ab. del.* 'practical']'

155.9 common . . . ['practical' *del.*]
tasks] *insrtd. for del.* '*material
physical & prac [*ab. del.* 'material
things']'

155.10 forms;] *aft. del.* 'forms,'

155.10 ²world] *aft. del.* 'moral world
the'

155.10–11 ethical judgments∧] (*semicolon omitted in error*); *ab. del.*
'moral relations,'

155.11 logic, of] *intrl.*

155.11 abstracted and] *in pencil ab.
pencil del.* 'each ['e' *ov. poss.* 'E']
with its 'laws,' and *all [*ab. ink del.*
'most of them'] *made ['of solely'
ink del.] [*ab. ink del.* 'containing
purely'] of [*intrl.*] conceptual ['and'
ink del.] objects, ['solely, abstracted
and' *ink del.*]'

155.12 instances,] *comma ov. period*

155.12–13 return again into] *in pencil
insrtd. for pencil del.* 'But all these
*different [*intrl.*] conceptual worlds
*relate themselves [*ab. ink del.*
'return in['to' *pencil del.*]']'

155.13 particulars] *in pencil ab. pencil
del.* 'world'

155.14 By . . . thises∧] ('apperceive'
alt. fr. 'apperceived'; *period omitted
in error*; 'By' *aft. pencil del.* '*All
[*ov.* 'As'] our *thises* are apperceived
as [*in pencil*]'); *insrtd. in pencil for
pencil and ink del.* 'Every [*ab. del.*
'All our'] *that*['s' *del.*] is [*undel. in
error; ab. del.* 'are'] apperceived *as
having some [*undel. in error; ab. del.*
'conceptually as *whats*, in their']
conceptual significance'

155.15 interpenetrate,] *comma added*

155.15 seem['s' *del.*]] *aft. del.* '*one another [*alt. fr.* 'each other'] each'

155.16 each] *ab. del.* 'the'

155.16 We] *ab. del.* 'Our experience'

155.16 ¹need['s' *del.*]] *bef. pencil del.* '& uses'

155.16 as] *aft. del.* 'as *much [*pencil del.*]'

155.16 we] *ab. del.* 'a man'

155.16 ²need['s' *del.*]] *bef. del.* 'and use['s' *del.*]'

155.17 our] *ab. del.* 'his'

155.17 By . . . informed] *ab. del.* 'The knowledge'

155.18 there;] (*semicolon added*); *bef. del.* 'is communicated *to us [*intrl.*] by sensation;'

155.18–19 know . . . *classing ['class' *in pencil*]] *ab. del.* '['learn' *del.*] know *when we have [*ab. del.* 'by'] *classing ['ing' *in ink ov.* 'ed [*ov.* 'ing']'] & **conceiving ['ing' *in ink undel. ab. ink del.* 'ed [*ov.* 'ing']'] [*pencil del.*]'

155.19 in [*ov. period*] . . . form.] *pencil insrtd.*

155.20 completeness.] *bef. del.* 'ˣ'

155.21 Aristotleˣ] 'ˣ' *in pencil*

155.21 philosophers] *aft. del.* 'most'

155.22 ˣSee . . . Metaphysics‸] (*period omitted in error*); *in pencil*

155.23 complete] *intrl.*

155.23 of fact,] *intrl. w. caret placed in error aft. instead of bef.* ¹'of'

155.24 sensational and] *aft. del.* 'the'; *bef. del.* 'the'

155.24 contribution.] *in pencil ab. pencil del.* 'factors.ˣ ['ˣ' *undel. in error*]'; *bef. pencil del. insrtd.* 'ˣThis ['ˣ' *undel. in error*] is the Aristotelian view, & may be found in Book I, Ch. II., of his Metaphysics.'

155.25 fact!] *exclm. mk. ov. semicolon*

155.25 facts] *final 's' del. then reinstated*

155.25 are] *insrtd. for del.* '*comes in [*ab. del.* 'are']'

155.27 soon] *ab. del.* '['fo' *del.*] ea'

155.28 so-called] *ab. del.* '['conceptual objects' *del.*] concepts'

155.28 meaning . . . abstract] ('concepts' *in pencil*); *ab. del.* ', so called, *of [*intrl.*] abstract qualities, and'

155.28 forms] 's' *in pencil ab. pencil del.* 's'

155.28 numbers,] *aft. del.* 'and'; *bef. del.* 'attributes [*intrl.*] and abstract'

155.29 relations,] (*comma added*); *aft. del.* 'of the'; *bef. del.* 'among them,'

155.29 were] *in pencil ab. pencil del.* 'was'

155.29 ²the] *intrl.*

155.30 mind] *final 's' del.*

155.30 decay] *ab. del.* 'perish and change'

155.31 vary.] *ab. del.* 'are variable.'

155.31 changes,] *bef. del.* 'having a'

155.32 such] *ab. del.* 'the same are always the same relations; unva'

155.33 terms] *ab. del.* 'terms'; *bef. del. insrtd.* 'intelligible forms'

155.33 found] *bef. del.* 'in'

155.35 and intelligibles,] *ab. del.* 'and that of particulars'

155.36 god-like,] *ab. del.* 'more'

155.36 to the knower,] *intrl.*

155.37 & . . . as] *ab. del.* 'as baser,'

155.37 base] *bef. del.* 'and contemptible.ˣ'

155.37 share] *in pencil ab. pencil del.* 'possess [*ab. ink del.* 'have'] in common'

155.38 with] *bef. del.* 'the'

155.39 ˣPlato['s' *del.*]] *aft. pencil del.* 'Aristotle's view may be found in Book I, Chapter II of his *metaphysics; [*semicolon added*] [', and in Book XI,' *ink del.*]'

155.39 places,] *ab. del.* 'passages,'

155.40 contrasts [*in pencil*] perceptual] *ab. pencil del.* 'in which'

155.40 knowledge] *bef. del.* 'of ['of' *del.*] particulars'

155.40 (δόξα)] *ab. del.* 'is contrasted'

155.41 true] *ab. del.* 'that of rational'

155.41 ἐπιστήμη] 'ι' *insrtd.*

156.4 R.] *aft. del.* 'Mal'

156.5 III & IV.] *possibly to be followed by pencil* 'Gratry: Conn. de l'Ame has an amusing quotation from the hegelian Michelet' *moved*

by unclear guideline from fol. 9ᵛ,
then pencil del.

156.5-6   The *platonic*] (*alt. in pencil
fr.* 'the *platonist*'); *aft. pencil del.*
'This is generally called'

156.6   [*pencil* 'so called' *pencil del.*]
doctrine . . . called,] *in pencil ab.
pencil del.* 'view, which'

156.6   in] *pencil insrtd. for pencil del.*
'and keeps its sway in'

156.6   that] *poss. ov.* 'the'

156.8   is] *in pencil ab. pencil del.* 'was'

156.9   rationalistic] *intrl. in pencil aft.
pencil del.* 'platonic'

156.9   philosophy.] *bef. pencil del.
illeg. letter in pencil*

156.12   As] *bef. pencil del.* 'these'

156.13   dream] *final* 's' *del.*

156.19   Plato] *cont. of fn. on fol.* 10
aft. del. text ' "Raise yourself,"
quotes Malebranche, [*line obliterated*]
perceptual [*ab. del.* 'sensational'] '

156.33-34   Italian . . . 1879.] *insrtd. in
mrgn.*

156.36   For] *insrtd. for del.* 'these ['t'
ov. 'T']'

156.36   writers] *bef. del.* 'had no'

156.36   knowledge] *bef. del.* 'had not
only an intrinsic value superior to
that of perceptual particulars, but
*its ['s' *added*] ['was wholly *indep
['p' *ov.* 'nd']' *del.*] value was independent of all'

156.36   the] *intrl.*

156.37   noble] *bef. del.* 'than'

156.37   knowledge,] (*comma added*);
bef. del. 'of perceptual particulars,'

156.37-38   it . . . perceptual] *orig.* 'it
had both an origin and a value independent of *its [*ov.* 'a'] relation to
*such [*intrl.*]'; *alt. to* 'its *region
[*ab. del.* 'origin'] was from above all
perceptual' *and then to* 'it . . . perceptual'

156.38   concepts] *aft. del.* 'id'

156.39   absolute] *intrl.*

156.40   worth,] *comma alt. fr. semicolon*

156.40-41   and . . . are,] *ab. del.* 'are
[*ov.* 'were'],'

156.41-42   as . . . practical] *ab. del.*

'by derivation from particular'

156.42   experience] *final* 's' *del.*

156.42-157.1   do . . . experience['s'
del.]] ('practical' *aft. del.* 'such' *and
bef. del.* 'perceptual'); *insrtd. for del.*
'are [*ov.* 'can'] ['be such' *del.*]
explained [*ab. del.* 'derived'].'

157.2   Understanding] *bef. del.* 'was
the'

157.8   But a ['A' *del.*]] *intrl. in pencil
aft. pencil del.* '[*ink del.* 'But this
*question of [*intrl.*] independent
origin of certain concepts need not
concern us here, the ['important'
del.] more important'] I will leave
this question of the['ir' *ink del.*]
origin *of concepts [*ab. ink del.* 'of
our concepts'] undiscussed *here:
[*colon added*] [*ink del.* 'in order to
emphasize the more strongly ['a
question ['to' *del.*] which ['little'
del.] has been too little' *del.*] the
question of their value and function']
['for there is another question which
in the present state of philosophic
opinion seems to me more important,'
ink del.] let ['l' *ov.* 'L'] the reader
believe, if he will, ['in the independent origin of' *ink del.*] that *they
[*in pencil ab. del.* 'concepts'] may
arise independent of perceptual
experience. The ['further and' *ink
del.*]'

157.8-9   than . . . their] *in pencil ab.
pencil del.* ', [*comma undel. in error*]
['remains' *del.*] ['as to *their ['ir'
added] value ['of' *del.*] and' *del.*]
of conceptual knowledge in'

157.9   and] (*underl. in pencil*); *ab. del.*
'or'

157.9   value:] (*colon added*); *bef.
pencil del.* 'of our concepts'

157.9   out] *in pencil ab. pencil del.*
'independent'

157.10   , or not?] (*comma added*; 'or'
ov. '?'; 'not?' *intrl.*); *in pencil*

157.10-11   knowledge] *bef. pencil del.*
'['per se' *ink del.*] significant per se'

157.11-14   self-sufficing . . . say:] *in
pencil except for* '*a better [*ov.* 'intellect [*in pencil*]'] understanding of'

157.11 a revelation] *ab. del.* 'significant'

157.12 in] *bef. del.* 'determ'

157.12 us] *intrl.*

157.12 to . . . of] *ab. del.* 'out in our dealings with'

157.14 Yes,] (*surrounding db. qts. added in ink then del.*; 'Y' *in ink ov.* 'y'); *in pencil bef. pencil and ink del.* 'though the concepts are windows through which *we look upon a higher world, known which is [*insrtd. for del.* 'our mind *sees [*ab. del.* 'looks upon'] a world of realities which being essential, immutable, and eternal are ['superior to ['the realities' *del.*] sense-particulars,' *del.*] superior to the ['real' *del.*] sense-world, and'] the object of a *give us a [*ab. del.* 'more honorable'] nobler kind of knowledge *than sense-knowledge, [*intrl.*] knowledge ['namely' *del.*] of ['what is' *del.*] essential, ['eternal and im' *del.*] immutable and eternal things, *of truth universal rather than [*intrl.*] ['and not' *del.*] of perishing particulars.'

157.14 concepts] 'c' *ov.* 'C'

157.14-15 they . . . a] *ab. del.* 'open upon a higher w'

157.15 show] *ab. del.* 'give'

157.15 being] *ab. del.* 'knowledge'

157.16 shows,] *insrtd.*

157.16 the realm of] *ab. del.* 'knowledge of truths'

157.16 ²of] *ab. del.* 'of'

157.17 facts] *aft. del.* 'particulars,'

157.17 of] *intrl.*

157.18 truth & right.] *ab. del.* 'reason.'

157.18 A] *alt. fr.* 'As a'

157.18-19 after ['setting' *del.*] exalting] *ab. del.* 'writes: *rating [*ab. del.* 'setting'] '

157.19-20 General . . . Transient] *all caps. ov. l.c.; each cap. triple underl. except* 'p' *of* 'particular' *db. underl.*

157.20 Transient] *ab. del.* 'perishable'

157.21 adds that] *ab. del.* 'says'

157.21-24 ‸if . . . limitation‸‸] (*period omitted in error*); *db. qts. del.*

157.21 unable] *bef. del.* ', not only'

157.22 or] *ab. del.* 'but'

157.23 that since] *intrl.*

157.24 such] *aft. del.* 'and tha'

157.25 VII,] *aft. del.* 'vol'; *bef. del.* 'p.'

157.28 To] *ab. del.* 'As against'

157.28 opinion] *ab. del.* 'view'

157.29 that] *bef. del.* 'concepts have'

157.29 consists] *ab. del.* 'is'

157.30 in their] *intrl.*

157.30 relation] 'on' *ov.* 've'

157.30 Made of percepts] *orig.* 'Framed after the analogy *of such particulars, they [*alt. to* 'of percepts'] ' *then* 'Framed after' *del. in pencil and* 'Made of' *intrl. in pencil*

157.31 percepts,] *ab. del.* 'such particulars,'

157.31 apply itself] *ab. del.* 're-descend'

157.32 to] *alt. fr.* 'into'

157.32 of percepts] *intrl. bef. del.* 'of *sense experience [*ab. del.* 'particulars'] '

157.32 command] *ab. del.* 'intelligence'

157.32 ['some' *del.*] ²the] *ab. del.* 'the particular ['situation' *del.*] perceptual'

157.33 there.] *bef. del.* '[¶] All that has preceded has *been but preliminary to [*ab. del.* 'had the purpose of preparing the reader's mind for'] the *defence ['c' *ov.* 's'] of this ['empiricist' *del.*] thesis. I will ['preface' *del.*] begin the ['said' *del.*] defence by asking a *question. [*period added*] ['of' *del.*] The ['T' *ov.* 't'] answer to *this question [*ab. del.* 'which'] will put into our hands *a [*ab. del.* 'an important methodological'] principle *of interpretation [*intrl.*] which we ['ha' *del.*] shall have frequent opportunity to use in the course of this book. The question is: In what may the meaning'

157.35 this] *ov.* 'the'

157.35 better,] *intrl. in error aft. comma; in pencil*

157.36 concept] *bef. del.* 'between [*pencil del.*] its content'

157.37 may intrinsically] *intrl.*

157.37 consist] *final* 's' *del.*

157.37 from] *in pencil ab. pencil del.* 'and'

157.37 may exert] 'may' *intrl.*; *final* 's' *of* 'exerts' *undel. in error*

157.38 other] *ab. del.* 'such'

157.38 by] *intrl.*

157.38 our . . . is] *ab. del.* 'the'

157.39 constituted.] ('d' *ov.* 's'; *period added*); *bef. del.* 'the mind's experience.'

157.39–158.2 The . . . representative] *insrtd. in pencil for pencil del.* '*The **concept [*in pencil ov.* 'notion'] [*intrl.*] 'Man' for example, ['as' *ink del.*] is not only *a [*ab. ink del.* 'that'] word, *and [*in pencil*] an [*ab. del.* 'but [*pencil del.*] ['carries the image of a certain *visible [*pencil del.*]' *ink del.*] is also a representative'] image, [*comma ov. period bef. ink del. comma*] *which possesses [*ab. ink del.* 'It [*intrl.*] connotes ['es' *ov.* 'ing'] certain visible and tactile facts, and *has [*ov.* 'having'] an'] intrinsic ['value *as a form [*ab. ink del.* 'in the way'] of' *ink del.*] beauty & dignity, *but has [*intrl. in pencil*] *in addition **a [*in pencil; undel. in error ab. del.* 'to its'] represen-|***tative [*undel. in error*] or [*ink del.*] [*ab. ink del.* 'as well as a func-' ‖]'

157.39–40 three . . . verbal] *ab. pencil del.* 'an'

157.40 itself.] (*period ov. semicolon*); *bef. pencil del.* 'not only that, however,'

157.40 2. It] *insrtd. for pencil del.* 'for *the word [*ab. del.* 'it']'

157.40 with it] *ab. pencil del.* 'with it a suggested meaning, in the shape of'

157.40 vague] *ab. pencil del.* 'generic'

158.1 may] *intrl.*

158.1 have] *alt. fr.* 'has'

158.2 dignity.] (*period ov. comma*); *bef. pencil del.* 'but *more than this too, [*ab. del.* 'this is not all, for it']'

158.2 3. It] *insrtd. for pencil del.* 'but *more than this too, [*ab. pencil del.* 'this is not all ['for it has only this

*aether, [*doubtful*]' *del.*] for it']'

158.3 function['al' *pencil del.*]] ('func' *insrtd.*); *bef. pencil del.* 'value'

158.3 naming *other [*in pencil*]] *ab. del.* '['leading' *del.*] denoting'

158.3 whom] *in pencil ab. pencil del.* '['whom' *ink del.*] which'

158.4 treatment] *aft. del.* 'consequences'

158.4 occasion] *aft. del.* 'the'

158.5–7 'cosine.' . . . lead] *insrtd. in pencil for pencil del.* ''cosine.' *They have two values: **one substantive [*intrl. in pencil*] as [*ov.* 'an'] ['intrinsic one' *del.*] ***words & [*in pencil*] [*intrl.*] as [*ov.* 'As'] images, *but also [*intrl. in pencil*] *['and' *del.*] a functional one ['as additional to *that [*ov.* 'their'] of their' *ink del.*] [*ab. ink del.* 'they have an intrinsic value as well as a function'] *whenever they [*in pencil ab. del.* 'in'] lead['ing' *del.*]'

158.5 their] *intrl.*

158.6 a] *ab. del.* 'their'

158.8 the *'image' [*in pencil ab. pencil del.* 'non-verbal'] . . . whose] *ab. del.* 'whose intrinsic'

158.8 content] ('¹'t' *ov.* 'c'); *bef. del.* 'apart [*intrl.*] or'

158.9 faint,] *ab. del.* 'dim or slight'

158.9 be functional.] *in pencil ab. pencil del.* 'consist in *the fact **that [*ov.* 'they'] they can lead [*ab. ink del.* 'their function, *the function [*intrl.*] of leading'] to consequences.'

158.10 'number‸'] (*comma omitted in error*); *intrl.*

158.10 'soul,' [''man,''' *del.*]] *intrl.*

158.10 suggest] *in pencil ab. pencil del.* 'are *words [*ab. ink del.* 'concepts'] ['to' *del.*] which *envelope [*intrl. in pencil*]'

158.11 sense-images,] *alt. in pencil fr.* 'sensible image attaches,'

158.11 their] *alt. fr.* 'the'

158.11 seems] *final* 's' *added in pencil*; *aft. pencil del.* 'of which *would ['w' *ov.* 's']'

158.12 further turn ['w' *del.*]] *ab.*

del. 'consequences'

158.12 they *may give [*in pencil aft. pencil del.* 'give'] ... or] *ab. del.* 'follow from them in'

158.13 the] *final* 'ir' *pencil del.*

158.13–14 of their substance] *pencil intrl.*

158.16 Now,] *ab. del.* 'Obviously,'

158.17 substantive] *in pencil ab. pencil del.* 'intrinsic'

158.17,18 may] *ab. del.* 'might'

158.19 held] *pencil insrtd. for pencil del.* 'considered'

158.19 may] *alt. fr.* 'many'

158.19–20 lie [*in pencil*] either] *ab. pencil del.* 'be consequences *solely [*ink del.*]'

158.20 or] *bef. del.* 'they may be consequences'

158.20 conduct] *aft. del.* 'practical'

158.21 these] *alt. in pencil fr.* 'them'

158.21 concept] *bef. del.* 'signi'

158.22 whether] *ab. del.* 'whatever'

158.22 substantive] *in pencil ab. pencil del.* 'intrinsic'

158.22–23 an *independent [*ab. del.* 'intrinsic'] ... own] *in pencil ab. pencil del.* 'a value of its own'

158.24 method] *aft. del.* 'definite'

158.25 concepts,] *comma in pencil*

158.25 name of] *bef. del.* 'th'

158.26 PRAGMATIC RULE] *alt. in pencil fr.* 'PRAGMATIST POSTULATE'

158.28–29 ˣ['Note on pragmatic' *pencil del.*] See ... Peirce.] *in pencil*

158.29 C.] *aft. pencil del.* 'Cha'

158.31 The *pragmatic rule [*alt. fr.* 'pragmatist postulate'] is that] *in pencil*

158.35 know] *ab. del.* 'understand'

158.38 may] *ab. del.* 'does'

159.1 to] *intrl.*

159.1 onlooking] *ab.* 'contemplation [*undel. in error*]'

159.4 prima facie] *intrl.*

159.4 his] *aft. del.* 'this'

159.9 under] *aft. del.* 'as'

159.12 all] *aft. del.* 'however'

159.15 how] *bef. del.* 'it goes'

159.17 such as size,] *ab. del.* 'which conception synonyms here *may

[*intrl.*] analyze['s' *del.*] out afterwards and isolate. It *contains [*ab. del.* 'has'] extent and'

159.18 interest] *ab. del.* 'and *interest [*ab. del.* 'roundness [*doubtful*]'] pleasantness or the *reverse, [*comma undel.* so can follow 'interest'] color and ['sp' *del.*] shape or'

159.18–19 quality ... shape,] *moved by guideline fr. bef.* 'complexity'

159.19–20 interestingness ... opposites] *ab. del.* 'pleasantness or disagreeableness'

159.20–21 leave it *its [*ab. del.* 'this sole'] unbroken] *ab. del.* 'don't keep it from ['p' *del.*] being its one'

159.21 boundary] 'y' *ov.* 'ies'

159.22 ran out of] *insrtd. for del.* '*came from [*ab. del.* 'runs into']'

159.22 past] *ab. del.* '['more' *del.*] behind it'

159.22 future] *bef. del.* 'in front of it *without [*undel. in error*] a cut ['or break' *del.*] between it and its other. It is part of a *continuum*. Who says 'continuum' in psychology'

159.24–25 ['knowing how' *del.*] per[c]eiving ... neighbor's.] *ab. del.* 'knowing where it ends or begins and its other begins or ends.'

159.26 free of] *insrtd. for del.* 'with no'

159.26 Bounds *intervene*] *ab. del.* 'Make a bound and it belongs to both parts bounded. A bound is something *that intervenes [*ab. del.* 'between']'

159.27 nothing intervenes] *ab. del.* 'there *is [*ab. del.* 'are'] no between['s' *insrtd. then del.*], and'

159.30 and these] *insrtd. for del.* 'in which'

159.30–31 whatever ['parts w' *del.*]] *ab. del.* '['the whole' *del.*] all that'

159.31 & isolate] *intrl.*

159.31 ['ideally,' *del.*] conceptually, is] *ab. del.* 'compenetrates, telescopes into are'

159.31 found] *ab. del.* 'found'

159.32 ¹and] *ab. del.* 'flow together,'

159.32 into ['into each other' *del.*]] *intrl.*

159.33 If my] *ab. del.* 'The ['field of' *del.*] sensible life of the'

159.33-34 can . . . and] *ab. del.* 'at this moment, if he can'

159.34 his] *bef. del.* 'sensib'

159.34 sensible] *bef. del.* 'f'

159.35 at . . . he] *ab. del.* 'discarding all conceptual interpretations,'

159.37 ¹as . . . is] *ab. del.* '[*del.* 'in which *the **harmonious [ab. del.* 'simultaneous'] [*intrl.*] manyness and oneness *& boundlessness

[*intrl.*] combine with'] ['of which is perfectly transparent alive & evident' *del.*] as [*undel. in error*] devoid of contradiction as it is alive and evident.'

159.37-38 evidently] *alt. fr.* 'evident. [*period undel. in error*]'

159.38 'much-|] *bef. del.* 'at once ness'

160.2 the] *aft. del.* 'that'; *bef. del.* 'harmonious'

160.6 lectures] *aft. del.* 'po'

160.7 values] 'v' *ov.* 'w'

b. Fragment of a Rejected Section

161.14 all] *insrtd.*

161.15 relation] *aft. del.* 'logical bridge'

161.16 logical] *ab. del.* 'bridge or'

161.16 medium] *bef. del.* '['of a *logical [ab. del.* 'logical'] passage' *del.*] of a logical kind'

161.17 for] *ab. del.* 'to'

161.17 intellect∧] *colon del.*

161.17 ¹to . . . other.] *intrl.*

161.18 As] *opp. mrgn.* '¶'

161.18 the] *ab. del.* 'this'

161.18 mystery∧] *comma del.*

161.18 should be at all∧] *orig.* 'at all should be [*comma del. by guideline*]'

161.19 thus] *intrl.*

161.19 this] (*alt. fr.* 'the'); *bef. del.* 'confession of their'

161.19 helplessness] *bef. del.* 'here, all'

161.20 confession of] *intrl.*

161.20 empiricism] ('ism' *ab. del.* 'al'); *bef. del.* 'element'

161.20 their systems.] *ab. del.* 'philosophies.'

161.21 for every system] *intrl.*

161.21 a gift] *aft. del.* 'a fact,'

161.22 intellectually . . . ¹or] *ab. del.* '['ex' *del.*] undermine or circumvent or envelope intellectually, or'

161.23 stand] *aft. del.* 'find, and'

161.24 dissect] *insrtd. for del.* '['dis-' | or 'des-' | *del.*] analyze'

161.27 no one] *ab. del.* 'neither'

161.27-28 look down upon] *ab. del.* 'impute demerit to'

161.28 his] *insrtd. for del.* 'its'

161.29 that] *ab. del.* 'which'

161.30 he . . . ['sparingly' *del.*] skilfully] *ab. del.* '*and he ['one' *del.*] begs ['a kind of' *del.*] more economically who [*ab. del.* 'from the point of view intellectual economy']'

161.30 and economically] *insrtd.*

161.31 the] *ab. del.* 'a'

161.34 If] *opp. mrgn.* '¶'

161.34 world] *ab. del.* 'list'

161.34 are some] *ab. del.* 'things'

161.35 grounds] *aft. del.* 'the'

161.35 for *others, ['s,' *added*]] *aft. del.* 'of'; *bef. del.* 'things'

161.35 clear] *ab. del.* 'obvious'

161.36 ['deepest' *del.*] ['widest' *del.*] deepest] *intrl.*

161.36 farthest:—the] 'st' *ov. poss.* 'rs'; *colon insrtd.*; *dash ov. period bef. del.* '*for all [*intrl.*]'; 't' *of* 'the' *ov.* 'T'

161.37 Thus he] *ab. del.* 'He'

161.37,38 begged] *alt. fr.* 'begs'

161.38 'Space'] 'S' *ov.* 's'

161.38 would] *intrl.*

161.38 have] *alt. fr.* 'has'

161.39 would have] *ab. del.* 'has'

161.41 merely] *intrl.*

161.41 must] *aft. del.* 'but'

161.42 ²the] *insrtd. for del.* '*he [*undel. in error*] gets [*insrtd. for del.* 'the']'

161.42 comes] *ab. del.* 'comes'

162.1   technical] *insrtd. for del.* 'elegant'

162.2   *ontological*] *aft. del.* 'assumption'

162.8   immediately] *intrl.*

162.8   their] 'ir' *added*

162.8   highest,] *alt. fr.* 'higher'; *comma undel. in error*

162.8   possible term,] *intrl.*

162.9   all] *intrl.*

162.10   ['terms' *del.*] things which ['the' *del.*]] *ab. del.* 'is things that'

162.10   ²which] *aft. del.* 'the objects ['that' *del.*] that'; *bef. del.* 'the'

162.10   Mind] 'M' *ov.* 'm'

162.10   among] *ab. del.* 'as'

162.11   given . . . . In] *ab. del.* 'due by implication. Out of'

162.12   be involved,] *ab. del.* 'come,'

162.12   out of] *insrtd.*

162.12   you] *intrl.*

162.12   evolve] *aft. del.* 'get [*ab. del.* 'give birth to']'

162.13   greater‸] *comma del.*

162.13   farther] *orig.* 'acts of farther' *alt. to* 'farther acts of' *then* 'acts of' *del.*

162.13   defined] *ab. del.* 'considered'

162.14   the] *ov.* 'a'

162.14   representing] 'ing' *ab. del.* 'ing' *ov.* 'ation'

162.15   virtualities,] *insrtd. for del.* 'potencies, [*insrtd. for del.* 'possibilities,']'

162.15   ['may' *del.*] thus ['also' *del.*]] *ab. del.* 'also begs 'Nature' *(in [*intrl.*] idealistic['ally,' *del.*] form) [*intrl.*] as a *transparently possible [*intrl.*] logical consequence. But whoso merely begs 'matter,' even though it *were [*ab. del.* 'be'] brain-matter, does not beg 'mind' by any *similarly ['ly' *added*] transparent [*ab. del.* 'logical'] implication. Mind ['exceeds' *del.*] falls outside of matter's logical definition.'

162.18-19   in . . . of] *ab. del.* 'such a thing as'

162.21   matter] *aft. del.* 'brain'

162.21   must] *aft. del.* 'know the fact by pure experience, we'

162.22   postulate] *ab. del.* 'assumption'

162.23   get] *ab. del.* 'find'

162.23   out] *ov.* 'in'

162.23   of] *insrtd.*

162.23   assumption.] *ab. del.* '['assumption.' *del.*] postulate.'

162.24   not] *bef. del.* 'only'

162.24   only] *intrl.*

162.25   ²things] *aft. del.* 'some'

162.27-28   one . . . hand.] *ab. del.* 'each | *other [*undel. in error*]'

162.30   whole . . . its] *ab. del.* 'whole organism'

162.30   included.] *ab. del.* 'also, *up to [*ab. del.* 'and'] the whole organism.'

162.31   Similarly] 'Sim-' *ov.* 'So' *and* 'ilarly' *intrl.*

162.32   going to] *insrtd. for del.* 'assuming'

162.33   a] *ab. del.* 'the'

162.33   bubble] *aft. del.* 'soap-'

162.33   ²whole] *intrl.*

162.33   of rain,] *ab. del.* 'of rain'

162.35   a] *aft. del.* 'it is'

162.35   'elegant'] *alt. fr.* ''elegance''

162.36   theory] *ab. del.* 'notion, to'

162.36   supposes] *final* 's' *added*

162.36-37   our . . . universe] *ab. del.* 'the entire world'

162.37   may lean['s' *del.*]] 'may' *intrl.*

162.37   existence‸] *comma del.*

162.38   a] *aft. del.* 'an [*ab. del.* 'the'] organic'

162.38-39   another. [*period added*] . . . view] *ab. del.* ', so that'

162.39   this] *alt. fr.* 'the'

162.39   world] *ab. del.* 'universe,'

162.40   assume] *ab. del.* 'begs'

162.41   assume] *ab. del.* 'beg'

162.41   starts with] *ab. del.* 'begs'

162.42   by itself,] *ab. del.* 'in his ignorance,'

163.1   —only . . . ignorance:—] (*dashes doubtful*); *alt. fr.* 'is because he is so ignorant.'

163.2   know] *bef. del.* 'about'

163.2-3   all . . . are] *insrtd. for del.* '*that nothing less than [*insrtd. for del.* 'the whole to be involved and reflected in it.']'

163.3 in] *ab. del.* 'by'

163.4 view] *intrl.*

163.4 one] *aft. del.* 'just'

163.4 of [*ov.* 'our'] picturing ['ing'
ov. 'e']] *aft. del.* 'in which we *make
[*alt. fr. poss.* 'mark'] '; *bef. del.* 'of'

163.4 whole] *intrl.*

163.4 world] *bef. del.* 'whole'

163.5 pattern] *aft. del.* 'analog'

163.5 one] *insrtd.*

163.5 especially.] (*period added*); *aft.
del.* ', or with which we happen to
be'; *bef. del.* 'acquainted.'

163.6 shows] *alt. fr.* 'has shown'

163.6 many] *aft. del.* 'so'

163.7 took] *aft. del.* 'supposed to'

163.8 and . . . our] ('universalize' *alt.
fr.* 'generalize'); *ab. del.* 'so [*insrtd.
for del.* 'that'] we tend to *generalize ['alize' *undel.*] the'

163.9 existence] *aft. del.* 'whole'

163.10 or on] *ab. del.* 'or'

163.10 that] *bef. del.* 'ice will float
on water,'

163.14 these] *ov.* 'they'

163.14–15 in a moment.] *ab. del.*
'later.'

163.15 the *begging [*ab. del.* 'doctrine']] *aft. del.* 'what we are
concerned with is'

163.15 directly] *ab. del.* 'immediately'

163.19 facts,] *insrtd. for del.* 'relations,'

163.20 school] *bef. del.* '['know as'
del.] known as that'

163.21 Absolute,] *comma ov. period*

163.21 so-called,] *intrl.*

163.21 a transcendental] *ab. del.*
'an['d' *del.*] absolute'

163.22 takes] *bef. del.* 'the form of
saying that'

163.23 & neccessitates] (2'c' *in
error*); *intrl.*

163.23 within it,] *ab. caret formed
fr. orig. comma*

163.24 get] *aft. del.* '['gra' *or* 'gro'
del.] think'

163.25 to] *bef. del.* 'infer'

163.27 thus] *intrl.*

163.28 stably] *bef. del.* 'and reasonably'

163.28 or . . . ima-] *insrtd. for del.*
'and reasonably ima-' |

163.29 contradiction] *aft. del.*
'implicit'

163.29 you . . . your] *alt. fr.* 'a
philosopher formulates his'

163.30 you] *ab. del.* 'he'

163.30 thing] *intrl.*

163.31 —or] (*dash intrl.*); *bef. del.*
'or the first'

163.31 Erebus_] (*comma del.*); *aft.
del.* 'Chaos,'

163.31 2or] *bef. del.* 'the first'

163.31 3or] *bef. del.* 'or the first was'

163.32 is . . . is] ('yourself' *alt. fr.*
'himself'); 'is . . . think-' | *moved fr.
bef.* '[| 'ing, or the first' *del.*] was
Abraham, or' [163.31] ; | 'ing, or
*is [*intrl.*] ' *insrtd.*

163.32 your] *ab. del.* 'this'

163.32 writing,—] *dash intrl.*

163.33 difference; for in] *semicolon
insrtd. for del. period*; 'for in' *ab.
del.* 'in ['i' *ov.* 'I']'

163.34 identically] *aft. del.* 'and the
same'

163.34 begotten,] *comma ov. period*

163.34 as] *aft. del.* 'This [*alt. fr.*
'The'] ['one and' *del.*] only possible
Universe will be required'

163.35 and only possible] *intrl.*

163.35 the] *ab. del.* 'what ever'

163.38 is not,] *aft. del.* 'world [*ab.
del.* 'verse']'; *bef. del.* 'as'

163.38 rational] *intrl.*

163.39–40 of fact,] *insrtd.*

163.40 Only] ('O' *ov.* 'o'); *aft. del.*
'He ['cannot' *del.*] can deduce'

163.41 can . . . him] *intrl.*

164.1–2 mutually [*insrtd.*] . . .
external, ['to one another,' *del.*]]
ab. del. 'irreducible,'

164.2 of them,] *intrl.*

164.2 fewer] *ov.* 'less'

164.2–3 so . . . see_] (*comma omitted
in error*); *intrl.*

164.3 2the] *final* 'ir' *del.*

164.3 of things] *intrl.*

164.4 of] *intrl.*

164.5 determinations] *intrl.*

164.5 facts] *ab. del.* 'things'

164.5　simply] *intrl.*

164.7　¹the['ir' *del.*]] *aft. del.* 'laws'

164.7　of objects.] ('of' *ov. period*); *ab. del.* 'things [*insrtd.*]'

164.9　certain] *aft. del.* 'the originally'

164.10　was] *ab. del.* 'is'

164.10　an in-] *ov.* 'in *an [*doubtful*]'

164.10　now] *intrl.*

164.10　has] *bef. del.* 'now [*intrl.*]'

164.12　reason] *bef. del.* 'for which'

164.12　for it] *intrl.*

164.16　see.] *alt. fr.* 'so [*doubtful*], but'

164.17–18　if . . . intelligence] *ab. del.* 'to a supreme intelligence'

164.18　would] *ab. del.* 'must'

164.18–19　to . . . remains] ('a' *ab. del.* 'an absolutely'); *insrtd. for del.* '*as an **absolutely ['ly' *added*] ['block-unit' *del.*] closed unit, admitting of neither more nor less, [*ab. del.* 'as such to a supreme intelligence, remains']'

164.20　No] *ab. del.* 'A [*insrtd. for del.* 'His']'

164.20–21　can['not' *del.*] . . . question] 'decide . . . question' *ab. del.* 'decide this matter'

164.21　one's intellectual] *ab. del.* 'our *own [*intrl.*]'

164.22　regions∧] *comma doubtfully smudged out*

164.23　those . . . in] *intrl.*

164.24　less unaware] *ab.* 'aware [*undel. in error*]'

164.24　their] *ov.* 'its'

164.26　kind of] *intrl.*

164.26　thoroughgoing] *bef. del.* 'unity of'

164.30　irreducibly] ('y' *ov.* 'e'); *bef. del.* 'kinds'

164.30　intensities] *aft. del.* 'sizes and collocations of things, and quantities'

164.31　sizes∧] (*comma del.*); *ab. del.* 'quantities'

164.31　individual] *aft. del.* 'determinations'

164.33　prevalence ['of' *del.*] in Nature] *ab. del.* 'fact'

164.34　causation.] (*period added*); *bef. del.* 'in nature.'

164.35,36　systems] *ab. del.* 'groups'

164.35　within each of] *ab. del.* 'of'

164.36　one] *aft. del.* 'each'

164.37　by] *ov.* 'in'

164.37　Mars . . . earth,] *ab. del.* 'Planets,'

164.39　But] *bef. del.* 'so long as the centre of gravity of each remains unaltered,'

164.39　in Mars] *intrl.*

164.40　position] *aft. del.* 'planets centr'

164.40　earth's] *ab. del.* 'planets'

164.41　¹the] *bel. del.* 'this'

164.42　in] *insrtd. for del.* 'to'

164.42　Mars's] ''s' *added*

164.42　orbit] *intrl.*

164.42　centres] ('s' *added*); *aft. del.* 'Earth's [*ab. del.* 'earth's']'

165.1　originates . . . globe,] *ab. del.* '*happens on or in [*ab. del.* 'men can do can alter the earth's centre of gravity by reason of ['its' *del.*] intrinsic forces,']'

165.2　do∧] *comma del.*

165.3　a . . . to] ('a' *intrl. in error aft.* 'cycle' *and bef.* 'disparate [*ab. del.* 'a ['different' *del.*]']'); *ab. del.* 'of causation from'

165.4　motion] *alt. fr.* 'perturbation'

165.4　described] *bef. del.* 'completely'

165.5　to imagine] *intrl.*

165.5　identical] *final* 'ly' *del.*

165.6　worlds] ('s' *added*); *aft. del.* 'a'

165.7　an . . . histories.] 'an' *undel. in error*; 'ies.' *ov.* 'y.'

165.8　sort] *aft. del.* 'irrelevance'

165.8　railway] 'way' *ov.* 'roads'

165.9　can] *ab. del.* 'may'

165.10　without . . . any] *alt. fr.* 'which ['leave the' *del.*] make no'

165.10–11　whatever] 'w' *ov.* 'a'

165.11　time-] *aft. del.* 'determin-' |

165.12　an external] *ab. del.* '['oth' *del.*] another'

165.13　Similarly] *aft. del.* '[*del.* 'Every household has *a [*intrl.*] history ['y' *ov.* 'ies'] with which ['the intimates of' *del.*] other households have nothing to do, ['and' *del.*] which unrolls itself for reasons ['that are' *del.*] intrinsic.'] Similarly it makes no difference in the unrolling of'

165.13 the] *ab. del.* 'what'

165.13 that] *insrtd.*

165.13 a ['Paris' *del.*] ['Berlin' *del.*] Moscow] *ab. del.* 'the'

165.13 household] *bef. del.* '['of a citizen' *del.*] of a bourgeois of *Paris ['P' *ov.* 'p']'

165.14 the occurrences] *ab. del.* 'those that occur'

165.15 New York] *aft. del.* '['New York,' *del.*] Boston,'

165.15 and~ . . . street~] *commas del.*

165.15 can] *intrl.*

165.16 one another] *alt. fr.* 'each other'

165.17 In] *opp. mrgn.* '¶'

165.17 fact of] *intrl.*

165.17 independent] ('t' *ov.* 'ce'); *bef. del.* 'of the'

165.20 it] *ab. del.* 'the process'

165.21 ²and] *bef. del.* 'not on'

165.22 even] *intrl.*

165.22 though] *bef. del.* 'these'

165.22 very] *intrl.*

165.25 Now it] *ab. del.* 'It'

165.25 of course] *intrl.*

165.25 such] *ab. del.* 'these'

165.25 examples.] *(period added)*; *bef. del.* 'hypothetically.'

165.26 might [*ov.* 'may'] conceivably] *intrl.*

165.26 would] *ab. del.* 'does'

165.27 men] 'e' *ov.* 'a'

165.28 Moscow] *ab. del.* 'Paris'

165.29 sunny . . . together] *ab. del.* '['rain' *del.*] sun came'

165.29 two thirds] *ab. del.* 'half'

165.30 third,] *ab. del.* 'half,'

165.30 no] *ab. del.* 'the'

165.31 be gathered;] *ab. del.* 'not eventuate,'

165.31 some] *aft. del.* 'Science will enable men *that [*intrl.*]'

165.31-32 thanks . . . a] *ab. del.* 'to get a'

165.32 upon] *ab. del.* 'of'

165.32 energy] *init.* 'e' *ov.* 'a'

165.33 perturb] *aft. del.* 'to'

165.33 In] *aft. del.* 'In *a more [*intrl.*] general ['it may be sai' *del.*]'

165.33-34 and dogmatic] *intrl. aft.* 'way' [165.34] *in error*

165.34 said~] *comma del.*

165.34 cycles] *aft. del.* 'mutually'

165.37 world] *ab. del.* 'tree'

165.37 which] *aft. del.* 'and'

165.37 necessitating] 'ing' *ov.* 'es'

165.38 binds] *ab. del.* 'makes of'

165.38 together into] *ab. del.* 'an'

165.40 much] *aft. del.* 'little independ'

165.40 the['y' *del.*] one] 'one' *ab. del.* 'directly'

165.41 the] *ab. del.* 'each'

165.42 I] *aft. del.* 'as'

166.6 readily.] *period insrtd. bef. del.* 'and clearly.'

166.8 weigh the] *ab. del.* 'consider'

166.9 alternatives.] *period insrtd. bef. del.* 'or [*ab. del.* 'and'] weighing them in the balance.'

166.9 To this] 'To' *insrtd.*; 'T' *of* 'This' *unreduced in error*

166.9 we are] *ab. del.* 'is'

166.13 can] *aft. del.* 'successfully'; *bef. del.* 'aim at here'

166.14 fact~] *comma del.*

166.16 be] *insrtd.*

166.16 given] *bef. del.* 'him'

166.18 who] *bef. del.* '['mer' *del.*] on'

166.18 must beg['s' *del.*]] 'must' *ab. del.* 'but'

166.26 nor] 'n' *added*

166.27 that] *insrtd.*

166.28 ['de[*poss.* 'ta']' *del.*] cut off] *ab. del.* 'it be removed'

166.29 entire body] *ab. del.* 'whole body'

166.29 here] *intrl.*

166.30 the half] *ab. del.* 'a portion'

166.30 the seed] *aft. del.* 'by'

166.31 unless] *ab. del.* 'without having'

166.31 bubble] *aft. del.* 'soap-'

166.32 shower] *bef. del.* '. shall'

166.34 elements] *aft. del.* 'organic'

166.34-35 ²of . . . to] *ab. del.* 'that they could not'

166.35 our] *ab. del.* 'the'

166.36 philosophic] | 'sophic' *ab. del.* | 'sophic'

166.38 in . . . beggars.] *ab. del.* 'beggars.'

166.39 I] *aft. del.* 'Rationalism,'

166.39 already] *intrl.*

166.40 than] 'n' *ov.* 't'

167.1 existence] *aft. del.* 'separate'; *bef. del.* ', but in the whole'

167.2 kept in being] *ab. del.* 'supported'

167.2 supporting] *aft. del.* 'mutually'

167.2-3 one . . . mutually.] *ab. caret formed fr. orig. period*

167.5 just] *intrl.*

167.5 of] *bef. del. poss. start of* 'th'

167.5 can,] *comma insrtd. bef. del.* 'be nothing'

167.6 monism] *aft. del.* 'rationalistic'

167.7 finds] 's' *added; aft. del.* 'can'

167.8 making] *aft. del.* 'for'

167.12-13 Or . . . *the ['t' ov.* 'T']] 'Or they show' *intrl.*

167.13 of] *ab. del.* '['they s' *del.*] of its h'

167.13 human] *insrtd.*

167.13 to] *aft. del.* 'they show'

167.13 ['b' *del.*] result] *ab. del.* '['be t' *del.*] depend'

167.14 from] *ov.* 'on'

167.14 ²the] *intrl.*

167.15 once . . . fell] *ab. del.* 'fell'

167.17 creature,] *ab. del.* 'element,'

167.18 entirely] *aft. del.* 'some'

167.18 Clover] *aft. del.* 'Cats permit'; *opp. mrgn. del.* '*Other examples needed [in pencil]*'

167.18 will] *intrl.*

167.19 depend] *final* 's' *del.*

167.19 cats,] *comma ov. period bef. del.* 'The'

167.19 ticks] ('T' *unreduced in error*); *bef. del.* '['depend on' *del.*] in New Zealand depend'

167.19 existence] *aft. del.* 'their'

167.19 sort] *underline del.*

167.20 interdependance] *ab. del.* 'thing'

167.20 well] *insrtd.*

167.20-21 so . . . mind] *ab. del.* '['and if we w' *del.*] our perception'

167.21 perceive] *ab. del.* 'see that'

167.22 actual] *intrl.*

167.22 to be an] *ab. del.* ', as we experience it, was one'

167.23 fraction] *alt. fr.* 'portion'

167.23 altered] *ab. del.* 'changed in the slightest degree'

167.23 alteration] (*alt. fr.* 'modification'); *aft. del.* 'the'

167.24 entire] *ab. del.* 'whole'

167.25 annihilated] *aft. del.* 'removed without'

167.26 were] *ab. del.* 'should be'

167.28 (*twice*) member] *insrtd. for del.* 'element'

167.28 universe] *ab. del.* 'world'

167.28 is] *bef. del.* 'one of'

167.29 of] *bef. del.* '*all the [intrl.]*'

167.29 a] *insrtd. for del.* 'the'

167.30 itself taking] *ab. del.* 'as if it were making'

167.31 understanding,] *aft. del.* 'insight'; *bef. del.* '*were made, [intrl.]*'

167.31 harbors] *ab. del.* 'feels'

167.31 other ['other' *del.*] minds] *ab. del.* 'those'

167.32 which] *ov.* 'who'

167.32 insight.] *bef. del.* 'Nevertheless it is only a *conjectural [alt. fr.* 'conjecture,'] vision, [*intrl.*] a projection of the known upon the unknown, and there are other known facts of which an entirely'

167.34 and beautiful] *intrl.*

167.34 be] 'b' *ov.* 'w'

167.36 all] *aft. del.* '['every' *del.*] every'

167.36 objections.] 's.' *ov. period*

167.38 colours] *ab. del.* 'light'

167.41-42 the . . . things] *ab. del.* 'their distances'

167.43 nature.] *period aft. del. period*

168.1 laws,] *ab. del.* 'habits,'

168.1 trace] *bef. del.* 'them back to previous data,'

168.3 plural] *aft. del.* 'a mass of data rather'

Appendix III

Annotations in TMs¹ᵇ by F. C. S. Schiller

All annotations are in lead pencil unless otherwise indicated. For the conventions of single and twin daggers see the headnote to the Alterations in the Manuscript. All daggers used with entries before 53.19 where TMs¹ is the copy-text refer to the Emendations; those used with entries after 53.19 where the manuscript resumes refer to the Historical Collation.

31.17 to a wider] *in* πTMs¹ᵇ *blue pencil bkt. bef.* 'to'; *blue intrl.* '? more precisely to a more *complexly discriminated* ['ly discriminated' *added in lead*] '

32.4 ¹discrete] *blue underl.*; 'but meaning isn't' *intrl.*

32.7 it . . . means] *blue bktd.*; 'any one can mean with it' *intrl.*

32.10 as such,] *underl.*; '(? abstraction) [*intrl.*]' *added*

32.10 means] '(though it conveys all one meaning' *blue intrl.*

32.13 conception] '? judgment' *blue intrl.*

32.24 we . . . ideal.] 'then there isn't any 'it' until we make them' *intrl.*

32.31 attention carves] '& selection' *intrl. ab.* WJ *del.* '& conception'; 's' *in* 'carves' *bktd.*

32.32 identifies] 'for future recognition' *intrl.*

32.32 forever] *bktd.*; *qst. mk. intrl.*

††32.39 pp. 282-28] '82-28' *underl.*; '?' *added*

33.4-6 The . . . comes.] *ab. is note* 'Doesnt that leave out the return to perception, the application of the concept, the verification of our thinking?'

33.10 arrest] *bktd.*; 'may be made' *intrl.*

33.19 book] 'thought' *intrl.*

33.31 gave] *bktd.*; 'took from Hume' *added*

33.34 ²the] *del.*; 'a['n' *del.*]' *in mrgn.*

34.2 worlds of logic] *underl.*; 'No!

logic has to describe actual thinking' *intrl.*

34.7 other.] 'But why?' *intrl.*

34.8-9 We . . . both] 'Bec. Knowl. is the interpretation of perception by thought' *intrl.*

34.10 frankly] *underl.*; *qst. mk. intrl.*

††34.14 plosophers] 'hi' *intrl.*

††35.29 Italien] 'a' *ab. del.* 'e'

35.32 1909.)] *bel. is note* 'Might n't you refer to Studies i. H. ch ii here?'

36.25 concept] *aft. intrl.* '? So called'

36.27-28 instrument for symbolizing] *opp. qst. mk.*

37.18 directly] *aft. intrl.* 'may be used'; *bef. intrl.* 'to'

37.29 names.] *intrl. w. caret ov. period* 'for the purpose in hand'; '(there must be a [*illeg. letter*]! difference, e. g. bec. the—words sound different, but the logˡ import of the rule is that this ought to have no logˡ. conseqˢ.' *added*

38.2 ¹some] *bef. intrl.* '(logˡ)'

38.4 important] '(logˡ)' *intrl.*

38.14 concept's meaning] *underl.*

41.6 perception] *marked w. preceding asterisk and underl. for note* 'But is there not something more? A choosing of the likeness or the unlikeness as essential (= important) & ∴ affirming an *identity* or denying it.'

44.30-31 an . . . world] *alt. to* 'the only real world entirely separate from the illusion of sense-perception'

45.38 only ministerial] 'only' *underl.*;

'What more shd they be? Copies?'
intrl.

45.38 falsify] *underl.*; '? fail to serve:
but then do we not select another
concept to do the job?' *intrl.*

45.39 understand.] 'only on the copy
theory of their function' *added*

46.26 out,] *bef. intrl.* 'as by Plato'

†46.32 substitute . . . for] '(otherwise
than from eternally)' *intrl.*

47.9 concept.] '(& meant to be)' *intrl.*

†48.10 give . . . back.] '[assuming that
you want it back wh. on the functional view you don't]' *intrl.*

50.4 worst] '? 'most hideous' or 'obtrusive'' *intrl.* (*See* Historical
Collation)

50.25-26 nobody . . . thing.] *bel. is*
'Yes but is not the prag^c question
'what do they concretely mean
when they say this?''

51.6-7 back . . . came.] *bel. is* 'It is all
misconception of the function of
cognition'

51.38 connects] *underl.*; '? does he—
isn't that where he fails?' *intrl.*

52.19-20 holding . . . feeling] *bel. is*
'Surely they all do in a way'

52.34 is, he says.] '& all its difficulties
must be swallowed with a final gulp
(Mind 74 p. 156)' *intrl.*

††52.37 top of the ladder] 'the
ladder' *bktd.*; 'it' *in mrgn.*

52.37 non-intellectualist] 'If H. is n't
an intellectualist what meaning
remains in the word.' *added bel.*

53.2-3 The . . . lines.] *mrgn.* '? ?'

53.4 one prejudice] *underl.*; 'many'
intrl.

53.11 conceptual form] *underl.*; 'No
I think it is only its misuse.' *intrl.*

53.28 taking . . . all] *bktd.*; 'reproduc-
tion of external' *intrl.*

53.29 by] 'in' *intrl.*

54.24-25 finds no representation]
'(isnt meant to)' *intrl.*

54.30-55.2 Properly . . . understanding]
mrgn. 'hear hear!'

54.40 founded.] *period del.*; 'as in a
'ground.'' *added*

†55.9-13 For . . . grows.] *mrgn.* '^xI

shd say 'insists on getting the sheep
to enter the fold, & is not content
with a fold too ideal to be contami-
nated by containing *actual [intrl.]
sheep^xx | ^xxxH. V. K. here suggests
a 'manifold' which is empty'

††55.33-56.1 Concepts . . . way.]
mrgn. 'but not in the same way'

56.1-2 definition] '(of one sense of
real)' *intrl.*

56.3-4 in any way] '? what are the
ways of 'reality' *intrl.*

56.6 enjoy] '? claim' *intrl.*

56.8 Philosophy] *aft. intrl.* 'And after
all our concepts are *not* eternal.'

56.11 strung upon] 'based on the
assumed stability of' *intrl.*

56.13 involves] 'generates' *intrl.* (*See*
Historical Collation)

56.13 all] *mrgn.* '& alters'

56.16 ^1means] *aft. intrl.* 'claims to'

56.17 self-sameness] *aft. intrl.*
'assumption of the'

56.31 substituted . . . things] *underl.*;
mrgn. 'quite true'

56.35 name] 'also a 'common'
*pragmatic measuring [orig.
'measuring pragmatic'] for [ov.
doubtful '&'] 2 or more persons'
intrl.; *ital. added*

††57.5 (a)] *mrgn.* 'never I think'

57.6-7 we . . . operations] *underl.*;
mrgn. 'always'

57.7-8 without . . . result] *bktd.*; 'to
satisfy a purpose' *intrl.*

57.8-9 these . . . meanings] *alt. to*
'this . . . meaning'

††57.22 we admit] 'then' *intrl. aft.*
'we'

57.23 meaning?] *underl.*; *ab. is note*
'Is it not rather the fact that the
identities are always constructed ad
hoc & rest on the setting aside of
perceived differences'

57.26 element] '? complex' *intrl.*

57.26 -quality] 'ies' *intrl.*

††57.27 shall inalterably] *bktd.*;
'serves to' *intrl.*

57.28 this quality] *alt. to* 'these
qualities'

57.30 that . . . quality] *alt. to*

'these . . . qualities'

57.32 to . . . so] *bef. intrl.* '& only
by this act'

57.34 Half] *underl.*; '? All' *intrl.*

57.34 impossible] *aft. intrl.*
'physically'

57.38 may be] *bktd.*; 'are' *intrl.*

58.1 the same white] *bktd.*; '? a
reference to a relatively stable group
of perceptual qualities' *intrl.*

58.3 over?] *mrgn.* '[The sense is that
if our aim is to copy reality the real
has changed]'

58.14 excentric] 'c' *ab. del.* 'x'

†58.17-19 I . . . together.] *mrgn.*
'then why their antithesis?'

58.20 evaporations] *underl.*; '?
carvings' *intrl.*

58.20 bosom] *underl.*; 'wax' *intrl.*

58.21 into] 'with' *intrl.*

58.21 condense] 'fuse' *intrl.*

††58.36 1979] *alt. to* '1879' *by mrgn.*
'8'

59.12 think] *aft. intrl.* 'are aroused to'

59.27 hourly] *bef. del.* 'practical' *ab.
del.* 'human'

†59.32-33 reflectively] *aft. intrl.* 'a'

†60.4 Dich . . . allermeist] *fn. to* WJ's
TMs *error* 'Tich *prüfe [*umlaut
doubtful*] du nur allermeiss'

†60.22-26 moment . . . Will,] *mrgn.*
line marking passage and 'expand'

60.26 relation] 'creation &' *intrl.*

††60.26 perceptively] *aft. mrgn.* 'a
relation'

60.29 happened] *del.*; 'interfered'
intrl.

60.34 undermined] 'discredited' *intrl.*

60.35 when . . . up] 'when . . . point'
bktd.; 'Consistently ['logically' *del.*]
interpreted acc. to its theory the
concept necessarily dissolves in' *intrl.*

A Note on the Editorial Method

The Text of
Some Problems of Philosophy

Apparatus
Emendations
Textual Notes
Historical Collation
Alterations in the Manuscript
Word-Division

A Note on the Editorial Method

These volumes of THE WORKS OF WILLIAM JAMES offer the critical text of a definitive edition of his published and unpublished writings (letters excepted). A text may be called 'critical' when an editor intervenes to correct the errors and aberrations of the copy-text[1] on his own responsibility or by reference to other authoritative documents, and also when he introduces authoritative revisions from such documents into the basic copy-text. An edition may be called 'definitive' (a) when the editor has exhaustively determined the authority, in whole or in part, of all preserved documents for the text; (b) when the text is based on the most authoritative documents produced during the work's formulation and execution and then during its publishing history; and (c) when the complete textual data of all authoritative documents are recorded, together with a full account of the edited text's divergences from the document chosen as copy-text, so that the user may reconstruct these sources in complete detail as if they were before him. When backed by this data, a critical text in such a definitive edition may be called 'established' if from the fully recorded documentary evidence it attempts to reconstruct the author's true and latest intention, even though in some details the restoration of intention from imperfect sources is conjectural and subject to differing opinion.

The most important editorial decision for any work edited without modernization[2] is the choice of its copy-text, that docu-

---

[1] The copy-text is that document, whether a manuscript or a printed edition, chosen by the editor as the most authoritative basis for his text, and therefore one which is reprinted in the present edition subject only to recorded editorial emendations, and to substitution or addition of readings from other authoritative documents, judged to be necessary or desirable for completing James's final intentions.

[2] By 'modernization' one means the silent substitution for the author's of an entirely new system of punctuation, spelling, capitalization, and word-division in order to bring

mentary form on which the edited text will be based. Textual theorists have long distinguished two kinds of authority: first, the authority of the words themselves—the *substantives*; second, the authority of the punctuation, spelling, capitalization, word-division, paragraphing, and devices of emphasis—the *accidentals* so-called— that is, the texture in which the substantives are placed but itself often a not unimportant source of meaning. In an unmodernized edition like the present, an attempt is made to print not only the substantives but also their 'accidental' texture, each in its most authoritative form. The most authoritative substantives are taken to be those that reflect most faithfully the author's latest intentions as he revised to perfect the form and meaning of his work. The most authoritative accidentals are those which are preferential, and even idiosyncratic, in the author's usage even though not necessarily invariable in his manuscripts. These characteristic forms convey something of an author's flavor, but their importance goes beyond aesthetic or antiquarian appreciation since they may become important adjuncts to meaning. Thus, advanced editorial theory agrees that in ordinary circumstances (and especially in a posthumous text like *Some Problems of Philosophy*) the best authority for the accidentals is that of the holograph manuscript or, when the manuscript is not preserved, whatever typed or printed document is closest to it, so that the fewest intermediaries have had a chance to change the text and its forms. Into this copy-text—chosen on the basis of its most authoritative accidentals—are placed the latest revised substantives, with the result that each part of the resulting eclectic text is presented in its highest documentary form of authority.[3]

---

these original old-fashioned 'accidentals' of the text thoroughly up to date for the benefit of a current reader. It is the theory of the present edition, however, that James's turn-of-the-century 'accidentals' offer no difficulty to a modern scholar or general reader and that to tamper with them by 'modernization' would not only destroy some of James's unique and vigorous flavor of presentation but would also risk distortion of his meaning. Moreover, it would be pointless to change his various idiosyncrasies of presentation, such as his increasing use of 'reform' spellings and his liking for the reduction of the capitals in words like *darwinism*. Hence in the present edition considerable pains have been devoted to reprinting the authoritative accidentals of the copy-text and also by emendation to their purification, so far as documentary evidence extends. For a further discussion, see below under the question of copy-text and its treatment.

[3]The use of these terms, and the application to editorial principles of the divided authority between both parts of an author's text, was chiefly initiated by W. W. Greg, "The Rationale of Copy-Text," *Studies in Bibliography*, 3 (1950–51), 19–36. For extensions of the principle, see Fredson Bowers, "Current Theories of Copy-Text," *Modern Philology*, 68 (1950), 12–20; "Multiple Authority: New Concepts of Copy-Text,"

The previously received text of *Some Problems* has been the first edition of 1911 prepared by Horace Kallen. The discourse on the text in the present volume shows in sufficient detail how various corruptions entered through the series of documents that intervened between James's manuscript (largely unknown to Kallen) and the final printed result. As a consequence, in some important respects the text of the present edition differs from that found in the first edition. Partly these differences arise because the manuscript has been chosen as copy-text and an attempt made to reproduce James's intentions, as found in it, modified only by his revisions added to the two copies of the initial typescript made by his daughter from the manuscript. Thus the essentially sophisticating form of Kallen's preparation of a later and corrupt typescript for the press, assisted by the attentions, also, of Henry James, Jr., and through him of Ralph Barton Perry, has been removed, including such important features as the restoration here of James's original chapters from Kallen's altered divisions and the dropping of Kallen's unauthoritative sidenotes. In the process of purification a number of readings found in the first edition have also been changed to more authoritative forms drawn from documents either not accessible to or not fully utilized by Kallen.

The scrupulous attention that James himself would have given to a printed form of *Some Problems* if he had lived to see it through the press, including a further revision of the important fourth chapter that had caused him so much difficulty, would have resulted in a considerably different text, both in substance and in form, from that found either in Kallen's edited first edition or in the present radical departure from that edition in a text based directly on the manuscript. No reconstructed text can attempt to produce a version that could correspond to what the book would have been like if James had supervised its revision and publication. Hence it has seemed best in the present edition to bring scholars and students into direct contact with the most authoritative form of the text that can be derived from the preserved original documents and to set aside, except in trivia, an attempt to imitate a completed authorially supervised printed book. However, since the 1911 first edition has for several generations been the only studied norm, a full record of all its variants is found in the

The Library, 5th ser., 27 (1972), 81–115; "Remarks on Eclectic Texts," *Proof*, 4 (1974), 31–76, all reprinted in *Essays in Bibliography, Text, and Editing* (Charlottesville: University Press of Virginia, 1975). See also "Greg's 'Rationale of Copy-Text' Revisited," *Studies in Bibliography*, 31 (1978), 90–161.

apparatus so that any detail of the present text can be related to it and the source of Kallen's variation identified. The final section of the textual discourse treating of "The Editorial Problem" will fill in many details about the treatment of the source documents that has shaped the present eclectic text intended to reproduce the latest revised form of the work so far as James had carried it before his death.

Except for the small amount of silent alteration listed below, every editorial change in the copy-text has been recorded, with the identification of its immediate source and the record of the rejected copy-text reading. An asterisk prefixed to the page-line reference (always to this edition) indicates that the alteration is discussed in a Textual Note. The formulas for notation are described in the headnote to the list of Emendations, but it may be well to mention here the use of the term *stet* to call attention in special cases to the retention of the copy-text reading. Textual Notes discuss certain emendations or refusals to emend. The Historical Collation lists all readings in the collated authoritative documents that differ from the edited text except for those alterations recorded in the list of Emendations, which are not repeated in the Historical Collation. The principles for the recording of variants are described in the headnote to this Collation, including the special notation for cross-reference to the list of Alterations in the Manuscript.

The rejected variants of the manuscript will be recorded in the Emendations according to the finally inscribed readings of the text. However, James's manuscripts are likely to be much rewritten both during the course of composition and in the process of review while he struggled to give shape to his thought, creating variants that are of particular concern to the scholar. Since this edition is bound to the principle that its apparatus should substitute for all authoritative documents, special provision is made by a list of Alterations in the Manuscript for the analysis and description of every difference between the initial inscription and the final revision. Alterations which are included in the Emendations (set off by a special warning sign) as part of the final manuscript reading there recorded as a variant are not repeated in the list of Alterations in the Manuscript. Occasionally James made a simple error in MS, as in putting a caret in the wrong position to indicate an interline, or in failing to omit a word or punctuation mark in an otherwise deleted passage, or in deleting a word or punctuation mark in error as part of a revision and not restoring it. Such mistakes, if linked to an alteration, are recorded in the entry for the passage in the Alterations list instead of in the Emendations.

A special section of the apparatus treats hyphenated word-compounds, listing the correct copy-text form of those broken between lines by the printer of the present edition and indicating those in the present text, with the form adopted, that were broken between lines in the copy-text and partake of the nature of emendations. Consultation of the first list will enable any user to quote from the present text with the correct hyphenation of the copy-text.

Manuscripts that are reproduced or are quoted in this edition are transcribed in diplomatic form,[4] without emendation, except for two features. As with many writers, James's placement of punctuation in relation to quotation marks was erratic, sometimes appearing within the marks as in the standard American system for commas and periods, sometimes outside according to the sense as in the British system, and sometimes carelessly placed immediately below the quotation mark. To attempt to determine the exact position of each mark would often be impossible; hence all such punctuation is placed as it would be by an American printer, the system that James in fact seems to have employed himself when he thought of it. Second, the spacing of ellipsis dots has been normalized. As part of this normalization the distinction is made (James's spacing usually being variable and ambiguous) between the closeup placement of the first of four dots when it represents the period directly after the last quoted word and the spaced placement (as in three dots) when the ellipsis begins in mid-sentence and the fourth dot thus represents the final period. According to convenience, manuscripts may be transcribed in their final, or clear-text, form, with all alteration variants recorded systematically in an appendix apparatus list, or on occasion they may be transcribed with a record of their alteration variants placed within the text. An abstract of the major features of the formulaic

---

[4] A diplomatic transcript reproduces exactly the final form of the original, insofar as type can represent script, but with no attempt to follow the lining of the original or visually—by typographical devices—to reproduce deletions, interlineations, additions, or substitutions. It follows that no emendation is attempted in such a transcript and all errors in the text are allowed to stand without correction, although a sparing use of square brackets for addition or clarification has been permitted. Errors that clearly result from James's alterations, however, are transferred to the list of Alterations in the Manuscript that, as necessary, may follow the particular transcript.

system for recording alterations, especially when they are described within the transcript of the text, may be found in the headnote to the Alterations in the Manuscript.[5]

In this edition of THE WORKS OF WILLIAM JAMES an attempt has been made to identify the exact edition used by James for his quotations from other authors and ordinarily to emend his carelessnesses of transcription so that the quotation will reproduce exactly what the author wrote. All such changes are noted in the list of Emendations. On some occasions, however, James altered quotations for his own purposes in such a manner that his version should be respected. Such readings are retained in the text but recorded in the list of Emendations (with the signal *stet*), and the original form is provided for the information of the consulting scholar. The general principles governing the treatment of emendation are as follows. As a rule, the author's accidentals are inserted from the original to replace variants created in the normal course of James's copying without particular attention to such features, or of compositorial styling. For substantives, James faced the usual problem of a quoter in getting at the meat of the quotation by judicious condensation. Major omissions he was likely to mark by ellipsis dots. On the other hand, he was by no means invariably scrupulous in indicating a number of his alterations. Thus to condense a quotation he might silently omit material ranging from a phrase to several sentences. Major omissions that would require excessive space to transcribe in the list of Emendations are indicated in the text by editorially added dots, recorded as emendations. For minor condensing omissions, James's text is ordinarily allowed to stand without the distraction of ellipsis dots, and the omitted matter is recorded as part of a *stet* entry in the list of Emendations. However, James's treatment of quotations could be more cavalier. Sometimes to speed up the quotation, but occasionally to sharpen its application to his own ideas, he paraphrased a word or phrase, or a major part of a sentence. Since alteration of this nature was consciously engaged in for literary or philosophic purposes, James's text in such cases is allowed to stand but the original reading is given as part of a *stet* entry in the Emendations. (Rarely, he paraphrased a whole quotation although enclosing it within quotation marks, in which case the marks are editorially removed as an emendation.) More troublesome are the minor variants in wording that seem to have no purpose ideologi-

---

[5] For full details of this system, see F. Bowers, "Transcription of Manuscripts: The Record of Variants," *Studies in Bibliography*, 29 (1976), 212–264.

cally or as condensations. When in the opinion of the editor these represent merely careless or inadvertent slips in copying, on a par with James's sometimes casual transcription of accidentals, the originals are restored as emendations. Within James's quotations, paragraphing that he did not observe in the original has not been restored or recorded and final dots have not been added editorially when he ends a quotation short of the completion of a sentence. Variation from the original in James's choice whether to begin a quotation with a capital or lower-case letter has also not been recorded. Similarly, James's syntactical capitalization or use of lower case following ellipsis has been ignored wherever by necessity it differs from the original.

Although James's own footnotes are preserved in the text in the form in which he wrote them save for the correction of positive error (the only footnotes allowed in the present edition), the citations have been expanded and corrected as necessary in Professor Skrupskelis' Notes to provide the full bibliographical detail required by a scholar, this ordinarily having been neglected in James's own sketchy notation. The Notes also provide full information about quotations in the text that James did not footnote.

References to McDermott (McD) are to the "Annotated Bibliography," *The Writings of William James*, ed. John J. McDermott (New York: Random House, 1967).

Silent alterations in the text concern themselves chiefly with mechanical presentation. For the purposes of the present edition, anomalous typographical conventions or use of fonts may be normalized including roman or italic syntactical punctuation, which here has been made to conform to a logical system. The minutiae of the accidentals of footnote reference have not been recorded as emendations or as rejected readings. For example, in the footnotes book titles are silently italicized from whatever other form present in the copy-text, as within quotation marks; periods are supplied after abbreviations and the forms of abbreviations are made consistent; the use of roman or italic fonts is normalized as is the general system of punctuating bibliographical references. In short, such matters involving the reference system have been silently brought into conformity with the printing practice of the time, and usually conform to that found in the styling of the period. When unusual features call for unusual treatment, special notice is always given. Two exceptions to this rule occur: the emendation of James's frequent use of lower case instead of capitals in titles and the normalizing of French titles to standard usage. Emendations of James's sometimes inaccurate use of ellipsis dots is done silently as is the purely typographical substitution of superior numbers for his own footnote markers. James's frequent double underlines of proper names in MS are also silently removed.

All line numbers keyed to the text include section numbers and subheadings but do not include spaces. James's references to pages within this volume are silently adjusted to the present edition; references to other volumes already published in the WORKS are added in brackets after James's original page numbers.

The intent of the editorial treatment both in large and in small matters, and in the recording of the textual information, has been to provide a clean reading text for the general user, with all specialized material isolated for the convenience of the scholar who wishes to consult it. The result has been to establish in the wording James's latest intentions in their most authoritative form, divorced from verbal corruption whether in the copy-text or in subsequent documents. To this crucial aim has been added the further attempt to present James's final verbal intentions within a logically contrived system of his own accidentals that in their texture are as close to their most authoritative form as controlled editorial theory can establish from the documentary evidence that has been preserved for each work.

The aid offered by this edition to serious scholars of William James's writings is not confined to the presentation of a trustworthy, purified, and established text. Of equal ultimate importance are the apparatuses and appendixes devoted to the facts about the progress of James's thought from its earliest known beginnings. Most of the materials here made available for close study of the development and refinement of James's ideas—almost literally in the workshop—have not previously been seen by scholars except in the James Collection of the Houghton Library, and then they could not be studied in detail without tiresome collation (here fully recorded in the apparatus). In other texts the refinements of thought between journal articles and book collection are of particular interest; but in *Some Problems of Philosophy* scholars may find more fascinating and fruitful for study the record of the manuscript and of the typescripts which—as they are reprinted in this edition or can be reconstructed from its apparatus—offer material for scholarly analysis of the way in which James shaped the thought itself as well as its expression, if the two can indeed ever be separated. As this edition progresses, the entire collection of manuscripts and of annotated journals and books at Harvard will be brought to philosophers, wherever they may live, for analysis and research in the privacy and convenience of their own studies.

It is the belief of the editors of the WORKS, and the Advisory Board, that this living historical record of the development of James's philosophical ideas and their expression, as found in the apparatus and appendixes, is as significant a part of the proposed 'definitive edition' for the purposes of scholarly research as is the establishment of a text closer to James's own intentions than is customarily represented by any single preserved document, including even his carefully worked-over books.

F. B.

The Text of *Some Problems of Philosophy*

I. THE HISTORY

The date for the actual start of *Some Problems of Philosophy* is provided by James's diary entry of Sunday, March 28, 1909, "I begin my Introduction to philosophy," underlined for emphasis. The length of the postponement of the project from some years before, and the genesis and development of the idea of a textbook like *Some Problems*, is a difficult question to approach. For over twenty years James had been promising himself a book that would not be a collection of articles and addresses. As early as April 17, 1896, he wrote to his brother Henry that he was giving "The Will to Believe" at Yale, that it would be the title essay of a collection, "and then I think [I shall] write no more addresses, of which the form takes it out of one unduly. If I do anything more it will be a book on general Philosophy" (Harvard, bMS Am 1092.9, #2767). Six years later, on April 23 (misdated April 24), 1902, writing to F. C. S. Schiller to urge that James Ward, not Schiller, review *Varieties of Religious Experience*, James sugared the request by adding, "['You' del.] I engage you for my next book which will be philosophical and constructive!" (James to Schiller letters courtesy of Stanford University Libraries). A few months later James commented to Schiller on August 6, 1902, "But they make me feel the sore need of a *systematic* and radical metaphysics affirming that whole point of view with *as [*intrl.*] classical rotundity as the Object, *the Universe, [*intrl.*] which is no rounded or finished whole as yet, admits of. Pray spend the *flower [*ab. del.* 'rest'] of your young life in composing such a thing, while I will *similarly [*intrl.*] spend the dregs of mine" (Stanford). Within the month, on August 25, 1902, after discussing *Varieties of Religious Experience* and its reception with Mrs.

Elizabeth Glendower Evans, James added, "I want now if possible to write something serious, ['logical and' *del.*] systematic, and syllogistic, I've had enough of the squashy popular-lecture style" (Schlesinger Library, Radcliffe College).

James's philosophy courses, and the syllabi he wrote for them, had an important influence on shaping the form of the book to be. He wrote to Schiller on November 27, 1902, "I am for the 1st time in my teaching life, trying to construct a universe before the eyes of my students in systematic lectures with no text. Es geht schlecht, but I get some instruction out of it myself. I have to refute Royce (as well as Bradley) to his own pupils; and sooth to say his *reasonings* are almost inconceivably bad, so the task is so easy that I am afraid to ['press' *del.*] bear on lest I should tumble through altogether" (Stanford). Schiller wrote to James on February 4, 1903, after receiving such a syllabus and discussed a number of points in it.

In an important letter to Schiller on April 8, 1903, James wrote: "But lord! how I do want to read as well as write, and with so much left undone, I am getting really anxious lest I be cut off in the bud. Another pathetic Keats case! I have just composed the first sentence of my forthcoming book—the only one yet *written [*ab. del.* 'composed']: 'Philosophy is a queer thing—at once the most sublime and the most contemptible of human occupations.'[1] There is nothing like having made your start! I shouldn't be surprised if the rest were like rolling down hill. I am sure that a book of a systematic sort *can* be written—a philosophy of pure experience, which will immediately prove a centre of crystallization and a new rallying point of opinion in philosophy. The times are fairly crying aloud for it. I have been extraordinarily pleased at the easy way in which my students this year assimilated the attitude, and reproduced the living pulse of it in their examination and other written work. It is the first time I ever tried to set it forth *ex cathedrâ*. My success makes me feel very sanguine." Schiller responded on April 22: "You can do far more for the world by writing that metaphysic than by any amount of lecturing to undergrad[s]. It is good news that composition has actually commenced & I applaud the beginning! May I suggest the 2nd sentence? 'Phil[y] is queer but phil[ers] are queerer, ['th' *del.*] & it is they who render phil[y] contemptible. For the queerest thing of

---

[1] This first sentence for a proposed book eventually found its way into the first lecture of *Pragmatism*, written out in October–November 1906: "Philosophy is at once the most sublime and the most trivial of human pursuits. It works in the minutest crannies and it opens out the widest vistas" (*Pragmatism*, WORKS [1975], p. 10).

all is that *so many of [*intrl.*] the most contemptible of men sh^d feel attracted towards what ought to be the sublimest of human occupations.' And then you can quote Plato to the same effect" (bMS Am 1092, #870). Three months after writing Schiller, James sent much the same information to J. Mark Baldwin on July 3, 1903: "I am little by little clearing my life of all odd jobs, so as to be able to do what I vitally wish to, ere the destroyer comes. I have just got some obstructions out of the way, and feel extraordinarily hearty and hopeful in consequence, intending as soon as I get back to Chocorua (next Tuesday) to write the 1st sentence of my system of philosophy already composed in my head, as follows 'Philosophy is a queer thing, at once the most sublime and the most contemptible of human occupations(!)' " (bMS Am 1092.1, typed copy). Because of the close connection of James's teaching with his plans for the book, it is possible that the metaphysic is referred to in a November 15, 1903, letter to Schiller, "I have written almost nothing of my own stuff, but my Seminary is helping me to get it into shape, and it will doubtless prove a good ally to your efforts" (bMS Am 1092, #3702). On November 29, 1903, he wrote to Giulio Cesare Ferrari: "I have a big treatise on general philosophy *in petto* but the interruptions are so incessant that I don't get any of it on paper. I feel as if it were more important than any of my previous works, but that may only be a symptom of paretic dementia" (courtesy of C. A. Ferrari di Valbona, Rome, Italy). James wrote to Henry on April 1, 1904, "I have written in all just 32 pp. of the MS. of my book since the term began" (bMS Am 1092.9, #2917). The same statement is made to Schiller on June 12, "I have been so frustrated that *32* (!) pages of MS. is all I have to show for my winters work. It is infamous!" On the same day in a letter to François Pillon about his ill health he adds: "I expected to have written at least 400 or 500 pp. of my magnum opus,—a general treatise on philosophy which has been slowly maturing in my mind,—but I have written only 32 pages! That tells the whole story" (bMS Am 1092.9, #3511). The last reference for two years comes in a letter of September 28, 1904, to James from Edward L. Thorndike, who had been encouraging James to revise the Briefer Course *Psychology*, "I trust that you are very well and that the *'Philosophy'* [*qts. added and 'p' triple underl. in ink, probably by* Thorndike] is making progress" (bMS Am 1092, #1140).

James's metaphysic, the systematic general treatise on philosophy which he was actively planning in 1903 would seem to be different only in its scope—his magnum opus—from the more modest textbook with much the same aims that seems to have taken shape as the result of his syllabus for the philosophy course he gave at Stanford University in the spring semester of 1906. Whether James ever had progressed beyond the thirty-two pages he had composed in the spring of 1904 is not to be determined. It is uncertain, indeed, whether the draft chapters and numerous notes for a book scattered through the manuscripts in the James Collection represent some such plan as that mentioned in 1904, or else a later modification, or both. At any rate, no identifiable unit of thirty-two pages is present in such manuscripts.

Schiller seems to have equated James's Stanford syllabus with the book so often mentioned. In a letter to James on April 3, 1906, he acknowledges receipt of a copy of the syllabus and adds, "But I hope it will have hastened & not delayed your Metaphysics" (bMS Am 1092, #908). However, unknown to Schiller, the syllabus—and perhaps the need for money—had turned James's thoughts towards shaping the treatise in the form of a textbook. The first indication of this change appears in a letter of May 21, 1906, to the Italian pragmatist Giovanni Papini, which links James's journal essays on radical empiricism, and his proposal at the time to publish them, with the project of a textbook:

> To tell the plain truth about your proposal to translate these recent essays of mine: it frightens me. I cannot believe that they could possibly have a market success, being, as they are, highly technical, polemical['l' *del.*], abstract, and unnatural[x] [*mrgn. note*: [x]I except from the *description [*intrl.*] the single essay pub[d] originally under the title "Philosophical Conceptions," etc, and reprinted as "the Pragmatic Method."'] for the most part. I expect to publish them some day in english, with one or two others still *in petto mio*, but only as a sort of appendix volume containing the *indigestibilities* of my system, after I have published a digestible and popular volume intended as a text-book for students, & sketching the Universe of radical empiricism *à grands traits*. Pray *don't* translate this indigestible stuff now! You ought to be doing original writing—not spending your time and talent over other people's words. When my text book comes out, if it ever does *(it [*paren ov. comma*] is composed in my head, but not a line written) it will be time to think of translating *it* first—and *then, [*intrl.*] only as an after-possibility, the Essays (Signora Paolo Casini, Florence, Italy).

It is interesting to find here in 1906 the same statement that the book is composed in his head that he had made to J. Mark Baldwin in the letter of July 3, 1903, although that may refer to the first sentence about the sublimity and contemptibility of philosophy (the modification is ambiguous).

The 1904 magnum opus clearly had ties ·with his Harvard teaching, as shown by the 1903 syllabus that he prepared; but his

Philosophy 1a and Philosophy 9, courses in a general introduction to philosophy and in metaphysics culminating in the detailed syllabus he prepared for his general course at Stanford early in 1906, shaped the interest in a textbook. In fact, the Stanford syllabus was later drawn on for *Some Problems*. That this syllabus was more than just a teaching tool in his view may be suggested by Schiller's letter of April 3 after receipt of a copy, and by a postcard of April 24, 1906, to Papini: "Since you are writing so much now on pragmatism, I send you the sheets of a 'syllabus' which I have had printed for my 250 students here. *You ['Y' *ov.* 'I'] may possibly find some suggestive points on certain pages. The class was one of beginners, and we used Paulsen's Introduction to Philosophy as a text-book. Of course the syllabus covers only some points wh. I wished particularly to make clear" (Signora Paolo Casini). Ralph Barton Perry is perhaps only slightly over-emphatic in his association of this course and its syllabus with *Some Problems*: "The course played an important part in James's philosophical development. It led to the writing of the unfinished volume, published after James's death but in accordance with his instructions, on *Some Problems of Philosophy*, considerably over one half of which follows the printed syllabus verbally as well as in the order of topics. This course also forced James to think of his philosophy as a whole, and was more comprehensive than any one of his published works. It can be looked upon as an essay in systematization" (*Thought and Character of William James*, II, 445). The syllabus is, of course, not the book, and Perry does not take sufficient account of James's linking his Harvard courses in 1903–4 with the writing of the general systematic philosophy magnum opus. Moreover, as James's letter of January 14, 1905, to President Jordan accepting the Stanford offer reveals, he had already planned his book on the basis of his Harvard Philosophy 1a:

I can['t' *del.*] only give three hours a week of instruction, the course being a general introduction *to [*ab. del.* 'of'] philosophy on what I call "radically empirical" principles. It will be a repetition of a course I am giving this year and expect to give next year here. I may say (though this should go no farther at present) that there is a possibility that I may be called to give this course at the Sorbonne in Paris in 1906['90' *ov.* '67']–7, and that I expect to get it into book form and published in 1907. This is why I must stick to it, in spite of the fact that it may possibly fly a little ['of' *del.*] over the heads of some of my younger hearers with you. . . . The course, as given this year, is more successful in awakening serious interest than any course I have ever given (Stanford University Archives).

Obviously, the formulation of his beginning course in the 1906 syllabus marked a step in the progress of the book in his mind, but it did not initiate it.

One may assume that the same book was in his mind when on September 10, 1906, he wrote to Henry about his "apprehension lest the Avenger should cut me off before I get my message out. Not that the message is particularly needed by the human race, which can live alomg perfectly well without any one philosopher; but objectively I hate to leave the volumes I have already published without their logical complement. It is an esthetic tragedy to have a bridge begun, & stopt in the middle of an arch" (bMS Am 1092.9, #2932). It may be significant that the same image of the uncompleted arch reappears in the note on *Some Problems*, written in England on July 26, 1910, when James had given up the idea of finishing the book and was writing instructions for Horace Kallen to edit the work for the press: "Say that I hoped by it to round out my system, which now is too much like an arch built only on one side." A brief mention comes in a letter of September 8, 1907, to Henry (bMS Am 1092.9, #2938) that he wants to write a work that will be less popular but more original than *Pragmatism*, and again, on October 6, 1907: "I am going to settle down to the composition of another small book, ['the most' *del.*] more original and ground-breaking than anything I have yet put forth(!) which I expect to print by the spring, after which I can lie back and write at leisure more routine things for the rest of my days" (bMS Am 1092.9, #2939). James's personal statement to him that he proposed a final formulation and completion of his thought in *Some Problems* was reported after his death by Julius Goldstein, the translator of *A Pluralistic Universe*: "Aber mit dem neuen Werke, das er unter der Feder hatte, einer Einleitung in die Philosophie, hoffte er eine neue Epoche seines Schaffens zu beginnen, die ihm die ruhige Sicherheit der Verfündung, die endgültige Formulierung seiner Gedanken bringen sollte" (Goldstein, "William James," *Deutsche Rundschau*, 145 [Oct.-Nov.-Dec. 1910], 455). The Hibbert Lectures that became *A Pluralistic Universe* diverted James's energies in 1908, as he foresaw in a letter to Théodore Flournoy of January 2, 1908, when he remarked that he was doomed to another round of the popular lecture form, whereas "What I wished to write this winter was something ultra dry in form, impersonal and exact" (*Letters*, II, 300).

The first mention of the textbook by name comes in a letter to

John F. Boodin of September 26, 1906: "I cease teaching after this year, and only wish I hadn't postponed it so long. My vital energy is lowering, and if I wish to save anything from the Destroyer's hand, I must not waste time. I have next year a big elementary course in Paulsen, during which I shall hardly have strength to write, but I want to write an *Introduction to Philosophy* similar in some ways to his (partly as a market venture) partly to popularize the pragmatic method; and after that to write some more essays on difficult points in radical empiricism and collect the lot into a volume" (Boodin, "William James as I Knew Him," *The Personalist*, 23 [1942], 289-290). This is the title in James's letter of December 19, 1908, to Henry announcing that he proposed to start the book within a month (bMS Am 1092.9, #2956). Article writing intervened, however, so that on March 20, 1909, James was still awaiting the opportunity to make a start, as he wrote in a letter to James Ward: "My family is very well, but my own precordial pain is a great impediment to every sort of exertion. It gets no *worse*, however, which is a great point; and I hope now, having got certain other tasks out of the way, to get at writing (very slowly) my little 'introduction to philosophy'" (bMS Am 1092.9, #3850). Eight days later, on March 28, the underlined diary entry records the actual start.

Thereafter the diary notes the steady progress, interrupted only by spells of ill health or of article writing. On Monday, March 29, the next day, he entered "Wrote Introd.," the same entry also appearing on March 31. Small tasks intervened but on April 5 he noted, "Pretty good day[.] Wrote on Introduction." After a lapse, on Saturday, April 24, he recorded, "Slept well[.] Got writing Introduction again"; the next entry does not appear until May 18, "Wrote Introd." Not every day that he worked on the book seems to have been entered in the diary, however, for the next record, on May 19, "Wrote on 'Being,'" refers to the third chapter.

On October 6, 1909, James wrote to Henry that he had done no work (bMS Am 1092.9, #2963), and on October 30 to Schiller, after an account of his bad health, "I have written only 26 pp. of MS. in the past month, and nothing before that for six months, but my brain has now 'struck' entirely, and I am to lie by and 'isolate' myself for many weeks." However, the diary entries resume on November 10, "Wrote in bed," repeated on November 14, with the addition of the note "Lost my chapter on 'pragmatist rule,'" referring to a portion of what is Chapter IV in this edition. This writing in bed may not have been on *Some Problems*, of course, since two weeks later James was finishing "Bradley or

Bergson?" and two weeks later than that "The Moral Equivalent of War." It is clear, however, that the book is the subject of the January 8, 1910, entry, "Recommenced writing," and of the identical entries "Wrote" that appear on January 9, 10, 11, 14, and 16; on January 13 it was "Wrote on book." On January 16 James wrote to Schiller: "If you could see a chapter I have just been writing on 'percept and concept,' I think you would be satisfied with my vindication of the conceptual function. I make it 'consubstantial' with perception. I have just re-opened a page to copy a phrase or two of your letter (you *didn't ['n't' *intrl.*] say it was copyrighted!) and to refer to your article on Thought & Immediacy which I have just re-read. I found it all marked up by my pencil, but quite forgotten!" The addition here referred to may be identified as fol. 65½ of the manuscript's typewriter paper leaves (59.11–15).

The diary resumes with "Wrote" on January 21, 22, 23, 25, 26, 27, 28, 29, 30 ("Wrote, feeling extraordinarily well"), 31, and on to February 1, 2, 3, 4. On February 4 in a letter to Henry, James remarked that he wrote fairly steadily (bMS Am 1092.9, #2967). In the diary on February 5 and 6 he noted, "Didn't write" but on February 7 "Wrote a little." On February 8 he "Wrote 5 pp" and on February 9 "Stayed in bed & wrote 5 pp." Again there is a gap in the entries, but on February 11 he was reading in preparation for tackling the subject of the infinite, as indicated by the note, "Spent a.m in bed, reading B. Russell" and "Read Russell" on February 12. On February 17 he was "Still reading about infinite" and on the 18th comes the single word "Infinite!" He recommenced writing on February 19 and on the 20th "I wrote 4 pp. on Infinity." "Wrote a bit" on February 21, "Wrote well" on the 22nd, "Wrote pretty well" on the 23rd, "Wrote well, but nervous ('infinite')" on the 24th, but "Didn't write" on the 25th. On February 26 he was "Still reading on Infinit!" and on February 27 "Reading morning," the subject not stated. The deleted entry "Tea & wrote on infinite" on February 28 represents a mistaken page since "Tea, & infinite" comes on March 1, followed on March 2 by "Coffee, & infinite, whose business I think I finisht up." This is the last record of *Some Problems of Philosophy* to appear in the diary.

On January 16 James had written to Schiller, "If you could see a chapter I have just been writing on 'percept and concept,'" to which Schiller responded on February 1: "As regards your chapter on percept & concept you say 'If you cd see' Well why not send it to me?" (bMS Am 1092, #965). James did not send a typescript, however, until April 22, 1910, from Lamb House in Rye: "Since you are at work on a logic, I have yielded to the temptation to send you some pages on 'percepts & concepts' from the MS. of my introduction to Metaphysics. Heaven forbid that you should assume ['that' *del.*] the labor of *commenting* on the stuff—it simply occurred to me that [*comma del.*] you might possibly find some of the statements helpfully simple. Return at your leisure, but don't let the stuff get used for lighting your fire!" Then in a P.S.: "My MS. consists of about 200 pp. so far—I hope about ½ of the book" (Stanford). Schiller started to annotate the type-script and sent James a letter, now lost, about the chapter, for on April 27 James responded from Lamb House:

What you write of my Ms. makes me see again how much more radically and deeply you & Dewey place your-|['self' *del.*] selves than I do. [I believe that your thought in this matter is absolutely congruent with Dewey's.] The problems I started with were more superficial and I have kept closer to their neighborhood. Of course I see the splendid sweep of your program and what your letter says makes me red-hot for the publication of your logic. . . . There may be an advantage, from the point of view of converting the public, in our working at different levels. E.g. in a book for College use like mine (I want it to *sell*) the 'eternal' view of concepts *can [*ab. del.* 'can may'] do no *particular [*intrl.*] harm, for they are *relatively* eternal (and some of them actually so, so far as we yet know) and the distinguishing of them as such is a rather definite stage in tho't, practically attained by opinion [*comma del.*] concerning them, on which the student can start easily and keep step with you. . . . I send you herewith the introductory pp. of my chapter, which [*comma del.*] I spared you before on acc⸍ of their relative triteness. You *can [*intrl.*] see how easy it would be for me to put myself quite on your ground by developing *here [*intrl.*] at greater length the notion of "meaning," and thereafter making ['ever' *del.*] all boundaries more fluid, as you do. But I question whether, for didactic purposes (as well as *for [*intrl.*] your priority rights!) I had n't better keep my level, and leave yours to you. I shall make use of some of your marginal scribblings, and altogether I have found this last letter of yours a very eye opening communication (Stanford).

James wrote again from Lamb House on May 4, 1910:

I shall also profit by the annotations on the pp. of my MS. wh. you return, and by your accompanying letter. I understand entirely what you are driving at, and the last Appendix (C?) of my pl. U. will show you that I have caught the meaning of the fluidity of concepts long since. ['But' *del.*] Also have I always known that percepts (in the plural) *are [*ab. del.* 'were'] just as much artefacts as any 'concept' is. But ever since ['the' *del.*] your 'Axioms as Postulates' you have been on much more fundamental ground, *didactically*, than I have ever placed myself on. You have aimed at *describing [*intrl.*] the whole process of knowledge, from an initial zero. I start (especially in this book for students) from the common sense level at which, as you admirably say, "many discriminations of proved pragmatic value have already been effected." It is important to show the public that the function of concepts is practical; but it disconcerts the beginner to be told that the very concepts you use in doing so are themselves deliquescent; and after all, our experience ought to have by this time establisht *some* of them in pragmatic solidity. I therefore assume the eternity of ['a' *del.*] 'realities' ['ies' *ov.* 'y'] independent of my belief, of the meaning 'same,' and of ['the' *del.*] the usual mathematical and logical objects, for no one can foresee any imminent probability of their not serving inalterably. I thus pedagogi[c]ally insert the thin end of the wedge *with [*ab. del.* 'of'] which you and Dewey are engaged in splitting up the whole thickness of the cake of epistemology. There is room for both of our methods; but the result of your notes and criticisms will be to make me confess more explicitly to the provisionality of my forms of statement (Stanford).

On May 6 Schiller responded with "Many thanks for your letter & the MS" and then devoted much space to a further discussion of concepts and percepts (bMS Am 1092, #972). This is the last letter about the book except for the postscript after James's death when Schiller wrote on January 17, 1911, to Mrs. James: "It is also good news that the 'Introduction to Philosophy' was advanced enough to be published. It may possibly want annotation in places, & if so I have told Mr Kallen who I understand is to do the editing, he can consult me in difficulties" (bMS Am 1092, #975). No evidence is preserved that such consultation took place. However, Henry James, Jr., noted two of Schiller's corrections to the book in his private copy although he did not use them in the plate alterations he ordered.

II. THE DOCUMENTS

In the James Collection, the Houghton Library, Harvard University, the file bMS Am 1092.7 contains in a series of folders the textual documents for *Some Problems of Philosophy*, comprising the preserved portion of the original manuscript (MS); the ribbon and carbon copies of the typescript (TMs[1]), both of which James revised by hand (TMs[1b] was taken abroad but TMs[1a] left in Cambridge); the second typescript (TMs[2]), made from the first, which was the printer's copy after being corrected and annotated by Horace Kallen; a set of proof sheets (I[p]); and certain memoranda and letters by William James, his son Henry James, Jr., and Horace Kallen.

In the main file are also found fourteen leaves of a rejected draft for a section of Chapter III, "The Problem of Being." A draft for the beginning of Chapter IV, "Percept and Concept," is preserved in bMS Am 1092.9, #4519. Both of these draft documents have been transcribed, with their variants, in Appendix I.

THE MANUSCRIPT

The manuscript of *Some Problems of Philosophy*, as preserved in bMS Am 1092.7, begins with eighty-six leaves of typewriter-size paper written chiefly in ink, corrected in ink and in small part in pencil, concluded in a notebook.

Chapter I, "Philosophy and its Critics," utilizes thirty-six sheets of wove typewriter paper (278 × 215 mm.) watermarked with a G in a shield surmounted by an arm brandishing a scimitar, counter-marked L. L. Brown Co. The leaves are foliated in the upper left corner [1] 2-11 12(11) 13(12) 14 14½ 15 16(17) 17(16) 18(17) 19-21 22(21) 23-35. Deleted matter appears on fols. 2^v, 12^v, and 16^v.

Folio 9 (11.22 *Shepherd . . . them.* 11.29) is a part-page and hence presumably a substituted revision. Folio 11 (12.4 *Only . . . and* 12.14) appears to be an original leaf since deleted matter at its foot links with a few words of unexcised text on fol. 12^v that represents an abandoned trial. That fols. 12 and 13 are numbered over original 11 and 12 respectively seems therefore to betray a slip on James's part and not a concealed textual disruption. Folio 14½ (13.10 *It . . . etc.*^{x}[plus fn.] 13.20) is marked for insertion on preceding fol. 14 as an afterthought. Folio 15 (13.30 *Spencer . . . moral* 14.8) was originally continued on a sheet numbered 16 at the left, but the top portion of the latter was deleted, the page was renumbered 17 in the center, and an expansion of the text begun on a new sheet numbered 16. This was broken off after a footnote (fn. 3, later written on fol. 18), deleted, and a briefer connecting passage of text (14.8 *speculations . . . better* 14.13) numbered 17 in error and then 16 was written on its verso. The revision can be placed as occurring after the inscription of fol. 18 (14.23 *I refer . . . very* 14.37), which was renumbered from 17, but before normally numbered 19. Before fol. 23 was inscribed, the first few words of fol. 21 (and the last 2½ lines of fol. 20) were deleted, the sheet was renumbered 22, and a part-page 21 (15.27 *If . . . . 'Sympathetic*$_\wedge$ 15.33) was inserted before it as an expansion. The chapter ends normally on fol. 35.

Chapter II, "The Problems of Metaphysics," continues the foliation with 36 on the same lot of L. L. Brown paper. The eleven leaves in this chapter are foliated 36–46 and appear to have been written without any disruption.

Chapter III (misnumbered 'II'), "The Problem of Being," begins on fol. 47 and continues the same L. L. Brown paper. Its foliation for fourteen leaves is 47–54 55(54) 56 57(53) 58(54?) 58½ 59. Deleted matter from what seems to have been a rejected section or chapter, otherwise preserved in fragmentary form in a folder of loose sheets, appears foliated in the upper right corner: 38 on 50^v, 37 on 51^v, 31 on 52^v, and 23 over 22 on 57^v. The deleted text on these four verso leaves is reprinted in its proper place in Appendix I arranged in sequence with the preserved loose draft sheets, some of which are themselves revisions written on the backs of earlier sheets in this discarded sequence. These loose draft sheets are also from the run of L. L. Brown paper, which ends with Chapter III; the use of the backs of four of these discarded draft leaves for the final inscription of Chapter III suggests some close connection in time, and it is possible to speculate that the writing-out of present Chapter III replaced a chapter now known only from the fragmentary text of the collected draft leaves and these four deleted versos. Excised text on four other versos of the Chapter III MS belongs within the present chapter: that on part-page fol. 58^v is numbered 52, has some reference to a few sentences on fol. 53 and also on 55(54), but seems to be part of an earlier sequence beginning in revised form with present fol. 50; 54^v originally continued the deleted foot of 55(54) and relates to the text near the head of present part-page 54; 56^v (starting a new paragraph) is related to the second sentence on present part-page 56; and 59^v is a trial continuing 57(53) and was thus intended as the start of original 54, now 58.

The text of this chapter starts out normally with fols. 47, 48, and 49; but deleted text beginning a paragraph at the foot of fol. 49 links with no text at the head of any present page. Instead, fol. 50 begins quite a different paragraph and is manifestly the substituted start of a considerable textual revision. Folio 50 (27.1 *One . . . only* 27.13) is written on the back of a discarded leaf from a rejected section (like 51^v, 52^v, and 57^v), a coincidence that is very likely not fortuitous. Moreover, deleted text at the foot of fol. 52 (27.27 *don't . . . mystery.* 28.1) is continued, deleted, at the head of fol. 57 (28.31 *in the . . . on the* 29.8), altered from 53. Thus the text of the four leaves on the backs of the draft was originally consecutive, and fols. 53–56 represent an expansion within the revision starting on fol. 50. The expansion was itself expanded, incidentally, since deleted text at the foot of fol. 53 (28.1 *Some . . . existence.'*[plus fn.] 28.12) is continued by deleted text at the head of fol. 55 (28.18 *or . . . with* 28.28), altered from 54. James then wrote fol. 54 (now renumbered to 55)[2] down to *most abstract of all* (28.27) with its footnote. Below this footnote he started a new paragraph with *The ontological state of mind is easy*, which he continued on what is now 54^v but abandoned this after two lines, turned the sheet over, and on what is now 54 he continued (omitting *to* in error) *produce in one's self*. At this point he stopped, deleted this phrase and the start of the sentence at the foot of 55(54) and began fol. 54 afresh with *It is mere*, joining the sheet with *The anselmian* (28.12–18) to the top of former 54 (deleting *The anselmian* at its head) and renumbering 54 to 55 to take account of inserted 54. He then wrote the start of a new paragraph on what is now 56^v but rejected it and turned the sheet over and, starting the new sentence in the vacant space after the last sentence and its footnote on fol. 55(54), with *This is somewhat in line with* he continued it on fol. 56 (28.28 *Kant's . . . 'being'* 28.31) which thus hitched in with the text (after a short deletion) at the head of 57(53), an original leaf. Heavily revised fol. 58 (29.8 *on the whole . . . how* 29.19) had been numbered 54 (itself an alteration perhaps of 52). The first line of 58 which links it with the foot of fol. 57 is an addition, a trial for this revision being present on fol. 59^v, rejected when James decided to alter fol. 58 instead of copying out its new start. However, the original now-deleted text at the head of fol. 58 does not link with the text at the foot of any preserved leaf. On the verso of this fol. 58 is a part-page trial foliated 52, which would have followed the original lost 51 (not the present revised substitute). Some of the phrasing is found on fol. 55(54) (28.24–25) but the context of 58^v is clearly allied to that on fol. 53 (28.3–8) and gives an early compressed discussion of the ontological proof of God's existence, followed by the evolutionary position, the order of the discussion then being reversed in the expansion following fol. 49. Folio 58½ (29.19 *the coming . . . airs.* 30.3) is a revision of deleted matter at the head of fol. 59. At its foot is pasted in a slightly revised clipping from the syllabus that he had printed for the course he gave at Stanford in 1906. However, the original deleted matter heading fol. 59 (itself a revision of the deleted foot of fol. 58) was

---

[2]The figure 54 on the recto, particularly the 4, seems to be traced over some other lines, but the earlier numbering—if it existed—cannot be recovered. The 5 of the original foliation 54 for present 55 is also odd looking.

then deleted and begun afresh on 58½. This last sheet 59 ends with deleted text that concludes a sentence; since the page is full, one cannot know whether the chapter originally continued beyond the present point.

Chapter IV, "Percept and Concept," begins a different lot of wove typewriter paper (266 X 203 mm.) watermarked with a pagoda, the date 1908, and the words Chinese Linen. The first leaf is unnumbered and so is the part-page second leaf, both of which are substitutes, or, more precisely, additions. However, the original text for the lost first page of "Percept and Concept" can be recovered from the typescript copies, both of which contain it, without chapter heading, independently revised by hand in each but then retyped in a version drawn instead from the revised first two leaves of the present manuscript. After the second unnumbered leaf the manuscript is wanting and does not begin until fol. 51 (53.19 *all . . . content.*[x] [plus fn.] 53.25), using the same Chinese Linen paper. The foliation for this chapter in the MS, then, is [1–2] [*wanting*] 51–53 53½ 54–61 61½ 62 62½ 63–65 65½ 66–69.

Folio 53½ (54.8 *only . . . possumus*, 54.14) was originally 53, but the ½ was added when present fol. 53 (54.2 *He . . . found* 54.8) was inserted to revise the deleted upper half of what is now 53½. On fol. 54 we first encounter the use of subheadings (another feature differentiating Chapter IV from I–III), these written in red ink. Originally, at 54.16 in a deep indention of the paragraph James wrote in lead pencil 'Corollaries' but then over it, in red ink, he wrote 'Corollary I' and above it squeezed in between the lines, in red ink, 'Some Corollaries' double underlined. On fol. 56 the text between 55.3 and 55.13 (*makeshift* [for *abstract*] *. . . experience.* [*grows.*]) at the head has been deleted by a vertical blue line, concluding with a horizontal blue line under the paragraph. The text below the deletion, beginning with *Empiricist* (55.13), heads typescript page 102; the blue deletion is to mark off matter already typed and to point the typist to the text indicated by the pencil note at the foot of p. 101(54) 'Continue copying *MS p. 56*'. Similar deleting lines in blue are found in the early pages of the Chapter VII text in the Partridge and Cooper notebook where they indicate pages that have been typed.

Folios 58–59 appear to be normal except that fol. 60 (56.15) completely alters the deleted start of the Third Corollary at the foot of fol. 59; moreover, both leaves are foliated in the upper right corner whereas fol. 60 reverts to the centered numbering. A chance exists, then, that the text of fols. 58–59 (55.29 *is quite . . . besides.* 56.14) is a revision. On fol. 61 James pasted in a nine-line printed quotation from James Mill (56.24 *"Every . . . mystical* 56.32) and himself copied only the opening and closing words. Folio 61½ (57.7. *without . . . 'white'* 57.23) does not reflect revision but instead a mistake in numbering two sheets as 61 repaired by the addition of ½. Although 62½ (57.34 *not . . . flux.* 58.5) expands the deleted upper half of fol. 63, the text at the foot of 62 does not link with the deleted (or undeleted) text at the head of fol. 63; thus it is possible that 62–63 are not originals. Folio 65½ (59.11 *Perception . . . immediacy.ˣ [perception.³⁴]* 59.15) is an insertion replacing the deleted upper part of fol. 66. (A letter to Schiller dates this as an addition on January 16, 1910.) The chapter ends normally, two-thirds of the way down on fol. 69.

The rest of the manuscript is contained in a hardcover notebook of unlined blue wove leaves (245 × 200 mm.) watermarked Wm. Partridge & Cooper, Chancery Lane. After three leaves of notes, on the rectos, the text begins on the fourth leaf with the heading 'One & Many' but without chapter number. Henry James, Jr.'s, memorandum states: "The first ms of what followed these pages [the destroyed leaves mentioned above] is found in the blue paper note-book (written from both ends)." The writing is ordinarily on the rectos, the versos being saved for additions and revisions. The first leaf is unnumbered but the second is numbered 2 and so on in the right corner. In TMs¹ᵃ (but not in TMs¹ᵇ) James changed the title to 'The One and the Many' and added the word 'Chapter' but did not fill in a number.

[Chapter V] is foliated [1] 2–34 in ink in the upper right corner except for fols. 14 and 15, which are in pencil, and fol. 29 numbered in the upper left corner. Folio 25 (69.17 *From . . . abstraction. Once* 70.25) consists of pasted-in slips from the printed Stanford Syllabus considerably revised by annotation, with more annotated paste-ins from this Syllabus on fols. 29–30 (72.1 *the other . . . belief.ˣ* 73.37), fol. 29 being numbered in the upper left corner when annotation had taken up the space in the upper right. Folio 34 (75.4 *of view . . . word?* 75.10) has deleted text at the foot promising a next chapter on the problems of being. Below this is a circled note, also deleted, 'Insert loose sheets 47–59' (59 *over* 58). The reference is to Chapter III, "The Problem of Being" (misnumbered II in MS), which occupies fols. 47 (26.1) to 59 (30.7) on L. L. Brown paper. This rejected proposal to insert

Chapter III after "The One and the Many" may help to explain James's alteration of the chapter number next succeeding the note, on fol. 60, to V from original IV. This intention to insert manuscript leaves 47–59 also accounts for the gap in the notebook foliation between the end of present Chapter V on fol. 34 and the start of present Chapter VI on the next leaf numbered (silently) as 60. When James changed his plan on fol. 33^v and revised the end of Chapter V, he mentioned the discussion of Being at the end of Chapter III as a datum or gift that must be begged, a clear-cut reference to 30.2–7 and also an indication that by the time he wrote this substituted ending he had clarified in his mind the arrangement of chapters and so recognized that Chapter II should in fact be III. It is worth notice, also, that present Chapter VI begins with a reference to Chapter III (76.8) by its correct number. This proposal to transfer what was to become Chapter III, and especially the gap in the foliation left for it (in its draft form, however) before the start of Chapter VI, indicates that even though the first chapter in this notebook was unnumbered, its composition was later than the inscription of the L. L. Brown draft leaves for Chapter III that were subsequently reworked into their present form in the MS.

Chapter VI, "The Problem of Novelty," is foliated [60] 61–68, its chapter number altered from IV to V. On the verso of fol. 60 are two deleted lines 'The problem is a complicated one and had better be treated in two chapters.', which may at one time have been intended for insertion on fol. 61 somewhere after 76.7–9, 'We are thus brought back to the problem with which Chapter III left off.' The text continues normally, with occasional verso additions, through the upper part of fol. 68, whereupon after *reality grows.* (79.2) the lower part of the page is deleted as is all of fol. 69, the revised ending of the chapter being written on fol. 67^v and 68^v, in pencil. Following deleted fol. 69 which ends in mid-sentence is the stub of an excised leaf, and then fol. 71, which has deleted text ending about halfway down the page, followed by 'Chapter VI | Concerning Causation:'. Between these two lines James had written and then deleted in pencil 'Second Sub-problem:' and to the right after 'Causation:' the addition 'I. The conceptual view.' as part of the chapter heading. This is all deleted, however. Immediately below the deleted heading is a line brought over from the verso of the excised page 70 as a guide to the position of some addition, now lost, that had appeared there.

This disruption was caused by a change of plan. On fol. 67^v, brought by a guideline to come before the opening words of the sentence on the first line of fol. 68 'Conception knows no way' (78.32–33), is a deleted ink passage promising to divide the discussion of the perceptual and the conceptual view into two chapters. On fol. 69^v moved by a guideline over to a deleted addition on the upper half of fol. 71 (and thus written after the excision of fol. 70) is the deleted note 'Rest of chapter to be found at other end of book, p. 70^a'. Finally, on fols. 67^v and 68^v, in pencil, a revised conclusion to Chapter VI (79.3 *It may . . . Infinite.* 79.18) is added, remarking that at this point James will interrupt his discussion of novelty at large in order to get out of the way the minor problem of the Infinite. Following this new ending is the pencil note 'Begin this new chapter at the other end of the book, p. 70^a'. It seems obvious that after starting what was to be his Chapter VI on Causation and very likely proceeding some distance with its text (possibly even as far as the end of the inscription in ink on fol. 107 [*a farther problem.*^{x} 109.1]), James found that he wanted to precede it with added material. The inflexibility of composition in a notebook thus forced him to turn the book end for end, reversing it, and to start the new material at its beginning. The proposal to incorporate this major addition after the chapter ending, revised, on fol. 68^v enabled him to utilize excised leaf 70 as his basic identification by adding letters for each leaf to the number.

[Chapter VII], "First sub-problem | The Infinite and the Continuum," starts on fol. 70^a in the reversed notebook and ends with a short horizontal line on fol. 70^{xx} in the second alphabet. The dates for the writing of this material on the Infinite are set by his diary as February 19 to March 2, 1910. Although this new matter is not given a chapter heading, it is promised as a chapter at the end of revised fol. 68^v, which concludes the preceding Chapter VI; moreover, its heading is double underlined in the manner that James adopted to indicate chapter titles. The assignment in this edition of Chapter VII seems justified by the evidence. Folios 70^a and 70^b are written on both recto and verso, the versos being a revision of deleted 70^b and the deleted top of 70^c. Beginning with 70^c, James used the rectos only, save when he added text or wrote revisions on the versos as needed. Folios 70^a–70^f are deleted by single vertical strokes with a blue pencil: the intent is certainly not to delete the text but instead to mark the completion of the typing. After fol. 70^z the next alphabet begins with 70^{aa}, but a large deletion starts after four lines on 70^{aa}

(88.27 *infinite . . . these* 88.29) plus a revised ending on 70^z verso (. . . *mystification.* 88.31) to the undeleted section on 70^{aa}. This deletion covers all of 70^{bb} and 70^{cc} and the top eight lines of the next leaf, which is then numbered 70^{bb} to take account of the deleted pages and so carries on the sequence with 70^{cc} next and so on. Similarly, an unnumbered deleted leaf is skipped in the foliation and the next leaf, only three lines of which are undeleted (89.15 *The 'new . . . growing* 89.17), is numbered 70^{dd}. The text on fols. 70^{mm} and 70^{nn} (91.20–21 *exposers*[*expounders*] . . . *infinitely nu-* 91.35–36) is written on the versos of 70^{ll} and the following unnumbered recto as a revision of deleted text on the three unnumbered rectos after 70^{ll} before 70^{oo} picks up the text from 70^{nn}. The text of 70^{pp}, 70^{qq}, and 70^{rr} (92.11 *It . . . case.*^{x} [plus fn.] 93.3) is written on the versos of 70^{oo} and the two un-numbered rectos following it as a revision of their deleted text. Footnote 16 starts on 70^{rr} and concludes on 70^{ss} verso, despite James's note on 70^{rr} that it is continued on 70^{tt}. Footnote 15, starting at the foot of 70^{qq} is completed at the head of 70^{tt} recto after being continued on 70^{ss} recto. The chapter continues 70^{ss} with text on the rectos to end on 70^{xx} with the statement that before James continues with the perceptual account he proposes to get out of the way the problem of causality.

[Chapter VIII], like Chapter VII, is unnumbered, and like VII its heading 'Second Sub-problem | Cause and Effect' is double underlined. It provides a new beginning to what had been num-bered as Chapter VI, the 'Second Sub-Problem: Concerning Causation', deleted on fol. 71. There can scarcely be a question, then, that this should be numbered as a new chapter. This chapter begins on an unnumbered recto after 76^{xx} and continues on a second unnumbered recto, at the foot of which James wrote the circled note 'Turn to page 71 at other end of book'. This leaf is followed by 43 blank leaves. The reference is, of course, back to the interrupted start of what James had numbered as Chapter VI on fol. 71 in the original sequence of leaves starting with the real beginning of the notebook. The inscription proceeds normally, with occasional additions on the versos, to end the text on fol. 95 with 104.3–4 'originally was found.' But the decision to add a lengthy footnote caused some difficulty about space. The note was started about a third of the way down on fol. 94^v and then continued on the remaining space at the foot of fol. 95 below the text. The continuation with a new paragraph on fol. 95^v may be an afterthought. At the end of the addition as presently constituted, eight lines of text are deleted and the remaining eight lines (*scientific . . . 374–8).*) are marked 'transfer to p 111' where they are inserted in footnote 3 as 110.11–17.

Chapter IX (James's Chapter VII), "Causation: II. The perceptual view," begins on fol. 96 and proceeds in sequence. Folio 101 is largely occupied by a clipping (only slightly altered) from James's "The Experience of Activity" in its *Psychological Review* form (McD 1905:1), comprising 106.40 *The . . . name.* 107.19. Beginning on fol. 107 with the footnote 2 and the text words 'With this' (109.1), James switched to a lead pencil. The pencil (with some alterations made in ink) continues to the end of the present book on fol. 112.

THE FIRST TYPESCRIPT (TMs[1a])

Henry James, Jr.'s, memorandum, after stating that his sister Margaret (M.M.J.) copied on the typewriter the manuscript, specifically the blue notebook, continues: "Two copies were made. One he corrected and left here. One, uncorrected, was taken abroad and one copy of the last pages was mailed after him. A few corrections and notes were added in Europe." Like most of Henry's statements about this book, the facts are not altogether accurate, for more than 'a few' revisions were made in the copy of the typescript taken abroad, which we may call TMs[1b]. The other copy, retained in Cambridge, we may identify as TMs[1a]. It is contained in another folder, or envelope, in the file and is prefaced by the typed statement:

> This is the manuscript of the unfinished volume published under the title: "Some Problems of Philosophy." The different copies of the manuscript show several stages of correction and the syllabus material should be treated as part of this manuscript material as it was used in the preparation of the manuscript. During my father's last journey he carried one copy of the manuscripts about with him in the leather portfolio in which it remains.

This is subscribed, in a strange hand, 'From Henry James's letter to Mr. Lane, Dec. 15, 1925'. (Mr. Lane was the librarian of the Philosophical Library in Emerson Hall, Harvard. The letter has not been located.)

A ragged manila envelope has James's own note, written vertically, 'My unfinisht book | MS.' with a pencil note beneath in another hand, 'Copy left in Cambridge.' As preserved in the envelope the first twenty-one leaves of the manuscript (text ending 15.33 *'Sympathetic*) precede the incomplete typescript, thus substituting the manuscript for the first fourteen missing leaves, since TMs[1a] begins only with p. 15 (15.28 *yam.*). Starting with this fifteenth leaf, the typescript is the carbon, on the paper watermarked Chinese Linen used for Chapter IV of the manuscript, up to p. 41 (29.19 *logical . . . speak* 30.3), which is an isolated ribbon-copy leaf on the Chinese Linen paper, possibly a revision of the nature of ribbon pp. 92–93 (see below) in the carbon sequence. The first leaves from 15 to 23 are numbered by hand, 15–19 in the upper left corner but 20–23 centered. Pages 24, 25, and 27 are unnumbered. Typed numbering starts with p. 26 and continues to the end on 221, pp. 31, 172–221 with periods. (The number for p. 6 is written over typed 5, and 9 over typed 8.) In this typescript leaf 33½ (misnumbered 34½ in TMs[1b]) is wanting.

Pages 42 and 43, which comprise the last few lines of Chapter III and the beginning of Chapter IV up to 32.2 are ribbon-copy revises on L. L. Brown typewriter paper used early in the manuscript and later in the typescript starting with p. 98(51). When the original typing of Chapter IV returns, it continues the Chinese Linen paper and the carbon copy, but the numbering is in an independent sequence different from Chapters I–III (15–42), commencing with ink 1–3 before the typed sequence then takes over with 4 to end on 54 (. . . *experience.* [*grows.*] 55.13). The first and highly revised page of the original beginning of Chapter IV is preserved (numbered 1) but not the numbered end (which would have been 42) of the original ending of Chapter III (30.3 *disdainfully . . . why.* 30.7). The revised text of p. 1 of Chapter IV ends on a part-page 43 (typed number) of the Brown paper, with a slight overlap of the text with the original p. 2 on Chinese Linen paper that follows. The early independent numbering of Chapter IV has been deleted at a later time and the sequential foliation added in pencil. Page 52, originally 9½, is a holograph insertion (35.15 *We . . . the world* 35.23). Reference within this addition is made back to typed p. 6 and forward to typed p. 20 of Chapter IV, indicating that the insertion was comparatively late; afterward, as part of a general review of the typescript James added 58 above 20, a reference to Corollary II of the MS fol. 58 (55.32 ff.) and a clear indication that at the moment of addition this corollary on TMs p. 103 had not yet been typed. The inserted page 9½ is written on the back of an undeleted trial. Although the brief text of this trial cannot be identified as a draft for any preserved leaf, it may seem probable that it represents a start for 9½, broken off, the leaf reversed and turned over for the inscription of the final version. Another such holograph leaf, also on Chinese Linen paper, is inserted as 10½ renumbered to 54 (36.16 *concepts . . .* content. 36.24), but its verso is blank. In both cases text in the typescript is deleted before and after the insertion, except that before the insertion of 10½ some text (*Certainly . . . our* 36.15–16) has been added to the foot of page 10. A third such leaf is 20½ or page 65 (40.36 *our faculty . . . worlds* 41.7), including what is now footnote 14.

In Chapter IV, for reasons that will be discussed in Section IV below, James himself typed pp. 1(43)–12(56) and the first line of 13(57), as well as the substitute pages 25½(71), 28(74), and 46(93). This gives the typescript of 31.8 *concepts . . . importance.* 37.23; 43.32 *Emerson . . . Love.)* 43.42; 44.14 [*compli*]*cation . . . insults of* 44.24; and 51.23 *Bradley . . . compenetra-* 52.8 an especial authority, including all handwritten corrections and revisions.

A serious mix-up in the typing occurs between original pages 25–30 (renumbered 70–76). By some mistake Peggy must have typed sheets out of order so that she started 29 numbered 25 and continued with 30 numbered 26. These two pages were later abstracted and put in their proper position, a new hand numbering from 25–30 replacing typed 27–29 by 25–27. However, the trouble seems to go deeper than a simple error. Page 24 ends with a completed paragraph a few lines short. The first sentence of p. 27 (renumbered 25[70]), which seems to follow normally, is deleted and James wrote 'run in' in the margin, above a paragraph sign before the second sentence that now starts the paragraph (42.35 *Ideality often*). A footnote (now numbered 16) on p. 27 refers only to Royce, but James wrote after it, 'Add 25½', an insert that appears typed by James on L. L. Brown paper numbered by hand, continuing the note with the quotation from Emerson. Since James's reference is to 25½, the addition was made after p. 27 had been renumbered as 25 but before it was renumbered as 70 in the final continued sequence. Another addition was made, perhaps at the same time. Page 29 (renumbered 27[73]) originally ended a paragraph at 44.13 *sense of the term.* However, by hand James added 'They are an unfortunate compli-' and the sentence is continued in his own typing on Chinese Linen paper, hand numbered 28, later changed to 74. This change, then, was also made after the pages had been renumbered following the discovery of the misplacement of 26–27. This part-page 28(74) is shown to be a later addition by the fact that it is written on the obverse of a discarded (ribbon) trial, undeleted, that would have followed the typed text at the foot of p. 29(73), material now found on p. 75

(renumbered from 25, 29).[3] The part-page 28(74) links with the hand alteration at the foot of 73 and continues with the text on transposed 25 (renumbered 29, 75). Since the part-page has no typed numbering and so was first inserted when the sequence had been renumbered to take account of the transposition of pages, it seems probable that a fairly early repair of this mistake was made and at the same time the opportunity was taken for revision. That a deeper revision may underlie the whole is only a suspicion, fostered by the fact that both p. 24(69) which ends the text before the start of the mistaken numbering and p. 26(30, 76) which concludes the transposition and the renumbered sequence (. . . *to be happy.*" 45.18) are a line short. Normality is restored with p. 31(77), continuing to 35(81), which James renumbered as 81[a] and added in the margin the note '*x*Note on next page', a reference to the added holograph footnote 19 (47.23–42) on leaves of L. L. Brown paper numbered 81[b] and 81[c]. Page 81[c] is a revision written on the back of original deleted autograph text, also numbered 81[c]. The text then continues with 82(36) to 89(43). Here an added footnote in James's hand, on Chinese Linen paper is numbered 43½, later 90, with a reference to its original numbering at the head, 'Note to p. 43.' Some abridgement of the text is shown by ribbon part-pages 92–93 between normal carbon 91(44) and 94(47). Page 92 (51.21 *wrote . . . here.*[x] [plus fn.] 51.23) has the typed number 45 but page 93 is numbered 46 in ink (51.23 *Bradley . . . compenetra-* 52.8). This part-page 93 links with the text on 94(47) only after the deletion of the first three lines, the beginning of the deleted text following no preserved page. Starting with page 98(51), the beginning of the MS with fol. 51 (53.19 *all future . . .*), the typescript switches for the remainder from a carbon to become the ribbon copy, this accompanied by a change in the paper from Chinese Linen to L. L. Brown, the paper also found in the TMs[1b] carbon. Beginning with the next page, pp. 99–101(52–54) are numbered in the upper left corner instead of the usual centering, which resumes on p. 102.

At the foot of p. 101(54) James wrote in pencil, 'Continue copying *MS. p. 56*'. The ribbon copy on Brown paper continues on p. 102 (the numbering once more centered) but at this point the typist knew about the hand renumbering of the leaves of this chapter since the typed number is 102 and the altered numbering ceases. The pagination is normal to p. 122, which has an 'a' added

---

[3]The text of p. 74[v], a draft of 44.11–15, may be found along with the texts of other TMs deleted versos at the end of the Alterations in the Manuscript.

in ink, with footnote 5 of "The One and the Many" chapter
starting in the margin in James's autograph, continued on a typed
page hand-numbered 122^b ('b' *over* 'a'), the paper watermarked
L C Smith & Sons Typewriter Co. Made in U.S.A., not otherwise
appearing in this typescript. (This addition is missing in TMs^{1b}.)
The leaf had originally been a note, for on the verso scrawled in
pencil, vertically, is James's 'Unity Cf. Plato & Plotinus in Bakewell', a memorandum applying to footnote 6 in Chapter IV
"Percept and Concept," and to the text at 62.38. Beginning with
172 (as well as on 169 previously), the typist placed periods after
each centered number, and so to the end on 221. Page 180 (91.18
quarter-inches . . . false. 91.38) originally continued with now
deleted 'This amounts to imply-' which was continued on original
typed 181. However, on a sheet of Brown paper paged 181 James
wrote out an addition (91.38 *For each . . . disappear.*^{x} 92.10)
which was typed as new 181, revising materially the upper deleted
third of old 181, now ink-renumbered 182.[4] Original typed p. 181
is renumbered 182 in ink; but this change must have been made
before p. 183 was typed since its typed number is correct as 183,
allowing for added 182. Thereafter everything is regular to the end
of the typescript on p. 221. This TMs^{1a} is complete except for
missing page 33½ and the first fourteen pages.

---

[4]Someone has transferred this leaf from TMs^{1a}, where it belongs, to the folder
containing the MS. Its text may be transcribed as follows:

For *each & [*intrl.*] every *point traversed [*ab. del.* 'position occupied'] by *the
tortoise [*ab. del.* 'Achilles'] there *is one [*ab. del.* 'is a'] [*intrl.* 'corresponding' *del.*]
*point traversed [*ab. del.* 'position occupied'] by Achilles, [*del.* '*to to each of [*ab. del.*
'and both'] these [*insrtd.*] *pairs of points [*ab. del.* 'sets of positions'] ['coincide with'
del.] there is one *corresponds [*final* 's' *ov.* 'ing'] [*intrl.* 'to' *del.*] more in s to one
point on the time scl scale corresponds'] at the corresponding ['point' *del.*] point [*ab.
insrtd. del.* 'moment'] of [*insrtd.*] time; and the *exact [*ab. del.* 'one-to-one'] correspondence, ['of point these three sets of *to [*intrl.*] point['s' *del.*] in each' *del.*] point
by point, of either one of these *three [*intrl.*] sets of points with both the others, makes
*of [*intrl.*] them similar and equally copious *sets [*comma del.*] [*intrl.*] from [*ov.* 'in']
the numerical point of view. There *is [*ab. del.* 'can'] thus ['be' *del.*] no *recurrent
[*intrl.*] 'remainder' of the tortoise's *head-start [*ab. del.* 'path,'] with which Achilles
[', owing to his back-starting handicap at the *outset [*alt. fr.* 'outside'],' *del.*] can't
catch up, which he can reduce indefinitely, but can't annul. The last point in Achilles
path, ['is rated with' *del.*] the last *point [*insrtd. for del.* 'one'] in the tortoises, and
['both are rated to' *del.*] the *last time- [*ab. del.* 'same'] instant of ['time—' *del.*] the
race ['mathematically coincide' *del.*] are terms which mathematically *coincide. [*period
ov. comma*] ['so that ['and' *del.*] the puzzle' *del. ab. del.* 'The paradox'] ['thus
disappears.^{x}' *del.*] With [*ab. del.* 'In'] this, which seems to be Mr. Russell's way of
analyzing the situation, the puzzle quite disappears.

II. The Documents: TMs[1b]

THE FIRST TYPESCRIPT (TMs[1b])

The second copy of the typescript, distinguished here as TMs[1b], is prefaced by James's handwritten title page on Chinese Linen paper: '*Some Problems of Philosophy [triple underlined] | An introductory text-book for students in metaphysics | by | William James | Longmans, Green, & Co.' It begins with the ribbon copy on sheets of laid paper 266 × 206 mm., watermarked Gloria Linen. Since the first fourteen pages of TMs[1a] are wanting, TMs[1b] at the start is the only witness to the typescript text and to James's revisions in the typescript. The first leaf is unnumbered, and the chapter number I has been supplied in ink. Pages 2-15 are numbered in ink as usual in the upper left corner (except p. 2, numbered twice, once in the center). Starting with p. 15 the paper shifts to that watermarked Chinese Linen, and with p. 16 the hand numbering is regularly centered (except 24 and 25, marked in the upper left corner). Page 20 is altered from 21 and 21 from 22. The typed numbers, as in TMs[1a] of course, start with 26 (27 marked only in ink) and carry on regularly, in the left upper corner until the end of Chapter III. Page 33½ concluding Chapter II (not present in TMs[1a]) was misnumbered 34, probably by a slip and has been wrongly repaired by adding an ink ½ to this 34 instead of altering to 33½. Page 40 of Chapter III (29.1-2 *the following . . . leave* 29.19) is missing. Variants in typed TMs[2] at 29.12 and 29.16-17 are assumed to derive from James's marking of the lost page.

Before Chapter IV, "Percept and Concept," Henry James, Jr., inserted a sheet on which he had written: 'The interlined pencil notes, hereafter, some in blue pencil, some in black, are Schiller's.' Then below a short rule he added at a diagonal, 'MEMO to keep at beginning of Chapter on Percept & Concept in ms. taken abroad.' The extensive Ferdinand Schiller notes (for which see Appendix III) are confined to this Chapter IV.

As in TMs[1a], the original typed page for the first Chinese Linen sheet of Chapter IV is present in TMs[1b], revised, and the typed revision with the end of the preceding chapter, on L. L. Brown paper, typed numbering 42 and 43. However, in Chapter IV the chapter pagination has not been altered in pencil, as it was in TMs[1a], to follow in sequence the numbering of the first three chapters. The number for page 6 is written in ink over typed 5 and 9 over typed 8; 10-12 are supplied in ink. Leaves 9½ and 10½ found in TMs[1a] are wanting, but, like TMs[1a], a handwritten 20½ is inserted although with slightly different text and without footnote

14. The carbon of typewritten 25½ is also inserted, in this case on the back of a typewritten start of the Emerson quotation at the head of the recto. At the foot of 25½ is the carbon reverse of this trial, created when the carbon paper was put in the typewriter facing the wrong way, the reason why the trial was abandoned. After 25½ the transfer of 25-26 enforces the renumbering in ink of 27 as 26 (6 *over* 5) and so on as in TMs^{1a}. The undeleted text, a draft for 44.11-15, is typed on the verso of page 28 (TMs^{1a} 74^v) as the carbon copy. The two handwritten pages of footnote 19 on TMs^{1a} pages 81^b, 81^c are not present, nor is the handwritten footnote 21 added in TMs^{1a} on page 90(43½).

The two typescripts diverge momentarily at TMs^{1b} page 46 (51.23 *Bradley* . . . *compenetra-* 52.8) as the result of an accident. The typing of 46 in TMs^{1a} is the original (as was 45), but the carbon of 46 was reversed so that the impression was offset on TMs^{1a} page 93(46) verso, and thus blank TMs^{1b} page 46 had to be retyped. With page 51(98) and the shift from Chinese Linen to L. L. Brown paper, TMs^{1b} becomes the carbon. After page 54 the typed number sequence changes to 102, the numbering of the whole typescript. Typed page number 110 has had a superior 'a' added in ink and also a note after its eleventh line, 'Insert here page 110^b—', a handwritten page on Brown paper numbered 110^b (58.33 *The world* . . . *elements.* 59.9) not present in TMs^{1a}. Similarly, page 111 is renumbered 111^a and an insertion on Brown paper (59.16 *Later* . . . *suffice.* 59.23) is written on page 111^b, not present in TMs^{1a}. The verso of 111^b has a deleted trial continuation of the insert on 110^b, numbered 110^c. The typed page 122^a added to TMs^{1a} is not present in TMs^{1b} but thereafter no physical differences mark the two typescripts save for James's separate holograph revisions.

THE REVISION OF TMs^{1a}, TMs^{1b}

In his memorandum Henry James, Jr., writes: "Two copies were made. One he corrected and left here. One, uncorrected, was taken abroad and one copy of the last pages was mailed after him. A few corrections and notes were added in Europe." Part of this statement is inaccurate in that TMs^{1b}—the typescript taken abroad— was not in an uncorrected state at the time of James's departure. That the latter part of the book (TMs pp. 192-221) had not been typed before he left and so was not revised in TMs^{1a} is textually of considerable importance. The last revision in TMs^{1a} was made by James at the head of page 191: the addition of interlined

conceptual translation before considering them at 96.17, followed
at 97.4 by the enclosure of *efficient* in single quotation marks, and
finally by the addition of single quotation marks about *that . . .
itself.* (97.6-7), typed without underlining but italicized by an
underline in the manuscript. Although minor corrections (not
revisions) appear in Peggy's hand between pages 192 (97.13 *1. No
effect . . .*) and the end on 221, they are ordinarily repeated in
TMs^{1b} in the same form and hence were made before the delayed
shipment abroad of what seems to have been TMs pages 192-221.[5]
This is to assume that when on August 19 James returned to the
United States on the point of death he had neither the time nor
the ability in the single week remaining to him to return to TMs^{1a}
after page 191, nor indeed to TMs^{1b}, so that the (unfortunately)
few revisions in TMs^{1b} after page 192 would need to have been
made abroad. Even though very inadequately in the latter part of
the two typescripts, then, James had reviewed the whole text in a
preliminary and, in part, even in an intermediate stage. In this
connection the relation between the revisions made in each copy
of the typescript assumes a particular importance.

First, it must be recognized that a number of simple corrections,
such as of run-together words, misspellings, transposed letters, and
the like, appear in TMs^{1a} in the newly typed pages that James
could not have overseen because he was abroad, these including as
well the addition of missing letters, hyphens, and sometimes of
punctuation at the ends of lines caused by the lack of a margin
release on the typewriter. Such corrections cannot be attributed
to James (except in the few pages that he typed himself), and
since they occur in both typescripts from the very beginning, as
well as in this section, and seem to be made in the same hand and
the same medium in both copies, they must represent some early
non-authorial stage of correction by the typist before the pages
were submitted to James. In cases when corrections of this sort
appear in one copy but not the other, it may be that James made
the changes or that Peggy was careless in marking only one copy
and not the other. In addition to these mechanical changes, a very
few verbal and some mechanical corrections have been made
throughout both TMs's in Peggy's hand with a thick-nibbed pen

---

[5] From Bad Nauheim James wrote to Peggy on May 29, 1910: "I got as a surprise
your finely typed copy of the rest of my MS., the other day. I thank you for it; also for
your delightful letters. The type-writing seems to set free both your & Aleck's genius
more than the pen. If you need a new ribbon it must be got from the agency in Milk S!
just above Devonshire—but you'll find it hard work to get it into its place" (bMS Am
1092.9, #3113).

and very black ink. For example, in TMs[1b], p. 14, the sentence *Injuring the substitute, you thus* [error for *then*] *made him suffer correspondingly.* (15.24–25), omitted by mistake in the typescript, has been supplied (TMs[1a] is missing here); on p. 15 the omitted words *the thought* (15.36) are written in both copies. Perhaps half a dozen or more similar corrections appear in both copies, like the insertion of omitted *Who can tell off-hand?* (30.1), or the correction earlier on the same page of typed 'consumed,' to 'conserved,' (29.27), or on page 99(52) the substitution of interlined *truth* for deleted *touch* (54.7), or on p. 218 the change of typed *provision* to *consideration* (109.38). The pen, hand, and ink are the same and the changes are always made in both copies. Peggy must have read through the typescript and its carbon, and when obvious difficulty appeared consulted the manuscript when it was available. She missed more errors than she discovered, however, and the correction was very limited in its extent: certainly nothing like a thorough collation of the manuscript was involved. The Schiller suggestions written in Chapter IV of TMs[1b] are in quite a different category. If he had lived, James might well have altered readings in this chapter with reference to Schiller's remarks and queries; but as it is, they were not incorporated (except for one at 50.4, adopted by Kallen in TMs[2]) and caused no authorial revisions. These suggestions are recorded in Appendix III.

Since the first fourteen pages of TMs[1a] (corresponding to the Gloria Linen paper) are wanting, comparison of the two typescripts TMs[1a] and TMs[1b] can start only with p. 15 (15.28 *yam.* . . .). James's revisions in TMs[1a] are in various stages as represented by dark ink, light ink, probably a medium ink, and by pencil, whereas those in TMs[1b] are ordinarily in one ink, with a few in pencil. The early pages of TMs[1b] through Chapter III are normally revised. In TMs[1a] except for a few mechanical pencil corrections like the capitalization of *The* wrongly typed as *the* on p. 16 (16.5,8) wanting in TMs[1b] the first authorial revision comes on p. 17: first the pencil alteration of *everyone's belief* to *everyone* (16.28), and then the change to *lives* (in the form of *lifes*) from *life's work* (16.31), and finally the substitution of *deliver the whole of* for *carry the torch Of* (16.31–32). None of these changes is present in TMs[1b]. Authorial changes then follow on p. 18 of TMs[1b] but not in TMs[1a] up to the start of Chapter III on p. 34. Both typescripts have a number of joint small alterations, probably not by James, involving questions of capitalization or lower case, underlining, and punctuation in Chapter III on p. 34 (26.1 *How . . . conceivable* 26.16) and others on p. 35 (26.17 *existence* . . . *no* 27.9) that seem to be made with the thick-nibbed pen that Peggy at one time used for correction. Another of these is made on p. 36, but James had nothing to do after p. 17 with Chapter III of TMs^{1a} (although TMs^{1b} is worked over) until on ribbon p. 41, its last full page, he added in TMs^{1a} footnote 4 (29.37–39) and a few other changes, none of these being present in TMs^{1b}.

Starting with Chapter IV, however, James revised TMs^{1a} very thoroughly in dark ink and added, in this chapter alone, subheadings in red ink not present in TMs^{1b}. (The last of these ink subheadings comes on p. 96(49); starting on p. 102, they are typed.) Certain of these dark-ink revisions are also found in TMs^{1b} although TMs^{1a} holds numerous major alterations in this ink not transferred to TMs^{1b}, such as the addition to footnote 6 (35.33–39), the added page 52(9½), or the handwritten addition starting at the foot of p. 53(10) and continuing on 54(10½) (36.16 *concepts . . . content.* 36.24). Later changes in different inks such as the addition on p. 53(10) of *Emerson . . . . And* (35.25–36.2) also were not transferred. In this area TMs^{1b} shows, of course, a few alterations made abroad that could not be represented in TMs^{1a}. However, in this chapter the main thrust of the revision, in several stages, is found in TMs^{1a}, including late alterations in pencil such as the addition of single quotation marks about *no . . . restraint.* and *you . . . fear,* and *you . . . sequences,* (38.25–28), or the addition of *our mental* (39.10). It is possible that these pencil revisions were made at the time the pages of Chapter IV in TMs^{1a} were renumbered in pencil to follow the sequence established in Chapters I–III. Ordinarily, revisions in the varying inks in TMs^{1a} are found transferred to TMs^{1b} in a uniform ink as if at one time; yet sporadic late transfers are infrequently found in pencil, as in the pencil addition in both of *an abstract* (41.22) or of *concrete* (44.33), or of light-ink changes made also in the light ink in TMs^{1b} such as the deletion of *Such an idealization of concepts is extremely natural* which in typed form had begun the paragraph at 42.35. These were obviously made at the same time in both typescripts. But the opposite may as readily occur, as the inscription in TMs^{1b}'s normal ink of the light-ink interlineation *and what is lost when* (43.22) in TMs^{1a}. Hence the evidence suggests that at some point James made an effort to bring Chapter IV in TMs^{1b} up to date with his master copy TMs^{1a} but that he continued later with extensive further revisions in TMs^{1a} that with only a few exceptions were not transferred to the other copy. The order of transfer is clearly from TMs^{1a} to TMs^{1b}, according to various pieces of evidence such as the TMs^{1a} interlineation of *contents of feeling* (46.19) in which *of* was written after deleted *and*, but in TMs^{1b} only the final form is inscribed. The complex series of alterations in TMs^{1a} for *could make* (for which see the Emendations list for 47.2) is a better example, since the penultimate form *might make* was transferred to TMs^{1b} before the final change in TMs^{1a} to *could make*.

The amount of revision in both typescripts falls off after the start of the Summary section of Chapter IV on p. 98(51) (53.26 ff.),[6] but toward the end of the chapter James made an important expansion in TMs^{1b} as a consequence of a marginal note he had written there opposite the paragraph beginning at 59.10. If this were done abroad, as seems almost certain, James took with him a supply of L. L. Brown paper, since this is used for the handwritten p. 110^b (58.33 *The world . . . elements.* 59.9) inserted in renumbered 110^a and for p. 111^b (59.16 *Later . . . suffice.* 59.23) inserted in p. 111^a. Otherwise, TMs^{1b} is less revised than TMs^{1a} and not many changes were made independent of TMs^{1a}.

However, TMs^{1b} contains one important addition. In this typescript after the late insertion of retyped pages 42–43 revising the beginning of Chapter IV is added a leaf numbered 43A, a footnote indicator, and in Horace Kallen's hand the bracketed footnote: *[At this point the author inserted the following memorandum which it seems fitting to reprint—Ed.]*. Below, in the hand of Henry James, Jr., is the memorandum: 'This note wh. belongs in the ms. at the beginning of the Chap. on Percept & Concept was not used in the printed book'. William James's note was written on the rectos of two leaves of blue paper, numbered 1 and 2 centered.

We think of not-being as if that were easy, but of being as if it argued ingenuity and *a way for perpetrating [*ab. del.* 'means for bringing out'] the trick. [*in left margin, pencilled* 'Blood']

[*in left margin, pencilled* 'To go in as note to beginning of *Percept & Concept*. H. M. Kallen.'] ^{x}Begin the Chapter on Concepts etc. by a fuller description of non conceptual experience and immediate reaction on stimuli. But the stimuli get emphasized, individuated, recognized, & named as the *same*. "Discursification" begins, and proceeds indefinitely as analysis of the given advances. The concepts that bear the same name may or may not alter their

---

[6]This page marks the beginning of the MS and thus of typing directly from it instead of the various expedients that had marked the preceding pages of Chapter IV (for which see below under Section IV).

meaning as they continue to be used. *Schiller^x [*pencil* 'x' *in text; in left margin, pencilled* 'xThe pencil notes hereafter are his'] is mainly struck by the alterations in the meaning, the lapse of concepts that have grown useless, and the production of new ones for new uses that arise. Meanwhile, to measure changes from, at least, it remains useful to keep certain meanings absolutely the same, and our discursification of experience ['depends' *del.*] consists mainly of the interplay between our absolute meanings, our denotative or designative concepts, and our sensible flux. The absolute concepts have relations which are eternal; the designative ones change their connotation and their denotation as experience enlarges; the flux never stays the same. [*in left margin opposite* 'eternal' *is the word* ' "perdurable." ', *in ink, possibly but not certainly in James's hand. Facing this, on the verso of the first leaf, is the note* 'find illustrations of this' *with an arrow drawn to the lower part of the second page.*]

James's correspondence with F. C. S. Schiller indicates that this note for a proposed addition was written in England after May 4, 1910, when James acknowledged the return of his typescript of "Percept and Concept" with Schiller's notes, and thus it was never part of the manuscript but only a memorandum for a future revision that was never accomplished.

Chapter V, "The One and the Many," shows a few common corrections in pencil between the two typescripts that may be James's although they are of a largely mechanical nature, but in addition two definite pencil transfers in TMs^{1b} of an ink alteration in TMs^{1a}—the addition of *are* (67.24) (an MS omission), and the alteration of the typed error *goods* to *grades* (70.8), a special case. The few other TMs^{1b} revisions in this chapter were made independently, in one case altering an unsatisfactory phrase *as what* (67.13) (see emend 67.12-13) to a version different from the TMs^{1a} revision that had not been entered in TMs^{1b}. Similar independent alteration is found with TMs^{1b} *in one* but TMs^{1a} revision *linked* (72.40), and *smallest* but *least* (74.14), and in the addition of footnote 5 at 64.22-45. In Chapter VI, "The Problem of Novelty," TMs^{1b} alteration is confined to a single change, the pencil addition of *led* for an omitted word, which TMs^{1a} correctly supplies with *brought* as in the manuscript (76.8). In Chapter VII, "The Continuum and the Infinite," James wrote-in, in pencil, on p. 159 part of a mathematical equation that had not been fully typed, although with a variant from TMs^{1a} (82.5), and he made a few later changes in pencil. On page 161, TMs^{1b} inserts the ink transfer of *may be regarded* (82.35) from after *objective existence* (82.34). Starting on p. 168 with the alteration of *involving* to *demanding* (86.7-8), James's alterations in TMs^{1b} shift to a black ink and are more frequent, with only a few in pencil. It is evident that at this point James undertook a relatively thorough independent revision of TMs^{1b} that involved considerable rewriting. Since TMs^{1a} is also heavily revised in this area, it would seem that James found the text unsatisfactory when he went over it while abroad and that he was not satisfied with the few TMs^{1a} changes that had been transferred or with his pencil notes made earlier. This extensive revision stops abruptly at the end of the First Sub-Problem. From p. 190 on and the start of the Second Sub-Problem—in this edition assigned the chapter number VIII—the revision in TMs^{1b} sinks to the level of casual improvements in ink and in pencil. This is the more unfortunate since the pages concerned, starting probably with 192 (97.13) represent the section typed after James had left Cambridge and so are authorially unrevised in TMs^{1a}.

THE SECOND TYPESCRIPT (TMs^{2})

In the folder in which TMs^{1b} is preserved is placed a leaf identified by Henry James, Jr., as torn from a notebook. On this leaf William James had written in a feeble hand, from his brother Henry's house at Rye, England:

The MS *in this pocket of the portfolio [*intrl.*] is the duplicate of that wh. Peggy has charge of. Ask Kallen to edit it for 250 dollars, comparing the two copies, for different corrections are in each. Say it is fragmentary and ['insufficiently' *del.*] unrevised. Call it: "A beginning of an introduction to Philosophy." Say that I hoped by it to round my system, which now is *too much [*intrl.*] like ['an only' *del.*] ['arch only begun, by' *del.*] ['of w' *del.*] an arch built only on one side. Tell Kallen to confine his emendations of the text to obvious obscurities or carelessnesses, and to make his annotation (if any) very scanty.   W.J.

Rye, July 26th *1910 [*alt. fr.* '1900']

In his memorandum of April 22, 1911, Henry James, Jr., elaborates:

Both type-written copies and the note book were given *to [*intrl.*] Kallen with a copy of one of them made again by M. M. J. for his use. He brought *these [*intrl.*] back finally having entered in this third copy what he thought best. When I came to go over it I found a number of omissions to slight changes which W. J. had made in one or other of the type-copies, and so I went through his copy myself comparing with the two copies which had passed under W. J.'s own hand. I found it necessary to make a number of small changes in the matter of italics etc, and retored the original reading in almost all of the few changes which Kallen had made. Later in reading the proof I referred several times to the note book ms. and am afraid that ['Kallen did not' *del.*] this *ought ['ou' *ov.* 'was'] to have been but was not referred to throughout in preparing the book for press.

Kallen supplied most of the marginal titles.

Peggy's typing of TMs[2] exhibits fewer of the misspellings and mechanical errors that characterize her first typescript, but in the process of copying she was not invariably accurate. Kallen caught and supplied some of her skips, but in general her less obvious departures from copy went unnoticed and were perpetuated in the book. The preserved copy of TMs[2] annotated by Kallen and in some part by Henry James became the printer's copy and contains numerous markings for the press. The dedication to Renouvier is written out in Henry James's hand and was never typed before setting. In the folder for TMs[1b] is a reconstruction of William James's headings as found in the manuscript, this copy in the hand of his wife, Alice; and in the same folder is Kallen's written-out Contents list which reflects his original headings and sidenotes added to TMs[2]. (See Section III below for an account of the rearrangement of chapters from James's own plan.) Before the conference with Kallen mentioned in Henry's memorandum, Henry went over these TMs[2] subheadings (perhaps at the suggestion of Ralph Barton Perry who had objected to the chapter headings) and in the typescript moved the early subheadings, sometimes with verbal revision, to their position as sidenotes as found in the book.[7] The new sidenotes were then typed out for the printer as the topics in a revised Contents list, present in the TMs[2] folder. Later in the text of TMs[2] Kallen himself moved the subheadings to their new positions and added a few sidenotes of his own.

In preparing the copy for the printer Kallen marked off the footnotes, which had been typed within the text, and corrected the various mishaps and mechanical errors in the typing. The typewriter's underline key had not been used; hence Kallen had to judge for himself what words to underline that had escaped James's alterations in the two copies of TMs[1] (although on Henry James's testimony he was not very careful about this part of the preparation). He styled James in such matters as capitalizing German nouns, italicizing the titles of books, and in general making a more professional job of the bibliographical references in the footnotes. By turning over the leaves of TMs[1a] and TMs[1b]

---

[7]These sidenotes and their originals in TMs[2] are listed in the Historical Collation. The exact position in relation to the paragraph they concern may vary between TMs[2] and the printed book since not all of TMs[2]'s paragraphs are followed in (I) or the present book and hence is much a question of convenience and of typographical style. For simplicity's sake they are noted in the HC as if they came opposite the first line of the paragraph concerned in TMs[2].

he was able to transfer the majority of James's hand revisions to the typed TMs^2 copy although he missed a number of small and some few larger items. There is no evidence that he ever consulted the manuscript which he had been given. From Henry James's account this seems to have been only the Partridge and Cooper blue notebook starting with Chapter V, "The One and the Many"; Henry never mentions the loose sheets of the manuscript that were the copy for TMs^1 Chapters I–IV and it may be that at the time he was not aware of them (except perhaps for fols. 1–18 that may have been substituted for pp. 1–14 of TMs^{1a}). It follows that Kallen had no idea of the departures from manuscript that Peggy had made in TMs^1 that were not recognized and corrected by James (except perhaps in fols. 1–18), and especially he had no idea of the departures from TMs^1 copy in the typescript of TMs^2, variants which occur with some frequency. He seems to have accepted this typescript as his ultimate authority save for his consultation of the autograph revisions in TMs^{1a} or TMs^{1b} that, depending upon the copy for TMs^2, had not been transcribed.[8] As a rule Kallen followed James's instructions and did not tinker with the text; but in a dozen or so places he did interfere—not always when the occasion warranted—with attempts at 'improvement' of syntax or expression.

According to the memorandum, Kallen brought the marked TMs^2 back to Henry James, Jr., who checking it over added some further revisions from TMs^{1a} or TMs^{1b} that had been overlooked. For most, but not all, of Kallen's own unauthoritative emendations Henry underdotted the typescript reading and marked *stet* in the margin in order to restore the original. The care given by Kallen and Henry James made the printer's copy a superficially correct document for typesetting, although it had the serious defects of its two transmissional stages that had never been set right by collation.

We know nothing of the first fourteen pages of TMs^{1a}, but for the following pages up to the start of Chapter IV there is scarcely an independent William James annotation in this copy nor had James transferred to TMs^{1a} the numerous revisions he had made in TMs^{1b}, the ribbon copy. (For instance, not even Peggy had corrected Chapter II.) It was most efficient, therefore, for Peggy to transcribe revised TMs^{1b} up to p. 41 for the first three chapters in her retyping that made up TMs^2. However, starting with Chap-

---

[8] Peggy typed TMs^2 Chapters I–III, pp. 1–40, from TMs^{1b}, but the rest of the typescript starting with p. 41 was copied from TMs^{1a}; see below.

ter IV, "Percept and Concept" (actually with p. 41, the next to the last page of Chapter III), the situation changed and TMs^{1a} on the whole became the more heavily revised copy. At this point, then, Peggy shifted and the rest of TMs^2 is transcribed from TMs^{1a}, including its alterations.

As remarked, although Kallen had been given TMs^2, and copies of TMs^{1a} and TMs^{1b}, he made no attempt to collate the text against the TMs^1 copy and instead contented himself with adding by hand most of James's alterations he observed when he scanned whichever typescript copy it was that had not served as the basis for Peggy's retyped transcript and thus had not had James's variant autograph alterations in it included in the typed TMs^2. Occasionally revised readings slipped through his net, some of which Henry James, Jr., restored—according to his testimony chiefly in such accidentals as the omission of underlining for italics, and, perhaps, in some of William James's revisions in the punctuation. When the same typescript reading had been differently altered in TMs^{1a} and TMs^{1b}, Kallen almost invariably chose the TMs^{1b} form and altered TMs^2 by hand accordingly (in the sections typed from TMs^{1a}) without considering whether the TMs^{1b} reading was independent or derived.

In the alterations that Kallen made by hand in TMs^2, the most serious problem concerns those that appear in the area where the first fourteen pages of TMs^{1a} are missing and where TMs^{1b} (Peggy's copy) is the only witness for what could have been James's typescript revisions in the alternate copy, if it existed. Although the working hypothesis for this edition is that Peggy never made a carbon copy of the first fourteen pages typed on the Gloria Linen paper, the case is not demonstrable and the possibility must be considered that these alterations were written by Kallen in TMs^2 when he compared a lost set of the TMs^{1a} carbon pages with the revisions in TMs^{1b} that had been used as copy for TMs^2 and hence that they could reflect James's authoritative revisions that should be adopted in the text. The odds against such a hypothesis are very long, however. Of major importance is the fact that in the preserved pages of TMs^{1a} Chapters I–III from page 15 to page 40 James made only two sets of substantive annotations (only one of which was adopted by Kallen in revising TMs^2), both of which appear on the same page 17. Hence, although James freely revised ribbon TMs^{1b} for the first three chapters for both substantives and accidentals, he made only two substantive changes by hand (both in pencil and hence probably late) in carbon TMs^{1a}, one at 16.28 and the other at 16.31–32, neither of which appears in the alterations in TMs[1b]. Two pencil accidental changes (also not transferred to TMs[1b]) at 16.5,8 on the preceding page, both simply raising a wrong lower-case 'the' at the start of a sentence to 'The', are probably James's as well. The status of the pencil deletion of the 's' in typed 'tumerisc' (15.28-29) is more doubtful, in part because the same change was made in ink in TMs[1b] but chiefly because the error *tumeric* for MS *turmeric* was allowed to stand during the correction of the other error.

In addition there are some distinctive features of the Kallen handwritten changes in TMs[2] in the area of the first fourteen pages of TMs[1] that cause certain of these to differ from the two known authorial changes in TMs[1a] pages 15-40 and also from the more copious changes in later chapters. An analysis of the seventeen changes that Kallen made by hand in TMs[2] that differ from TMs[1b] may be useful. First, six of these are in the accidentals and constitute such normal correction of TMs[1] errors as to be readily attributable to Kallen himself (on all sorts of similar evidence elsewhere) without the necessity of assuming authorial intervention. Some, like the addition of a hyphen between *race heritage* (9.15), the expansion of *Prof.* to *Professor* (10.26), and the addition of a necessary omitted quotation mark (11.39) are so neutral as to offer evidence only of Kallen's own interference, particularly when at 9.22 he changed James's typical *german* to a capital or at 11.39 inserted the quotation mark at a slightly different place from its position in MS. At 11.6 the TMs[1] comma after *Aristotle* was manifestly wrong and needed to be removed, as was Peggy's wrong capitalization of *principle* at 15.9. The removal of a bibliographical reference from the text at 14.23-24 to a footnote was a normal editorial cleaning up of an informally written text.

The substantive alterations divide conspicuously between those which restore the MS reading and those for which there is no known authority. In the first group come the rather obvious change at 9.1 of *facts* to *fact* and possibly the obviously required underlining for italic of *whence* and *whither* at 10.11. But others are by no means obvious, such as the addition, as in MS, of *human* at 9.2 (part of the phrase also corrected by *fact* from *facts*), the alteration of '*thinking*' at 14.25 to '*thinking*, thinking' (although this change may have been suggested by a wrong correction in TMs[1b] [see the Textual Note]), but especially by the addition as in MS of an entire omitted sentence, *It has sought by hard reasoning for results emotionally valuable.* (11.14). Moreover, the omission of *Socially considered* at 11.23 has some authority in the

MS. As against at least three significant returns to MS readings, we have the unsupported changes of *commonly* for *generally* (10.13) and the alteration of *defining such high and abstract concepts and discriminating between them* (11.27-29) to *defining the high and abstract concepts of the philosopher, and discriminating between them.*

The first point to notice is that the evidence of James's changes throughout both typescripts indicates that he did not consult MS when he found something wrong. Sometimes by chance, or necessity, he altered TMs[1] back to the MS reading, but just as often he paraphrased according to what seemed to be required. Hence such a case as his restoration verbatim of a missing sentence (and one that leaves no obvious gap) is most unusual if it had been an authorial correction in a now lost TMs[1a]. (For his usual treatment of omissions, see 12.10-11, described in footnote 16.) Secondly, the two changes made by Kallen which differ from MS are not beyond his abilities as shown by his other editorial tinkering with the text. Why *commonly* would be considered superior to *generally* is not clear; but the change at 11.27-29 unquestionably improved the coherence, for *such high and abstract concepts* is not immediately referable to its antecedent *philosophic study* and James's sentence as in MS and TMs is certainly rather sloppy. With these one may perhaps compare demonstrable Kallen sophistications and 'improvements' such as may be found, for example, later at 16.5 where Peggy had mistyped MS *The cold, the hot, the wet, the dry* as *The hot, the wet, the cold the dry* and Kallen on his own responsibility rearranged as *The hot, the cold, the wet, the dry*; or his fussy change of *knowledge* to *knowing* (22.6); of *embalmed* to *petrified* (24.24); or of *that* to *the agency* (33.35). In short, whereas these independent alterations at 10.13 and at 11.27-29 might be authorial, they need not be so.

Since the changes that restore the MS reading are in a different category from those that are independent of MS, the case for Kallen's transcript of the independent readings from authorial revision in lost TMs[1a] pages runs into the truly serious problem of physical evidence that suggests the contrary. This evidence is of two kinds: first, the serious imbalance between the number of authorial revisions that must be posited within the first fourteen pages as against the almost complete lack of such revisions in TMs[1a] pages 15-40, combined with the unusual nature of some of the readings that restore those in the MS. Second, the physical evidence strongly suggests that these pages never existed: in TMs[1] the fourteen pages are a unit, typed early on a paper used nowhere else in the typescript, and succeeded after the interval of typing much of Chapter IV by a resumption of the typing, on a different paper, with page 15. Obviously this history could have no connection with any discrimination in the pile of TMs[1a] sheets used by Kallen in a manner to require the hypothesis that he had access to a now lost set of the carbon pages. The normal evidence is that these pages never existed.

Even though one may speculate that certain of the changes were not beyond Kallen's independent ministrations, the fact remains that those readings that deliberately restore the MS, and especially the missing complete sentence, must have come to him from some authoritative source. If this source were not a now lost marked copy of TMs[1a], pages 1-14, the only alternative is the MS itself. One may observe that in spite of the preservation of the almost complete MS as well as a number of its discarded draft pages, Henry James, Jr., was almost certainly unaware of the sheets written on typewriter paper before the start of James's inscription in the Partridge and Cooper blue notebook. It is, thus, most unlikely (and there is no evidence in favor of the hypothesis) that Kallen through Henry had access to the loose sheets of the whole MS as a source of comparison. However, it must be observed that as the file of materials is now constituted, the first twenty-one folios of the MS are placed to substitute for the missing fourteen pages of TMs[1a], the first line of fol. 21 agreeing with the last sentence on the last line of TMs[1b] page 14.

The unanswerable question is whether these manuscript pages had already been substituted for the lack of a carbon of TMs[1a] when Kallen was given the retyped TMs[2] and the two copies of TMs[1] to assist his preparation of final marked copy for the printer. An intercalation of manuscript sheets and typed pages in a similar manner is found in "The Moral Equivalent of War," and for *Some Problems of Philosophy* appears to be the only explanation that will satisfy the curious evidence that Kallen seems to have seen a copy of MS and made from it a few changes in typed TMs[2] in the area of the missing TMs[1a] pages but not elsewhere—this on the assumption that his annotation of TMs[2] to agree with MS did not derive from James's own corrections in a lost set of TMs[1a] pages, a proposition already suggested to be an unlikely one for several reasons. (See the Textual Note for 11.23 for further evidence.) The textual consequences of this working hypothesis adopted for the present edition are as follows: the markings that Kallen made in TMs[2] between 9.1 and 15.9 are taken to be authoritative only when they agree with MS; among the unauthoritative annotations only the expansion of *Prof.* at 10.26 is accepted as a useful editorial contribution: the rest, whether substantive or accidental, are rejected on the same basis as Kallen's later tinkerings with the text when the complete documents show these to have been without authority.

Copy sent to the printer that is preserved in the file includes not only TMs² but also a typed and hand-revised copy of Henry James, Jr.'s, "Prefatory Note" as well as the typed copy of the Contents and the handwritten (by Henry James, Jr.) dedication to Renouvier. The copy for the Appendix was the marked-up printed Syllabus, from Stanford, preserved, but the copy for the Index, which Kallen made up later, is not preserved. In the file, also, is a projected Prefatory Note in Kallen's hand which Henry discarded in favor of his own. Kallen's Note reads:

Prefatory Note

The manuscript from which this book is printed is a first draft, fragmentary and unrevised. In its completed form it would have been the expression of William James's final opinion on the most fundamental problems philosophy ['faces' *del.*] knows. "Say," he writes, in the directions for the disposal of the manuscript, dated Rye, July 26th, 1910, "that I hoped by it to round out my system which now is too much like an arch built only on one side."

Those who *are accustomed to [*ab. del.* 'knew'] the limpid clearness and flowing ease of the Master's finished work can hardly realize with what numerous and laborious corrections, what infinite pains even his first drafts were prepared. Unrevised fragment though this book be, its editing has involved hardly anything more than the ordering of its contents. The responsibility for the arrangement of the book, for *most [*ov.* 'many'] of its subdivisions into topics and chapters, is the editor's.

Cambridge, March 1, 1911   H. M. Kallen

PROOFS FOR THE BOOK (I[p])

The text of the book is preserved in a set of page-proofs which, being the duplicate set to those returned to the printer, is mostly unmarked by Henry James, Jr., only a few corrections having been transferred from the master on pp. 15, 29, 56, 124, 133, 152, 176. For the entire book the returned printer's proofs have not been preserved, and the sets that we have, whether marked or not, are the duplicates. In addition, the page-proofs for Henry James, Jr.'s, "Prefatory Note" containing a few transferred revisions are found in the file, as well as the page-proofs for the Contents, in which some alterations in the pagination of Chapters III–IV have been marked. Finally, galley-proofs of the Index, heavily corrected by

Kallen, accompany an unmarked set of page-proofs made from the galleys.

A letter in the file from Kallen to Henry James, Jr., written on a Harvard Union letterhead and dated April 7, 1911, begins: "I had been wondering when the galley-proof was to come in. You are very good to have wished to spare me the task of reading it, but I should have read it joyfully, the more as it is part of my task. However, I shall be glad to get the page-proof and do the index as soon as you send it in." The preserved page-proofs for the text are too clean to represent anything but revises, and indeed from this letter we know that the proofs were first read in galley by Henry James and then returned for paging. Although the page-proofs are almost entirely unmarked, the alterations in the set returned to the printer (perhaps mixed in with anything further noted in the revises) may be recovered by collation of the proofs against the book's text. These alterations seem to represent Kallen's corrections and revisions (according to the letter) even though further changes by Henry are quite possibly included. Most of the changes from the page-proofs to the book concern the details of the footnote bibliographical references; a minority deal with misprints and the improvement of accidentals such as the reduction of capitals to lower case. Except for the correction of typos and the alteration of bibliographical minutiae in the footnotes and sidenotes, which are made silently, these variants between proofs and book are recorded in the Historical Collation as I(p) when not accepted as necessary corrections of MS and listed in the Emendations.

THE BOOK (I)

Under A 286890 the book was entered for copyright in the Library of Congress following its publication on May 29, 1911, in the name of Henry James, Jr. Two advertisements in the *Publishers' Weekly* appeared. To the first, on May 20, 1911 (79, 2093–94), noting future publication, was appended the statement:

William James did not live to complete what may be considered as his greatest work, which develops still further the author's great pragmatic programme. What he has written offers a lucid and original restatement and solution of the chief problems of all philosophy, and as it is complete in itself, it will be published this spring. "Say," he wrote in the memorandum directing its publication, "that I had hoped by it to round out my system, which is now too much like an arch built only on one side." The Longmans will publish this work shortly.

The second, on June 10, announces publication (79, 2313) and adds: "For several years before his death Professor William James cherished the purpose of stating his views on certain problems of metaphysics in a book addressed particularly to readers of philosophy. What is now published is all that he had succeeded in writing before he died in August, 1910."

The title page reads: 'SOME PROBLEMS | OF PHILOSOPHY | A BEGINNING OF AN INTRODUCTION | TO PHILOSOPHY | BY | WILLIAM JAMES | [leaf orn.] | LONGMANS, GREEN, AND CO. | FOURTH AVENUE & 30TH STREET, NEW YORK | LONDON, BOMBAY, AND CALCUTTA | 1911'. The pagination formula is [i-vi] vii [viii] ix-xi [xii], [1-2] 3-27 [28] 29-36 [37] 38-45 [46] 47-73 [74] 75-96 [97] 98-111 [112] 113-133 [134] 135-145 [146] 147-152 [153] 154-164 [165] 166-187 [188] 189-206 [207] 208-218 [219-220] 221-230 [231-232] 233-236 [237-240], the gatherings in 8's with the final in 6. The Contents are: pp. i-ii: blank; p. iii: title; p. iv: 'COPYRIGHT, 1911, BY HENRY JAMES JR. | ALL RIGHTS RESERVED'; p. v: dedication; p. vi: blank; p. vii: 'PREFATORY NOTE', subscribed 'HENRY JAMES, JR. | CAMBRIDGE, March 25, 1911.'; p. ix: 'CONTENTS'; p. 1: hf. title 'SOME PROBLEMS OF | PHILOSOPHY'; p. 2: blank; p. 3 'CHAPTER I | PHILOSOPHY AND ITS CRITICS'; p. 29: 'CHAPTER II | THE PROBLEMS OF METAPHYSICS'; p. 38: 'CHAPTER III | THE PROBLEM OF BEING'; p. 47: 'CHAPTER IV | PERCEPT AND CONCEPT—THE IMPORT | OF CONCEPTS'; p. 75: 'CHAPTER V | PERCEPT AND CONCEPT— THE ABUSE | OF CONCEPTS[1]'; p. 98: 'CHAPTER VI | PERCEPT AND CONCEPT—SOME | COROLLARIES'; p. 113: 'CHAPTER VII | THE ONE AND THE MANY'; p. 135: 'CHAPTER VIII[1] | THE ONE AND THE MANY (*continued*)— | VALUES AND DEFECTS'; p. 147: 'CHAPTER IX | THE PROBLEM OF NOVELTY'; p. 154: 'CHAPTER X | NOVELTY AND THE INFINITE—THE | CONCEPTUAL VIEW[1]'; p. 166: 'CHAPTER XI[1] | NOVELTY AND THE INFINITE—THE | PERCEPTUAL VIEW'; p. 189: 'CHAPTER XII[1] | NOVELTY AND CAUSATION—THE | CONCEPTUAL VIEW'; p. 208: 'CHAPTER XIII | NOVELTY AND CAUSATION—THE | PERCEPTUAL VIEW'; p. 220: blank; p. 221: 'APPENDIX | FAITH AND THE RIGHT TO BELIEVE[1]'; p. 232: blank; p. 233: 'INDEX'; p. 238: 'The Riverside Press | CAMBRIDGE. MASSACHUSETTS | U. S. A.'; pp. 239-240: blank.

The book is bound uniformly with the rest of the Longmans, Green volumes of James's works.

In England Longmans, Green issued the American sheets with the variant title page and imprint 'LONGMANS, GREEN, AND CO. | 39 PATERNOSTER ROW, LONDON | NEW YORK, BOMBAY, AND CALCUTTA | 1911'. This title page is a cancellans. The British Library statutory copy (2236.b.7) is date-stamped 3 June 1911 and has been rebound. The London Library has two copies of this first English issue, one in the original binding of green-brown buckram and a paper label on the spine: '[double rule] | SOME | PROBLEMS | OF | PHILOSOPHY | BY | WILLIAM JAMES | [double rule]'. The Bodleian Library statutory copy (date-stamped 5 June 1911) is the American edition (2657.e.338). Bound with it is the spine of the original dust-jacket on buff paper: '[double rule] | SOME | PROBLEMS | OF | PHILOSOPHY | BY | WILLIAM JAMES | [double rule] | Price | $1.25 net | LONGMANS'.

The American edition went through a succession of printings, the second in July 1911, the third in August 1916, the fourth in September 1919, the fifth in February 1921, and the sixth in April 1924, the last that has been examined for possible plate changes. A series of changes authorized by Henry James, Jr., was made in the plates of the second printing, and five further changes in the third. Thereafter the plates remained invariant. Henry James, Jr.'s, marked copy of the first printing at Harvard (*AC85. J2376.911s) contains on various pages a total of thirty-eight corrections and notes or queries. The source for these is given in only a few places. On the inside back cover, below the list of page numbers sent to the printer for correction, James wrote '183 - Phil. of Math. for Princip of Math. also in other places says Perry—', a reference to 89.40 and 93.17,34. In the top margin of the text of p. 9, referring to the quotation in 11.37-40, he adds, 'Esther Carpenter writes attributing this to Lord Bowen, making the correction with which my memory agrees and wh. is certainly an improvt. on the text.' The correction is the change of *black cat* to *black hat*. Finally, in reference to *eintheilung* at 10.1, he notes, 'Schiller writes the "modern" spelling omits the *h*', and at 107.39 he writes about the first appearance of *causes*, 'Schiller suggests that this sh'd read "antecedents." The ms. reads *causes*.' The two references to Schiller do not exclude the possibility that other of the corrections came from him as well perhaps from Kallen,[9]

---

[9]Kallen was very likely responsible for the suggested addition to the index of 'Dreams 125' and 'Toleration, 225', changes that in fact were not made in the plates because of the difficulties of adding lines.

Perry, and various friends. As in the reference to 107.39 James seems to have consulted the manuscript to verify whether the queried readings were misprints or mistranscriptions. In marking the insertion of *parts* after *worlds*, changed to *world's*, at 68.8 he added, 'This word appears in the orig. MS in the copy book but was omitted in the type copy—H.J.Jr.' At 89.13 in adding *un* before *criticized* [i.e., *unanalyzed*] he noted, 'The first ms. reads "unanalyzed." '; in altering *it* to *its* at 101.33, 'correction accords with orig. ms.'; and at 104.32 in altering *hypothesis* to *hypotheses* he wrote, 'The ms reads *hypotheses*'.[10] Two annotations have no relation to correction. Opposite the start of the paragraph *Philosophy, beginning in wonder* (11.6) he noted, 'This ¶ is surprisingly like a passage in the Nation editorial (Sept. 21. '76)';[11] and opposite 106.40–107.6 he noted in the left margin, 'Quoted from Pluralistic Univ.—p. 376'.[12] For the rest, as recorded in the Historical Collation he corrected errors in German, Latin, and French, in the spellings of authors' names, and other misprints and typescript errors. On the back pasted-down flyleaf under '*Corrections*' he gave a list of page numbers and to the right of a brace wrote 'Directed the Press to make these corrections in the 2nd 2000 copies June 29. 1911. H.J. Jr.' Since some of the annotations were not corrective, not all of the comments were listed; but twenty-seven corrections were made in the plates of the July second printing, two of these of readings and pages not marked in James's copy: the correct alteration of *on* at 41.14 to *upon*, and of *Science* to *science* at 93.44 in (I), an unauthoritative bibliographical reference added by Kallen and removed from the present text (see Historical Collation). Certain of the alterations marked

---

[10] Since at this time Henry knew only the blue notebook which began with Chapter V, "The One and the Many," he could not verify earlier queries. For instance, at 13.34 he bracketed *passings* and noted 'passions?' but did not order the alteration of the plates (until the third printing, in 1916). The MS reading is somewhat scrawled, which accounts for the original mistyping, but if Henry had indeed consulted it he ought to have been able to see that *passions* was the reading. He seems to have entered various of these notes with a question mark and then deleted the query when he verified the correction. He did not, of course, need the manuscript confirmation before he deleted the query after the misprint *1609* and its correction to *1690* at 13.36. When someone suggested, and he recorded, that at 15.9–10 *metaphysical* and *theological* (mistyped in that order and so printed) should be exchanged, he added the note '*obviously*' when he accepted the query, but the MS would have given him the necessary evidence if he had seen it.

[11] This is "The Teaching of Philosophy in Our Colleges," reprinted in *Essays in Philosophy*, WORKS (1978).

[12] Consultation of the MS would have shown him here that for the text William James had pasted in a clipping from "The Experience of Activity" in the *Psychological Review*.

in the copy do not appear in the list of page numbers at the back and are not represented in the second-printing plate-changes. At 17.21 the *sine* was altered to *cosine* (in ink instead of the usual pencil) and at 20.8 *fulfill-|ment* was marked as *fulfil-|ment*, two changes that were delayed until the third printing of August 1916 when they appear in the plates. The note about Perry's report that Bertrand Russell's *Philosophy of Mathematics* should be *Principles of Mathematics* in the book's pp. 183 and 174 that was written at the back below the page numbers led James to mark the text at this page, but the changes do not appear in the second printing and (presumably by oversight) were not made in the third printing when the alterations at 13.34, 17.21, 20.8, and 99.4 (plus Index) (also presumably received too late for inclusion in the list to the printer of June 29) were added. Schiller's suggestion about the spelling of *eintheilung* at 10.1 was never sent to the printer nor was his suggestion that the first *causes* at 107.39 should read *antecedents*, although in this latter case the page number 214 occurs in the list at the back of the book but is followed by a question mark and is then deleted. The query about the misreading *passings* at 13.34 was not resolved until the third printing; that about *Absn.* at 103.41 was never made although the page is listed. The alteration of the misspelling of *Geulincx* marked in the text at 99.4 is also listed at the back among the page numbers sent to the printer but was not instituted until the third printing (its second alteration marked in the book in the Index is not present in the page list). A query whether *science* in a French title at 89.39 should not be capitalized did not produce an alteration and, perhaps again by oversight, the marking in the same title of a grave accent for the mistake *hypothese* was not made in the plates. Outside of the four late entries mentioned that were delayed until the third printing, no further attempt was made to correct the book.

III. KALLEN'S REARRANGEMENT OF THE CHAPTERS

The problem of the constitution of the chapters is complicated by the fact that James seems to have written some of them (or their drafts) out of sequence and to have given the chapters only a provisional numbering, or no numbering at all, proposing no doubt to order the typescript made from his manuscript on a final survey before it was sent to the printer.

Faced with the problem of James's uncertain numbering, Horace

III. Kallen's Chapter Rearrangement

Kallen organized the chapter headings into Problems, according to the hint of James's own title for the book. The first two chapters were treated as preliminary. James's third chapter became First Problem—The Problem of Being, James's fourth, the Second Problem—Percept and Concept, James's fifth, the Third Problem—The One and the Many, and James's overall sixth (comprising the first and second sub-problems of Chapters VII–IX), the Fourth Problem—Novelty. James's own chapter titles thus being used as Problem headings, Kallen invented his own descriptive titles for the chapters he carved out of the text under each Problem. In ink, then, he altered Chapter III to '*First Problem*. The Problem of Being. | Chapter III Being and Non-Being'.[13] Each new chapter repeated the Problem heading above its title, as '*Second Problem* | Percept and Concept[x] | Chapter IV, Their Nature and Relations'. The text of the Second Problem (James's Chapter IV) was then subdivided into three further chapters: 'Chapter V The Import of Concepts' (38.36 *The first thing to notice* . . .), 'Chapter VI—The Abuse of Concepts' (44.6 *In spite of this obvious need* . . .), 'Chapter VII—Some Corollaries' (54.17 I. *The first corollary* . . .), this latter using James's subheading as the chapter title. James's unnumbered chapter "The One and the Many," becoming the Third Problem, was divided into two chapters, 'Chapter VIII Monism *versus [*ab. del.* 'and'] Pluralism' (61.1 *The full nature* . . .), which in his handwritten Contents list prefixed to TMs[1b] Kallen changed to 'Pluralism *versus* Monism'; and 'Chapter IX The Values and Defects of Monism and Pluralism' (70.32 *We might dismiss* . . .). James's Chapter V (properly Chapter VI), "The Problem of Novelty," was the Fourth Problem called simply 'Novelty', which Kallen made into four chapters, beginning 'Chapter X ['The Meaning of' *del.*] Novelty and the Infinite' (76.1 *The impotence to explain* . . .), which in the Contents list he altered to 'Novelty & the Infinite: The Rationalist View'. Originally, at the point where James introduced his first sub-problem (80.1 *The problem is as to* . . .) Kallen started a Chapter XI but gave it no title (perhaps adopting 'First Sub-Problem . . . Infinite') and assigned The Problem of Novelty wrongly as Problem III (an error he also made and then corrected at 76.1), but he then deleted the entry and included the section under his Chapter X. James had run on his text at 85.18 (*Kant's and Renouvier's dealings* . . .)

---

[13] The quoted headings are from the formal handwritten Contents list that Kallen prefixed to TMs[1b]. This list reprints in more orderly form the combination of his handwritten additions and the typed titles in the headings of the chapters of TMs[2].

without even a subheading; but Kallen at this point interpolated his reassigned 'Chapter XI—The Pragmatic *Solution [*ab. del.* 'Treatment'] of *Problem of [*intrl.*] the Infinite', which in his list was copied correctly as 'the Problem of'. James's Second Sub-Problem of Cause and Effect (96.1 *If reality changes . . .*) became Kallen's 'Chapter XII Novelty and Causation: The Conceptual View', which led into his final 'Chapter XIII Novelty and Causation: The Perceptual View' at 105.1 (*Most persons remain . . .*). In the Contents list above Chapter XII Kallen wrote 'Fifth Problem' but deleted the insertion; no indication appears in TMs^2 of any Problem other than the fourth.

In his memorandum Henry James, Jr., states: "Kallen supplied most of the marginal titles. His division into chapters, again divided into 'problems' in the table of contents, did not seem quite satisfactory; and R. B. Perry, who read the manuscript, suggested an arrangement substantially like that finally adopted after a morning's conference *which I had [*intrl.*] with Kallen." Perry's hand does not appear in TMs^2; thus his suggested rearrangement must have been in the form of a note which Henry James, Jr., followed when he himself altered Kallen's version in TMs^2. The rearrangement in the form as was then printed in the first edition was not at all drastic and consisted chiefly of scrapping Kallen's four headings of Problems and restoring the original chapter titles, in the process deleting one of Kallen's chapter divisions and restoring another. Henry James in ink crossed out Kallen's additions and moved the original typed chapter titles to follow the chapter number. When he came to Chapter IV, he deleted 'Their Nature and Relations' and added 'Percept and Concept—The Import of Concepts'. Kallen's arbitrary Chapter V, "The Import of Concepts," starting at 38.36 was removed. However, the rest of Kallen's chapter divisions were accepted and thus Kallen merely renumbered them up to XI where the two numberings joined. Kallen's Chapter VI became 'Chapter V—Percept and Concept The Abuse of Concepts'; at a later time, in pencil, Kallen added a footnote signed 'Ed.' stating that this and the following chapter did not appear separately in the manuscript (the note reads 'following chapters' but the book has the singular). Kallen's interpolated Chapter IX, by mistake not renumbered as VIII, becomes 'The One and the Many (Continued) Values and Defects'. Kallen's previously deleted chapter at 80.1 was reinstated so that James's 'First sub-problem: The Continuum and the Infinite' becomes 'Novelty and the Infinite—[The] Conceptual View' with the pencil footnote giving James's original title and the information that in the manuscript this chapter and the succeeding ones were labeled sub-problems. Kallen also altered Chapter XI to the new title 'Novelty and the Infinite—The Perceptual View' adding the footnote that this was not a separate chapter in the manuscript. In ink Kallen added 'The Conceptualist View' to his original Chapter XII title and then in pencil deleted the heading 'Fourth Problem', removed 'ist' from 'Conceptualist', and added a footnote pointing out that in the manuscript the chapter was given the heading of 'Second Sub-problem—Cause and Effect'. The alterations to restore the typed Chapter XIII heading were carried out in pencil.

The initial changes made by Kallen and Perry's suggested modifications conveyed to James have no authority. It follows that the present new text of *Some Problems of Philosophy*, based on the ultimate authority of James's manuscript as revised in the two copies of TMs¹, properly goes back to James's own demarcation of his chapters, with the exception that the divisions of Chapters VII and VIII, introduced in the present edition, appear to follow James's intentions in the manuscript even though he did not formally mark the final version of the manuscript at these places with chapter headings.

IV. THE FIRST TYPESCRIPT: A RECONSTRUCTED HISTORY

In a memorandum dated April 22, 1911, contained in the file of *Some Problems* in the Houghton Library, Henry James, Jr., states that "The first pages were destroyed after M. M. J. [Peggy James] had typewritten them." Other references by William's son indicate that when he was seeing the book into print he was unaware of any manuscript except that in the blue notebook containing Chapters V–IX. Thus his remark about the destruction of the manuscript was based on hearsay and was intended to cover all of the manuscript before the notebook (possibly excepting the substitute MS leaves at the start of TMs¹ᵃ), with no specific reference to the first fifty missing pages of the manuscript of Chapter IV. These unaccounted-for pages offer a serious problem, the answer to which unlocks a curious sequence of events in the production of the first typescript (TMs¹).

To start at the beginning, one must notice the coincidence that the first fourteen pages of TMs¹ᵇ (ribbon copy) have been typed on a laid paper watermarked Gloria Linen, that these pages are not present in the copy of TMs¹ᵃ in the file (MS leaves acting as a substitute), and that TMs¹ᵃ (carbon) begins with p. 15 when in both typescripts the paper has changed to the wove sheets water-marked Chinese Linen. The Gloria Linen paper is found nowhere else in the *Some Problems* typescript (nor had it appeared in the manuscript). However, Gloria Linen is the paper of the draft typescript that Peggy prepared of an early form of the essay "The Moral Equivalent of War," a typescript that James expanded by the addition of autograph pages on Chinese Linen paper, this in an article finished on December 13, 1909. In the interval between November 1909 and the diary entry for January 8, 1910, "Recommenced writing," James had been busy with the three essays— "Bradley or Bergson?," "The Moral Equivalent of War," and "A Suggestion about Mysticism," which according to James's diary were completed respectively on November 28, December 13, and December 17, 1909, written in a blue Partridge & Cooper notebook (bMS Am 1092.9, #4519) that had been reversed after starting with notes and a draft of part of Chapter IV, "Percepts and Concepts." The incomplete evidence suggests that the use of the Gloria Linen paper in the draft typescript of "The Moral Equivalent of War" was earlier than James's use of the Chinese Linen paper expanding it (not vice versa). It is thus a normal assumption that the fourteen sheets of Gloria Linen paper beginning the typescript of *Some Problems* represent Peggy's initial stint of typing, the earliest preserved and presumably the earliest in fact, started probably in December 1909.

The evidence is conflicting as to how far Peggy had progressed in this start of her typing the book before she broke off. The natural conclusion would be that she stopped at the point where the ribbon copy on Gloria Linen stops, that is, after fourteen pages, and that she resumed work on p. 15 with Chinese Linen paper and a carbon on the same sheets at some later time (to be specific, after she had typed part of Chapter IV). One slight difficulty in accepting this hypothesis comes in the evidence of the pagination. The first chapter's number is left blank in the heading, and the pages are not numbered on the typewriter for the whole Gloria Linen sequence. However, when typing was resumed on Chinese Linen with p. 15, the pages were not numbered on the typewriter either, until 26, then unnumbered 27 follows, and then typed 28 and so forth in order. Peggy herself seems to have numbered pp. 1–15 by hand in the left corner, James to have taken over with centered numbering at 16, although it is possible that Peggy resumed, with centered numbering, at 22 and 23 but at least she returned to number 24 and 25 in the left corner. It might be possible, thus, to hypothesize that Peggy kept on typing after the Gloria Linen stock had run out by turning to Chinese Linen, and that she broke off at p. 25, the last of the unnumbered sequence (except for skipped 27), when she came to a natural stopping place with the last line of Chapter I heading p. 25 and the first page of Chapter II below it. This is possible if James had been satisfied with Chapter I, in its early form, but was in process of revising Chapters II and III. The more attractive hypothesis, however, limits the early typing to Gloria Linen paper and a ribbon copy on the speculation that for what at the start would have been considered a draft typescript (to be retyped after correction and revision) no carbon was at first thought necessary and thus pp. 1–14 are wanting in TMs[1a] (carbon) since they were never made. The account that follows of the chequered history of Chapter IV also reinforces the theory that Peggy did not return to type p. 15 of Chapter I until she had worked on Chapter IV. The lack of numbering at the beginning of the resumed typing with p. 15 is not too difficult to explain: all we need suppose is that Peggy continued the unpaged sheets she had found in her early stint until it became apparent that she was indeed working with Chapter I and that the pages could be numbered. (It is possible that James did not add the 'I' by hand to typed 'CHAPTER' until he had firmly decided on "Percept and Concept" as Chapter IV and thus on the order of the early sequence, although the 'I' seems to be original in the manuscript and the subject could only constitute the first chapter.)

One further piece of evidence may seem to support the case that the typing of pp. 15–42 (to the end of Chapter III) was not continuous with that of 1–14. At first inspection it seems odd that p. 14 ends only one three-letter word short of the completion of a sentence although there would seem to have been room for this one short word (*yam* 15.28) to have completed the last line if the typist had known at the time that p. 14 was to be the temporary end of a stint. Oddly, also, when p. 15 was started on a different paper, and at a later time, Peggy did not begin with this word *yam* but instead indented seven spaces before starting the next sentence. This opening was less than her usual paragraph indention, but it seems to have been designed in order to leave space for the insertion at some later time of text carried on from the preceding page, as if Peggy had started to type p. 15 without a precise memory of just where in the sentence she had ended p. 14. Moreover, when *yam* was added on the typewriter within the indented opening, it was itself indented two spaces from the left margin either because of an irregularity in the insertion of the paper or perhaps in order not to leave too wide a space between its period and the first word of the next sentence beginning seven spaces in from the margin. The weight of this evidence for the later insertion on p. 15 of this last word of the sentence running on from p. 14, added to the evidence of the change in paper and the probable reason for the lack of a carbon copy, seems to suggest very strongly that typing was not continuous. It follows that there was a delay between the suspension of this initial typing (perhaps in December 1909) and the start of the next stint. Interestingly, according to the working hypothesis adopted, another section of the typescript—Chapter IV—intervened before Peggy resumed Chapter I on p. 15.

Before the start of Chapter V in a blue notebook, the manuscript of *Some Problems* consists of sheets of typewriter paper, Chapters I-III written on a paper watermarked L. L. Brown, and Chapter IV (so much as is found in the file) on paper watermarked Chinese Linen. In contrast, the typescript after its first fourteen pages on Gloria Linen paper shifts to the Chinese Linen with p. 15 in Chapter I and continues with this paper through p. 97(50) of Chapter IV. Beginning with p. 98(51) the L. L. Brown paper enters TMs[1] and continues to the end. The use of Brown paper for the interpolated additions of typed p. 25½(71) and the autograph leaves 81b and 81c within the sequence of Chinese Linen indicates the order beyond all question. On the other hand, in the manuscript it is clear that the L. L. Brown paper of Chapters I-III precedes the use of the Chinese Linen paper of Chapter IV. Whatever may have been the medium (as perhaps a notebook) in which the earliest discarded drafts of Chapters I-III were written, the preserved text of present Chapter III on the L. L. Brown paper is worked over from a draft on the same paper, which had been a favorite with James who had used it for the manuscript of *A Pluralistic Universe* two years before. Although we have no means of knowing what was the text of Chapter III before fol. 23(22) of these fragmentary draft leaves (see Appendix I), this draft could not have included Chapter I, which is thirty-six leaves in the present MS, but it may well have included present Chapter II and its eleven leaves.[14] Whatever the text, however, it is clear that the

---

[14]Chapters in the MS were not commonly numbered, as one sees, for example, in "Percept and Concept" and "The One and the Many"; the numbering of Chapters I-III on L. L. Brown paper occurs on pages that were a late revision. One should note that a chapter on the problems of being (i.e., Chapter III) is promised in deleted text at the foot of fol. 34 of the notebook MS of "The One and the Many" (Chapter V), an example of the fluidity with which James early contemplated the arrangement of his

numbering of the draft leaves did not take into account the present Chapter I and, like "Percept and Concept," this discussion of Being in the Chapter [II-] III draft seems to have been written with independent pagination, not in any series.

The L. L. Brown paper could have not been used continuously for the inscription of MS Chapters I-III and then for the typing of TMs[1] pp. 98-221, of course. The link seems to be established between the use of Chinese Linen paper in the expansion of the Gloria Linen typescript of "The Moral Equivalent of War," the inscription of the final form of fols. 51-69 (and the addition of fols. 1-2) of MS "Percept and Concept," and then the typing of the start of the fourth chapter followed by the revived typing of Chapters I-III beginning with p. 15, all these using the same Chinese Linen paper. The inference is, then, that Peggy's typing of Chapter I was suspended while she devoted her attention to other material. One may have a strong suspicion, though no proof, that the coincidence of the Gloria Linen paper in the early type-script of "The Moral Equivalent of War" and the first fourteen pages of Chapter I indicates that these Chapter I pages were typed just before or just after the completion of "The Moral Equivalent"

---

chapters. Yet he seems to have had in mind at least some tentative arrangements; hence it may be that the misnumbering of Chapter III as II as late as the present MS revised form need not be a slip and could reflect the numbering of the draft in its lost pages, or else James's original proposal for its position. The whole question is extremely obscure. For instance, whether the fragmentary draft of Chapter III included what is now Chapter II, so that present II was carved out of its early part, or whether each was originally indicated as a separate chapter is not to be demonstrated. A useful hint may be found in "The One and the Many," however, to suggest that the draft of present Chapter III was not sixty pages long, as indicated by its last preserved folio number in the odd sheets. Following the deleted promise of a chapter on Being at the foot of the last folio of "The One and the Many" is a circled note to insert loose sheets 47-59, which refers to the fourteen leaves, including 58½, of the manuscript and its pagination of the revised present Chapter III. But this must be a later note, taking account of the revision of Chapter III (and its separation from Chapter II), since a gap of twenty-five pages follows between the notebook numbering of "The One and the Many" and the start of "The Problem of Novelty," a space that would be filled exactly by the twenty-five combined manuscript pages of the final form of Chapters II and III. This fact seems to support the possibility, already suggested by the misnumbering of the heading for present Chapter III, that the abnormal brevity of II and III—which together make up about the length of a normal chapter—resulted from the separation into two parts of what had originally been planned in the draft as a single unit. It also suggests that even after the two were separated, James continued to think of them as a unit that could be transferred together and only later changed his mind when he specified merely the pages of Chapter III. The proposal, even though dropped, to shift this material from its early position to follow "The One and the Many" offers an interesting sidelight on the lack of an arbitrary plan in James's mind for the order of his chapters.

on December 13, 1909. The scattered references in the diary do not conflict with such a hypothesis. It seems clear from the diary entry "Wrote on 'Being,'" of May 19, 1909, that follows the next day after "Wrote Introd." of May 18 that what are now Chapters I–II were considered to be his Introduction. According to James's letters of October 6 to his brother Henry and to Schiller on October 8, a gap of some months had intervened in his writing (probably from late May to early or mid-September) so that only twenty-six pages had been written in the month before October 8. One may speculate, however, that he had completed Chapter III (although not necessarily its revision) by this date and had made some progress on a draft of material that was to go in Chapter IV, since after resuming work on November 10 he noted in his diary that he had lost his chapter on the 'pragmatist rule.' Work on the three articles then intervened, and it was not until January 8, 1910, that James recorded his resumption of writing. By January 16 he had finished the manuscript of "Percept and Concept," in the form now known, for on that date he 're-opened' a page to add a reference to Schiller, which may be identified as fol. 65½ (59.10–14 [*plus fn.*]) added on Chinese Linen paper to the manuscript only four pages before the end of the chapter.

This reference shows that on January 16, Peggy's typing had not yet reached p. 110 of the typescript, where the text of the addition on MS 65½ starts.

The diary entry that James had lost his chapter on the 'pragmatist rule' is especially puzzling. A hardcover notebook of blue paper sporadically watermarked Partridge & Cooper is preserved as bMS Am 1092.9, #4519 in the James Collection in which (fortuitously reversed as shown by the label on the inside back cover, the only mark on front or back) James began initial inscription on two now excised leaves preserved only by the stubs, then a leaf numbered 2 containing a pencil note on Perry's 'equality of all interests' (very likely of different date), followed by eighteen stubs of abstracted leaves and then a draft text of the beginning of Chapter IV, without chapter number and headed merely 'Concepts etc', written in ink on the rectos of nineteen numbered leaves, corrected in pencil, with pencil notes for additions on the versos of the first four leaves and the twelfth. (This draft is transcribed in Appendix I.) Stubs of abstracted leaves (the margins showing some ink letters) occur twice within the text. This manuscript ends at the foot of fol. 19 with the ink heading 'THE PRAGMATIST POSTULATE.[x]' and footnote indicator, altered in pencil to 'THE PRAGMATIC RULE.[x]' Below this heading the text continues—

in pencil, however—with 'The *pragmatic rule [*alt. in pencil fr.* 'pragmatist postulate'] is that' (37.17), the last line on the page. There follow eighty-six stubs until one comes to a page of pencil notes for *Some Problems* including material for a footnote that was later added by hand to TMs¹ª (44.35–38) on page 73(27). This page in the notebook has been pasted over with a blank piece of paper, obviously to avoid any confusion with the text on its reversed verso containing the last page of the article "A Suggestion about Mysticism," completed on December 17, 1909, the last of the three articles written in the notebook from the other end, the notebook reversed from the Chapter IV draft to accommodate the beginning of the first article on its initial page. (This reversal fortuitously restored the correct position of the notebook as shown by a Partridge & Cooper label pasted on the inside of the original front cover before the first article.) The evidence of the paste-over suggests that this leaf was not removed from the notebook with its eighty-six predecessors since it contained the last page of the article's text, in which case the leaves were cut out at some date later than December 17, 1909, when "A Suggestion" had been finished. That they had been written before December 17, 1909, however, is certain, given the physical evidence of the notebook and also the diary entries that suggest that the discussion of Percept and Concept was started at least as early as November 10.

These pieces of evidence, and their dates, make the November 14 diary entry "Lost my chapter on 'pragmatist rule,'" difficult to explain in any precise detail. (One should notice that James refers to the unrevised form of the heading for the first word but the revised for the second.) If James thought of this chapter-to-be as constituting the pragmatist rule, then it is possible that he had mislaid the notebook and found it later. On the other hand, so many odd coincidences cluster about the removal of the leaves immediately after the text for the pragmatic rule heading, including the effect, apparently, on the typescript (TMs¹) later to be made from them, that it is tempting to believe that for some purpose James cut out the leaves and either mislaid or permanently lost them. In this connection one may remark the two sets of leaves removed in the preceding text, the gaps repaired by pencil revision. This pencil bridging suggests that the leaves were not cut out during the course of composition but instead during the later revision of the whole of the preserved text in pencil. In this connection it may be significant that the first sentence beginning the section on the pragmatic rule at the foot of the last preserved leaf was written in pencil, although the heading was in ink, revised in pencil, the pencil text itself being similarly altered in pencil. This fact suggests that James did not immediately begin the section on the rule after writing its heading but instead had completed a stint with the heading. This conjecture seems to be strengthened by the addition, also in pencil, of the footnote on the facing verso which refers to the ink footnote indicator of the heading. It may be, therefore—although the evidence is slim—that James stopped temporarily on fol. 19 with the heading and at some later time returned to revise the leaves in pencil and only at that time continued the text in pencil. The remaining text of "Percept and Concept" would fit into the eighty-six missing leaves and perhaps leave some room for supplementary notes such as seem to be represented on the last page in pencil under the paste-over. Since the substance of the note about Wallace on this pasted-over page was transferred by hand as an added footnote in the typescript on p. 73(27) (44.35–38), it has no bearing on how far the text had progressed by this last leaf, particularly since the end of the preceding note continued from the removed stub just before this leaf is repeated on the first page of the original typescript of Chapter IV, later revised and changed. It would be a natural assumption that the whole of the discourse had been sketched in, although we have no means of ascertaining the facts.

It is an oddity that the MS of the book starts "Percept and Concept" with two unnumbered leaves of the Chinese Linen paper (breaking with the L. L. Brown paper of manuscript Chapters I–III), and then is wanting leaves until the text begins in mid-sentence on fol. 51 with *all future time* after the deletion of the initial words *wading through* (53.19). The oddity is compounded in that *all future time* are the opening words of TMs[1] on p. 51, renumbered 98 in sequence, the page where the typescript changes from Chinese Linen to L. L. Brown paper and the carbon of TMs[1a] becomes the ribbon copy. Chance cannot be expected to encompass such an extraordinary coincidence, the more especially when it is considered that fifty-one pages of manuscript text on the Chinese Linen paper would have amounted to considerably less than fifty-one pages of typescript. Moreover, the first two unnumbered leaves of the MS are substitutes, not originals, and the second is only a part-page. This anomaly is also transferred to the typescript TMs[1]. Originally the start of this chapter had been typed by James himself without a heading ("Percept and Concept" being supplied later by hand but without a chapter number) on Chinese Linen paper, unnumbered, its text varying from the notebook draft in its first two sentences although agreeing with the very end of the first note under the paste-over after the stubs. The text of this first page was also somewhat revised by hand. Subsequently, a revised version was typed by Peggy on L. L. Brown paper, the text of the first paragraph drawn from the substitute manuscript leaf and a half, and then, continuing from James's revised typed pages, this substitute begun on p. 42 (headed Chapter 4) under the last five lines concluding Chapter III and continuing on a new part-page 43 that ends with the last three lines of text still further revising the hand-revised text of the top three lines of the original typescript hand-numbered as p. 2. The revised opening takes account of the final placement as Chapter IV of this section. The use of L. L. Brown paper for the revision indicates that the substitution was made at some point after L. L. Brown paper had entered the typescript later in Chapter IV with p. 51, renumbered 98.

It now seems possible to attempt a conjectural reconstruction of the course of events. Chapter IV is not only the longest chapter in the book but in a sense is its heart and the most important section. It seems to have given James the greatest trouble in composition and revision and in the end he was forced to leave further revision to a note written in England about expanding the opening. Kallen admitted that the section was flawed and would have been different if James had lived to perfect it. James did not put it through several versions, as he had done with Chapter III, for example, on the evidence of Chapter III's draft leaves and complete rewriting on L. L. Brown paper; but instead he started to type the section himself on Chinese Linen paper, rewriting it in the process from his copy of the preserved draft leaves in bMS Am 1092.9, #4519. James's typing is distinguishable from Peggy's in three particular respects. The most prominent difference is that he often uses an ampersand as in his handwritten copy whereas Peggy never does. It is interesting to see, as an example, the disappearance of the ampersands in James's typed p. 93(46) when Peggy had to retype it to provide a copy for TMs[1b] because of a reversed carbon paper. Second, since the typewriter had no margin release, a typist had to become expert at estimating the length of words when approaching the right margin and planning whether to break them with a hyphen or to leave an extra wide space at the right and begin the word in the next line. Peggy was fairly adept at this judgment but James was not and hence he frequently found himself up against the right margin with several letters of a word still to go, which he had to supply by hand. Third, he was ordinarily a good speller (although prone to omit or double letters in typing), whereas Peggy's spelling could be uncertain. The use of typed ampersands and the difficulties in ending words before the right margin are both exemplified in the typescript of "W. James's Statement" transcribed in *The Meaning of Truth*, pp. 293–296 and illustrated on p. 294, in the present edition of the WORKS. Both typescripts are clearly James's.

James typed the original first page of the chapter, later revised and then retyped by Peggy, continued through p. 12 (p. 56 of the renumbering), and stopped after completing a sentence at the end of the first line of p. 13 (. . . *its importance.* 37.23). Pages 4–9 and 13 have typed centered numbers; the other pages are numbered in ink by hand, probably when James gave these pages an extensive revision in ink. Page 8 has a hyphen before and after the number and page 13 an asterisk and a hyphen, whereas Peggy, in this typescript at least, never uses such hyphens. Later in the chapter, after Peggy had taken over the typing with the second line of p. 13, James himself typed added pages 25½ (43.32 *Emerson . . .* Love*). 43.42), 28 (44.14 |cation on . . . insults of* 44.24), and 46 (51.23 *Bradley . . . compenetra-|* 52.8). The text of pp. 1–12 comprised all of the preserved manuscript in the notebook in #4519 (much rewritten as it was typed) plus the completion of the sentence broken at the foot of notebook fol. 19 followed by another sentence.

That Peggy took over the typing with the sentence beginning the second line of p. 13 (the first line had contained an ampersand) seems to be indicated by the lack of any further ampersands on the page and by her more skillful treatment of the right margin. Moreover, the first line of the typescript (and its carbon) on p. 13 seems to be typed with a heavier pressure than the rest of the page. Numbering each page in the center she continued the typing on Chinese Linen paper through her typed p. 50, renumbered 97 (. . . *wading through* 53.19). Starting with the next page, 51(98), the L. L. Brown paper makes its first appearance in the typescript, and TMs[1b], the previous ribbon copy, becomes the carbon and TMs[1a] the ribbon. As remarked, the coincidence of these changes with the beginning of MS fol. 51 and TMs[1] p. 51 with the same text cannot be chance, and an explanation is required. The simplest, and almost certainly the correct answer (although necessarily conjectural) is that fols. 1–50 of the MS inscribed on typewriter paper never existed except for the first page and a half added as a revision to the typed pages.

James was a reluctant and inexpert typist who preferred to

conduct his extensive correspondence in longhand or (especially when he was ill) by dictation, usually to his wife, Alice. Thus some unusual circumstances must have called forth his taking over the typewriter for the first twelve pages of the fourth chapter. What these were is subject only to speculation, of course. It may have been that Peggy was unavailable; it may have been that he thought that since he was going to need to rewrite extensively his draft in the notebook, he might as well type it and provide a better foundation for even more revision rather than writing it out in longhand. The first may seem to be the better guess, on the evidence that he was prepared to rewrite Chapter III in longhand. However, if he could provide acceptable copy, Peggy would not need to retype his pages and thus her time could be saved. It may be pertinent that when James finished "Bradley or Bergson?" on November 28, 1909, he recorded in his diary on the next day, "Type-wrote & mailed my article." If this means what it says, then Peggy was not used, as she was in the next article, "The Moral Equivalent of War," but, instead, James typewrote the printer's copy himself. Moreover, in his diary for December 17, 1909, he noted "Copy & mail mysticism article." The copy could have been in longhand, of course (or Peggy's typescript), but it may also have been a James typescript, such as "Bradley or Bergson?" A possible date at which James could have typed these pages of Chapter IV is difficult to assign. But if, as seems likely, Peggy took over from James after the first line of typed p. 13, the most probable date would be late December or, perhaps more likely, early January 1910, a date that would still give James a chance to deal with the problems of the text in typed pages 13–50, to write MS fols. 51–69, and report to Schiller on January 16 in terms that indicate he had completed the manuscript part of the chapter, just possibly on January 13.

The question then arises of the nature of the copy when Peggy took over the typing, for James had left off only a sentence beyond the point at which the last leaf of the notebook #4519 preserves the draft text of the chapter's start. Once again we are back at the enigma of the November 14 diary entry noting that James had written in bed, with the added entry, "Lost my chapter on 'pragmatist rule.'" The preservation of the last page of notes for *Some Problems* in the notebook, only because it was on what was then the verso of the last page of "A Suggestion about Mysticism," completed on December 16–17, indicates that these notes, at least, were cut out of the notebook after mid-December. It seems possible to associate the removal of the text of the section, beginning with the Pragmatic Rule, with the removal of pages within the preceding text as part of a general revision made in pencil, although such a hypothesis is not at all certain if, as seems perhaps even more likely, the explanation for the continuation of the Pragmatic Rule section in pencil is that it was written after the general pencil revision of the earlier text. Speculation seems idle whether James had cut out the leaves of the text as a part of this revision, leaving notes that he removed later, or abstracted them after December 17, in which case the diary entry about the loss of the 'chapter' on the Rule is even more inexplicable. The motive for removing the leaves is also speculative. The most natural explanation would be that James wished to preserve in the notebook only text that was in a state suitable for typing after further revision. (The deleting strokes on fols. 1–5, 7–13, 15–19 are not intended to remove the text but to mark the completion of its typing.) On the evidence, he was able to revise the text in the first nineteen folios while typing it himself. That his typing should stop so close to the point where fol. 19 ended may seem to present a more than natural coincidence—such as that he became weary of the labor and Peggy was then available. It may seem probable also that something in the nature of the copy could have dictated the decision, and nothing is more natural than to associate this difference with the loss of the section reported on November 14.

A very speculative working hypothesis can be constructed, therefore, that assumes a change in James's working methods starting with the text of the second line on the typescript p. 13. We have no means of knowing whether the lost leaves were ever found, although one may assume that they were. What is evident, however, is that instead of rewriting them or handing the originals (or an already rewritten version of the originals) to Peggy to type, James worked very closely with Peggy, probably right beside her, dictating at least some of the text and probably having her type other parts from the copy when he did not need to revise. Whatever the copy was like from which they worked, it may seem to have been more malleable to this treatment than the ending of the chapter, which James was forced to write out in longhand on Chinese Linen paper after this method of typing had concluded with typed p. 51. According to this working hypothesis, then, MS pp. 1–50 never existed written out on typewriter paper like the rest of the manuscript. Whatever copy James dictated from, or Peggy copied, was separate and was discarded as typed, perhaps giving rise to Henry James, Jr.'s, report about the destruction of the manuscript before the notebook text of Chapter V. This process relieved James of the labor of typing or of copying out a revision, such as he engaged himself to beginning with MS fol. 51, whether because of a change in the nature of the copy that enforced greater care or because the dictating cum copying process proved to be too inefficient. The hypothesis of dictation, combined with copying, is not strictly necessary but it is very useful in helping to explain the fact that James wrote out the revised copy on Chinese Linen paper only after typing had stopped at p. 51. Moreover, there are a few hints that dictation may have resulted in Peggy's misspelling unfamiliar words. A typist not entirely wedded to the touch system may introduce her own misspellings despite correct copy if her eyes are on the keyboard instead of the manuscript and she is transferring memorized text to the machine. Such a procedure could explain a misspelling like *juxterposed* found at 49.1,3 and 49.15; but the extraordinary *sea-enemiey* (for *sea-anemone*) at 39.12 may seem more likely to have come from spelling by sound, as well as the mishearing of *its roots* for *which brutes* (39.24) on the same typed page, or *some mations* for *summation*[*s*] (48.7), and possibly such corrections as *sole* typed over *soul* (39.39). Memorial error in typing is difficult to distinguish from evidence of dictation; hence *That A and B are equal,* ['*mean*' typed del.] *for example, means either* (38.16–17) could signify only the common sort of anticipation to which Peggy was prone, but other examples may be more suggestive, such as *constructed, new* ['*system*' typed del.] *relations are* (40.33) where, far enough above not to be retained in a typist's memory, the text had read the *concepts in the explanatory system* (40.29–30) or, a few lines later, *In another book I have* ['*shown*' typed del.] *tried to show* (40.35); or *by thinking that know*['*ledge*' typed del.]*ing the latter* (47.22); or *it is impossible to*['*make*' typed del.] *construe by their means* (46.32 further revised by hand later). Typed-out words of this sort are not found elsewhere in Peggy's share of the typescript. One may add that Peggy began the second line on p. 13 with *if* (later corrected by hand to *If*), a natural mistake if she had started from dictation. On the other hand, her typing very likely proceeded from a mixture of dictation and transcription of passages from the lost manuscript draft. As an example, the typing mistake *move and move* corrected by hand to *more and more* (41.18) would seem to suggest misreading of James's handwriting, as would *one path* corrected to *our path* (42.11), or *leave* and *discover* corrected to *learn* and *discourse* (47.21,22).

Further evidence exists that a holograph on the Chinese Linen sheets was never present for pp. 1–50. For instance, James added subheadings in red ink in typed pp. 4–49; and in the subsequent part of MS, after p. 51, similar headings were either added in red ink or (what had not been done before) written-in as integral parts. Yet with the start of typing from MS after p. 51 these subheadings appear in the typed copy, an indication that the earlier pages of TMs[1] and of MS were continuous. Internal references to numbering constitute lesser evidence. For example, in TMs[1a] in the added handwritten p. 9½(52) James writes, *We shall see on a later page (p. 20) that the various conceptual universes referred to on page 6 can be considered in complete abstraction from perceptual reality* (35.15–17), in which the references to pp. 6 and 20 are to the typescript (33.21–34.5; 40.31–41.12). However, revising this sentence, James at some later time altered *on a later page* to *in later places* and added the figure 58 above 'p. 20'. This 58 cannot be referred to the typescript page but instead is concerned with the second corollary found on fol. 58 of the MS (55.32), later to be typed as TMs[1] p. 103. On p. 19(63) of TMs[1] James added a marginal pencil note, later deleted, *Possibly the note on Stallo etc, on p. 51* ['51' alt. fr. '52'] *below ought to come in this place.*, a note keyed to a pencil asterisk footnote indicator added after *perceive* (40.19). This refers to a deleted marginally added footnote on MS fol. 51 mentioning Stallo, with other references, that had originally been attached to *grasp* (53.23), in a sentence typed on TMs[1] p. 51(98). These internal references are not inconsistent with the hypothesis that typed TMs[1] pp. 1–50 and MS fols. 51–69 were chronologically continuous but all that they demonstrate, in fact, is that each was added in TMs[1] by revision while MS fol. 51 was in existence but before it was typed. More to the point is the interesting anomaly that the note about Wallace made on the last leaf of notebook #4519 and now found under the paste-over blank forms part of a footnote added by hand not in the MS (which was not in existence) but in TMs[1] on p. 73(27)'.

We are now in a position to reconstruct conjecturally the history of TMs[1] as a whole and of the MS of Chapter IV, "Percept and Concept." The association of the paper watermarked Gloria Linen in Peggy's typescript of the draft of "The Moral Equivalent of War" with the same paper in pp. 1–13 of TMs[1] Chapter I makes it probable that both were typed at about the same time. The evidence suggests the possibility that the typing of TMs[1] was suspended after p. 13 not to allow Peggy to assist James with Chapter IV (since she seems to have taken over immediately after James had typed one line of Chapter IV's p. 13) but to permit her to work on the typing of "The Moral Equivalent of War." James's use of the paper watermarked Chinese Linen to add handwritten leaves to the draft typescript of "The Moral Equivalent" links this draft also with the Chinese Linen paper with which he started the typing of Chapter IV. He worked on this typing for the first twelve pages and the first line of p. 13, rewriting and copying from the draft of the text in #4519. Peggy then took over the typing with the same paper and seems to have worked from a combination of dictation and selected passages of the lost copy (possibly the abstracted leaves from the notebook, a revision of these, or both) and proceeded as far as TMs^1 p. 50(97). At this point while James continued the reworking of the text in manuscript on p. 51 to prepare for further typing, Peggy returned to the early part of TMs^1, resumed typing from MS with p. 14 on the same Chinese Linen paper, and continued with this paper through preserved p. 40 (and then ribbon p. 41, possibly a retyped revision), and then on to the end of Chapter III on lost original p. 42. By this time James had finished the preparation of the final part of the MS for Chapter IV, which he had begun with fol. 51, following typed p. 50; Peggy then picked up the typing of Chapter IV (probably after an interval) with TMs p. 51(98), copying the first page of the MS fol. 51, but at this point switching to L. L. Brown paper and disposing the ribbon copy (then or later) with the typed sheets of the carbon TMs^{1a}. The numbering of p. 51(98) was centered, but pp. 52(99)–54(101) were numbered in the upper left corner, the position she had adopted for Chapters I–III although she had followed James's centered numbering when she picked up Chapter IV with pp. 13–14 through 51. It seems probable that James was simultaneously revising the typescript of Chapter IV and renumbering it by hand in sequence with Chapters I–III to provide continuous pagination, in the process abstracting the first typed page of Chapter IV and substituting a page and a half (the second numbered 44) of manuscript for a revised beginning. (These two pages Peggy at some later time typed up on the L. L. Brown paper by retyping the end of Chapter III on p. 42 and placing the start of Chapter IV—now numbered for the first time—below it, ending the substitution two-thirds of the way down on newly typed p. 43.) It may well be that Peggy delayed her typing after finishing p. 54(101) of Chapter IV to allow James to complete the revision of the rest of the manuscript. To indicate where she was to start afresh, James cancelled the text on MS fol. 56 with a vertical blue-pencil stroke through the word *experience* (55.13), the original ending of the sentence at the foot of typed p. 54(101), and continued it horizontally to the right margin. At the foot of typed p. 54 (now renumbered 101) he wrote in lead pencil, below this last sentence, 'Continue copying *MS p. 56*', thus insuring that there would be no overlap or skip when Peggy resumed typing. Since at this time he had completed the revision and renumbering of the typescript, Peggy was able to start p. 102 with typed 102 in the final sequence, centered like James's renumbered pagination for the chapter. From this point, without visible signs of delay, she completed the typescript on the L. L. Brown paper up to the last page of the chapter. At various times before he renumbered the pages of typed Chapter IV, James himself, to save time perhaps, added revisions by typing pp. 25½(71), 28(74), and 46(93), the first on L. L. Brown paper (late), the other two earlier on Chinese Linen.

With the beginning of Chapter V, the typescript was copied directly from the blue notebook containing the last part of the text, and no problems of sequence arise.

V. The Editorial Problem

The materials on which the text of *Some Problems of Philosophy* must be based have been described in the preceding sections. It remains to detail the editorial treatment suitable for dealing with the special problems raised by the transmission of the text. As sketched in A Note on the Editorial Method, the classic theory of copy-text calls for a critical text to be based on the *accidentals*— that is, the spelling, punctuation, capitalization, paragraphing, word-division, and methods of emphasis—of the preserved document closest to the author's holograph. Any authorial revisions, whether in these *accidentals* or in the *substantives*—that is, the words themselves—established from these documents, or to be conjectured as occurring in intermediate lost documents, are then inserted in the generally authoritative accidental texture by emendation, or to be more precise, by selection.

This classic rationale of copy-text is completely applicable to the special situation of the *Problems*. Except in the portion that is wanting, James's manuscript is the sole generally authoritative document for accidentals and for substantives and it yields in this authority only to his subsequent revisions of details within the typescripts. Save for the few pages that James himself typed, the typescript and its carbon (TMs[1a] and TMs[1b], each in some part both ribbon and carbon) that his daughter Margaret typed is only a transcript of this manuscript, more or less faulty whenever she misread the handwriting, suffered memorial error, or else to a slight degree imposed her own system of accidentals. The problems she encountered in interpreting the much revised inscription were serious; it is probable that from time to time she required James's advice to straighten out ambiguities of words and their positions in heavily worked-over passages. On the whole, however, the typescript was a naive but relatively acceptable document (save for her neglect of the underlining key) to serve as the basis for James's correction and revision.

Except for the start in which a revised leaf and a half are preserved, any copy that may have existed for Chapter IV, "Percept and Concept" (whatever it was), was discarded as typed up to the fifty-first page (31.9 *and our life . . . wading through* 53.19). In this area the copy-text perforce becomes TMs^1, which is the most authoritative preserved document, especially for pp. 1[43]–12(56), 25½(71), 28(74), and 46(93), containing the text for 31.8–37.22 (*concepts . . . understanding*), 43.32–42 (*Emerson . . . Love*).), 44.14–24 (*|cation . . . insults of*), and 51.23–52.8 (*Bradley . . . compenetra-|*), all of which James typed himself from the draft in #4519. For editorial purposes the basic typescript in this area of missing manuscript, corrected but unrevised, is taken as the copy-text, and not its revised form, for several reasons. First, insofar as it may be a faithful transcript of the copy, it maintains consistency in representing in surrogate form the original holograph which, when present, has been this edition's copy-text. (In James's own typed pages, the extensive reworking of the draft text in #4519 promotes the typescript in that area to prime copy-text authority. From p. 13 to p. 50 [except for his additions] only the pages typed under James's direction are present, and despite his supervision the copy-text authority is less.) The text James himself typed has been identified above and is indicated in the apparatus by notes at the beginning and end.

Whenever the manuscript is present elsewhere and thus is chosen as the copy-text, the mechanical aberrances of the derived typescript have not been recorded when by no meaningful definition of the terms could they come under the heading of either substantive or accidental. Thus no mechanical errors in TMs^1 are noted when MS is copy-text even when they have been corrected in one or both copies. The procedures necessarily change when the MS is wanting and the typescript (whether by James or by Peggy) is the sole authority and copy-text. When the typescript is the copy-text, the recording corresponds in general to that given elsewhere to the details of the manuscript but with due regard for the fact that the significance of some alterations varies from those in manuscript, such as hitting the wrong key or omitting a strike of the space bar between words. Hence, the following special procedures have been adopted for dealing with the typescript in the area of Chapter IV where (in the absence of MS) it becomes the copy-text. First, it was necessary to decide what to record. All final handwritten revisions in either typescript are listed in the Emendations either as accepted or as rejected authorial alterations. Rejected revisions are also noted in the Historical Collation when the acceptance of an alternate variant from one or other typescript has been listed under the *stet* form of entry in the Emendations. Also, all corrections (as opposed to revisions) made in only one typescript have been recorded, with the original TMs reading as represented in the opposite typescript. In a handful of cases, some errors which would normally be construed as mechanical typist errors and which are corrected in both copies are recorded on the chance that they may reflect authorial revision during dictation (see emend 39.11), or may constitute evidence for such dictation as emend 49.1,3,15. Alterations changing one word to another made by typing over the original are listed in the Historical Collation. Finally, errors of any nature, no matter how mechanical, are recorded, with the editorial emendation, when they remain uncorrected in both typescripts.

Second, certain alterations made by hand or by typing are not recorded. Prominent among these are the filling out of the last letters of a word by hand when the right-hand margin prevented the word from being completed on the typewriter. All mechanical corrections made during typing are unlisted with the single exception of false starts on a different word. Similarly, all mechanical errors corrected by hand in both typescripts—including Peggy's misspellings—are not recorded on the principle that the corrected, and not the uncorrected, typescript is most properly the copy-text. Hand underlining present in both typescripts is not recorded as an emendation since the uncertain use of what passed for an underlining key made for very few words underlined in the original. As in the transcript of the MS, the variable position of punctuation in relation to quotation marks has been normalized in the text and not noted in the apparatus, and the ampersand has been silently transcribed as *and*. Within the apparatus, however, both forms of variants are transcribed when they occur.

Neither TMs[1a] nor TMs[1b] has been made the copy-text but instead their corrected composite. The revisions being divided between both typescripts, neither copy is more authoritative than the other except as revised; hence a selection of one, including its revisions, as copy-text would have introduced an unwarranted denigration of the authority of the other. Moreover, if a revised TMs[1] (either as a single copy or as a conflation of the two) had been made the copy-text, the recording of its revisions would have been inconsistent with that of the same kind of revisions when the manuscript is present, for they would need to have been moved to the Historical Collation from their natural place in the list of Emendations. Thus in the absence of the manuscript, the basic and original typescript, as *corrected* in both copies (apart from *revisions*) becomes the copy-text, and the revisions made in TMs[1a] and TMs[1b] are treated consistently whether or not the manuscript is present.

The evidence suggests that from time to time as Peggy completed sections of the typescript she read it over to correct the more obvious errors of omission and commission. In general, this correction seems to have been made without reference to the manuscript except in cases of serious omissions or corruptions that could not be rectified without its assistance. The majority of these corrections are of mechanical matters, however—transposed letters, dittographic mistakes, clearly omitted or impossible punctuation, and the more obvious misspellings. It would seem that this correction was ordinarily made simultaneously in both ribbon and carbon copies. Since they preceded James's reading over the typescript and since they were usually written-in without reference to manuscript, these markings—however necessary in most cases—introduce a non-authoritative element into the handwritten annotation of the typescripts. Indeed, in the nature of the case many of these unauthorial alterations are indistinguishable from James's own corrections and revisions: the inscriber of a comma, for example, cannot usually be identified. Especially in Chapter IV, many of James's own alterations were transferred from one copy to another (particularly in the area of his own typing); thus the simple criterion whether a mechanical correction appears in both copies is not an automatic means of identifying a non-Jamesian marking, although it may be helpful especially when the correction is made in the same medium. (At an early stage James seems to have brought a small part of TMs[1b] into general conformity with TMs[1a] but not simultaneously and hence without a distinguishable ink or pencil.) The record of alterations in the typescript thus may ascribe to James a small number of corrections that originated with another source. It is hoped that little real damage is done to his intentions, however, especially since he always had the option—which he exercised from time to time—of rejecting the changes that Peggy had made by hand.

At the start of his revision James selected the ribbon copy TMs^{1b} for the first three chapters and worked on it exclusively except for the two pencil substantive changes and the few pencil accidental corrections in TMs^{1a} detailed above. (Owing to what may have been a retyping, p. 41 of TMs^{1a} close to the end of Chapter III is a ribbon instead of a carbon copy, and James chose that for more revisions, not transferred to carbon TMs^{1b} of this page. He continued to work over the ribbon copy of revised and retyped TMs^{1a} pp. 42–43 ending the chapter.) Hence it may not be of any crucial import that the first fourteen pages of carbon TMs^{1a} are missing for some uncertain reason or, as is the working hypothesis for this discourse, never existed. The alterations that James made in TMs^{1b} in these first three chapters (up to p. 41) are almost certainly early and written in Cambridge, although the possibility must exist that some could be additions from the period when he carried this copy abroad. With the retyped end of Chapter III in the ribbon pages and then in Chapter IV James's main work in Cambridge shifted to the revision of TMs^{1a}. Since this copy of the typescript never left the United States, its revisions are all to be assigned to this period. The evidence suggests that the revision of TMs^{1a} was not uniform but that James looked it over on various occasions and further revised already annotated pages. The alterations made in pencil appear to be close to the last. In at least one of these stages James made an attempt to transfer his Chapter IV alterations from TMs^{1a} to TMs^{1b} although such joint revisions by no means outweigh the unique alterations that he then continued to make in TMs^{1a} and those that, later, were written into TMs^{1b} abroad.[15]

---

[15] One of the various examples occurs at 40.12 where TMs^1 originally was typed as *logically congruous with*. First this was changed in both copies to *formed to* and then finally, in both, to *agreeable to*. At 41.30 TMs^1 read *is the various* but both copies were revised to *being those*. At 42.19–20 TMs^{1a} first added to the typescript the phrase *into which we translate nature* but then altered *nature* to *our experience*. The phrase in the revised form was added to TMs^{1b}. These go well beyond the possibility of independent revision at different times in Cambridge and abroad. On occasion after having entered a revision in both copies James subsequently revised one without altering the other. An example occurs at 39.5 in which TMs^1 originally read *thus sticks* (an error), corrected in both to *thus sinks* but later altered in TMs^{1a} to *may thus often sink*. Another example occurs at 46.32 where TMs^1 had read *construe by their means*, revised in both copies by hand to *identify them with*. However, at a later time James further revised TMs^{1a} alone to read *substitute them for*.

V. The Editorial Problem

The amount of annotation that James gave independently to these two typescripts varies from part to part and dwindles in TMs[1b] as his health declined abroad. Editorial theory requires that his intentions to revise the readings of his manuscript as evidenced by the typescripts he was using as copy should be respected and that these second, third, and fourth thoughts should form part of the final critical text otherwise based on the manuscript. James himself was conscious of the fact that he had created problems by revising both copies separately, and in his note of July 26, 1910, from Rye, he asked Kallen to compare "the two copies, for different corrections are in each." Kallen attempted to perform this duty but missed various of James's changes in one or the other typescript.

When James made an alteration in TMs[1b] abroad he was not aware whether he had revised TMs[1a] left in Cambridge for safekeeping, and it would seem that the possibility had no effect on the changes that he wrote-in. Ordinarily this independent revision presents no problems since one copy retains the original typescript reading whereas the other alters it. In these cases the present editor, following James's request to Kallen, has attempted to incorporate all such typescript revisions whether appearing in TMs[1a] or TMs[1b], or in both so long as they are the same. However, an exception is made when the revision resulted from the repair of a TMs[1] error for a reading that was correct in the MS. Almost every time that James altered TMs[1] when it was clearly in error, he did not consult the MS. Under these circumstances although his altered reading is chronologically later than the inscription of the MS, the intention to revise the MS is wanting, for no evidence exists that James in these circumstances would have touched the reading if TMs[1] had faithfully transcribed it from the MS. The change, then, is not a revision of the MS reading but the correction of the TMs[1] error; and since it will often vary inadvertently from the MS because James was merely making present sense without knowledge of what he had actually written at first, sound editorial practice suggests that one should ignore the alteration and return to the perfectly correct original.[16]

---

[16] For example, at 12.10–11 in the area where TMs[1a] is missing, TMs[1] omitted the MS phrase *theoretic progress, and shows no* which in TMs[1b] James by hand supplied as *progress & has no*, a reading which there is no need to prefer to that of MS. At 55.8 MS *any essential novelty* was mistyped as *an essential novelty*. But the phrase making imperfect sense, James merely deleted the *an* in TMs[1a] without referring to the original MS reading.

An occasional problem arises when in the transfer to TMs^{1b} of a revision in TMs^{1a} James further revised the reading. When such a situation can be identified as in fact a transfer and not two different revisions arrived at independently, the later or TMs^{1b} reading must be accepted as representing a conscious revisory intention, even though James did not at the same time alter the TMs^{1a} revision to conform to the new version.[17] The only really serious problems occur, however, when both TMs^{1a} and TMs^{1b} are revised in a different manner, each independently of the other, a situation occurring when James had taken the TMs^{1b} copy abroad and found he was dissatisfied with a passage but, of course, had no evidence whether he had revised it already in TMs^{1a} and, if so, in what form. Here the matter of chronology is of no significance and an editor is thrown back on his judgment as to the reading that best fulfills James's stylistic or expository intentions. In different cases the reading in either typescript may be thought superior to the other.

The easiest readings to decide are those in which one copy merely tinkers with the original whereas the other makes a thoroughgoing revision, which obviously must represent a more highly fulfilled intention. For example, at 60.17 MS and TMs^1 read *so far as the*, which in TMs^{1a} is altered to *so far as that* but in TMs^{1b} to the more drastic and preferable *on them for the*. In reverse, at 60.18, just below, MS and TMs^1 read, incorrectly, *endow*, which James in TMs^{1b} corrected to *endows* (probably the intention of the MS) but which in TMs^{1a} he had revised (not corrected) to *has now endowed*. In TMs^1 at 48.7 the text originally read *time and matter*, which in TMs^{1a} James subsumed by revising to *motion*. That abroad he added *space* to make the phrase into *time*[,] *space and matter* makes for a less thoroughgoing revision in TMs^{1b} than

---

[17]It is possible at 40.12 (noted above in footnote 15) when James altered both copies from TMs^1 *logically congruous with* to *formed to* and then finally to *agreeable to* that back alteration of the one typescript from the one revised was present, but evidence is wanting. A small example of TMs^{1b} revision by transfer of a TMs^{1a} revision comes at 42.16. The typescript had read *theses* which James at first altered in TMs^{1a} to *things* but then to *thises* (all in roman). When this reading was transferred to TMs^{1b} it was italicized. A better case comes at 48.23 in which during the process of copying in TMs^{1b} an extended addition in TMs^{1a}, *rationalist* became *rationalistic*, a more characteristic adjective. At 52.26 the typescript read *never attain to a* which in TMs^{1a} was changed to *never show a* but in the process of transfer to TMs^{1b} was further altered to *show no*. At 92.6 where in both copies James made an extensive autograph addition, one sentence in TMs^{1a} read *The books balance to the end* but when he recopied the passage in TMs^{1b} James preferred *The books balance perfectly*, obviously a conscious choice.

that in TMs^{1a}'s condensation, and since it substantially retains the original, it is less preferable than the reading of TMs^{1a}. On the other hand, at 52.21 TMs^{1a} had revised original *the immediate feeling* simply by dropping *the*, but in TMs^{1b} James also dropped *immediate* to produce a more comprehensive final reading. So with 67.12-13. Here MS and TMs^1 had read *together as what an abstract collective noun denotes*, which in TMs^{1a} James slightly amplified as *together, for that is all that an abstract noun denotes*, at the same time deleting *abstract* of *abstract susceptibility* at 67.12. But when in TMs^{1b} he altered to the summary *together and named by a collective noun* and retained *abstract susceptibility* his radical revision produced the superior reading.

The ordinary test of the authority of revision is the editor's estimate of an author's 'final intention,' a phrase that covers more slippery theory than can properly be analyzed here.[18] If it can be demonstrated that James was aware of the TMs^{1a} reading when he came to produce a TMs^{1b} variant, final intention is in no doubt so long as we qualify the phrase by indicating that James's revision of the typescripts was by no means so thorough as it would have been if he had lived to prepare copy for the printer and to make his final revision of the text in galley proof in his customary manner. But given the early stage at which he had to break off his revision, at least one can properly note final intention on a relative basis if the evidence shows that he consciously made a revision in TMs^{1b} when aware of a revision of the same material earlier in TMs^{1a}. However, if evidence is wanting that would point to the conscious improvement of an earlier revision, 'final intention' comes to be too misleading a term to employ. The chronologically later *and named by a collective noun* is stylistically superior and more comprehensive in sense than *for that is all that an abstract noun denotes* as a revision of *as what an abstract noun denotes*. If one could show (what cannot be shown) that James had TMs^{1a} before him when he made this TMs^{1b} revision, it would be proper to think of it as representing his final intention insofar as he was able to revise TMs^1. But since it is as possible that he wrote-in the succinct phrase when he was abroad and without knowledge of his previous tinkering with the passage, one must appeal instead to what may be called the 'principle of superior (or radical) development' as applied to independent revision, a principle illustrated by

---

[18]The most comprehensive survey to date is by G. Thomas Tanselle, "The Editorial Problem of Final Intention," *Studies in Bibliography*, 30 (1976), 167-211.

the various examples above that work in both directions in the two copies of the typescript.

The test of 'superior (radical) development' as a guide to editorial judgment may lead in rare cases to an estimate of authorial intention and in turn to editorial selection that attempts to produce artificially the conditions of conscious or 'final' intention. These are exceptions, of course, and do not bulk so large in practice as to affect the main lines of textual theory. An example occurs at 83.40–41. Here MS followed by TMs[1] read *given, which is finite, and an infinite*. In TMs[1a] James contented himself with restoring *part* which in the revision of MS before typing had been deleted after *given* and after *infinite*. However, in TMs[1b], without knowledge of what he had done in TMs[1a], he revised to *phenomenal given which is finite, and a conditioning infinite*. This is an improvement, but in his preparation of TMs[2], when Kallen came to compare James's revisions in both copies of TMs[1], he seems to have considered that James's intention to restore the two original MS readings *part* should be honored but not to the exclusion of the superior TMs[1b] revision in other respects. The present editor is inclined to agree with him that in a critical text James's fullest (or most developed) intentions are reconstructed under the peculiar circumstances of this text by the conflated eclectic reading *phenomenal given part which is finite, and a conditioning infinite part*.[19]

Various minor matters connected with the imperfect state of the documents create some problems. Although the typewriter used for TMs[1] and TMs[2] had an underlining key, it was used only occasionally and in a handful of examples, these occurring either in the pages that James typed himself or in the area of TMs[1] conjectured to represent Peggy's typing largely from dictation. Almost all underlining for italic, therefore, was introduced by hand. When this underlining was part of a mechanical correction that Peggy gave the typescript, she copied the underlines only partially and erratically. James's own underlinings that can be identified in both TMs[1a] and TMs[1b] are sketchier than in MS since he seems never to have consulted the manuscript in his corrections and revisions; those that he made sometimes reproduce what he had done in MS but sometimes he added underlines not present in that document.

---

[19]'Superior development' is a principle to be treated with some caution, however, if the revision has some relation to a typescript error. For an example, see the Textual Note to *instantaneous act* at 92.30–31.

Of course, when MS is present and words are not underlined in either typescript, the authority of the manuscript is supreme. One may suspect, however, that some of the revisory underlinings found in either typescript but not in MS might not have been introduced if James had been reading a transcript that throughout reproduced the MS underlines. Nevertheless, an editor has no option, it would seem, but to honor whatever additional italics James chose to insert in the typescripts. A conflict sometimes occurs as to whether a word or phrase should be in single quotation marks or in italics for emphasis. Peggy often omitted the single quotation marks of the MS; thus when James came to read the typescripts and to find that he needed some form of emphasis, he was as likely as not to italicize words that in MS, but not in TMs[1], were enclosed in quotation marks, or else he could put quotation marks about roman words in TMs[1] that had been italicized in the MS. Changes of this nature made in ignorance of the forms in the MS can scarcely be considered as revisions to be followed; hence, whenever MS is present its forms rule over those of the altered TMs[1] unless James deleted his (or Peggy's) underlines or quotation marks or otherwise altered forms in which MS and TMs[1] had agreed.

In the MS James was inconsistent in the bibliographical details of his footnote references. He started by double underlining authors' names for setting in small caps but gradually abandoned the form. He might put book titles in roman, in roman with quotation marks, or in italic. He sometimes capitalized references to book, volume, and chapter, but sometimes not, and his abbreviations are often inconsistent. He generally used full roman numerals for volume numbers but sometimes altered them to lower case. Since all these details have nothing to do with the expression of his meaning, they have been normalized—mostly in silence—to what seems to have been his generally observed practice in this manuscript, but all book titles have been italicized. In general, therefore, the footnotes agree with standard methods of reference for the time as in their first-edition form.

In his letter of April 7, 1911, to Henry James, Jr., about correcting the proofs, Horace Kallen took polite issue with Henry's Prefatory Note for having quoted without context William James's own note beginning, "Say it is fragmentary and unrevised":

I cannot agree with you about the condition of the book. The chapter on Percept and Concept certainly would have had much more revision and some complete changes—that I know from conversations your *Father ['F' *ov.* 'f'] and I had just before he left for Europe. And the chapter on Cause, magnificent as it is, would have received considerable elaboration. I cannot think *either [*intrl.*] that "fragmentary and unrevised" apply to the mere incompleteness of the book. If he had meant that, he would have said, incomplete. But I have the feeling that each chapter would have been subjected to considerable revision, in the end. He had a great plan in mind, touching subjects on which he was himself not altogether certain, and he was experimenting—if our conversations are anything to go by—a good deal by the way. However, as your note quotes *his [*alt. fr.* 'him'] memorandum fully, in addition to giving your interpretation of the condition of the Ms., it will do well enough. And then you know *so [*insrtd.*] much better than I what the Master's working methods were, that I *must seem [*ov.* 'will not'] to [*insrtd.*] put *the [*ov.* 'thing'] thing dogmatically.

It is a hard way to steer between over-interpretation and over-literalness, isn't it[.]

That James would have completed the book had he lived goes without saying, for he had advanced it much further than the abortive earlier book on philosophical subjects that is scattered through the different envelopes of former Box F in the James Collection, manuscripts that will be transcribed in a later volume of the WORKS. That the part we have—admittedly not all that had been planned (James wrote to Schiller that it represented about a half)—would have been revised more extensively in typescript before printing is certain: heavily revised as a few parts of TMs^{1a} and TMs^{1b} are, the alterations are far from systematic and they do not equal the revisions which comparison of the common readings of book and *Hibbert Journal* reveals were characteristic of the alterations he added in the typescript of *A Pluralistic Universe*. Again, if we may take *A Pluralistic Universe* as a control, the even more extensive revision which James made in its galley proof (as he had done for parts of *Pragmatism* and *The Meaning of Truth* where comparison with copy is possible) would have vitally altered the style, if not the content, had *Some Problems of Philosophy* been put into type and reworked by him.

What we have preserved in the multiple evidence of the documents, therefore, is a work that is not only incomplete but by James's standards was in only the preliminary stages of revision. By reference to the preserved pages of the manuscript an editor can purify the text of the typescript on which James was working and thereby remove Peggy's departures from copy that were not detected in the revision and were mostly perpetuated in the printed book as a consequence. Moreover, by his conflation of the separate revisions made in the two copies of the typescript he can make certain that James's maximum revisory intentions are preserved. When the joint revisions of both copies differ by reason of James's conscious revision while copying in TMs^{1b} some of the alterations already made in TMs^{1a}, the chronological progression of authority can be observed and the latest form of each revision can be selected. When the same words or passages are revised independently in both copies, an editor can select the more highly developed version as better representing James's presumed wishes than a more elementary change closer to the original text, regardless of the order of their inscription and of the copy in which they appear. False revisions—that is, attempted corrections of typescript errors made without consultation of the manuscript and differing from the manuscript text—can be removed and the purity of the original reading restored.

These systematic editorial procedures have not previously been applied to the text. When Kallen accepted TMs^2 (Peggy's transcript of TMs^{1b} for most of the first three chapters, but thereafter of TMs^{1a} starting with p. 41), he did not consult the manuscript to remove the errors of this second transmissional stage, as well as the overlooked errors of the first typing, as Henry James, Jr., ruefully observed when he made a few such explorations while reading proof. James also found that Kallen had been insufficiently careful in transferring from both typescripts the minor alterations of such matters as quotation marks, underlinings, and the like, which appear to represent William James's own wishes. Collation discloses, also, that Kallen missed some substantive handwritten variants that he should have added to his own basic typescript. Moreover, when TMs^{1a} and TMs^{1b} differed in their revision of the same material, Kallen ordinarily chose the readings of TMs^{1b} on a purely arbitrary basis, perhaps because he believed that it represented James's final intentions—a view only partly justified and then only under strictly controlled conditions that he did not recognize. As a result, the most highly developed revisory alterations were not always selected owing to the lack of a rational principle of choice: even the selection of TMs^{1b} in cases of doubt is not always observed when its readings may be superior. Worst of all, perhaps, was the reliance on the authority of TMs^2 without an investigation of the transmissional history. As a result, the copy sent to the printer contained not only Peggy's departures in TMs^1 from MS that James had overlooked but also the further departures of TMs^2 both in substantives and in accidentals from TMs^1 so that an unwelcome level of real corruption was passed on to the printed text. Most, but not all, of Kallen's own sophistications of the text in an attempt to improve it were noticed and removed in TMs^2 before printing by Henry James, Jr.

Texts of William James in the present series such as *Pragmatism*, *The Meaning of Truth*, and *A Pluralistic Universe* have been based on James's carefully worked-over book versions as copy-texts and so have not differed very strikingly in substance from the first editions although there has been some useful refinement of the texture of presentation by reference to James's manuscripts, as the lists of Emendations reveal. The case is altered for *Some Problems of Philosophy* where the manuscript being the copy-text—or the first typescript when the manuscript is wanting—the texture of the so-called 'accidentals' differs considerably and there is an unusually high ratio of substantive differences from the book-text that Kallen edited. Many of the differences are exposed in the Historical Collation but others are contained in the list of Emendations since in this volume for special reasons the two lists are not mutually dependent as in the earlier volumes of this series.

In previous volumes the choice of the book-text as copy-text on the grounds that it represented James's own controlled final form both for substantives and for accidentals made the list of Emendations chiefly a record of *corrections*, whereas the Historical Collation by its record of transmission from the earliest preserved documents up to the final highly worked-over book-text enabled a scholar to reconstruct the stages by which the text developed through every authoritative document. On the contrary, the line of authority is radically different for *Some Problems of Philosophy*, since only the manuscript (and in its absence the typescript[20]) has authority save for the autograph revisions that James irregularly entered in TMs[1a] and TMs[1b]. The further textual documents represented by TMs[2] and the book (I) contribute nothing to the establishment of the text. Since the earliest and only fully authoritative document, the manuscript, becomes the copy-text, the list of Emendations is considerably expanded by the record of each alteration that James made in the typescript, not to be understood without the notation of the original MS reading; the TMs[1] reading inherited from it, which usually but not invariably is the reading of the unrevised copy of TMs[1]; and the rejected alternative re-

---

[20] As remarked, when MS is not present after the start of Chapter IV, the first twelve pages of typescript (including the sentence finished on the first line of the thirteenth [. . . *importance.* 37.23], but excluding the beginning of the chapter [31.1–31.9] which has MS authority) were typed by James and thus have substantially the same authority as his manuscript would have possessed, and greater authority except in a detail or two than the draft in #4519. The remaining part of the typescript, continued by Peggy up to p. 51 (53.19) where MS begins, is the sole authority but is less pure because of its transmitted nature.

vision when both copies of TMs[1] were revised. At this point in normal procedure duplication would enter the Historical Collation. However, in the present volume, owing to the lack of authority of the later documents—TMs[2], the book-proof, and the first edition—it has seemed wasteful to duplicate in the Historical Collation each record of textual emendation fully provided in the Emendations. Thus the nature of the apparatus has been modified. The Historical Collation entries are confined exclusively to those variants in TMs[1], TMs[2], (I[p]) and (I), including the second and third printings, that have been rejected in the critical text and are not otherwise noted in the Emendations section. On the other hand, the readings of all documents are provided for each entry in the Emendations list whenever it results (as usually) from James's revision in TMs[1] or from editorial necessity, so long as the MS copy-text has been altered for the purposes of the present new critical text. This procedure concentrates in the list of Emendations the full record of the transmissional history of revisory or corrective alterations to the generally authoritative manuscript. Readers interested in observing the differences between the present and the previously received text will find this information in the Historical Collation.

The complexity of the transmissional history of revision poses various problems for the reader who needs to identify the different forms of the documents according to the particular circumstances in which they contribute to the overall textual transmission. Hence some new and special conventions have been invented for the apparatus. The building blocks are, of course, the sigla for the manuscript (MS), the first typescript (TMs[1])—identified by copies as TMs[1a] retained in Cambridge and TMs[1b] taken abroad—the second typescript (TMs[2]), which was the printer's copy, the proof-sheets (I[p]), and the first edition (I) with its three printings to which plate-changes apply, identified as (I[1]), (I[2]), and (I[3]). James's handwritten alterations are noted as WJ/ and appear as WJ/TMs[1a] and WJ/TMs[1b]. Similarly, Kallen's alterations in the TMs[2] type-script are noted as K/TMs[2]; when identifiable, Henry James, Jr.'s, changes are HJ/TMs[2]. If the agent making the alterations is unknown, the sigil would be (?)/TMs[1a] or (?)/TMs[1b] (or in both as [?]/TMs[1a-b]), although ordinarily these should be taken to represent Peggy's changes, identified as PJ/TMs[1]. Whenever TMs[1] or TMs[2] is cited without further identification, it is to be taken that the reference is to material in them that has not been altered in any copy. A typical entry would be

65.2   philosophers] TMs[1]+; filosofers MS

In this case the present editor has rejected the MS spelling-reform *filosofers* since on the evidence of James's other articles and book publications he would not have altered the normal spelling that had been set in proof. In this case Peggy had normalized the spelling on her own responsibility in typing her first transcript TMs^1, which is thus assigned as the historical source for the emendation of the copy-text *filosofers*. Since in this entry TMs^1 is not distinguished as ^{a} or ^{b}, it represents the original and unaltered typescript reading. The plus sign, as always, indicates the concurrence of all subsequent collated documents with the TMs^1 reading. The original of TMs^1 becomes identified as $TMs^1(u)$—i.e., unrevised—in all cases when alteration occurs both in TMs^{1a} and in TMs^{1b}, but never in this generic form if only one of the two has been revised.

30.4   Fact] WJ/$TMs^{1a-b}+$; the fact $TMs^1(u)$; fact MS

In this entry James corrected the typescript error *the fact* to the MS reading *fact* in both copies of TMs^1 but in the process capitalized it. Thus capitalized *Fact* is repeated in TMs^2 and (I). Similarly, if Kallen made a change in TMs^2, the original unrevised reading becomes $TMs^2(u)$.

On the other hand, when only one of the two copies of TMs^1 has been annotated, the generic $TMs^1(u)$ is insufficiently precise or informative, and the fact that the opposite copy agrees with the original TMs^1 reading (whenever it does) must be noted in another manner.

18.22   telephones] WJ/$TMs^{1b}+$; and telefones MS;
and telephones $TMs^1(u)^a$

This entry describes how James deleted *and* in TMs^{1b} but left untouched in TMs^{1a} the original typescript reading *and telephones*, Peggy's normalization of MS *and telefones*. Since in this area TMs^2 was copied from TMs^{1b}, its original typing repeats the TMs^{1b} revised reading which is thereupon passed on to the book. The special form $TMs^1(u)^a$ is adopted since it adds to the basic sigil for the uncorrected first typescript the information that TMs^{1a} has not been altered and thus reads with the original typing. The form $TMs^1(u)$ would be anomalous here, for it would imply that TMs^{1a} had also been revised to another reading (see below). In reverse, for a TMs^{1a} unique revision, one may read:

87.23   here] WJ/$TMs^{1a}+$; *om.* MS,$TMs^1(u)^b$

James had added in TMs^{1a} the word *here*, wanting in MS and in TMs^1, and this omission was also found in TMs^{1b}.

Further refinement may be needed to meet more complex situations, as when the opposite typescript is also revised but in a different manner.

> 90.12   decreed] WJ/TMs^{1b},K/TMs^2,I; conceived
> WJ/TMs^{1a},TMs^2(u); *om.* MS,TMs^1(u)

From other evidence in nearby revisions it seems evident that in adding a word at this point not present in the MS or in TMs^1, James was entering in TMs^{1b} some revisions he had made earlier in TMs^{1a}; hence in TMs^{1b} when he added *decreed*, one may take it that he intended to revise further the original addition in WJ/TMs^{1a} of *conceived*. Since TMs^2 was copying TMs^{1a} here, it too read *conceived*, but Kallen changed this to *decreed* by hand, and the reading was passed on to (I). In the next example below, James altered the roman word *What* to make it italic in TMs^{1a}; but here he was not aware of what he had done in TMs^{1a} when he revised roman *What* in TMs^{1b} to roman *Which*. When Kallen changed TMs^2 italic *What* by interlining *ich* above deleted *at*, he did not under-line the substituted letters, but neither did he cross out the underlined part *Wh* and it is probable that he intended the revised *Which* to be italic. Since James was not aware in revising TMs^{1b} that he had italicized the original word in WJ/TMs^{1a}, the present editor takes it that a conflated emendation best serves James's intentions at this point, and the critical text accepts the emendation to italic *Which*, attributing the reading to Kallen:

> § 74.30   *Which*] K/TMs^2,I; *rom.* WJ/TMs^{1b}; *What* WJ/TMs^{1a},
> TMs^2(u); What ['W' *ov.* 'w'] MS;TMs^1(u)

Further refinements may prove necessary to deal with more complex situations:

> 90.24–25   useful conceptual bridge] WJ/TMs$^{1a(r2)}$+;
> conceptual bridge WJ/TMs$^{1a(r1)}$; bridge useful
> MS,TMs^1(u)^b

This entry records the initial revision in TMs^{1a} of *bridge useful* to *conceptual bridge* and then, as a further revision, the restoration of *useful*. (The superior $^{(r)}$ indicates *revised*.)

> 90.37–38   any ... one] WJ/TMs^{1b}; any one and every
> K/TMs^2,I; any one MS,WJ/TMs$^{1a(r2)}$,TMs^1(u),
> TMs^2(u); *any one* WJ/TMs$^{1a(r1)}$

This difficult but logical entry records the fact that MS read *any one* (in roman) and that this is also the reading that Peggy typed. But James at first revised the roman by underlining it (WJ/

$TMs^{1a[r1]}$) and then changed his mind and deleted the underline to restore the $TMs^1(u)$ reading ($WJ/TMs^{1a[r2]}$). In this form it was transcribed into TMs^2. However, in revising TMs^{1b} James altered the $TMs^1(u)$ roman *any one* to read *any and every one* in roman. When Kallen compared the typescripts he saw that the TMs^{1b} revision should be added to TMs^2; but in entering it by hand he placed *and every* differently from James's and this faulty reading was thereupon transmitted to the book. The present text prints James's original revision as found in TMs^{1b}, of course. In this entry since the revision of TMs^{1a} affected the TMs^1 reading itself, the necessary distinction is made between $WJ/TMs^{1a(r2)}$, finally revised, and $WJ/TMs^{1a(r1)}$, initially revised, and the information must be given as to what the $TMs^1(u)$ reading was before James made his first, or $TMs^{1a(r1)}$ alteration. The principles of notation apply identically to TMs^2. Since TMs^2 had copied TMs^{1a} starting with Chapter IV, Kallen attempted to follow James's wishes by entering in $TMs^2(u)$ the authorial revision in TMs^{1b}, even though he got it wrong.

Condensed entries may sometimes be possible for these stages of revision. For example, $WJ/TMs^{1a(r1)-b}$ would mean that whereas a revision in TMs^{1a} had itself been revised subsequently, James had entered the initial stage of his revision in TMs^{1b} but had not further altered it so that WJ/TMs^{1b} agrees with $WJ/TMs^{1a(r1)}$, not with $WJ/TMs^{1a(r2)}$. In reverse, $WJ/TMs^{1a-b(r1)}$ would signify that James's revision of TMs^{1a} had been entered by hand in TMs^{1b} but at some later stage had been independently revised to a different reading, which would be listed as $WJ/TMs^{1b(r2)}$. If in both copies a revised reading had been further revised, the identical first stage of the joint revision would be expressed as $WJ/TMs^{1a(r1)-b(r1)}$; the no doubt variant final readings would be recorded respectively as $WJ/TMs^{1a(r2)}$ and $WJ/TMs^{1b(r2)}$, but if identical, then as $WJ/TMs^{1a(r2)-b(r2)}$.

Revisions within a revision in one or other copy of TMs^1 may be handled as above, or in a formulaic manner when the alterations were made during the course of writing-in the revision and not in stages that can be distinguished as (r1) and (r2):

> 45.25 the . . . terms;] WJ/TMs^{1b}; the [*ab. del.* 'its'] discreteness
> *of ['what' *del.*] its **elements [*ov.* 'separ'] ; [*intrl.*]
> $WJ/TMs^{1a}+$; its discreteness; $TMs^1(u)$

The details of such formulaic transcription will be found in the headnote to the list of Alterations in the Manuscript. What happened here was that in this area where MS is missing and TMs^1 is the copy-text, the typescript read *its discreteness;*. James deleted *its* and interlined *the*. With a guideline pointing to follow *discreteness* he then interlined *of what* but crossed out *what* and added *its*; he then started to write *separate* or *separateness* but got as far as *separ* before he stopped and altered the reading by inscribing *elements;* over the incompleted false start. When he came to add this change to TMs^{1b} he found that he preferred *terms* to *elements* and so wrote-in the phrase as *of its terms;*. Unfortunately, Kallen did not see the significance of the fact that TMs^{1b} derives immediately from TMs^{1a} in this revision and hence that its variant is a conscious alteration that reflects James's later intention. Thus he did not alter TMs^2 (which had copied WJ/TMs^{1a}), and the intermediate stage of the revision got into the text as a consequence.

Minor variations in the form of entries may take account of special circumstances. For instance, the first fourteen pages of TMs^{1a} are not known and hence the readings of the revised typescript are preserved only through the handwritten annotations in TMs^{1b}. Since in these pages TMs^{1a} would have agreed with TMs^{1b} in the readings of the typescript itself, there is no problem in identifying these. Yet possible revisions in the missing pages of TMs^{1a} cannot be ignored in the notation, and an entry like 9.21 be] $WJ/TMs^{1b}+$; are $MS,TMs^1(u)^a$ would be improper, for no one can guarantee that at this point TMs^{1a} (if it existed) was itself unrevised as this entry would indicate. Thus in this area the rejected readings to the right of the bracket must be $MS,TMs^1(u)^b$.

In a few places in either TMs^{1a} or TMs^{1b} or in both, James added handwritten passages that expanded the text with new material. Ordinarily revisions within a handwritten annotation to the typescript are handled by the conventions of $WJ/TMs^{1(r1)}$ and $WJ/TMs^{1(r2)}$ as described above; but this notation, and also the formulaic transcription as in the illustration for 45.25 above, are possible only with original typescript readings and their revisions. In the case of these handwritten additions, changes made during the course of composition are not always identifiable as against those made later on review; hence the two classes must be treated as one and the same and on a different basis from revisions made in an established typescript text. The presence of these added passages is always noted in the Emendations list as text that is not present in the MS copy-text or in TMs^1, as in

58.33–59.9 The . . . elements.] $WJ/TMs^{1b},K/TMs^2,I$;
om. $MS,TMs^1(u)^a,TMs^2(u)$

which tells the reader that the passage was added by hand in the

TMs^{1b} copy and was transcribed by Kallen as an addition to the TMs^2 typescript which had followed its copy TMs^{1a} in omitting the passage. After this main entry for the entire passage, James's alterations, additions, and deletions are described as if they were the apparatus to a clear-text manuscript:

> 58.33 practically] *ab. del.* 'concretely'
> 59.5   associating] *aft. del.* 'while [*ab. del.* 'and'] They connect
> *as they associate [*intrl.*] it with *the [*intrl.*] remoter
> percepts, so also with which'

In such a case when the passage is added in only one document, no sigil is necessary, for the entries can apply only to the single copy. If a passage is copied out in both typescripts, then the differences in the variants between the two copies are identified.

As in other volumes in which a manuscript has been present, when an entry in the apparatus covers a reading in MS that has been altered in its inscription, the information of its different readings in MS is provided in connection with the entry and is thereupon omitted from the separate list of Alterations in the Manuscript. Such entries are flagged by the arbitrary sign § which warns that information about the alteration of MS readings is present. In previous volumes, when the manuscript was not the copy-text, the MS readings of this sort were noted in the Historical Collation, signaled by §; but since the MS is the copy-text in the present volume, the information is necessarily moved to the Emendations list, where it would appear as:

> §59.11 awakens] WJ/TMs^{1b}; prompts [*ab. del.* 'evokes']
> our [*intrl.*] MS,TMs^1(u)$^{a+}$

This entry records the fact that the present critical text contains James's revision *awakens* which he substituted in TMs^{1b} for the TMs^1 (and MS) reading *prompts our*, that in MS this phrase was revised from *evokes*, that Kallen failed to transfer the TMs^{1b} revision to TMs^2 and as a consequence it and (I) read *prompts our* like the copy TMs^{1a}.

It should also be noted that a rejected manuscript reading which is part of an alteration in the list of Alterations in the Manuscript is signaled by a prefixed ‡ to the page-line reference. These occur when it is impossible to transfer the entire alteration to the Emendations.

The dedication that James wrote as part of his text in the present Chapter VII (printed in the first edition as part of a footnote) Henry James, Jr., prefixed to the book, as in the present volume. Henry James, Jr.'s, Prefatory Note, which he substituted for one by Kallen, is preserved as part of TMs^2, revised by hand. Its emendations, including those made in the proof, are recorded heading the list of Emendations. The Contents list that Kallen made up for Henry's revision which was printed in the book is not suited for the present volume since it reflects the rearrangement into chapters made by Kallen that does some violence to William James's plan as reconstructed in the present volume. However, its list of the subjects in the chapters is valuable as a conspectus, and these have been retained although arranged under the chapter headings in the contents list chosen for this edition. The relation of the new chapters in the present edition to the ones in the 1911 edition has been worked out above under the changes made by Kallen and Henry James, Jr., in TMs^2; for convenience a parallel listing is offered in the Foreword.

FREDSON BOWERS

Emendations

Every editorial change from the copy-text is recorded for the substantives, and every change in the accidentals as well save for such silent typographical adjustments as are remarked in A Note on the Editorial Method. The reading to the left of the bracket, the lemma, represents the form chosen in the present edition, usually as an emendation of the copy-text. (A prefixed superior 1 or 2 indicates which of any two identical words in the same line is intended.) The sigil immediately following the bracket is the identifying symbol for the earliest source of the emendation, followed by the sigla of any later agreeing documents or by a plus sign should all succeeding documents agree with the earliest source. Readings in parentheses after sigla indicate a difference in the accidental form of the source from that of the emended reading to the left of the bracket. A semicolon follows the last of the sigla for emending sources. To the right of this semicolon appear the rejected readings of the copy-text and of any other recorded documents, followed by their sigla. The rejected readings are not necessarily listed chronologically but are usually presented in an order which most clearly relates revisions to the edition reading adopted as an emendation. The copy-text is MS, the holograph manuscript found at Harvard, from which TMs[1], the typescript drawn up by Margaret James (Peggy) under her father's supervision, was copied. This typescript exists in two copies, each serving as ribbon or carbon at various points. TMs[1a], which was retained in Cambridge, and TMs[1b], which was taken abroad, not only shared authorial revisions but underwent independent revision as well. TMs[1] in turn served as copy for TMs[2], also typed by Peggy and edited after James's death by Horace Kallen and Henry James, Jr. TMs[2] became printer's copy for the book (I), the proof-sheets of which are designated as I(p). Unless otherwise noted, I(p) is assumed to agree with (I). If no indication of printing is given, the assumption is that the reading in (I) is invariant in all impressions from the original plates. A superior number identifies the exact printing in case of need, as I[1] for the May 1911 first printing and I[3] for August 1916. Emendations marked as H (Harvard) are editorial and are not drawn from any authoritative document. The word *stet* after the bracket calls special attention to the retention of a copy-text reading. It may be employed to key a Textual Note, as marked by an asterisk before the page-line number. In a quotation it may indicate that James's version (differing from the source in some respect) has been retained in the edited text. It may also be used in rare instances to indicate that a possibly questionable or unusual reading has been retained in the text.

For convenience, certain shorthand symbols familiar in textual notation are employed. A wavy dash ($\sim$) represents the same word that appears before the bracket and is used exclusively in recording punctuation or other accidental variants. An inferior caret ($_\wedge$) indicates the absence of a punctuation mark (or of a footnote superscript) when a difference in the punctuation constitutes the variant being recorded, or is a part of the variant. A vertical stroke (|) represents a line ending, sometimes recorded as bearing on the cause of an error or fault. The page of preliminary typescript found at the beginning of Chapter IV is designated as $^{\pi}$TMs^1. The abbreviation *s.n.* for *sidenote* is found in both the Emendations and Historical Collation.

For a full discussion of the special conventions adopted in the apparatus to identify the different forms of textual transmission in the various documents and their uses, see The Text of *Some Problems of Philosophy*, pp. 271-277. The sigil WJ/TMs^{1a} or WJ/TMs^{1b} identifies James's handwritten revisions in TMs^{1a} and TMs^{1b}, respectively. The sigil PJ/ similarly represents Peggy James's handwritten corrections or revisions of her own typing when recorded. Likewise, K/TMs^2 or HJ/TMs^2 signifies Kallen's or Henry James, Jr.'s, changes in TMs^2. When a revision has been made in one typescript as WJ/TMs^{1a}, the original typescript reading is given as TMs^1(u)^b. If revisions occur in both typescripts, as WJ/TMs^{1a-b}, the unrevised typescript reading appears simply as TMs^1(u). On the same principle, when a K/TMs^2 reading appears, there must always be a corresponding TMs^2(u) reading. If two or more layers of revision appear in any reading, they are set out as, for example, TMs^1(u)^b (original typescript reading), WJ/TMs$^{1a(r1)}$ (first revision), WJ/TMs$^{1a(r2)}$ (second revision), etc., as the circumstances dictate. When James adds handwritten passages to one or both of the typescripts that are not easily described by the conventions outlined above, it is easier to describe their revisions by formulaic transcription or by a list of alterations immediately following the emendation entry for the whole handwritten passage (see, for example, Emendations entry 58.33-59.9 and the alterations entries following it).

Other arbitrary symbols employed in the Emendations include § and ‡. The mark § indicates that the variant is included wholly or in part in an alteration in the MS, the description of which has been removed to the Emendations list from the list of Alterations in the Manuscript. The double dagger (‡) indicates that the variant in the MS is part of a larger alteration not easily transferable to the Emendations list, the details of which can be found in the Alterations in the Manuscript.

For conventions of the description of alterations see the headnote to the list of Alterations in the Manuscript.

[TMs^{1a} *missing*]

9.0 Its] H; its MS,TMs^2(u); ITS TMs^{1b}, K/TMs^2,I

§9.6 variations] WJ/TMs^{1b}+; odd [*intrl.*] variations MS;TMs^1(u)^b

9.11 meaning] WJ/TMs^{1b}+; *om.* MS, TMs^1(u)^b

‡9.13 relish, . . . admiration,] WJ/TMs^{1b}+; ~$_\wedge$ . . . ~$_\wedge$ MS,TMs^1(u)^b

9.14 the . . . proclaim] WJ/TMs^{1b}+; their wisdom MS,TMs^1(u)^b

9.15 forms . . . totality] WJ/TMs^{1b}, K/TMs^2,I; forms MS,TMs^1(u)^b, TMs^2(u)

9.16 learning.] WJ/TMs^{1b},K/TMs^2,I; learning, if taken in its totality. MS, TMs^1(u)^b; learning in its totality. TMs^2(u)

*§9.18-19 and . . . excluded,] and [*insrtd.*] . . . explained [*caret deletes comma in error*] *special . . . excluded, [*by guideline fr. aft.* 'however,'] *stet* MS; special sciences are today *excluded, [*poss.* 'excluded;'] and for reasons presently to be explained TMs^1(u)^b; special . . . excluded, ['and,' *del.*] for . . . explained; WJ/TMs^{1b}+

9.19 explained,] TMs^1(u)^b; ~$_\wedge$ MS (*error*); ~; WJ/TMs^{1b}+

9.19 to-day] I; ~ ̬ ~MS; today
 TMs^{1b-2}

9.21 man ̬] WJ/TMs^{1b}+; ~, MS,
 TMs¹(u)^b

9.21 be] WJ/TMs^{1b}+; are MS,TMs¹(u)^b

9.22 text-book] H; textbook MS+

10.1 and] WJ/TMs^{1b}+; *om.* MS,TMs¹(u)^b

§10.3 after] TMs^{1b}+; after *wards [*intrl.*]
 MS (*error not del.*)

‡10.7 sciences,] WJ/TMs^{1b}+; ~ ̬ MS,
 TMs¹(u)^b

10.10 gods] WJ/TMs^{1b}+; Gods MS
 (*cap. doubtful*); TMs¹(u)^b

10.11-12 cosmic] WJ/TMs^{1b}; whole
 cosmic MS,TMs¹(u)^b,TMs²,I

‡10.13 action–] WJ/TMs^{1b}+; ~, MS;
 ~ ̬ TMs¹(u)^b

*10.13 generally] *stet* MS,TMs^{1b},
 TMs²(u); commonly K/TMs²

10.14 *excellence;*] WJ/TMs^{1b}+; ~,
 MS,TMs¹(u)^b

10.16-18 'the . . . knowledge.']
 WJ/TMs^{1b}+; ̬~. . . ~. ̬ MS,
 TMs¹(u)^b

‡10.19 large,] WJ/TMs^{1b}+; ~ ̬ MS
 (*error*),TMs¹(u)^b

‡10.20 at;] WJ/TMs^{1b}+; ~, MS,TMs¹(u)^b

§10.20 so] WJ/TMs^{1b}+; thus [*alt. fr.*
 'this'] MS; TMs¹(u)^b

‡10.23 -embracing, . . . itself.]
 WJ/TMs^{1b}+; -embracing. MS,TMs¹(u)^b

10.24 tho] H; though MS+

‡10.25 *weltanschauung*] H; *rom.* MS;
 weltanschaung TMs¹(u)^b(*rom.*),
 WJ/TMs^{1b},TMs²(u); *Weltanschauung*
 K/TMs²; *Weltanschauung* I

10.26 life.] K/TMs^{2(r2)},I; ~, MS (*error*),
 TMs^{1b}; ~ ̬ TMs²(u); ~; K/TMs^{2(r1)}

10.26 Professor] K/TMs²,I; Prof. MS,
 TMs²(u); Prof, TMs^{1b}

10.27 ²that] WJ/TMs^{1b}+; *om.* MS,
 TMs¹(u)^b

10.28 purpose,] Bradley; ~ ̬ MS+

10.29 will ̬] *stet* Bradley, MS,TMs¹(u)^b;
 ~, WJ/TMs^{1b}+

10.29 boundaries] *stet* MS+; exact
 boundaries and contents Bradley

10.33 themselves,] WJ/TMs^{1b}+; ~ ̬
 MS,TMs¹(u)^b

10.34 indeed,] WJ/TMs^{1b(r2)}+; in
 fact, is WJ/TMs^{1b(r1)}; in fact ̬ is
 MS,TMs¹(u)^b

10.35 is] WJ/TMs^{1b}+; *om.* MS,TMs¹(u)^b

10.39 Compare the] WJ/TMs^{1b}+; *om.*
 MS,TMs¹(u)^b

10.39 article] TMs^{1b}+; Article MS

10.39 'Philosophy'] I; 'philosophy' MS;
 ̬ philosophy ̬ TMs^{1b},TMs²(u);
 "~" K/TMs²,I(p)

10.39-40 *Dictionary . . . Psychology*]
 K/TMs²,I; *l.c. rom.* MS,TMs^{1b},
 TMs²(u)

11.4-5 anything . . . seen,]
 WJ/TMs^{1b(r2)}+; things, any
 different . . . seen, WJ/TMs^{1b(r1)};
 things, MS,TMs¹(u)^b

§11.7 sees] WJ/TMs^{1b}+; *can [*ov.* 'is']
 ['able to' *del.*] [*ab. del.* 'sees'] see
 [*insrtd.*] MS;TMs¹(u)^b

11.13 science] TMs^{1b}+; Science MS
 (*cap. doubtful*)

‡11.15 some] WJ/TMs^{1b}+; enough
 MS,TMs¹(u)^b

‡11.15 influence,] WJ/TMs^{1b}+; ~ ̬
 MS,TMs¹(u)^b

‡11.17 minds;] WJ/TMs^{1b}+; ~,
 MS,TMs¹(u)^b

11.18 scientific;] WJ/TMs^{1b}+; ~,
 MS,TMs¹(u)^b

§11.20 from philosophy] WJ/TMs^{1b}+;
 *['from' *del.*] philosophy's ['s'
 added] [*intrl.*] MS;TMs¹(u)^b

*§11.20 a liberal] a liberal['izing' *del.*]
 stet MS; livlier TMs¹(u)^b; a livlier
 TMs²(u); a livelier WJ/TMs^{1b},
 K/TMs²,I

11.21 mental] WJ/TMs^{1b}+; *om.* MS,
 TMs¹(u)^b

11.22 thee,] K/TMs²,I; ~ ̬ MS,TMs^{1b},
 TMs²(u)

*§11.23 A] K/TMs²,I; *Socially con-
 sidered, a [*ab. del.* 'A'] MS;WJ/TMs^{1b},
 TMs²(u); ~~ ̬ ~ TMs¹(u)^b

11.28 concepts ̬] WJ/TMs^{1b}+; ~,
 MS,TMs¹(u)^b

11.29+ *no space*] I; *space* MS,TMs^{1b},
 TMs²

11.36 dialectics,'] WJ/TMs^{1b}+; ~ ̬'
 MS,TMs¹(u)^b

‡§11.37 With] WJ/TMs^{1b}+; The [*aft.
 del.* 'Philosophic'] philosopher with
 MS;TMs¹(u)^b

11.38 the philosopher] WJ/TMs^{1b}(The)+;
 om. MS,TMs¹(u)^b

§ 12.2-3 "systematische . . . Terminolo-
gie."] WJ/TMs¹ᵇ; ˏ~. . .~. ˏ
TMs¹(u)ᵇ; *'~. . .~.' [*moved fr. aft.*
'described ['as the 'der' *del.*]' [11.40]]
MS;K/TMs²,I(p),I (*ital.*);' ~. . .~.ˏ
TMs²(u)

12.2 Missbrauch] I²; misbrauch
MS,TMs¹ᵇ,TMs²(u); Missbrauch
K/TMs²,I(p),I¹ (*ital.*)

12.4 to] WJ/TMs¹ᵇ+; in MS,TMs¹(u)ᵇ

12.7+;18.27+;19.12+;19.30+ *space*] H;
no space MS+

12.8-9 *Objection 1.* | ¶Whereas] H (*as
subh.*); ¶*Objection I.* Whereas MS+
(*I*ˏ TMs¹ᵇ)

*12.11 shows] *stet* MS; has WJ/TMs¹ᵇ+

12.14 answered,] WJ/TMs¹ᵇ+; ~ˏ
MS,TMs¹(u)ᵇ

12.18 more] WJ/TMs¹ᵇ+; *om.* MS,
TMs¹(u)ᵇ

*12.22 encyclopaedic] I (encyclopædic);
encyclopedic MS-I(p)

*12.25 need] *stet* MS; needs TMs¹ᵇ+

12.28 sages] WJ/TMs¹ᵇ+; ones MS,
TMs¹(u)ᵇ

12.31 B.] TMs¹ᵇ+; ~ˏ MS

12.34 time,] TMs¹ᵇ+; ~ˏ MS

§ 12.37 *Summa,*] H; 'Summa,'
WJ/TMs¹ᵇ+; ˏSummaeˏˏ TMs¹(u)ᵇ;
'Summaeˏ' [*alt. fr.* ' 'Summa' ']
['Theologiae,' *del.*] MS

12.38 century] TMs¹ᵇ+; *cap.* MS
(*doubtful*)

13.13 reason,] WJ/TMs¹ᵇ+; ~ˏ MS,
TMs¹(u)ᵇ

‡13.16 , determinable,] WJ/TMs¹ᵇ+;
ˏ~, TMs¹(u)ᵇ; ˏ~ˏˏ MS (*error*)

‡13.16 element;] TMs¹ᵇ+; ~, MS

13.17 determiningˏ] WJ/TMs¹ᵇ; ~,
MS,TMs¹(u)ᵇ,TMs²,I

‡13.22 *a priori*] I; *rom.* MS-TMs²

13.22 scholasticism] TMs¹ᵇ+; *cap.* MS
(*doubtful*)

13.22 Suárez's] H; Suarez's MS+

§ 13.24 Descartes,] WJ/TMs¹ᵇ+; ~ˏ
[*comma del.*] MS; TMs¹(u)ᵇ

‡13.31 'the] WJ/TMs¹ᵇ+; "~ MS,
TMs¹(u)ᵇ

13.31 redistribution] *stet* MS+;
continuous redistribution Spencer

‡13.35-36 *Essay . . . Understanding,*]
H; ˏ~. . .~,ˏ (*rom.*) MS,TMs¹ᵇ,

TMs²(u); '~. . .~,' (*rom.*)
K/TMs²,I

13.35 *Concerning*] TMs¹ᵇ+; *l.c.* MS

13.36 1690,] TMs¹ᵇ,I²; 1690ˏ MS;
1609, TMs²,I¹

13.38 Thomas] TMs¹ᵇ+; Thos. MS

§ 13.38 M.] H; *illeg. ov. illeg. letter*
MS; J. TMs¹+

§ 14.2 developed;] WJ/TMs¹ᵇ+; ~,
[*comma insrtd.*] MS;TMs¹(u)ᵇ

14.6 'from . . . slumber,'] WJ/TMs¹ᵇ+;
'~. . .~,ˏ MS; ˏ~. . . ~,ˏ
TMs¹(u)ᵇ

14.7 'philosophy'] WJ/TMs¹ᵇ+; ˏ~ˏ
MS,TMs¹(u)ᵇ

14.9 time,] WJ/TMs¹ᵇ,K/TMs²,I; ~ ˏ
MS,TMs¹(u)ᵇ,TMs²(u) (~ˏ |)

§ 14.9 our] WJ/TMs¹ᵇ+; ['American'
del.] MS;TMs¹(u)ᵇ

14.11-12 exclusively, . . . philosophy.']
WJ/TMs¹ᵇ+ (Philosophy TMs²);
exclusively. MS,TMs¹(u)ᵇ

§ 14.18 philosophical.] TMs¹ᵇ+;
~ [*alt. fr.* 'philosophy']ˏ MS (*error*)

14.19 momentous] *stet* MS; monotonous TMs¹(u)ᵇ; meritorious WJ/TMs¹ᵇ+

‡14.19 kantian] H; Kantian MS+

14.20 in order] WJ/TMs¹ᵇ+; *om.* MS,
TMs¹(u)ᵇ

§ 14.21 take . . . the] WJ/TMs¹ᵇ+; still
*['envisage' *del.*] consider the [*ab.
del.* 'keep hold of'] objective cosmic
situation *and [*insrtd. for del.* 'with
its problems of'] the MS;TMs¹(u)ᵇ

§ 14.22 to-day] TMs¹ᵇ+; ~ˏ~ [*intrl.*]
MS

14.23-24 *Introduction to Philosophy*] I;
rom. MS-TMs²

14.24 *Philosophy.*] TMs²; ~ˏ MS,
TMs¹ᵇ; ~, I

*‡14.25 *thinking,* thinking] *stet* MS,
K/TMs²,I; thinkingˏ | thinking
TMs¹(u)ᵇ; | thinking PJ?/TMs¹ᵇ;
thinking TMs²(u)

14.29-30 something] WJ/TMs¹ᵇ+; *om.*
MS,TMs¹(u)ᵇ

14.31 to-day] TMs²,I; today MS,TMs¹ᵇ

14.34 it] TMs¹ᵇ+; *om.* MS (*error*)

14.39 (1895)] WJ/TMs¹ᵇ+; *om.*
MS,TMs¹(u)ᵇ

14.40 *Aristotle* (1864), chap. iv.] H;
Aristotle. MS,TMs¹(u)ᵇ; Aristotle

(1864)‸ Chapter IV. WJ/TMs[1b];
TMs[2](4); ~(~), chap. 4. I (chapter 4. I[p])

§15.6 described‸] TMs[1b]+; ~ [*underline del.*], MS (*error*)

15.9 'Spiritus rector'] TMs[2]; 'spiritus
~' MS; ‸spiritus ~' TMs[1](u)[b];
"~ ~' WJ/TMs[1b]; '*spiritus rector*' I

*15.10-11 positive,] *stet* MS,TMs[1b];
~‸ TMs[2],I

15.11 theory‸] TMs[2],I; ~, MS,TMs[1b]

‡15.16 diseases,] TMs[1b]+; ~‸ MS

15.19 oneself] TMs[1b]+; ones self MS

§15.19 'Sympathetic magic']
WJ/TMs[1b]+; ['Sympath' *del.*]
‸~ ~‸ ['was the gr' *del.*]
MS;TMs[1](u)[b] (Sympathic)

*15.25 then] *stet* MS; thus PJ/TMs[1b]+

§15.25 rain] WJ/TMs[1b]+; rain *or wind
[*intrl.*] MS;TMs[1](u)[b]

15.26 ground,...you] WJ/TMs[1b]+;
ground‸ or MS,TMs[1](u)[b]

‡15.27 If] WJ/TMs[1b]+; This If MS,
TMs[1](u)[b](*error*) [*see* Alterations
entry 15.33-34]

§15.27 would have yams] WJ/TMs[1b]+;
wish['ed' *del.*] yams to MS;TMs[1](u)[b]
[*begin* TMs[1a]]

15.28 Would...jaundice,] WJ/TMs[1b]+;
If you wish to cure jaundice‸
MS,TMs[1](u)[a]

15.29 look yellow;] WJ/TMs[1b]+; yellow,
MS,TMs[1](u)[a]

15.30 head,] WJ/TMs[1b]+; ~ ‸ MS,
TMs[1](u)[a]

§15.30-31 'doctrine of signatures‸'] I;
[*sg. qt. del.*] ~ ~' ~ ‸' MS; ‸~ ~
'Signatures,' TMs[1](u)[a]; '~ ~Signa-
tures,' WJ/TMs[1b]; '~ ~ ~,'
TMs[2],I(p)

*15.32 'mancies and 'mantics‸] *stet*
MS; '~' ~ '~,' TMs[1],TMs[2](u);
'-~' ~ '-~,' K/TMs[2],I(p),I
('-mantics‸')

15.32-33 [2]in...incipient] WJ/TMs[1b]+;
and witchcraft and MS,TMs[1](u)[a]

15.37 thoughts] TMs[1]+; tho'ts MS

15.39 Paris (1830-1842).] WJ/TMs[1b];
Paris, 18 MS; paris‸ TMs[1](u)[b];
~ . ‸~-~‸. TMs[2],I (Paris,)

15.40 Mulford's...type.] WJ/TMs[1b];
Mulford MS,TMs[1](u)[a](~.); Mulford's

and others of the 'New thought' type.
TMs[2] (*caret aft.* Mulford's); Mulford
and...'new thought' type. I

15.40 —For] WJ/TMs[1b]; ‸For the
MS,TMs[1](u)[a],TMs[2](u); ‸For
K/TMs[2],I

16.1 'positive'] H; '~‸ MS; ‸~‸
TMs[1]+

§16.7 heavens] K/TMs[2],I; Heavens
[*alt. fr.* 'Heavenly'] ['bodies' *del.*]
MS; Heaven TMs[1],TMs[2](u)

*16.13 held‸] TMs[1]+; ~,MS

‡16.14 brought] TMs[1]+; bro't MS

*16.14 etc.[7]] H; *om. fn. sign* MS,TMs[1],
TMs[2](u); *placed aft.* 'arm' [16.10]
K/TMs[2],I

16.18 seventeenth] TMs[1]+; XVIIth. MS

16.18 century] K/TMs[2],I; *cap.* MS-
TMs[2](u)

16.24 motion‸] TMs[1]+; ~, MS

16.27 five thousand] TMs[1]+; 5000 MS

‡16.28 everyone] WJ/TMs[1a](*pencil*);
everyone's belief MS+ (every one's I)

16.31-32 deliver...into] WJ/TMs[1a]
(*pencil*) (deliver ['transmit' *del.*] the
whole of it *into ['in' *ab. del.* 'in']);
K/TMs[2],I; carry the torch of it into
MS,TMs[1](u)[b](Of),TMs[2](u)

16.34-35 the...etc.;] WJ/TMs[1b]; J.
Jastrow: *Fact & Fable*, etc., chapter
on Analogy; MS; J. Jastrow...etc.‸
Chapter on Analogy, TMs[1](u)[a]; in J.
Jastrow; Fact, Fable, etc. the chapter
on Analogy, TMs[2](u); in...Fact and
Fable, in Psychology,...Analogy;
K/TMs[2]; J. Jastrow in *Fact and Fable
in Psychology*, the chapter on Analogy;
I (in J. Jastrow: *Fact* I[p])

16.35 *the*] I; the WJ/TMs[1b-2]; *om.*
MS,TMs[1](u)[a]

16.36 Marett] I[2]; Marrett MS-I[1]

16.37 *The*] I; the MS; the TMs[1-2]

16.37 vol. xvi, p. 357.] WJ/TMs[1b-2],I(p)
(*all* 16; vol‸ WJ/TMs[1b]); xvi, 357‸ MS,I
(357.); 16, 357. TMs[1](u)[a]

17.20 Descartes'] K/TMs[2],I; Descartes‸
MS,TMs[1]; Descartes's TMs[2](u)

*17.20-21 sine to sine] *stet* MS-I[2]; sine
to cosine I[3]

17.24 variations,] WJ/TMs[1b]+; ~‸
MS,TMs[1](u)[a]

18.4 two thousand] TMs[1]+; 2000 MS

18.4 ¹answer‸] WJ/TMs¹ᵇ,TMs²(u);
answer‸ that MS,TMs¹(u)ᵃ; ∼, that
K/TMs²,I

‡18.6 paragraph] TMs¹+; paragraf MS

18.7-8 three hundred] TMs¹+; 300 MS

18.8 is] WJ/TMs¹ᵇ+; is probably MS,
TMs¹(u)ᵃ

‡18.11 mathematical,] TMs¹+; ∼‸ MS

‡18.12 question,] WJ/TMs¹ᵇ+; ∼‸
MS,TMs¹(u)ᵃ

18.21-22 little things, the] WJ/TMs¹ᵇ+;
om. MS,TMs¹(u)ᵃ

‡18.22 telephones] WJ/TMs¹ᵇ+; and
tele**fones** MS; and telephones TMs¹(u)ᵃ

*‡18.22 and details] WJ/TMs¹ᵇ+; the
details MS; and the details TMs¹(u)ᵃ

18.26 'critical‸'] TMs²,I; '∼,' MS,
TMs¹; '∼‸‸ I(p)

18.27 in.] TMs¹+; ∼‸ MS (*error*)

18.28 *Objection 2.*] H; *rom. subh.*
MS–TMs²(u); ¶*Objection 2.*
K/TMs²,I (*in text*)

18.34 established] TMs¹+; establisht
MS

§18.34-35 claiming infallibility]
WJ/TMs¹ᵇ+; which *have [*ab. del.*
'were'] claimed *to be [*intrl.*]
infallible [*alt. fr.* 'infallibility']
MS;TMs¹(u)ᵃ

18.35 accepted . . . only] WJ/TMs¹ᵇ(r2)+;
taken or left only WJ/TMs¹ᵇ(r1); taken
or left MS,TMs¹(u)ᵃ

18.38 excellent] WJ/TMs¹ᵇ+; admirable
MS,TMs¹(u)ᵃ

19.2 dogmatists‸] WJ/TMs¹ᵇ+; dogmatic
minds, MS,TMs¹(u)ᵃ

*19.7-8 whatever‸] *stet* MS; whatsoever‸
WJ/TMs¹ᵇ+; whatfvfeever, TMs¹(u)ᵃ

19.10 philosophy] WJ/TMs¹ᵇ+; she
MS,TMs¹(u)ᵃ

19.13 *Objection 3.*] H; Objection 3‸
(*subh.*) MS (*db. underl.*),TMs¹,
TMs²(u); ¶ ∼∼. K/TMs²,I (*in text*)

19.31-32 *Conclusion.* | ¶ In] H (*as
subh.*); ¶ *Conclusion.* In MS; Con-
clusion. (*subh.*) | ¶ In TMs¹,TMs²(u);
In [*added* HJ] Conclusion‸ (*subh.*) |
¶ In K/TMs²; ¶ *In conclusion.* In I

19.34 the latter] WJ/TMs¹ᵇ+; them
MS,TMs¹(u)ᵃ

19.35 science] WJ/TMs¹ᵇ+; them
MS,TMs¹(u)ᵃ

§19.35 Herbert] I; H. [*intrl.*] MS;
TMs¹⁻²

‡19.35-36 ‸system of '*completely-*] H;
'∼∼ ‸completely‸ MS+

19.35-36 *completely-unified*] Spencer;
completely‸ unified MS+

19.38 Defined] I; defined MS–TMs²

20.5 defined] WJ/TMs¹ᵇ+; discriminated
and defined MS,TMs¹(u)ᵃ(refined)

‡21.1 possible, and to] WJ/TMs¹ᵇ+;
possible. To MS; ∼. to TMs¹(u)ᵃ

21.3 means] WJ/TMs¹ᵇ+; is MS,TMs¹(u)ᵃ

§21.4 the] WJ/TMs¹ᵇ+; other [*ab. del.*
'the'] MS;TMs¹(u)ᵃ

§21.5 left . . . were;] WJ/TMs¹ᵇ+; *left
over*; [*ab. del.* 'very'] MS; left over;
TMs¹(u)ᵃ

‡21.6 them‸] TMs²,I; ∼, MS,TMs¹

§21.8 examples‸ . . . order,] WJ/TMs¹ᵇ
-I(p); ∼,. . .∼, I; ∼, taken at
random, [':–' *del.*] MS;TMs¹(u)ᵃ

21.10-11 What . . . connected?]
WJ/TMs¹ᵇ+; What do we mean when
we say 'reality'? MS,TMs¹(u)ᵃ

21.12 'truth'?] WJ/TMs¹ᵇ+; 'truth'?
[¶] What is the meaning, character,
or significance of Nature, taken as a
whole? MS,TMs¹(u)ᵃ

21.13 facts] WJ/TMs¹ᵇ+; things MS,
TMs¹(u)ᵃ

21.14-15 ¶How . . . been?] WJ/TMs¹ᵇ+;
¶How . . . all? |Might . . . been?
MS,TMs¹(u)ᵃ (¶Might)

21.14 might] H; *cap.* MS+

21.17 all] WJ/TMs¹ᵇ+; *om.* MS,TMs¹(u)ᵃ

21.17 universe?] WJ/TMs¹ᵇ+; continuous
world? MS,TMs¹(u)ᵃ

21.18 unity‸ or diversity] TMs²,I; ∼,
∼∼ WJ/TMs¹ᵇ; the unity, or the
diversity of things MS,TMs¹(u)ᵃ

21.20-21 (our . . . example)] WJ/TMs¹ᵇ+;
, ∼. . .∼, MS,TMs¹(u)ᵃ

22.5 beings] WJ/TMs¹ᵇ+; entities
MS,TMs¹(u)ᵃ

§22.12 'beauty‸' and 'good‸']
WJ/TMs¹ᵇ+; ‸∼‸‸ [*ab. del.* 'truth']
∼‸∼‸‸ MS; '∼,' ∼ ‸Good,'
TMs¹(u)ᵃ

22.13 what] TMs¹+; what what MS
(*error*)

22.14 ‸Such] *stet* MS,TMs¹(u)ᵃ,I; – ∼
WJ/TMs¹ᵇ,TMs²

22.24 science] K/TMs^2,I; Science
MS–TMs^2(u)

22.29 generalized] WJ/TMs^{1b}(*pencil*)+;
general MS; 'General TMs^1(u)^a

§22.29 can act only] WJ/TMs^{1b}+;
$_\wedge$['can' *del.*] only act MS;TMs^1(u)^a
(, $\sim \sim$)

‡22.32-33 *the separate single*]
WJ/TMs^{1b}+ (*rom.*); *separate* MS,
TMs^1(u)^a (*rom.*)

§22.35-36 separate ... untouched]
WJ/TMs^{1b}+; *of the [*intrl.*] separate
questions of metaphysics MS; TMs^1(u)^a

22.37 problems] WJ/TMs^{1b}+; questions
MS,TMs^1(u)^a

22.37-38 but ... ^{1}them] WJ/TMs^{1b}(r2)+;
so far as they do not WJ/TMs^{1b}(r1);
they do not MS,TMs^1(u)^a

22.38 'Things,'] I; $_\wedge \sim,_\wedge$ MS; $_\wedge \sim _{\wedge\wedge}$
TMs^1(u)^a; '$\sim _\wedge$' WJ/TMs^{1b},TMs^2

23.10 power–so] H; $\sim$,–$\sim$ MS; $\sim$. So
TMs^1+

23.11 for him] WJ/TMs^{1b}+; *om.*
MS,TMs^1(u)^a

23.11 this] WJ/TMs^{1b}+; this division
MS,TMs^1(u)^a

23.14 $_\wedge$ with Spencer$_\wedge$] WJ/TMs^{1b}
(*pencil*)+; , along with Spencer,
MS,TMs^1(u)^a

23.14 mode] WJ/TMs^{1b}+; of the three
modes MS,TMs^1(u)^a

23.17 self-contradictory] TMs^1+;
$\sim _\wedge \sim$ MS

‡23.22 either ... disproof] WJ/TMs^{1b}+;
of proof MS,TMs^1(u)^a

‡23.26 learning.^{1}] WJ/TMs^{1b}+; $\sim._\wedge$
MS,TMs^1(u)^a (MS,TMs^1[u] ^{a} *place fn.
aft.* 'ourselves.' [23.27]. TMs^1[u]^a
also has a fn. indicator in error aft.
'classing' [23.24].)

23.33 meant] H; mean MS (*error*);
means TMs^1+

‡23.34 exists$_\wedge$] WJ/TMs^{1b}+; $\sim$,
MS,TMs^1(u)^a

§23.36-37 Democritus and Protagoras]
WJ/TMs^{1b}(r2)+; later thought
WJ/TMs^{1b}(r1); rival [*ab. del.* 'later
european'] thought MS;TMs^1(u)^a

§23.37 had] WJ/TMs^{1b}+; should [*ab.
del.* 'might'] MS;TMs^1(u)^a

23.37-38 either ... names] WJ/TMs^{1b}+;
Democritus or Protagoras MS,TMs^1(u)

§23.39 *Principes* ... ii.] WJ/TMs^{1b}
(*rom.* WJ/TMs^{1b}–TMs^2)+; Cours$_\wedge$
[*ab. del.* 'Introductio'] MS; Cours.
TMs^1(u)^a

23.39 *métaphysique*] H; *cap.*
TMs^{1b}–I

‡24.2 universals,] WJ/TMs^{1b}+;
$\sim _\wedge$ MS,TMs^1(u)^a

‡24.6 archrationalist,] TMs^1,K/TMs^2,I;
$\sim _\wedge$ MS (*error*),TMs^2(u)

§24.7 in] WJ/TMs^{1b}+; in a *higher
[*intrl.*] world of MS;TMs^1(u)^a

‡24.17 life,] WJ/TMs^{1b}+; $\sim _\wedge$
MS,TMs^1(u)^a

‡24.17 Hegel,] I; $\sim _\wedge$ MS–I(p)

24.24 embalmed] WJ/TMs^{1b},
HJ/TMs^2(r2),I; petrified K/TMs^2(r1);
embalmed and enclosed MS,TMs^1(u)^a

24.25 building on] WJ/TMs^{1b}+;
proceeding from MS,TMs^1(u)^a

§24.27 reached ... method] WJ/TMs^{1b}
(*pencil*)+; which the method *may
have [*ab. del.* 'gives at'] reached [*alt.
fr.* 'reaches'] MS;TMs^1(u)^a

24.31 etc.);] TMs^1; $\sim _\wedge$);MS; $\sim$.)$_\wedge$
TMs^2,I(p); $\sim$.), I

24.34 F.C.S.] WJ/TMs^{1b}+; J.C.S. MS;
J$_\wedge$C.S. TMs^1(u)^a

24.40 strong] WJ/TMs^{1b}(*pencil*)+;
marked MS,TMs^1(u)^a

§25.3 enter] WJ/TMs^{1b}(*pencil*)+;
proceed ['by' *del.*] into MS;TMs^1(u)^a

25.3-4 discussing ... problems]
WJ/TMs^{1b}(*pencil*),K/TMs^2,I; taking
some special problems in succession
MS,TMs^1(u)^a; discussing some special
problems TMs^2(u)

25.4 inquiry;] WJ/TMs^{1b}(*pencil*)+; $\sim$,
MS,TMs^1(u)^a

25.8 Sentiment of Rationality] TMs^1+;
l.c. MS

25.8 Rationality,] WJ/TMs^{1b}+; $\sim _\wedge$
MS,TMs^1(u)^a

25.9 1897] H; 1899 MS+

25.10 *Pluralistic*] TMs^1(*rom.*),TMs^2
(*rom.*),I; *l.c.* MS

§26.0 III$_\wedge$] TMs^1(3),TMs^2,I; II.
[*triple underl.*] MS

26.3-22 "Apart ... chord."] TMs^1;
"$\sim$ ... man,$_\wedge$ ... $_\wedge$no ... $\sim$." MS;
all sg. qts. TMs^2,I

26.5 conscious$_\wedge$] *stet* MS (*comma

probably del.); ∼, TMs^1+

*26.10-11 him ...] I; 5 *dots* MS; 7 *dots* TMs^1; 9 *dots* TMs^2

26.16 conceivable$_\wedge$] ∼$_\wedge$ | TMs^1(u), WJ/TMs^{1b}(r2)+; ∼ , MS, WJ/TMs^{1a-b}(r1)

§26.22 Giovanni] TMs^1+; ['Gi' *del.*] Juan MS

26.23 'On] I; 'on MS-TMs^2

§27.2 there,] PJ/TMs^{1a-b}+; ∼$_\wedge$ [*comma del. in error*] MS;TMs^1(u)

§27.3 says),] WJ/TMs^{1b},K/TMs^2,I; ∼)$_\wedge$ [*paren ov. comma in error*] MS;TMs^1(u)^a,TMs^2(u)

‡27.4 one's] TMs^1+; ones MS (*error*)

27.7 that] TMs^1+; *om.* MS

27.8 from nothing to] WJ/TMs^{1b}+; between nothing and MS,TMs^1(u)^a

§27.9 bridge] WJ/TMs^{1b}+; relation *to bridge over the [*ab. del.* 'but *plain [*intrl.*]'] mutual exclusion. [*period insrtd. bef. del.* '*which the terms present. [*ab. del.* 'nor any ['logical' *del.*] bridge from the one notion to the other [*doubtful period*]']'] MS;TMs^1(u)

§27.12 the contrast] WJ/TMs^{1b}+; *a contrast [*ab. del.* '['at large of a re-' | *del.*] re[*insrtd.*]lation'] MS;TMs^1(u)^a

27.14 shape,] WJ/TMs^{1b}+; ∼$_\wedge$ MS,TMs^1(u)^a

27.16 primordial] WJ/TMs^{1b}+; primal MS,TMs^1(u)^a

27.21-23 beginning; ... measured;] WJ/TMs^{1b}+; ∼, ... ∼, MS,TMs^1(u)^a

‡27.31 part$_\wedge$] WJ/TMs^{1b}+; ∼ , MS (*error*),TMs^1(u)^a

§27.36 no ... founded.] K/TMs^2(r1); can ['found' *del.*] no genuine problem *can be founded. [*ab. caret formed fr. orig. period*] MS; can no genuine problem be founded TMs^1,TMs^2(u), K/TMs^2(r2),I

27.36 curtly] WJ/TMs^{1b}+; briefly MS, TMs^1(u)^a

§‡27.38-39 [1]"why ... triangle?"] H; "∼ ... myself?$_\wedge$ [*qst. mk. ov. comma*] or $_\wedge$why ... ∼?$_\wedge$ MS; *all sg. qts.* TMs^1+

27.40 Rationalistic] I; Rationistic MS-I(p)

27.40 sought] TMs^1+; soght MS (*error*)

§28.2 or] WJ/TMs^{1b}+; *del.* MS; *om.* TMs^1(u)^a

28.4 whatever] TMs^1+; ∼ | ∼ MS

*28.5 imperceptible] *stet* MS+

‡28.10-12 "The ... existence."] H; *all sg. qts.* MS+

28.13 and] WJ/TMs^{1b}+; *om.* MS, TMs^1(u)^a

28.24 therefore] TMs^1+; therfore MS

28.25 way,] H; ∼$_\wedge$ MS+

28.26 if ...] H; if $_\wedge$ MS+

28.26 God$_\wedge$] *stet* MS+; ∼ , Hegel (Wallace)

28.27 very] Hegel (Wallace); *om.* MS+

§28.27 all."] H; all.$_\wedge$^{x} | [*fn.*] *Smaller ['S' *double underl.*] Logic MS; all.$_\wedge$ (smaller logic) TMs^1(u)^a (*in text*); all.$_\wedge$ WJ/TMs^{1b}; ∼ .' TMs^2,I

28.30 *Logic*] H; Logic MS; logic TMs^1+

28.37 Deane] H; Doane MS+

28.38 *Pure*] TMs^2(*rom.*),I; pure MS, TMs^1

§28.38 *Transcendental*] WJ/TMs^{1b} (*rom.*)+; Tr. [*intrl.*] MS;TMs^1(u)^a

28.39 proof,' etc.] H; ∼ ,$_\wedge$ ∼. MS, TMs^1; ∼ , ∼.' TMs^2,I

[TMs^{1b} *missing*]

29.3 'polar'] TMs^2,I; "∼" MS; $_\wedge$∼' TMs^{1a}

*29.12 all things have] TMs^2,I; things MS,TMs^{1a}

29.12 shaped] TMs^1+; soaped MS

29.16-17 say; ... grams;] TMs^2,I; ∼, ... ∼, MS,TMs^{1a}

[TMs^{1b} *resumes*]

29.21 understood.[4]] WJ/TMs^{1a}+; ∼.$_\wedge$ MS,TMs^1(u)^b

§29.23 philosophers] TMs^1+; filosofers[[1]'f' *ov.* 'ph'] MS

29.24 God,] WJ/TMs^{1a}+; ∼$_\wedge$ MS,TMs^1(u)^b

29.26 orthodox ... that the] WJ/TMs^{1a}+; *om.* MS,TMs^1(u)^b

[*begin* Stanford Syllabus clipping *pasted on* MS]

29.32 grow] WJ/SS(*clipping*)+; *grow* SS(*clipping*)

29.32 recurs] WJ/SS(*clipping*)+; recurs about experience SS(*clipping*)

[*end* Stanford Syllabus clipping]

29.37-39 [4]In ... elusive.] WJ/TMs^{1a}, PJ/TMs^2,I; *om.* MS,TMs^1(u)^b,TMs^2(u)

29.37 In more] 'In' *insrtd. bef.* 'More
['M' *unreduced in error*]'
29.37 technical] *final* 'ly' *del.*
29.37 language,] *ab. del.* 'exprest,'
29.38 The] *ab. del.* 'Its'
29.38 its appearance] *ab. del.* 'coming
are'
29.39 are] *insrtd.*
29.39 2when] *ab. del.* 'elusive in the'
[*begin* Stanford Syllabus clipping
pasted on MS]
30.1 can tell off-hand] WJ/SS(*clipping*),
PJ/TMs1a–b,TMs2,I; knows SS(*clipping*)
30.2 philosophy] TMs1+; *cap.* SS(*clipping*)
30.2 here, and no] WJ/SS(*clipping*)
(& No)+; here. No SS (*clipping*)
30.2 school] WJ/SS(*clipping*)+; school,
whether rationalist or empiricist,
SS(*clipping*)
30.3 another . . . airs.]
WJ/SS(*clipping*)(r1),(r3)+; another.
WJ/SS(*clipping*)(r2); another or give
itself airs. SS(*clipping*)
[*end* Stanford Syllabus clipping]
‡30.4 Fact] WJ/TMs1a–b+; the fact
TMs1(u); fact MS
*30.6–7 *whence* or *why*] H; Whence or
Why WJ/TMs1b(*pencil*),K/TMs2(r2),I;
Whence or Why K/TMs2(r1); That
TMs1(u)a; *That* TMs2(u); *that* MS
[*begin* WJ *typing* πTMs; PJ *typing* TMs]
31.0 Chapter IV] *stet* MS,TMs1+; *om.*
πTMs1
31.1 *Their difference.*] WJ/πTMs1a(*red*);
om. MS,πTMs1(u)b,TMs1(u)b,TMs2(u);
rom. WJ/TMs1a (∼ ∼.–); *s.n.*
K/TMs2,I
§31.2–8 The . . . contrast, but]
WJ/TMs1a(r2)(*pencil*),TMs2,I(*all
omit* use); *om.* πTMs1; The problem
most convenient . . . authors⌃ . . .
have myself . . . contrast⌃ *which
[*intrl.*] we are considering. ['is
embodied.' *del.*] But ['sense and ['I'
del.] idea' *del.*] things and thoughts
are strangely interlaced in our experience; MS;TMs1(u)b (experience;. ;
omits use); The . . . contrast. But . . .
experience; WJ/TMs1a(r1)(*ink*)
31.7 use] *stet* MS; *om.* TMs1+

[MS *missing*]
31.8 concepts] WJ/πTMs1a(r2),
TMs2,I; MAN'S ['thinking life' *ink
del.* WJ/πTMs1a(r1)–b] conscious
life is the interplay of his percepts
*and [*pencil*; *ab. del.* 'with'
WJ/πTMs1a(r1)–b] his concepts.
Concepts πTMs1; [*subh.*] Percept
and Concept. Their difference. |
[¶] Concepts TMs1(u)b; Concepts
WJ/TMs1a
31.8 and . . . again,] WJ/πTMs1a–b
(again. WJ/πTMs1b)+; 7 flow back
πTMs1(u) ('7' *error for* '&')
31.9 they . . . interlaced,] WJ/TMs1a
(*pencil*)+; *om.* πTMs1,TMs1(u)b
31.9 and . . . on] WJ/πTMs1a+; The
two are of homogeneous nature,
& we use πTMs1(u)b
31.10 undiscriminatingly,]
WJ/πTMs1a+; ∼⌃ πTMs1(u)b
31.10 it is ['usually' *del.*] often]
WJ/πTMs1a+; I have always found
it πTMs1(u)b
31.11 quickly to beginners]
WJ/πTMs1a+; to students who are
beginners in philosophy πTMs1(u)b
31.11 the difference meant]
WJ/πTMs1a+; what the distinction
means πTMs1(u)b
31.11–13 Sensation . . . independently.]
WJ/πTMs1a(r2)+; The difference is
that between our merely sensitive
experience & the ['ideas or' *del.*
WJ/πTMs1a(r1)–b] thoughts or ideas
that are grafted on it. πTMs1(u)b
31.14 their] WJ/πTMs1a–b,WJ/TMs1a+;
the πTMs1(u),TMs1(u)b
31.15 either . . . more] WJ/TMs1b
(*pencil*),K/TMs2,I; less πTMs1,
TMs1(u)a,TMs2(u)
31.15–16 must have been] WJ/TMs1a+;
is πTMs1,TMs1(u)b
31.16 originally] WJ/TMs1a; originally
& essentially πTMs1(u),
WJ/πTMs1a(r2),TMs1(u)b; essentially
WJ/πTMs1a(r1)–b
31.17 function,] WJ/πTMs1a–b+;
∼⌃ | πTMs1(u)
31.18 Some parts] WJ/πTMs1a+; Parts
πTMs1(u)b
31.19 exciting] WJ/πTMs1a–b+;

exciting in $^{\pi}$TMs^{1}(u)

31.20 ourselves;] WJ/$^{\pi}$TMs^{1a-b}+; $\sim_{\wedge}$ | $^{\pi}$TMs^{1}(u)

31.22 them,] WJ/$^{\pi}$TMs^{1a-b}+; the | $^{\pi}$TMs^{1}(u)

31.22–32.1 react ... using] WJ/$^{\pi}$TMs^{1a} (intellectually$_{\wedge}$),TMs^{1}(u)^{b}(them, intellectually$_{\wedge}$),WJ/TMs^{1a}+; use $^{\pi}$TMs^{1}(u); react upon them intellectually, & use WJ/$^{\pi}$TMs^{1b}

32.1 adjectives,] WJ/TMs^{1a}+; $\sim_{\wedge}$ $^{\pi}$TMs^{1},TMs^{1}(u)^{b}

32.1 them] WJ/TMs^{1a}+; them by $^{\pi}$TMs^{1},TMs^{1}(u)^{b}

[end $^{\pi}$TMs and PJ *typing; begin* WJ *typing* TMs]

32.4–5 ^{2}discrete ... *being,*] WJ/TMs^{1a-b}+; *psychologically* discrete, TMs^{1}(u)

32.7 just] WJ/TMs^{1a-b}+; *om.* TMs^{1}(u)

32.8 that,] WJ/TMs^{1b},K/TMs^{2},I; $\sim_{\wedge}$ TMs^{1}(u)^{a},TMs^{2}(u)

32.10 as such,] WJ/TMs^{1a-b}+; *om.* TMs^{1}(u)

32.10 nothing, and is but] WJ/TMs^{1a-b}+; nothing$_{\wedge}$ but TMs^{1}(u)

32.11 be] WJ/TMs^{1a-b}(*pencil*)+; may be TMs^{1}(u)

32.13 isolate,] WJ/TMs^{1a-b},K/TMs^{2},I; $\sim_{\wedge}$ TMs^{1}(u); isolate& TMs^{2}(u)

32.14 intend] WJ/TMs^{1a-b}+; mean TMs^{1}(u)

32.14 It shows duration,] WJ/TMs^{1a-b}+; *om.* TMs^{1}(u) (*error*)

32.16 a] WJ/TMs^{1a-b}+; the TMs^{1}(u)

32.17 occupies a] WJ/TMs^{1a}+; has its TMs^{1}(u)^{b}

32.21 are overflowed by] WJ/TMs^{1a-b}+; overflow into TMs^{1}(u)

32.21 separate,] WJ/TMs^{1a-b}+; $\sim_{\wedge}$ | TMs^{1}(u)

32.22 whatever] WJ/TMs^{1a-b}+; what TMs^{1}(u)

32.23 perceptually to] WJ/TMs^{1a-b}+; t | TMs^{1}(u)

32.29 all] WJ/TMs^{1a-b}+; *om.* (*end of line*) TMs^{1}(u)

32.30 *The ... order.*] WJ/TMs^{1a}(*red; Conceptual*),TMs^{2}(u) (*init. caps*); *om.* TMs^{1}(u)^{b}; *s.n.* K/TMs^{2}(*moved fr. subh. to s.n.* HJ?),I

32.31 this] WJ/TMs^{1a-b}+; the TMs^{1}(u)

32.31 attention] WJ/TMs^{1a-b}+; attention & conception TMs^{1}(u)

32.32 then] WJ/TMs^{1a-b}+; *om.* TMs^{1}(u)

32.33 'Idea,' 'thought,'] WJ/TMs^{1b},I; '$\sim_{\wedge}$' & '$\sim_{\wedge}$' TMs^{1}(u),TMs^{2}(u); '$\sim_{\wedge}$' & '$\sim_{\wedge}$' WJ/TMs^{1a}; '$\sim_{\wedge}$' '$\sim_{\wedge}$' K/TMs^{2}

32.34 and] K/TMs^{2},I; *om.* TMs^{1}–TMs^{2}(u)

32.34 'intellection$_{\wedge}$'] TMs^{2},I; 'Intellection.' TMs^{1}(u); 'Intellection,' (*moved by guideline fr. line below*) WJ/TMs^{1a-b}

32.34 synonymous] I; synomous TMs^{1}; synonomous TMs^{2}

32.34 'concept.'] WJ/TMs^{1a-b}('$\sim.\,_{\wedge}$ *error*),K/TMs^{2},I; 'concept$_{\wedge}$–likewise 'Intellection.' TMs^{1}(u); $_{\wedge}\sim.\,_{\wedge}$ TMs^{2}(u)

32.37 synonymous] TMs^{2},I; synomnymous TMs^{1}

32.39 *Universe*] WJ/TMs^{1b}(*rom.*)+; universe TMs^{1}(u)^{a}

32.39 288] I; 28 TMs^{1},TMs^{2}(u); 88 K/TMs^{2}

33.1 beach,'] WJ/TMs^{1b}+; $\sim_{\wedge}$' TMs^{1}(u)^{a}

33.2 'days'] WJ/TMs^{1b},K/TMs^{2},I; '$\sim_{\wedge}$ TMs^{1}(u)^{a},TMs^{2}(u)

33.3 these] WJ/TMs^{1a-b}+; these parts TMs^{1}(u) (*error*)

33.4 *whats*] WJ/TMs^{1b}+; whats WJ/TMs^{1a}; parts TMs^{1}(u)

33.4 *concepts.*^{3}] WJ/TMs^{1a-b}+ (*rom.* TMs^{2},I); *concepts.*^{x} [¶] In the adult mind trains of concepts unmixed with percepts grow frequent; & parts of these conceptual trains arrest our attention just as parts of the perceptual train did, giving TMs^{1}(u)

33.4 *The* (*no* ¶)] WJ/TMs^{1a-b}, K/TMs^{2}; ¶ TMs^{1}(u),TMs^{2}(u),I

33.5 *his substituting*] WJ/TMs^{1a-b}; *the substitution of* TMs^{1}(u); *his substitution of* TMs^{2},I

33.6 *his*] WJ/TMs^{1a-b}+; *om.* TMs^{1}(u)

33.6 But before] WJ/TMs^{1a-b}+; Before TMs^{1}(u)

33.18 conjunctions] WJ/TMs^{1a-b}+; conjunctives TMs^{1}(u)

33.20 concept,] WJ/TMs¹ᵃ⁻ᵇ+; ~ˌ
TMs¹(u)

33.24-26 Sir ... Book I;] WJ/TMs¹ᵃ+
(*all* Book ii); *om.* TMs¹(u)ᵇ

33.26 Book I] H; Book ii WJ/TMs¹ᵃ+

33.28 *L'Évolution ... générales*] H;
l'Evolution des Idées Generales TMs¹
(*rom.*)+ (*Générales* I)

33.29 *l'évolution ... jugement*] H;
l'Evolution ... Jugement TMs¹(*rom.*)+

33.30 *philosophie*] H; *Philosophie*
TMs¹(*rom.*)+

33.33 *disconnectedness*] WJ/TMs¹ᵇ;
rom. TMs¹(u)ᵃ+

33.34 apperception';] WJ/TMs¹ᵇ;
~,' TMs¹(u)ᵃ+

33.34-35 definite connexions]
WJ/TMs¹ᵃ+ (connections TMs²,I);
particular form of connexion
TMs¹(u)ᵇ

33.35 synthetizing] TMs²,I; synthetising TMs¹

33.36-40 "Die ... Verstandeshandlung."] H; *sg. qts.* TMs¹,K/TMs²⁽ʳ¹⁾,
K/TMs²⁽ʳ³⁾,I; ˌ~...~.' TMs²(u);
"~...~.' K/TMs²⁽ʳ²⁾

33.36 *conjunctio*] Kant; *rom.* TMs¹+

33.36 überhaupt kann] Kant; kann
Uberhaupt TMs¹-I¹ (überhaupt I²+)

33.37 kommen, und] WJ/TMs¹ᵃ⁻ᵇ+;
~ˌ Und TMs¹(u)

33.37 Form] Kant, I²+; form
TMs¹-I¹

33.38 zugleich] WJ/TMs¹ᵃ⁻ᵇ+; *cap.*
TMs¹(u)

33.38 Aktus] Kant; Actus TMs¹+

33.38-39 Spontaneität]
WJ/TMs¹ᵃ⁻ᵇ⁽ʳ²⁾+; Spontanëit
WJ/TMs¹ᵇ⁽ʳ¹⁾; Spontaneit TMs¹(u)

33.39 Vorstellungskraft] Kant;
Einbildungskraft TMs¹+

33.39 Unterschiede] WJ/TMs¹ᵃ⁻ᵇ+;
unterschiede TMs¹(u)

33.40-41 *Krit. d. reinen Vernunft*] H;
K.d.r.V. TMs¹+

33.41 –The] WJ/TMs¹ᵇ; ˌ~
TMs¹(u)ᵃ+

33.42 actual experience] WJ/TMs¹ᵃ+;
living consciousness TMs¹(u)ᵇ

33.43-44 *Philosophy of Reflection*,] I;
'philosophy of reflectionˌ' TMs¹,
TMs²(u); '~~~ˌ' K/TMs²

34.2 etc.ˌ] H; ~ ., TMs¹+

34.2 –all] WJ/TMs¹ᵇ; ˌ~
WJ/TMs¹ᵃ+; *om.* TMs¹(u)

34.3 long-forgotten] H; ~ˌ~
TMs¹+

34.3 instancesˌ] WJ/TMs¹ᵃ⁻ᵇ; ~,
TMs¹(u),TMs²,I

34.3-4 from ... out–] WJ/TMs¹ᵇ(out
[*comma del.*] –); from ... out,
WJ/TMs¹ᵃ+; *om.* TMs¹(u)

34.4 return] WJ/TMs¹ᵃ⁻ᵇ+; return
again TMs¹(u)

34.5 again in] WJ/TMs¹ᵃ⁻ᵇ+; into
TMs¹(u)

34.9 to walk with] WJ/TMs¹ᵃ⁻ᵇ+; in
walking TMs¹(u)

34.11 indispensability,] WJ/TMs¹ᵃ⁻ᵇ+;
~ ˌ TMs¹(u)

34.12 For] WJ/TMs¹ᵃ⁻ᵇ+; A TMs¹(u)

34.13 particulars] WJ/TMs¹ᵃ⁻ᵇ+;
particular | TMs¹(u)

34.14 philosophers] TMs²,I;
plosophers TMs¹

34.16 forms,] WJ/TMs¹ᵃ⁻ᵇ+; ~ ˌ |
TMs¹(u)

34.16-17 relations,] WJ/TMs¹ᵇ; ~ ˌ
TMs¹(u)ᵃ+

34.18 perceptions] WJ/TMs¹ᵃ⁻ᵇ+;
sense perceptions TMs¹(u)

34.19 termsˌ] WJ/TMs¹ᵃ⁻ᵇ+; ~,
TMs¹(u)

34.23 that] WJ/TMs¹ᵃ⁻ᵇ+; *om.* TMs¹(u)

34.24 more ... with] WJ/TMs¹ᵃ⁻ᵇ+;
leaves us like TMs¹(u)

34.25 ⁵See ... *Metaphysics.*]
WJ/TMs¹ᵃ⁻ᵇ; *om.* TMs¹(u); ˣSee ...
Aristotle's TMs²(u); See ...
Aristotle's *Interpretations of Poetry
and Religion,* p. HJ/TMs²,I (*om.* p.)

34.25 example,] K/TMs²,I; ~ ˌ TMs¹,
TMs²(u)

34.26 VII] WJ/TMs¹ᵃ+; VI | TMs¹(u)ᵇ

34.27 real] WJ/TMs¹ᵃ⁻ᵇ+; true
TMs¹(u)

34.29 *und*] K/TMs²,I; u. TMs¹,
TMs²(u)

34.29 –For] WJ/TMs¹ᵃ⁻ᵇ,TMs²(u);
ˌ~ TMs¹(u),K/TMs²,I

34.29 other] WJ/TMs¹ᵇ; *om.*
TMs¹(u)ᵃ+

34.30 read] WJ/TMs¹ᵇ; read the
passage from TMs¹(u)ᵃ+

34.30 *Source Book*] H; Source-book
TMs¹,TMs²(u); ∼-*book* K/TMs²,I

34.31 *Traité*] WJ/TMs¹ᵃ(*rom.*)+;
Traite TMs¹(u)ᵇ

34.31 *connaissance*] H; *Connaissance*
TMs¹(*rom.*)+

34.32 *A*] K/TMs²,I; a TMs¹,TMs²(u)

34.32 *Concerning ... Immutable*] H;
l.c. ital. K/TMs²,I(*amd*); on concerning eternal and immutable TMs¹
(*error*), TMs²(u) (*omit* on)

34.33 III] WJ/TMs¹ᵃ⁻ᵇ+; I | TMs¹(u)

34.33 "Plato," ... "thought] H; *all sg.
qts.* TMs¹+

34.35 and] Santayana; to TMs¹+

34.35-36 distortions, disappearances,]
Santayana,WJ/TMs¹ᵃ⁻ᵇ+; ∼ˏ ∼ˏ |
TMs¹(u)

34.36 multiplications] Santayana,
WJ/TMs¹ᵃ⁻ᵇ+; multiplication TMs¹(u)

34.36 ephemeral] *stet* TMs¹+; earthly
Santayana

34.37-38 essence, ... exist, but] *stet*
TMs¹; essence, but TMs²,I; essence.
As Plato said, they are never anything
fixed but Santayana

34.38 always,] Santayana,
WJ/TMs¹ᵃ⁻ᵇ+; ∼, TMs¹(u)

34.38 arising] *stet* TMs¹+; becoming
Santayana

34.38 be.] *stet* TMs¹+; be what we
think them. Santayana

34.40 multiform] *stet* TMs¹+;
manifold Santayana

34.40 trait, ... another,] Santayana;
∼, ... ∼, TMs¹+

34.41 reminds ... reality,] *stet* TMs¹+;
lights up that vague and haunting idea,
Santayana

34.41 ²us] TMs²,I; as TMs¹(*error*)

34.42 We, ... universe,] Santayana;
∼ˏ ... ∼ˏ TMs¹+

34.42 in the] *stet* TMs¹+; by the
passionate Santayana

34.43 to lose] *stet* TMs¹+; by the
radical need of losing Santayana

34.43 all] Santayana; and all TMs¹+

34.44 honour] Santayana; honor TMs¹+

34.44 the] Santayana; a TMs¹+

34.44 birthright;] Santayana,
WJ/TMs¹ᵃ+; ∼, TMs¹(u)ᵇ

35.1 *Two ... knowledge.*]

WJ/TMs¹ᵃ(*red*; Two [*ab. del.* 'The
Rationalist']),TMs²(u) (*rom.*); *om.*
TMs¹(u)ᵇ; Conceptual Knowledge. |
1. The Rationalist View K/TMs²(r1);
*Conceptual Knowledge,—the Ration-
alist View* K/TMs²(r2),K/TMs²(r3)
(*moved fr. subh. to s.n.*),I

35.5 truth,] WJ/TMs¹ᵃ⁻ᵇ+; truth,
ri[ght, *ink*] TMs¹(u)

35.7 of] WJ/TMs¹ᵃ⁻ᵇ+; of our TMs¹(u)

35.8 , and ... ['one' *del.*] view,]
WJ/TMs¹ᵃ+; *om.* TMs¹(u)ᵇ

35.11 *that*] WJ/TMs¹ᵃ+; *rom.*
TMs¹(u)ᵇ

35.12-13 knowledge] WJ/TMs¹ᵃ+;
knowle | TMs¹(u)ᵇ

35.13 its] WJ/TMs¹ᵃ+; it | TMs¹(u)ᵇ

35.15-23 We ... the world]
WJ/TMs¹ᵃ(r2),TMs²(u) (ethics,); [¶]
Rationalists say, Yes. For, as we ...
(page 58), the various ... reality, and
when ... parts. From these the ...
ethics, ... world K/TMs²,I (page 68);
[¶] Rationalist writers say Yes.
Concepts, they think, admit us to a
*higher [*del.* WJ/TMs¹ᵃ(r1)] diviner
world & show us an altogether higher
realm of knowledge, *the realm [*del.*;
ab. is intrl. 'knowledge' WJ/TMs¹ᵃ(r1)]
TMs¹(u)ᵇ

35.15 in later places] *alt. fr.* 'on a later
page'

35.15 pages 40, 55] H; p. 20 58
WJ/TMs¹ᵃ (*see* Textual Introduction,
pp. 255-256 *above*); p. 58 TMs²;
page 58 I(p) (*uncorrected*); page 68
I(p),I

35.15-16 conceptual] *intrl.*

35.16 universes] *bef. del.* 'of thought
which were'

35.17 they are] *intrl.*

35.17-18 considered,] *bef. del.* 'they
['form' *del.*] are self-sufficing, and
form the objects of *our [*intrl.*]
so-called a priori ['knowledge' *del.*]
truth ab'

35.18 among] *aft. del.* 'by'

35.19 *a priori*] I; 'a priori' TMs¹ᵃ⁻²

35.20 the] *alt. fr.* 'these *two [*intrl.*]'

35.20 two] *intrl.*

35.21 thus] *ov.* 'then'

35.22 by] (*ov.* 'to'); *intrl.*

35.22 been . . . admitting] *alt. fr.*
'*been said [*ab. del.* 'seemed'] to
admit'

35.24 immutable] TMs[2],I; inmutable
WJ/TMs[1a]; i mutable TMs[1](u)[b]

35.25-36.2 Emerson . . . . And a]
WJ/TMs[1a]+; A TMs[1](u)[b]

35.25-36.2 "Generalization . . . it."] H;
'∼ . . . ∼ .ₐ TMs[1a]; '∼ . . . ∼ .'
TMs[2],I

35.26 [1]a] WJ/TMs[1a]+; or TMs[1](u)[b]
(*error*)

35.26 clouds∧] Santayana,TMs[1](u)[b];
∼ , WJ/TMs[1a]+

35.27 If] Santayana; And if TMs[1]+

35.27 away∧] Santayana; ∼ , TMs[1]+

35.28 much immersed] Santayana;
unversed TMs[1]+

35.29-30 'Platonic . . . *Religion*,]
K/TMs[2],I (some): Platonism in the
Italian Poets. WJ/TMs[1a](Italien
TMs[1][u]b), TMs[2](u)

35.30 1900.)] H; 1896.∧ TMs[1](u)[b],
TMs[2](u); 1896.) WJ/TMs[1a],I; 1896∧)
K/TMs[2]['For a sketch of Platonism,
see E. Lass' *typed-del.* TMs[1]]

35.30-32 This . . . 1909.)]
WJ/TMs[1a-b]+; *om.* TMs[1](u)

35.31 said] *ab. del.* 'added' TMs[1a-b]

35.31 its profundity] *alt. in pencil fr.*
'it' TMs[1a]

35.31 challenged] *bef. del.* 'in our day'
TMs[1a]

35.32 *Plato's Doctrine*] K/TMs[2];
Plato's Doctrine TMs[1a-b],TMs[2](u);
Plato's *Doctrine* I

35.33-39 Aristotle . . . divine."]
WJ/TMs[1a]+; *om.* TMs[1](u)[b]

35.33 Aristotle∧] TMs[2],I; ∼,
TMs[1a](*error*)

35.33 found] *ab. del.* 'altho he finds'

35.33 treatment] *ab. del.* 'doctrine'

35.33 as] *aft. del.* ', fully'

35.34 to] *aft. del.* 'th'

35.34 of] *bef. del.* 'cont'

35.34 or] *aft. del.* 'life'

35.35 In] *aft. del.* 'Cont'

35.35 chapters] K/TMs[2],I; Chapters
[*insrtd. for del.* 'Sections']
TMs[1a];TMs[2](u)

35.35 Book] *aft. del.* 'Cha'

35.35 *Nichomachean Ethics*] K/TMs[2],I;

rom. TMs[1a],TMs[2](u)

35.36 as alone] *ab. del.* 'as [*ov.* 'at']
the highest'

35.40 *Essay Concerning*] H; *Essay
concerning* TMs[2],I; *l.c. rom.* TMs[1]

35.41 *sensations*] *stet* TMs[1](u)[b],
TMs[2](u)(*both rom.*); Sensations
WJ/TMs[1a];K/TMs[2],I (*ital.*)

35.41 Helvétius's] H; Helvetius's TMs[1]+

35.42 work∧] WJ/TMs[1a(r2)-b(r2)],
TMs[2](u); ∼ : WJ/TMs[1a(r1)-b(r1)];
∼ , TMs[1](u) (*doubtful*), K/TMs[2],I

35.42 *De*] K/TMs[2], I; de TMs[1],TMs[2](u)

35.42 *Human*] TMs[2],I; human TMs[1]

36.1 [1]the] *intrl.*

36.1 mind. Hence] Emerson; ∼ :
hence TMs[1a]+

36.3-4 "the . . . Transient,"] H; *all sg.
qts.* TMs[1]+

36.7 particular] WJ/TMs[1a](*misplaced
after* 'such')+; *om.* TMs[1](u)[b]

36.7 'how'] WJ/TMs[1a-b]+; ∧∼'
TMs[1](u)

*36.7 knowledge] *stet* TMs[1](u)[a]+;
ital. WJ/TMs[1b]

36.8 strictly so called,] WJ/TMs[1b(r1)];
∼∼∼∧ WJ/TMs[1b(r2)]; ∼∼-∼ ,
WJ/TMs[1a]+; *om.* TMs[1](u)

36.8 defect.] WJ/TMs[1a-b]+; limitation
TMs[1](u)

36.9 *The . . . view.*] WJ/TMs[1a](*red*),
TMs[2](u); *om.* TMs[1](u)[b]; *Conceptual
Knowledge—The Empiricist View.
(s.n.)* K/TMs[2](*moved fr. subh. to
s.n.*),I

36.10 opinion] WJ/TMs[1a],TMs[2](u),
K/TMs[2(r2)],I; opinion I oppose
TMs[1](u)[b]; opinion has been opposed
K/TMs[2(r1)]

36.12 has ['usually' *del.*] been opposed]
WJ/TMs[1a],K/TMs[2(r2)],I; *om.*
TMs[1](u)[b],K/TMs[2(r1)]

36.13 their] WJ/TMs[1a-b]+; their office
TMs[1](u)

36.13 , it . . . said,] WJ/TMs[1a]+; *om.*
TMs[1](u)[b]

36.14 coalesce with] WJ/TMs[1a-b]+;
condense themselves into TMs[1](u)

36.14 bringing] WJ/TMs[1a(r2)-b(r2)]+;
and to bring WJ/TMs[1a(r1)-b(r1)]; to
bring TMs[1](u)

36.14 into] WJ/TMs[1a-b]+; to TMs[1](u)

36.15-24 Certainly ... *content.*]
WJ/TMs¹ᵃ⁺; *om.* TMs¹(u)ᵇ

36.16 whenever] *ab. del.* 'if'

36.17 flocking with] *ab. del.* 'in'

36.17 and] *ab. del.* 'companions only'

36.19 conceptual] *aft. del.* 'that'

36.19 to be] *ab. del.* 'is'

36.20 empiricists] *aft. del.* 'association'

36.21 by] *aft. del.* 'where'

36.21 combining it with] *ab. del.*
'inserting it into'

36.22 mediating] *ab. del.* 'mor [*intrl.*]
discriminating'

36.22 this book] *ab. del.* 'we'

36.24 now ... to] *intrl.*

36.25 ¶ The] WJ/TMs¹ᵃ⁺; [¶] To
understand *this [alt. fr.* 'the'
TMs¹ᵃ⁻ᵇ] empiricist contention
better let us begin by distinguishing
the *function* of concepts from their
content. [*no* ¶] The TMs¹(u)ᵇ

36.25 to ... example,] WJ/TMs¹ᵃ⁺;
for example‸ TMs¹(u)ᵇ

36.25 things:] I; ∼ ; TMs¹-I(p)

36.25-26 the word] WJ/TMs¹ᵃ⁻ᵇ⁺; a
verbal object by TMs¹(u)

36.26 form‸] WJ/TMs¹ᵃ⁻ᵇ⁺; ∼ ,
TMs¹(u)

36.26 has] WJ/TMs¹ᵃ⁻ᵇ⁺; may have
TMs¹(u)

36.27 not] WJ/TMs¹ᵃ⁻ᵇ⁺; dignity
TMs¹(u)

36.27-28 an ... symbolizing]
WJ/TMs¹ᵃ⁻ᵇ(symbolizing *pencil*
TMs¹ᵃ)⁺; a representative use in
naming TMs¹(u)

36.28 certain] WJ/TMs¹ᵃ,K/TMs²,I;
other TMs¹(u)ᵇ; *om.* TMs²(u)

36.28 which] WJ/TMs¹ᵃ⁻ᵇ(*pencil in*
TMs¹ᵃ)⁺; *om.* TMs¹(u)

36.30 have] WJ/TMs¹ᵃ⁻ᵇ⁺; thei
TMs¹(u)

36.34 'God,'] TMs²,I; ‸∼,' TMs¹

36.34 'cause,'] WJ/TMs¹ᵃ⁻ᵇ(‸∼,')⁺;
'number,' ‸Cause,' TMs¹(u)

36.35 *De*] K/TMs²,I; de TMs¹,TMs²(u)

36.36 *âme*] H; *Âme* K/TMs²,I; Ame
TMs¹,TMs²(u)

36.36 similar] WJ/TMs¹ᵃ⁺; claim of
similar TMs¹(u)ᵇ

36.37-39 , and ... *Morality.*]
WJ/TMs¹ᵃ⁺; *om.* TMs¹(u)ᵇ

36.38 *Concerning*] H; on TMs¹ᵃ,
TMs²(u); *on* K/TMs²,I

36.38-39 *Eternal... Morality*]
TMs²,I; *l.c. rom.* TMs¹ᵃ

37.1 picture;] WJ/TMs¹ᵃ⁻ᵇ⁺; ∼ ,
TMs¹(u)

37.2 significance] TMs²,I; signifixcance
TMs¹(u) (*corr. in pencil in* TMs¹ᵇ *by
Schiller*)

37.4 thought.⁹] WJ/TMs¹ᵃ⁺; ∼ .‸
TMs¹(u)ᵇ

37.4 form] WJ/TMs¹ᵃ⁻ᵇ⁺; being form
TMs¹(u)

37.5 'circle'] WJ/TMs¹ᵃ⁻ᵇ⁺; ‸∼‸
TMs¹(u)

37.7-8 important] WJ/TMs¹ᵃ⁽ʳ²⁾⁺;
ital. WJ/TMs¹ᵃ⁽ʳ¹⁾⁻ᵇ; *rom.* TMs¹(u)

37.10 making us think,] WJ/TMs¹ᵃ⁻ᵇ
(think‸ WJ/TMs¹ᵇ)⁺; thought‸
TMs¹(u)

37.10 making us act] WJ/TMs¹ᵃ⁻ᵇ⁺;
conduct TMs¹(u)

37.16 *The ... rule.*¹⁰] WJ/TMs¹ᵃ,
TMs¹(u)ᵇ (*rom.*),TMs²(u); *the
Pragmatic Rule.*ˣ (*in text*) K/TMs²,I

37.21-22 "What ... make?"] H;
'∼ ... ∼?' WJ/TMs¹ᵃ⁻ᵇ,I;TMs²,
I(p) (what); ‸∼ ... ∼?‸ TMs¹(u)

37.23 for] WJ/TMs¹ᵃ⁻ᵇ⁺; for discover-
ing TMs¹(u)

[*end* WJ *typing*]

37.23 If,] WJ/TMs¹ᵃ⁻ᵇ⁺; if‸ TMs¹(u)

37.32 philosophy] I; *cap.* TMs¹⁻²,I(p)

37.32 ill-defined] K/TMs²,I; ∼‸∼
WJ/TMs¹ᵃ⁻ᵇ,TMs²(u); illdefined
TMs¹(u)

37.36-37 ⁹On ... 1870).] WJ/TMs¹ᵃ
(1890)‸)⁺; *om.* TMs¹(u)ᵇ

37.36 **H.**] *ov.* 'I'

37.38 ii] WJ/TMs¹ᵃ(II)⁺; II?
TMs¹(u)ᵇ

37.38 *Dictionary*] WJ/TMs¹ᵇ(*rom.*)⁺;
dictionary TMs¹(u)ᵃ

38.3-4 know, ... claiming,] WJ/TMs¹ᵇ;
∼‸ ... ∼‸ TMs¹(u)ᵃ⁺

38.5 verify] WJ/TMs¹ᵃ⁻ᵇ⁺; varify
TMs¹(u)

38.5 claim] WJ/TMs¹ᵃ⁺; alternative
TMs¹(u)ᵇ

38.9 existed,] WJ/TMs¹ᵃ⁺; were there,
TMs¹(u)ᵇ

38.10 the ... reality] WJ/TMs¹ᵃ⁻ᵇ⁺;

reality of other parts TMs^1(u)

38.10-11 'Idealism'] WJ/TMs^{1a}+; 'idealism' WJ/TMs^{1b}; ˄idealism˄ TMs^1(u)

38.11 tho] H; though TMs^1+

38.14 a] WJ/TMs^{1a}+; the TMs^1(u)^b

38.17 'equal,'] WJ/TMs^{1a-b}+; ˄ ∼ ,˄ TMs^1(u)

38.17-18 'you . . . difference'] WJ/TMs^{1a}+; ˄ ∼ . . . ∼ ˄ TMs^1(u)^b

38.19-20 'you . . . times.'] WJ/TMs^{1a} (*pencil*)+; ˄ ∼ . . . ∼ .˄ TMs^1(u)^b

38.20 'Substance'] WJ/TMs^{1a-b}+; ˄ ∼ ˄ TMs^1(u)

38.20-21 'a . . . recur.'] WJ/TMs^{1a} (*pencil*)+; ˄ ∼ . . . ∼ .˄ TMs^1(u)^b

38.21 'Incommensurable'] WJ/TMs^{1a-b}+; ˄ ∼ ˄ TMs^1(u)

38.21-22 'you . . . remainder.'] WJ/TMs^{1a}+; ˄ ∼ . . . ∼ .˄ TMs^1(u)^b

38.22 that,] WJ/TMs^{1a-b}+; ∼ ˄ TMs^1(u)

38.23 'you . . . whole.'] WJ/TMs^{1a}+; ˄ ∼ . . . ∼ .˄ TMs^1(u)^b

38.24 'less'] WJ/TMs^{1a-b}+; 'Less' TMs^1(u)

38.25 'no . . . restraint.'] WJ/TMs^{1a} (*pencil*)+; ˄ ∼ . . . ∼ .˄ TMs^1(u)^b

38.26 'your . . . one.'] WJ/TMs^{1a}(*pencil*)+; ˄ ∼ . . . ∼ .˄ TMs^1(u)^b

38.27 'you . . . fear,'] WJ/TMs^{1a}(*pencil*)+; ˄ ∼ . . . ∼ ,˄ TMs^1(u)^b

38.27 fear,] WJ/TMs^{1a-b}+; theory, TMs^1(u)

38.28 'you . . . sequences,'] WJ/TMs^{1a} (*pencil*)+; ˄ ∼ . . . ∼ ,˄ TMs^1(u)^b

38.28 etc.,] H; etc.˄ TMs^1+

38.29 book;] WJ/TMs^{1a-b}+; ∼ , TMs^1(u)

38.32 be] WJ/TMs^{1a-b}+; is TMs^1(u)

38.33 question,] WJ/TMs^{1a-b}+; ∼ ˄ | TMs^1(u)

38.35 *The . . . utility.*] WJ/TMs^{1a}(*red*; 'their' *ab. del.* 'practical'),TMs^2(u) (*del.*); *om.* TMs^1(u)^b; *The *Import* [*ab. del.* '*Utilitarian Origin*'] *of Concepts* K/TMs^2(r1); ['*The utilitarian*' *del.*] *Origin* ['*O*' *ov.* '*o*'] *of concepts in their utility.* (*s.n.*) K/TMs^2(r2),I

39.4,5 percept] WJ/TMs^{1a}+; instance TMs^1(u)^b

39.4 or certainly] WJ/TMs^{1a-b}+; *om.* TMs^1(u)

39.5 immediacy] WJ/TMs^{1a}+; perceptual immediacy TMs^1(u)^b

39.5 may thus often sink] WJ/TMs$^{1a(r2)}$+; thus sinks WJ/TMs$^{1a(r1)-b}$; thus sticks TMs^1(u)

39.6 ^{1}the] *stet* TMs^1(u),WJ/TMs$^{1a(r2)-b(r2)}$+; *del.* WJ/TMs$^{1a(r1)-b(r2)}$

39.8 connexions] H; connections TMs^1+

39.8 a] WJ/TMs^{1a-b}+; the TMs^1(u)

39.9 order,] WJ/TMs^{1a-b}+; ∼ ˄ TMs^1(u)

39.10 our mental] WJ/TMs^{1a}(*pencil*)+; the TMs^1(u)^b

39.10 panorama.] WJ/TMs^{1a}(*pencil period*)+; panorama of our world. WJ/TMs^{1b} (*pencil del. in* WJ/TMs^{1a}); panorama and perspective of our world. TMs^1(u)

39.11 should] WJ/TMs^{1a-b}; wshould TMs^1(u)

39.12 anemone] WJ/TMs^{1a-b}+; eneminy TMs^1(u)

39.13 concepts,] WJ/TMs^{1b}; ∼ ˄ TMs^1(u)^{a}+

39.19-20 handling . . . meeting] WJ/TMs$^{1a(r2)}$; *both ital.* WJ/TMs$^{1a(r1)-b}$+; banding . . . meeting TMs^1(u)

39.19-20 the perceptual flux] WJ/TMs^{1a-b}+; *om.* TMs^1(u)

39.20 it;] WJ/TMs^{1a-b}+; the perceptual flux; TMs^1(u)

39.24 which brutes] WJ/TMs^{1a-b}+; its roots TMs^1(u)

39.24-26 We . . . ends.] WJ/TMs^{1a}+; *om.* TMs^1(u)^b

39.27 *The . . . concepts.*] WJ/TMs^{1a} (*red*),TMs^2(u) (*theoritic*); *om.* TMs^1(u)^b; *s.n.* K/TMs^2(*moved fr. subh. to s.n.*),I

39.29 *understand*] WJ/TMs^{1b}; *rom.* TMs^1(u)^{a}+

39.30 'understand'] WJ/TMs^{1a}(*pencil*), WJ/TMs^{1b},K/TMs^2,I; ˄ ∼ ˄ TMs^1(u),TMs^2(u)

39.31 better] WJ/TMs^{1a}(*pencil*)+; more TMs^1(u)^b

39.32 *tell . . . it*] WJ/TMs¹ᵇ,K/TMs²,I;
  rom. TMs¹(u)ᵃ,TMs²(u)

39.33 *what*] WJ/TMs¹ᵇ,K/TMs²,I;
  rom. TMs¹(u)ᵃ,TMs²(u)

39.36 I.] H; J. TMs¹+

39.38 *Psychology*] TMs²,I; Phsychology
  TMs¹(*corr. in pencil in* TMs¹ᵇ *by
  Schiller*)

40.2 spatial,] TMs²,I; ∼‸ | TMs¹
  (spacial)

40.3 philosophical] WJ/TMs¹ᵃ⁻ᵇ+;
  cap. TMs¹(u)

40.4 a thing] WJ/TMs¹ᵃ⁻ᵇ+; things
  TMs¹(u)

40.5 'the cat'] WJ/TMs¹ᵃ(*pencil*),
  WJ/TMs¹ᵇ+; ‸∼ ∼‸ TMs¹(u)

40.6 a causally] WJ/TMs¹ᵃ+; an
  TMs¹(u)ᵇ

40.7 Clerk‸] H; Clerk- WJ/TMs¹ᵃ⁻ᵇ+;
  Clark TMs¹(u)

*40.7 -elasticity] *stet* TMs¹;
  -electricity TMs²,I

40.8 imaginary] WJ/TMs¹ᵃ⁻ᵇ+; *om.*
  TMs¹(u)

40.9 in . . . a] WJ/TMs¹ᵃ⁻ᵇ+; *om.*
  TMs¹(u)

40.11 valid] WJ/TMs¹ᵃ⁻ᵇ+; valid so
  TMs¹(u)

40.12 its existence probable,]
  WJ/TMs¹ᵃ⁻ᵇ+; it real existence
  probable‸ TMs¹(u)

40.12 with] WJ/TMs¹ᵃ⁻ᵇ+; gives it
  TMs¹(u)

40.12 agreeable to]
  WJ/TMs¹ᵃ(r2)-ᵇ(r2)+; formed to
  WJ/TMs¹ᵃ(r1)-ᵇ(r1); logically con-
  gruous with TMs¹(u)

40.13 produce] WJ/TMs¹ᵃ⁻ᵇ+; produced TMs¹(u)

40.14 type,] WJ/TMs¹ᵇ; ∼‸
  TMs¹(u)ᵃ+

40.16-17 hypothetically]
  WJ/TMs¹ᵃ⁻ᵇ+; *om.* TMs¹(u)

40.18 *what . . . that*] WJ/TMs¹ᵃ+;
  rom. TMs¹(u)ᵇ

40.19 perceive.‸] *stet* TMs¹(u)ᵇ,
  TMs²(u),K/TMs²(r2); ∼ .ˣ (*undel.
  pencil fn. indicator*) WJ/TMs¹ᵃ,
  K/TMs²(r1); *in* TMs¹ᵃ *opp. a pencil
  del. marg. memo in pencil:* 'Possibly
  the note on Stallo etc, on *p. 51 ['1'

ov. '2'] below ought to come in in
this place' (*The reference is to the fn.
added in the marg. of* MS p. 51, *and
keyed to* 53.23 'grasp.' *The fn. and
key were then del. and a revised
version adopted as fn.* 21 *at* 51.25.)

40.22 opening] WJ/TMs¹ᵃ⁻ᵇ+; utility
  opening TMs¹(u)

40.23 of] WJ/TMs¹ᵃ⁻ᵇ+; *om.* TMs¹(u)

40.23 consequences] WJ/TMs¹ᵃ⁻ᵇ+;
  consequence TMs¹(u)

40.25 things,] WJ/TMs¹ᵇ; ∼‸
  TMs¹(u)ᵃ

40.28 *The . . . sciences.*] WJ/TMs¹ᵃ
  (*red*),TMs²(u); *om.* TMs¹(u)ᵇ;
  In the a priori sciences. (*s.n.*)
  K/TMs²(*moved fr. subh. to s.n.*),I

40.33 sorts] WJ/TMs¹ᵃ⁻ᵇ+; orders
  TMs¹(u)

40.33 constructed] WJ/TMs¹ᵇ; abstracted or constructed TMs¹(u)ᵃ+

40.33 then] WJ/TMs¹ᵃ⁻ᵇ+; also
  TMs¹(u)

40.34 intimate,] WJ/TMs¹ᵃ+; ∼‸ and
  TMs¹(u)

40.34-35 'rational,' and unchangeable]
  WJ/TMs¹ᵃ+; 'rational‸' | WJ/TMs¹ᵇ;
  ‸rational‸ TMs¹(u)

40.36-41.7 our . . . worlds]
  WJ/TMs¹ᵃ(r2),WJ/TMs¹ᵇ(r2),TMs²,
  I; of [*error*] our sense of 'more'
  faculty of comparison and mathematics mainly establishes equations,
  substitutes equals for equals; logic
  has been defined as the substitution
  of similars; and in general one may
  say that the perception of likeness
  and unlikeness generates the whole
  of 'rational' or 'necessary' truth.
  Nothing happens in the worlds
  TMs¹(u); our [*pencil* TMs¹ᵃ; *ink*
  TMs¹ᵇ] faculty of comparison and
  of our sense of 'more.' Mathematics . . . *equals; [semicolon aft.
  del. semicolon*] . . . defined as a
  'substitution of similars'; . . .
  happens . . . worlds WJ/TMs¹ᵃ(r1),
  WJ/TMs¹ᵇ(r1)

40.36 our] *aft. del.* 'of' TMs¹ᵃ

40.36-37 comparison] TMs¹ᵃ+;
  comparison | son TMs¹ᵇ(*error*)

40.38 so-called] TMs1b+; ~∧~ TMs1a

40.38 sciences] TMs1a+; *cap.* TMs1b

40.38 of] *bef. del.* 'classification' TMs1a

40.38 mathematic] *final* 's' *del.* TMs1a(*see* HC *entry*)

41.1,37–39 logic.14] WJ/TMs1a+; *om. fn.* TMs1(u)b

41.1 these sciences express] *ab. del.* 'the' TMs1a; 'express' *ab. del.* 'trace' TMs1b

41.1 relations] *bef. del.* 'which mathematic['s' *del.*] traces are those' TMs1a

41.1-2 and identification] TMs1a [*intrl.*]+; *om.* TMs1b

41.2-3 , for ... certain] TMs1a [*comma insrtd.*; 'for ... certain' *ab. del.* 'form']+; first define certain TMs1b

41.3 then] *intrl.* TMs1a

*41.5 'the substitution] TMs1b; ∧~ '~ TMs1a,K/TMs2,I; ∧~ ∧~ TMs2(u)

41.7 happens] TMs1a+; *rom.* TMs1b

41.9 in these worlds] WJ/TMs1a-b+; of these TMs1(u)

41.9 propositions] WJ/TMs1a-b+; proposition TMs1(u)

41.10 character:] WJ/TMs1a+; ~ . TMs1(u)b

41.10-11 , e.g.,] WJ/TMs1a(*pencil*)+; *om.* TMs1(u)b

41.11 terms,] WJ/TMs1a-b+; ~∧ TMs1(u)

41.13 vast] WJ/TMs1a-b+; mast TMs1(u)

41.13 universals] WJ/TMs1b; universal terms TMs1(u)a+

*41.14 33] H; 6 WJ/TMs1a-b,TMs2(u); six TMs1(u); 48 K/TMs2,I(p) (*changed in ink to* 68); 56 I

41.15 or are] WJ/TMs1a-b+; or one TMs1(u)

41.18 (*twice*) more] WJ/TMs1a-b+; move TMs1(u) (*error*)

41.19 established] TMs2+; establisht TMs1

41.20 hand,] WJ/TMs1b; ~∧ TMs1(u)a+

41.22 an abstract] WJ/TMs1a-b(*pencil*)+; *om.* TMs1(u)

41.22 four; what] WJ/TMs1a+; ~. What TMs1(u)b

41.23 container] WJ/TMs1a-b+; contained TMs1(u) (*error*)

41.24 be made] TMs2,I; made be made TMs1 (*error*)

41.24 made; equals] WJ/TMs1a+; ~ . Equals TMs1(u)b

41.26 possess; the] WJ/TMs1a-b+; ~ . The TMs1(u)

41.27 of] WJ/TMs1a+; on TMs1(u)b

41.27 advance; if] WJ/TMs1a-b+; ~ . If TMs1(u)

41.30 etc.,] H; ~∧, WJ/TMs1a-b; ~ .∧ TMs1(u)+

41.30 etc.;] TMs2,I; ~ ∧; WJ/TMs1a-b; *om.* TMs1(u)

41.30 the] WJ/TMs1a-b+; The TMs1(u)

41.30 being those] WJ/TMs1a-b+; is the various TMs1(u)

41.33-35 terms. . . . ¶ The] WJ/TMs1a+ (*see next entry*); terms; and the TMs1(u)b

41.34 What ... physics.] WJ/TMs1a (*red*),TMs2(u)(*rom.*); *om.* TMs1(u)b; *And in physics.* (*s.n.*) K/TMs2(*moved fr. subh. to s.n.*),I

*41.35 consists] *stet* TMs1(u),K/TMs2, I; consisting WJ/TMs1a-b,TMs2(u)

41.36 first] WJ/TMs1b; *om.* TMs1(u)a+

41.37-39 14The ... (1874).] WJ/TMs1a+; *om.* TMs1(u)b

41.37 abstract] *intrl.*

42.1 conceptual] WJ/TMs1a-b+; rational TMs1(u)

42.3 gas-pressure] WJ/TMs1a-b+; ~∧~ TMs1(u)

42.4 hypothetic] WJ/TMs1a+; *om.* TMs1(u)b

42.4 molecules] WJ/TMs1a+; moecules TMs1(u)b (*error*)

42.5 frequent] WJ/TMs1a-b+; pregnant TMs1(u)

42.11 senses] WJ/TMs1a-b+; sense TMs1(u)

42.11 2our] WJ/TMs1a-b+; one TMs1(u)

*42.14 concepts] WJ/TMs1a+; images TMs1(u)b

42.16 co-ordinate] H; coördinate TMs1+

42.16 *thises*] WJ/TMs1b+; thises

WJ/TMs¹ᵃ(r2); things WJ/TMs¹ᵃ(r1);
theses TMs¹(u)

42.17 *whats*] WJ/TMs¹ᵃ⁻ᵇ+; *what*
TMs¹(u)

42.17 the ideal . . . be.¹⁵]
WJ/TMs¹ᵃ⁻ᵇ+; an ideal manifold.ˣ
TMs¹(u)

42.18 conquest] WJ/TMs¹ᵃ⁻ᵇ+;
contest TMs¹(u)

42.19-20 into . . . experience]
WJ/TMs¹ᵃ(r2)⁻ᵇ+; into which we
translate nature WJ/TMs¹ᵃ(r1);
om. TMs¹(u)

42.24 *Concepts . . . values.*]
WJ/TMs¹ᵃ(*red*),TMs²(u); *om.*
TMs¹(u)ᵇ; *s.n.* K/TMs² (*moved fr.
subh. to s.n.*),I

42.25 as] WJ/TMs¹ᵇ; such TMs¹(u)ᵃ+

42.27 *revalue*] WJ/TMs¹ᵃ+; *rom.*
TMs¹(u)ᵇ

42.28 indeed] WJ/TMs¹ᵃ⁻ᵇ+;
om. TMs¹(u)

42.28 by preparing] WJ/TMs¹ᵃ⁻ᵇ+;
by gu | preparing TMs¹(u)

42.29 it . . . addition] WJ/TMs¹ᵃ⁻ᵇ+;
in addition to this use it also endows
TMs¹(u)

42.30 splendor‸] WJ/TMs¹ᵇ; ~ ,
TMs¹(u)ᵃ+

42.30 interesting . . . itself]
WJ/TMs¹ᵃ⁻ᵇ+; occupation with
which is ['fit' *del.*] enough TMs¹(u)

42.30 to occupy] WJ/TMs¹ᵃ+;
to fill TMs¹(u)ᵇ

42.32 mere] WJ/TMs¹ᵃ⁻ᵇ+; *om.*
TMs¹(u)

42.32 is] WJ/TMs¹ᵃ⁻ᵇ+; is of itself
TMs¹(u)

42.33 good: . . . new] WJ/TMs¹ᵃ⁻ᵇ+;
good. New TMs¹(u)

42.33-34 admiration,] WJ/TMs¹ᵃ⁻ᵇ+;
~ ‸ are aroused– TMs¹(u)

42.35 ¶ Ideality] WJ/TMs¹ᵃ⁻ᵇ(r2)+;
[¶] Such an idealization of concepts
is extremely natural. Ideality
TMs¹(u); It is that Such . . . .
Ideality WJ/TMs¹ᵇ(r1)

42.35 clings . . . are] WJ/TMs¹ᵃ⁻ᵇ+;
seems to cling to a thing only when
it is TMs¹(u)

42.35 thus] WJ/TMs¹ᵃ+; *om.* TMs¹(u)ᵇ

*42.36 'Causes,'] TMs²(u); "causes,"

TMs¹; "Causes," WJ/TMs¹ᵃ,
WJ/TMs¹ᵇ(*pencil*); " ~ ,‸ K/TMs²,I

42.39 *über*] WJ/TMs¹ᵃ (*rom.*)+;
uber TMs¹(u)ᵇ

43.2 Loyalty] WJ/TMs¹ᵇ; *l.c.*
TMs¹(u)ᵃ+

43.2 order‸] WJ/TMs¹ᵇ; ~ ,
TMs¹(u)ᵃ+

43.3 'momentous issue,'] H;
" ~ ~ ," WJ/TMs¹ᵇ; " ~ ~ ‸"
TMs¹(u)ᵃ; ' ~ ~ ‸ ' TMs²,I

43.4 ‸poor scraps,‸ 'mere . . . suc-
cesses.'] H; " ~ ~, ~ . . . ~."
WJ/TMs¹ᵃ,K/TMs²; " ~ ~, ~ . . . ~.'
WJ/TMs¹ᵇ; " ~ ~," ~ . . . ~.
TMs¹(u); ' ~ ~,' ~ . . . ~. TMs²(u);
' ~ ~, ~ . . . ~.' " I

43.9 *Concepts . . . parts*] WJ/TMs¹ᵃ
(*underl. red*)+; *rom.* TMs¹(u)ᵇ

43.10 provide] WJ/TMs¹ᵇ,K/TMs²,I;
furnish TMs¹(u)ᵃ,TMs²(u)

43.11 which map,] WJ/TMs¹ᵇ; which,
TMs¹(u)ᵃ+

43.11 tho] H; though TMs¹+

43.12 now‸] WJ/TMs¹ᵇ; ~ ,
TMs¹(u)ᵃ+

43.13 practically.] WJ/TMs¹ᵇ; ~ ;
TMs¹(u)ᵃ+

43.16 emphasis.] WJ/TMs¹ᵇ; ~ ;
TMs¹(u)ᵃ,I; ~ , TMs²,I(p)

43.19 'eternal'] WJ/TMs¹ᵃ+; *om.*
TMs¹(u)ᵇ

43.20 ‸truths‸] *stet* TMs¹(u)ᵃ+; ' ~ '
WJ/TMs¹ᵇ

43.21 annihilated] WJ/TMs¹ᵇ+;
annhiliated TMs¹(u)ᵃ

43.22 thus] WJ/TMs¹ᵃ⁻ᵇ+; now
TMs¹(u)

43.22-23 and . . . translated]
WJ/TMs¹ᵃ(r2) (lost by ['by' *undel.
in error*]),WJ/TMs¹ᵇ+; and what is
lost by translating percepts
WJ/TMs¹ᵃ(r1); by the translation
of percepts TMs¹(u)

43.24 now] WJ/TMs¹ᵃ⁻ᵇ+; the now
TMs¹(u)

43.27 concrete] WJ/TMs¹ᵃ,TMs²(u),
K/TMs²(r2),I; *concrete* K/TMs²(r1);
solid TMs¹(u)ᵇ

43.28 We . . . weigh] WJ/TMs¹ᵃ⁻ᵇ(r2)+;
It is but to weigh WJ/TMs¹ᵇ(r1); It is
a case for weighing TMs¹(u)

43.29 and . . . that] WJ/TMs^{1a–b}+;
and TMs¹(u)

43.31 J. . . . 1908,] WJ/TMs^{1a}+;
Compare J. . . . 1908, passim,
TMs¹(u)^b

[*begin* WJ *typing*]

43.32 —Emerson writes:]
WJ/TMs^{1a(r2)}; ∧∼∼: WJ/TMs^{1b};
More beautifully does Emerson
write: TMs¹(u),WJ/TMs^{1a(r1)} (still
does); ¶ Emerson writes: TMs²,I

43.32–42 "Each . . . yesterday."] H;
'∼ . . . ∼ .' TMs¹+

43.33 looks] WJ/TMs^{1a}+; look |
TMs¹(u)^b

43.37 Every thing] Emerson;
Everything TMs¹+

43.37 point of view] *stet* TMs¹+;
point Emerson

43.38 truth. But] Emerson; ∼ , but
TMs¹+

43.40 ideal,] Emerson,WJ/TMs^{1a}+;
∼∧ TMs¹(u)^b

43.41 joy] Emerson; Joy TMs¹+

43.41 joy.] WJ/TMs^{1a}(Joy)+; Joy∧
TMs¹(u)^b

43.41 cleaves] Emerson; clings TMs¹+

43.41 names,] Emerson; ∼∧ TMs¹+

43.42 (Essay on 'Love.')] H;
(∼∼∧∼∧∧). TMs¹; (*Essay on*
∧*Love*∧∧). K/TMs²,I [∧*Love*∧.)]

[*end* WJ *typing*]

44.1 off-hand] H; ∼∧ ∼ TMs¹;
offhand TMs²,I

44.5 *The* . . . *creed.*] WJ/TMs^{1a}(*red*),
TMs²(u) (*rom.*); *om.* TMs¹(u)^b; *s.n.*
K/TMs²,I

44.6 In spite] TMs²,I; Inspite TMs¹

44.6 fast∧] WJ/TMs^{1a–b}+; ∼ , TMs¹(u)

44.8–9 as the more] WJ/TMs^{1a–b}+
(*more* K/TMs^{2[r1]}); alone as the
TMs¹(u)

44.9 knowledge.¹⁷] WJ/TMs^{1a}+;
∼.∧ TMs¹(u)^b

44.9 platonizing] H; Platonising TMs¹;
Platonizing TMs²,I

44.10 ever] WJ/TMs^{1a–b}+ (*ital.*
K/TMs^{2[r1]}); always TMs¹(u)

44.10 supersede] WJ/TMs^{1a–b}+;
supercede TMs¹(u)

44.13–14 They . . . compli-|]
WJ/TMs^{1a–b}+; *om.* TMs¹(u)

[*begin* WJ *typing*]

44.16 "Your . . . "are] H; *all sg. qts.*
TMs¹+

44.16 Your] WJ/TMs^{1a–b}+; your
TMs¹(u)

44.16 these] WJ/TMs^{1a}+; them
TMs¹(u)^b

44.20–21 [reason].] WJ/TMs^{1a–b},
K/TMs²,I; reaso | TMs¹(u);
(reason). TMs²(u)

44.21 confound] TMs²,I; confund
TMs¹(u) ('f' *typed ov.* 'o')

44.24 threats . . . insults of]
WJ/TMs^{1a–b}+; threat |. . . insults |
TMs¹(u)

[*end* WJ *typing*]

44.32 lit] WJ/TMs^{1a–b},K/TMs²,I; let
TMs¹(u),TMs²(u)

44.33 concrete] WJ/TMs^{1a–b}(*pencil*)+;
former TMs¹(u)

44.35–38 ¹⁷The . . . 29).] WJ/TMs^{1a}+;
om. TMs¹(u)^b

44.36 the] *intrl.*

44.36–37 "special . . . better"] H; *all
sg. qts.* TMs^{1a}+

44.39 Malebranche:] WJ/TMs^{1a–b}(*pencil*)+; *om.* TMs¹(u)

44.39 *métaphysique*] H; *cap.* TMs¹+

44.39 3me. Entretien] WJ/TMs^{1a–b}+;
3rd entretien TMs¹(u)

45.2 "was] WJ/TMs^{1a–b}(*pencil*),
K/TMs²; ∧∼ TMs¹(u); '∼ TMs²(u),I

45.2 kindness] *stet* TMs¹+; demon-
stration of kindness Plutarch

45.3 citizens] *stet* TMs¹+; citizens,
also, Plutarch

45.4 reformation,] Plutarch; ∼∧
TMs¹+

45.5 ruled] WJ/TMs^{1a–b}+; rule TMs¹(u)

45.5 prevailed] Plutarch; reigned TMs¹+

45.6 himself also behaving] Plutarch;
also behaving himself TMs¹+

45.8 insomuch] Plutarch; so much so
WJ/TMs^{1a–b}+; so much TMs¹(u)

45.8 reported,] Plutarch,WJ/TMs^{1a–b}+;
∼∧ TMs¹(u)

45.10 [in the sand].] WJ/TMs^{1a–b},
K/TMs²; *om.* TMs¹(u); (∼∼∼).
TMs²(u); ∧∼∼∼∧. I ([∼∼∼].
I[p])

45.10 Some] *stet* TMs¹+; Others
Plutarch

45.12 Syracuse] *stet* TMs[1]+;
Sicily Plutarch

45.12 numerous army] *stet* TMs[1]+;
a numerous land-army Plutarch

45.13 city,] *stet* WJ/TMs[1a-b]+; city of
Syracuse, Plutarch,TMs[1](u)

45.13-14 now, ... sophister,]
Plutarch,I; $\sim_\wedge \ldots \sim_\wedge$ WJ/TMs[1a-b],
TMs[2],I(p); $\sim_\wedge \ldots \sim$, TMs[1](u)

45.14 inveigling] Plutarch,WJ/TMs[1b],
I; inveighing TMs[1](u)[a]-I(p)

45.15,16 10,000] *stet* TMs[1]+; ten
thousand Plutarch

45.15 400] *stet* TMs[1]+; four hundred
Plutarch

45.19 *Defects* ... ['*system.*' *del.*]
translation.] WJ/TMs[1a](*red*),
TMs[2](u); *om.* TMs[1](u)[b]; *s.n.*
K/TMs[2](*moved fr. subh. to s.n.*),I

45.21 shortcomings] WJ/TMs[1a],
K/TMs[2],I; $\sim$-$\sim$ TMs[1](u)[b];
forthcomings TMs[2](u)

45.22 map:] WJ/TMs[1a],TMs[2](u);
$\sim$. TMs[1](u)[b],K/TMs[2],I

*45.23 them, ... value.] WJ/TMs[1b];
$\sim$, ... $\sim$; WJ/TMs[1a](*in pencil
except for ink semicolon*); *them,
and some of them we even transfigure.* TMs[1](u)

45.23-24 But ... remains]
WJ/TMs[1b(r2)](['*whole*' *del.*] map);
but ... remains WJ/TMs[1a(r2)]+;
But when we substitute concepts for
the continuous flow of our perceptual *nows* [*rom.* TMs[1](u)[a]],
[*comma added* WJ/TMs[1a(r1)-b(r1)]]
our acquaintance with *these
[*insrtd. for del.* 'the nows'
WJ/TMs[1a(r1)-b(r1)]] grows TMs[1](u)

45.24 the abstractness] WJ/TMs[1a-b]+;
its abstractions TMs[1](u)

45.25 the ... terms;] WJ/TMs[1b]; the
[*ab. del.* 'its'] discreteness *of
['*what*' *del.*] its **elements [*ov.*
'separ'] ; [*intrl.*] WJ/TMs[1a]+; its
discreteness; TMs[1](u)

45.25-26 the whole ... rational,]
WJ/TMs[1a-b] (['*substitution*' *del.*]
operation WJ/TMs[1b]; ['substitution,'
del.] operation WJ/TMs[1a])+; and, so
far from rationalizing the flux, as we
keep hoping it will, the substitution

TMs[1](u)

45.26 quite] WJ/TMs[1a]+; many
TMs[1](u)[b]

45.27 Conceptual] WJ/TMs[1a-b]+; My
thesis then is that conceptual TMs[1](u)

45.27 ['*in short*' *del.*] forever]
WJ/TMs[1a-b],K/TMs[2],I; *om.* TMs[1](u),
TMs[2](u)

45.29-30 universals$_\wedge$ ... -names,]
WJ/TMs[1b],K/TMs[2],I; universals,
TMs[1](u)[a],TMs[2](u)

45.33 even when] WJ/TMs[1a]+; as long
as TMs[1](u)[b]

45.37 it,] WJ/TMs[1a-b]+; $\sim_\wedge$ TMs[1](u)

46.2-3 creatures$_\wedge$ ... adaptations$_\wedge$]
WJ/TMs[1b]; $\sim$, ... $\sim$, TMs[1](u)[a]+

46.5 *this,* ... *this,*] WJ/TMs[1a-b]+;
that$_\wedge$ ... *that*$_\wedge$ TMs[1](u)

46.6-7 world, ... portions.]
WJ/TMs[1a-b](grouping [*ab. del.*
'complex arrangement'] WJ/TMs[1a])+;
world. TMs[1](u)

46.8 'colour'] H; 'color' TMs[1]+

46.12 rarefied] WJ/TMs[1a]; rarified
TMs[1](u)[b]+

46.13 'bright' and 'loud.'] WJ/TMs[1a]+;
$_\wedge\sim_\wedge \sim_\wedge \sim \cdot_\wedge$ TMs[1](u)[b]

46.14 once] WJ/TMs[1a-b]+; *om.*
TMs[1](u)

46.18 given] WJ/TMs[1a-b]+; give
TMs[1](u)

46.19 contents of feeling,]
WJ/TMs[1a(r2)-b]+; essences and
properties, WJ/TMs[1a(r1)]; essences
of properties, TMs[1](u)

46.28 *Why* ... *inadequate.*]
WJ/TMs[1a](*red*), TMs[2](u); *om.*
TMs[1](u)[b]; *s.n.* K/TMs[2](*moved fr.
subh. to s.n.*),I

46.29 that] WJ/TMs[1a]+; *om.* TMs[1](u)[b]

46.30 substitute their] WJ/TMs[1a-b]+;
think that the TMs[1](u)

46.30 too.] WJ/TMs[1b](too. ['must
also be' *del.*]); also. [*period added*]
['must be the more real.' *del.*]
WJ/TMs[1a]+; of the concepts must
obtain in the perceptual world.
TMs[1](u)

46.31 of static] WJ/TMs[1a-b]+; purely
static, being those of TMs[1](u)

46.32 substitute them for] WJ/TMs[1a]
('substitute' *ab. del.* 'identify'; 'for'

insrtd. *for del.* 'with')+; identify
them with WJ/TMs^{1b}; ['make' *typed
del.*] construe by their means
TMs^1(u)

46.33 conceptual] WJ/TMs^{1a-b}+;
conceptual field is one of continuous
change, while the conceptual scheme
consists of discontinuous unchanging
terms the conceptual TMs^1(u)

46.33-34 scheme, . . . terms,]
WJ/TMs^{1a-b}+; $\sim_\wedge$ . . . $\sim_\wedge$ TMs^1(u)

46.34 discontinous] WJ/TMs^{1a},
K/TMs^2,I; discontinuous unchanging
TMs^1(u)^b; continuous TMs^2(u)

46.35 spots$_\wedge$] WJ/TMs^{1a-b}+; $\sim$,
TMs^1(u)

46.35-36 full . . . ^{1}of] WJ/TMs^{1a-b}+;
equivalent for TMs^1(u)

46.36 flux] WJ/TMs^{1a}+; immediate
flux TMs^1(u)^b

46.36 escaping] WJ/TMs^{1a-b}+; escape
TMs^1(u)

46.37 put . . . place.] WJ/TMs^{1a-b}+;
substitute concepts for it. TMs^1(u)

47.1 actions;] WJ/TMs^{1a}+; $\sim$,
TMs^1(u)^b

47.2 could make] *could ['might' *del.*]
make [*ab. del.* 'introduce' *ab. del.*
'*preserve both [*ab. del.* 'could
maintain'] some *activity and some
[*intrl.*] continuity *in [*ab. del.*
'in']'] WJ/TMs^{1a}+; might make
WJ/TMs^{1b}; could maintain some
continuity in TMs^1(u)

47.2 active.^{19}] WJ/TMs^{1a}+; active.$_\wedge$
WJ/TMs^{1b}; *om.* TMs^1(u)

47.4 tho] H; though TMs^1+

47.4-5 that . . . act not, . . . activities;]
WJ/TMs$^{1b(r2)}$(activities.); $\sim$ . . . do
not *act, [$\sim$; TMs^2(u)] . . . $\sim$;
WJ/TMs$^{1a(r2)}$+; of the flux that
move WJ/TMs$^{1a(r1)-b(r1)}$; of the
flux which moves TMs^1(u)

47.8 'change,'] WJ/TMs^{1a-b}+;
$_\wedge\overset{-}{\sim}$,$_\wedge$ TMs^1(u)

47.9 changed,] WJ/TMs^{1a-b}+; $\sim_\wedge$
TMs^1(u)

47.10 from;] WJ/TMs^{1a-b}+; $\sim$,
TMs^1(u)

47.13-14 differences] WJ/TMs^{1a-b}+;
difference TMs^1(u)

47.14 as] WJ/TMs^{1a-b}+; as an TMs^1(u)

47.14 relations] WJ/TMs^{1a-b}+;
relation TMs^1(u)

47.15 *Origin of intellectualism.*]
WJ/TMs^{1a}(*red*),TMs^2(u); *om.*
TMs^1(u)^b; *s.n.* K/TMs^2(*moved fr.
subh. to s.n.*),I

47.16 'define'] WJ/TMs^{1a-b},TMs^2;
$_\wedge\sim_\wedge$ TMs^1(u),I

47.17 ^{1}define] WJ/TMs^{1a-b}+;
redefine TMs^1(u)

47.18 'this is motion,'] WJ/TMs^{1a-b}+;
"$\sim\sim\sim$,$_\wedge$ TMs^1(u)

47.19-20 'being . . . time.']
WJ/TMs^{1a-b}+; $_\wedge\sim$ . . . $\sim._\wedge$ TMs^1(u)

47.20 what . . . is] *stet* TMs^1(u),
WJ/TMs^{1a}(*underl. del.*)+; *both ital.*
WJ/TMs^{1b}

47.21 learn] WJ/TMs^{1a-b}+; leave
TMs^1(u)

47.22 discourse] WJ/TMs^{1a-b}+;
discover TMs^1(u)

47.22-48.1 always] WJ/TMs^{1a-b}+;
practically TMs^1(u)

47.23-42 ^{19}Prof. . . . knowledge.]
WJ/TMs^{1a}+; *om.* TMs^1(u)^b

47.23 *Philosophical*] H; Philosophic
TMs^{1a},TMs^2(u); *Philosophic*
K/TMs^2,I

47.23 Prof.] *alt. fr.* 'Professor'

47.23 *Review,*] *intrl.* (*rom.*)

47.25 he] ['th' *del.*] he

47.25-26 "The . . . continuous,"] H;
'$\sim$ . . . $\sim$,' TMs^{1a}+

47.26 thought is] *stet* TMs^{1a}+; our
thought Hibben

47.26-27 proves it by] *ab. del.* 'appeals
to'

47.27 example of the] *ab. del.*
'['calculus ['ca' *ov.* 'di']' *del.*] differ-
ential'

47.27 calculus.] *period insrtd.*

47.27 I reply that] *insrtd. for del.* 'to
prove it. It seems to me that Prof.
Hibben does n't sufficiently distinguish between the *designative [*ab.
del.* '*denotative*'] and the function
of concepts and their representative
*or copying [*intrl.*] function.'

47.27 calculus, in substituting] *alt. fr.*
'calculus substitutes'

47.28 lets . . . changes] *ab. del.* 'which
bring us out with the same result.

We *follow* ['the' *del.*] a [*insrtd.*]
curve'

47.29 point,] point, ['but we dont
[*illeg. del.*] duplicate it except for
the so as to but' *del.*]

47.29 thus] *insrtd. aft. del.* 'from this
point of view'

47.29 ¹their] *ab. del.* 'its'

47.29 not their] *ab. del.* '['not its' *del.*]
in no way its'

47.29-30 any change] *ab. del.* 'the
curve'

47.30 felt] *ab. del.* 'saw'

47.30 ²it] *intrl.*

47.30 ¹lead] *ab. del.* 'only ['bring'
del.]'

47.30 ²to] *intrl.*

47.30 ²lead] *ab. del.* 'bring'

47.31 practically] *intrl.*

47.31 cannot] *ab. del.* 'does nt'

47.31 I am] *ab. del.* 'the critics of
logic'

47.32 contending] 'ing' *added*

47.32 of reality] *aft. del. intrl.* 'here'
ab. del. 'of the perceptual life'

47.32-33 ²part . . . content of] *ab. del.*
'element in'

47.33 Hibben] *aft. del.* 'Mr.'

47.33 believe] *ab. del.* 'imply'

47.34 if only] *ab. del.* 'when'

47.34 might] *ab. del.* '['is suffic' *del.*]
['is' *del.*] will'

47.34-36 "It . . . intellect."] H; *all sg.
qts.* TMs¹ᵃ+

47.35 philosophy,] *stet* TMs¹ᵃ+; ∼ ,
moreover, Hibben

47.36 claims] *aft. del.* 'consequently'

47.38-39 ˌa priori˄] I; '∼ ∼' TMs¹ᵃ,
TMs²

47.39 world is] *alt. fr.* 'worlds are'

47.39 they . . . and] *intrl.*

47.39 that] *aft. del.* 'the [*intrl.*]'

47.39 no] *intrl.*

47.40 reader] *final* 's' *del.*

47.40 accuse . . . identifying] TMs²,I;
*accuse me to ['trying to make' *del.*]
identifying [*ab. del.* 'steer clear of
the tendency to regard absolute']
TMs¹ᵃ

47.40 with] *insrtd. for del.* 'as consisting of'

47.40 perception] 'ion' *added*

47.41 ¹conception] 'ion' *added*

47.41 Perception gives] *ab. del.* 'The
one gives the element of'

47.41 conception gives] *insrtd. for del.*
'the other that of'

47.42 our] *aft. del.* 'reality'

47.42 knowledge.] TMs²,I; ∼ ˄ TMs¹ᵃ

48.1 the] WJ/TMs¹ᵃ⁻ᵇ+; *om.* TMs¹(u)

48.1 mere] WJ/TMs¹ᵇ; *om.* TMs¹(u)ᵃ,
TMs²,I

48.2 datum.] WJ/TMs¹ᵇ(*pencil*); [*del.*
'form. [¶] As our first definitions
are always inadequate, we build
them out by more qualifying concepts, and continuing to seek for
truth in concepts upon concepts
with limit, we confirm the habit of
turning our attention away from the
perceptual *type of experience;
[*undel.* TMs¹ᵃ]'] TMs¹(u); type of
experience; TMs²(u); type of experience. K/TMs²,I

48.3 'intellectualism'] WJ/TMs¹ᵃ⁻ᵇ+;
˄ ∼ ˄ TMs¹(u)

48.5 *Inadequacy of intellectualism.*]
WJ/TMs¹ᵃ(*red*),TMs²(u); *om.*
TMs¹(u)ᵇ; *s.n.* K/TMs²(*moved fr.
subh. to s.n.*),I

48.7 motion] WJ/TMs¹ᵃ+; time space
and matter WJ/TMs¹ᵇ; time and
matter TMs¹(u)

48.7 it . . . parts] WJ/TMs¹ᵃ+; them as
some mations of points, instants, or
parts TMs¹(u)ᵇ,WJ/TMs¹ᵇ (summa-
tions)

48.7-8 *ad infinitum*] WJ/TMs¹ᵃ⁻ᵇ+;
ad infinitem TMs¹(u)

48.8 insufficiency] WJ/TMs¹ᵃ+;
impossibilities TMs¹(u)ᵇ

48.8 Altho] H; Although TMs¹+

48.8 continuum] *stet* TMs¹(u)ᵇ,
WJ/TMs¹ᵃ(r2)+; continuous movement WJ/TMs¹ᵃ(r1)

48.9 given, you] WJ/TMs¹ᵃ(you | you
in error)+; given to your perception,
you WJ/TMs¹ᵇ; given˄ you | you
TMs¹(u)

48.9 make] WJ/TMs¹ᵃ⁻ᵇ+; make discontinuous TMs¹(u)

48.9 *ad libitum*] WJ/TMs¹ᵃ⁻ᵇ+; ad
libortum TMs¹(u)

48.9 enumerating] WJ/TMs¹ᵃ+;

summing TMs[1](u)[b]

48.10 continuum] *stet* TMs[1](u)[a]+; *continuous perception [ab. del. 'time, space, or matter'] WJ/TMs[1b]

48.11 admits] WJ/TMs[1a-b]+; has to meet TMs[1](u)

48.11 that the] TMs[2],I; the the TMs[1] (*error*)

48.12,14 concepts,] WJ/TMs[1a-b]+; ~_ TMs[1](u)

48.12 blames] WJ/TMs[1a-b]+; blaims TMs[1](u) (*error*)

48.14 to ... indefinitely.] WJ/TMs[1a(r2)-b(r2)] (indefinitely.[x] [*fn. indicator originally for fn.* 20])+; indefinitely, to be ['added' *del.*] strung out.[x] WJ/TMs[1a(r1)]; indefinitely to be strung out. WJ/TMs[1b(r1)]; indefinitely prolonged.[x] TMs[1](u)

48.14 When] WJ/TMs[1a]+; But when TMs[1](u)[b]

48.15 a completed sum,] WJ/TMs[1a(r2)]+; completion, WJ/TMs[1a(r1)-b]; completion_ TMs[1](u)

48.16 is ... thinkers] WJ/TMs[1a]+; has to be sought TMs[1](u)[b]

48.16 of the] TMs[2],I; ofthe TMs[1]

48.17 Kant lodges] WJ/TMs[1a]+; Some, like Kant, lodge TMs[1](u)[b]

48.18 'things in themselves';[20]] WJ/TMs[1a]+; '~ ~ ~,'[x] WJ/TMs[1b]; _~ ~ ~,_ TMs[1](u)

48.18 others] WJ/TMs[1a]+; while others TMs[1](u)[b]

48.19 'Absolute'] WJ/TMs[1b]; _absolute_ TMs[1](u)[a],TMs[2](u); _Absolute_ K/TMs[2],I

48.19 Mind] WJ/TMs[1a-b]+; mind TMs[1](u)

48.20 Green ... Royce] WJ/TMs[1a]+; Hegel, Royce TMs[1](u)[b]

48.21-22 by such philosophers] WJ/TMs[1a-b]+; *om.* TMs[1](u)

48.23-24 they ... also,] WJ/TMs[1a(r2)-b(r2)]±; both they and it the reality are static, TMs[1](u), WJ/TMs[1a(r1)-b(r1)] (and the) (*See Emendation entries at* 48.23)

48.23 all] *ab. del.* 'platonic' TMs[1a]

48.23 rationalistic] TMs[1b]; rationalist TMs[1a]+

48.23 authors] *insrtd. for del.* 'philosophers' TMs[1a]

48.25 over with] WJ/TMs[1a-b]+; over | TMs[1](u)

48.26 Examples ... translation.] WJ/TMs[1a](*red*),TMs[2](u); *om.* TMs[1](u)[b]; *Examples of* ['*the*' *del.*] ... ['*the*' *del.*] *conceptual translation.* (*s.n.*) K/TMs[2](*moved fr. subh. to s.n.*),I

48.27 great a number] WJ/TMs[1b]; many TMs[1](u)[a]+

48.29 'known'] WJ/TMs[1a]+; _~_ TMs[1](u)[b]

48.29 sense_] WJ/TMs[1a-b]+; sense) TMs[1](u) (*error*)

48.32 are] WJ/TMs[1a-b]+; *and* TMs[1](u)

48.33 them. Nothing] WJ/TMs[1a-b]+; ~ : nothing TMs[1](u)

48.33 happens] WJ/TMs[1a-b]; *rom.* TMs[1](u),TMs[2],I

48.34-49.1 the concept ... crow.] WJ/TMs[1a](['A conceptual' *del.*] The)+; *om.* TMs[1](u)[b]

48.36 *Krit. d. reinen Vernunft*] I[2]; K/TMs[2],I[1](*Reinen*); K.D.R.V. TMs[1-2](u)

49.1 Concepts ... [1]and] WJ/TMs[1a]+; concepts TMs[1](u)[b]

49.1,3,15 juxtaposed] WJ/TMs[1a-b]+; juxterposed TMs[1](u)

49.1-2 Concepts ... compared.] WJ/TMs[1a](*moved by guideline to follow added* [1]'the ... crow.' [48.34-49.1]); *follows* 'therein:' [48.34] TMs[1](u)[b],TMs[2],I (Concepts *all l.c. except* TMs[2][u])

49.3 two] WJ/TMs[1a]+; two sequent TMs[1](u)[b]

49.3 phenomena;] WJ/TMs[1a-b], TMs[2](u); ~ , TMs[1](u); ~ : K/TMs[2]; ~ . I

49.4 adjacency,] K/TMs[2],I; ~_ TMs[2](u),WJ/TMs[1a(r2)-b(r2)]; juxtaposition_ WJ/TMs[1a(r1)-b(r1)]; juxterposition TMs[1](u)

49.5 reality] WJ/TMs[1a(r2)-b]+; phenomenon WJ/TMs[1a(r1)]; phenomena TMs[1](u)

49.6   disguise, and our] WJ/TMs$^{1a(r2)}$+;
$\sim$; $\sim$ $\sim$ WJ/TMs$^{1a(r1)}$-b; $\sim$. Our
TMs^1(u)

49.6   successions] WJ/TMs^{1a}+; places
TMs^1(u)^b

49.7   Lotze] WJ/TMs^{1a-b}+; Lotzei
TMs^1(u)

49.8   'influencing'] WJ/TMs^{1a-b}+;
$_\wedge$$\sim$$_\wedge$ TMs^1(u)

49.9   concept;] WJ/TMs^{1a},TMs^2(u);
$\sim$, TMs^1(u)^b,K/TMs^2,I

49.9   , as such,] WJ/TMs^{1a-b}+;
$_\wedge$$\sim$ $\sim$$_\wedge$ TMs^1(u)

49.13   But] WJ/TMs^{1a-b}+; but
TMs^1(u)

49.13   etc., etc.–] H; $\sim$$_\wedge$, $\sim$$_\wedge$– TMs^1;
$\sim$·$_\wedge$$\sim$·– TMs^2(u); and so forth, and
so forth [', And so *they go [*alt. fr.*
'it goes'] on.' *del.*] K/TMs^2;I

49.14   of] WJ/TMs^{1a-b}+; and TMs^1(u)

49.16   out of] WJ/TMs^{1a-b}+; out from
TMs^1(u)

49.18-19   concept,] WJ/TMs^{1a-b}+;
$\sim$$_\wedge$ TMs^1(u)

49.25   *conceptually*] WJ/TMs^{1a}+;
conceptualy TMs^1(u)^b (*error*)

49.26   are] WJ/TMs^{1a-b}+; and TMs^1(u)

49.26   concepts,] WJ/TMs^{1a-b}+; $\sim$$_\wedge$
TMs^1(u)

49.27   plurality of] WJ/TMs^{1a-b}+;
plurality, of which the terms are
TMs^1(u)

49.29   scheme] WJ/TMs^{1a-b}+; view
TMs^1(u)

49.30   a . . . melt] WJ/TMs^{1a-b}+;
$_\wedge$soul$_\wedge$ or $_\wedge$ego$_\wedge$ to run TMs^1(u)

49.30   collective] WJ/TMs^{1a-b}+;
om. TMs^1(u)

49.32   and] WJ/TMs^{1a-b}+; *om.* TMs^1(u)

49.32   puzzles] WJ/TMs^{1a-b}+;
incomprehensibilities TMs^1(u)

49.34   of] WJ/TMs^{1a-b}+; *om.* TMs^1(u)

49.34   rationalists] WJ/TMs^{1a-b}+; the
theorists TMs^1(u)

49.34   refuse the] WJ/TMs^{1a}+;
refusethe TMs^1(u)^b

49.35   in its] WJ/TMs^{1a-b}+; us in the
TMs^1(u)

49.35   form] WJ/TMs^{1a-b}+; flux
TMs^1(u)

49.36   Perception] *bef.* WJ *del. intrl.*

'indee [*doubtful*] ' TMs^{1a}

49.37   pulsewise] TMs^2,I; $\sim$ - $\sim$
[*hyphen typed ov.* 'w'] TMs^1

49.37-38   each . . . bounds.]
WJ/TMs^{1a-b}+; and melt into one
another. TMs^1(u)

49.38   translation, . . . continuum]
WJ/TMs^{1a}+; $\sim$$_\wedge$ . . . $\sim$ WJ/TMs^{1b};
translation, continuity TMs^1(u)

50.12   no] WJ/TMs^{1a-b}+; on TMs^1(u)
(*error*)

50.13   Defined . . . by] WJ/TMs^{1a-b}+;
Living as it does between TMs^1(u)

50.13   ending,] WJ/TMs^{1a-b}+; $\sim$$_\wedge$
TMs^1(u)

50.16   going, . . . future,] WJ/TMs^{1a-b}+;
$\sim$$_\wedge$ . . . $\sim$$_\wedge$ TMs^1(u)

50.18   *No . . . once*] WJ/TMs^{1a}+; *rom.*
TMs^1(u)^b

50.19   , for example,] WJ/TMs^{1a-b}+;
$_\wedge$$\sim$ $\sim$$_\wedge$ TMs^1(u)

50.19   both] WJ/TMs^{1a-b}+; *om.*
TMs^1(u)

50.20   if,] WJ/TMs^{1a-b}+; $\sim$$_\wedge$ TMs^1(u)

50.21   and predicating]
WJ/TMs$^{1a(r2)}$-b+; , you predicate
WJ/TMs$^{1a(r1)}$; and predicate
TMs^1(u)

50.24   not-A] WJ/TMs^{1a},K/TMs^2,I;
not$_\wedge$A TMs^1(u)^b; not be A TMs^2(u)

50.25   be,] WJ/TMs^{1a-b}+; be, and
glorious their 'dialectic' remedies,
TMs^1(u)

50.25-26   disbelieves . . . thing.]
WJ/TMs^{1a-b}('see' *ab. del.* '['can'
del.] know' WJ/TMs^{1a})+; believes
that the many-in-oneness of his
perceptual impressions is not
genuine. TMs^1(u)

50.29   concept;] WJ/TMs^{1a-b}+; $\sim$,
TMs^1(u)

50.34-36   *The . . . -contradictory*]
WJ/TMs^{1a}+; *The . . . thinking* | (*all
ital.*) WJ/TMs^{1b} (itself . . . -contra-
dictory *all rom.*); *rom.* TMs^1(u)

50.34-35   *judgments, . . . itself,*]
WJ/TMs^{1a-b}+; $\sim$$_\wedge$ . . . $\sim$$_\wedge$ TMs^1(u)

50.36   ready-made] WJ/TMs^{1a-b}+;
$\sim$$_\wedge$ $\sim$ TMs^1(u)

50.37   we] TMs^2,I; *typed del. in error*
TMs^1

50.38 sweet,] WJ/TMs¹ᵃ+; ∼₍ₐ₎
TMs¹(u)ᵇ

51.1 described,] WJ/TMs¹ᵃ+; ∼₍ₐ₎
TMs¹(u)ᵇ

51.2 nor] WJ/TMs¹ᵃ⁻ᵇ+; now
TMs¹(u) (*error*)

51.2 description, is] WJ/TMs¹ᵃ⁻ᵇ+;
description₍ₐ₎ of it is at all TMs¹(u)

51.2,25-35 comprehensible.²¹]
WJ/TMs¹ᵃ+; *om. fn.* TMs¹(u)ᵇ

51.3 *Relation . . . difficulties.*]
WJ/TMs¹ᵃ(*red*),TMs²(u); *om.*
TMs¹(u)ᵇ; *Attitude* [*ab. del.*
'*Relation*'] *. . . difficulties. (s.n.)*
K/TMs²(*moved fr. subh. to s.n.*);I

51.4 inconceivability,] WJ/TMs¹ᵃ⁻ᵇ+;
∼₍ₐ₎ TMs¹(u)

51.6 continuum] WJ/TMs¹ᵃ⁻ᵇ+;
continuity TMs¹(u)

51.7 came.] WJ/TMs¹ᵃ⁻ᵇ+; was
made. TMs¹(u)

51.8-9 impossible . . . intellectually.]
WJ/TMs¹ᵃ+; intellectually impossible to construe. TMs¹(u)ᵇ

51.10 seriously;] WJ/TMs¹ᵃ⁻ᵇ+; ∼ ,
TMs¹(u)

51.11 greek] H; Greek TMs¹+

51.11 lain] WJ/TMs¹ᵃ+; lain hid
TMs¹(u)ᵇ

51.15 only,] WJ/TMs¹ᵃ⁻ᵇ+; ∼ ₍ₐ₎
TMs¹(u)

51.16 Sceptics] WJ/TMs¹ᵃ⁻ᵇ+;
l.c. TMs¹(u)

51.17 writers] WJ/TMs¹ᵃ⁻ᵇ+; ones
TMs¹(u)

51.18-19 a . . . all.] WJ/TMs¹ᵃ+;
radical solutions. TMs¹(u)ᵇ

51.20 Sceptics] H; *l.c.* TMs¹+

[*begin* WJ *typing* TMs¹ᵃ]

51.23 and Bergson] WJ/TMs¹ᵃ
(*retyped* TMs¹ᵇ)+; *om.* TMs¹(u)ᵃ

[*end* WJ *typing* TMs¹ᵃ]

51.25 conceptual puzzles] *ab. del.*
', contradictions'

51.25 ²have] *aft. del.* 'the'

51.26 but the ['cur' *del.*]] *ab. del.*
'through the notion that only out
of concepts can deeper truth be
wrung. The'

51.26 current in] *ab. del.* 'of'

51.26 have] *aft. del.* 'which have to be
used together'

51.26 also] *intrl.*

51.27 (altho . . . philosophy)] *parens
over commas*

51.28 such] *aft. del.* 'after all'

51.28 notions] *ab. del.* 'concepts'

51.28 unconditional] *ab. del.* 'deeper'

51.29 the concepts] *ab. del.* 'notions
[*ab. del.* 'such concepts'] '

51.30 not . . . ['intimate' *del.*] hidden]
ab. del. 'less revelations of natures
intimate'

51.30 realities] 'ies' *ov.* 'y'

51.30 in nature] I; in Nature TMs¹ᵃ
(*intrl.*), TMs²,I(p)

51.30 as] *ab. del.* 'than'

51.31 after-] TMs²,I; after₍ₐ₎ [*ab. del.*
'when we have'] TMs¹ᵃ

51.31 substitution] 'ion' *ov.* 'ed'

51.31 of] *intrl.*

51.31-32 considered] *intrl.*

51.32 like . . . yard.] *intrl.*

51.33 *Physics*] K/TMs²,I; physics'
TMs¹ᵃ; Philosophy TMs²(u)

51.34 is] *aft. del.* 'may be referred to'

51.34 Mach] *aft. del.* 'Other authors
are'

51.34 Ostwald,] *comma added bef.
del.* '(Naturphilosophie, *(1902)
[*parens del.*] pp. 308-311),'

51.35 H.] *intrl.*

51.35 are] *ab. del.* 'and'

51.35 other] *final* 's' *del.*

51.35 of . . . sort.] *insrtd.*

51.36 Herbart] WJ/TMs¹ᵃ⁻ᵇ+;
Herbert TMs¹(u)

51.37 history] K/TMs²,I; History
TMs¹,TMs²(u)

51.37 *sub voce*] WJ/TMs¹ᵃ+; *rom.*
TMs¹(u)ᵇ

51.41-52.36 Compare . . . Dialectic.']
WJ/TMs¹ᵃ⁻ᵇ+; *om.* TMs¹(u)

51.41 e.g.,] TMs¹ᵃ+; *e,g* TMs¹ᵇ

51.41-42 *The . . . Spirit*] TMs²,I;
the . . . spirit TMs¹ᵃ⁻ᵇ(*all rom.*)

51.42 Essay,] TMs¹ᵃ,TMs²(u); ∼ ₍ₐ₎
TMs¹ᵇ; ∼ ; K/TMs²,I

51.42 The] H; on the TMs¹ᵃ⁻ᵇ,TMs²;
On the K/TMs²,I

51.42 Element] 'E' *ov.* 'e'

[*begin* WJ *typing* TMs¹ᵃ]

52.1 *Bradley . . . concept.*]
WJ/TMs¹ᵃ(*red*),TMs²(u) (*percepts*

and concepts); *om.* TMs¹(u)ᵇ; *s.n.*
K/TMs² (*moved fr. subh. to s.n.*),I
52.5   'encounter'] WJ/TMs¹ᵃ(*retyped*
TMs¹ᵇ)+; ‸~' TMs¹(u)ᵃ
52.8   ideas,] WJ/TMs¹ᵃ(*retyped*
TMs¹ᵇ)+; ~‸ TMs¹(u)ᵃ
52.8-9   compenetration] WJ/TMs¹ᵃ-ᵇ+;
compenetra-| [p. 94(47)] related
together, or *they [*ov.* 'their'] are
[*intrl.*] abstract designative words;
and in neither case do we get back
what we started from, namely *that
[*alt. fr.* 'the'] harmonious compenetration TMs¹(u)
[*end WJ typing* TMs¹ᵃ]
52.9   -in-] WJ/TMs¹ᵃ-ᵇ+; ‸and‸
TMs¹(u)
52.9-10   feeling . . . possible.]
WJ/TMs¹ᵃ-ᵇ+; immediate feeling
gave. TMs¹(u)
52.10   Concepts indeed extend]
WJ/TMs¹ᵃ-ᵇ(r2)+; Relational
thought ['indeed' WJ/TMs¹ᵇ(r1)]
extends TMs¹(u)
52.10   lose] WJ/TMs¹ᵃ-ᵇ+; loses
TMs¹(u)
52.10-11   lose . . . its] *stet* TMs¹(u)ᵇ,
WJ/TMs¹ᵃ(r2)+; violates the inner
WJ/TMs¹ᵃ(r1)
52.11   wholeness;] WJ/TMs¹ᵃ+; ~,
TMs¹(u)ᵇ
52.11   when ideal] WJ/TMs¹ᵃ-ᵇ+;
Bradley confesses that when TMs¹(u)
52.13   due entirely] WJ/TMs¹ᵃ(r2)+;
wholly due WJ/TMs¹ᵃ(r1); due
TMs¹(u)ᵇ
52.14   that one] WJ/TMs¹ᵃ-ᵇ+; a man
TMs¹(u)
52.15   clearly] WJ/TMs¹ᵃ-ᵇ+; well
TMs¹(u)
52.16   does, would] WJ/TMs¹ᵃ-ᵇ+;
does‸ to TMs¹(u)
52.16   philosophy] K/TMs²,I; *cap.*
TMs¹,TMs²(u)
52.17   works,] WJ/TMs¹ᵃ-ᵇ+; ~‸
TMs¹(u)
52.19   tho] *stet* TMs¹(u)ᵃ; tho'
WJ/TMs¹ᵇ; though TMs²,I
52.21   feeling] WJ/TMs¹ᵇ; immediate
feeling WJ/TMs¹ᵃ+; the immediate
feeling TMs¹(u)
52.21   'philosophy'] WJ/TMs¹ᵃ+;

‸~‸ TMs¹(u)ᵇ
52.22-23   "For . . . philosophy."] H;
all sg. qts. TMs¹+
52.22   or for] WJ/TMs¹ᵃ-ᵇ+; off or
TMs¹(u)
52.22   stands] Bradley; stays TMs¹+
52.23   of] Bradley; *om.* TMs¹+
52.25   'ideally' . . . concepts)]
WJ/TMs¹ᵃ+; *'ideally' . . .* concepts)
WJ/TMs¹ᵇ; ‸ideally‸ TMs¹(u)
52.25   'ideas'] WJ/TMs¹ᵃ-ᵇ+; ‸~‸
TMs¹(u)
52.26   show no] WJ/TMs¹ᵇ,K/TMs²,I;
never show a WJ/TMs¹ᵃ,TMs²(u);
never attain to a TMs¹(u)
52.27   living] WJ/TMs¹ᵇ; the living
K/TMs²,I; the aboriginal TMs¹(u)ᵃ
(*alt. fr.* 'aborige['ne' *typed del.*]nal');
TMs²(u)
52.28   only goes] WJ/TMs¹ᵇ,K/TMs²,I;
can only go TMs¹(u)ᵃ,TMs²(u)
52.29-31   assumes, . . . perspective,]
WJ/TMs¹ᵃ-ᵇ+; ~‸ . . . ~‸ TMs¹(u)
52.31   reality,] WJ/TMs¹ᵃ-ᵇ+; ~‸|
TMs¹(u)
52.32   intellectual] *del. but restored*
WJ/TMs¹ᵇ
52.32   shall] WJ/TMs¹ᵃ-ᵇ+; *om.*
TMs¹(u)
52.34   is, he says.] WJ/TMs¹ᵇ;
~ ‸ ~~. K/TMs²,I; *is.*
TMs¹(u)ᵃ,TMs²(u)
52.35   the . . . metaphysic]
WJ/TMs¹ᵃ-ᵇ+; Bradleyan ['and'
typed del.] philosophy TMs¹(u)
(²'a' *of* 'Bradleyan' *typed ov.* 'y')
52.36   Hegelian] K/TMs²,I; *l.c.* TMs¹
52.36   Dialectic.'] TMs¹ᵃ+; ~.‸ TMs¹ᵇ
52.36   the ladder] WJ/TMs¹ᵃ-ᵇ+; *om.*
TMs¹(u)
52.37   top,] WJ/TMs¹ᵃ(~.)+; top of
the ladder. (Compare, e.g. H. W.
Dresser) TMs¹(u)ᵇ; top of it‸
WJ/TMs¹ᵇ
53.1   *Criticism of Bradley.*]
WJ/TMs¹ᵃ(*red*),TMs²(u); *om.*
TMs¹(u)ᵇ; *s.n.* K/TMs²(*moved*
fr. subh. to s.n.),I
53.3   But,] WJ/TMs¹ᵃ(r2)-ᵇ(r2) (*ov.*
typed |'ley,' *of* 'Brad|ley,')+; To
insist on an 'immediate unity which
comes in feeling' *flutters ['u' *ab.*

del. 'a' WJ/TMs^{1a}(r1)–b(r1)] all the Kantian dovecotes; yet when one exhibits at the same time a virulent anti-empiricist *temper [*ab. del.* 'to tender' WJ/TMs^{1a}(r1)–b(r1)], Kantians can't well throw one out. To my own mind, Mr. Bradley, TMs^{1}(u)

53.4 Mr. Bradley] WJ/TMs^{1a-b}+; *om.* TMs^{1}(u)

53.4 uncriticized–] WJ/TMs^{1a}(r2)–b, TMs^{2}(u); ~ : WJ/TMs^{1a}(r1),K/TMs^{2}; ~ . I; He simply *won't* look back. For him ['the content of' *del.* WJ/TMs^{1a-b}] feeling *simply must [*insrtd. for del.* 'has to' WJ/TMs^{1a-b}] be got away from. *Final truth [*ab. del.* 'The final *truth, [*comma added*]' WJ/TMs^{1a}] *he [*ov.* 'the' WJ/TMs^{1a}; *ov.* 'his' WJ/TMs^{1b}] thinks, must lie [*ab. del.* 'lay forward,' WJ/TMs^{1a-b}] ever farther *forward [*insrtd.* WJ/TMs^{1a-b}] away [*insrtd.* WJ/TMs^{1a}] from *perception, [*comma added* WJ/TMs^{1b}] till the *trans-[*ab. del.* 'terms' WJ/TMs^{1a-b}]conceptual and *super-relational [*period del.* WJ/TMs^{1a-b}] 'Absolute,' [*sg. qts. added* WJ/TMs^{1b}] in whose inner form he though that the lost unity of feeling must 'somehow' wake up again, [*comma added* WJ/TMs^{1a-b}] gets [*insrtd. for del.* 'was' WJ/TMs^{1b}; 'is' *insrtd. for del.* 'was' WJ/TMs^{1a}] reacht. TMs^{1}(u)

53.4-5 perception ... 'truth.'] WJ/TMs^{1b}('p' *ov.* 'P'); perception ['p' *ov.* 'P'] 'untransmuted' ['must not, *he insists [*intrl. in pencil*] cannot, enter' *del.*] he ['h' *ov.* 'b'] believes, *must not, [*intrl.*] cannot, shall not, enter into final 'truth.' WJ/TMs^{1a},TMs^{2}(ˏtruth.' TMs^{2}[u]), I(Perception 'untransmuted,' K/TMs^{2},I); *om.* TMs^{1}(u)

53.7 pathetic: concepts] WJ/TMs^{1a-b}+; ~ . Concepts TMs^{1}(u)

53.8 pursued; percepts] WJ/TMs^{1a-b}+; ~ . Percepts TMs^{1}(u)

53.9 anti-sensationalism] WJ/TMs^{1b}; ~ˏ ~ WJ/TMs^{1a}; antisensationalism

TMs^{2}; ~-|~ I; platonic-rationalistic superstition TMs^{1}(u) (superstitution TMs^{1}[u]^{a})

53.9 an] WJ/TMs^{1a}(r3)+; a mere WJ/TMs^{1a}(r2); an WJ/TMs^{1a}(r1); a mere TMs^{1}(u)^{b}

53.12 contradictions] WJ/TMs^{1a}, K/TMs^{2},I; puzzles and paradoxes TMs^{1}(u)^{b}; conditions TMs^{2}(u)

53.12 sensible] WJ/TMs^{1a-b}+; *om.* TMs^{1}(u)

53.13 help,] WJ/TMs^{1a-b}+; ~ˏ TMs^{1}(u)

53.14 hinder,] WJ/TMs^{1a},TMs^{2}(u); ~ˏ TMs^{1}(u)^{b},K/TMs^{2},I

53.17 There] WJ/TMs^{1a}+; Though there TMs^{1}(u)^{b}

53.17 but] WJ/TMs^{1a}+; *om.* TMs^{1}(u)^{b} [*resume MS*]

53.21 tho] H; though MS+

53.26 *Summary.*] H; *rom. subh.* TMs^{1}, TMs^{2}(u); *in text* MS (*red*); *s.n.* K/TMs^{2} (*moved fr. subh. to s.n.*),I [*end MS*]

53.34 s.,] WJ/TMs^{1b}(*cap.*); ~ .ˏ TMs^{1}(u)^{a}+

53.34 his] WJ/TMs^{1a}+; his Logic, *Bk. I. Ch. I [*typed ov.* 'Chap. I'] & II and his TMs^{1}(u)^{b} [*resume MS*]

53.39 vol. vii, no. 2.] WJ/TMs^{1a}(Vol. viiˏ Nº 2ˏ)+; *om.* MS,TMs^{1}(u)^{b}

‡54.14 out,] I; ~ˏ MS (*error*),TMs$^{1-2}$

54.18 *empiricism,*] WJ/TMs^{1a-b}+; ~ˏ MS,TMs^{1}(u)

§54.22 that] WJ/TMs^{1a}+; which [*comma del.*] [*insrtd.*] MS;TMs^{1}(u)^{b}

§54.24 concrete] WJ/TMs^{1a}+; genuine [*intrl.*] MS;TMs^{1}(u)^{b}

§54.25-26 abstracted] WJ/TMs^{1a}+; always [*del.* 'ready-made *affairs [*ab. del.* 'terms,'] and can ['gr' *del.*] foretell the new only in terms'] drawn, after the fact, MS;TMs^{1}(u)^{b}

54.26 seen or] WJ/TMs^{1a}+; *om.* MS,TMs^{1}(u)^{b}

§54.27 can ... but] WJ/TMs^{1a}+; *can **do so [*insrtd. for del.* 'do so'] ['paint it' *del.*] [*intrl.*] only MS;TMs^{1}(u)^{b}

54.31 extend] WJ/TMs^{1a}+; even extend MS,TMs^{1}(u)^{b}

‡54.31 even a] WJ/TMs¹ᵃ; a
MS,TMs¹(u)ᵇ,TMs²(u); an even
K/TMs²,I

54.33-34 vii, 4.] K/TMs²,I; *space* MS;
om. TMs¹,TMs²(u)

§55.3 abstract] WJ/TMs¹ᵃ+;
makeshift [*ab. del.* 'skeleton or
abstract'] MS;TMs¹(u)ᵇ

55.8 possible,] *stet* MS,TMs¹(u)ᵇ;
~ ₐ WJ/TMs¹ᵃ,K/TMs²(possib |
TMs²[u]),I

*55.11 and . . . into] *stet* MS (*see
Historical Collation for* TMs,I
variants)

§55.12-13 as our . . . grows.]
WJ/TMs¹ᵃ+; *as we [intrl.]* ['by'
del.] *['['following' *del.*] sharing in'
del.] share in [*ab. del.* 'partaking of
the'] perceptual *experience. [*ab.
del.* 'life.'] MS;TMs¹(u)ᵇ

§55.24 altho] H; although [*ab. del.*
'are only'] MS+

55.26 regarded ₐ] TMs¹+; ~ , MS
(*error*)

‡55.33 paragraph] TMs¹+; paragraf MS

55.37 *The*] K/TMs²,I; 'the MS–TMs²(u)

55.38 E. D.] WJ(?)/TMs¹ᵇ,K/TMs²,I;
A. D. MS,TMs¹(u)ᵃ,TMs²(u)

56.2 anything] TMs¹+; any thing MS

‡56.3 of which . . . account]
WJ/TMs¹ᵃ+; which . . . account of
MS,TMs¹(u)ᵇ

§56.8 thus] WJ/TMs¹ᵃ+; then [*intrl.*]
MS;TMs¹(u)ᵇ

56.8 many] *stet* MS,TMs¹(u)ᵃ,TMs²,I;
many interpenetrating WJ/TMs¹ᵇ

‡56.9 reality] WJ/TMs¹ᵃ+; reality in
the universe, MS,TMs¹(u)
(universe ₐ),WJ/TMs¹ᵇ(universe.)

56.9 which . . . interpenetrate.]
WJ/TMs¹ᵃ+; which interpenetrate.
MS,TMs¹(u); *del.* WJ/TMs¹ᵇ

§56.10 logic,] TMs¹+; ~ ₐ [*alt. fr.*
'logical,'] MS (*error*)

§56.19 based;] WJ/TMs¹ᵃ+; ~ ,
[*comma ov. period*] MS;TMs¹(u)ᵇ

56.27 ²common,] H; ~ ; MS
(*clipping*)+

56.37 , p. 51.] K/TMs²,I; ₐ but I
cannot recover the page. ['and
passage.' *del.*] MS;TMs¹,TMs²(u)
(; but)

56.37-38 On . . . *Mathematics.*]
K/TMs²(Nature),I(p)(Nature of
ₐlogicalₐ), I(nature of ₐlogicalₐ);
om. MS,TMs¹(u)ᵇ; Logical reality
Cf. Russell etc. WJ/TMs¹ᵃ(*pencil;
marginal note opp.* What . . . 'real'?
[56.1]),TMs²(u)

§56.39 *Human Mind*] TMs²,I; human
mind [*comma del.*] MS;TMs¹;
Phenomena of the ~ ~ Mill

56.39 (1869), vol. i, p. 249.]
WJ/TMs¹ᵃ(Volₐ I); (18) vol I MS;
(18) Vol I. TMs¹(u)ᵇ; (1869)
Vol I, P. 24 TMs²(u); (1869),
vol i, pₐ 249. K/TMs²; (1869), i,
249. I

‡57.16 'white';] WJ/TMs¹ᵃ+; ₐ~ ,ₐ
MS,TMs¹(u)ᵇ

57.19 (which . . . know)] WJ/TMs¹ᵃ+;
om. MS,TMs¹(u)ᵇ

57.22 therefore] WJ/TMs¹ᵃ+; *om.*
MS,TMs¹(u)ᵇ

§57.26 colour-] TMs¹⁻²; color- [*ab.
del.* 'coul colour'] MS;I

57.27 we mean that] WJ/TMs¹ᵃ+;
om. MS,TMs¹(u)ᵇ

57.29 irrelevant,] WJ/TMs¹ᵃ+; ~ ₐ
MS,TMs¹(u)ᵇ

§57.31 applied] WJ/TMs¹ᵃ+; ['we'
del.] predicated [*final* 'd' *added*]
['it' *del.*] MS;TMs¹(u)ᵇ

57.35 things–] H; ~ , MS,TMs¹,
TMs²(u); ~ ,– K/TMs²,I

57.35 zeros] TMs²,I; zero's MS,TMs¹

§57.38-39 which . . . cue)]
WJ/TMs¹ᵇ; of which the mind
*appoints [*ab. del.* 'possesses'] the
standard, MS;TMs¹(u)ᵃ,TMs²,I

§57.39-40 which . . . disguises.]
WJ/TMs¹ᵇ,K/TMs²,I; and ['of' *del.*]
of [*insrtd.*] which it can *['recognize' *del.*] mean the kind [*ab. del.*
'detect the physical pretence']
under all *the [*added in ink* TMs²]
modifications that ['changing
condit' *del.*] physical conditions
bring. MS;TMs¹(u)ᵃ,TMs²(u)

57.40-58.1 white . . . white]
WJ/TMs¹ᵇ,K/TMs²,I; kind . . . kind
MS,TMs¹(u)ᵃ,TMs²(u)

§58.1 altho] H; although [*ab. del.*
'when' MS] MS+

Emendations

58.3-4 it . . . -identically;] WJ/TMs^{1b}, K/TMs^{2},I; there shall be no difference in it; MS,TMs^{1}(u)^{a},TMs^{2}(u)

§58.4 is false of] WJ/TMs^{1a}, TMs^{2}(u),HJ/TMs$^{2(r2)}$,I; applies *never [ab. del. 'not'] to MS;TMs^{1}(u)^{b},K/TMs$^{2(r1)}$

58.5 and . . . of] WJ/TMs^{1a},TMs^{2}(u), HJ/TMs$^{2(r2)}$,I; but only to MS,TMs^{1}(u)^{b},K/TMs$^{2(r1)}$

‡58.7 singulars,] WJ/TMs^{1a-b}+; ∼$_∧$ MS; singular$_∧$ TMs^{1}(u)

‡58.7 ^{1}that] WJ/TMs^{1b},K/TMs^{2},I; and MS,WJ/TMs^{1a} [possibly intrl. 'i' ab. del. 'that'] ,TMs^{2}(u); and that TMs^{1}(u)

§58.7 is] WJ/TMs^{1b},K/TMs^{2},I; del. MS; om. TMs^{1}(u)^{a},TMs^{2}(u)

58.11 rationalism,] WJ/TMs^{1a}+; ∼$_∧$ MS,TMs^{1}(u)^{b}

§58.18 kind of] WJ/TMs^{1a}+; *kinds of [intrl.] MS;TMs^{1}(u)^{b}

58.19 otherwise] TMs^{1}+; other wise MS (doubtful spacing)

§58.24 much,] WJ/TMs^{1a}+; ∼$_∧$ MS [comma del.];TMs^{1}(u)^{b}

§58.24 intellect,] WJ/TMs^{1a}+; memory and intellect[', goes out to meet it,' del.] MS;TMs^{1}(u)^{b}

‡58.29-30 indefinitely;] WJ/TMs^{1a}+; ∼ , MS,TMs^{1}(u)^{b}

§58.33 joint.] WJ/TMs^{1a-b}+; joint ['t' ov. 'ed [ov. 's'] '], ['the other,' del.] the [alt. fr. 'they'] whole [insrtd. for del. 'lock [ab. del. 'fuses into *a [undel. in error]']'] *forms such a [intrl.] unity. MS;TMs^{1}(u)

58.33-59.9 The . . . elements.] WJ/TMs^{1b},K/TMs^{2},I; om. MS,TMs^{1}(u)^{a},TMs^{2}(u) (insrtd. in TMs^{1b} opp. mrgn. note 'This ought to be expanded | The entire world that we dwell in & deal with is a world in which it is impossible to disentangle (except by theoretic analysis) the contributions of intellect from those of sense. [begin pencil] They are inextricably wrapped & netted with each other and they ['never' del.] work together when they work at all')

58.33 practically] ab. del. 'concretely'

58.33 is one] aft. del. 'and deal with'

58.34 by theoretic] 'by [ab. del. 'in'] theoretic' intrl.

58.34 retrospection)] bef. del. 'and *in [ab. del. 'by'] theory)'

58.37 and] WJ/TMs^{1a}+; and the MS,TMs^{1}(u)^{b}

59.1 They] 'y' added; bef. del. 'latter'

59.2 together] ab. del. 'in the former'

59.2 the mountains] ab. del. 'a ravine'

59.3 echo] aft. del. 'reverberating'

59.3 reverberative] 've' ov. 'on'

59.3 clamor.] intrl.

59.3 Even] aft. del. 'The intellectual reverberations'

59.3 do] ab. del. 'the'

59.4 enlarge and] *enlarge ['spread' del.] and [ab. del. 'spread out and']

59.4 prolong] bef. del. 'and make significant'

59.4-5 experience] aft. del. 'conta'

59.5 associating] aft. del. 'while [ab. del. 'and'] They connect *as they associate [intrl.] it with *the [intrl.] remoter percepts, so also with which'

59.5 parts] aft. del. 'associated'

59.6 existence.] period added in red

59.6 And . . . these] *And [red] **the ideas of [black] these [red] [ab. del. 'which again,']

59.6 work] ab. del. ', work'

59.6 those] ab. del. 'the'

59.7 that] insrtd.

59.7 pick out partial] ab. del. 'that *emphasize ['e' ab. del. 'ing' ov. 'e'] particular'

59.7 partial] (error of repetition); ab. del. 'over' of 'overtones'

59.7 sounds. They] sounds. [period in red aft. red del. comma] [del. intrl. 'and'] They [intrl. in red]

59.8 our . . . parts] *our ['the' del.] percept['s' del.] ['structure' del.] into parts [ab. del. '['its' del.] into its own elements']

59.8-9 ^{2}and . . . elements.] alt. fr. '*and isolate the elements **of its immediacy. [alt. fr. 'it may *consist [ov. 'contain'] of'] [insrtd. for del. verso of 111^{b}, numbered 110^{c}: 'and isolate ['these latter.' del.] the elements it may contain.']

306

‡59.10   The] WJ/TMs^{1b},K/TMs^2,I;
Even so do the MS,TMs^1(u)^a,
TMs^2(u)

59.10   thus play] WJ/TMs^{1b}(r2),
K/TMs^2,I; play MS,TMs^1(u)^a,
TMs^2(u); $\sim\sim$ incessantly
WJ/TMs^{1b}(r1)

§59.11   awakens] WJ/TMs^{1b}; prompts
[*ab. del.* 'evokes'] our [*intrl.*]
MS;TMs^1(u)^a+

59.11-12   perception] WJ/TMs^{1b}; our
perception MS,TMs^1(u)^a+

‡59.12   see,] WJ/TMs^{1a}+; $\sim_{\wedge}$
MS,TMs^1(u)^b

‡59.12   think;] WJ/TMs^{1a-b}+; $\sim$,
MS,TMs^1(u)

‡59.12   while] WJ/TMs^{1b},
K/TMs^2(r2),I; and MS,TMs^1(u)^a,
TMs^2(u),K/TMs^2(r1)

‡59.13   think,] WJ/TMs^{1a}+; $\sim_{\wedge}$
MS,TMs^1(u)^b

59.13   immediate] WJ/TMs^{1b},
K/TMs^2(r2),I; perceptual MS,
TMs^1(u)^a,TMs^2(u),K/TMs^2(r1)

59.14   the detail, . . . significant]
WJ/TMs^{1b},K/TMs^2(r2)(detail$_{\wedge}$),I
(detail$_{\wedge}$); *om.* MS,TMs^1(u)^a,TMs^2(u),
K/TMs^2(r1)

§59.15   our perception.]
WJ/TMs^{1b}(r2),K/TMs^2(r2),I; what
we life through. WJ/TMs^{1b}(r1);
our [*intrl.*] immediacy.
MS;TMs^1(u)^a,TMs^2(u),K/TMs^2(r1)

59.16-23   ¶ Later . . . suffice.]
WJ/TMs^{1b},K/TMs^2,I (*no* ¶); *om.*
MS,TMs^1(u)^a,TMs^2(u)

59.17   momentous] *ab. del.* 'important
this'

59.18   through] *ab. del.* 'by'

59.18   wrapping] *ab. del.* 'envelop-
ment'

59.18   our] *intrl.*

59.18   whole] *ab. del.* 'whole'

59.19   of both] *ab. del.* 'that'

59.22   the] *ab. del.* 'our'

59.22   stage] *ab. del.* 'point'

59.22 ^{1}of] *ov.* 'in'

59.22   our] *insrtd. for del.* 'the'

59.22-23   mention of it] *ab. del.*
'indication'

59.24-25   , however important]
WJ/TMs^{1b}; *om.* MS,TMs^1(u)^a+

59.25-26   may . . . they] WJ/TMs^{1b};
om. MS,TMs^1(u)^a+

59.26   secondary$_{\wedge}$ . . . ministerial$_{\wedge}$]
TMs^1+; $\sim$, . . . $\sim$, MS

§59.26   and ministerial$_{\wedge}$] WJ/TMs^{1b};
*and on the whole [*ab. del.* 'and']
imperfect, *& ['on [*ov.* 'min'] the
whole' *del.*] ministerial, [*intrl.*]
MS;WJ/TMs^{1a}+ (*no commas*);
and . . . imperfect$_{\wedge}$ ministerial$_{\wedge}$
TMs^1(u)

§59.32-33   and . . . experience.]
WJ/TMs^{1a}+; *and ['to have' *del.*]
given ['back' *del.*] a ['good' *del.*]
reflectively good [*ab. del.* '*restored
[*ab. del.* 'married'] a good [*ab. del.*
'restore a good conscience']']
conscience to our instinctive
*dealings [*intrl. for del.* '*attitudes
towards [*ab. del.* 'relations to']']
*with immediate experience. [*ab.
del.* 'reality.']' MS;TMs^1(u)^b ('a'
added)

59.35   p. 234] K/TMs^2,I(p)(9, p. 234),
I(234); 9 WJ/TMs^{1b}; *om.* MS,
TMs^1(u)^a,TMs^2(u)

‡59.35-40   —The . . . formation.]
marked as fn. WJ/TMs^{1b};K/TMs^2,I
($_{\wedge}$The); *as text* MS,TMs^1(u)^a,
TMs^2(u) (*all* $_{\wedge}$The)

59.37   are enabled to] WJ/TMs^{1b};
om. MS,TMs^1(u)^a+

59.39   repeat] WJ/TMs^{1a}+; say
MS,TMs^1(u)^b

‡59.39   be] WJ/TMs^{1a}; ever be
MS,TMs^1(u)^b+

59.39   *full*] WJ/TMs^{1a}+; full
MS,TMs^1(u)^b

60.1   "Other . . . world,"]
WJ/TMs^{1a-b},TMs^2; "Other world?"
. . . "there . . . world,$_{\wedge}$ TMs^1(u);
'Other world?" . . . 'there . . . world,'
MS; *all sg. qts.* I

60.2   one, namely,] WJ/TMs^{1a}+;
om. MS,TMs^1(u)^b

‡60.2   biographies] TMs^1+;
biografies MS

60.2-5   "Natur . . . seist."] H;
'Natur . . . Schale,' . . . $_{\wedge}$Alles . . .
seist.' MS; 'Natur . . . seist.' TMs^1+

60.3   Kern noch] *stet* MS+;
Kern | Noch   Goethe

60.4   Male.] WJ/TMs^{1a–b}+; ∼ :
MS,TMs¹(u)

60.4   Dich . . . allermeist,] Goethe,
K/TMs²,I; Erprüfe du am allermeist_∧
MS,WJ/TMs^{1a},TMs²(u); Erprüfe du
an allermeist_∧ TMs¹(u)^b

60.4   Ob] Goethe,I; ob MS–TMs²

60.4   ²du] Goethe,TMs¹+; *du* MS

60.6   sensibly] WJ/TMs^{1a}; *om.*
MS,TMs¹(u)^b,K/TMs²,I; feel
sensibly TMs²(u)

60.6   squeeze] WJ/TMs^{1b},K/TMs²,I;
pinch MS,TMs¹(u)^a,TMs²(u)

60.6   life,] WJ/TMs^{1a–b}+; ∼_∧
MS,TMs¹(u)

60.7   or] WJ/TMs^{1a}+; and
MS,TMs¹(u)^b

60.8   to] TMs¹+; *om.* MS (*error*)

60.10   ¶But] WJ/TMs^{1a(r2)}+;
no ¶ MS,TMs¹(u)^b; –But
WJ/TMs^{1a(r1)}

60.13   ¹is] TMs¹+; *om.* MS

‡60.14   cows] WJ/TMs^{1a}+; dogs
MS,TMs¹(u)^b

‡60.15;62.14   established] TMs²,I;
establisht MS,TMs¹

‡60.17   on . . . the] WJ/TMs^{1b},
K/TMs²,I; , so far as that WJ/TMs^{1a},
TMs²(u); , so far as the MS,TMs¹(u)

60.17   "reality"] I; '∼' MS–I(p)

§60.17   with] WJ/TMs^{1b},K/TMs²,I;
goes [*comma del.*] with [*intrl.*] MS;
goes, with TMs¹(u)^a,TMs²(u)
(*comma undel. in error* K/TMs²)

§60.18   reasoning] WJ/TMs^{1b},
K/TMs²,I; reasonings [*alt. fr.*
'reasoning'] MS;TMs¹(u)^a, TMs²(u)

‡60.18   has now endowed] H; have
now endowed WJ/TMs^{1a},TMs²(u);
endow MS,TMs¹(u); endows
WJ/TMs^{1b},K/TMs²,I

60.20   have to] WJ/TMs^{1a–b}+; to
TMs¹(u); ['have *had to* [*intrl.*]'
del.] MS

§60.20   employ] WJ/TMs^{1a}+; employ
['ed' *del. ab. del.* 'ed'] them *no less
when* [*ab. del.* 'both in our']
attempting['ing' *added*] to undermine MS;TMs¹(u)^b

60.20   even] WJ/TMs^{1a}+; than
MS,TMs¹(u)^b

60.23   *designative*;] WJ/TMs^{1a}+;

designative, MS,TMs¹(u)^b(*rom.*)

60.24–25   perception,] WJ/TMs^{1a}+;
∼_∧ MS,TMs¹(u)^b

60.26   Will,_∧] WJ/TMs^{1a}+ (∼ , ['a
relation' *del. intrl.*] K/TMs²); ∼ ,^x
MS,TMs¹(u)^b

§60.26   *perceptively experienced*,³⁵]
WJ/TMs^{1a}+; ∼ ∼ ,_∧ (*rom.*) [*insrtd.*]
MS;TMs¹(u)^b(*rom.*)

60.29   concepts] I; *cap.* MS (*unreduced in error*),TMs^{1–2}

§60.29   can] WJ/TMs^{1b},K/TMs²,I;
can *thus* [*intrl.*] MS;TMs¹(u)^a,
TMs²(u)

60.30   concepts_∧] WJ/TMs^{1a–b}+; ∼ ,
MS,TMs¹(u)

§60.30   is one of . . . functions]
WJ/TMs^{1b(r2)}(*red*);K/TMs²(of
['the' *del.*]);I; and re-locate
them[': thus [*colon ov. period*;
't' *ov.* 'T'] *del.*] we have seen to
be ['part of' *del.*] their ['map-making
function' *del.*] great practical function. MS;TMs¹(u) (them,
WJ/TMs^{1a–b}[r1],TMs²[u])

60.37–38   'The . . . Reality.'] TMs²;
all l.c. MS,TMs¹; "∼ . . . ∼.' I

60.39   *Pluralistic*] TMs²,I; pluralistic
MS,TMs¹

‡61.0   *Chapter* . . . Many] WJ/TMs^{1a},
TMs²(u)(*both omit chap. number*),
HJ/TMs^{2(r2)}(VII), I(VII); One &
Many MS,TMs¹(u)^b; *Third Problem*
['*III*' *del.*] –THE ONE AND THE
MANY. | Chapter VIII Monism
versus [*ab. del.* 'and'] Pluralism
K/TMs^{2(r1)}

61.1   , as . . . amount,] WJ/TMs^{1a}+;
om. MS,TMs¹(u)^b

‡§61.2   _∧ to be given] WJ/TMs^{1a},
K/TMs²+; , to be given TMs²(u);
, is ['only' *del.*] found MS;TMs¹(u)^b

61.2   But_∧ tho] H; But tho' WJ/TMs^{1a};
But, though TMs²,I; Tho MS,
TMs¹(u)^b

‡61.5   disconnection] TMs²,I;
disconnexion MS,TMs¹

§61.9–10   (provisionally . . . rate)]
WJ/TMs^{1a(r2)}+; _∧∼ . . . ∼_∧
TMs¹(u)^b; , *∼ . . . ∼ , [*intrl.*]
MS;WJ/TMs^{1a(r1)}

‡61.14   notion_∧] WJ/TMs^{1a}; ∼ ,

MS,TMs¹(u)ᵇ+

§61.19 entire universe,] WJ/TMs¹ᵃ+;
world [*ab. del.* 'universe'] , MS;
TMs¹(u)ᵇ

61.21 *un seul fait*] *stet* MS+ (*rom.*
TMs¹⁻²); qu'un fait unique
d'Alembert

§62.2 collectively?–] WJ/TMs¹ᵃ+;
~‸‸ TMs¹(u)ᵇ; ~ ?‸ [*qst. mk.
ab. del. comma*] MS

§62.5 *cuncti,*] I; ~ ? [*qst. mk. over
comma*] MS;TMs¹⁻²

62.5 *sämmtliche,*] H; ~‸ WJ/TMs¹ᵃ+;
~ ? MS,TMs¹(u)ᵇ

62.9-10 between ... assumes]
WJ/TMs¹ᵃ+; *om.* MS,TMs¹(u)ᵇ

62.12-13 *anything ... anything*]
WJ/TMs¹ᵃ+; *both ital.* MS; *rom.*
TMs¹(u)ᵇ

‡62.12-13 infinitesimal,] TMs¹+;
~‸ MS (*error*)

62.13 enough,] WJ/TMs¹ᵃ+; ~‸
MS,TMs¹(u)ᵇ

62.16-17 'no disconnection,']
WJ/TMs¹ᵃ+; '~' [*final qt. typed ov.*
'n'] ~‚‸ TMs¹(u)ᵇ; '~' ~ , MS

62.19 bank-account] WJ/TMs¹ᵃ+;
~‸ ~ MS,TMs¹(u)ᵇ

§62.22 in ... believes,] WJ/TMs¹ᵃ,
K/TMs²,I; which it believes,
TMs²(u); which [*insrtd.*] it
believes *in, [*comma over period*]
MS;TMs¹(u)ᵇ

62.26 the ultimate] WJ/TMs¹ᵃ⁽ʳ²⁾+;
the deep WJ/TMs¹ᵃ⁽ʳ¹⁾; its
MS,TMs¹(u)ᵇ

62.30-31 of them] Plotinus
(Bakewell); *om.* MS+

62.35 ¹overflows‸] *stet* Plotinus
(Bakewell),MS,TMs¹(u)ᵇ; ~ ,
WJ/TMs¹ᵃ+

62.36 How] *stet* MS+; How then
Plotinus (Bakewell)

62.38 , then,] Plotinus (Bakewell);
‸~‸ MS+

62.39 *Source Book*] H; source book
MS,TMs¹; Source book TMs²(u);
Source-book K/TMs²; *Source-Book* I

63.1-2 *Bhagavad-gita*] H; Bhagavat-gita
MS+

63.6 universe,–] Bhagavad-gita
(Thomson); ~‸– MS+

63.7 'Om!'] Bhagavad-gita(Thomson);
'~‸' MS+

63.21 God] WJ/TMs¹ᵃ+; god
MS,TMs¹(u)ᵇ

63.24 But this] TMs²,I; But This
WJ/TMs¹ᵃ; This MS,TMs¹(u)ᵇ

63.25 for ... explicit,]
WJ/TMs¹ᵃ⁽ʳ²⁾+; for ... talkative,
or explicit, WJ/TMs¹ᵃ⁽ʳ¹⁾; *om.*
MS,TMs¹(u)ᵇ

‡63.27 philosophic] TMs¹+;
filosofic MS

63.29 -370,] TMs¹+; - ~‸ MS

63.29 M. N.] H; F. MS+

63.30 translation.] TMs¹+; ~‸ MS

63.31 ix] H; VI MS,TMs¹;
6 TMs²-I(p); iv I

‡63.32 mystic,] TMs¹+; ~‸ MS

‡§63.33-40 "Allah ... asked.'"] H;
'~ ... *~.‸' [*sg. qt. ov. db. qt.*]
MS+

‡63.33 Allah] *stet* MS+; He Macdonald

‡§63.36 obedience, and] Macdonald;
~ . [*period alt. fr. semicolon*] And
['A' *ov.* 'a'] MS+

‡63.36 Fire‸] Macdonald; ~ , MS+

‡63.37 Prophet,] Macdonald; ~ : MS+

‡63.38 'These ... not.'] Macdonald;
"~ ... ~ ." MS+

‡§63.38 Garden‸] Macdonald; ~ ,
['G' *triple underl.*] MS+

‡63.39 Allah‸] Macdonald; ~ ,
the MS+

‡63.39 Reality;] Macdonald; ~ . MS+

‡63.39-40 'He ... asked.']
Macdonald; ‸~ ... ~ .‸ MS+

63.40 Macdonald's] Macdonald;
MacDonald MS+

‡63.40 translation,] K/TMs²,I;
Translation, WJ/TMs¹ᵃ,TMs²(u);
Translation‸ MS,TMs¹(u)ᵇ

63.41 *The*] K/TMs²,I; the
MS–TMs²(u)

64.3-4 *Ens ... existendum*]
WJ/TMs¹ᵃ+; *rom.* MS,TMs¹(u)ᵇ

64.3-4 *tamquam*] TMs¹+; tanquam MS

‡64.4 'substance'] WJ/TMs¹ᵃ+;
‸~‸ MS,TMs¹(u)ᵇ

64.4 first] WJ/TMs¹ᵃ+; *om.*
MS,TMs¹(u)ᵇ

64.5 distinguished] TMs²,I;

distinguisht MS,TMs[1]

§64.5-6 'accidents' (which . . . inhesion—] WJ/TMs[1a]+; '~,' ~ . . . *~ ([*paren ov. comma*] MS;TMs[1](u)[b]

64.6 *cujus . . . inesse*] WJ/TMs[1a]+; *rom.* MS,TMs[1](u)[b]

§64.6 *inesse*) . . . identified] WJ/TMs[1a]+; inesse), ['and' *del.*] identified MS;TMs[1](u)[b]

64.8 for . . . into] WJ/TMs[1a]+; as MS,TMs[1](u)[b]

64.9-10 individual,] TMs[1]+; ~ ₍ MS (*error*)

§64.11 *a se*;] WJ/TMs[1a]+; ~ ~ , [*comma ov. period*] MS;TMs[1](u)[b]

64.12 also] WJ/TMs[1a]+; *om.* MS,TMs[1](u)[b]

§64.13 exist] TMs[1]+; *exist*['ed' *del.*] MS

64.13 tho . . . *se*.] WJ/TMs[1a]+; *om.* MS,TMs[1](u)[b]

‡§64.13 , for scholasticism,] WJ/TMs[1a]+; ₍ ~ ['For ['F' *ov.* 'f']' *del.*] ~ ₍ MS;TMs[1](u)[b]

64.17 *Ethics*] H; 'Ethics' MS+

64.20 *Metaphysics*] K/TMs[2],I; *rom.* TMs[1],TMs[2](u); *rom. l.c.* MS

64.20 A.] TMs[1]+; ~ ₍ MS

64.21 *Metaphysicae*] K/TMs[2],I; *rom.* TMs[1],TMs[2](u); *rom. (l.c. doubtful)* MS

64.22-32 [5]Spinosa . . . type:—] WJ/TMs[1a](type₍₍)+ (*see* Historical Collation *entry* 64.22); *om. fn.* MS,TMs[1](u)[b]

64.22 expressed] TMs[2]+; exprest TMs[1a]

64.22 Part I of] ('of' *ov. period*); *moved by guideline fr. aft.* '*Ethics*:' [64.22] *to aft.* 'in' [64.22] *in error, and then correctly to aft.* 'to' [64.22]

64.23-29 "I . . . potentiality."] H; *all sg. qts.* TMs[1a]+

64.23 now] *ab. del.* 'thus'

64.23 he says,] *intrl.*

64.31 out of] *ab. del.* 'by'

64.32 type:—] K/TMs[2],I; ~:₍ TMs[2](u); ~ ₍₍ TMs[1a]

64.32-44 "The . . . Universe."] TMs[1a](". . . . The [*ink* 'T' *ov.* 't'])+;

om. MS,TMs[1b]

64.43-44 Universe."] TMs[2],I; ~.₍ TMs[1a]; ~₍ " WJ/TMs[1a]

64.44-45 (Solomon . . . -13.)] WJ/TMs[1a](-13₍; *ov. pencil note* 'Silberstein')+; *om.* TMs[1](u)[b]

64.44 J.] *intrl.*

64.45 1896,] H; 1906. [*final paren del.*] TMs[1a];TMs[2](u); 1906, K/TMs[2],I

65.2 philosophers] TMs[1]+; filosofers MS

65.2-3 spinosistic] H; spinozistic WJ/TMs[1a]+; *om.* MS,TMs[1](u)[b]

65.9 clear] *stet* MS+; *clear* Locke

65.9 all . . .] H; ~ , MS+

65.9-10 *supposition . . . what*] *stet* MS; *all rom.* Locke,TMs[1]+

65.10 *what* . . .] H; ~ , MS; what, TMs[1]+

65.10 substratum] *stet* MS+; *ital.* Locke

65.10 support,] Locke; ~ ₍ MS+

§65.12 self- . . . minds.] WJ/TMs[1a]+; *our different mind's [ab. del.* 'our'] self-sameness. ['Rather' *del.*] MS; TMs[1](u)[b]

65.13 *Experientially*,] WJ/TMs[1a]+; ~ ₍ MS;TMs[1](u)[b](*rom.*)

‡65.13 said,] TMs[1]+; ~ ₍ MS

65.14 and perceptible] WJ/TMs[1a]+; *om.* MS,TMs[1](u)[b]

65.17 'being,' in general,] H; 'being₍'~ ~ , WJ/TMs[1a-2]; "being₍" ~ ~ , I; 'being₍₍~ ~' TMs[1](u)[b]; '*being, in general*,' MS

§65.19 *material substance*,] Berkeley; 'material substance,' WJ/TMs[1a-2]; "material substance," I; ₍material [*intrl.*] substance,₍ MS;TMs[1](u)[b]

65.20 Suppose] *stet* MS+; Suppose— what no one can deny possible— Berkeley

§65.21 bodies,] Berkeley; *~₍ ['(i.e. *corporeal [ab. del.* 'material'] substances)' *del.*] MS+

65.22 or ideas] Berkeley; *om.* MS+

65.22 order₍] Berkeley; ~ , MS+

65.26 thing?] Berkeley; ~ . MS+

§65.26-27 *grouped sensations*] WJ/TMs[1a]+; grouped [*intrl.*] sensations MS,TMs[1](u)[b]

§65.29 that it denotes] WJ/TMs¹ᵃ+; to ['desig' *del.*] denote MS;TMs¹(u)ᵇ

65.32 means] WJ/TMs¹ᵃ+; causes MS,TMs¹(u)ᵇ

§65.37 but the] WJ/TMs¹ᵃ+; *as so many [*in pencil ab. pencil del.* 'are'] MS;TMs¹(u)ᵇ

65.37 so many] WJ/TMs¹ᵃ(*moved fr. bef.* 'names')+; *om.* MS,TMs¹(u)ᵇ

‡65.38 be, . . . rather] WJ/TMs¹ᵃ+; be‸ MS,TMs¹(u)ᵇ

‡65.39 hidden] WJ/TMs¹ᵃ,K/TMs²,I; *om.* TMs²(u); buried MS,TMs¹(u)ᵇ

65.40 *Concerning*] H; concerning WJ/TMs¹ᵃ+ (*ital.* TMs²,I); conc. MS,TMs¹(u)ᵇ

65.40 *Human Understanding*] K/TMs²,I; *l.c. rom.* WJ/TMs¹ᵃ, TMs²(u); H. J. MS,TMs¹(u)ᵇ

65.41 *Ibid.*] WJ/TMs¹ᵃ,K/TMs²,I(p); *rom.* MS,TMs¹(u)ᵇ,TMs²(u),I

65.42 *Human*] I; human MS-TMs²

§66.5 , calling it 'mine.'] WJ/TMs¹ᵃ+; past. [*period aft. del. comma*] ['at every moment.' *del.*] MS;TMs¹(u)ᵇ

‡66.7 permanently . . . cluster] WJ/TMs¹ᵃ(r2)+; spatially . . . cluster MS;TMs¹(u)ᵇ(spacially); spatially . . . permanent cluster WJ/TMs¹ᵃ(r1)

66.10 "We] H; ‸ ~ MS (*error*); '~ TMs¹+

66.10 have] *stet* MS+; have therefore Hume

§66.13–15 ideas, . . . imagination, . . . them,] Hume; ~‸ . . . ~‸ . . . ['to' *del.*] ~‸ MS+

§66.15 recal] *stet* MS[*final* 'l' *del.*] (recall TMs²,I)+; recal, either to ourselves or others, Hume

66.16 Hume's‸] TMs¹+; ~ , MS (*error*)

‡66.18 name,] TMs¹+; ~‸ MS

‡66.21 intelligible‸] TMs¹+; ~ , MS

‡66.25 *principle,*] TMs¹+ (*rom.*); ~‸ MS (*error*)

‡66.26–27 *specific . . . connexions*] WJ/TMs¹ᵃ+; *rom.* MS,TMs¹(u)ᵇ

§66.32 easily conceive] WJ/TMs¹ᵃ+; *easily frame a [*intrl.*] concept [*alt. fr.* 'conceive'] MS; easily frame a conception TMs¹(u)ᵇ

66.35 *of*] H; on MS-TMs²(u); *on* K/TMs²,I

66.36 *Critique . . . Reason*] K/TMs²,I; Critique of pure reason WJ/TMs¹ᵃ, TMs²(u); K.d.r.V. TMs¹(u)ᵇ; K.d.r.V. MS (*in MS fn.* 11 *occurs in two separate entries, the first* ['K. . . . Experience.'] *keyed to* intelligible [66.19–20], *the second* ['For . . . synonymous.'] *to word* [66.22]. *The two are amalgamated in* TMs¹ᵃ, *keyed to* word *but keyed in error to* intelligible *in* K/TMs²,I)

66.37 *System*] TMs²,I; system MS,TMs¹

67.1 even] WJ/TMs¹ᵃ+; *om.* MS,TMs¹(u)ᵇ

‡67.2 another,] WJ/TMs¹ᵃ+; ~‸ MS,TMs¹(u)ᵇ

‡§67.5 diversity,] TMs¹+; *['coexistence' *del.*] ~‸ [*ab. del.* 'together'] MS

‡67.5 however;] WJ/TMs¹ᵃ+; ~ , MS,TMs¹(u)ᵇ

‡67.6 the . . . them] WJ/TMs¹ᵃ+; they MS,TMs¹(u)ᵇ

67.12 abstract] *stet* MS,TMs¹(u)ᵇ; *del.* WJ/TMs¹ᵃ+

‡§67.12–13 together‸ . . . noun] WJ/TMs¹ᵇ(*pencil*); ~ , . . . ~ K/TMs²,I; together *as what [*ab. del.* '[', of' *del.*] or ['forming ['a collective' *del.*] an abstract' *del.*] being the object of'] an abstract collective noun ['may' *del.*] denotes. ['s' *added*] MS;TMs¹(u); together, for that is all that an abstract collective noun denotes WJ/TMs¹ᵃ, TMs²(u)

‡67.14 perceived,] H; ~‸ MS+

‡67.15 fact,] WJ/TMs¹ᵃ+; ~‸ MS,TMs¹(u)ᵇ

‡67.16 'world'] WJ/TMs¹ᵃ+; ‸~‸ MS,TMs¹(u)ᵇ

67.20,22,23 *gravitation . . . chemically . . . physical*] WJ/TMs¹ᵃ+; *rom.* MS,TMs¹(u)ᵇ

‡67.23–24 connexions‸ are] WJ/TMs¹ᵃ⁻ᵇ+; connexions, TMs¹(u); connexions‸ MS (*error*)

67.27 many,] WJ/TMs¹ᵃ+; ~‸ MS,TMs¹(u)ᵇ

67.28 towards] WJ/TMs¹ᵃ+; to MS,TMs¹(u)ᵇ

67.36 well-] TMs²,I; ['p' *del.*]
well‸ ['w' *ov.* 'p'] WJ/TMs¹ᵃ;
om. MS,TMs¹(u)ᵇ

67.37 ¹the . . . manyness]
WJ/TMs¹ᵃ(r2)+; oneness or
manyness WJ/TMs¹ᵃ(r1); *om.*
MS,TMs¹(u)ᵇ

67.38 attribute] WJ/TMs¹ᵃ+; *om.* MS,
TMs¹(u)ᵇ

68.12 heterogeneity] TMs²,I;
heterogenity MS,TMs¹

§68.20 at one stroke] WJ/TMs¹ᵃ+;
at once [intrl.] MS;TMs¹(u)ᵇ

68.21 part] WJ/TMs¹ᵃ+; single part
MS,TMs¹(u)ᵇ

68.21 post-kantian] H; post-Kantian
MS; *om.* TMs¹+

68.23 Substance] WJ/TMs¹ᵃ+; *l.c.*
MS,TMs¹(u)ᵇ

68.25 one] WJ/TMs¹ᵃ+; One
MS,TMs¹(u)ᵇ

‡68.33 According . . . everything]
WJ/TMs¹ᵃ+; Everything MS,
TMs¹(u)ᵇ

68.33 known‸] WJ/TMs¹ᵃ+; ~,
MS,TMs¹(u)ᵇ

68.35 act–] H; ~,– MS+

68.36-37 and Z possibly] WJ/TMs¹ᵃ+;
Z MS,TMs¹(u)ᵇ

§68.37 A again,] WJ/TMs¹ᵃ+; A,
['A' *ov.* 'a'] again *(or not)
[parens ov. commas]* MS;TMs¹(u)ᵇ

68.38 ‸concatenated‸] WJ/TMs¹ᵇ
(pencil); '~' MS,TMs¹(u)ᵃ+

68.39 ‸consolidated‸] WJ/TMs¹ᵇ
(pencil); '~' MS,TMs¹(u)ᵃ+

§69.1 supposed . . . the] WJ/TMs¹ᵃ+;
*exercised by the supposed [ab.
del.* '['of the' *del.]* an'] MS;
TMs¹(u)ᵇ

‡69.3-4 is . . . others.] WJ/TMs¹ᵃ+;
others know. MS,TMs¹(u)ᵇ

69.5 systems of concatenation]
WJ/TMs¹ᵃ+; concatenated systems
MS,TMs¹(u)ᵇ

69.5 besides] TMs¹+; beside MS

§69.5-6 noetic concatenation.]
WJ/TMs¹ᵃ+; *noetic system. [ab.
del.* 'noetic sy network of
knowing.'] MS;TMs¹(u)ᵇ

69.10-12 telephone . . . telephones]
TMs¹+; telefone . . . telefones MS

69.16 love] WJ/TMs¹ᵇ*(pencil)*,
K/TMs²,I; affection MS,TMs¹(u)ᵃ,
TMs²(u)

[begin Syllabus proof]

69.18-20 so . . . . Gravitation]
WJ/MS(s)+; conforming to the
concatenated type of union.
Gravitation ['but g' del.; 'G'
underdotted WJ/MS(s)] MS(s)

69.19 are] WJ/TMs¹ᵇ*(pencil)*,
K/TMs²,I; get MS(s),TMs¹(u)ᵃ,
TMs²(u)

69.19 can] *bef. del.* '['get ['onto' *or*
'contra' *del.*] on to another' *del.*]
usually get'

69.19 be] WJ/TMs¹ᵇ*(pencil)*,K/TMs²,
I; get MS(s),TMs¹(u)ᵃ,TMs²(u)

69.19 something else,] WJ/TMs¹ᵇ,
K/TMs²,I; some *thing else,
[insrtd. for del. 'other,'] MS(s);
TMs¹(u)ᵃ,TMs²(u)

69.20 ever] *intrl.*

69.20 your] *ov.* 'this'

69.20-21 positively known]
WJ/MS(s)+; *om.* MS(s)

69.22 monistic] WJ/MS(s)+; through
and through MS(s)

69.22 *mass*] WJ/MS(s); 'mass'
WJ/TMs¹ᵃ,K/TMs²,I; ‸mass‸ MS(s),
TMs¹(u)ᵇ,TMs²(u)

69.22-23 anywhere,] WJ/MS(s)+;
~ ‸ MS(s)

69.25 Teleological] H; ['5.' *del.*]
Unity of Purpose, Meaning, Story.—
Teleological MS(s),TMs¹,TMs²(u);
Unity of Purpose, Meaning [', *Story*,'
del. HJ?] *(s.n.)* K/TMs²*(moved fr.
subh. to s.n.)*;I

69.25 other forms] WJ/MS(s)+; one
form MS(s)

69.26 That] WJ/MS(s)+; But that
MS(s)

69.27 form] WJ/MS(s)+; should form
MS(s)

69.27 inclusive story] WJ/TMs¹ᵃ+;
history MS(s),TMs¹(u)ᵇ

69.28 the monistic] WJ/MS(s)+; a
pure MS(s)

69.28 *seem*] WJ/TMs¹ᵃ+; *rom.* MS(s),
TMs¹(u)ᵇ

69.28 , meanwhile, simply]
WJ/MS(s)+; *om.* MS(s)

69.29 alongside] WJ/TMs^{1a}+; $\sim_\wedge\sim$ MS(s),TMs^1(u)^b

69.29 other–] WJ/TMs^{1a}+; $\sim$, MS(s),TMs^1(u)^b

69.29 or,] WJ/TMs^{1a}+; $\sim_\wedge$ MS(s), TMs^1(u)^b

69.30 to mutual frustrations–] WJ/TMs^{1a}+ (frustrations,–); either to frustrations or to mutual compromises, WJ/MS(s) (compromises. MS[s]), TMs^1(u)^b

69.30-31 so . . . view.] WJ/MS(s)+; On pp. 20–21 of this syllabus we saw how hard it is to find one single harmonious story in the world. MS(s)

69.31 this . . . view] WJ/TMs^{1a}+; the [*ov.* 'this'] purposive [*intrl.*] point of view. ['of purpose.' *del.*] MS(s); TMs^1(u)^b

69.32 It] H; ['6.' *del.*] *Unity of Origin.*–It MS(s),TMs^1,TMs^2(u); *Unity of Origin.* (*s.n.*) K/TMs^2 (*moved fr. subh. to s.n.*),I

69.35 absolute] WJ/MS(s)+; *cap.* MS(s)

69.36 results] WJ/MS(s)+; atoms or 'monads,' results MS(s)

69.36 , atoms$_\wedge$ or monads,] WJ/MS(s); , $\sim$, $\sim\sim$, WJ/TMs^{1a}, TMs^2,I; , $\sim$, $\sim\sim_\wedge$ | TMs^1(u)^b; *om.* MS(s)

69.37 But] WJ/MS(s),TMs^1,I; But we saw (Syllabus, p. 5) that MS(s); Bur TMs^2

70.2 here] WJ/MS(s)+; well MS(s)

70.2 question,] WJ/MS(s)+; $\sim$. It seems a question to be solved empirically rather than rationalistically; MS(s)

70.2 tho] H; though MS(s)+

70.5 These] H; *Conclusion.*–These MS(s),TMs^1,TMs^2(u); *Conclusion.* K/TMs$^{2(r1)}$(*moved fr. subh. to s.n.*); Summary (*s.n.*) HJ?/TMs$^{2(r2)}$,I

70.5 *known-as*] WJ/TMs^{1a}+; $\sim_\wedge\sim$ MS(s);TMs^1(u)^b(*rom.*)

70.7 of these ways] WJ/TMs^{1a}+; one of these way TMs^1(u)^b; one of these ways MS(s)

70.7 be no chaos$_\wedge$] WJ/MS(s); be, not a chaos, MS(s); $\sim\sim\sim$, TMs^1+

70.8 The grades . . . . The] WJ/MS(s), WJ/TMs^{1a-b}(TMs^{1b} *pencil*)+; The

goods . . . . The TMs^1(u); Its MS(s)

70.8 e.g.,] TMs^1+; *ital.* MS(s)

70.10 gravitate; . . . heat;] WJ/TMs^{1a}+; $\sim$, . . . $\sim$, MS(s), TMs^1(u)^b

70.10 or know . . . another,] WJ/MS(s)+; *om.* MS(s)

70.12-13 consists . . . and] WJ/TMs^{1a}+; *om.* MS(s),TMs^1(u)^b

70.14 rationalistic minds,] WJ/TMs$^{1a(r2)}$,WJ/MS(s)$^{(r1)}$(minds$_\wedge$), TMs^2,I; the rationalistic mind, WJ/TMs$^{1a(r1)}$,MS(s)(mind$_\wedge$), WJ/MS(s)$^{(r2)}$(mind$_\wedge$); rationalistic mind$_\wedge$ TMs^1(u)^b

70.14 habitually] WJ/TMs^{1a}+; *om.* MS(s),TMs^1(u)^b

70.14 despise] WJ/TMs^{1a}, WJ/MS(s)$^{(r1)}$,TMs^2,I; despises TMs^1(u)^b,MS(s),WJ/MS(s)$^{(r2)}$

70.15 Such minds insist] WJ/MS(s)+; It insists MS(s)

70.16 absolute] TMs^1+; *cap.* MS(s)

70.16 'each . . . each,'] WJ/MS(s)+; *db. qts.* MS(s)

70.18 may be] WJ/MS(s)+; seems MS(s)

70.18 usual] WJ/MS(s)+; rationalistic MS(s)

70.18 abstractions,] WJ/MS(s)$^{(r2)}$+; abstractions. It may be WJ/MS(s)$^{(r1)}$; $\sim$. It is MS(s)

70.20 features] WJ/TMs^{1a}+; vigor, good digestion and sleep, etc., MS(s), TMs^1(u)^b

70.20 'face,'] I; '$\sim_\wedge$' WJ/TMs^{1a}, TMs^2,I(p); 'healthiness,' MS(s), TMs^1(u)^b

70.21 features] WJ/TMs^{1a}+; vigor, good sleep, etc., MS(s),TMs^1(u)^b

70.22 the face] WJ/TMs^{1a}+; healthiness MS(s),TMs^1(u)^b

70.24 , if] WJ/TMs^{1a}+; $_\wedge$ for MS(s), TMs^1(u)^b

70.25 is] WJ/TMs^{1a}+; *om.* MS(s), TMs^1(u)^b

70.25 Once] WJ/MS(s)+; *om.* MS(s)
[*end* Syllabus *proof*]

70.25 we are] WJ/TMs^{1a}+; *om.* MS,TMs^1(u)^b

§70.26 view,] WJ/TMs^{1a}+; $\sim_\wedge$ [*ab. del.* 'discrimination,'] MS;TMs^1(u)^b

70.28 in short only] WJ/TMs^{1a}+; eminently MS,TMs^1(u)^b

70.28 observation] WJ/TMs^{1a}+; science MS,TMs^1(u)^b

70.29 down,] WJ/TMs^{1a}+; $\sim_\wedge$ MS; $\sim_\wedge$ | TMs^1(u)^b

70.31 *The monistic theory.*] WJ/TMs^{1a}(*red*),TMs^2(u); *om.* MS,TMs^1(u)^b; *The Monistic theory* (*s.n.*) K/TMs^2,I

70.32 subject] WJ/TMs^{1a}+; matter MS,TMs^1(u)^b

‡70.32 these words,] WJ/TMs^{1a-b}, TMs^2(u); $\sim \sim_\wedge$ MS,TMs^1(u); the preceding chapter$_\wedge$ K/TMs^2,I

70.34 ^{2}of ... pluralism] WJ/TMs^{1a}+; *om.* MS,TMs^1(u)^b

70.37 precedes,] WJ/TMs^{1a}+; $\sim_\wedge$ MS,TMs^1(u)^b

70.37 'The ... Many'] K/TMs^2,I; 'the ... Many' TMs^1,TMs^2(u); "the ... Many$_\wedge$ MS

71.5 through-and-through] WJ/TMs^{1a}+; $\sim_\wedge \sim_\wedge \sim$ MS,TMs^1(u)^b

71.6 in some quarters] WJ/TMs$^{1a(r2)}$+; by many thinkers WJ/TMs$^{1a(r1)}$; *om.* MS,TMs^1(u)^b

§71.7 might we believe] WJ/TMs^{1a}+; *might a ['the' *del.*] [*ab. del.* 'could ['c' *ov.* 'w'] an all-']knower *find ['realize' *del.*] out [*ab. del.* 'perceive'] MS;TMs^1(u)^b

§71.10 'irrational';] WJ/TMs^{1a}+; '$\sim$,' [*comma possibly del.*] MS;TMs^1(u)^b

71.11 partly alogical, or] WJ/TMs$^{1a(r2)}$; $\sim \sim_\wedge \sim$ TMs^2,I; alogical, or WJ/TMs$^{1a(r1)}$; *om.* MS,TMs^1(u)^b

§71.11 -rational,] H; -$\sim_\wedge$ [*alt. fr.* 'irrational'] MS+

§71.12 intellectual] WJ/TMs^{1a}+; ['intellectual or' *del.*] logical MS;TMs^1(u)^b

§71.13 ^{1}the] WJ/TMs^{1a}+; ['the' *del.*] MS; *om.* TMs^1(u)^b

§71.13 the more] WJ/TMs^{1a}+; the [*ab. del.* 'more'] MS;TMs^1(u)^b

‡71.17 With] WJ/TMs^{1a}+; Like MS,TMs^1(u)^b

‡71.17 monism] TMs^1+; Monism MS (*error*)

‡71.17 likes to believe] WJ/TMs^{1a}+; believes MS,TMs^1(u)^b

‡§71.19-20 angles. The ... not] WJ/TMs^{1a}+; angles [*comma del.*] the whole *yielding ['explain['s yielding' *del.*]ing here' *del.*] [*ab. del.* 'explaining'] the parts [*del. intrl.* '['then' *del.*] here'] and not MS;TMs^1(u)^b (angles, ... parts,)

71.23 by monistic writers] WJ/TMs$^{1a(r2)}$+; by these writers WJ/TMs$^{1a(r1)}$; *om.* MS,TMs^1(u)^b

71.24 -rationality-] WJ/TMs^{1a}+; -$\sim$, MS,TMs^1(u)^b

71.24 philosopher] TMs^1+; philosofer MS

71.26 *absolute idealism*] WJ/TMs^{1a}+; *rom.* MS,TMs^1(u)^b

71.31 and in which] WJ/TMs^{1a}+; so that MS,TMs^1(u)^b

‡71.32 so far] TMs^1+; sofar MS

§71.33 so ... are] WJ/TMs^{1a}+; and may *thus [*insrtd.*] be considered MS;TMs^1(u)^b

71.35 an] TMs^1+; a MS (*error*)

‡71.35 connexion] TMs^1; connection MS,TMs^2,I

71.36 without exception.^{13}] WJ/TMs^{1a}+; *om.* MS,TMs^1(u)^b

71.38-39 ^{13}In ... representative.] WJ/TMs^{1a}+; *om.* MS,TMs^1(u)^b

71.38 prophet] *alt. fr.* 'prophetic' [*begin* Syllabus]

72.1 Yet, on] WJ/TMs^{1a}+; $\sim_\wedge \sim$ WJ/MS(s),TMs^1(u)^b; On MS(s)

72.1-2 , like ... out,] WJ/MS(s)+; *om.* MS(s)

72.3 follows:-] WJ/MS(s)+; $\sim:_\wedge$ MS(s)

72.5 but] WJ/TMs^{1a}+; except MS(s), TMs^1(u)^b

72.9 woes] WJ/TMs^{1a}+; pain MS(s), TMs^1(u)^b

72.10-11 and ... knowing] WJ/MS(s), WJ/TMs^{1a}+; and ... knowings TMs^1(u)^b; additional to It and knowing *differently* from It MS(s)

72.12 It] WJ/MS(s)+ (*rom.*); *Monism* MS(s)

72.13 ^{1}the] WJ/MS(s)+; a MS(s)

72.13 of ... it] WJ/MS(s)+; *om.* MS(s)

72.14 source] WJ/TMs^{1a}+; *cap.*

MS(s),TMs^1(u)^b

72.19-20 *perceptually experienced*]
WJ/TMs^{1a}+(*rom.*); experienced
TMs^1(u)^b; *experienced perceptually*
WJ/MS(s); *experienced by us* MS(s)

72.20 change] WJ/TMs^{1a}+; *cap.*
MS(s),TMs^1(u)^b

72.20-21 There is] WJ/TMs^{1a}+; It has
a MS(s),TMs^1(u)^b

72.24 the sense-] WJ/MS(s)$^{(r2)}$+; our
sense- WJ/MS(s)$^{(r1)}$; our MS(s)

72.28 human] WJ/MS(s)+; our
human MS(s)

72.29 necessary,] WJ/MS(s)+; $\sim_\wedge$
MS(s)

72.30 monists pretend] WJ/MS(s)+;
monism pretends MS(s)

72.36 *addable*] WJ/TMs^{1a}+ (*rom.*);
added TMs^1(u)^b; *added* MS(s)

72.36 addable] WJ/TMs^{1a}+; added
MS(s),TMs^1(u)^b

72.38 ambiguous . . . this . . . that]
TMs^1+; *each ital.* MS(s)

72.38 i.e.] TMs^1+; *ital.* MS(s)

72.40 common sense] *stet* MS(s),
TMs^1(u)^b; $\sim$-$\sim$ WJ/TMs^{1a}+

72.40 linked] WJ/TMs^{1a},TMs^2(u),
K/TMs$^{2(r2)}$,I; given in one
WJ/TMs^{1b}(*pencil*),K/TMs$^{2(r1)}$;
given together MS(s),TMs^1(u)

73.1 can be] WJ/TMs^{1a}+; is MS(s),
TMs^1(u)^b

73.1 for] WJ/MS(s)+; and MS(s)

73.1-4 to . . . reason.] WJ/TMs^{1a}+;
it is repugnant to our reason to
*attribute [*bel. del.* 'suppose'] an
additive constitution to reality.
WJ/TMs^{1b}(*pencil*); an additive
constitution is repugnant to *our
reason. [*insrtd. for del.* 'the world.'
WJ/MS(s)] MS(s);TMs^1(u)

73.3 'plus,'] TMs^2,I; *ital.* TMs^{1a}

73.5-8 Pluralism . . . world]
WJ/MS(s)+; *om.* MS(s)

73.6 face-value] WJ/TMs^{1a-b}+;
$\sim_\wedge\sim$ MS(s),TMs^1(u)

73.6 difficulties] *ab. del.* 'troubles'

73.7 ideas in] *aft. del.* 'conceptions in'

73.7 vacuum . . . abstractions.]
WJ/TMs^{1a}+; conceptual vacuum.
MS(s),TMs^1(u)^b

73.8 , it admits, cannot] WJ/TMs^{1a}+;

$_\wedge$ indeed$_\wedge$ can't MS(s),TMs^1(u)^b

73.9 , it says,] WJ/TMs^{1a-b}+; $_\wedge\sim\sim_\wedge$
WJ/MS(s),TMs^1(u); *om.* MS(s)

73.9 seems] WJ/TMs^{1a}+; *rom.* MS(s),
TMs^1(u)^b

73.10 conceptually] WJ/MS(s)+; *om.*
MS(s)

73.11 genuine novelties] WJ/MS(s)+;
a genuine novelty MS(s)

73.11-12 if . . . came.]
WJ/TMs$^{1a(r2)}$+; we could *experience
that* *one [*insrtd. for del.* 'it'
WJ/MS(s)] came$_\wedge$ if it did come.
MS(s),TMs^1(u)^b(*all rom.*); we
could experience *that* one came, if
it did come. WJ/TMs$^{1a(r1)}$

73.12-13 We . . . . Our] WJ/TMs^{1b}
(*pencil*),K/TMs^2,I; *om.* MS(s),
TMs^1(u)^a,TMs^2(u)

73.13 perceptual experience]
WJ/TMs^{1b},K/TMs^2,I; Perceptual
experience WJ/MS(s),TMs^1(u)^a,
TMs^2(u); Experience MS(s)

73.13 our] WJ/TMs^{1b}(*pencil*),
K/TMs^2,I; *om.* MS(s),TMs^1(u)^a,
TMs^2(u)

73.13 conceptual] WJ/MS(s)+;
om. MS(s)

73.14 reason: the] WJ/MS(s)+; $\sim$.
The MS(s)

73.14 common-sense] WJ/TMs^{1a}+;
$\sim_\wedge\sim$ MS(s),TMs^1(u)^b

73.16-18 Free-will . . . free-will] H;
$\sim_\wedge\sim$ . . . $\sim_\wedge\sim$ MS(s)+

73.17-18 accepts . . . of] WJ/TMs^{1a}+;
goes with MS(s),TMs^1(u)^b

73.23 Real."] WJ/MS(s)+; $\sim_\wedge$ "
(PAULSEN, p. 252). MS(s)

73.24 is . . . exert] WJ/TMs^{1a}+;
usually exerts MS(s),TMs^1(u)^b

73.27,38-39 risk.^{14} | ^{14}For . . . x.]
WJ/TMs^{1a}+; *om. fn.* MS(s),TMs^1(u)^b

73.27 world$_\wedge$] WJ/MS(s),WJ/TMs^{1a}+;
$\sim$, TMs^1(u)^b; real world, actually
MS(s)

73.30 , on . . . hand,] WJ/MS(s)+;
om. MS(s)

73.34 lack of balance] WJ/MS(s)+;
tension MS(s)

73.36-37 usually . . . belief.^{15}]
WJ/MS(s)+; will usually let this
determine their preference.$_\wedge$ MS(s)

73.38 expression] *ab. del.* 'statement'
[*end* Syllabus]

§74.3 advantages:—] WJ/TMs¹ᵃ+; ~.
[*period insrtd. bef. del.* '['to pit
against its disadvantage of' *del.*] to
set off against its ['emot' *del.*]
aesthetic and religious inferiority.']
MS; ~:ᴧ WJ/TMs¹ᵇ; ~ᴧᴧ TMs¹(u)

§74.6 disjunctions] WJ/TMs¹ᵃ⁻ᵇ+;
disjunction['s' *del.*] MS;TMs¹(u)

‡74.10 is] WJ/TMs¹ᵃ+; is strictly MS,
TMs¹(u)ᵇ

‡74.14 if] WJ/TMs¹ᵃ+; as soon as
MS,TMs¹(u)ᵇ

‡74.14 least] WJ/TMs¹ᵃ,TMs²(u);
smallest WJ/TMs¹ᵇ,K/TMs²,I;
minutest MS; *om.* TMs¹(u)

74.29 singly or] WJ/TMs¹ᵃ+; *om.*
MS,TMs¹(u)ᵇ

§74.30 *Which*] K/TMs²,I; *rom.*
WJ/TMs¹ᵇ; *What* WJ/TMs¹ᵃ,TMs²(u);
What ['W' *ov.* 'w'] MS;TMs¹(u)

74.30 are] TMs¹+; *ital.* MS

‡74.30 which] WJ/TMs¹ᵇ(*pencil*),
K/TMs²,I; what MS,TMs¹(u)ᵃ,
TMs²(u)

74.30 *when*] WJ/TMs¹ᵃ+; *rom.*
MS,TMs¹(u)ᵇ

74.30 *when*ᴧ] H; ~, MS+

§74.32 an exact] WJ/TMs¹ᵃ+; the
scientific [intrl.] MS;TMs¹(u)ᵇ

§74.33 in . . . example] WJ/TMs¹ᵃ+;
, for example, *in [bef. del.* 'for' *ab.
del.* 'are'] perception [*alt. fr.* 'perceptually'] MS;TMs¹(u)ᵇ

74.33-34 another,] TMs¹+; ~; MS

74.34 while] WJ/TMs¹ᵃ (*insrtd. aft.* 'in'
in error)+; *om.* MS,TMs¹(u)ᵇ

§74.35-36 monistic . . . being,]
WJ/TMs¹ᵇ(*pencil*),K/TMs²,I;
indivisible [*ab. del.* 'entitative']
block *of being, [*intrl.*] as monism
claims it ['is,' *del.*] is, MS;TMs¹(u)ᵃ,
TMs²(u)

75.7 —Is] WJ/TMs¹ᵇ(*pencil*); ᴧ ~
MS,TMs¹ᵃ+

‡75.8 is it] *stet* MS,TMs¹(u)ᵃ+; *om.*
WJ/TMs¹ᵇ

‡75.8 goes?] TMs¹+; ~, MS

‡75.8-9 —which . . . original,]
WJ/TMs¹ᵃ+; ᴧor what is the same
thing, is it originalᴧ MS;TMs¹(u)ᵇ (or,)

‡75.9 thingᴧ] TMs²,I; ~, MS,TMs¹

‡§75.12 III] K/TMs²,I; iii [*alt. fr.*
'III:'] MS;TMs¹,TMs²(u)

75.13 we] WJ/TMs¹ᵃ+; *om.*
MS,TMs¹(u)ᵇ

‡§75.14 ²beg . . . or] WJ/TMs¹ᵃ(r2)+;
[*del. intrl.* 'can he beg it'] piece
meal, ['and' *del.*] MS;TMs¹(u);
piecemeal WJ/TMs¹ᵃ(r1)⁻ᵇ

§76.0 *Chapter* . . . Novelty] TMs¹(IV),
K/TMs²(r3)(IX); Chapter V. [*alt. fr.*
'IV.'] | *The problem of [*in pencil
ab. pencil del.* 'Can there be real']
Novelty [*triple underl.*] MS; Chapter
IV | The Problem of Novelty.
TMs²(u); Chapter VI. | Problem III—
The Problem of Novelty. K/TMs²(r1);
Fourth Problem: Novelty. | Chap-
ter X ['The Meaning of' *del.*]
Novelty and the Infinite K/TMs²(r2)

76.5 Possibly,] WJ/TMs¹ᵃ+; ~ᴧ
MS,TMs¹(u)ᵇ

§76.7 provokingly.] TMs¹+;
provkingly. [*period insrtd.*] MS
(*error*)

‡76.8 brought] *stet* MS,WJ/TMs¹ᵃ+;
led WJ/TMs¹ᵇ; *om.* TMs¹(u)

*76.8 III] *stet* MS,TMs²(u); iii TMs¹;
VII K/TMs²,I

76.15 in only] WJ/TMs¹ᵃ+; only in
MS,TMs¹(u)ᵇ

76.19; 77.24 Delbœuf] I [Delboeuf
in I(p) *at* 77.24]; Delboeuf
MS–TMs²

77.9 dissimilar, . . .] TMs¹(~, - - -);
TMs²-I(~,–); dissimiler, . . . MS
('e' *doubtful*)

77.9-10 may be] WJ/TMs¹ᵃ+; is
MS,TMs¹(u)ᵇ

77.17 supposed to be] WJ/TMs¹ᵃ+;
om. MS,TMs¹(u)ᵇ

77.17 and,] WJ/TMs¹ᵃ+; ~ᴧ
MS,TMs¹(u)ᵇ

‡77.18 grasped] TMs²,I; graspt
MS,TMs¹

77.23 things.²] TMs¹+; *no placement
of fn.* MS

77.24 J.] WJ/TMs¹ᵃ+; F. MS,TMs¹(u)ᵇ

77.24 *philosophique*] H; *cap.* MS+
(*rom.* MS,TMs¹)

‡77.24 infinite] TMs¹+; infinit MS

‡77.25 *Introduction . . . Philosophy*]

K/TMs^2,I; *l.c. rom.* MS,TMs^1, TMs^2(u)

77.28   explanation,] TMs^1+; $\sim_\wedge$ MS

‡77.32-33   , and deny] WJ/TMs^{1a}+; $_\wedge$ by denying MS,TMs^1(u)^b

77.34   *Überwindung*] Ostwald; Ueberwindung MS,WJ/TMs^{1a}, TMs^2(u); *Ueberwindung* K/TMs^2,I; Neberwindung TMs^1(u)^b

‡77.37   vanished] TMs^2,I; vanisht MS, TMs^1

‡77.39   When,] TMs^1+; $\sim_\wedge$ MS

77.43   'La ... mixte,'] H; 'La ... Mixte,' K/TMs$^{2(r2)}$,I; *La ... Mixte,* K/TMs$^{2(r1)}$; $_\wedge$La ... Mixte,$_\wedge$ TMs^2(u); $_\wedge$la ... Mixte,$_\wedge$ MS,TMs^1

77.43   *philosophie*] H; Philosophie MS+ (*ital.* K/TMs^2)

78.7   conceptual] WJ/TMs^{1a}+; *om.* MS,TMs^1(u)^b

78.11   tho] *stet* MS,TMs^1(u)^b; tho' WJ/TMs^{1a}; though TMs^2,I

*78.14   *as it is*] *stet* MS; *rom.* TMs^1(u)^b; as it *is* WJ/TMs^{1a}+

§78.17   tho] TMs^1(u)^b; tho' [*bef. del.* '['their' *del.*] conditions of their appearance should have to be sought in'] MS;WJ/TMs^{1a}; though TMs^2,I

‡78.18   Biography] WJ/TMs$^{1a(r2)}$+; Biografy or life MS; Biography of life TMs^1(u)^b; Biography, or life, WJ/TMs$^{1a(r1)}$

‡78.19   stuff$_\wedge$] TMs^1+; $\sim$, MS (*error*)

‡78.20   biographies,] WJ/TMs^{1a}+; biografies$_\wedge$ MS; biographies$_\wedge$ TMs^1(u)^b

78.25   science] TMs^1+; *cap.* MS (*error*)

§78.27   biographies] WJ/TMs^{1a}+; biographificsl ['sl' *typed-del.*] TMs^1(u)^b; biografies [*alt. fr.* 'biografical'] ['impression' *del.*] MS

78.27   anyone] H; any one MS+

§78.27   and] WJ/TMs^{1a}+; *del.* MS; *om.* TMs^1(u)^b

§78.36   IV] H; III [*alt. fr.* 'II'] MS;TMs^1,TMs^2(u); VII K/TMs$^{2(r1)}$; VI K/TMs$^{2(r2)}$,I(p)(u); V I(p)(c),I

§78.37   *name*] WJ/TMs^{1a}+; name [*ab. del.* 'designate'] MS;TMs^1(u)^b

78.37   them] WJ/TMs^{1a}+; *doubtfully pencil del.* MS; *om.* TMs^1(u)^b

§78.38   matter.–] TMs$^{1-2}$; $\sim_\wedge$– [*dash over period*] MS; $\sim._\wedge$ I

78.39   *L'Évolution de la matière.*] H; l'Evolution de la Matiere. MS(Matiere$_\wedge$)+ (*L'Évolution de la Matière.* K/TMs^2,I [L'Evolution I(p)])

79.6 ^{2}continuity] TMs^2,I; Continuity MS (*doubtful cap.*); Continuity ['C' *typed ov.* 'c'] TMs^1

‡79.7   'infinitely'] WJ/TMs^{1a}+; $_\wedge\sim_\wedge$ MS,TMs^1(u)^b

§79.9   non-existence] WJ/TMs^{1a} ($\sim$- | $\sim$); impossibility [*in pencil ab. pencil del. pencil* 'denial'] MS;TMs^1(u)^b; nonexistence TMs^2,I

80.0   *Chapter ... Infinite*] WJ/TMs^{1a}, TMs^2(u)(*both read* Chapter V *and* Problem:); First sub-problem. The Infinite and the Continuum MS (*pencil db. underl.*); Chapter V | First Sub-Problem: | The Infinite and the Continuum TMs^1(u)^b; Problem III–The Problem of Novelty | Chapter XI | First Sub-Problem: | The Continuum and the Infinite K/TMs$^{2(r1)}$; Chapter X. | *Novelty and the Infinite–Conceptual View*^{x} | [*fn.*] ^{x}[In the authors manuscript this chapter and the succeeding chapters were labelled "sub-problems," and this ['particular' *del.*] chapter was entitled "The Continuum and the Infinite." Ed.] K/TMs$^{2(r2)}$;I (*all sg. qts.*; –The Conceptual)

80.1   problem] WJ/TMs^{1a}+; question MS,TMs^1(u)^b

‡80.1 ^{2}is] WJ/TMs^{1a}+; be MS, TMs^1(u)^b

80.4   etc.,] TMs^1+; $\sim_{\wedge\wedge}$ MS

‡80.5   all,] WJ/TMs^{1a}+; $\sim_\wedge$ MS,TMs^1(u)^b

80.8   Just as] WJ/TMs^{1a}+; As MS,TMs^1(u)^b

‡80.8   half- or quarter-] WJ/TMs^{1a}+; ½ or ¼ MS,TMs^1(u)^b

80.10   etc.,] TMs^1+; $\sim_\wedge$, MS

§80.12   minimal amounts] WJ/TMs^{1a}+; minima, ['of time' *del.*] or atoms, MS;TMs^1(u)^b

80.13   actually] WJ/TMs^{1a}+; really

MS,TMs¹(u)ᵇ

80.14 nothing,] WJ/TMs¹ᵃ⁺; ∼ₐ
MS,TMs¹(u)ᵇ

80.14 or] TMs¹⁺; or of MS (*error*)

80.15 there] WJ/TMs¹ᵃ⁺; *om.*
MS,TMs¹(u)ᵇ

80.16 'threshold.'] TMs¹⁺; "∼."
MS

§80.17 content, of no] WJ/TMs¹ᵃ⁺;
*contentₐ or [*pencil*] ['space,'
pencil del.] no [*intrl.*] MS;TMs¹(u)ᵇ

§80.17 perceptible] WJ/TMs¹ᵃ⁺;
['date' *or* 'datu' *del.*] definite
MS;TMs¹(u)ᵇ

80.19 of perception] WJ/TMs¹ᵃ⁺;
om. MS,TMs¹(u)ᵇ

81.1 For if] WJ/TMs¹ᵃ⁺; If
MS,TMs¹(u)ᵇ

81.3 If,] TMs¹⁺; ∼ₐ MS

81.9 *ad infinitum*] K/TMs²,I; *rom.*
MS,TMs¹,TMs²(u)

‡81.10 ₐfacts,ₐ] WJ/TMs¹ᵃ⁺;
'∼ₐ' MS,TMs¹(u)ᵇ

81.13-14 *problem of the Infinite*] I
(*infinite*); *problem of* the Infinite
MS (*error*); *rom.* TMs¹⁻²,I(p)

81.16 heads.¹ But] K/TMs²,I;
∼,ˣ But WJ/TMs¹ᵃ; ∼,ˣ but
MS,TMs¹(u)ᵇ,TMs²(u)

81.17 How] I; *l.c.* MS-TMs²

81.20 motion,] WJ/TMs¹ᵃ⁺; ∼ₐ
MS,TMs¹(u)ᵇ

81.21 apparently] WJ/TMs¹ᵃ⁺;
om. MS,TMs¹(u)ᵇ

81.23-24 , not . . . place,]
WJ/TMs¹ᵃ⁽ʳ²⁾⁺; , (∼. . .∼)ₐ
MS,TMs¹(u)ᵇ; ₐ(∼. . .∼)ₐ
WJ/TMs¹ᵃ⁽ʳ¹⁾

81.27 existsₐ notₐ] *stet* MS;
∼, ∼ₐ TMs¹(u)ᵇ; ∼ₐ∼,
WJ/TMs¹ᵃ⁺

81.28 in] WJ/TMs¹ᵃ⁺; *rom.*
MS,TMs¹(u)ᵇ

81.32 head-start] WJ/TMs¹ᵃ⁺; ∼ₐ∼
MS,TMs¹(u)ᵇ

81.34 starting-point] H; ∼ₐ∼ MS+

81.34,35 half] TMs²,I; ½ MS,TMs¹

81.36 Calderwood's] K/TMs²,I;
Calderwoods MS-TMs²(u)

81.37 discussed,] WJ/TMs¹ᵃ⁺; ∼ₐ
MS,TMs¹(u)ᵇ

81.37 shown] WJ/TMs¹ᵃ,K/TMs²,I;

om. MS,TMs¹(u)ᵇ,TMs²(u)

§81.38 *Philosophers*] TMs²,I;
Philosophy ['P' *ov.* 'F'] MS;TMs¹
('y' *ov.* 'e'; 'rs' *typed-del.*)

81.39 'Le] K/TMs²,I; 'le MS-TMs²(u)

81.39 Concept] H; *l.c.* MS+

81.39-40 *philosophique*] H;
Philosophique MS,TMs¹,TMs²(u);
cap. K/TMs²,I

§82.1 etc., so that] H; etc.ₐ [*intrl.*]
*so that [*ab. del.* 'We can plot the
race as follows,'] MS; etc. So that
TMs¹⁺

§82.1-2 occupied . . . form]
WJ/TMs¹ᵃ⁺; ['success' *del.*] simultaneously occupied by the runners
['being in succession 1 inch, ½ in,
¼ in., ⅛ in, ¹⁄₁₆ in, . . . ¹⁄ₙ from'
del.] form['ing' *del.*] MS;TMs¹(u)ᵇ
(forming)

82.3 inches,] WJ/TMs¹ᵃ⁺; ∼ₐ
MS,TMs¹(u)ᵇ

82.5 $\frac{1}{\infty}$] WJ/TMs¹ᵃ⁺; *om.* MS,TMs¹(u)ᵇ

‡82.6 divisible . . . so,] WJ/TMs¹ᵃ⁺;
∼; but if soₐ MS,TMs¹(u)ᵇ

‡82.7 all] WJ/TMs¹ᵃ⁺; *om.*
MS,TMs¹(u)ᵇ

*82.9 last] TMs¹⁺; *last* MS

§82.10 altho] H; although ['al'
insrtd.] MS+

‡82.17 exhaust,] WJ/TMs¹ᵃ⁺; ∼,
complete, MS,TMs¹(u)ᵇ

82.17 one by one,] WJ/TMs¹ᵃ⁺;
om. MS,TMs¹(u)ᵇ

‡82.19 to come never] WJ/TMs¹ᵃ⁺;
never to come MS,TMs¹(u)ᵇ

§82.24 entire] WJ/TMs¹ᵃ⁺; integral
[*intrl. aft. del.* 'unitary' *ab. del.*
'one'] MS;TMs¹(u)ᵇ

82.27 , composed] WJ/TMs¹ᵃ⁺;
om. MS,TMs¹(u)ᵇ

82.32 *Critique . . . Reason*] H; *rom.*
MS-TMs²; '∼. . .∼' (*rom.*) I

‡82.33 follows:—] I; ∼. MS-I(p)

83.5 tho] H; though MS+

83.7 definite] TMs¹⁺; definit MS

83.8 ₐinfinityₐ] WJ/TMs¹ᵃ⁺; '∼'
MS,TMs¹(u)ᵇ

83.10 complete] WJ/TMs¹ᵃ⁺; *om.*
MS,TMs¹(u)ᵇ

83.13 given,] WJ/TMs¹ᵃ⁺; ∼ₐ
MS,TMs¹(u)ᵇ

83.14-15 the . . . conditions]
WJ/TMs^{1b}(*pencil*); its parts
MS,TMs^1(u)^a+
83.14 which] H; wh. TMs^{1b}
§83.16 the . . . also] WJ/TMs^{1a}+;
[*del.* 'all' *ab. del.* 'the'] previous
time must MS;TMs^1(u)^b
§83.18 enumeration:] WJ/TMs^{1a}+;
~ — [*dash over period*] MS;TMs^1(u)^b
§83.19 grow . . . less,] WJ/TMs^{1b}
(*pencil*); are ['conceptually' *del.*] . . .
less$_\wedge$ MS;TMs^1(u)^a+
83.19 *ad infinitum*] I; *ad in-*|*finitum*
MS (*error*); *rom.* TMs$^{1-2}$
§83.20-21 regressive$_\wedge$ . . . has a]
WJ/TMs^{1a}+; regressive, and the
'whole' of *an infinite [*ab. del.*
'such a'] series never can *exist.
[*ab. del.* 'be given.'] *Such ['S'
ov. 's'] a series has a [*ab. del.*
'Mathematically ['it is a' *del.*]']
MS;TMs^1(u)^b
83.21 ^{1}a] *ab. del.* 'the'
83.24 (by . . . above)] WJ/TMs^{1a}
(*intrl.* '(by *the [*intrl.*] principle *1
above) [*ab. del.* '['1, above).' *del.*]
just stated)']')+; *om.* MS,TMs^1(u)^b
83.31 'idealism,'] WJ/TMs^{1a}+; $_\wedge$~,$_\wedge$
MS,TMs^1(u)^b
83.31 philosophy] TMs^1+; filosofy MS
‡§83.34 existence, for *actual*] H;
~, ~ actual WJ/TMs^{1b}(*pencil*);
existence. *Actual* WJ/TMs^{1a},K/TMs^2;
~. *Actual [*aft. del.* 'To our
perception the conditions are
always'] MS;TMs^1(u),TMs^2(u)
83.34 phenomena,] WJ/TMs^{1a-b}+;
~$_\wedge$ MS,TMs^1(u)
§83.35-36 , as . . . moment;]
WJ/TMs^{1a}; , as . . . any given
moment; TMs^2,I; *at any given
moment, [*insrtd. for del.* '['and the
subdivision' *del.*] but we can go on
to subdivide them or add to them
indefinitely, and our reason forces us
to the endless task.'] MS;TMs^1(u)^b
83.36 infinite] TMs^1+; infinit MS
83.39 itself,] WJ/TMs^{1a}+; ~$_\wedge$
MS,TMs^1(u)^b
83.39 our] WJ/TMs^{1a-b}+; the MS;
om. TMs^1(u)
§83.40-41 phenomenal given . . . part]

K/TMs^2,I; given ['part' *del.*], which
is finite, and | and an infinite ['part'
del.] MS;TMs^1(u) (given$_\wedge$ . . .
finite, and an); given part which is
finite, and an infinite part
WJ/TMs^{1a},TMs^2(u) (an indefinite);
phenomenal given which is finite,
and a conditioning infinite
WJ/TMs^{1b}(*pencil*)
83.41 to . . . hereafter] WJ/TMs^{1a}+;
om. MS,TMs^1(u)^b
83.42 part,] WJ/TMs^{1a}+; ~$_\wedge$
MS,TMs^1(u)^b
‡§83.43 *gegeben* . . . extant).]
WJ/TMs^{1a}+; *gegeben*, or *already
extant. [*ab. del.* 'existent. ['in
determinate amount.' *del.*]']
MS;TMs^1(u)^b(*rom.*)
84.3 synthesis$_\wedge$'] WJ/TMs^{1a}+; ~,'
MS,TMs^1(u)^b
§84.4 collection$_\wedge$] TMs^1+; ~, [|'col'
insrtd. for del. 'col-' | ; *comma
undel. in error*] MS
84.5 or have existed] WJ/TMs^{1a}+;
om. MS,TMs^1(u)^b
§84.7 in . . . whole sum,] H; in . . .
whole *sum, [*intrl.*] MS; *rom.*
TMs^1+
84.7-8 logical situation] WJ/TMs^{1a}+;
logic MS,TMs^1(u)^b
§84.10-11 The . . . taken] WJ/TMs^{1a}+;
Things can be conceived WJ/TMs^{1b}
(*pencil*); Things ['T' *ov.* 't'] can be
taken MS;TMs^1(u)
§84.11 talked] WJ/TMs^{1b}(*pencil*);
*can be [*insrtd.*] talked MS;
TMs^1(u)^a+
84.12-13 equally well] WJ/TMs^{1a}+;
om. MS,TMs^1(u)^b
84.15 series$_\wedge$] WJ/TMs^{1a}+; ~,
MS,TMs^1(u)^b
§84.15 distributively,] WJ/TMs^{1a}+;
piecemeal or *distributively,
[*comma ov. period*] MS;TMs^1(u)^b
‡84.16 none] WJ/TMs^{1b}(*pencil*);
none of them·MS,TMs^1(u)^a+
84.16-17 one . . . conditions]
WJ/TMs^{1a}+; condition MS,TMs^1(u)^b
84.17 therefore] WJ/TMs^{1a}+;
om. MS,TMs^1(u)^b
§84.21 harvested and] WJ/TMs^{1a}+;
completed, ['and' *del.*] MS;TMs^1(u)^b

84.23-24 puzzles and incomprehensi-
bilities] WJ/TMs^{1a}+; antinomies
MS,TMs^1(u)^b

§ 84.30 –the . . . it–] WJ/TMs^{1a}+;
$_\wedge \sim$ [*sg. qt. del.*; *alt. fr. doubtful*
'le'] . . . $\sim$, MS;TMs^1(u)^b

84.31;86.10 4,] TMs^1+; $\sim_\wedge$ MS

84.31 'infinith'] WJ/TMs^{1a},TMs^2;
$_\wedge$infinite$_\wedge$ MS,TMs^1(u)^b;
'infinite' I

‡84.37 opaque] TMs^1+; opake MS

§ 85.1-2 things . . . composition.]
WJ/TMs$^{1a(r2)}$+; things [*ab. del.*
'an'] infinite *in ['series' *del.*]
form, having yet been [*ab. del.*
'which'] paid in [', given,' *del.*]
and completed. MS;TMs^1(u)^b
(things, . . . paid-in WJ/TMs$^{1a[r1]}$)

85.1 altho] H; although TMs^{1a}+

§ 85.4 freedom,] TMs^1+; and *freedom,
[*comma ov. period*] MS

85.7 distinguished] TMs^1+;
distinguisht MS

85.12 'seventies'] H; $_\wedge \sim$ TMs^2,I;
'70-s MS; $_\wedge$70-s TMs^1

85.15 , in short,] WJ/TMs^{1a}+; *om.*
MS,TMs^1(u)^b

‡85.16 this] WJ/TMs^{1a}+; my
MS,TMs^1(u)^b

§ 85.22 experience;] H; $\sim$;^{x} | [*fn.*]
^{x}For *an ['n' *added*] ['fuller' *del.*]
account of ['ide' *del.*] idealism the
reader is referred to chapter – below.
MS;TMs^1(Chapter); K/TMs^2,I (*both*
chapter$_\wedge$ below; *both add* [Never
written. Ed.])

85.29 *critique générale*] H; *init. caps.*
MS,TMs^2; Critique Generale
TMs^1(u)^b; Critique Générale
WJ/TMs^{1a}

85.29 1854-1864] K/TMs^2,I; 18 ,
MS,TMs^1,TMs^2(u)

85.30 *Le*] TMs^1(*rom.*)+; *le* MS

85.31-32 *systématique . . . philosophiques*$_\wedge$] H; *des Systèmes*, [*comma
undel. in error*] MS; des Systemes,
TMs^1,TMs^2(u); *des Systèmes*$_\wedge$
K/TMs^2,I

85.32 cette conclusion] H; ces
conclusions MS–I

‡85.32-33 autobiographic] TMs^1+;
autobiografic MS

85.34 eighty-eight] TMs^2,I; 88
MS,TMs^1

86.1 sub-classes] WJ/TMs^{1a}+;
subclasses MS,TMs^1(u)^b

86.7-8 demanding . . . for] WJ/TMs^{1b},
K/TMs^2,I; involving . . . in MS,
TMs^1(u)^a,TMs^2(u)

86.10 several] WJ/TMs^{1b},K/TMs^2,I;
om. MS,TMs^1(u)^a,TMs^2(u)

86.12 would then] WJ/TMs^{1b},
K/TMs^2,I; will MS; *om.* TMs^1(u)^a;
need TMs^2(u)

86.13 would find] WJ/TMs^{1b},
K/TMs^2,I; finds MS,TMs^1(u)^a,
TMs^2(u)

86.17 *class*] WJ/TMs^{1b}; *rom.*
MS,TMs^1(u)^a+

§ 86.19 determinate] WJ/TMs^{1b};
terminated [*ab. del.* 'fixed']
MS;TMs^1(u)^a+

86.21 keep] WJ/TMs^{1a-b}+; keep to
MS,TMs^1(u)

86.31 $_\wedge$How,$_\wedge$] H; '$\sim$,' MS+

86.34 , one may think,] WJ/TMs^{1b};
, $\sim \sim \sim_\wedge$ K/TMs^2,I; *om.*
MS,TMs^1(u)^a,TMs^2(u)

86.35 then$_\wedge$] WJ/TMs^{1a}+; $\sim$,
MS,TMs^1(u)^b

86.36 , we are told,] WJ/TMs^{1a}+;
om. MS,TMs^1(u)^b

§ 86.37 , therefore,] WJ/TMs^{1a}+;
$_\wedge \sim_\wedge$ [*ab. del.* 'also'] MS;TMs^1(u)^b

§ 86.37-38 gross, . . . two.]
WJ/TMs^{1a}+; gross. [*period ab. del.*
comma] [*del.* 'and amounts to
saying that ['whatever has' *del.*] if
['time' *del.*] past time has one 'end'
it must have two–a ['purely' *del.*]
verbal confusion between 'end'
and'] MS;TMs^1(u)^b

86.38 bound] *ab. del.* 'end'

§ 86.39-40 is . . . implied.]
WJ/TMs^{1a-b}+ (*only* K/TMs^2,I); *is
logically the only [*ab. del.* 'no
other'] beginning *implied. [*insrtd.
for del.* 'follows. [*ab. del.* 'is
*logically [*intrl.*] involved. [*period
insrtd.*] ['in the facts.' *del.*]']']
MS;TMs^1(u)

§ 86.41 were] WJ/TMs^{1b},K/TMs^2,I;
be [*ab. del.* 'were'] MS,TMs^1(u)^a,
TMs^2(u)

86.42 'negative'] WJ/TMs^{1a}+; ˄ ~ ˄
MS,TMs¹(u)^b

87.1–2 'growing measure' ... 'standing
bulk'] *stet* MS+ (˄growing measure˄
TMs¹[u]); standing measure ...
growing bulk Locke

87.2 some time] WJ/TMs^{1b},K/TMs²,I;
om. MS,TMs¹(u)^a,TMs²(u)

‡87.2 a] WJ/TMs^{1b},K/TMs²,I; the
MS,TMs¹(u)^a,TMs²(u)

87.3 finished or finited] WJ/TMs^{1b}
(*pencil*),K/TMs²,I(finite); finite
MS,TMs¹(u)^a; infinite TMs²(u)

87.4 But this] WJ/TMs^{1b},K/TMs²,I;
This MS,TMs¹(u)^a,TMs²(u)

87.4 again˄] TMs¹+; ~, MS

87.5 given as] WJ/TMs^{1a}+; *om.*
MS,TMs¹(u)^b

87.8 probably] WJ/TMs^{1a}+; *om.*
MS,TMs¹(u)^b

‡87.9 infinite] TMs¹+; infinit MS

87.14 wish to] WJ/TMs^{1b},K/TMs²,I;
om. MS,TMs¹(u)^a,TMs²(u)

87.19 succession] WJ/TMs^{1a} (*intrl.*
bef. del. intrl. 'sue')+; series
MS,TMs¹(u)^b

§87.19–20 be ... out.] WJ/TMs^{1a},
TMs²(u); have been *successively*
counted out WJ/TMs^{1b},K/TMs²,I;
have *terminated. [*insrtd. for del.*
'come to an end and been
exhausted.'] MS;TMs¹(u)

87.21 small;] WJ/TMs^{1a}+; ~,
MS,TMs¹(u)^b

87.21 event˄] WJ/TMs^{1a–b}+; ~,
MS,TMs¹(u)

87.21–22 unrolling itself] WJ/TMs^{1a}+;
taking place MS,TMs¹(u)^b

87.22–23 *ad infinitum*;] K/TMs²,I;
rom. WJ/TMs^{1a–b},TMs²(u); ad
infinitum, MS,TMs¹(u)

87.23 here] WJ/TMs^{1a}+; *om.*
MS,TMs¹(u)^b

§87.23 proceed] WJ/TMs^{1a}+;
proceed *here [*intrl.*] MS;TMs¹(u)^b

‡87.24 (or ... units)] WJ/TMs^{1a}+;
, ~ ... ~, WJ/TMs^{1b}; , ~ ... ~˄
MS,TMs¹(u)

‡87.24 or by] WJ/TMs^{1b},K/TMs²,I;
or MS,TMs¹(u)^a,TMs²(u)

87.27 *in succession*] WJ/TMs^{1b}
(*pencil*)+; *rom.* MS,TMs¹(u)^a

87.27 'all'] WJ/TMs^{1b},K/TMs²,I;
˄ ~ ˄ MS,TMs¹(u)^a,TMs²(u)

87.28 a conception] WJ/TMs^{1a}+;
conceptually MS,TMs¹(u)^b

§87.29 count] WJ/TMs^{1a}+; finish
[*insrtd.*] counting ['ing' *added*]
MS;TMs¹(u)^b

§87.29–30 and ... end.] WJ/TMs^{1a}+;
inclusive. [*intrl.*] MS;TMs¹(u)^b

87.33–88.1 it ... and] WJ/TMs^{1a}+;
here MS,TMs¹(u)^b

‡87.37–38 *piecemeal ... collecti-*
bility] WJ/TMs^{1a–b}+; *rom.*
MS,TMs¹(u)

88.1 add,] WJ/TMs^{1a–b}+; ~ ˄
MS,TMs¹(u)

‡88.2 paid-in] H; ~ ˄ ~ MS+

‡88.2 in,] WJ/TMs^{1b}; ~ ˄ MS,
TMs¹(u)^a+

§88.3 end .... Starting] WJ/TMs^{1a}+;
cancelling [*ab. del.* 'end'] of the
*debt can be [*ab. del.* 'series is']
accomplisht. We start MS;TMs¹(u)^b
(accomplished)

‡88.4 we have] WJ/TMs^{1a}+; which
therefore has WJ/TMs^{1b}; which has
MS,TMs¹(u)

88.6 other case,] WJ/TMs^{1a}+; case˄
MS,TMs¹(u)^b

88.7 is,] WJ/TMs^{1b}; ~ ˄
MS,TMs¹(u)^a+

§88.7 *aufgegeben:*] WJ/TMs^{1a}+;
aufgegeben [*alt. fr.* '*aufgeben*'] ;
MS;WJ/TMs^{1b}; ~ ; (*rom.*) TMs¹(u)

‡88.7 *task*–] WJ/TMs^{1a}; ~ ;–
MS,TMs¹(u)^b; task– TMs²,I

‡88.9 entire ... agent] WJ/TMs^{1a}+;
end of it. He MS,TMs¹(u)^b

§88.11–12 , with ... don't catch up]
WJ/TMs^{1a}; ˄ with ... cannot catch
up WJ/TMs^{1b}; ˄ with ... do not
catch up TMs²,I; ˄ even [*intrl.*] the
interest of which we can't catch up
with MS; ˄ even ... cannot catch
up with TMs¹(ũ)

88.13 *Infinitum ... nequit,*] *stet*
MS,WJ/TMs^{1b}; ' ~ ... ~ ,' (*all rom.*)
WJ/TMs^{1a}; ˄ ~ ... ~ ,˄ (*all rom.*)
TMs¹(u); ' ~ ... ~ ,' TMs²,I

88.14 gradually] WJ/TMs^{1a}+; *om.*
MS,TMs¹(u)^b

88.14 conceived] WJ/TMs^{1a}+; conceived and defined MS,TMs^1(u)^b

88.16 conception] WJ/TMs^{1a}+;
definition MS,TMs^1(u)^b

‡88.19 fall] TMs^1+; falls MS (*error*)

‡88.19 at once] WJ/TMs^{1b},K/TMs^2,I;
successively MS,TMs^1(u)^a,TMs^2(u)

88.22 84–85] K/TMs^2,I(p)(165–166);
I (164–165); *om.* MS,TMs^1,TMs^2(u)

‡88.27–28 naif.... *Naif*] WJ/TMs^{1a},
TMs^2,I(p); *naïf.... Naïf* I; *rom.*
MS,TMs^1(u)^b

88.28;90.39 (*first*) tho] H; tho' MS;
though TMs^1+

88.30 as] WJ/TMs^{1b},K/TMs^2,I;
om. MS,TMs^1(u),TMs^2(u)

88.35 or other difference]
WJ/TMs^{1b},K/TMs^2,I; *om.*
MS,TMs^1(u)^a,TMs^2(u)

88.39 of collections] WJ/TMs^{1a}+;
om. MS,TMs^1(u)^b

§88.39–40 between one another]
WJ/TMs^{1a}+; *[*'among' *del.*]
between each [*ab. del.* 'between
one'] another MS; between each
other, TMs^1(u) (other$_\wedge$ WJ/TMs^{1b})

89.1 halves,] WJ/TMs^{1b}; $\sim_\wedge$
MS,TMs^1(u)^a+

§89.8 these ... cuts] WJ/TMs$^{1a(r2)}$+;
the same numbers of these cuts
WJ/TMs$^{1a(r1)}$; the['se' *del.*]
[*intrl.*] numbers, [*comma ov. period
undel. in error* MS; *comma del.*
WJ/TMs$^{1a(r1)-b}$] *of these cuts
[*insrtd.*] MS;TMs^1(u)^b

‡§89.8 their number] WJ/TMs^{1a}+;
the number of *their [*alt. fr.*
'these'] numbers MS;TMs^1(u)^b

89.9–10 "Of ... disappears,"] H;
sg. qts. MS+ ($_\wedge$ Of TMs^1(u)^b)

89.9–10 'unity in multiplicity,']
TMs^1(u)^b; " $\sim \sim \sim$," MS,
WJ/TMs^{1a}+

89.12 sensible] WJ/TMs^{1b}; *om.*
MS,TMs^1(u)^a+

89.13 view,] WJ/TMs^{1a}+; $\sim_\wedge$
MS,TMs^1(u)^b

89.13–14 "mass ... dogma."] H;
all sg. qts. MS+

89.13 unanalyzed] *stet* Russell,
MS,WJ/TMs^{1b}; uncriticized
WJ/TMs^{1a}; criticized TMs^2,I;
unequalized TMs^1(u)

§89.13 prejudice$_\wedge$"] H; $\sim_\wedge$' TMs^2,I;
$\sim$,' [*sg. qt. and comma insrtd. for
del. sg. qt. and period bef. del.* 'x']
MS;TMs^1

89.13–14 by Russell, or] WJ/TMs^{1b},
K/TMs^2,I; *om.* MS,TMs^1(u)^a,
TMs^2(u)

89.15 So ... ^{2}for] WJ/TMs^{1a}+;
om. MS,TMs^1(u)^b

89.15 number-continuum] I; $\sim_\wedge \sim$
TMs^{1a-2}

§89.15–16 the 'new infinite,' that]
H; ' $\sim \sim \sim$,' $\sim$ WJ/TMs^{1a};
' $\sim \sim \sim$;' $\sim$ TMs^2,I(p)(infinite';));
' $\sim \sim \sim$ ': $\sim$ I; The ['notion of the'
del.] 'new infinite$_\wedge$' MS; The $_\wedge$new
infinite$_\wedge$' TMs^1(u)^b

[*begin different typing* TMs^{1b}]

89.17 entirety,] WJ/TMs^{1a}+; $\sim_\wedge$
MS,TMs^{1a}(u),TMs^{1b}

89.18 it,] WJ/TMs^{1a},WJ/TMs^{1b};
$\sim_\wedge$ MS,TMs^{1a}(u),TMs^{1b}(u)

89.19–20 No ... is] WJ/TMs^{1a}+;
The part is not MS,TMs^{1a}(u),TMs^{1b}

‡89.21 taken;] WJ/TMs^{1a}+; $\sim$,
MS,TMs^{1a}(u),TMs^{1b}

89.21 any ... them] WJ/TMs^{1a}+;
it MS,TMs^{1a}(u),TMs^{1b}

89.23 its ... every] WJ/TMs^{1b}; *each*
of its elements and *each* MS,
WJ/TMs^{1a}(*rom.* TMs^{1a}[u] –
TMs^{1b}[u])+

89.24 the part and the] WJ/TMs^{1b};
part and MS,TMs^{1b}(u),TMs^{1a}+

89.24 what ... call] WJ/TMs^{1a}+;
om. MS,TMs^{1a}(u),TMs^{1b}

89.25 'class,'] WJ/TMs^{1a}+; ' $\sim_\wedge$'
MS,TMs^{1a}(u),WJ/TMs^{1b}; $_\wedge \sim_{\wedge\wedge}$
TMs^{1b}(u)

89.27–28 ^{2}and ... *überhaupt*,]
WJ/TMs^{1b} ('*überhaupt*,' *ab. del.*
'in general');K/TMs^2,I (*überhaupt*$_\wedge$);
om. MS,TMs^{1a},TMs^{1b}(u),TMs^2(u)

89.29 such] WJ/TMs^{1b},K/TMs^2,I;
om. MS,TMs^{1a},TMs^{1b}(u),TMs^2(u)

89.30 , for instance,] WJ/TMs^{1b},
K/TMs^2,I; *om.* MS,TMs^{1a},TMs^{1b}(u),
TMs^2(u)

89.31 *ad infinitum*] WJ/TMs^{1a}(*rom.*)+;
ad libitum MS,TMs^{1a}(u)(*rom.*),
TMs^{1b}(*rom.*)

89.31–32 , queerer-sounding still,]

WJ/TMs1b('queerer-' *ab. del.* 'odder-'),K/TMs2,I; *om.* MS,TMs1a, TMs1b(u),TMs2(u)

89.32 , odd or even,] WJ/TMs1a+; *om.* MS,TMs1a(u),TMs1b

§89.33 the ... alone] WJ/TMs1a, TMs2(u); the ... thus produced [*comma del.*] WJ/TMs1b;K/TMs2,I; odd [*ab. del.* 'even'] numbers MS;TMs1a(u),TMs1b(u)

89.35 whole] WJ/TMs1b,K/TMs2,I; *om.* MS,TMs1a,TMs1b(u),TMs2(u)

§89.36 ¶ These paradoxical] WJ/TMs1a+; ['This was long judged abs' *del.*] These (*no* ¶) MS,TMs1a(u), TMs1b

[*end different typing*]

89.39 *La*] K/TMs2,I; La TMs1, TMs2(u); la MS

89.40;93.17 *Principles*] H; Philosophy MS,TMs1,TMs2(u); *Philosophy* K/TMs2,I

90.1 series] WJ/TMs1b,K/TMs2,I; *om.* MS,TMs1(u)a,TMs2(u)

90.2 ever] WJ/TMs1b,K/TMs2,I; *om.* MS,TMs1(u)a,TMs2(u)

‡90.3 But (*no* ¶)] WJ/TMs1a+; ¶ MS,TMs1(u)b

90.9 now] WJ/TMs1b,K/TMs2,I; *om.* MS,TMs1(u)a,TMs2(u)

90.9 the conception of] WJ/TMs1a+; *om.* MS,TMs1(u)b

90.11 numbers‸'] WJ/TMs1b; ~,' MS,TMs1(u)a+

90.11-12 *created by definition*] WJ/TMs1a+; *rom.* MS,TMs1(u)b

90.12 decreed] WJ/TMs1b,K/TMs2,I; conceived WJ/TMs1a,TMs2(u); *om.* MS,TMs1(u)

90.14-15 *after ... addition*] WJ/TMs1b(r2),K/TMs2,I; *after all the numbers formed by such addition* WJ/TMs1b(r1)(*rom.* TMs1[u]), TMs2(u); *after all the numbers formed by such addition* WJ/TMs1a; *after* all the numbers formed by such addition MS

§90.16 'Omega'] WJ/TMs1a+; ‸omega‸[*ab. del.* 'ω'] MS;TMs1(u); *omega* WJ/TMs1b

90.17 would,] TMs1+; ~‸ MS

90.19-20 Or ... terminate.]

WJ/TMs1a+; *om.* MS,TMs1(u)b

90.20 counting] *ab. del.* 'enumeration'

90.21 miles away] WJ/TMs1a-b+; the distance MS,TMs1(u)

90.21 parallel lines] WJ/TMs1a, K/TMs2,I; parallels MS,TMs1(u)b; parallels lines TMs2(u)

§90.22 do] WJ/TMs1a+; *can* [*ab. del.* '*could*'] MS; could TMs1(u)b

‡90.23 one;] WJ/TMs1b; ~, MS,TMs1(u)a

§90.23-24 useful conceptual bridge] WJ/TMs1a(r2)+; conceptual bridge WJ/TMs1a(r1); *bridge useful [*ab. del.* 'useful conception ['in' *del.*] for simplifying ['mathematical' *del.*] formulas. ['s.' *insrtd. for del.* | 'tion']'] MS;TMs1(u)b

90.24 range of facts] WJ/TMs1a+; fact MS,TMs1(u)b

90.25 sort of] WJ/TMs1a+; *om.* MS,TMs1(u)b

§90.26-27 above ... as] WJ/TMs1a (175 WJ/TMs1a,TMs2,I[p] ; 173 I)+; on [*ov.* 'in'] ['p. [*ov.* '§'] 000' *del.*] as MS; in as TMs1(u); above as WJ/TMs1b

90.27 infinitely repeated] WJ/TMs1b, K/TMs2,I; *om.* MS,TMs1(u)a, TMs2(u)

90.28 1the] WJ/TMs1b,K/TMs2,I; such MS,TMs1(u)a,TMs2(u)

§90.29 The ... taken] WJ/TMs1b, K/TMs2,I; That [*intrl.*] taken ['t' *ov.* 'T'] MS;TMs1(u)a,TMs2(u)

90.32 distances,] WJ/TMs1a+; ~‸ MS,TMs1(u)b

90.34-35 should stop ... would cease] WJ/TMs1b,K/TMs2,I; stops ... ceases MS,TMs1(u)a, TMs2(u)

§90.36 'all] WJ/TMs1b; ‸~[*intrl.*] MS;TMs1(u)a+

90.36 come] TMs1(u); '~ MS, PJ/TMs1a-b+

§90.36-37 definitely limited] WJ/TMs1b,K/TMs2,I; definite ['logical' *del.*] MS;TMs1(u)a, TMs2(u)

‡90.37-38 any ... one] WJ/TMs1b; any one and every K/TMs2,I; any one MS,WJ/TMs1a(r2),TMs1(u),

TMs^2(u); *any one* WJ/TMs$^{1a(r1)}$

90.38　by definition to] WJ/TMs^{1b},
K/TMs^2,I; *om.* MS,TMs^1(u)^a,TMs^2(u)

90.38　*before*] WJ/TMs^{1a}+; *rom.*
MS,TMs^1(u)^b

§90.39　comes−] WJ/TMs^{1a}+; ∼, [*ab.
del.* 'does,'] MS;TMs^1(u)^b

90.39　they . . . whole, and] WJ/TMs^{1b};
they . . . whole$_\wedge$ and K/TMs^2,I;
om. MS,TMs^1(u)^a,TMs^2(u)

90.39　^{2}and] WJ/TMs^{1b},K/TMs^2,I;
and even MS,TMs^1(u)^a,TMs^2(u)

90.40–41　The . . . entire numbers.]
WJ/TMs^{1a}('entire numbers$_\wedge$' *ab. del.*
'integers$_\wedge$ [*bel. del.* ' 'natural'
numbers$_\wedge$']')+; *om.* MS,TMs^1(u)^b

90.40–41　ordinal$_\wedge$] TMs^2,I; ∼, ['but
a cardinal' *del.*] TMs^{1a}(*comma error*)

90.41　continue] TMs^2,I; con- | tue
TMs^{1a} (*error*)

§91.2　Omega . . . defined.]
WJ/TMs^{1a}+; *omega, [comma over
period*] just defined. [*ab. del.* 'ω.^{x}']
MS;TMs^1(u),WJ/TMs$^{1b(r2)}$; omega,
just created by definition, and the
value of the limit can be substituted.
for that of the series. WJ/TMs$^{1b(r1)}$

§91.3　multitude; thus] WJ/TMs^{1b},
K/TMs^2,I; * ∼ ['quantity' *del.*]
[*ab. del.* 'infinite'] −[*dash over
period*] thus ['t' *ov.* 'T'] MS; ∼.
Thus TMs^1(u)^a,TMs^2(u)

‡91.4　practically . . . limit)]
WJ/TMs^{1a}+; equated MS,TMs^1(u)^b

‡§91.5　fixed; thus] WJ/TMs^{1b},K/TMs^2,
I; ∼. [*period insrtd. aft. del. comma
over period*] Thus MS;TMs^1(u)^a,
TMs^2(u)

91.5　circumvent] WJ/TMs^{1b},K/TMs^2,
I; short-circuit MS,TMs^1(u)^a,
TMs^2(u)

91.5–6　addition$_\wedge$ or division,] H;
∼, ∼ ∼$_\wedge$ WJ/TMs^{1b};K/TMs^2
('division' *aft. del.* 'addition');I;
addition, MS,TMs^1(u)^a,TMs^2(u)

91.7　constructable] WJ/TMs^{1a-b}+;
construable MS,TMs^1(u)

§91.8–10　may . . . be.] WJ/TMs$^{1b(r2)}$,
K/TMs^2,I; may . . . small it may
appear. WJ/TMs$^{1b(r1)}$; now [*intrl.*]
measures any ['& every part of a'
del.] continuous finite quantity,

*however small. [*intrl.*] MS;TMs^1(u)
(continuous quantity, WJ/TMs^{1a},
TMs^2[u])

§91.11　¶When] WJ/TMs$^{1b(r2)}$,
K/TMs^2,I; The points in an inch['e'
del.] or the fractions between one &
zero have an exact one-to-one correspondence with the several units *of
[*insrtd.*] which it ['consists.' *del.*]
must consist. [¶] When MS;TMs^1(u);
The . . . units of which the inch or
the one is the limit. [¶]When
WJ/TMs$^{1b(r1)}$; The . . . units each of
which it must include. [¶]When
WJ/TMs^{1a},TMs^2(u)

‡91.12–13　the 'new infinite']
WJ/TMs^{1a}+; novelty MS,TMs^1(u)^b

‡§91.14–16　any . . . half-inch,]
WJ/TMs^{1a},TMs^2(u),K/TMs$^{2(r2)}$
(every point K/TMs$^{2[r1]}$),I; any
point in an imaginary inch is conceivable as ['match' *del.*] matching
some point in a quarter-inch or
half-inch, MS;TMs^1(u)(quarter$_\wedge$inch);
every point in an imaginary inch is
conceivable as being matched by
some point in a quarter inch or
half-inch, WJ/TMs$^{1b(r2)}$; every
point in an imaginary quarter inch
or half-inch is conceivable as being
matched by some point in a whole
inch, WJ/TMs$^{1b(r1)}$

91.16　'similarity'] WJ/TMs^{1b},
K/TMs^2,I; $_\wedge$∼$_\wedge$ MS,TMs^1(u)^a,
TMs^2(u)

91.18　mathematically] WJ/TMs^{1b},
K/TMs^2,I; *om.* MS,TMs^1(u)^a,
TMs^2(u)

‡91.20　scientifically] WJ/TMs^{1b},
K/TMs^2,I; practically MS,TMs^1(u)^a,
TMs^2(u)

‡91.20–21　expounders] WJ/TMs^{1b},
K/TMs^2,I; exposers MS,WJ/TMs^{1a}
(*pencil*),TMs^2(u); exposer's TMs^1(u)

91.24–25　Achilles-puzzle] WJ/TMs^{1a}
(*pencil*)+; ∼$_\wedge$∼ MS,TMs^1(u)^b

‡91.26–28　(measured . . . time)]
WJ/TMs^{1a}+; , ∼...∼,
MS,WJ/TMs^{1b}; $_\wedge$∼...∼, TMs^1(u)

‡91.26　measured] WJ/TMs^{1b},
K/TMs^2,I; taken MS,TMs^1(u)^a,
TMs^2(u)

91.27 then] WJ/TMs^{1b},K/TMs^2,I; *om.* MS,TMs^1(u)^a,TMs^2(u)

§91.27 consist] WJ/TMs^{1b},K/TMs^2,I; consist['ing' *del.*] severally [*intrl.*] MS;TMs^1(u)^a,TMs^2(u)

§91.28 points] WJ/TMs^{1b},K/TMs^2,I; the [*insrtd.*] ['serial' *del. ab. del.* 'with'] points MS;TMs^1(u)^a,TMs^2(u)

91.28 common] WJ/TMs^{1a}+; *om.* MS,TMs^1(u)^b

‡91.29 if . . . not] WJ/TMs^{1a}+; unless they be MS,TMs^1(u)^b

91.31 How$_\wedge$ then,] WJ/TMs^{1a-b}; $\sim$, $\sim$, TMs^2,I; How, MS,TMs^1(u)

91.34 Russell$_\wedge$ (if . . . him),] WJ/TMs^{1a}(if [*ov.* 'as'] I *rightly [*intrl.*]); Russell, if . . . him, TMs^2,I; Russell, as I apprehend him, WJ/TMs^{1b}; Russell, MS,TMs^1(u)

91.35 the points] WJ/TMs^{1a}; all the sets of points WJ/TMs^{1b}; the sets of points K/TMs^2,I; the points TMs^2(u); all the points MS,TMs^1(u)

91.36 in both paths] WJ/TMs^{1a}+; *om.* MS,TMs^1(u)^b

§91.38 false.] WJ/TMs$^{1a(r2)-b}$+; false. This amounts to *implying [*ab. del.* 'saying'] that remainders of continua may be neglected, from the ['number' *del.*] point of view of number. Two *infinite [*intrl.*] continua will 'balance,' no matter how much *finite [*intrl.*] you may add *or subtract. [*ab. del.* 'to *either. [*ab. del.* 'to one or subtract from the other. Numerically, the limit of']'] [*del. intrl.* 'Since, in short,'] Achilles' [*alt. fr.* 'Achille's'] path and the reptile's ['is the same.' *del.*] have the same numerical 'limit' (namely omega); [*del.* 'the race can easily be *won. [*ab. del.* 'run.'] [¶] It seems to me that in how'] *so, no matter how [*insrtd.*] many inches 'longer' the one is than the other, the *time in which they are traversed may be the same.^{x} [*ab. del.* 'race can easily be won.'; *fn.* 'x' *orig. keyed to fn.* 14] MS;TMs^1(u)(*except* $_\wedge$balance,$_\wedge$ . . . omega)$_\wedge$ So, . . . $_\wedge$longer$_\wedge$); false. This amounts to implying that 'remainders' may be neglected, from

the point of view of number, when continua are compared. Two infinite continua will 'balance,' no matter how much finite ['distance' *del.*] quantity you may add to either. Achilles' path and the reptile's have the same numerical 'limit' (namely Omega); so, no matter how many inches 'longer' the one is than the other, the time in which they are traversed may be the same. The ['number of' *del.*] positions occupied simultaneously by the two runners, and the ['number of' *del.*] instants of time with which they coincide form ['['an' *del.*] a' *del.*] three absolutely congruent number-series, which begin and end together, so the overtaking ['must occur.' *del.*] judged impossible by Zeno must in point of fact occur. WJ/TMs$^{1a(r1)}$

91.38-92.10 For . . . puzzle] TMs^{1a} (*handwritten*)+; *om.* MS

91.38 each and] *intrl.*; 'and' *written as* '&'

91.38 point traversed] *ab. del.* 'position occupied'

91.38 the tortoise] *ab. del.* 'Achilles'

91.38-39 is . . . traversed] *ab. del.* 'is a *corresponding [*intrl.*] position occupied'

91.39 Achilles$_\wedge$ at a] WJ/TMs^{1b}; $\sim$, at the TMs^{1a}(*handwritten*), TMs^1(u)^a+

91.39 at] *aft. del.* '[*del.* 'and *to ['to' *del.*] each of these pairs of points [*ab. del.* 'both sets of positions'] ['coincide with' *del.*] there ['is one' *del.*] corresponds ['s' *ov.* 'ing'] ['to [*intrl.*] more ins' *del.*]'] to one point on the time ['scl' *del.*] scale corresponds'

91.39 point of] ('point' *ab. del.* 'moment' *aft. del. insrtd.* 'point'); *insrtd.*

92.1 exact] *ab. del.* 'one-to-one'

92.1 correspondence,] *comma insrtd. bef. del.* 'of ['point' *del.*] these three sets *to [*ab. del.* 'of'] point['s' *del.*] in each'

92.2 three] *intrl.*

92.2 ²of] *intrl.*

92.3 sets [*comma del.*]] *intrl.*

92.4 is] *ab. del.* 'can'

92.4 no] *aft. del.* 'be'

92.4 recurrent] *intrl.*

92.4 head-start] *ab. del.* 'path,'

92.5-6 can't . . . can't] *stet* TMs¹ᵃ (*handwritten*); cannot . . . cannot TMs¹ (. . . can not TMs¹[u] ᵃ)+

92.5 can't] *aft. del.* '[', owing to his back-start,' *del.*] handicap at the *outset [*alt. fr.* 'outside'],'

92.5 up–] WJ/TMs¹ᵇ; ~, TMs¹ᵃ (*handwritten*),TMs¹(u)ᵃ+

92.6 The . . . perfectly.] WJ/TMs¹ᵇ; The books balance to the end. WJ/TMs¹ᵃ+; *om.* TMs¹ᵃ(*handwritten*),TMs¹(u)

92.7 Achilles'] TMs¹; ~ₐ TMs¹ᵃ (*handwritten*); Achilles's TMs²,I

92.7 ¹the] *aft. del.* 'is mated with'

92.7 point] *insrtd. for del.* 'one'

92.7 tortoise's] TMs¹+; tortoises TMs¹ᵃ(*handwritten*)

92.7 ³the] *aft. del.* 'both are mated w'

92.7 last time-] *ab. del.* 'same'

92.8 of] *stet* TMs¹ᵃ(*handwritten*); in TMs¹+

92.8 the race] *aft. del.* 'time–'; *bef. del.* 'mathematically coincide'

92.8 coincide.] (*period over comma*); *bef. del.* '*so that ['and' *del.*] the puzzle [*intrl.*] ['The paradox thus disappears.ˣ' *del.*]'

92.8 With] *ab. del.* 'In'

92.9 to me] WJ/TMs¹ᵇ; to be TMs¹ᵃ(*handwritten*),TMs¹(u)ᵃ+

92.10 is . . . disappear] WJ/TMs¹ᵇ, K/TMs²,I; quite disappears TMs¹ᵃ(*handwritten*),TMs¹(u)ᵃ, TMs²(u); *om.* MS

92.10 disappear.¹⁴] WJ/TMs¹ᵃ (*pencil*; quite disappears.)+; ~.ₐ TMs¹ᵃ(*handwritten*),TMs¹(u)ᵇ

92.11 , however,] WJ/TMs¹ᵇ; ₐ~ₐ K/TMs²,I; *om.* MS,TMs¹(u)ᵃ, TMs²(u)

92.11 statements dodge] WJ/TMs¹ᵃ+; treatment dodges MS,TMs¹(u)ᵇ

92.13 varietyₐ] WJ/TMs¹ᵇ; ~, MS,TMs¹(u)ᵃ+

§92.14-15 assumes . . . thinks]

WJ/TMs¹ᵇ;K/TMs²,I(runₐ); supposes ['es' *ov.* 'ing'] that the race is already runₐ and MS;TMs¹(u)ᵃ,TMs²(u)

‡92.15 remainsₐ] WJ/TMs¹ᵃ⁻ᵇ+; ~, MS,TMs¹(u)

§92.15 numerically] WJ/TMs¹ᵃ⁻ᵇ+; numerical['ly' *del.*] ['*one of [*ab. del.* 'measur']' *del.*] MS;TMs¹(u)

§92.17 attends] WJ/TMs¹ᵇ,K/TMs²,I; haunts [*ab. del.* 'concerns'] MS; TMs¹(u)ᵃ,TMs²(u)

‡§92.20 intervalₐ . . . traversed firstₐ] WJ/TMs¹ᵇ(r2),I; ~, . . . ~ ~, WJ/TMs¹ᵇ(r1); ~ₐ . . . ~ ~, K/TMs²; ~, . . . crossed *first, [*ab. del.* '['first' *del.*] recurrently and'] MS;TMs¹(u)ᵃ,TMs²(u) (*both* intervalₐ)

92.22 quantum] *stet* MS,TMs¹(u)ᵃ, TMs²(u),I; *ital.* WJ/TMs¹ᵇ,K/TMs²

*92.24 produced] *stet* MS; *om.* TMs¹(u); created WJ/TMs¹ᵃ⁻ᵇ+

92.25 in it] WJ/TMs¹ᵇ,K/TMs²,I; *om.* MS,TMs¹(u)ᵃ,TMs²(u)

§92.27-28 so, . . . once.] WJ/TMs¹ᵇ(r2) (soₐ);K/TMs²,I; *so, for our imagination, ['at a stroke.' *del.*] all at once. [*ab. del.* 'all at once in that peculiar *form. [*ab. del.* 'shape.']'] MS; WJ/TMs¹ᵇ(r1) (imaginationₐ TMs¹[u]ᵃ,TMs²[u])

92.28-29 a single decree,] WJ/TMs¹ᵇ, K/TMs²,I; *om.* MS,TMs¹(u)ᵃ, TMs²(u)

92.30 actually] WJ/TMs¹ᵇ,K/TMs²,I; *om.* MS,TMs¹(u)ᵃ,TMs²(u)

*§92.30-31 instantaneous act.] *stet* MS ('act.' *ab. del.* 'process.'); PJ/TMs¹ᵃ(*pencil*),TMs²(u); continuous act. TMs¹(u); process ['inst' *del.*] continuous in the mathematician's sense. WJ/TMs¹ᵇ;K/TMs²,I (mathematical)

92.31 occupied] WJ/TMs¹ᵇ,K/TMs²,I; *enumerated* MS; enumerated TMs¹(u)ᵃ,TMs²(u)

*‡92.34 ₐneglect.ₐ] WJ/TMs¹ᵇ; '~.' K/TMs²,I; '~ₐ' (Cf. above, p. 70¹¹). MS;TMs¹(u)ᵃ,TMs²(u) (p. 70¹¹)ₐ)

92.34 ∧ in short∧] WJ/TMs¹ᵇ;
, ∼ ∼, K/TMs²,I; *om.* MS,TMs¹(u)ᵃ,
TMs²(u)

§92.35 method of occupation∧]
WJ/TMs¹ᵇ⁽ʳ²⁾(occupation,),K/TMs²,
I; 'law of formation,' or method of
occupation, WJ/TMs¹ᵇ⁽ʳ¹⁾; 'law['' of
['production' *del.*] generation in
growth' *del.*] of formation' MS;
TMs¹(u)ᵃ,TMs²(u)

92.35-36 implied in the famous]
WJ/TMs¹ᵇ,K/TMs²,I; occupied in
Zeno's MS,TMs¹(u)ᵃ,TMs²(u)

‡§92.38-39 finds . . . convenient to]
WJ/TMs¹ᵇ,K/TMs²,I; paraphrases
the puzzle, *so [*intrl.*] I MS;
TMs¹(u)(puzzle∧); has *had [*ov.*
'to'] paraphrase the puzzle, so I
have *had [*ov.* 'to'] to WJ/TMs¹ᵃ;
has paraphrased the puzzle, so I
have had to TMs²(u)

93.1-2 "the . . . mystery,"] H;
sg. qts. MS+ (mystery,∧ TMs¹)

93.1-2 *without enumeration*] *stet* MS;
rom. Russell,TMs¹+

93.6 page] I; p. MS; Page TMs¹⁻²

‡93.6 tho] H; though MS+

93.8 Evellin∧ and others,] WJ/TMs¹ᵃ+;
∼, ∼ ∼∧ MS,TMs¹(u)ᵇ

93.10 if] *stet* MS,TMs¹(u)ᵇ,
WJ/TMs¹ᵃ⁽ʳ²⁾+; when the
WJ/TMs¹ᵃ⁽ʳ¹⁾

93.11 which . . . were] WJ/TMs¹ᵃ,
TMs²,I; be MS,TMs¹(u)ᵇ

§93.11-12 if . . . could] WJ/TMs¹ᵃ,
TMs²,I; *if [ab. del. 'were'] this *be
[*intrl.*] the only way of reaching it,
['could' del.] can [insrtd.]* MS;
TMs¹(u)ᵇ(*rom.*)

93.13 therefore,] *stet* MS,WJ/TMs¹ᵃ,
TMs²(u); ∼ ∧ TMs¹(u); therefore,
in these cases, WJ/TMs¹ᵇ,K/TMs²
(cases;),I(cases;)

93.14 reached] TMs¹+; reacht MS

93.14 in . . . cases] WJ/TMs¹ᵃ+;
om. MS,TMs¹(u)ᵇ

93.15 finite and] WJ/TMs¹ᵇ,
K/TMs²,I; *om.* MS,TMs¹(u)ᵃ,
TMs²(u)

93.15 approach−] WJ/TMs¹ᵃ+; ∼,
MS,TMs¹(u)ᵇ

93.16 wholly∧] WJ/TMs¹ᵃ⁻ᵇ+; ∼,

MS,TMs¹(u)

93.21 may be] WJ/TMs¹ᵇ; is MS,
TMs¹(u)ᵃ,TMs²,I

93.24 hypothesis . . . infinity]
WJ/TMs¹ᵇ⁽ʳ²⁾; hypothesis of a
growing physical infinity
WJ/TMs¹ᵇ⁽ʳ¹⁾; physical hypothesis
MS,TMs¹(u)ᵃ,TMs²,I

93.24-25 *"if . . . task."*] H; *sg. qts.*
MS+

93.24-25 *T. S. lives . . . doesn't weary*]
stet MS+; he had lived . . . not
wearied Russell

93.26 made. The] WJ/TMs¹ᵇ; ∼ :
the MS,TMs¹(u)ᵃ,TMs²,I

93.34 *Principles*] H; *Philosophy* MS+
(*rom.* TMs¹[u]ᵇ)

93.35 *mathématiques*] H; *cap.* MS+
(*rom.* TMs¹ᵇ; *no accent* TMs¹ᵃ)

93.36 'The . . . Order,'] H; *l.c.*
MS(The);TMs¹,TMs²(u)(The
Continuum; [*ital.* WJ/TMs¹ᵃ]);
∧*The Continuum as a Type of
Order,*∧ K/TMs²,I

93.36-37 *Mathematics*] TMs¹(*rom.*
TMs¹ᵇ; *ital.* WJ/TMs¹ᵃ)+; *l.c.* MS

‡93.38 ¹the] TMs¹+; *ital.* MS

93.41(*second*),42,43 vol.] WJ/TMs¹ᵇ;
om. MS,TMs¹(u)ᵃ,TMs²,I

93.42 S. Waterlow . . . 1910;]
WJ/TMs¹ᵇ(*pencil*);K/TMs²,I(Water-
ton); *om.* MS,TMs¹(u)ᵃ,TMs²(u)

93.42 J.] H; *space* MS,TMs¹; *om.*
TMs²,I

93.46 S.] H; MS+

94.1 nature] WJ/TMs¹ᵇ,K/TMs²,I;
constitution MS,TMs¹(u)ᵃ,TMs²(u)

94.2 by] *stet* MS,TMs¹(u),
WJ/TMs¹ᵇ⁽ʳ³⁾,K/TMs²,I; either by
WJ/TMs¹ᵃ⁻ᵇ⁽ʳ¹⁾,TMs²(u); as by
WJ/TMs¹ᵇ⁽ʳ²⁾

‡94.2 amounts∧] WJ/TMs¹ᵇ; ∼,
MS,TMs¹(u)ᵃ,TMs²,I

94.3 we . . . it] WJ/TMs¹ᵇ,K/TMs²,I;
om. MS,TMs¹(u)ᵃ,TMs²(u)

§94.4 it by . . . repeating]
WJ/TMs¹ᵇ⁽ʳ²⁾,K/TMs²⁽ʳ²⁾,I; *it
retrospectively [ab. del. 'them
subsequently'] by ['abstract
repetition of' del.]* indefinite
repetition of MS;TMs¹(u)ᵃ,TMs²(u);
it by our conception retrospectively

and indefinitely repeating
WJ/TMs 1b(r1); it by our later
conception when it indefinitely
repeats K/TMs 2(r1)

§94.4-5 subdividing] WJ/TMs 1b,
K/TMs 2,I; subdividing *in conception [*intrl.*] MS;TMs 1(u)a,TMs 2(u)

‡94.6 treatment;] WJ/TMs 1a+; ∼,
MS,TMs 1(u)b

‡94.15 consummation] WJ/TMs 1a+;
summation MS,TMs 1(u)b

94.15 units∧ . . . points')∧]
WJ/TMs 1b,K/TMs 2[points'),],I
[points'),] ; units, MS,TMs 1(u);
units∧ WJ/TMs 1a,TMs 2(u)

94.16-17 (such as 'space')]
WJ/TMs 1b,K/TMs 2,I; *om.*
MS,TMs 1(u)a,TMs 2(u)

94.18 absurd] WJ/TMs 1a+; absurd
and self-contradictory MS,TMs 1(u)b

‡94.19 (p. 88)] H; (p.   ) MS; *om.*
TMs 1+

§94.21 accept,] WJ/TMs 1a+; ∼∧
[*bef. del.* 'here, [*ab. caret formed
fr. orig. comma*]'] MS;TMs 1(u)b

‡94.21 data] WJ/TMs 1a+; datum
MS,TMs 1(u)b

‡94.22 concepts] WJ/TMs 1a+; the
concept MS,TMs 1(u)b

94.23 'problem . . . infinite,']
TMs 1+; *db. qts.* MS

§94.25-26 complaint . . . method]
WJ/TMs 1a+; ['other' *del.*] charge
*against the intellectualistic method
[*intrl.*] that it MS;TMs 1(u)
(method, WJ/TMs 1b)

‡94.26 (above, p. 46)] H; (above p.   )
MS; (above page)TMs 1,TMs 2(u)
[*del.* K/TMs 2; *om.* I]

94.28 change,] WJ/TMs 1b; ∼∧
MS,TMs 1(u)a+

§94.29 mathematic['s' *del.*]] *stet*
MS,WJ/TMs 1b; mathematics
TMs 1(u)a+

‡94.30-37 "Weierstrass . . .
quotients"] H; *all sg. qts.* MS+

94.32 flight,] Russell,I; ∼∧ MS-I(p)

94.32 *op.*] I; Op. MS,WJ/TMs 1a-b,
TMs 2; Opus TMs 1(u)

94.33-34 *state . . . .* "Motion] H;
state of motion. Motion MS,
TMs 1(u), Russell(*state*); "state of

motion." Motion WJ/TMs 1b; ∧state
of motion,' he ['continues:' *del.*]
says elsewhere: 'Motion WJ/TMs 1a,
TMs 2(u) (elsewhere; 'motion
K/TMs 2,I)

94.38 *dis*continuum] WJ/TMs 1b;
rom. MS,TMs 1(u)a+

94.40-43 —It . . . case.] WJ/TMs 1b
(Russell∧s),K/TMs 2(∧It),I(∧It);
om. MS,TMs 1(u)a,TMs 2(u)

94.41 of . . . etc.,] *intrl.*

94.41 mathematical] *aft. del.*
'*logical and [*intrl.*]'

94.41 world] *final* 's' *del.*

94.42 charge] *ab. del.* 'suppose'

95.6 novelty,] WJ/TMs 1a+; ∼∧
MS,TMs 1(u)b

96.0 *Chapter . . .* View] H; Second
Sub-problem | Cause and Effect. MS
(*db. underl.; see* Alterations 96.18),
TMs 1(u)b; Second Sub-problem: Cause
and Effect. WJ/TMs 1a(*db. underl.*),
TMs 2(u); *Fourth Problem*: ['III—
The Problem of' *del.*] *Novelty* |
*Chapter XII Novelty and Causation:
The Conceptualist View* K/TMs 2(r1);
*Chapter XII Novelty and Causation:
The Conceptual View*x | [*fn.*] x[In
the authors manuscript this chapter
bore the heading—"Second
Sub-problem: Cause and Effect.∧
Ed.] K/TMs 2(r2),I (Causation— . . .
author's . . . 'Second Sub-problem—
. . . Effect.' [Effect∧— I(p)])

96.3 Being∧] WJ/TMs 1a+; ∼,
MS (*error*),TMs 1(u)b

‡96.4 large,] TMs 1+; ∼∧ MS

96.6 we] TMs 1+; be MS (*error*)

96.10 read'] I; ∼" K/TMs 2; ∼∧
MS,TMs 1,TMs 2(u)

96.17 considering] WJ/TMs 1a+;
taking MS

‡96.22 *Metaphysics*] K/TMs 2,I;
rom. TMs 1,TMs 2(u); *l.c. rom.* MS

97.4 'efficient'] WJ/TMs 1a+; ∧∼∧
MS,TMs 1(u)b

97.6-7 ∧that . . . *itself.*∧] *stet* MS;
'∼. . .∼.' (*all rom.*) WJ/TMs 1a+;
∧∼. . .∼.∧ (*all rom.*) TMs 1(u)b

97.11 sub-principles] WJ/TMs 1a+;
∼∧∼ MS(*hyphen doubtful*),
TMs 1(u)b

‡97.13 No . . . cause.] TMs¹+;
   ital. MS
97.29 *non*] K/TMs²,I; non TMs¹,
   TMs²(u); not MS
97.30 *Causa*] PJ/TMs¹ᵃ⁻ᵇ(*rom.*),
   TMs²,I(p); *causa* MS,TMs¹(u)
   (*rom.*),I
97.39 a] H; A MS+
97.41 cause,] *stet* MS+; cause,
   then, Mill
98.21 rationalistic] K/TMs²,I;
   rationistic WJ/TMs¹ᵇ; monistic
   MS,TMs¹(u)ᵃ,TMs²(u)
§98.30 conditions‸] *stet* MS(*comma
   del.*)+; ~, Mill
98.36 William] TMs¹+; Wm. MS
98.36 What] TMs¹+; what
   Hamilton,MS
98.37 phænomenally] Hamilton;
   phenomenally MS+
98.39 know] *stet* MS+; come to know
   Hamilton
§99.2 'God'] WJ/TMs¹ᵇ,K/TMs²,I;
   the ['word' *del.*] 'God' MS;
   TMs¹(u)ᵃ,TMs²(u)
99.4 Geulincx] I³; Geulinx MS;
   Genlinx TMs¹,TMs²(u); Guelincx
   K/TMs²,I¹⁻²
99.8 of . . . are] WJ/TMs¹ᵇ(*pencil*),
   K/TMs²,I; are MS,TMs¹(u)ᵃ,
   TMs²(u) (*see* HC 99.8 *for* TMs²
   readings)
‡99.15 pre-established] K/TMs²,I;
   pre establisht MS; preestablished
   TMs¹,TMs²(u)
*‡99.15 so called] H; ~ - ~MS+
99.17 continuity,] K/TMs²,I; ~‸
   MS–TMs²(u)
99.24 'the] TMs¹+; " ~ MS
99.25 *Treatise . . . Essays,*] H; 'treatise
   on human nature‸' . . . 'essays,' MS;
   'treatise on . . . nature,' . . . 'Essays,'
   TMs¹,TMs²(u); *init. caps.* (*except
   'on'; all rom.*) K/TMs²,I
§99.28 we] WJ/TMs¹ᵇ,K/TMs²,I;
   [*del.* 'our imagination' *ab. del.* 'we'
   not restored in error] MS; *om.*
   TMs¹(u)ᵃ,TMs²(u)
*§99.28–29 isolate . . . from] *stet*
   isolate any *'energy' ['transitive'
   del.] transennt from [*ab. del.*
   'dynamic relation passing ['from'

del.] over from what we call']
   MS; isolated ('isolatr' TMs¹[u])
   'energy' transmit from TMs¹(u),
   PJ/TMs¹ᵃ⁻ᵇ(r1),TMs²(u); isolate
   the 'energy' transmitted from
   WJ/TMs¹ᵇ(r2),K/TMs²,I
99.29 trans-sent] H; transennt MS;
   transmit TMs¹(u)ᵃ,TMs²(u); transmitted WJ/TMs¹ᵇ,K/TMs²,I
99.30–100.13 "All . . . other."] H;
   all sg. qts. MS+
99.30 deriv'd from,] Hume; derived
   from‸ MS+
99.31 impression,] Hume; ~‸ MS+
99.33 any thing] Hume; anything MS+
99.37 *seems*] Hume; seems MS+
99.37 be,] Hume; ~‸ MS+
99.39 reasonings, or] Hume; ~‸ or
   in MS+
‡99.40 ‸"Nothing] TMs¹(‸ '~)+;
   . . . ' ~ MS
‡99.40 evident,] Hume; ~‸ MS+
‡99.40 mind] *stet* MS+; human mind
   Hume
‡100.1 objects,] Hume; ~‸ MS+
‡100.1 betwixt] Hume; between MS+
‡100.2 efficacy,] Hume; ~‸ MS+
100.7 we are] *stet* MS+; the mind is
   Hume
100.7–8 the first one] *stet* MS+; one
   event Hume
100.8 believe,] Hume; ~‸ MS+
100.9 imagination . . .] H; ~‸ MS+
100.10 impression,] Hume; ~‸ MS+
§100.11 case." "A] H; *~.' . . .*'A
   [*ov.* 'a'] [*qts. added*] MS; ~‸' . . .
   '~ PJ/TMs¹ᵃ⁻ᵇ,TMs²(u); '~‸' . . .
   ‸~ TMs¹(u); ~‸‸ . . . '~ K/TMs²;
   ~.' '~ I
100.11 cause] *stet* MS+; CAUSE
   Hume
100.12 it,] Hume; ~‸ MS+
100.13 determines . . .] H; ~‸ MS+
100.17 free-will] H; free will MS;
   freewill TMs¹+
100.20 Of . . . Necessity] H; *l.c.*
   MS(on)+
§100.36 of,] TMs²,I; of, [*intrl.*]
   MS;TMs¹
‡101.7;‡101.13 short,] TMs¹+; ~‸
   MS
101.8 tho] H; though MS+

‡101.10-13 "All . . . *connected.*"] H; *all sg. qts.* MS+

‡101.11 writes,] TMs¹+; ∼ ∧ MS

101.12 another;] Hume; ∼ , MS+

‡101.14 anything] TMs¹+; any thing MS

101.25 *Critique*] H; *rom.* MS+

101.37 expressions] TMs¹+; expression MS (*error*)

101.38 The] TMs²,I; the MS,TMs¹

§101.39 *Krit. d. reinen Vernunft*] H; ['C' *del.*] ['K.d.r.V.' *del.*] Critique of pure reason MS; *Critique of Pure Reason* TMs¹(*rom.*)+

102.1 *Verstand*] TMs²,I; *rom.* MS,TMs¹

102.13 yet!'] TMs¹+; ∼ !.' MS (*period error*)

102.19 in] WJ/TMs¹ᵇ,K/TMs²,I; it MS,TMs¹(u)ª,TMs²(u)

102.20-21 the earth . . . everything−] WJ/TMs¹ᵇ(¹earth's); K/TMs²,I; of the earth's attraction− MS,TMs¹(u)ª, TMs²(u)

102.20 it.] *ab. del.* 'the air.'

§102.22 generalize facts,] WJ/TMs¹ᵇ, K/TMs²,I; coordinate & correlate *phenomena [ab. caret formed fr. orig. comma*] MS;TMs¹(u)ª,TMs²(u)

‡102.23 them.⁸] H; ∼ ∧ MS+

102.27 member,] K/TMs²,I; ∼ ∧ MS,TMs¹,TMs²(u)

*§102.38 humian] *stet (alt. fr.* 'humean' *or* 'humaan') MS; human TMs¹-I¹; humean I²+

102.38 *flounders,*] TMs¹+(*rom.*); ∼ ; MS

102.40 *Logic,*] K/TMs²,I; ∼ : MS,TMs¹,TMs²(u)

§103.19-24 "Consciousness . . . reality"] H; *all sg. qts.* MS(reality ∧ [*db. qt. del.*])+ (reality, I[p])

103.26 satisfactorily] TMs¹+; satisfactory MS (*error*)

103.41 Abschn.] H; Absn. MS+

*104.5-6 is confused] H; , is, as I called it on p. 71, confused MS; TMs¹,TMs²(u)(71 ∧); , is, as I have called it before, confused K/TMs²,I

104.9-17 "Mathematicians . . . 'relations.' "] H; '∼ . . . ∧ ∼ ∧∧' MS; ∧ ∼ . . . ∧ ∼ ∧ ' ∧ TMs¹(u); ∧ ∼ . . .

'∼ ∧ ' ∧ PJ/TMs¹ᵃ⁻ᵇ,TMs²,I ('relations.' ∧)

104.10-11 'function.'] H; "∼ ." MS; ∧ ∼ · ∧ TMs¹+

104.11 *a*=f[*b*]] Jerusalem; *a*=f[*b*] MS(*error*); A equals B TMs¹+

*104.17 'relations.'¹²] I; *no fn. indicator; fn. is text within parens* MS-TMs²

104.22 appellation] I; appelation MS-TMs²(*error*)

§104.22-23 ∧ an "unearthly . . . categories."] H; *"∼ [poss. sg. ov. db. qt.*] ∧ ∼ . . . ∼ .' MS; '∼ ∧ ∼ . . . ∼ .' TMs¹+

‡§104.32 'non fingo hypotheses,'] K/TMs²; *non fingo* *hypotheses,' [²'e' ov. 'i'*] MS; nonfingo 'hypothesis,' TMs¹;TMs²(u) (non fingo); *non fingo* ∧ hypothesis,' I¹(*all rom.* I[p]); '*non fingo* ∧ ∼ ,' I²+

§105.0 *Chapter . . .* View] H; Chapter VII | Causation: II. The perceptual view. MS (*triple underl.*),TMs¹, TMs²(u); *Fourth Problem:* ['III.− The Problem of' *del.*] *Novelty* | Chapter XIII Novelty and Causation: The perceptual view. K/TMs²(r1); Chapter XIII *Novelty and Causation: The perceptual view.* K/TMs²(r2),I (CAUSATION−)

‡105.3 naive] H; *ital.* MS; *om.* TMs¹+

§105.4-5 "Le . . . discours ∧ "] H; '∼ [*sg. qt. ov. db. qt.*] . . . ∼ ,' MS(discours ∧)+

105.9 'will'] *stet* MS,PJ/TMs¹ᵃ, TMs²,I; "∼ " PJ/TMs¹ᵇ; ∧ ∼ ∧ TMs¹(u)

§105.11-13 arouse; we . . . ; we] I; ∼ ; We . . . ; We [*semicolons ov. poss. periods; caps. unreduced in error*] MS; ∼ ; We . . . ; we TMs¹, K/TMs²(arouse ∧ | TMs²[u])

105.14-15 extinguished] TMs¹+; extinguisht MS

‡§105.16 cooperant] TMs¹; ['the [*ab. del.* 'a']' *del.*] co operant [*alt. fr.* 'co existing'] MS; ∼ - | ∼ TMs²;I

‡105.18 *close*] *stet* MS; close TMs¹(u)ª,TMs²(u); 'close' WJ/TMs¹ᵇ, K/TMs²,I

106.20 accomplished] TMs^1+;
accomplisht MS

106.28 ^{2}a] TMs^1+; an MS (*error*)

§106.39 appear] TMs^1+; appears ['s' *added*] MS

[*begin* P^{34}]

106.40 $_\wedge$The] *stet* MS(P^{34}),TMs^1(u),I;
"The PJ/TMs^{1a-b},TMs^2,I(p) ('$\sim$)
(PJ/TMs^{1b} *prefixes* 'Printed ¶')

106.40 situation] WJ/MS(P^{34})+;
situation possesses all that the idea
contains. He MS(P^{34})

107.1 triumph,] WJ/MS(P^{34})+; $\sim_\wedge$
MS(P^{34})

107.3 colour] TMs^1; color MS(P^{34}),
TMs^2,I

107.6 The] WJ/MS(P^{34})+; If we
suppose activities to go on outside
of our experience it is in forms like
these that we must suppose them,
or else give them some other name;
for the MS(P^{34}) [*in margin of* MS
is del. pencil note 'own personal']

107.9 ¶No] WJ/MS(P^{34})(*not marked*)+; ¶Were this the end of the
matter, one might think that when-
ever we had successfully lived
through an activity-situation we
should have to be permitted,
without provoking contradiction,
to say that we had been really
active, that we had met real resistance and had really prevailed.
Lotze somewhere says that to be an
entity all that is necessary is to
gelten as an entity, to operate, or be
felt, experienced, recognized, or in
any way realized, as such. In our
activity-experiences the activity
assuredly fulfils Lotze's demand. It
makes itself *gelten*. It is witnessed at
its work. No MS(P^{34})

107.9 'efficacies'] WJ/MS(P^{34})+;
$_\wedge$activities$_\wedge$ MS(P^{34})

107.10 universe] WJ/MS(P^{34})+;
universe of ours MS(P^{34})

107.13 obstacles,] WJ/MS(P^{34})+; $\sim$;
MS(P^{34})

107.19 causal agency] WJ/MS(P^{34})+;
activity MS(P^{34})

[*end* P^{34}]

107.20 that] WJ/TMs^{1b}(*intrl. aft.*
'our' *in error*);K/TMs^2,I; *om.*
MS,TMs^1(u)^a,TMs^2(u)

§107.20 continue] WJ/TMs^{1b},
K/TMs^2,I; continue [*intrl.*] into
MS;TMs^1(u)^a,TMs^2(u)

*107.39 ^{1}causes] *stet* MS+

108.39 1904] H; 1894 MS+

109.25–26 as . . . dissolved]
WJ/TMs^{1b},K/TMs^2,I; like salt
dissolved in water MS,TMs^1(u)^a,
TMs^2(u) [WJ/TMs^{1b} *in error fails to delete* TMs^1(u) 'in water']

109.30 so-called] I; $\sim_\wedge \sim$ MS,I(p);
socalled TMs$^{1-2}$

110.6 *of*] TMs^1(of)+; of | of MS
(*error*)

110.7 activity,] Hodgson; $\sim_\wedge$ MS+

110.9 *nothing*] Hodgson; *rom.* MS+

§110.11–17 "causality . . . -existent"]
H; '$\sim$ . . . *$_\wedge \sim$' [*period del.; sg. ov. poss. db. qt.*] MS; '$\sim$ . . . -existamt'
TMs^1,TMs^2(-existant); *sg. qts.* I

110.11 . . . has] H; $_\wedge \sim$ MS+

110.12 common-sense] Hodgson,I;
$\sim_\wedge | \sim$ MS; $\sim_\wedge \sim$ TMs^1,TMs^2(u);
commonsense K/TMs^2,I(p)

110.16 recognised,] Hodgson;
recognized$_\wedge$ MS+

110.17 non-existent] Hodgson,
TMs^1+; $\sim_\wedge \sim$ MS

110.17 375] H; 378 MS+

§110.20 'Mental Activity']
K/TMs^2,I; $_\wedge \sim \sim_\wedge$ TMs^1,TMs^2(u);
mental [*intrl. in ink*] 'Activity$_\wedge$ MS

§110.21 *Pluralistic Universe*] TMs^1
(*rom.*)+; ['a' *del.*] pluralistic universe
MS

APPENDIX

111.0 *Appendix*] K/TMs^{1b}(S),I; *om.*
TMs^{1b}(S)

111.1 'Intellectualism'] K/TMs^{1b}(S),I;

¶ PAULSEN'S chapter on Knowledge
and Faith shows a certain courage,
for in Germany Intellectualism is

today in the ascendent. | [¶] 'Intel-
lectualism' TMs^{1b}(S)
112.26 'passive'] I; "∼" TMs^{1b}(S)
112.32 natural] *stet* TMs^{1b}(S),I; *ital.*
Paulsen
112.32 ¹order] *stet* TMs^{1b}(S),I; order
of the world Paulsen
112.32 moral] *stet* TMs^{1b}(S),I; *ital.*
Paulsen
112.37 'evidence'] I; "∼" TMs^{1b}(S)
113.2 'faith-ladder'] I; "∼-∼"
TMs^{1b}(S)
113.4 -contradictory;] I; -∼.
TMs^{1b}(S)
113.20 'come true.'] I; "∼ ∼."
TMs^{1b}(S)
113.22-23 'pluralistically' . . .
'melioristic'] I; *all db. qts.* TMs^{1b}(S)
113.22-23 universe . . . above,]
K/TMs^{1b}(S),I; universe (the "melioristic" universe of p. 30, above)
TMs^{1b}(S)
113.29 of] I; or TMs^{1b}(S),I(p)
113.37 'Probability' . . . 'possibility']
I; *db. qts.* TMs^{1b}(S)

114.2-3 'bare' . . . 'grounded'] I;
db. qts. TMs^{1b}(S)
114.14;115.6 Insurance-companies] H;
∼ ∼ TMs^{1b}(S),I
114.22 1-5000] I; 1−5000 TMs^{1b}(S),
I(p)
114.23 'long run'] I; "∼ ∼" TMs^{1b}(S)
115.16 e.g.] H; *e.g.* TMs^{1b}(S),I
115.17,37 prevail.¹] K/TMs^{1b}(S),I;
prevail. | [¶] Read here W. JAMES'S
Essays entitled "The Will to Believe,"
and "The Sentiment of Rationality,".
pp. 90–110 (not for examination).
TMs^{1b}(S)
115.19 'melioristic' universe] I; "∼"
universe of p. 30 of this syllabus
TMs^{1b}(S)
116.29 pattern ever] I; patter ever
TMs^{1b}(S); patter never I(p)
116.32-35 'vicious . . . vicious.'] I;
all db. qts. TMs^{1b}(S)
117.6-7 *Religion . . . Forecast,*] H;
ˏReligion, a criticism and a forecast,ˏ TMs^{1b}(S); "∼ . . . ∼," I
(*rom.*) (*like text* I[p])

Textual Notes

9.18–19 and . . . excluded,] This is the first of a number of examples in which James's corrections of faults in the typescript take a different form from the readings of MS that Peggy had mistyped. Since James did not consult the MS when he was working over TMs[1], in either copy, he was likely to try to guess what reading Peggy had corrupted or else he wrote-in some different but obvious way of straightening out the tangle. In such cases it is conservative editorial policy to retain the reading of the MS: since the case was one of correction, no evidence is present that James was in fact revising the reading. The assumption is that he would not have altered TMs[1] if the MS reading had been correctly transcribed.

10.13 generally] This is the first of what appear to be certain of Kallen's unauthoritative changes in TMs[2] for which there is no preserved physical evidence of authority. Another, and more important, is found at 11.28 (see Historical Collation, entry 11.28 concepts). For the discussion of the textual situation in the first fourteen pages of TMs[1] in which TMs[1a] is wanting, see the textual introduction, pp. 243–246.

11.20 a liberal] James's manuscript here is so heavily revised that Peggy made sad work of the typescript and James did not consult the MS when he worked over TMs[1b]. Thus a small problem is raised when Peggy misread altered 'a liberal' (substituted for 'the liberalizing' with the interlined 'a' difficult to read) and typed 'livlier'. Without thought James 'corrected' this 'livlier' by interlining what he thought must have been a missing 'e' and supplying the necessary article as 'a'. Peggy also seems to have confused the second interlined 'ought to get' with the first interlined 'ought to get' and so omitted the repeated phrase which James did not notice and so did not add.

11.23 A] This sentence originally read in MS, 'A man . . . possible companions, socially considered.' James first deleted the final phrase and moved it to the start of the sentence, reducing the capital 'A', to produce the reading, 'Socially considered, a man'; later, dissatisfied with the inverted phrase, he altered 'companions' to 'social mates' but neglected to delete the now repetitious opening. Since the change to 'social mates' appears to be the latest, Kallen's alteration of TMs[2] is desirable, and has been adopted. Although it is true that faced with a manifestly unsatisfactory sentence Kallen had a fifty per cent chance of revising it according to what appear to be James's true intentions; nevertheless, if it is true, as suggested, that in this area he occasionally consulted the MS leaves that had been abstracted in order to complete TMs[1a], the alterations that James made in MS would have assisted him to arrive at the correct solution, to delete 'Socially considered,' and thus to return to the original form of the MS sentence save for the change of 'companions' to 'social mates'.

12.11 shows] By an eyeskip Peggy omitted in TMs[1] the MS phrase 'theoretic progress, and shows' which James supplied by hand as 'progress and has no'. Since this correction was made without reference to manuscript, the original reading has the greater authority.

12.22 encyclopaedic]   MS reads 'encyclopedic', but for the form with *ae*, see 13.25.

12.25 need]   James first wrote 'needs' but then deleted the final 's', a change that Peggy did not observe when she typed the plural in TMs[1] and so established the wrong reading. She did the same with the deleted 's' of 'problems' a few words later.

14.25 *man thinking*, thinking]   The lemma here represents the MS reading, in which James took the time-honored definition and then modified it by the distinction between generalities and particulars. When TMs[1] was typed, as seen in TMs[1b]—the only copy here—Peggy followed MS in the repetition of the word 'thinking' but her omission of the important comma was matched by her usual practice of not underlining words as in MS. Moreover, the end of a line in TMs[1] intervened between the repetition. The absence of a comma and the separation by the end of the line made the result look like an obvious case of dittography, and someone deleted the first 'thinking' at the line ending. The authority of the change comes in question. The pen that made the deletion is probably the same as the one that earlier in the same line had deleted a false start 'of' after 'sense' and it appears to differ in its relative fineness from the various mechanical changes that James himself seems to have made on this page 12 in connection with four substantive revisions or additions. In short, James seems to have read over the page carefully, and if he did not approve of the change (conjecturally assigned to Peggy), he could have altered it. (One cannot of course guarantee that he did not himself delete the first 'thinking'.) If he made the change or 'approved' of Peggy's change, the question then arises whether this is a case of a revision or correction made as a consequence of a typescript error without knowledge of the true reading of the MS. In other cases of this occurrence, the editorial policy ordinarily rejects the alteration in the typescript and accepts the original MS reading on the ground that if the satisfactory MS reading had been known, the typescript would only have been altered to agree with it and not to some other form. This would be the situation with the present reading if one could be certain that, say, in passing Peggy's mistaken correction of an apparent dittographic error he had forgotten the more emphatic twist he had given in MS to the apothegm. The obscuring of the apothegm by the change is not necessarily an improvement that one could feel reasonably certain was a Jamesian revision. On the whole, however, it seems the conservative procedure to retain the MS reading as against the marking of TMs[1b]. Although some lingering doubt may always be present, Kallen's restoration in TMs[2] by hand of the MS reading, complete with italics, is conjectured to derive directly from his consultation of the MS sheet at this point and hence has no connection with the authority or non-authority of the alterations made by hand in TMs[1b], even though it would appear that, in fact, he came to the correct decision.

15.10–11 positive,]   The punctuation of this series should not be in question. At the end of the first element 'theological' in MS, an extension of the final upper stroke of the last 'l' deletes the upper dot of a semicolon to form a comma. At the end of 'metaphysical' a horizontal stroke makes a similar deletion. Probably influenced by this last, Peggy mistook the deletion strokes and typed them as dashes. They were not removed by James and so continued through into the book text.

15.25 then] Peggy dropped the line 'Injuring . . . correspondingly.' (15.24-25) because of an eyeskip when typing TMs[1b]. She then added the line by hand, and when referring back to MS, she misread 'then' as 'thus'.

15.32 'mancies and 'mantics] Since James inscribed each apostrophe in MS as if it were a single quotation mark, his intention is not perhaps demonstrable. At any rate, what he proposed (and an apostrophe seems the best guess) was misinterpreted by Peggy and only partly straightened out in TMs[2] and (I).

16.13 held‸] The MS comma originally preceded 'etc.' and was not removed when James deleted the 'etc.' and interlined 'if . . . near, etc.'

16.14 etc.[7]] James neglected to insert an asterisk as a key to his footnote, an error repeated in TMs[1]. TMs[2] added the number after 'arm' at 16.10 without authority. James customarily added his footnotes in MS immediately below the line in which he had placed the asterisk. Thus the present placement has the best authority, for in MS the footnote follows the end of the paragraph.

17.20-21 sine to sine] See Professor Skrupskelis' Note on this phrase.

18.22 and details] The two changes that James made in this series in TMs[1b] may have been partly due to a reworking of Peggy's error in memorial expansion whereby she typed 'and the details' for 'the details'; but on the whole it would seem that James was trying to clarify an ambiguity in the MS reading (although he certainly did not have the MS before him when he worked over TMs[1b]). In MS 'the details of the sciences,' seems to be but is not in apposition to 'microscopes, electric lights, and telefones', a revised reading. The original went, 'it would be the details and practical applications'. Although without knowing it, by adopting Peggy's unauthoritative 'and' before 'the details', James altered TMs[1b] to produce a series in which 'details' was coordinate with the examples of 'practical applications' as in the first version.

19.7-8 whatever] James's correction 'whatsoever' without a comma, for Peggy's mistyping 'whatfveever,' of MS 'whatever' was made without knowledge of his reading in MS and hence may be taken as of lesser authority.

26.10-11 him . . .] In this manuscript, as in his other holographs, James had no fixed number of dots for indicating ellipsis. Since the exact random number he used in MS, and the different number Peggy typed or was typed in TMs[2], is of no significance, variants in the indication of ellipsis will not be recorded after this point unless a question of meaning is involved.

28.5 imperceptible] MS has no dot over the first 'i' and thus—in James's hand—could as readily be 'unperceptible' as 'imperceptible', which is the reading of TMs[1] that James did not alter when he read over the page. The reading 'imperceptible' is probably the intended one, on the basis of the close parallel 'foisted or shaped themselves imperceptibly into existence' (29.12-13).

29.12 all things have] TMs[1b] p. 40 (29.1-2 *the following . . . leave* 29.19) is not present in the file and must have been accidentally lost along with whatever annotations James made in it. Since TMs[1b] is assumed to have been the copy for TMs[2] at this point, and since the TMs[2] variant is not normal for Peggy to have typed without authority, it is a reasonable assumption that the TMs[2] text reflects a now lost James alteration in the TMs[1b] page. On the basis of this hypothesis, the reading of TMs^2 is accepted as very probably reflecting authority.

30.6-7   *whence* or *why*]   MS read '*what* than with its *that*', which in TMs^1 appears as 'What than with its That'. When in TMs^{1b} James came to revise the sentence's ending, he was aware only of the TMs^1(u) form, and so he wrote 'whence' and 'why' in roman, without underlines, and then with three strokes marked each for initial capitalization so that they would agree with Peggy's mistake, TMs^1 'What . . . That'. This inscription of the accidentals, being based on a misconception and thus departing from the authority of the MS, may be editorially emended to restore the italic form used for original MS '*that*'.

36.7   knowledge]   Examination of the alterations in TMs^{1b} discloses that James first underlined 'knowledge' for emphasis; later, in a different ink which agrees with various other alterations on the page he interlined 'strictly so called,' (probably to follow his identical revision in TMs^{1a}) which removed the reason for the underline although James neglected to delete the marking for italic. Since an anomaly of a sort is created by the interlineation substituting for the underline, and the failure to remove the underline seems accidental, the original TMs^1 reading has been followed to correct the situation.

40.7   -elasticity]   In typing TMs^2 Peggy made the error '-electricity' which was thereupon transferred to (I) and has persisted through all printings.

41.5   'the substitution]   Since this part of an autograph revision in both typescripts substituting for deleted TMs text was copied in TMs^{1b} from TMs^{1a} (although in an intermediate state of revision), the shift in the single quotation mark from before 'substitution' in TMs^{1a} to before 'the' in TMs^{1b} presumably reflects James's final intention.

41.14   33]   The reference in TMs^1 is to 33.21-34.5. K/TMs^2 altered the reference in terms of its own numbers to p. 48, which is p. 52 in (I). Somehow, the reference got shifted in (I) to p. 56 (i.e., 35.15-25). This latter is appropriate enough, but it does not reproduce James's intention.

41.35   consists]   The revision in TMs^1(u) 'consists' to 'consisting' in TMs^{1a-b} was appropriate for TMs^{1b}, but the original should have been restored when at a later time James in TMs^{1a} inserted the subheading at 41.34 and altered the sentence to begin a paragraph below the subheading.

42.14   concepts]   When in TMs^{1a} James altered 'images' to 'concepts' we cannot know whether he had observed his use of concepts earlier in the sentence and intended to alter that, too, but inadvertently let the reading stand. Kallen took the bull by the horns and on his own authority changed the first to read 'ideal constructions', which makes sense and might well have been accepted by James but is a form of emendation forbidden in an edition like the present. An editor has the choice, therefore, of reverting to the original TMs^1 reading 'concepts . . . images' on the grounds that at least this was what James wrote at first and that it is difficult to accept only one half of a necessary emendation in the alteration of 'images' to 'concepts'. The logic of such a position is certainly defensible. But James was right to be dissatisfied with 'images', which is too close in meaning to 'sensations' or 'percepts' and suggests 'pictures' which was not what he meant. The difficulty came when he revised 'images' to 'concepts' without either changing the earlier use (as Kallen ventured to do) or else distinguishing the second use more clearly from the first. The distinction is in fact attempted by the word 'alone': 'made out of its concepts alone'. But the word cannot carry the weight James assigns to it. The 'concepts' that first result from our sensations or perceptual flow are in isolation, or 'alone'; that is, as James states in 41.36–42.1 the concrete terms of perceptual fact are assimilated 'one by one, to so many terms of the conceptual series'. This 'one by one' seems to be what James means by 'alone'. But these terms of the conceptual series having been assimilated then become a 'static arrangement' or overall 'concept' of a quite different and more comprehensive sort, one that can serve to interpret or transform our 'sense-order into a more rational equivalent'. Just before (42.1–3) James has defined this rationalization after the assimilation, as 'assuming that the relations intuitively found among the latter [the conceptual series] are what connect the former [the perceptual fact] too.' Dr. Burkhardt provides an illustration: I look out of my window, and perceive or sense something (a "this") which registers as a "bird" (image, "concept" in isolation, "alone") and then gets related to a whole scheme or "arrangement" of ornithological concepts which provide meaning depending upon how complex my conceptual bird-lore arrangement is. Since 'images' is not really a satisfactory word for the one by one assimilation of percepts to an equal number of terms in a conceptual series, an editor may therefore follow James in abandoning it in favor of 'concepts'. One must recognize, however, that James's distinction between the static arrangement which the mind makes out of the 'concepts alone' and the 'concepts alone' themselves which first arise from percepts is not an easy one given his retention of 'concepts' in the phrase 'in the shape of concepts'; but difficult as the repetition of the same word in two senses makes the thought, the exact sense is better served by adopting James's partial revision than by reverting to his original reading.

42.36 'Causes,'] In correcting TMs^2 Kallen made a serious error by which he mistook a mark in TMs^{1a-b} as a deletion of the quotation marks after 'Causes' whereas it seems (in TMs^{1a}) to have been no more than an attempt by James to clarify a bad spacing on the typewriter of quotation mark and comma. As a consequence, Kallen took it that the whole passage from 'Causes' to 'successes' (43.4) was the quotation from Royce, and this error was printed in (I).

45.23 them, . . . value.] In this case a pencil alteration in TMs^{1a} appears to have been continued at a later time in ink by the writing of an ink semicolon over a pencil period, and the sentence then was continued in ink. Since it appears that in this page TMs^{1b} copied its revisions from TMs^{1a}, the TMs^{1b} form of 'value. But' seems to represent James's later preference over TMs^{1a} 'value; but'.

55.11 and . . . into] Peggy misread a much altered manuscript at this point and produced an important difference in meaning which James largely compounded when he altered TMs^{1a} and TMs^{1b}. For the revisions that led to the misreading, see the list of Alterations in the Manuscript, and for the TMs^1 and subsequent readings, see the Historical Collation.

76.8 III] This reading of MS is correct, as shown by the same reference ending the preceding chapter at 75.12. When Kallen altered TMs^2 to read 'VII'—the emendation not of James's chapter on "The One and the Many" but of his own artificial division of James's longer chapter—he was misled by the text at 70.23–30.

78.14   *as* it is]   This would appear to be a typical case of James varying in his revision of TMs[1a] from MS since MS underlines for italic were not typed in TMs[1]; thus in his revision of the typescript he had to underline what at the moment he felt to be the intended sense, without regard for the manuscript form. Unless clearer evidences of altered intention are present than in this example, the MS emphasis seems to be preferred when the revision was made without consultation of the original reading and its meaning.

82.9   last]   MS originally underlined '*last* point' and continued with the opposition '*next* point'; but when the latter was deleted as part of a longer revision, 'a further point' was interlined without italics. It would appear, then, that—the contrast having been removed—the original 'last' should revert to roman.

92.24   produced]   Because the typescript omitted the MS word 'produced' at this point, James filled in the gap by writing 'created' in TMs[1a] and TMs[1b]. This repair of an error without consultation of the MS cannot be called a revision; thus the original MS reading is to be preferred.

92.30-31   instantaneous act]   A typing error in which 'continuous' appeared in TMs[1] for MS 'instantaneous' caused James trouble here. In the relatively late stage of pencil revision, he (or Peggy) altered TMs[1a] alone to read with the MS; but, abroad, when revising TMs[1b] he had to make what sense he could of 'continuous'. A circled question mark in the margin suggests that he was not satisfied with what he had done, as indeed he should not have been, for his change made less than the required sense in context. In TMs[1b] he first interlined 'process' before 'continuous', an interesting word since in MS it had been the original reading, altered to 'act' by interlineation. After 'process' he started 'inst', an indication that his intention was to substitute 'instantaneous' for 'continuous'; but he then broke this off and after deleting 'act' he continued to the final reading 'process continuous in the mathematician's sense'. In the next sentence, however, the phrase 'must be occupied in its due order of succession' does not illustrate the revised statement in TMs[1b] whereas it follows naturally on the original MS reading. Hence the text is returned to MS and WJ(PJ?)/TMs[1a], and the TMs[1b] mistaken revision, followed by Kallen (with the substitution of 'mathematical' for 'mathematician's') is rejected.

92.34   neglect.]   The reference to MS fol. 70[ll] in MS and TMs[1](u) was excised in WJ/TMs[1b], presumably because the pertinent text in the MS there had been removed as part of a revision. For the original text, see the Alterations listing for 91.14-15 'Because . . . some'.

99.15   so called]   James only sporadically observed a distinction between adverb without hyphen and hyphenated adjective. Two earlier occurrences of the adverbial form were unhyphenated; emendation to remove the hyphen here is called for to preserve consistency.

99.28-29   isolate . . . from]   This phrase interestingly shows several levels of revision between TMs[1a] and TMs[1b] owing to original faults in the transcript of MS in TMs[1]. In the initial review of both copies, the misprint 'isolatr' for MS 'isolate' was probably changed by Peggy in each to 'isolated', what seemed to be a necessary correction since TMs[1] had not typed 'we' (which remained deleted in error in MS after its interlined substitute 'our imagination' had been rejected and excised). This alteration made superficial sense. At a later stage, apparently, James returned to TMs[1b] and recognized that something was wrong. By adding the necessary 'we' he was then forced to alter 'isolated' back to 'isolate' and to supply some missing word before 'energy'. Without reference to MS he chose the obvious 'the' (for MS 'any') and then, to complete the revision of the syntax, altered 'transmit' to 'transmitted'. However, MS had had the odd preterite 'transennt' (presumably for 'trans-sent') which Peggy had misread and typed as 'transmit', so that in forming the necessary preterite James unwittingly accepted the corruption 'transmitted'. The whole range of error was initiated, perhaps, by the mistake in MS of not restoring 'we', which James recognized in his later revision of TMs[1b]; but thereafter in the correction of the faulty typescript he was led to readings that differed from the perfectly correct originals in MS. Under these circumstances it seems to be proper editorial theory to revert to MS, for there is no indication that these readings would have been altered had they been faithfully transferred to TMs[1].

102.38 humian] The writing of this word in MS is not certain; however, the evidence suggests that James first wrote 'humean' but then altered it clumsily to 'humian', the adjectival form of Hume with the lower case that James preferred. Peggy misread the word as 'human', a reading that persisted into (I) and was not corrected until it was included among the plate changes of the second printing (I[2]), then altered to 'humean'. Either 'humean' or 'humian' would be acceptable, but James seems to have preferred the forms in '-ian'. See humian (for 'Humian') in *Essays in Radical Empiricism*, 22.25, and 'Lockian' in *The Meaning of Truth*, 13.18.

104.5-6 is confused] James's reference to page 71 of his manuscript applies to an inserted passage that continued writing he had begun on the verso of fol. 70, now remaining only as a stub. This insertion was included in the original conclusion of Chapter VI before James decided to turn the notebook end for end and insert the new Chapter VII. He therefore rewrote the ending for Chapter VI in order to accommodate his change of plan, thus deleting the original conclusion on fols. 68-71, including the insertion referring to the situation among contemporary thinkers being 'confused and unsatisfactory' (see Alterations entry 96.18). The reference now being an empty one, it is removed entirely from the present text.

104.17 'relations.' "[12]] The first edition was correct in placing this reference footnote at the foot of the page instead of in the text within parentheses as in MS-TMs[2]. The text from 104.5-23 is an addition, written on fol. 95[v] of the notebook and in a much smaller hand in order to crowd it in. Clearly, the original text had ended on fol. 95 with 'found.' (104.4) and its footnote, and the new chapter 105.1 ff. had been written before James added the new ending on fol. 95[v]. Since he was pressed for space, it would seem that he placed the reference in the text, in a manner uncharacteristic of this manuscript, purely in order to save the space required by the usual footnote notation written on a separate line.

107.39 [1]causes] In his marked copy of the first edition (*AC85.J2376. 911s) Henry James, Jr., notes that Schiller queries whether the reading should not be 'antecedents' but that the manuscript reads 'causes'. Emendation does not seem required. The key discussion comes on pp. 392-393 of Mill's *Logic*, with special reference to "We may define, therefore, the cause of a phenomenon, to be the antecedent, or the concurrence of antecedents, on which it is invariably and *unconditionally* consequent. Or if we adopt the convenient modification of the meaning of the word cause, which confines it to the assemblage of positive conditions without the negative, then instead of 'unconditionally,' we must say, 'subject to no other than negative conditions' " (p. 392).

Historical Collation

This list comprises the substantive and accidental variant readings that differ from the edited text in the authoritative documents recorded for the book. The reading to the left of the bracket is that of the present edition. The rejected variants in the noted documents follow in chronological order to the right of the bracket. Any collated texts not recorded are to be taken as agreeing with the edition-reading to the left of the bracket: only variation appears to the right, except for the special case of emphasis when the origin of an accepted reading to the left is a handwritten correction or revision by the typist, Peggy James, designated as PJ/TMs[1] and added in order to distinguish her autograph changes from her father's. The noting of variant readings is complete for the substantives and for the accidentals. In order to save space, however, neither substantive nor accidental variants are repeated in the Historical Collation when the copy-text has been emended, since the details may be found in the list of Emendations. An exception to this rule is the repetition in the Historical Collation of all *stet* readings in the Emendations except for rejected readings of the sources for James's quotations. Trivial differences in the accidental bibliographical details of footnotes such as in the typography, punctuation, abbreviation, and forms of references and dates are ignored, and typographical differences as italic versus roman or lower case versus capitals among documents shown in the record of omitted sidenotes are also excluded. All I(p) variants are recorded except for internal references to pagination, simple mechanical slips as in running two words together, and the typographical differences in sidenotes and purely bibliographical references in footnotes just mentioned.

The headnote to the Emendations list may be consulted for general conventions of notation and for the documents and the forms of their sigla used to describe the textual transmission of this book. The Note on the Editorial Method outlines types of variants that are not recorded. One special feature appearing in the Historical Collation is the use of *et seq.* When this phrase occurs, all subsequent readings within the text are to be taken as agreeing with the particular feature of the reading being recorded (save for singulars and plurals and inessential typographical variation, as between roman and italic), unless specifically noted to the contrary by notation within the entry itself. Readings grouped together with multiple page-line references may also be concerned with only the particular feature being recorded and not with inessential types of variation. A plus sign signifies all collated texts later than the text identified by the sigil.

[*begin* Prefatory Note]

5.2 problems] fundamental problems TMs[2],I(p)(u)

5.3 readers of philosophy] philosophical readers TMs[2],I(p)(u)

5.4-5 'introductory . . . metaphysics,']
    db. qts. TMs[2],I(p)

5.6 at last] finally TMs[2],I(p)(u)

5.6 his] the author's TMs[2](u)

5.7 interfere,] ~ₐ TMs[2]

5.13 of phrase and detail] *om.* TMs²(u)

5.14 yet] yet had TMs²(u)

5.14-16 perhaps . . . book,] finished the book he would perhaps have made further and final revisions. TMs²(u)

5.15 further] *aft. del.* 'alte' HJ/TMs²

5.16 for in] In TMs²(u)

5.17-18 'Say . . . unrevised.'] "∼ . . . ∼." TMs²(u) (*unrevised.*₍∧₎), HJ/TMs²,I(p)

5.19 ¶This . . . continues,] *om.* TMs²(u)

5.19-21 'Call it "A . . . philosophy." . . . side.'] "∼ ∼'∼ . . . ∼.' . . . ∼." TMs²(u) (₍∧₎*Call*), HJ/TMs²,I(p)

6.3 incomplete] fragmentary and incomplete TMs²(u)

[*end* Prefatory Note; *begin text*]

[TMs¹ᵃ *missing*]

9.0 Chapter I] HJ/TMs²(r2); Introduction [*ink*] | Chapter I K/TMs²(r1)

9.1 fact] facts TMs¹ᵇ,TMs²(u)

9.2 human] *om.* TMs¹ᵇ,TMs²(u)

9.2 directions,] ∼₍∧₎ TMs¹(u)ᵇ

9.3 which they show] *om.* TMs¹ᵇ⁺

9.3 useful,] ∼₍∧₎ TMs¹ᵇ⁺

9.4 leaders,] ∼₍∧₎ TMs¹(u)ᵇ

9.4-5 setters . . . imitation] objects of envy or admiration, and setters of new ideals TMs¹ᵇ⁺

9.6 ff. *omit*] Philosophy and those who write it (*s.n.*) HJ/TMs²,I [*del. subh.*: *How philosophy arises* K/TMs²]

9.10 prophecies] prophesies TMs¹ᵇ

9.15 ff. *omit*] What *Philosophy ['P' *ov.* 'p'] is ['s' *ov.* 't'] (*s.n.*) HJ/TMs², I [*del. subh.*: *What* ['Phi' *del.*] *It Is* K/TMs²]

9.15 race heritage] ∼-∼K/TMs²,I

9.18 excluded] explained TMs¹(u)ᵇ

9.18-19 and . . . excluded,] special sciences are today excluded, and for reasons presently to be explained, TMs¹(u)ᵇ; special . . . excluded, for . . . explained; WJ/TMs¹ᵇ⁺

9.22 german] German K/TMs²,I

10.1 begriff und eintheilung,] ₍∧∼ ∼ ∼ ∼∧∧₎ (*rom.*) TMs¹(u)ᵇ; '∼ ∼ ∼,' (*rom.*) WJ/TMs¹ᵇ; 'begritt, und eintheilung,' TMs²(u);

'Begriff, und Eintheilung,' K/TMs²,I

10.1 *aufgabe und methode.*] ₍∧∼ ∼ ∼ ∼∧∧₎ (*rom.*) TMs¹(u)ᵇ; '∼ ∼ ∼.' (*rom.*) WJ/TMs¹ᵇ, TMs²(u); '*Aufgabe und Methode.*' K/TMs²,I

10.4 tho] though TMs¹ᵇ⁺

10.7 name] name of TMs¹ᵇ⁺

10.11 *whence . . . whither*] *rom.* TMs¹ᵇ

10.13 generally] commonly K/TMs²,I

10.14 'philosopher'] ₍∧∼₍∧₎ TMs¹ᵇ⁺

10.16 text-books] MS(∼-|∼); textbooks TMs¹ᵇ⁺

10.20 'philosophic'] ₍∧∼₍∧₎ TMs¹ᵇ⁺

10.22 proximate₍∧₎] ∼, TMs¹ᵇ⁺

10.24 philosophy,] ∼₍∧₎ TMs¹ᵇ⁺

10.27-30 "philosophy . . . off."] *no qts.* TMs¹ᵇ⁺ (Philosophy TMs¹ᵇ⁻²)

10.30 off."] *no fn. indicator* TMs¹(u)ᵇ

10.31 ¶To] *no* ¶ TMs¹ᵇ,TMs²(u)

10.31 ff. omit] Its Value (*s.n.*) HJ/TMs²,I [*del. subh.*: *What it is good for.* K/TMs²]

10.33 surely] *om.* I

10.34 of] of an TMs²(u)

10.36 'college'] ₍∧∼₍∧₎ TMs¹(u)ᵇ, TMs²(u)

10.38 first-rate] ∼₍∧₎∼ TMs¹ᵇ⁻²

10.39-40 *Psychology*, ii, 291.] psychology. TMs¹ᵇ,TMs²(u); *Psychology.* K/TMs²

11.2 'liberal culture.'] ₍∧∼ ∼.₍∧₎ TMs¹ᵇ⁺

11.5 atmosphere₍∧₎] ∼, TMs¹ᵇ⁺

11.6 Plato₍∧₎] ∼, TMs¹(u)ᵇ

11.6 Aristotle₍∧₎] ∼, TMs¹ᵇ,TMs²(u)

11.11 'dogmatic slumber'] ₍∧∼ ∼₍∧₎ TMs¹ᵇ⁺

11.12 a sort] a source WJ/TMs¹ᵇ(r1) (*del. and* 'a sort' *restored*)

11.14 It . . . valuable.] *om.* TMs¹ᵇ, TMs²(u)

11.18 speaks] appeals TMs²,I

11.20 ¶Both] *no* ¶ TMs¹ᵇ⁺

11.20 student] students TMs¹ᵇ,TMs²

11.20 a liberal] livlier TMs¹(u)ᵇ; a livlier TMs²(u); a livelier WJ/TMs¹ᵇ, K/TMs²,I

11.21 ought to get] *om.* TMs¹ᵇ⁺

11.21-22 "Hast ... Shepherd?"]
   $_\wedge\sim\ldots\sim?_\wedge$ TMs^1b; '$\sim\ldots\sim?_\wedge$
   TMs^2(u); '$\sim\ldots\sim?$' K/TMs^2,I
11.24 *no*] no TMs^1b+
11.28 such] the K/TMs^2,I
11.28 concepts] concepts of the
   philosopher$_\wedge$ K/TMs^2,I (philosopher,)
11.30 ff. *omit*] Its Enemies and their
   objections (*s.n.*) HJ/TMs^2,I
11.35-36 'Scholastic jargon,' ...
   dialectics,'] $_\wedge\sim\sim,_\wedge\ldots\sim_{\wedge\wedge}$
   TMs^1(u)^b
11.36;12.35 mediaeval] mediæval I
11.37-38 'obscure ... things$_\wedge$']
   $_\wedge\sim\ldots\sim,_\wedge$ TMs^1b+
11.39 'a blind] $_\wedge\sim_\wedge\sim$ TMs^1(u)^b,
   TMs^2(u); $_\wedge\sim$ '$\sim$ K/TMs^2,I
11.39 cat] hat I^2+
11.40 isn't] is not TMs^1b+
11.40 there.'] $\sim._\wedge$ TMs^1(u)^b,TMs^2(u)
11.40-12.1 'the ... $_\wedge$endlessly ...
   conclusion,'] $_\wedge\sim\ldots_\wedge\sim\ldots\sim,_\wedge$
   TMs^1(u)^b; $_\wedge\sim\ldots$'$\sim\ldots\sim,$'
   WJ/TMs^1b+
12.9 ff. *omit*] Objection that it is
   unpractical answered (*s.n.*)
   HJ/TMs^2,I; [*del. subh.*: *Philosophy
   contrasted with science* K/TMs^2]
12.9 'sciences'] $_\wedge$Sciences$_\wedge$ TMs^1b-I(p);
   $_\wedge$sciences$_\wedge$ I
12.9 progress,] $\sim_\wedge$ TMs^1b+
12.9-10 applications] aplications
   TMs^1b
12.10-11 theoretic ... no] *om.*
   TMs^1(u)^b; progress$_\wedge$ and has no
   WJ/TMs^1b(&)+
12.14 'scientific,'] $_\wedge\sim,_\wedge$ TMs^1(u)^b
12.15 'philosophy'] $_\wedge\sim_\wedge$ TMs^1(u)^b
12.15 to-day] today TMs^1b-2
12.21 ff. *omit*] This objection in the
   light of history (*s.n.*) HJ/TMs^2,I;
   [*del. subh.*: *The History of Philosophy Reviewed* K/TMs^2]
12.25 need] needs TMs^1b+
12.25-26 problem] problems TMs^1b+
12.27 India$_\wedge$] $\sim,$ TMs^1b+
12.27 men,] $\sim_\wedge$ |TMs^1(u)^b
12.29 greek] Greek I
12.31 600] six hundred TMs^1b-2,I(p)
12.31 Heraclitus] Heracleitus TMs^1b+

13.3 creator] *cap.* TMs^1b-2,I(p)
13.3 knower with known] Knower
   with known TMs^1(u)^b; the Knower
   with the known TMs^2,I(p),I
   (knower)
13.4 forms,] $\sim_\wedge$ TMs^1(u)^b
13.4 mind] PJ/TMs^1b; mind and
   TMs^1(u)^b
13.6 morals$_\wedge$] $\sim,$ TMs^1b+
13.7 principles] principals TMs^1(u)^b
13.10 ¶It] no ¶ TMs^1b+
13.13 scripture] *cap.* TMs^1b+
13.14 changes] change TMs^1(u)^b
13.16 form$_\wedge$] $\sim,$ TMs^1b+
13.19 was] could was TMs^1b
13.19 determinate] PJ/TMs^1b;
   determinable ate TMs^1(u)^b
13.20 ^1etc.,] $\sim._\wedge$ TMs^1b-2
13.21 century$_\wedge$] $\sim,$ TMs^1b+
13.23 the fashion] fashion TMs^2,I
13.23 'new philosophy'] $_\wedge\sim\sim_\wedge$
   TMs^1b+
13.25 encyclopaedic] encyclopædic I
13.26 now a days] nowadays TMs^1b+
13.27 *Cogito, ergo sum,*] $_\wedge\sim_\wedge\sim\sim_{\wedge\wedge}$
   TMs^1(u)^b(*rom.*); '$\sim_\wedge\sim\sim,$'
   WJ/TMs^1b(*rom.*); '$\sim,\sim\sim,$' TMs^2,I
   (*both rom.*)
13.28 'substances,'] $_\wedge\sim,_\wedge$ TMs^1b+
13.30 explained$_\wedge$] $\sim,$ TMs^1b+
13.31 motion$_\wedge$] $\sim,_\wedge$ TMs^1(u)^b;
   $\sim,$' WJ/TMs^1b+
13.33 the apparatus] apparatus TMs^2,I
13.34 passions] passings TMs^2,I^1-2
13.34 soul$_\wedge$] $\sim,$ TMs^1b+
13.34 connexion] connection TMs^1b+
13.38 Nature] *l.c.* TMs^2,I
14.2 altho] although TMs^1b+
14.3 up$_\wedge$] $\sim,$ TMs^1(u)^b
14.4 $_\wedge$Wolff$_\wedge$] , $\sim,$ TMs^1(u)^b
14.5 *everything*] *rom.* TMs^2,I
14.6 succeeded] succeded TMs^1b-2
14.10 of] PJ/TMs^1b; of the TMs^1(u)
14.18 what] *cap.* TMs^1b+
14.19 momentous] monotonous
   TMs^1(u)^b; meritorious WJ/TMs^1b+
14.19 how] *cap.* I (*l.c.* I[p])
14.20 possible?', so] $\sim?'.$ So
   TMs^1b-2; $\sim?'_\wedge$ So I
14.20 philosophy,] $\sim_\wedge$ TMs^1(u)^b
14.23-24 For ... *Philosophy*.]

beginning fn. 3 K/TMs²,I

14.23 readers] reader's TMs²

14.25 ff. *omit] Philosophy *is only [alt. to 'as' HJ] "man thinking" (s.n.) K/TMs²,I (sg. qts.)*

14.25 sense] PJ/TMs¹ᵇ; sense of TMs¹(u)ᵇ

14.25 *man thinking*, thinking] man thinking_∧ | thinking TMs¹(u)ᵇ; man | thinking PJ?/TMs¹ᵇ; man thinking_∧ TMs²(u)

14.36 It *(no ¶)*] ¶ TMs¹ᵇ,K/TMs²,I

14.38 ff. *omit] Origin of Man's present ways of thinking (s.n.) HJ/TMs²,I; [del. subh.: How Man's Present Ways of Thinking Originated. K/TMs²]*

15.1 'positive,'] '~_∧' *[sg. ov. db. qts.]* WJ/TMs¹ᵇ;TMs²

15.2 'theological'] _∧~_∧ TMs¹ᵇ+

15.2 theorizing_∧] ~, TMs¹ᵇ+

15.3-4 'metaphysical'] ('metaphysical') WJ/TMs¹ᵇ; _∧ ~ _∧ TMs²,I *[WJ/TMs¹ᵇ parens retained in error on deletion of similar parens around 'theological' and of line transposing the two words]*

15.4,6 stage_∧] ~, TMs¹ᵇ+

15.6 'positive'] _∧~_∧ TMs²,I

15.7 'laws'] _∧~_∧ TMs¹(u)ᵇ

15.8 nature] natures TMs²,I

15.9 theological,_∧] metaphysical,— TMs¹ᵇ-I¹; theological,— I²+

15.9 'principle] _∧Principle TMs¹ᵇ, TMs²(u)

15.10 ¹would be] *om.* TMs¹ᵇ+

15.10 metaphysical,_∧] theological,— TMs¹ᵇ-I¹; metaphysical,— I²+

15.10 squares_∧'] ~,' TMs¹ᵇ-²,I(p)

15.10-11 positive,] ~_∧ TMs²,I

15.15 especially] PJ?/TMs¹ᵇ; especially thiings TMs¹(u)ᵇ

15.17 *awful] rom.* TMs¹ᵇ+

15.22 resembled] ressembled TMs¹-²

15.22 enemy_∧] ~, TMs¹ᵇ+

15.24-25 Injuring . . . correspondingly.] PJ/TMs¹ᵇ; *om.* TMs¹(u)ᵇ

15.25 then] thus PJ/TMs¹ᵇ+ *[begin TMs¹ᵃ]*

15.28-29 turmeric] tumeric WJ/TMs¹ᵃ(*pencil*)-ᵇ+; tumerisc TMs¹(u)

15.30 seed vessels] seedvessels TMs¹, TMs²(u)

15.30 'head.'] _∧~._∧ TMs¹(u)

15.32 'mancies and 'mantics_∧] '~' ~ '~,' TMs¹,TMs²(u); '-~' ~ '-~,' K/TMs²,I(p);I ('-mantics_∧')

15.33 intermixed] mixed TMs¹+

15.33 'Sympathetic'] 'Sympathic_∧ TMs¹(u)ᵃ; 'Sympathic' WJ/TMs¹ᵇ; _∧Sympathetic_∧ TMs²(u)

15.34 things_∧'] ~,' TMs¹+

15.36 the thought] PJ/TMs¹ᵃ-ᵇ; *om.* TMs¹(u)

15.37 elsewhere] else where TMs¹

15.38 fulfilled.⁶] ~ .- TMs¹-²

16.1 little_∧] ~, TMs²,I

16.5 cold, . . . wet,] hot, the cold, the wet, K/TMs²,I; hot, the wet, the cold_∧ TMs²(u)

16.5 dry_∧] ~, TMs¹,TMs²(u)

16.6 warm,] ~_∧ TMs¹(u)

16.7 'natural'] _∧~_∧ TMs¹+

16.7 'violent.'] '~._∧ TMs¹; _∧~._∧ TMs²,I

16.8 'perfect.'] _∧~._∧ TMs¹+

16.12 putrefaction] putrifaction TMs¹,TMs²(u)

16.12 loadstone] lodestone K/TMs²,I

16.14 near,] ~_∧ TMs¹,TMs²(u)

16.16 *we*] we TMs¹+

16.19 attract] abstract TMs¹+

16.21-22 anyone] any one I

16.24 the air] air TMs²,I

16.28 astrology_∧] ~, TMs¹+

16.29 Galileo,] ~_∧ | TMs¹,TMs²(u)

16.30 Huyghens] Huygens TMs²,I

16.31 lives] life's work TMs¹(u)ᵇ, TMs²(u); lifes WJ/TMs¹ᵃ

16.31 witnessed_∧] ~, TMs¹+

16.37 Lóvejoy, in] Lovejoy: I (~, ~ I[p])

16.38 greek] Greek K/TMs²,I

17.1 readers] the readers TMs²,I

17.3 ff. *omit] Science *is [alt. to 'as' HJ] ['but' del. HJ] specialized Philosophy (s.n.) K/TMs²(moved fr. subh. to s.n. HJ),I*

17.3 ¶The] *no* ¶ TMs¹,TMs²(u)

17.10 astronomy_∧] ~, TMs¹+

17.11 parent stem] ~-~ WJ/TMs¹ᵇ(r1)

17.14 ferretted] ferreted I

17.15 search] PJ/TMs[1a-b]; control search TMs[1](u)

17.16 describe] describes TMs[1](u)[a]

17.17-18 *v* . . . *t* . . . *s* . . . *t*[2]] *caps.* TMs[1](u)[a]; *rom. l.c.* TMs[2]

17.19 height] heigth TMs[1](u)[a]; heigt WJ/TMs[1b]

17.20-21 sine to sine] sine to cosine I[3]

17.20-21 to sine‸] ∼∼, TMs[1](u)[a]

17.21 ray‸] ∼, TMs[1]+

17.23 only‸] ∼, TMs[2],I

17.25 showed] shewed TMs[2],I(p)

17.26 spheres] parts spheres TMs[2](u)

17.27 'science,'] ‸Science,' TMs[1](u)[a]; 'Science,' WJ/TMs[1b]+

17.28 'general philosophy,'] ‸General Philosophy,' TMs[1-2]; *init. caps.* I

17.29 ¶The] *no* ¶ TMs[1]+

17.29-30 ‸Down with philosophy!‸] '∼ ∼ ∼!' K/TMs[2],I

17.30-32 ‸Give . . . explain.‸] '∼ . . . ∼.' K/TMs[2],I

17.31 additions,] ∼‸ TMs[1](u)[b]

17.35 ff. *omit*] ['And' *del.* HJ] *Philosophy* ['P' *ov.* 'p' HJ] *is* [*del.* HJ] *the residuum of problems* *un-solved* ['un' *ab. del.* 'not' HJ] *by science* (*s.n.*) K/TMs[2](*moved fr. subh. to s.n.* HJ),I

17.37 credited] accredited TMs[2],I

17.37 'science,'] ‸∼,‸ TMs[1]; ‸∼‸‸ TMs[2],I

17.39-18.1 happening . . . a collective] a happening . . . collective I(p) (*error*)

18.3 follow that] follow, K/TMs[2],I

18.10 therefore‸] ∼, TMs[2],I

18.12 inquiry] enquiry TMs[2],I

18.14 spiritual] PJ/TMs[1b]; extreme spiritual TMs[1](u)[a]

18.15-16 have‸ . . . extent‸] ∼‸ . . . ∼, K/TMs[2(r2)]; ∼, . . . ∼, I; ∼‸ . . . ∼‸ I(p); To some extent, they have K/TMs[2(r1)]

18.16 In . . . indeed,] Although, in some respects, K/TMs[2(r1)]

18.16-17 'science'] ‸Science' TMs[1]; 'Science' TMs[2]

18.18 Aristotle‸ nor Descartes‸] ∼, ∼ ∼, TMs[1],TMs[2](u); ∼‸ ∼ ∼, K/TMs[2],I

18.23 awe-inspiring] aweinspiring TMs[1]

18.24 metaphysics‸] ∼, TMs[1]+

18.24-25 lecture-room] ∼‸∼ TMs[1]+

18.31 classes‸] ∼, TMs[1]+

18.31 analyzes] analyses TMs[2],I(p)

18.33 ff. *omit*] Philosophy need not be dogmatic (*s.n.*) HJ/TMs[2],I; [*del. subh.*: *Dogmatism not necessary to Philosophy* K/TMs[2]]

18.33 *Reply.*] *rom. subh.* TMs[1], TMs[2](u)

18.34 *a priori*] *rom.* TMs[1-2]; *à priori* I(p)

18.37 or] and TMs[1]+

18.39 XV (1890), p. 213] fifteen. TMs[1],TMs[2](u); 15, No lviii: "The Progress of Philosophy." K/TMs[2];I(p) (No.; *sg. qts.*);I (no.; *sg. qts.*)

19.6 man] men TMs[1]+

19.7-8 whatever‸] whatsoever‸ WJ/TMs[1b]+; whatfvfeever, TMs[1](u)[a]

19.12 them all.] them | TMs[2](u)

19.16 almost . . . have] have, almost without exception, TMs[1]+

19.21 first] HJ/TMs[2(r2)]; foremost K/TMs[2(r1)]

19.23 ff. *omit*] Nor is *it* [*insrtd.* HJ] divorced from reality (*s.n.*) K/TMs[2] (*moved fr. subh. to s.n.* HJ),I

19.23 *Reply.*] *rom.* TMs[1],TMs[2](u) (*subh.*)

19.25 developes] develops TMs[1]+

19.32 ff. *omit*] Phisophy as Meta-physics (*s.n.*) HJ/TMs[2](*moved fr. subh. to s.n.*); Philosophy as meta-physics (*s.n.*) I

19.32 acception] acceptation TMs[2],I

19.37 *Principles*‸] ∼, I; Principles, TMs[1-2]

20.6 metaphysics‸] ∼, TMs[1],K/TMs[2], I

20.8 fulfilment] fulfillment TMs[2],I[1-2]

20.9 to] *om.* TMs[1]

21.1 ff. *omit*] *Examples of Metaphysical Problems* (*s.n.*) K/TMs[2](*moved fr. subh. to s.n.* HJ),I

21.1 ‸metaphysics‸‸] '∼,' TMs[1], TMs[2](*comma doubtful*); '∼‸' I

21.9 questions:−] ∼:‸ TMs[2],I(p)

21.10 'thoughts‸'] '∼,' TMs[2],I

21.14 and‸] ∼, I

22.2 Do (*no* ¶)] ¶ TMs^2(u)

22.2 upon] on TMs^2,I

22.4 into] *om.* TMs^1+

22.6 knowledge‸] ∼, TMs^1, HJ/TMs$^{2(r2)}$; knowing, K/TMs$^{2(r1)}$

22.7 *at*] at TMs^1+

22.8 notions–are] ∼. Are TMs^1+

22.11 reason‸'] ∼,' TMs^1+

22.13 And‸] ∼, TMs^1+

22.14 ‸Such] − Such WJ/TMs^{1b},TMs^2

22.17 do?] know? TMs^2(u)

22.19 ff. *omit*] *Metaphysics defined* (*s.n.*) K/TMs^2(*moved fr. subh. to s.n.* HJ),I

22.22 actual] what is actual TMs^2,I

22.23-24 meaning‸ ... outcome,] ∼, ... ∼‸ TMs^1+

22.26 connexion] connection TMs^1+

22.27 'Principles‸'] '∼,' TMs^1-I(p)

22.27 *entities*] *rom.* TMs^1+

22.28 'souls';] '∼,'; TMs^2; '∼,' I

22.28 laws, like‸] ∼‸∼: TMs^1+

22.29 'things‸'] '∼' TMs^1

22.30 'science'] 'Science' TMs^1-I(p)

22.32-33 *The ... questions.*] *rom.* TMs^1+

22.33 severally] *om.* I (severally I[p])

22.34 rightfully] properly I (rightfully I[p])

22.37 ff. *omit*] ['The' *del.* HJ] *Nature of Metaphysical Problems* (*s.n.*) K/TMs^2(*moved fr. subh. to s.n.* HJ),I

22.39 ^{1}either] *om.* TMs^1+

23.1 they] *om.* TMs^2(u)

23.2-3 impossible‸] possible, TMs^1(u)^a

23.4 someone] some one I

23.5 proposed,] ∼‸ WJ/TMs$^{1b(r1)}$

23.6 do] does TMs^2,I

23.12 –and] ‸∼ TMs^1+

23.17 If (*no* ¶)] ¶ If TMs^1(u)^a

23.17 'what] ‸∼ WJ/TMs$^{1b(r1)}$

23.18 synthesis] syntheses I (synthesis I[p])

23.20 example‸] ∼, WJ/TMs$^{1b(r1)}$

23.21 nature] Nature TMs$^{1-2}$

23.23 *vacua*] vacua TMs^1+

23.28 ff. *omit*] *Rationalism and Empiricism in Metaphysics* (*s.n.*) K/TMs^2(*moved fr. subh. to s.n.* HJ),I

23.30 rationalist‸ ... empiricist]

∼, ... ∼ TMs^1-I(p) (*init. caps.* TMs^1[u]^a)

23.31 everyone] every one I

23.32 ^{2}aristotelian‸] ∼, TMs^1+

23.32 meant] means TMs^1+

23.33 platonist‸] platonistic, TMs^1-I(p)

23.33 altho] although TMs^1+

23.34 greek] Greek TMs^1+

24.5 wholes to parts] parts to wholes TMs^2(u)

24.5 goes] proceeds by going TMs^1+

24.6 archrationalist] arch | rationalist TMs^1(u)^a; arch-rationalist WJ/TMs^{1b}(*doubtful*),TMs^2

24.7 'ideas,'] ‸Ideas,' TMs^1(u)^a; 'Ideas,' WJ/TMs^{1b},TMs^2

24.8 'the good.'] ‸∼ '∼.' TMs^1+

24.8 Democritus and Protagoras] Protagoras and Democritus TMs^1+

24.9 former] latter TMs^1+

24.9 gods] Gods TMs^1-I(p)

24.14 to] prefer to TMs^1+

24.19 optimistic,] ∼‸ | TMs^1(u)^a

24.21;28.11 Spinosa] Spinoza TMs^1+

24.30 virtue] *om.* TMs^2,I

24.34 Dewey] J. Dewey TMs^1+

24.38 the present] this TMs^1+

25.2+ *no space*] *space* K/TMs^2,I

25.6-7 'ontological' problem,] '∼‸ ∼,‸ TMs^2(u); '∼‸ ∼,' K/TMs^2,I

25.7 anything] ∼-∼ TMs^1; ∼-|∼ TMs^2

25.8 'The ... Rationality,'] ‸∼ ... ∼,‸ TMs^1(u)^a

25.8 *The*] the I(p)

25.9 Longmans] Longman's TMs^1

26.0 *Chapter ... Being*] The Problem of Being TMs^2(u); *First Problem.* The Problem of Being. | Being and Non-Being K/TMs$^{2(r1)}$; Chapter III The Problem of Being. HJ/TMs$^{2(r2)}$

26.1 ff. *omit*] *Schopenhauer on the origin of the problem* (*s.n.*) K/TMs^2,I

26.4 ‸When] "∼ TMs^1(u)

26.5 conscious‸] ∼, TMs^1+

26.6 ^{2}for] For TMs^1(u)

26.7 reflexion] reflection TMs^1+

26.7 *wonder*] *rom.* TMs^2,I

26.9 wonder.–] ∼‸− TMs^1+

26.11 but] But TMs[1](u)

26.13 never stopping] neverstopping TMs[1-2]

26.15 as] is I(p)

26.22 philosophy] Philosophy TMs[1]-I(p)

27.2 [1]one's] PJ/TMs[1a-b]; ones's TMs[1](u)

27.2 being] existencebeing TMs[1](u)

27.4 character∧] (MS *comma del.*); ∼, PJ/TMs[1a-b](r1)

27.10 ff. *omit] Various treatments of the* ['*question.*' *del.*] *problem. (s.n.)* K/TMs[2],I

27.13 ∧indeed∧] , ∼∧ TMs[1]; , ∼, TMs[2],I

27.18 ¶But] *no* ¶ TMs[1]+

27.27 You (*no* ¶)] ¶ TMs[2],I

27.27 again] *om.* TMs[1]+

27.27 don't] do not TMs[1]+

27.28 into] onto TMs[2](u)

27.29 altho] although TMs[1]+

27.33 Zeno,] ∼; TMs[2],I

27.33 is, so] ∼. Hence K/TMs[2],I

27.33-34 is∧ is] ∼, ∼ K/TMs[2],I

27.34 [1]being−] ∼, TMs[1](u)[a]

27.34 ∧ in short∧] , ∼ ∼∧ TMs[1]; , ∼ ∼, TMs[2],I

27.34 Others,] Other∧ TMs[1](u)[a]; Others∧ TMs[2],I(p)

27.37-38 *grübelsucht*] grubelsucht TMs[1](u)[a],TMs[2](u); *rom.* WJ/TMs[1b]; *Grübelsucht* K/TMs[2],I

27.38 asking∧] ∼, TMs[2],I

27.38 (*twice*) why] Why I (why I[p])

27.40 ff. *omit] Rationalist and Empiricist treatments (s.n.)* K/TMs[2],I

27.40 however] *om.* TMs[1]+

28.1 Being] being I (Being I[p])

28.4 of] *om.* TMs[1](u)[a]

28.5 faintest,] *om.* TMs[2](u)

28.9 minimum] maximum TMs[2](u)

28.10 easiest] earliest TMs[1]+

28.10 *first*] First TMs[1],K/TMs[2],I; first TMs[2](u)

28.11 doesn't] does not TMs[1]+

28.11-12 contrary∧] ∼, TMs[1]+

28.16 power ... have.] powerful ... become. TMs[1]+ (becomeS∧ TMs[1][u][a])

28.19 criticized] criticised I

28.21 lack∧] ∼, TMs[1](u)[a]

28.22 God,] ∼∧ TMs[1](u)[a]

28.22 *Ens perfectissimum*] *rom.* TMs[1-2] (Perfectissimum TMs[2])

28.23 whatever∧] ∼, TMs[1]+

28.24-25 [1]*Ens ... perfectissimum*] *all rom.* TMs[1],TMs[2](u)

28.25 Hegel, (*no* ¶)] ¶ Hegel∧ TMs[1]+

28.25 lordly] lowly TMs[1](u)[a]

28.25 says∧ "it] ∼∧ 'it TMs[1]; ∼: 'It TMs[2],I

28.28 Kant's] Kanta's TMs[1](u)[a]

28.31 *mere*] *rom.* TMs[1]+

28.32 'nothing';] PJ/TMs[1b]; ∧∼∧∧ TMs[1](u)[a]

28.34 may be] PJ/TMs[1b]; *om.* TMs[1](u)[a]

28.35 Other still] Still other and K/TMs[2](r1)

28.37 *Proslogium*] Prosologium K/TMs[2],I[1]

28.38 V] %5 TMs[1]; p. 5 TMs[2](u),I; 5 K/TMs[2]

[TMs[1b] *missing*]

29.6 ff. *omit] The same amount of existence must be begged by all. (s.n.)* K/TMs[2],I

29.7 philosophers,] ∼∧ TMs[1a]

29.9 *fact*] fact K/TMs[2]

29.9-10 Nothing] nothing K/TMs[2](r1),I

29.11 beings,] ∼; TMs[2],I

29.14 philosopher] philosophers TMs[1a]

29.18 pretend.] pretend to leave. TMs[1a]

[TMs[1b] *resumes*]

29.18-19 You ... logical] The logical TMs[1](u)[b]; logical WJ/TMs[1a]

29.19 riddle∧] ∼, TMs[1](u)[b]

29.22 ff. *omit] Conservation vs. Creation (s.n.)* K/TMs[2](*moved fr. subh. to s.n.* HJ?),I

29.27 'conserved,'] PJ/TMs[1a-b]; 'consumed' TMs[1](u); ∧∼∧,∧ TMs[2],I

[*begin* Stanford Syllabus clipping *pasted on* MS]

29.30 *within experience*] *rom.* TMs[1]+

29.33 how] How I (how I[p])

29.33 being∧] ∼? TMs[1](u)

29.35 *call*] *rom.* TMs[1]+

29.35 don't] do not TMs[1]+

29.39 unforeseeable∧] ∼, I

30.1 Who ... off-hand?] PJ/TMs¹ᵃ⁻ᵇ;
   om. TMs¹(u)
30.1 Being] being TMs¹+
30.2 one] *om.* TMs²,I
[*end* Stanford Syllabus clipping]
30.4 *vorgefundenes*] rom. TMs¹(u)ᵇ,
   TMs²(u); *Vorgefundenes* K/TMs²,I
30.5 explain,] ∼ₐ TMs²,I
30.5 itselfₐ] ∼, TMs¹(u)
30.6 *what*] What TMs¹,TMs²(u),
   K/TMs²(r2),I; *What* K/TMs²(r1)
[*begin* WJ *typing* ᵗTMs; PJ *typing* TMs]
31.0 *Chapter IV*] *om.* ᵗTMs¹
31.0 *Chapter* ... Concept] Chapter 4. |
   Percept and Concept. Their differ-
   ence.– TMs²(u); *Second Problem* |
   Percept and Conceptˣ | Chapter IV,
   Their Nature and Relations
   K/TMs²(r1); *Chapter IV, Percept
   and Concept–the Import of Concept.*ˣ HJ/TMs²(r2),I
31.7 use] *om.* TMs¹+
[MS *missing*]
31.13 quadrupedal] quadrupal TMs¹,
   TMs²(u)
32.1 nouns,] *om.* TMs¹(u)ᵇ
[*end* ᵗTMs *and* PJ *typing; begin* WJ
   typing TMs]
32.8 doesn't] does not TMs²,I
32.11 is; and no] is. No K/TMs²,I
32.13 outₐ and] out, K/TMs²,I
32.28 -onceness] ₐ∼TMs²
32.34 'percept'] 'Percept' TMs²
33.19 book] HJ/TMs²(r2); discourse
   K/TMs²(r1)
33.26,28;34.33 (*first*) and] *om.*
   K/TMs²,I
33.27 G.J.] J.G. TMs²,I
33.30 2me.... Leçon] part 2, lesson
   12 K/TMs²,I
33.31 and] *om.* I
33.35 that] the agency K/TMs²,I
33.39 man] mann TMs²,I¹
34.14 greek] Greek I
34.18 facts] facts they found,
   K/TMs²(r1)
34.18-19 A ... varies] Compared
   with them, concepts never vary
   K/TMs²(r1)
34.30 viewₐ] ∼, K/TMs²,I
34.33 Santayana,] Santayana,

Interpretations of Poetry and
   Religion, p. K/TMs²(r1); *del.*
   HJ?/TMs²(r2)
34.41 celestial] *om.* TMs²(u)
35.10,11 as to] HJ/TMs²(r2); of
   K/TMs²(r1)
35.11 ¹to] t |TMs¹(u)ᵇ
35.11 value:] ∼; I
35.29 G. Santayana:] *om.* K/TMs²,I
35.30 This (*no* ¶)] ¶ TMs²,I
35.35 7 and 8] vii and viii I (7 and 8
   I[p])
35.36-39 "The ... divine."] *sg. qts.*
   K/TMs²,I
35.40 and] *om.* K/TMs²,I
35.41 *sensations*] Sensations WJ/TMs¹ᵃ;
   K/TMs²,I (*ital.*)
35.42 *Mind*ₐ] ∼, K/TMs²,I
36.1 ¹the] *om.* TMs²,I
36.4 Sensible,] ∼ₐ | TMs²,I
36.7 knowledge] *ital.* WJ/TMs¹ᵇ
36.18 thereforeₐ] ∼, TMs²,I
36.21-22 perceptual] perpetual
   TMs²(u)
36.25 ff. *omit*] *The Content and
   Function of Concepts.* (*s.n.*) K/TMs²
   (*moved fr. subh. to s.n.*),I
36.25-27 1.... 2.... 3.]
   ∼, ... ∼, ... ∼, I (*periods* I[p])
36.29 cosine,'] ∼,' K/TMs²,I
37.6 ff. *omit*] *The Pragmatic Rule*
   (*s.n.*) K/TMs²,I
37.13 not.] *In pencil* WJ/TMs¹ᵃ *adds
   and deletes a fn. indicator and the
   note* Compare Taine, *an early memorandum for fn. 9*
[*end* WJ *typing*]
37.30 complexity,] ∼ₐ |TMs²;I(p)
38.16 ff. *omit*] *Examples* (*s.n.*)
   K/TMs² (*moved fr. subh. to s.n.*),I
38.17 for] ['mean' *typed and ink del.*]
   for TMs¹
38.19 the other] another TMs²(u)
38.22 'Infiniteₐ'] '∼,' TMs²,I(p)
38.23 whole.'] whole to which it
   belongs.' K/TMs²(r1)
38.24 the] *om.* TMs²(u)
38.32 truth] reality K/TMs²,I
38.35+ *omit*] *Second Problem* ['II'
   del.]–*Percept and Concept* | *Chap-
   ter V–The Import of Concepts*

K/TMs$^{2(r1)}$; *del.* HJ/TMs$^{2(r2)}$

39.6 ^{1}the] *del.* WJ/TMs$^{1a(r1)-b(r1)}$

39.6 which] ['of' *typed-del.*] which TMs^1

39.35 the] *om.* TMs^2,I

39.39 sole] *typed ov.* 'soul' TMs^1

40.1 whats . . . whats] HJ?/TMs$^{2(r2)}$; *each ital.* K/TMs$^{2(r1)}$

40.7 -elasticity] -electricity TMs^2,I

40.9 context] contest TMs$^{2(u)}$

40.12 makes] both makes WJ/TMs$^{1b(r1)}$

40.15 nature,] $\sim_\wedge$ I

40.19 perceive.$_\wedge$] $\sim$.^{x} WJ/TMs^{1a}, K/TMs$^{2(r1)}$ (*see* Emendations)

40.33 relations] ['system' *typed-del.*] relations TMs^1

40.35 tried] ['shown' *typed-del.*] tried TMs^1

40.37 The (*no* ¶)] ¶ The I

40.38 mathematic] mathematics TMs^2,I

41.8 aesthetic] æsthetic I

41.14 upon] on I^1

41.16 relations] relation | TMs$^{2(u)}$

41.23 contained,] $\sim_\wedge$ | TMs^2;I

41.28 off one] one off TMs^2,I

41.30 first;] $\sim$, I

41.31-32 mathematic-] mathematics- I

41.35 consists] consisting WJ/TMs^{1a-b}, TMs$^{2(u)}$

41.39 english] English K/TMs^2,I

42.13 concepts] ideal constructions K/TMs^2,I

42.22 *truer*] '$\sim$' TMs^2

42.22 illusory,] $\sim_\wedge$ | TMs^2;I

42.26 Concepts] It is that Concepts WJ/TMs$^{1a(r1)}$

42.33 they arouse] they a | arouse TMs^2

42.39 Sechste Vorlesung] *ital.* K/TMs^2,I

43.3 Truth] truth I (Truth I[p])

43.9 ff. *omit*] *Summary* (*s.n.*) K/TMs^2 (*moved fr. subh. to s.n.*),I

43.9 in human life] *ital.* K/TMs$^{2(r1)}$

43.9 life:] $\sim$. I

43.14 new] *typed ov.* 'you' TMs^1 (*repaired* WJ/TMs^{1b})

43.16 emphasis] emphasis [*last* 's' *ov.* 'z'; *final* 'e' *typed-del.*] TMs^1

43.20 $_\wedge$truths$_\wedge$] '$\sim$' WJ/TMs^{1b}

43.28 We . . . to] *ital.* K/TMs$^{2(r1)}$

43.29 spread,] $\sim$;WJ/TMs$^{1a(r1)}$

43.29 and . . . that] *ital.* K/TMs$^{2(r1)}$

[*begin* WJ *typing*]

43.34 his] *om.* TMs$^{2(u)}$

43.41 Round . . . sing.] *del.* WJ/TMs$^{1a(r1)}$

43.41 Muses] muses TMs^2,I

[*end* WJ *typing*]

44.1 better,] $\sim_\wedge$ K?/TMs^2 (*error*),I

44.2 life?] $\sim$?^{x} WJ/TMs$^{1a(r1)}$

44.5+ *omit*] The intellectualist creed. TMs$^{2(u)}$ (*see* Emendations); *Second Problem*: ['II' *del.*] *Percept and Concept* | Chapter VI–*The Abuse of Concepts.* K/TMs$^{2(r1)}$; Chapter V– *Percept and Concept The Abuse of Concepts.*^{x} K/TMs$^{2(r2)}$, ('^{x}' *written by HJ when he ...ded ji.., see* HC 44.34+);I (V$_\wedge$ . . . Concept–)

44.6 percepts] percept | TMs$^{2(u)}$

44.10 intelligible] intelligent TMs$^{2(u)}$

44.13 $_\wedge$knowledge$_{\wedge\wedge}$] '$\sim$,' K/TMs^2,I

44.13 inalterable] unalterable K/TMs^2,I

44.13 the term] that term K/TMs^2,I

44.13-14 They . . . complication on] *ital.* K/TMs$^{2(r1)}$

[*begin* WJ *typing*]

44.22-23 touch and move] move and touch TMs^2,I

[*end* WJ *typing*]

44.28 confused."] $\sim$.' TMs^2,I

44.31-32 immortal] mortal TMs$^{2(u)}$

44.34+ *omit*] ^{x1}[This chapter and the following *chapters ['chapter' I^1] do not appear as separate chapters in the manuscript. Ed.] HJ/TMs^2,I

44.39 Entretien] Éntretien K/TMs$^{2(r1)}$

45.5 in] *om.* TMs^2,I

45.10 there$_\wedge$ . . . sand]. . . .] there' $_\wedge$in the sand.$_\wedge$ I (there$_\wedge$ . . . sand]. . . . I[p])

45.10-11 $_\wedge$professed] '$\sim$ I ($_\wedge\sim$ I[p])

45.18 happy."] $\sim$.$_\wedge$ TMs$^{2(u)}$; $\sim$.' I ($\sim$." I[p])

45.21 next] now TMs^2; *om.* I

45.25 operation . . . from] so far from operation, TMs$^{2(u)}$ (*error*)

45.26 becomes] become | TMs$^{2(u)}$

45.29 essences] essence | TMs$^{2(u)}$

45.31 ^{1}flux] flux [*typed ov.* 'flow'] TMs^1; flow TMs^2(u)

45.31 superseded, we] $\sim$. We K/TMs^2,I

45.35 ff. omit] The insuperability of sensation (*s.n.*) K/TMs^2,I

45.38 falsify] fail to serve K/TMs$^{2(r1)}$

46.9 red,] $\sim_\wedge$ I (*error*)

46.19 -bubble,] -$\sim_\wedge$ I

46.23+ *omit*] *Concepts give rise to* (*red*) WJ/TMs$^{1a(r1)}$

46.26–27 experience] ['opinio' *typed-del.*] experience TMs^1

46.37 its] HJ/TMs$^{2(r2)}$; their K/TMs$^{2(r1)}$

47.4 fixed,] $\sim_\wedge$ K/TMs$^{2(r1)}$

47.5;50.24 tho] though TMs^2,I

47.7 stationary] ['stat' *typed-del.*] stationary TMs^1

47.9 changed,] be changed, TMs^2(u)

47.19 positions] position | TMs^2(u)

47.20 what] *what* WJ/TMs^{1b}

47.20 is] *is* WJ/TMs^{1b}

47.22 knowing] know['ledge' *typed-del.*]ing TMs^1

47.29 can't] cannot TMs^2,I

47.35 writes,] $\sim_\wedge$ | TMs^2

47.37 so] *om.* TMs^2(u)

47.39 world] worlds TMs^2

48.7 parts] points TMs^2(u)

48.8 continuum] continuous movement WJ/TMs$^{1a(r1)}$

48.9 it$_\wedge$] $\sim$, I

48.10 won't] will not TMs^2,I

48.10 continuum] continuous perception WJ/TMs^{1b}

48.12 This,] $\sim_\wedge$ TMs^2

48.34 doesn't ... doesn't] does not ... does not TMs^2,I

48.35 $_\wedge$We ... Noumena,$_\wedge$] $_\wedge\sim$ ... $\sim$,' TMs^2; '$\sim$...$\sim$,' I

48.35–36 "in ... -knowledge"] '$\sim$...-$\sim$' TMs^2,I

48.37 sinnlichkeit] *cap.* K/TMs^2,I

49.3 phenomena; and later] $\sim$: Later K/TMs^2;I ($\sim$.)

49.5 same] *ital.* K/TMs$^{2(r1)}$

49.14 you can't possibly] it is not possible to K/TMs$^{2(r1)}$; you cannot possibly TMs^2(u),HJ/TMs$^{2(r2)}$,I

49.20 'transcendent'] 'transcendant'

TMs^1(u),TMs^2(u)

50.3 Eleatic$_\wedge$] $\sim$, TMs^2,I

50.4 worst] most obtrusive K/TMs$^{2(r1)}$ (*after* Schiller)

50.5 *naively*] naïvely I (*naively* I[p])

50.16 and] *typed ov.* 'all' TMs^1

50.19;52.4 can't] cannot TMs^2,I

50.19 me] me['n' *typed-del.*] TMs^1

50.21 and$_\wedge$] $\sim$, I

50.23–24 and be] and TMs^2,I

50.31 conceived] concieved I(p)

50.40 concept$_\wedge$] $\sim$, I

51.7 The] The The The WJ/TMs^{1a} (*error*)

51.14 have they] they have TMs^2,I

51.17 Bergson,] $\sim_\wedge$ WJ/TMs$^{1a(r1)}$

51.20 ff. *omit*] The Sceptics and Hegel (*s.n.*) HJ?/TMs$^{2(r2)}$,I; *Hegel and the Sceptics* (*subh.*) K/TMs$^{2(r1)}$

51.27 altho] although TMs^2,I

51.28 develope] develop I

51.30 force,'] $\sim_\wedge$' TMs^2

51.31–32 considered ... yard.] considered, like the kilogram or the imperial yard, 'artefacts,' not revelations. K/TMs^2('artefacts,$_\wedge$);I

51.33–34 (1882) ... is] (1882); pages 136–140 especially, are K/TMs^2,I

51.34 Pearson,] $\sim_\wedge$ I (*error*)

51.34 Milhaud] Milhand TMs^2(u)

51.35 Le Roy] LeRoy TMs^2,I

51.37–52.38 ^{23}See ... Pyrrho. | ^{24}Hegel ... tone.] *fns. reversed in* I(p)

51.37 $_\wedge$Pyrrho.$_\wedge$] '$\sim$.' K/TMs^2,I

51.39 least$_\wedge$] $\sim$, K/TMs^2,I

52.10–11 lose ... its] violates the inner WJ/TMs$^{1a(r1)}$

52.11 so] *om.* TMs^2,I

52.18 M.] Mr. TMs^2(u)

52.19 tho] tho' WJ/TMs^{1b}; though TMs^2,I

52.25 concepts)$_\wedge$] $\sim$), K/TMs^2,I

52.33 -in-unity] -$\sim_\wedge$ $\sim$ TMs^2,I

52.36 doesn't] does not TMs^2,I

52.37 may] HJ/TMs$^{2(r2)}$; might K/TMs$^{2(r1)}$

53.6 Such (*no* ¶)] ¶ TMs^2,I [*resume* MS]

53.21 abridgments] abridgements TMs^1(u)

53.22 purpose ... partial] *om.* TMs^2,I

53.32 philosopher,] $\sim_\wedge$ TMs^1(u)^b
53.32;54.5 altho] although TMs^1+
53.36 is] is in TMs^2,I
53.37 —For] $_\wedge\sim$ K/TMs^2,I
54.1-2 ideal symbols] the ideal symbol TMs^2,I
54.2 He (*no* ¶)] ¶ He TMs^1,TMs^2(u)
54.4 extracts] abstracts TMs^2(u)
54.5 wide] wider TMs^1+
54.7 truth] PJ/TMs^{1a-b}; touch TMs^1(u)
54.12 with freedom] and with freedom TMs^1+
54.14 *possumus*,] $\sim$. TMs^1
54.16+ *Some corollaries.*] *Second Problem* ['*II*' *del.*] *—Percept and Concept* | Chapter VII–SOME COROLLARIES. K/TMs$^{2(r1)}$; Chapter VI–*Percept and Concept* $_\wedge$ SOME COROLLARIES. HJ/TMs$^{2(r2)}$;I (Concept–)
54.17 ff. *omit*] 1. *Novelty becomes possible.* (*s.n.*) K/TMs^2,I
54.17 *I.*] *om.* TMs^1+
54.17 this conclusion] the conclusions of the foregoing chapter K/TMs^2,I
54.20 being . . . our knowledge] things . . . knowledge TMs^2(u)
54.20 In (*no* ¶)] ¶ In our TMs^2(u)
54.31 'mystical'] $_\wedge\sim_\wedge$ TMs^1(u)^b
54.33 favor] favour TMs$^{1-2}$,I(p)
54.33 this.] $\sim_\wedge$ I$^{1-2}$ (*error*) ($\sim$. I[p])
54.33 *Journal*] 'A Suggestion about Mysticism,' *Journal* K/TMs^2,I
54.38 considers,] $\sim$; K/TMs^2,I
55.1 preparations,] $\sim_\wedge$ | TMs^1(u)
55.6 aspired] tried aspire | TMs^2(u)
55.6 -in view] -$\sim$-$\sim$ TMs^2,I(p)
55.8 any] an TMs^1(u)^b (*del.* WJ/TMs^{1a}+)
55.8 possible,] $\sim_\wedge$ WJ/TMs^{1a}, K/TMs^2 (possib | TMs^2[u]),I
55.8 ruled-out] $\sim_\wedge\sim$ TMs^1+
55.9 empiricism] Empiricism TMs$^{1-2}$, I(p)
55.9 reality$_\wedge$] $\sim$, TMs^1(u)^b
55.10 confined by] *om.* TMs^1(u)
55.10 -fence.] -fence. Confined TMs^1(u)
55.11 alters; and . . . into] alters; may turn into novelties, and TMs^1(u); alters; it may . . . and WJ/TMs^{1a}, TMs^2(u); alters. It may . . . and

WJ/TMs^{1b},K/TMs^2,I
55.14 all-inclusive] $\sim_\wedge\sim$ TMs^1(u)^b
55.17 fulminating] formulating TMs^1+
55.32 *II. The . . . reality.*] subh. TMs^1, TMs^2(u) (*omit* '*II.*'); II. The Status of Conceptual Systems K/TMs$^{2(r1)}$; 2$_\wedge$ Conceptual . . . Reality. (*s.n.*) K/TMs$^{2(r2)}$(*moved fr. subh. to s.n.*), I
55.33 concepts] Concepts TMs$^{1-2}$,I(p)
55.34;56.18 $_\wedge$eternal$_\wedge$] '$\sim$' K/TMs^2,I
55.36 book$_\wedge$] $\sim$, I
56.4 way.'] $\sim$.$_\wedge$ TMs^1(u)^b
56.4 Concepts (*no* ¶)] ¶ TMs^2(u)
56.8 many] many interpenetrating WJ/TMs^{1b}
56.10 our] *om.* TMs^1+
56.10 aesthetics] æsthetics I
56.13 involves] HJ/TMs$^{2(r1)}$; generates K/TMs$^{2(r1)}$(*after* Schiller)
56.15 *III. The . . . objects.*] subh. TMs^2(u); *s.n.* (3$_\wedge$) K/TMs^2(*moved fr. subh. to s.n.*),I
56.22 can] rom. TMs^1+
56.24-33 "Every . . . nothing."] '$\sim$ . . . $\sim$.' I
56.29 common,] $\sim_\wedge$ TMs^2,I
56.30 it] is TMs^1
56.35 *name*] name TMs^1(u)^b
57.1 only] *om.* TMs^1+
57.1 called] rom. TMs^1+
57.2 *name*] name TMs^1+
57.5-6 $_\wedge a$) . . . $_\wedge b$)] (a) . . . (b) TMs^1+
57.10 colour] color I (colour I[p])
57.11 And] An TMs^1(u)
57.15 dirty$_\wedge$] $\sim$, TMs^1+
57.17 another,] $\sim_\wedge$ TMs^1+
57.26 colour-] color- I
57.27 *shall*] shall TMs^1(u)^b
57.30 whenever] when ever TMs^1, TMs^2(u) (MS *doubtful spacing*)
57.31-32 *mean . . . meanings*] *each* rom. TMs^1+
57.38 colour-quality] $\sim_\wedge\sim$ TMs^2; color$_\wedge\sim$ I
57.40 *That*] That TMs^1(u)^a
58.2 *be*] be TMs^1(u)^b,TMs^2,I
58.14 excentric] eccentric TMs^2,I
58.17 *IV. Concepts . . . consubstantial.*] subh. TMs^1,TMs^2(u); *s.n.* (4.) K/TMs^2(*moved fr. subh. to s.n.*),I

58.22 thing] things TMs[1]+

58.25 'book.'] 'book'? PJ?/TMs[1a]+

58.26 of the] of TMs[2](u)

58.32 continues] contrives TMs[1](u)

58.34 (except . . . retrospection)]
, ~ . . . ~, K/TMs[2],I

58.35 [2]of] of of TMs[2] (*error*)

58.36 1879] 1979 TMs[1-2]

58.38 —The] ₍ₐ₎~ TMs[1]+

58.38 nominalistic] nominalist TMs[2],I

58.39 (1872)] *om.* TMs[2]

59.5 envelope] envelop I (envelope
I[p])

59.13 see₍ₐ₎] ~, WJ/TMs[1a(r1)]–b(r1)

59.16 ¶ Later] *no* ¶ I

59.22 one,] ~₍ₐ₎ K/TMs[2],I

59.24 *V. An . . . to.*] *subh.* TMs[2](u);
s.n. (5.) K/TMs[2](*moved fr. subh. to
s.n.*),I

59.28 that,] ~₍ₐ₎ TMs[1](u)[b]

59.28 may] *om.* TMs[1]+

59.30–31 derealized] de-realized
K/TMs[2],I

59.35 interpenetration] interpretation
I

59.36 nothing₍ₐ₎] ~, TMs[1](u)

60.1 world,] ~. TMs[2] (*error*)

60.2 founded.₍ₐ₎] ~." TMs[1](u)

60.3 Kern . . . sie] kein TMs[1](u)

60.3 Schale,] ~. WJ/TMs[1a],TMs[2](u);
~; WJ/TMs[1b],K/TMs[2],I

60.3 writes Goethe,] *om.* TMs[1]+

60.3-4 mit einem Male] mit einem
male K/TMs[2],I; *om.* TMs[2](u)

60.4 prüfe] prufe I(p)

60.4 Kern] kern WJ/TMs[1a]; kein
TMs[1](u)

60.8 expel] expell TMs[1](u)[b],K/TMs[2]

60.12 own] *om.* TMs[1]+

60.21 instal] install I (instal I[p])

60.28,39 farther] further TMs[1]+

60.29 happened] interfered WJ/TMs[1b],
K/TMs[2(r1)]

60.31 concepts] percepts TMs[2](u)

60.33 won't] will not TMs[2],I

61.1 ff. *omit*] *Pluralism vs. Monism*
(*s.n.*) K/TMs[2],I

61.6 e.g.,] e.g.₍ₐ₎ TMs[1](u)[b], TMs[2](u);
e.g.₍ₐ₎ WJ/TMs[1a]

61.7 shut-off] ~₍ₐ₎~ TMs[2],I

61.8 what not] whatnot K/TMs[2],I

61.11 unrelated,] ~₍ₐ₎ TMs[1]+

61.11 related only] only related
TMs[2](u)

61.13 or] ['an' *typed-del.*] or TMs[1]

61.18 one ₍ₐ₎ another] ~-~ I (~₍ₐ₎~
I[p])

61.21 *un . . . vérité*] all rom. TMs[1-2]

61.21 *vérité*] *véritté* I(p)

62.1 altho] although TMs[2],I

62.3 *eaches . . . whole*] all rom.
TMs[1](u)[b]

62.4 *content*] *rom.* TMs[1]+

62.4 obtaining,] ~₍ₐ₎ TMs[1](u)[b]

62.5 latin . . . german] *init. caps.*
K/TMs[2],I

62.5 *omnes . . . sämmtliche*] all rom.
TMs[1](u)[b]

62.5 *omnes*₍ₐ₎] ~, TMs[2],I

62.6 alternative] alternatives K/TMs[2],I

62.10 beings] things TMs[2],I

62.11 contradicting] contradictory
TMs[1](u)[b]

62.11 *no*] no TMs[1](u)[b]

62.12 disconnection] disconnexion
TMs[1],TMs[2](u)

62.12 *outness*] *rom.* TMs[1]+

62.13 *any*] *rom.* TMs[1](u)[b]

62.17 for] *om.* TMs[1](u)[b]

62.19 the VIIth's] VII's I

62.21 bridged over] HJ/TMs[2(r2)];
built upon K/TMs[2(r1)]

62.23 *real*] real TMs[1]+

62.25 ff. *omit*] *Kinds of Monism* (*s.n.*)
K/TMs[2],I

62.25 ff. *omit*] *Mystical Monism* (*s.n.*)
K/TMs[2],I

62.27 *must*] must TMs[1]+

62.29-38 "The . . . it."] *sg. qts.* I

62.36 hypostasis] by postastis
TMs[1](u)[b]

62.38 This (*no* ¶)] ¶ I

63.1 hindoo] *cap.* I

63.1 *Brahman . . . Âtman*] *rom.* TMs[1]+

63.2 Krishna,] ~₍ₐ₎ TMs[2],I

63.2-14 "I . . . me."] *sg. qts.* TMs[1]+

63.3 whole] *om.* TMs[2],I

63.4 [1]am] a, TMs[1](u)[b]

63.6 this] the TMs[1]+

63.7 'Om!'] 'One' TMs[1](u)[b]

63.10 world).] ~)₍ₐ₎ I

63.13 worshiping] worshipping TMs[1]+

63.15 it$_\wedge$] $\sim$, TMs^1(u)^b

63.16 often] *om.* TMs^1+

63.16 accredits] credits TMs^1(u)^b

63.22 The (*no* ¶)] ¶ TMs^1+

63.27 ff. *omit*] *Monism of Substance* (*s.n.*) K/TMs^2,I

63.28 *substance*] *rom.* TMs^1(u)^b,I; Substance WJ/TMs^{1a},TMs^2,I(p)

63.29 books] book TMs^1

63.32 -Ghazzali] -Ghaggali TMs^1(u)^b

63.33 Allah] All TMs^1(u)^b

63.34 wills,] $\sim_\wedge$ TMs^1+

63.35 a] *om.* TMs^1(u)^b

63.38 ^{1}care not] cannot TMs^2(u)

63.38 Fire$_\wedge$] $\sim$, I

63.41 1910.)–] $\sim$.). TMs^1; $\sim$.)$_\wedge$ TMs^2,I

63.41 Compare$_\wedge$] $\sim$, TMs^1

64.1 middle ages] Middle Ages TMs^1+

64.2 *per se*] *rom.* TMs^1+

64.9 specific$_\wedge$] $\sim$, TMs^2

64.10 $_\wedge$ on this view$_\wedge$] , $\sim\sim\sim$, TMs^1+

64.11,13 *per . . . se*] *all rom.* TMs^1(u)^b

64.13 tho] though TMs^2,I

64.14 totality$_\wedge$] $\sim$, TMs^1+

64.16 *et seq.* Spinosa] Spinoza TMs^2,I

64.19 manual$_\wedge$] $\sim$, WJ/TMs^{1a}+

64.22 in . . . of] in Part I of the Appendix to TMs^2,I (*see* Emendations *entry* 64.22)

64.32 spinosistic] *cap.* TMs^2,I(p); spinozistic I

64.32 The (*no* ¶)] ¶ TMs^2,I(p)

64.32-44 "The . . . Universe."] *sg. qts.* I (". . . . The TMs^2(u); ' ". . . . The K/TMs^2)

64.37 unity] unit I

64.44 (Solomon [*no* ¶]] ¶ TMs^2,I

65.1-2 favored] favoured TMs^2

65.4 Berkeley$_\wedge$] $\sim$, TMs^1+

65.8 ff. *omit*] *Critique of Substance* (*s.n.*) K/TMs^2,I

65.8-11 "we . . . know."] *sg. qts.* WJ/TMs^{1a},TMs^2,I; "$\sim$ . . . $\sim$." TMs^1(u)^b

65.11 do] do not TMs^2,I

65.12 substances] substance I

65.15 Berkeley (*no* ¶)] ¶ I

65.17 $_\wedge$When I consider,$_\wedge$] *sg. qts.* TMs$^{1-2}$,I

65.17 $_\wedge$the] '$\sim$ TMs$^{1-2}$,I

65.18 '*supporting accidents*'] *rom.* TMs$^{1-2}$;I (*db. qts.*)

65.18 "which] $_\wedge\sim$ TMs$^{1-2}$,I

65.26 thing?"] $\sim$.' TMs^1+

65.27 *known-as*] *rom.* TMs^1(u)^b

65.33 experientially] experi['m' *typed-del.*]entia['a' *ov.* 'i']lly TMs^1; experimentally TMs^2,I

65.37 soul$_\wedge$'] $\sim$,' TMs^1+

65.42 *Knowledge*] *l.c. rom.* TMs$^{1-2}$

66.1 our] out TMs^1

66.4 and appropriate] appropriates TMs^1(u)^b

66.7-8 *certain . . . to*] *all rom.* TMs^1+

66.8 *belong together*] *rom.* TMs^1(u)^b

66.10 clearness:–] $\sim$. TMs^1+

66.10-15 "We . . . collection."] *all sg. qts.* TMs^1+

66.19 *necessarily*] *rom.* TMs^1(u)^b

66.23 ff. *omit*] *Pragmatic analysis of oneness* (*s.n.*) K/TMs^2(*moved fr. subh. to s.n.*),I

66.27 *et seq.* connexions] connections TMs^2,I

66.28-29 Suppose] *l.c.* TMs^1,TMs^2(u), K/TMs$^{2(r2)}$

66.37 Substance-] *l.c.* I (*cap.* I[p])

66.37 -concept$_\wedge$] -$\sim$, TMs$^{1-2}$

66.38 *being . . . substance*] *rom.* TMs^1+

67.5 conceive] *rom.* TMs^1+

67.10 'universe'] $_\wedge\sim_\wedge$ TMs^1+

67.12 abstract] *del.* WJ/TMs^{1a}

67.17 ff. *omit*] *Kinds of Oneness* (*s.n.*) K/TMs^2,I

67.19 *mechanically*] *rom.* TMs^1(u)^b

67.22 the] tho TMs^1(u)^b

67.23 electrical$_\wedge$] $\sim$, TMs^1+

67.24 *mean . . . oneness*] *all rom.* TMs^1+

67.28 *disconnected*] *rom.* TMs^1+

67.28-29 another,] $\sim_\wedge$ TMs^2,I

67.29 light$_\wedge$] $\sim$, TMs$^{1-2}$

68.1 practical] natural TMs^2(u)

68.3 *temporal . . . unity*] *all rom.* TMs^1(u)^b

68.4 *determinately sundering*] *rom.* TMs^1+

68.7 *generic oneness*] *rom.* TMs^1(u)^b

68.8 world's parts] world's TMs^1, TMs^2(u); worlds K/TMs^2,I^1

68.16 *noetic unity*] rom. TMs[1]+
68.18 such] *om.* TMs[1]+
68.23 Substance₌] ~, TMs[2],I
68.23 Subject] *l.c.* TMs[1](u)[b]
68.24 it₌'] ~,' TMs[1]+
68.27 amen] Amen TMs[1](u)[b]
68.28 *object*] rom. TMs[1]+
68.30 ff. *omit*] *Unity by concatenation*
      (s.n.) K/TMs[2],I
68.32 moment₌] ~, WJ/TMs[1a(r1)]
68.36 B,] ~. TMs[1](u)[b]
68.36 C . . .] ~--- TMs[1]; ~,– TMs[2],I
69.2 universe, . . . universe] universe₌
      TMs[2],I
69.3 [2]that] that a TMs[2]
69.5 ¶ There] *no* ¶ TMs[1](u)[b]
69.7 labor-] labour- TMs[2]
69.10,12 can't] cannot TMs[2],I
69.11 copper₌] ~, TMs[1](u)[b]
69.11 connexions₌] ~, TMs[1]+
[*begin* Syllabus *proof*]
69.25 aesthetic] æsthetic I
69.28 seem,] ~₌ K/TMs[2](*error*),I(p)
69.34 Universe] *l.c.* I (*cap.* I[p])
69.36 *primordia rerum*] rom. TMs[1](u)[b]
69.37 Being] being I (Being I[p])
69.39 come] came TMs[2],I
70.3 *economical*] rom. TMs[1]+
70.6 coherent] inherent TMs[2](u)
70.11 *cash-value*] rom. TMs[1]+
70.13 follows upon] *del.* WJ/TMs[1a(r1)]
70.14 which] who WJ/MS(S)[(r1)]
70.17 *prior condition*] rom. TMs[1]+
70.20 *is*] is TMs[1](u)[b]
70.21 *mean by*] rom. TMs[1](u)[b];
      mean by WJ/TMs[1a]+
[*end* Syllabus *proof*]
70.28 or] or of TMs[2],I
70.30+ *omit*] *Third Problem* ['*III*'
      del.] *–The One and the Many* |
      Chapter IX   The Values and
      Defects [*comma del.*] *of Monism*
      and Pluralism K/TMs[2(r1)]; *Chapter*
      IX[X] *The One and the Many*
      (Continued)₌ *Values and Defects*
      | [*fn.*] [X][This chapter was not indi-
      cated as a separate chapter in the
      manuscript. *Ed.*] HJ/TMs[2(r2)],I
      (CHAPTER VIII . . . (*continued*)–)
71.1 One] one I (One I[p])
71.2 *value*] rom. TMs[1]+

71.5 a] a ['conception of it' *typed-del.*]
      TMs[1]
71.7 *rationality*] rom. TMs[1]+
71.8 *belong*] rom. TMs[1](u)[b]
71.13 ff. *omit*] *The Value of* ['*Oneness*'
      del.] *Absolute Oneness (s.n.)*
      K/TMs[2],I
71.15 *that*] rom. TMs[1]+
71.21 *tight*] rom. TMs[1](u)[b]
71.21 *loose*] rom. TMs[1]+
71.22 whole] part TMs[2](u)
71.29 [1]of] *om.* TMs[1](u)[b]
71.34 ff. *omit*] *Its defects (s.n.)*
      K/TMs[2],I
71.38 Hegel] Hegel were K/TMs[2(r2)],I;
      Hegel are K/TMs[2(r1)]
71.39 Royce] Royce is K/TMs[2],I
72.1 favor] favour TMs[2]
[*begin* Syllabus]
72.4 *It . . . Consciousness.*] all rom.
      TMs[1]+
72.4 *doesn't*] does not TMs[2],I
72.4 *Consciousness*] *l.c.* K/TMs[2],I
72.6 *otherwise than*] rom. TMs[1]+
72.8 *without*] rom. TMs[1]+
72.10 Subject] *l.c.* I (*cap.* I[p])
72.11 *differently*] rom. TMs[1]+
72.12 *It . . . Evil*] all rom. TMs[1]+
72.12 *Evil*] *l.c.* TMs[2],I
72.13 *practical*] rom. TMs[1]+
72.14 *theoretical*] rom. TMs[1]+
72.14 –how,] –How, TMs[1-2];
      ₌How,– I(p); ₌How– I
72.17 *also*] rom. TMs[1]+
72.19-20 *It . . . experienced*] all rom.
      TMs[1]+
72.24 *mirage*] rom. TMs[1]+
72.26 *It is fatalistic*] rom. TMs[1]+
72.29 *is*] is TMs[1]+
72.30 Unit] *l.c.* I (*cap.* I[p])
72.36 or] or TMs[1](u)[b]
72.40 common sense] ~-~ WJ/TMs[1a]+
73.3 'with₌'] '~,' TMs[2],I
73.5 ff. *omit*] *The Value and Defects of*
      Pluralism (subh.) K/TMs[2(r1)]; *The*
      Pluralistic Theory (s.n.) K/TMs[2(r2)],I
73.10 can't] cannot TMs[2],I
73.10 *explain*] rom. TMs[1]+
73.10 *how*] how TMs[1](u)[b]
73.12 ₌ in fact₌] , ~ ~, K/TMs[2],I
73.14 *that . . . why*] rom. TMs[1](u)[b]

73.19 ff. *omit*] *Its defects (s.n.)*
 K/TMs²,I
73.22 *rationally*] *rom.* TMs¹+
73.23 "sees . . . -Real."] *sg. qts.* TMs¹+
73.27 A *(no ¶)*] ¶ I
73.31 *melioristic*ₐ] *rom.* TMs¹;
 melioristic, TMs²,I
73.31-32 *may . . . best*] *all rom.* TMs¹+
73.35-36 *peace . . . religious*] *all rom.*
 TMs¹+
[*end* Syllabus]
73.40 Lecture] lecture TMs¹+
74.1 ff. *omit*] *Its advantages (s.n.)*
 K/TMs²,I
74.15 *quite*] *rom.* TMs¹+
74.17 whatever₍] ∼, WJ/TMs¹ᵇ⁽ʳ¹⁾
74.30 absent,] ∼ₐ TMs¹+
74.36 ₐ at least₍] , ∼ ∼, TMs¹+
74.39 *novelty*] *rom.* TMs¹+
74.40 ff. *omit*] *Monism, pluralism, and
 novelty (s.n.)* K/TMs²,I
75.6 *chance*] *rom.* TMs¹(u)ᵇ
75.8 being? Or] ∼? or TMs¹,TMs²(u);
 ∼ₐ or K/TMs²,I
75.8 is it] *om.* WJ/TMs¹ᵇ
75.14-15 instalments?] ∼. TMs¹+
76.1 ff. *omit*] HJ/TMs²⁽ʳ²⁾; *Introduction* [*ab. del.* 'Perceptual Novelty']
 (s.n.) K/TMs²⁽ʳ¹⁾
76.4 powerlessness] power lessen
 TMs¹(u)ᵇ
76.5 empiricist] empiricist['s' *typed-
 del.*] TMs¹
76.8 brought] *om.* TMs¹(u); led
 WJ/TMs¹ᵇ
76.8 III] iii TMs¹; VII K/TMs²,I
76.11 Being] being K/TMs²,I
76.14 ff. *omit*] *Perceptual Novelty
 (s.n.)* K/TMs²,I
76.17 content] Content TMs¹-I(p)
 (MS *doubtful*)
76.17 never] ['which' *typed-del.*]
 never TMs¹
76.18 will never] never will TMs²(u)
76.19-77.10 "My . . . reversed."] *all
 sg. qts.* TMs¹+
76.23 graver] grave TMs¹+
77.1 Time] time TMs²,I
77.1-2 on births₍] ∼ ∼, TMs²,I
77.10 reversed."¹] ∼.'₍ I(p)
77.11 ff. *omit*] *Science and Novelty

(s.n.) K/TMs²,I
77.11-12 is so obvious] *om.* TMs¹(u)ᵇ
77.16 inalterable] unalterable K/TMs²,I
77.18 them,] ∼ₐ TMs¹(u)ᵇ
77.24 —On] ₐ∼ I
77.27 atomistic] Atomistic TMs¹+
77.28 Democritus₍] ∼, TMs¹+
77.35 *Materialismus*] Materialisms
 TMs¹,TMs²(u); *Materialisms*
 K/TMs²,I¹
77.35-41 "The . . . nonsense."] *sg. qts.*
 TMs¹+
77.36 and of] and I
77.39 all that] all TMs²,I
77.42 english] English K/TMs²,I
77.43 —Also] ₐ∼ TMs¹+
77.44 is] in TMs¹,TMs²(u)
78.1 ff. *omit*] *Biography and Novelty
 (s.n.)* K/TMs²⁽ʳ¹⁾; *Personal Experience and Novelty (s.n.)*
 HJ?/TMs²⁽ʳ²⁾,I
78.1 Nature] nature TMs²,I
78.9-10 ²our . . . are 'really' only]
 'really' our . . . are only WJ/TMs¹ᵃ+;
 'really' only our . . . are TMs¹(u)ᵇ
78.11 tho] tho' WJ/TMs¹ᵃ; though
 TMs²,I
78.11 of a] *om.* TMs¹(u)ᵇ
78.14 *as it is*] *rom.* TMs¹(u)ᵇ; as it *is*
 WJ/TMs¹ᵃ+
78.15-16 consciousness,] ∼ₐ TMs¹(u)ᵇ
78.16 *as such,*] *rom.* TMs¹+ (such₍
 TMs¹[u]ᵇ)
78.28 naively₍] ∼, TMs¹(u)ᵇ;
 naïvely₍ I (naïvely₍ I[p])
78.31 *live*] *rom.* TMs¹+
78.31 or] *om.* TMs²(u)
78.36 conceptualism₍] ∼, TMs¹+
79.1 own,] ∼ₐ TMs¹(u)ᵇ
79.3 ff. *omit*] *Novelty and the Infinite
 (s.n.)* K/TMs²,I
79.3 ¶ It] *no* ¶ TMs¹(u)ᵇ
79.3 this] the TMs¹+
79.13 novelty, however₍] ∼, ∼,
 TMs¹(u)ᵇ; ∼ₐ ∼ₐ TMs²,I
79.15 to . . . point] at this point to
 interrupt TMs¹+
79.18 Infinite] infinite TMs²,I
80.3 exists] exist TMs¹-I(p)
80.4 ff. *omit*] *The Discontinuity
 Theory (s.n.)* K/TMs²,I

80.4 theory of discontinuity] disconti-
nuity$_\wedge$ theory TMs^1(u)^b; $\sim$-$\sim$
WJ/TMs^{1a}+

80.8 atoms,] $\sim_\wedge$ TMs^1+

80.12 space$_\wedge$] $\sim$, TMs^1+

80.22 ff. *omit*] *The Continuity Theory*
(s.n.) K/TMs^2,I

80.23 *can*] *rom.* TMs^1+

81.2 inconceivable] conceivable
TMs^2(u)

81.7 *ad infinitum*] *rom.* TMs^1,TMs^2(u)

81.11 number] ['and' *typed-del.*]
number TMs^1; and number TMs^2,I

81.15 ff. *omit*] *Zeno's paradoxes (s.n.)*
K/TMs^2,I

81.15 -problem$_\wedge$] - $\sim$, TMs^1+

81.16 english] *cap.* TMs^2,I

81.21 numbers,'] $\sim_\wedge$' TMs^1

81.23,24 couldn't] could not TMs^2,I

81.27 exists$_\wedge$ not$_\wedge$] $\sim$, $\sim_\wedge$ TMs^1(u)^b;
$\sim_\wedge$ $\sim$, WJ/TMs^{1a}+

81.27 point,] $\sim$; TMs^2,I

81.38 chapter] *cap.* TMs^1-I(p) (MS
doubtful)

82.3 starting-point] $\sim_\wedge$ $\sim$ TMs^1+

82.3 Achilles. Measured] $\sim$; measured
TMs^1(u)^b

82.4 follows:—] $\sim$:$_\wedge$ I

82.5 $\frac{1}{8}$ ... $\frac{1}{n}$] *om.* TMs^1(u)

82.6 infinitely] infinitely divided
TMs^2(u)

82.13 *could*] *rom.* TMs^1(u)^b+

82.20 'Eleatic'] $_\wedge$$\sim$' TMs^1

82.21 *minima sensibilia*] '$\sim$ $\sim$'
(rom.) TMs^1+

82.23 *ad infinitum*] *rom.* TMs$^{1-2}$

82.31 infinite,] $\sim$. TMs^1(u)^b

82.33 ff. *omit*] *Kant's Antinomies*
(s.n.) K/TMs^2,I

82.34-35 must ... as] may be regarded
must be determinate existence as
TMs^1(u)

82.34 *determinate*] *rom.* TMs^1+

82.38 *infinitely long*] *rom.* TMs^1+

83.1 Pleiades] Pleides TMs^1(u)^b

83.4 number] numbers TMs^1+

83.6 *countable*] *rom.* TMs^1+

83.8 'that] $_\wedge$$\sim$TMs^1(u)^b

83.9 words$_\wedge$] $\sim$, K/TMs^2,I

83.11 'given$_\wedge$'] '$\sim$,' TMs^1+

83.17 etc.,] $\sim_\wedge$; TMs^1; $\sim$.$_\wedge$ TMs^2

83.28-29 *form ... fact*] *rom.*
TMs^1(u)^b

83.30 experience] ex-|istence perience
TMs^1(u)^b

83.32 can't] can not TMs^1; cannot
TMs^2,I

83.32 , he says,] $_\wedge$ $\sim$ $\sim_\wedge$ TMs^1(u)^b

83.32 *don't*] do not TMs^1+

83.33 independently,] $\sim_\wedge$ | TMs^1+

83.33 *an sich ... for us*] *rom.*
TMs^1(u)^b

83.33 'phenomena,'] $_\wedge$$\sim$,$_\wedge$ TMs^1+

83.38 doesn't] does not TMs^1+

83.38-39 already there] there already
TMs^2,I

83.39 'Experience,'] $_\wedge$$\sim$,$_\wedge$ TMs^1+

83.42 *aufgegeben*$_\wedge$ ... task),]
$\sim$, ... $\sim$)$_\wedge$ WJ/TMs^{1a};TMs^2(u)
(rom.); $\sim_\wedge$ ... $\sim$), *(rom.)*
WJ/TMs^{1b}*(pencil)*; $\sim_\wedge$ ... $\sim$)$_\wedge$
(rom.) TMs^1(u); $\sim$, ... $\sim$), K/TMs^2

84.1 ff. *omit*] *Ambiguity of Kant's*
statement of the problem (s.n.)
K/TMs^2,I

84.1 infinite,] $\sim_\wedge$ TMs^1(u)^b,TMs^2(u)

84.3-4 of ... words] the words of the
conditions$_\wedge$ TMs^1(u)^b; of the con-
ditions$_\wedge$ the words WJ/TMs^{1a},
TMs^2(u)

84.6 given$_\wedge$'] $\sim$,' I ($\sim_\wedge$' I[p])

84.12 each$_\wedge$'] $\sim$,' TMs^1(u)^a,TMs^2,I

84.12 'any.'] as 'any' K/TMs^2,I

84.12 treatment] statement TMs^2,I

84.16 'any,' 'each,'] '$\sim_\wedge$' | 'Each,'
TMs^1; '$\sim_\wedge$' '$\sim$,' TMs^2

84.16 'every$_\wedge$'] '$\sim$,' TMs^1(u)^b

84.18;90.39*(second)* tho] though
TMs^1+

84.19 the] *om.* TMs^2(u)

84.24 require,] $\sim_\wedge$ TMs^1(u)^b

84.26 ff. *omit*] Renouvier's solution
(s.n.) K/TMs^2,I

84.27 XIXth Century] 19 century
TMs^1(u)^b; 19th. century WJ/TMs^{1a};
19th century TMs^2; nineteenth
century I

84.29 *supra,*] Supra, TMs^1; Supra$_\wedge$
TMs^2; supra$_\wedge$ I(p); supra, I

84.30 'principe du nombre,'] *ital.* I

84.31 etc.,] $\sim$.$_\wedge$ | TMs^2

84.37 seem,] seem to be, TMs^1+

85.3 ff. *omit*] *It favors novelty (s.n.)*
K/TMs[2(r1)]; His solution *favors
novelty* K/TMs[2(r2)], I

85.4 unmediated] unmeditated I

85.9-17 [1]I . . . memory.] *set as start
of fn. 6 keyed to* 'last chapter.'
K/TMs[2], I

85.11 *characters*] *rom.* TMs[1]+

85.17 memory.[6]] ~., K/TMs[2], I

85.17+ *omit*] Chapter XI *Novelty and
the Infinite—The Perceptual View.*[1] |
[*fn.*] [1][This chapter was not indicated as a separate chapter in the
['author' *del.*] manuscript. Ed.]
K/TMs[2(r2)]; I; *Fourth Problem:*
['*III*' *del.*] —['*The Problem of*' *del.*]
Novelty | *Chapter XI—The Prag-
matic* *solution [*ab. del.* '*Treatment*'] *of* *Problem of [*intrl.*] *the
Infinite* K/TMs[2(r1)]

85.27 ¶ Proceeding] *no* ¶ TMs[2], I

85.29 [1]in] i | in TMs[1]; is in TMs[2], I

85.29 four,] ~ [*intrl.* 'vols.,' *del.*] ,
WJ/TMs[1a]

85.29 six,] ~, WJ/TMs[1a], TMs[2]
(*comma error*)

85.31 *classification*] *rom., cap.* TMs[1],
TMs[2](u); *ital., cap.* K/TMs[2]

85.32 Comment] comment TMs[1],
TMs[2](u)

85.32 arrivé à] arrive a TMs[1](u)[b]

85.33 His] *om.* TMs[2], I

85.36 say now] now say TMs[2], I

85.37 *inferring*] *rom.* TMs[1]+

85.39 won't] will not TMs[1]+

86.3-5 *standing . . . growing*] *rom.*
TMs[1](u)[b]

86.6 ff. *omit*] *The Standing Infinite
(s.n.)* K/TMs[2], I

86.8 If,] ~, TMs[1]

86.11;89.17 *n*] *rom.* TMs[1]+

86.11 numbers,] ~, TMs[1](u)

86.11 endlessly,] ~, WJ/TMs[1a-b]+

86.12 as you count,] *om.* TMs[1]+

86.14 numbered,] ~ ; K/TMs[2], I

86.14 this] thus TMs[2](u)

86.14 *in infinitum*] *rom.* TMs[1]-I(p)

86.15 was,] ~, WJ/TMs[1a], TMs[2](u)

86.16 numbers,] ~, | TMs[1]+

86.17 *each*] each TMs[1](u)[a], TMs[2], I

86.21 ff. *omit*] *Its pragmatic definition*

(s.n.) K/TMs[2], I

86.26 there,' ,we] ~,'—, ~ I(p);
~,'—,~ I

86.27 *all*] all TMs[1]+

86.28 there,'] ~,' TMs[1]+

86.31 asked,] ~, TMs[1]+

86.32 offer] differ TMs[2](u)

86.32 better men] HJ/TMs[2(r2)];
professional philosophers K/TMs[2(r1)]

86.33 moment,] moment, one may
think, WJ/TMs[1b(r1)]

86.33 an] in TMs[1](u)

86.33 'amount.'] ,~., TMs[1](u)[b]

86.37 finite] infinite TMs[1](u)[b]

86.37 —The] ,~ TMs[1]+

87.2 Any] And I

87.3 -series] *om.* TMs[1](u)[b]; *ab. del.
intrl.* 'a series' WJ/TMs[1a]

87.4 determination] determinations
TMs[1](u)[a], TMs[2](u)

87.5 'standing'] ,~, TMs[1](u)[b]

87.6 *each*] each TMs[1](u)[b]

87.6 date,] ~, | TMs[1]+

87.7 'bulk,'] '~,' I

87.8 ¶ But] *no* ¶ TMs[1]+

87.9 reason] ['probabl' *intrl. and del.*]
reason WJ/TMs[1a]

87.10 space,] ~, TMs[1](u)

87.11 *stupid*] *rom.* TMs[2], I

87.12 *so much*] *rom.* TMs[1]+

87.13 *be*] *rom.* TMs[1]+

87.15 finitist] finitest I

87.16 ff. *omit*] *The growing infinite
(s.n.)* K/TMs[2], I

87.16 ¶ If] *no* ¶ TMs[1](u)

87.18 *before*] *rom.* TMs[1]+

87.23 can't] can not TMs[1], TMs[2];
cannot I

87.26 can't] cannot TMs[1]+

87.26 *by this process*] *rom.* TMs[1](u)[b]

87.29 numbers,] ~, TMs[2], I

87.29 etc.,] ~., TMs[1]

87.29 'infinite,'] ,infinity,, TMs[1]+

87.35 [1]distributive] distribution
TMs[1](u)

87.37 this] the TMs[1](u)[b]

87.39 the] *om.* TMs[2], I

87.39 if in finite] of infinite TMs[1](u);
if in infinite WJ/TMs[1a]+

87.39 number] in number
WJ/TMs[1b(r1)]

87.41 all] All TMs[1]+

88.1 'more'] ˄more˄ WJ/TMs[1b];
˄move˄ TMs[1](u); note 'more'
TMs[2],I

88.2 of] or TMs[1](u)

88.3 Starting] to start WJ/TMs[1a(r1)]

88.5 words] word TMs[1]+

88.6-7 *aufgegeben*. In . . . [2]it]
aufgegeben. It TMs[2](u); ∼: In . . .
it K/TMs[2]; ∼: in . . . it I

88.6 the] that TMs[1](u)[a],K/TMs[2(r1)]

88.7 contrary,] ∼˄ TMs[1](u)[a]+

88.8 any] a | any TMs[1]

88.13 *Infinitum . . . nequit*,] '∼ . . . ∼,'
(*all rom.*) WJ/TMs[1a]; ˄∼ . . . ∼,˄
(*all rom.*) TMs[1](u); '∼ . . . ∼,'
TMs[2],I

88.13 ff. *omit*] *It must be treated as
discontinuous* (*s.n.*) K/TMs[2(r1)];
*The growing infinite must be treated
as discontinuous* K/TMs[2(r2)],I

88.17 taking] composed taking
TMs[1](u)

88.18 finite,] ∼˄ TMs[1](u)[a],TMs[2],I

88.23 [2]it] it a TMs[2](u)

88.24 ff. *omit*] Objections [*bel. del.*
'Contemporar'] (*s.n.*) K/TMs[2];I

88.27 bothers˄] ∼, TMs[1]+

88.30 which,] ∼˄ TMs[1](u)

88.32 ff. *omit*] ['in th' *del.*] *(1) The
Number continuum* (*s.n.*) K/TMs[2];
(1) The number-continuum I

88.34 (ἀριθμὸς . . . quantity] of all
*quantity˄ [*period del.* WJ/TMs[1a–b]]
(*arithmos* [*rom.* TMs[1](u)[b]] meaning
number). TMs[1]–I(p)

88.35 *quanta*] *rom.* TMs[1](u)[b]

88.36 been˄] ∼, TMs[1](u)

88.38 equivalent] system equivalent
TMs[1](u)[b]

89.1,5,8 cuts] cists TMs[1](u) (*error*)

89.4 made] *om.* TMs[1]+

89.3 etc.,] ∼.˄ TMs[1–2]

89.6 *ad infinitum*] *rom.* TMs[1],TMs[2](u)

89.7 gets at last] at last gets TMs[1]+

89.7 *full*,] full, WJ/TMs[1b]; full˄
TMs[1](u)

89.11 translations−] ∼˄ TMs[1](u);
∼: WJ/TMs[1a(r1)–b(r1)]; ∼,
WJ/TMs[1b(r2)]

89.13 unanalyzed] uncriticized

WJ/TMs[1a]; criticized TMs[2],I;
unequalized TMs[1](u)

89.14 "a kind] ˄a 'kind TMs[1]+

89.15 ff. *omit*] *and (2) the "new
infinite"* (*s.n.*) K/TMs[2(r1)]; *(2) the
"new infinite"* (*s.n.*) K/TMs[2(r2)];I
(*sg. qts.*)

89.16-17 indefinitely˄ growing]
∼-∼ TMs[1](u)[a],TMs[2],I

[*begin different typing* TMs[1b]]

89.18 numbers,] ∼˄ I

89.18-19 'prime' . . . 'square' numbers,]
or 'square' numbers, or 'prime' numbers, TMs[1b] (numbers˄ TMs[1b[u]])

89.19 a] *om.* TMs[1b(u)]

89.20 'equal'] *equal* WJ/TMs[1b];
˄equal˄ TMs[1a]+

89.21 whole,] ∼˄ | TMs[1a–b]+

89.22 whole,] ∼˄ TMs[1b]

89.23-24 whole, so] ∼. So TMs[1a–b](u)

89.25 Thus,] ∼˄ TMs[1b(u)]

89.36 ff. *omit*] *It is paradoxical* (*s.n.*)
K/TMs[2(r1)]; *The new infinite paradoxical* K/TMs[2(r2)],I

89.37 number-series] ∼˄∼ TMs[1b]

89.37-38 'growing'] ˄∼˄ TMs[1b]

89.38-90.1 *reductio ad absurdum*] *rom.*
TMs[1b]

89.39 *Science*] *l.c.* K/TMs[2],I

[*end different typing* TMs[1b]]

90.2 *in act*] *rom.* TMs[1]+

90.7 infinite] finite TMs[2](u)

90.8 finite] infinite TMs[1](u),
TMs[2](u)

90.11 ff. *omit*] *"Transfinite Numbers"*
(*s.n.*) K/TMs[2];I (*sg. qts.*)

90.11 concepts˄] ∼, I (∼˄ I[p])

90.13 *ad infinitum*] *rom.* TMs[1](u)[b]

90.18 him?−] ∼− TMs[1],I; ∼) TMs[2]

90.20 couldn't] could not TMs[2],I

90.22 ˄ in short˄] , ∼∼, K/TMs[2],I

90.25 ff. *omit*] *Their uses *and
defects [added]* (*s.n.*) K/TMs[2],I

90.26 number-continuum] ∼˄∼
TMs[1](u)[b]

90.30 be] be made TMs[1](u)[a],TMs[2],I

90.32 difference,] ∼˄ TMs[1](u)[b]

90.34 magnitudes,] ∼˄ TMs[2],I

90.34 content] contact TMs[1](u)

90.34 Moreover,] ∼˄ TMs[1](u)[a],TMs[2],I

90.37-38 any . . . one] any one and

every K/TMs[2],I

91.2   defined. Thus] ∼; thus K/TMs[2],I

91.7   , and] . Thus do we K/TMs[2(r1)]

91.11 ff.   *omit*] *and defects* (*s.n.*)
K/TMs[2(r1)](*del.* K/TMs[2[r2]])

91.11   of] of my TMs[1](u)[a],TMs[2],I

91.17   quanta,] ∼ₐ | TMs[1](u)[b]; *ital.* I
(*rom.* I[p])

91.18   [1]-inches,] -∼ₐ | TMs[1](u)[a]

91.21   'sophism ₐ'] '∼ₐₐ TMs[1];
'∼,' I

91.23 ff.   *omit*] *Russell's solution of
Zeno's paradox by their means*
(*s.n.*) K/TMs[2],I

91.23   don't] do not TMs[1]+

91.25   lay] *om.* TMs[1](u); consisted
WJ/TMs[1b(r1)]

91.26   runners] manners TMs[1](u)

91.26-27   ₐand . . . ₐcoincident]
(∼ . . . (∼ WJ/TMs[1a(r1)]

91.29-33   But . . . time?] Owing to the
tortoise's head-start, the tortoise's
path is only a part of the path of
Achilles. How, then, since the two
paths are of different lengths can the
longer path *not* take the longer time
if time-points are to be the medium
of measurement? K/TMs[2(r1)]

91.29   [2]they] the two paths I

91.31   Achilles.] ∼ₐ | TMs[1]

91.33   not] *ital.* TMs[2],I

91.34   remedy,] ∼ₐ TMs[1](u)[b],I

92.2   these] the TMs[2],I

92.4   head-start] ∼-|∼ TMs[1];
headstart TMs[2]

92.8   of] in TMs[1]+

92.11 ff.   *omit*] *The Solution Criticized*
(*s.n.*) K/TMs[2],I

92.15   that remains] which remains to
be solved K/TMs[2(r1)]

92.16   almost] always TMs[1](u)

92.17   *process of formation*] process
of *formation* WJ/TMs[1a],TMs[2],I;
rom. TMs[1](u)[b]

92.17   Moreover,] ∼ₐ TMs[1],TMs[2](u)

92.18   *two*] two TMs[1]+

92.19-20   isₐ . . . touching] is: How
can you touch K/TMs[2(r1)]; is: . . .
touching K/TMs[2(r2)]

92.22   quantum] *ital.* WJ/TMs[1b],
K/TMs[2]

92.23   *printed*] rom. TMs[1]+

92.24   one] a TMs[2],I

92.24   God,] ∼ₐ TMs[1](u)

92.24   produced] *om.* TMs[1](u); created
WJ/TMs[1a-b]+

92.26   *fiat*] rom. TMs[1](u)[a]

92.28   'Omegaₐ'] '∼,' TMs[1](u)[a],
TMs[2],I(p)

92.30   traverses] *rom.* TMs[1](u)[a]

92.30   continuumₐ] ∼, K/TMs[2],I

92.30-31   instantaneous act.] continuous act. TMs[1](u); process continuous
in the mathematician's sense.
WJ/TMs[1b]; K/TMs[2],I (mathematical)

92.36   saying,] ∼ₐ TMs[1](u)[a],TMs[2],I

93.4 ff.   *omit*] Conclusions (*s.n.*)
K/TMs[2],I

93.6   page 88] page 172 I; Page 173-4
WJ/TMs[1b],TMs[2],I(p); Page 70z
TMs[1](u)[a]; p. 70[z] MS

93.6-8   Irrelevant . . . others,]
HJ/TMs[2(r2)]; The criticisms . . .
others, (irrelevant . . . sort),
K/TMs[2(r1)]

93.10   *seriatim*] rom. TMs[1]+

93.10   if] when the WJ/TMs[1a (r1)]

93.13   therefore,] ∼ₐ TMs[1](u);
therefore, in these cases, WJ/TMs[1a];
K/TMs[2],I (cases;)

93.15-16   , or . . . them,] (∼ . . . ∼)
K/TMs[2(r1)]

93.22   nth] nth TMs[1],TMs[2](u); *nth* I
(*also* 93.22)

93.24-25   "if . . . task."] all *rom.*
TMs[1]+ (If)

93.24   *T.S.*] Tristram Shandy TMs[1]+

93.25   *for ever*] forever TMs[1]+

93.25   *doesn't*] does not TMs[1]+

93.26   'live for ever,'] '∼ forever,'
WJ/TMs[1b]; ₐ∼ forever,ₐ TMs[1](u)[a],
TMs[2],I

93.29   logically,] ∼ₐ TMs[1](u)

93.29   feel] fell TMs[1](u)[a],TMs[2](u)

93.31   —The] ₐ∼ TMs[2],I

93.33   Baldwin's . . . 'continuity';]
om. TMs[1]+

93.34   Couturat's] Conturat's
TMs[1]-I[1]

93.34   *mathématique*] *cap.* TMs[1]+
(*rom.* TMs[1b]; *no accent* TMs[1a])

93.35   of] *om.* TMs[1](u)[a],TMs[2],I

93.39 Hobson,] $\sim_\wedge$ TMs[1]+

93.40 —For] $_\wedge\sim$ TMs[1]+

93.44 with . . . titles.] , *La *Science [*Lc.* I[2+]] *et l'hypothèse*, Paris; *The Value of Science* (authorized translation by G. B. Halsted), New York, 1907; *Science et Méthode*, Paris, 1908. I

93.44 'Science'] 'science' TMs[1](u)[a], TMs[2]

93.44 —The] $_\wedge\sim$ TMs[1]+

93.45 synthesis$_\wedge$] $\sim$, TMs[2],I

94.2 by] either by WJ/TMs[1a–b(r1)], TMs[2](u); as by WJ/TMs[1b(r2)]

94.6 it] the treatment K/TMs[2],I

94.9 ff. *omit*] *Conceptual Transformation of Perceptual Experience turns* ['makes' *del.*] *the Infinite into a problem. (s.n.)* K/TMs[2(r1)]; K/TMs[2(r2)](1. *Conceptual*); I (1. Conceptual)

94.21 perception$_\wedge$] $\sim$, TMs[1]+

94.23 ff. *omit*] *It leaves the problem of Novelty where it was (s.n.)* K/TMs[2];I (2. It)

94.25–26 intellectualistic] intellectualist TMs[2],I

94.28 quanta] *ital.* I (*rom.* I[p])

94.28 motion] notion I

94.29 mathematic] mathematics TMs[1](u)[a],TMs[2],I

94.31 infinitesimals,] $\sim_\wedge$ TMs[1](u)[a], TMs[2],I

94.34 *merely*] *rom.* TMs[1]+

94.35 moment$_\wedge$] $\sim$, TMs[2],I

94.37 —The] $_\wedge\sim$ K/TMs[2],I

94.39 altho] although TMs[1]+

94.40 its] *om.* TMs[1](u)[b]

94.41 etc.,] $\sim._\wedge$ K/TMs[2],I

94.42 altho] although I

95.1–2 steps . . . number] discrete steps finite in number K/TMs[2(r1)]; (*change del.* HJ/TMs[2[r2]])

95.2 discrete$_\wedge$] $\sim$, K/TMs[2],I

95.3–4 this . . . chapter] these . . . chapters K/TMs[2(r2)],I; this . . . discussion K/TMs[2(r1)]

95.5 laid] had laid TMs[2],I

95.9 term,'] $\sim_\wedge$' TMs[1]+

95.13 settle] HJ/TMs[2(r2)]; settle down K/TMs[2(r1)]

95.14 'the . . . causality'] *del.* K/TMs[2], I

95.15 way.] way. This is the 'problem of *causation [ab. del.* 'causality'].' K/TMs[2];I

96.1 ff. *omit*] *The 'Principle of Causality' (s.n.)* K/TMs[2],I

96.3 Chapter] a Chapter TMs[1](u)[b]

96.3 *überhaupt*] uberhaupt TMs[1](u)[b]; *rom.* WJ/TMs[1a]

96.4 *intellect*] *rom.* TMs[1]-I(p)

96.7 eternal,] $\sim_\wedge$ TMs[1]+

96.9 creation$_\wedge$] $\sim$' K/TMs[2(r1)]

96.9 write] *om.* TMs[1](u)[b]

96.9 day] dawn K/TMs[2],I

96.10 Monism and Pluralism] *l.c.* K/TMs[2],I

96.17 conceptual . . . them] *om.* TMs[1](u)[b] (*intrl. aft.* 'them' *in error* WJ/TMs[1a])

96.18 ff. *omit*] *Aristotle on Causation (s.n.)* K/TMs[2],I

96.18 ¶ The] *no* ¶ TMs[1]+

96.18 The (*no* ¶)] ¶ I

96.20 brass] bronze TMs[1]+

96.20 [2]cause$_\wedge$] $\sim$, TMs[2],I(p)

96.22 [1]Book . . . gives] Book 2, or Book 5, Chapter 2, of his *Metaphysics*, *or [*intrl.* WJ/TMs[1a]] Chapter 3 of his *Physics* give TMs[1](*rom.*)-I ([2]book . . . chap. . . . chap. K/TMs[2],I)

97.1 child);] $\sim)_\wedge$ TMs[1]+

97.2 'exercises'] $_\wedge\sim_\wedge$ TMs[1]+

97.6 ff. *omit*] *Scholasticism on the Efficient Cause (s.n.)* K/TMs[2],I

97.6–7 $_\wedge$*that . . . itself.*$_\wedge$] *all rom.* TMs[1](u)[b]; '$\sim$ . . . $\sim$.' (*all rom.*) WJ/TMs[1a]+

97.11 supposes] is supposed TMs[1]+

97.13 ¶ 1. No] *no* ¶ TMs[1]+

97.15 *nothing can happen*] *rom.* TMs[1]+

97.21 some way] someway TMs[1]

97.22–28 ['Formally . . . cunning.]] ('$\sim$ . . . $\sim$.) TMs[1]+

97.27 tho] though TMs[1]+

97.29 *Nemo . . . habet*] *all rom.* TMs[1], TMs[2](u)

97.29 *habet*$_\wedge$] $\sim$, TMs[2]-I(p)

97.30;103.2 *Causa . . . effectum*] *all rom.* TMs[1],TMs[2](u)

97.30;103.2 *aequat*] *æquat* I

97.30 *effectum*$_\wedge$] $\sim$, PJ/TMs^{1a-b},
TMs^2,I(p)

97.31 sums . . . up] sums up the whole
of it TMs^1+

97.31 It (*no* ¶)] ¶ I

97.35 School-] *l.c.* I (*cap.* I[p])

97.35 causation] Causation TMs^1-I(p)

97.37,38 (*second*) the] The K/TMs^2,I

97.38 ^{2}causes] Causes TMs^1+

97.41-98.30 "The . . . negative,"] *sg.
qts.* TMs^1+

98.1 But (*no* ¶)] ¶ TMs^1,TMs^2
(*follows* K *note* 'no break')

98.1 *Quidquid*] Quid quid TMs^1,
TMs^2(u); *quid quid* K/TMs^2

98.1-2 *Quidquid . . . causa*] *all rom.*
TMs^1,TMs^2(u)

98.1 *effectu*] *effecta* TMs^1-I^1

98.4 unremittingly$_\wedge$ . . . illusion$_\wedge$]
$\sim$, . . . $\sim$, TMs^1+

98.8 aliquo modo] *ital.* K/TMs$^{2(r1)}$

98.8 *differ*] *rom.* TMs^1+

98.8-9;103.28;107.26 *aliquo modo*]
rom. TMs^1,TMs^2(u)

98.10 situation,] $\sim_\wedge$ TMs^1+

98.18-23 The . . . in.] *included in fn.* 4
aft. 'Metaphysics.)' [98.42] TMs^2,I

98.18 reason, the effect] $\sim_\wedge$ the effect
of TMs^2(u)

98.20 developes] develops TMs^1+

98.22 persistent] persistant TMs^1,
TMs^2(u)

98.22 being$_\wedge$] $\sim$, TMs^1+

98.24 ff. *omit*] *Occasionalism (s.n.)*
K/TMs^2,I

98.30 speaking,] $\sim_\wedge$ | TMs^1;TMs^2(u)

98.34 but] *om.* TMs^1+

98.35 considered] desired TMs^2,I

98.36 compactly:] $\sim$; TMs^1-I(p)

98.36-41 "What . . . surmise."] *sg. qts.*
TMs^2,I

98.38 [i.e. the amount]] ($\sim\sim\sim$)
TMs^1+

98.41 even] *om.* TMs^1+

99.1 body and mind] mind and body
TMs^2,I

99.1 'rational.'] $_\wedge\sim._\wedge$ TMs^1+

99.2 absurdities–he] $\sim$–He TMs^1;
$\sim$. He TMs^2,I

99.4-5 psychophysical] psychological
TMs^2,I

99.5-6 God . . . changes] There are
changes K/TMs$^{2(r1)}$ (change |
TMs^2[u])

99.5 them] then TMs^1

99.7 those] changes K/TMs$^{2(r1)}$

99.7 mind$_\wedge$] $\sim$, K/TMs^2,I

99.8 causes, . . . occasions.] causes,
but are in reality only the signals
or occasions. TMs^2(u); causes.
But they are *not causes, [*intrl.
in error aft.* 'But'] they are only
signals or occasions: the *immediate, [*intrl.*] real ['cause' *del.*]
and only cause is God. K/TMs$^{2(r1)}$;
causes, . . . occasions: (*colon error*)
K/TMs$^{2(r2)}$

99.9 ff. *omit*] *Leibnitz (s.n.)* K/TMs^2,I

99.9 Leibnitz (*no* ¶)] ¶ K/TMs^2,I

99.11 assistance] assistence TMs^1

99.11 him] Him TMs^1+

99.14 thereafter] there | after TMs^1

99.15 the] of the TMs^1(u)^a,TMs^2(u)

99.16 immediately] immediate
TMs^1(u)^a+

99.22 it] the theory K/TMs$^{2(r1)}$

99.22 true] not true TMs^2(u)

99.23 ff. *omit*] *Hume (s.n.)* K/TMs^2,I

99.23 common-sense] $\sim_\wedge\sim$ TMs^1,
TMs^2(u); commonsense K/TMs^2

99.24;99.35-36,37;100.1,4,11
connexion] connection TMs^1+

99.26 'efficacy' . . . 'power']
'$\sim_\wedge$ . . . '$\sim$' TMs^1; '$\sim_\wedge$ . . . $_\wedge\sim$'
TMs^2,I

99.28-29 isolate . . . from] isolated
('isolatr' TMs^1[u]) 'energy' transmit
from PJ/TMs$^{1a-b(r1)}$,TMs^2(u);
isolate the 'energy' transmitted from
WJ/TMs$^{1b(r2)}$,K/TMs^2,I

99.33 can, . . . scrutiny,] $\sim_\wedge$ . . . $\sim$,
TMs^1; $\sim_\wedge$ . . . $\sim_\wedge$ TMs^2,I

100.1-2 them, or] $\sim$. $\sim$ TMs^1,
TMs^2(u) (*error*); $\sim$. Or K/TMs$^{2(r1)}$

100.4 connexion,] $\sim_\wedge$ K/TMs^2,I

100.13 other."] $\sim._\wedge$ TMs^1(u)

100.15 made] makes TMs^1+

100.15 rattle] rattle | rattle TMs^1

100.20 Necessity$_\wedge$'] $\sim$,' TMs^1+ (*l.c.*)

100.21 tho] though TMs^1+

100.24 ff. *omit*] *Criticism of Hume
(s.n.)* K/TMs^2,I

100.29-30 prepositions . . . of] *om.*
TMs²,I

100.34 fact‸] ∼, TMs¹,TMs²(u)

100.36-37 *in . . . because.*] *all rom.*
TMs¹,TMs²(u)

100.37 *and, but*] but‸ and TMs¹; *but,
and* TMs²,I

100.37 *for*‸] ∼, TMs¹+

100.38 elements] element TMs¹(u)

100.40 *durcheinander*] *rom.* TMs¹(u)ᵃ

101.10 view‸] ∼, TMs¹+

101.12 tye] tie TMs¹+

101.13-14 *conjoined . . . connected . . .
belongs*] *rom.* TMs¹+

101.15 ¶ Thus] *no* ¶ TMs¹+

101.24 ff. *omit*] Kant *(s.n.)* K/TMs²,I

101.24 cause] Cause TMs¹+

101.27 where] when TMs¹-I(p)

101.30 common sense] commonsense
K/TMs²,I(p)

101.30 does,] ∼‸ | TMs²;I

101.31 only‸] ∼, TMs²,I

101.32 Hume,] ∼‸ | TMs²;I

101.33 its] it TMs¹-I¹

101.33-35 'objective,' . . . *Verstand.*‸]
'∼‸‸ | . . . ∼.‸ TMs¹,TMs²(u);
'∼,' . . . ∼.‸ K/TMs²(r1); '∼‸‸ . . .
∼.' K/TMs²(r2),I

101.34 law‸] ∼, TMs¹+

101.34-35 *Sinnlichkeit . . . Verstand*]
rom. TMs¹,TMs²(u)

101.36 *rule*] *rom.* TMs¹+

102.1 ff. *omit*] Criticism of Kant *(s.n.)*
K/TMs²*(del.)*

102.2 *understand*] *rom.* TMs¹+

102.9 ff. *omit*] Positivism *(s.n.)*
K/TMs²,I

102.11 lobsters,] ∼; TMs¹+

102.12 *Why*] *rom.* TMs¹+

102.13 not] Not I (not I[p])

102.16 ¹familiar‸] ∼, TMs¹+

102.18 the water] water TMs¹+

102.22 this] theif TMs¹; their TMs²,I

102.23 don't . . . them.⁸] do not
connect them in any intimate sense.
TMs¹+ (sense.ˣ TMs²,I keyed to fn.
8)

102.24 ff. *omit*] Deductive theories of
causation *(s.n.)* K/TMs²,I

102.26 *could . . . logic*] *all rom.* TMs¹+

102.27 the 'tie' . . . sequence] in the
particular sequence the 'tie' I (I[p]
like text)

102.27-28 unmistakeable]
unmistakable I (unmistakeable I[p])

102.29 *phenomenon*] *rom.* TMs¹+

102.29 'effect'),] '∼')‸ TMs¹+

102.31-38 *the observer . . . flounders*]
all rom. TMs¹+

102.31 case] single case TMs¹+
('single' *del.* MS)

102.33 —Or] ‸∼ TMs¹+

102.35 doesn't] does not TMs¹+

102.37 judgments] judgements TMs¹⁻²

102.38 humian] human TMs¹-I¹;
humean I²+

102.38 ‸ in short‸ *flounders,*] , ∼∼‸
flounders, TMs¹(u); , ∼∼, flounders
[*extra comma added in error and
del.*], PJ/TMs¹ᵃ⁻ᵇ+

102.40 expressions] PJ/TMs¹ᵃ⁻ᵇ;
impressions TMs¹(u)

102.42 ; K.] , and K. TMs¹+

103.2 *effectum*‸] ∼, TMs¹+

103.5 with] in K/TMs²(r1)

103.5-6 appearances‸ . . . conscious‸]
∼‸ . . . ∼, TMs¹,TMs²(u); ∼, . . .
∼, K/TMs²,I

103.8 *(twice)* real] *rom.* TMs¹+

103.10 ff. *omit*] Summary and Conclusion *(s.n.)* K/TMs²,I

103.16 *insulated*] *rom.* TMs¹+

103.18-104.1 , supposed . . . phenomenon,] (∼ . . . ∼) K/TMs²(r1)

103.18 *aliquo modo*] *rom.* TMs¹,
TMs²(u); '∼ ∼' K/TMs²

103.19 Couturat] Conturat TMs²,I¹

103.20 *unreal*] *rom.* TMs¹+

103.20 in] is TMs¹(u)ᵃ,TMs²(u)

103.21 in] and in TMs¹(u)

103.24 *Revue*] Révue WJ/TMs¹ᵃ⁻ᵇ;
Révue K/TMs²,I¹

103.24 *métaphysique*] *cap.*
TMs¹*(rom.)*+

103.27 for comfort] *om.* TMs²,I

103.28-29 nature, would of course]
∼, ∼, ∼∼‸ TMs¹-I(p);
∼‸ ∼, ∼∼, I

103.29 activity‸] ∼, TMs²,I

103.31 *ruthlessly*] *rom.* TMs¹+

103.34 atoms] Atoms TMs^1,TMs^2(u)

103.36 conceptual] Conceptual TMs^1, TMs^2(u)

103.36-37 chapter iv] Chapter 4 TMs^1,TMs^2(u); chapter 4 K/TMs^2; discussion I

103.37 logic] knowledge logic TMs^1(u)

103.39 cause] the cause TMs^2(u)

103.41 *wissenschaftlichen*] *cap.* TMs$^{1-2}$(*rom.*); *cap.* I(p)

103.42 88] 85 PJ/TMs^{1a}(88 PJ/TMs^{1b})+

104.7 identity-view] $\sim_\wedge \sim$ TMs^1+

104.11 $^1a \ldots {}^1b$] A ... B TMs^1+

104.12 *b ... a*] A ... B TMs^1+

104.13-14 dependences] dependencies TMs^1+

104.16 then has] has then TMs^1+

104.20 which,] $\sim_\wedge$ | TMs^2;I

104.21 is] PJ/TMs^{1a-b}; *om.* TMs^1(u)

104.27 *principle*] *rom.* TMs^1+

104.30 magnificently] magnificent TMs^1+

104.31-32 surface of] surface TMs^1+

104.32 eminently] evidently TMs^1+

104.34 *Philosophie*] *Philosophies* I(p)

104.34 145] 445 I(p)

105.1 ff. *omit*] Defects of the perceptual view *do not warrant scepticism [added; underl. of 'Defects ... view' del.] (s.n.)* K/TMs^2;I

105.3 activity] naive activity TMs^1, TMs^2(naif),I(p)(naif),I(naïf)

105.4-5 Le ... discours] *ital.* K/TMs^2(r1)

105.4 vie,] $\sim_\wedge$ TMs^2,I

105.6 also has] has also TMs^1+

105.9 'will'] $_\wedge\sim_\wedge$ TMs^1(u); "$\sim$." PJ/TMs^{1b}

105.11 *we*] *rom.* TMs^1+

105.14 causes,] $\sim_\wedge$ | TMs^1

105.15 draft$_\wedge$'] $\sim$,' TMs^1+

105.17 *unconditional*] *rom.* TMs^1+

105.17 antecedents] antecedants TMs$^{1-2}$

105.17 Venn] then TMs^1(u)^a,TMs^2(u)

105.18 *close*] close TMs^1(u)^a, TMs^2(u); 'close' WJ/TMs^{1b},K/TMs^2,I

105.19;109.23 antecedent] antecedant TMs^2

105.21 things,] $\sim_\wedge$ TMs^1-I(p)

106.1 ff. *omit*] *They do not warrant scepticism (s.n.)* K/TMs^2(*del.*)

106.3 begin to] *om.* TMs^1+

106.8 we falsely] falsely we TMs^1+

106.10 *elsewhere*] *rom.* TMs^1+

106.11 the other] other TMs^2,I

106.13 that] *om.* TMs^2,I

106.13 causation,] $\sim$. TMs^1,TMs^2(u)

106.13-14 *that ... thing*] all *rom.* TMs^1+

106.14 rightly$_\wedge$] $\sim$, TMs^1-I(p)

106.14 wrongly,] $\sim_\wedge$ TMs^1+

106.16 ff. *omit*] *The perceptual experience of causation (s.n.)* K/TMs^2,I

106.17 consciousness,] $\sim_\wedge$ TMs^1+

106.18 *result*] *rom.* TMs^1+

106.18-19 developes] develops I (developes I[p])

106.19 result$_\wedge$] $\sim$, I(p)

106.22 activity-situations] $\sim_\wedge\sim$ TMs^1+

106.22 'strive'] 'striv | TMs^1; 'stri | TMs^2(u)

106.26 to] as to I(p)

106.26 desire,] $\sim_\wedge$ | TMs^1+

106.26 either of] of either TMs^1-I(p)

106.26-27 resistance] resistence TMs^1

106.27 wrong;] $\sim$, TMs^1+

106.33 kind,] $\sim_\wedge$ | TMs^1+

106.38 'efficacy$_\wedge$'] '$\sim$,' TMs^1,TMs^2

106.38 *known-as*] *rom.* TMs^1-I(p)

106.40 ff. *omit*] *In it [added] 'Final' and 'efficient' causation coincide. ['in it' del.] (s.n.)* K/TMs^2;I ('final') [*begin* P^{34}]

106.40 $_\wedge$The] "$\sim$ PJ/TMs^{1a-b},TMs^2; I(p) ('$\sim$)

107.2 or] of TMs^2,I

107.5 ever can] can ever TMs^1+

107.7 ultimate *qualia*] ultima qualia TMs^1,TMs^2(u) (*ital.* K/TMs^2,I[p])

107.10 universe,] $\sim_\wedge$ TMs^1+

107.15 no one] noone TMs^1,TMs^2(u)

107.15 'sweet,'] '$\sim_\wedge$' TMs^1

107.16 eyes$_\wedge$] $\sim$, TMs^1+

107.16 and] and a TMs^1(u)

107.16-17 *percipi ... esse*] *rom.* TMs^1, TMs^2(u) [*end* P^{34}]

107.20 ff. *omit*] *And* ['*it finds*' *del.*]
 novelties *arise [*added*] (*s.n.*)
 K/TMs²;I
107.20 'fields'] ∧ ∼ ∧ TMs¹+
107.29,30 surprises] surprizes TMs¹
107.36 how] How I (how I[p])
108.2 says,¹] ∼∧∧ | TMs¹(u)ᵃ; ∼∧ˣ
 WJ/TMs¹ᵇ
108.8 Isn't] Is not TMs¹+
108.9 and] And TMs¹+
108.10 aught] ought TMs¹,TMs²(u)
108.15 ff. *omit*] *Perceptual causation*
 *sets [*ab. del.* '*puts*'] *a problem*
 (*s.n.*) K/TMs²;I
108.18 *close*] *rom.* TMs¹+
108.26 naively] naïvely I (naively I[p])
108.29 *kind*] *rom.* TMs¹+
108.30 is∧] ∼, TMs¹+
108.32 *fact ... there*] *rom.* TMs¹+
108.32 words,] ∼∧ TMs¹+
108.35-36 *nature ... facts*] *rom.*
 TMs¹+
109.1 (*twice*) farther] further TMs¹+
109.3 inquiring] enquiring TMs¹+
109.3-4 psychophysical] psychological
 TMs¹+
109.4 ff. *omit*] *This is [*added*] *the*
 ['*t*' *ov.* '*T*'] *problem of* *the [*ov.*
 '*mind*'] *relation of mind to brain*
 (*s.n.*) K/TMs²;I
109.4 Perception (*no* ¶)] ¶ TMs¹+
109.5 agency,] ∼∧ TMs¹+
109.6 such∧] ∼, TMs¹+
109.6 ¹,²such,] ∼; TMs²,I
109.6 finally∧] ∼, TMs¹+
109.12 ff. *omit*] *Conclusion* (*s.n.*)
 K/TMs²,I
109.13 'cause∧'] '∼,' TMs¹+
109.16 Thus] This TMs¹-I(p)
109.16 has] *om.* TMs¹+
109.17 once more had] once more
 has had TMs¹,TMs²(u),I; has had
 once more K/TMs²(r1)
109.20 'transitive'] ∧ ∼ ∧ TMs¹+
109.24-25 causality-] ∼∧ TMs¹(u)ᵃ
109.25 ¹flavors] flavours TMs¹⁻²
109.34 Cause-] With this cause- TMs¹+
109.37 altering,] ∼∧ TMs¹+
109.38 consideration] PJ/TMs¹ᵃ⁻ᵇ;
 provision TMs¹(u)
110.4-5 'thought,' ... 'category.']

PJ/TMs¹ᵃ⁻ᵇ; ∧ ∼, ∧ ... ∧ ∼·∧
 TMs¹(u); '∼,' ... ∧ ∼·' TMs²(u)
110.6 *Experience*] experience TMs¹
110.6-9 "What ... perceive"] *sg. qts.* I
110.11 causality] *cap.* TMs¹+
110.11 [why ... *se*?]] (∼ ... ∼?)
 TMs¹+
110.11 ²*per se*] *rom.* TMs¹(u)ᵃ,
 TMs²(u)
110.11-12 philosophical] philosophic
 TMs²,I
110.13 *post ... istud*] *all rom.*
 TMs¹(u)ᵃ,TMs²(u)
110.13 say,] ∼∧ TMs¹+
110.15 [i.e. ... merely]] (∼ ... ∼)
 TMs¹+
110.15-16 conditioning·∧ ... ∧It]
 ∼·∧ ... "∼ PJ/TMs¹ᵃ⁻ᵇ,TMs²(u);
 ∼·' ... ∧∼ K/TMs²; ∼·'∧∼ I
110.17 *per se*] *rom.* TMs¹-I(p)
110.17 375] 378 TMs¹+
110.17 The (*no* ¶)] ¶ TMs¹+
110.18 resembles] ressembles TMs¹,
 TMs²(u)
110.19 (see] '∼ TMs¹; , ∼ TMs²(u)
110.19 'activity∧'] '∼∧∧ TMs¹(u);
 'Activity,' TMs²(u); '∼,' K/TMs²,I(p)
110.19 'causality'] ∧ ∼ ∧ TMs¹(u)
110.20 Index] index TMs¹+
110.23 all our] all TMs¹+
110.24-25 imagine,] ∼∧ TMs¹+
110.25 false.] ∼, TMs¹,TMs²(u)
111.0 *Appendix*] PPENDIX I(p) (*error*)
111.0.1 Believe] Believe¹ | [*fn.*] ¹[The
 following pages, part of a syllabus
 printed for the use of students in an
 introductory course in philosophy,
 *were [*ov.* 'was'] found ['f' *ov.* 'F']
 with the MS. of this book, *with
 the words, [*ab. del.* 'with *a [*ov.*
 'the'] words note, in pencil, in *the
 author's [*insrtd. for del.* 'William
 James's'] hand:'] 'To be printed as
 part of the *Introduction ['I' *ov.* 'i']
 to Philosophy,' noted thereon in the
 author's handwriting.] K/TMs¹ᵇ(S);
 I (*adds* 'ED.')
111.5 Intellectualists] *l.c.* I (*cap.* I[p])
111.8 *et seq.* HEGEL ... ROYCE] *all
 names caps. and l.c.* K/TMs¹ᵇ(S),I
112.31-32 "the ... order."] *sg. qts.* I

113.12 *Sorites*] sorites I
113.22 organized∧] ∼, K/TMs¹ᵇ(S),I
113.23-24 Intellectualism] *l.c.* I (*cap.* I[p])
113.26 birthrights] ∼∧ | ∼ I(p); ∼- | ∼ I
114.16 houseowners] ∼-∼ I
114.23,30 befal] befall I
114.31;116.1 insurance-company] ∼∧∼ I (∼-∼ I[p])

114.34 Boston] Bostion I (*error*)
115.30-33 [Empiricism . . . categorical.]] (∼. . . ∼.) K/TMs¹ᵇ(S),I
115.35 that∧] ∼, K/TMs¹ᵇ(S),I
116.14,16 2nd] 2d I (2nd I[p])
116.16 3rd] 3d I (3rd I[p])
116.17-18 "*If* . . . perfected"] *sg. qts.* I
116.20-23 A . . . *per se* . . . its] *all ital.* K/TMs¹ᵇ(S);I (per se *rom.*)
117.7 1905.] ∼, I (∼. I[p])

Alterations in the Manuscript

All alterations made during the course of writing and of revision are recorded here except for strengthened letters to clarify a reading, a very few mendings over illegible letters, and false starts for the same word. The medium is the black ink of the original inscription unless otherwise specified. It is certain that many of the alterations were made *currente calamo* and others as part of one or more reviews. The two are ordinarily so indistinguishable in the intensity of ink or in the kind of pen, however, as not to yield to systematic recording by categories on the physical evidence. In the description of the alterations, when no record of position is given the inference should be that the change was made in the line of the text and during the course of the original writing. *Deleted* or *deletion* is given the abbreviation *del.*; *over* (*ov.*) means inscribed over the letters of the original without interlining; *above* (*ab.*) always describes an independent interlineation. When an addition is a simple interlineation, either with or without a caret, the description *intrl.* is used; when an interlineation is a substitute for one or more deleted words, the formula reads, instead, *ab. del.* 'xyz'. The word *inserted* (*insrtd.*) ordinarily refers to marginal additions or to squeezed-in letters, syllables, and words that also cannot properly be called interlines but are of the same nature. When reference is made to one or the other of two identical words in the same line of the present edition, some preceding or following word or punctuation mark is added for identification, or else the designated word is identified with a superscript [1] or [2] according as it is the first or second occurrence in the line. A superscript is also used to indicate which of more than one identical letter in the same word is referred to. A vertical stroke | signifies a line ending.

In order to ease the difficulty of reading quoted revised material of some length and complexity, the following convention is adopted. The quoted text will ordinarily be the final version in the manuscript, whereas the processes of revision are described within square brackets. To specify what words in the text are being affected by the description within square brackets, an asterisk is placed before the first word to which the description in brackets applies; thus it is to be taken that all following words before the square brackets are a part of the described material. For example, at 68.2 James altered 'one' to 'One' when he deleted four succeeding sentences. In the first sentence, which he subsequently may have independently deleted, he wrote 'We may mean' and then interlined 'for instance', following it with 'that' and a false start 'it is our' which he deleted. For the false start he substituted 'we treat the whole of it', deleted that, and wrote above it 'the whole of it can be taken', ending the sentence with 'as one topic of discourse.' He began the second sentence with 'We do this by the' which he deleted. He started again with 'Whenever we use the word 'universe' we' in which he wrote 'W' over 'w' in 'Whenever', interlined 'take it thus,' above deleted 'do this,', interlined 'for', continued with 'we mean that no item of reality shall', wrote 'escape' above deleted 'be left out', wrote 'from what' and inserted 'our word covers;' in the margin for deleted 'we point to,' which he inscribed above deleted 'is signified,'. He carried on beyond the semicolon with 'but this unity of abstract reference, altho it has been made much of by', crossed out 'some rationalists,' above which he wrote 'idealistic writers,' and ended with 'is insignificant in the extreme.'

In the third sentence James wrote 'It carries no', altered 'other' to 'further', continued with 'sort of connection with it, and would apply as well to', inter-lined 'any' above deleted 'an utter', and ended with 'chaos as to our actual world.' The final sentence reads 'Both would be *knowable-together* in the same barren way.' with 'the' written over 'this'. In formulaic terms the altera-tion entry is transcribed as 68.2 One] ('O' *ov.* 'o'); *bef. del.* '[*del.* 'We may mean *for instance [*intrl.*] that *the whole of it can be taken [*ab. del.* '['it is our' *del.*] we treat the whole of it'] as one topic of discourse. We do this by the'] Whenever ['W' *ov.* 'w'] we use the word universe we *take it thus, [*ab. del.* 'do this,'] for [*intrl.*] we mean that no item of reality shall *escape [*ab. del.* 'be left out'] from what *our word covers; [*insrtd. for del.* '*we point to, [*ab. del.* 'is signified,']'] but this unity of abstract reference, altho it has been made much of by *idealistic writers, [*ab. del.* 'some rational-ists,'] is insignificant in the extreme. It carries no *further [*alt. fr.* 'other'] sort of connection with it, and would apply as well to*any [*ab. del.* 'an utter'] chaos as to our actual world. Both would be *knowable-together* in *the [*alt.fr.* 'this'] same barren way.'

In formulaic transcriptions double asterisks can also be used to set off subsidiary alterations occurring between the single asterisk and the bracketed description that applies to this single asterisk, as, for example, 'In all these modes of union *some parts **of the world [*intrl.*] prove [*ab. del.* 'several aspects seem'] to be conjoined'. Inferior brackets clarify subsidiary bracketed descriptions within or before the main bracketed entry with or without the use of asterisks according to circumstances. (The full details of this system may be found in F. Bowers, "Transcription of Manuscripts: The Record of Variants," *Studies in Bibliography*, 29 (1976), 212-264.)

The lemmata (the readings to the left of the bracket) are ordinarily drawn from the present edition and represent the agreement of book and manuscript. To permit condensed entries, in some cases a single dagger prefixed to the page-line reference warns the user to refer to the Emendations for the exact manuscript reading in simple situations when the precise form of the alteration in words or accidentals is (a) not printed in the lemma, or (b) not specified in the descriptive part of the entry. For instance, at 91.28-29 the manuscript reads '-measure unless they be themselves' which has been inscribed above a deletion. The phrase 'unless they be' has been emended to 'if they be not', so that the daggered entry †91.28-29 -measure ... themselves] *ab. del.* '-limits without being' saves space by referring the user to the Emendations which reads ‡91.29 if ... not] WJ/TMs^{1a}+; unless they be MS,TMs^1(u)^b (the double dagger in turn cross-referencing to the Alterations entry). On the contrary, twin daggers warn the user that the lemma is not (as in every other circumstance) the reading of the edition-text but is instead that of the manu-script. This convention is employed only when the two readings are so similar that a user following the edition-text in the Alterations list will be able to identify with certainty the reading that is intended, without recourse to the Emendations. A simple example of an accidental difference occurs at 85.32-33 where the edition-text has been emended from the MS spelling-reform 'auto-biografic' to 'autobiographic'. The condensed entry reads ††85.32-33 an autobiografic] *alt. fr.* 'a biografical'. A simple substantive example appears at 85.16 where MS 'my text-book' reads 'this text-book' in the present edition. The alteration reads ††85.16 my text-book] *ab. del.* 'the volume'. It is worth emphasizing that whereas the device of twin daggers saves the reader from consulting the Emendations, the details of all such variants will nevertheless appear there should he wish to check them. There are two instances, however, in which a twin-daggered variant cannot be found in the Emendations list. If James has made an obvious error in MS which occurs because of an alteration, that error is silently emended and appears only in the Alterations entry instead of taking up space in the Emendations. Second, when the manuscript reading used in the lemma participates in the class of silent emendations indicated in A Note on the Editorial Method or in the headnote to the Emendations list, twin daggers do not refer to the Emendations but merely draw attention to the easily construed variant between text and MS.

Whenever practicable, alterations in the manuscript that also comprise textual variants complete in themselves appear in the Emendations instead of in the list of Alterations. For the details of these entries, see the headnote to the Emendations.

The use of three dots to the right of the bracket almost invariably indicates ellipsis rather than the existence of dots in the manuscript. This is the only violation of the bibliographical rule that material within single quotes is cited exactly as it appears in the original document. In order to avoid confusion with the asterisks used in formulaic description, James's footnote markers, which are frequently asterisks, are invariably indicated by a superior 'x'. One category of alteration not recorded here is James's changing in footnotes of lower-case roman numerals to roman capitals or vice-versa; it is often impossible to tell which form was his final intention, and as accidentals in footnote references are emended silently, these have not been considered of enough importance to record.

Deleted versos which do not apparently relate to revisions in the main body of the Alterations list or which are revisions of continuous deleted material already set out therein are transcribed in a separate section following the list of Alterations for the entire manuscript.

††9.0   CHAPTER I.] *double underl.*
††9.0   PHILOSOPHY AND ITS CRITICS.] ('and' *ov.* 'is'; *aft. del.* 'What'); *triple underl.*
9.1   progress] *aft. del.* 'whole of human'
9.1   society] *aft. del.* 'human'
9.1   the fact that] *ab. del.* 'certain'
9.1   vary] *final* 'ing' *del.*
9.2   human] *intrl.*
9.2   average] *bef. del.* 'of the tribe'
9.2   that the] *insrtd. for del.* '*that sometimes [ab. del. 'through ['their' del.] the force or attractiveness of their']*'
9.3   originality] *bef. del.* ', giving a new direction to'
9.3   often] *intrl.*
9.4   setters] *aft. del.* 'and'
9.5   and] *ov. period*

9.5   objects . . . imitation.] ('envy or' *intrl.; period insrtd.*); *moved fr. aft.* 'become' [9.4]
9.6   every] *aft. del.* 'there are men w'
9.6   produces] *ab. del.* 'there are'
9.7   individuals ['who' *del.*] exceptionally] *ab. del.* 'who['se' *del.*] are unusually'
9.7   Such men find] *ab. del.* 'they see'
9.12   regarded] *bef. del.* 'often [*ab. del.* 'usually']'
†9.12-13   an . . . admiration,] ('if' *aft. del.* 'or even w'); 'an . . . admi-'|*ab. del.* 'admi-'|
9.14   or] *insrtd. for del.* ', and *usually [intrl.]* with *an [ab. del. 'a certain']* indulgent relish even by those who do not'
9.14   much] *intrl.*

9.15   thus] *ab. del.* 'thus'

9.16   monstrously] *ab. del.* 'most'

9.22   abstract] *intrl.*

9.23   limited by usage,] *ab. del.* 'circum-
scribed,'

10.1   ¹its] *ab. del.* 'the *aufgabe und
methode*'

10.2   such displays ['would be' *del.*] are]
(*final* 's' *added to* 'displays'); *ab. del.*
'these things are unin-'|

10.2   usually unintelligible] 'usually unin'
insrtd.

10.2   beginners,] *comma insrtd. bef. del.*
'before [*ab. del.* 'until'] the book *has
[*alt. fr.* 'had'] been read,'

10.3   reading the book,] *ab. del.* 'it *has
[*alt. fr.* 'had'] been understood,'

10.3-4   ²to . . . chapter] ('to omit'
insrtd.); *ab. del.* 'to leave *it [*ab. del.*
'them'] out'

10.4   tho it] *ab. del.* 'as they'

10.4   might possibly be] *insrtd. for del.*
'may *often be [*ab. del.* 'be'] to *the
[*ab. del.* 'an'] be [*intrl.*] author *may
[*intrl.*] as *a [*intrl.*] summary memorandum['s' *del.*] of his own mental
achievement—what *is ['s' *ov.* 't'] to
follow.'

10.6   tarry a] ('a' *ab. del.* 'one'); *aft. del.*
'only'

10.6   , however,] *init. comma insrtd.*;
'however,' *intrl.*

10.6   matter] *aft. del.* 'definition'

10.7   Limited . . . of] *ab. del.*
'Circum-|*scribed by [*undel. in error*]
leaving out'

10.7   ²the] *bef. del. intrl.* 'facts &'

10.7   special] *aft. del.* 'laws [*ab. del.*
'truths'] of the'

10.7   the name] *ab. caret formed fr. orig.
comma*

10.7-8   philosophy] *bef. del.* ' 's material
*has [*insrtd.*] become['s' *del.*]
exceedingly ['general' *del.*] wider in
scope in these later times, and *correspondingly [*ab. del.* 'exceedingly']
narrow ['in content.' *del.*] in proportion as it has become narrower in
content.'

10.8   come] *intrl.*

10.8   to] *aft. del.* 'learned [*ab. del.* 'come']

to [*undel. in error*] confine itself'

10.8   denote ideas] ('denote' *ov.* 'mean');
ab. del. 'questions'

10.8   ['general' *del.*] universal] *ab. del.*
'universal'

10.9   exclusively.] *ab. del.* 'and universal
application.'

10.10   elements] *ab. del.* 'things'

††10.12-13   ²the . . . action,] ('most
general rules' *ab. del.* 'highest principles'); *ab. del.* 'the [*undel. in error*]
relation to them of what is known,'

10.13   furnish] *ab. del.* 'are'

10.15   finds] *ab. del.* 'has'

10.16   knowledge] *ab. del.* 'science'

10.16-17   in general] *ab. del.* 'universally'

10.18   such] *aft. del.* 'it.'

††10.18-19   of . . . large‿] *intrl. w. caret
placed in error aft. comma aft.* 'explanation,'

10.19   not] *ab. del.* 'rather than'

10.19   description] *bef. del. comma*

10.19   its details,] *ab. del.* 'the universe'

10.19   philosophy must] *ab. del.* 'it is
supposed to'

††10.20   at,] (*comma ov. period ov.
comma*); *bef. del.* '[*del.* 'and that details escape it. Human action is of
course included in the sum total of
things, so philosophy deals with the
ultimate principles of that also. In short,
a philosophical view of'] From'

10.20   and] *insrtd.*

10.22   or intermediate,] *intrl.*

††10.23   and all-embracing.] *ab. caret
formed fr. orig. period*

10.23   sweeping] *ab. del.* 'general'

10.24   it] *ab. del.* 'its may'

††10.25   is a weltanschauung,] *ab. del.* 'is'

††10.26   Prof.] *aft. del.* 'what the Germans
call a *Weltanschauung*;'

10.26   constitution] *aft. del.* 'actual'

10.27   philosophy] *aft. del.* 'a'

10.31   chief] *intrl.*

10.32   have heard] *ab. del.* 'understand'

10.32   some] *alt. fr.* 'something'

10.35   in . . . term] *intrl.*

10.36   Things] *ab. del.* 'Any subject'

10.37   dry] *aft. del.* 'a'

10.37   ways] 's' *added*

10.37   At a] *ab. del.* 'Your'

10.38 a man ... into a] (¹'a' *insrtd.*; 'man' *bef. del.* 'into a'); *ab. del.* 'can make a'

10.38 instrument] *bef. del.* 'of a man'

11.1 the] *ab. del.* 'that'

11.1-2 mind ... 'liberal] *ab. del.* 'intellect which ['such words' *del.*] the word'

11.2 culture.'] (*init. sg. qt. del.; period insrtd.*); *bef. del.* 'suggests. [*ab. del.* 'denotes.'] ['His' *del.*] Mentally'

11.2 He] 'H' *ov.* 'h'

11.3   , intellectually] *comma ov. period*; 'intellectually' *intrl.*

11.3-4 pinned ... subject,] ('his' *bef. del.* 'its'; 'subject,' *bef. del.* 'He'); *ab. del.* 'Solidly planted *in* his subject, his mind may be unable to play *round* it. It may be too'

11.5 mental] *intrl. in pencil*

11.6 Philosophy,] *alt. fr.* 'Philosophic'; *comma insrtd. bef. del.* 'study,'

11.6 Plato and] *intrl.*

11.6 said,] *alt. fr.* 'says,'

11.7 is ... fancy] 'is able to' *intrl.*; 'fancy' *alt. fr.* 'fancies'

11.7 everything] *ab. del.* 'that anything might be'

11.9 lay] *ab. del.* 'drop'

11.9 down again.] *intrl.*

11.9-10 Its ... that] ('that' *aft. del.* 'and can'); *ab. del.* 'Its ['s' *added*] brings air into the mind, makes it'

11.10 plays] ('s' *added*); *bef. del.* 'flexibly'

11.10-11 It ... prejudices.] ('native' *alt. fr.* 'natively'); *intrl.*

11.12 fecundation] *aft. del.* 'mutual'

11.14 emotionally] *bef. del.* '['and' *del.*] as well as practically'

†11.15 have ... it,] ('have' *bef. del.* 'had'); *ab. del.* 'dip into the p philosophy enough'

††11.15 its ['the' *del.*] influence‸] *ab. del.* '['som' *del.*] an inkling of its spirit'

11.16 literary ... students.] *insrtd. for del.* 'of the types of men whose antagonism pervades our institutions of learning. It stiffens up ['and br' *del.*] the soft and merely literary mind; it softens the heart'

11.16 poetry] (*alt. fr.* 'poetic'); *bef. del.* 'aspects'

††11.17 literary minds, but] *ab. del.* 'the literary minds *former ['fo' *ov.* 'la']* [*intrl.*] but it'

11.17 its logic] *insrtd.*

11.17 them] *intrl.*

11.17 and] *aft. del.* 'and braces them. ['by its' *del.*] By its their softness. By its logic it convin their minds'

11.18 speaks] *ab. del.* 'appeals'

11.18 the] *ov.* 're [*doubtful*]'

11.18-19 by ... aspects,] *intrl.*

††11.19 dry a technicality‸] ('dry' *alt. fr.* 'drily'; 'a' *ab. del.* 'a'; 'ity' *of* 'technicality' *ab. del.* 'ity'; *period omitted in error*); *bef. del.* 'a set of interests'

11.20 types ... get] 'types of students ['get' *del.*] ['gain' *del.*] ought to get' *ab. del.* 'get the'

11.20 a liberal] 'a [*intrl.*] liberal['izing' *del.*]'

11.21 ought to get] *ab. del.* '['their' *del.*] think with more thought gain'

11.23 men] *ab. del.* 'we all'

11.23 always] *intrl. aft. del. intrl.* 'all'

11.23 one another] 'one' *ab. del.* 'each'; 'another' *alt. fr.* 'other'

11.25 social mates.] *ab. del.* 'companions. [*period insrtd. for del. comma*] ['socially considered.' *del.*]'

11.26 what may be called] *ab. del.* 'what many persons would claim to be'

11.26 gymnastic] *ab. del.* 'sovereign'

11.27 purely] *ab. del.* 'purely'

11.27-28 power ... ¹and] ('power' *bef. del.* 'vigor'; 'high' *aft. del.* 'general and'); *ab. del.* 'ability gained by discipline of **dealing** with such highly'

11.28 and discriminating] *aft. del.* 'and defining their meaning,'

11.30 thus] *ab. del.* 'I am'

11.30 enumerated] *alt. fr.* 'enumerating'

11.31 systematic] *aft. del.* 'enemies, and nev'

11.31 they] *insrtd.*

11.31 were ... numerous] *ab. del.* 'never had ['m' *del.*] as many'

11.32 day.] (*period insrtd. for del. comma*); *bef. del.* 'When the ['remove' *del.*] confinement of the name philosophy'

11.32 definite conquests] *ab. del.* 'triumphs'

11.32-33 apparent] *aft. del.* 'povert'
11.33 indefiniteness] *ab. del.* 'poverty'
11.33 results] *aft. del.* 'assured'; *bef. del.* 'are'
11.33 account] *ab. del.* 'to blame'
11.34 to . . . ¹of] *ab. del.* 'and at all times'
11.34 rudeness] *ab. del.* 'laziness'
11.34 mind,] *comma insrtd.*
11.34 which ['finds' *del.*]] *ab. del.* 'has found a'
11.34-35 maliciously] 'ly' *added*
11.35 enjoys deriding] *ab. del.* 'satisfaction in making fun of'
††11.37-38 with . . . things'] *intrl.*
11.40 described] *bef. del.* 'as ['th' *del.*] 'der'
11.40 as] *aft. del.* 'or more mildly'
12.1 conclusion,'] *comma ov. period*
12.4 this] *aft. del.* 'this' |
12.5-6 order, . . . reply] *comma ov. period*; 'since to reply' *ab. del.* 'Replying'
12.9 the] *intrl.*
12.9 'sciences'] *final* 's' *added*
12.9-10 yield ['produce['s' *del.*] '*del.*] applications] *ab. del.* 'prove themselves to be'
12.12 unjustly founded,] *ab. del.* '*an unreal [*ab. del.* 'a false one']'
12.13 branches] *aft. del.* 'only [*intrl.*]'
12.13 tree] *aft. del.* 'original'
12.13 philosophy.] *bef. del.* 'As they grew voluminous and accurate they became so unwieldy and **technical that only** specialists could follow them.'
12.13 As fast as] ('fast' *aft. del.* 'when a'); *ab. del.* 'Whatever'
12.13 questions] *final* 's' *ab. del.* 's'
12.14 the] *aft. del.* 'were called scientific'
12.14 answers were] *final* 's' *added*; 'were' *ab. del.* 'was'
12.14 and] *bef. del.* 'only the as yet unanswered questions *have [*intrl.*] remained ['ed' *added*] to constitute the subject matter of philosophy in the modern sense of the word. The scientific | [*fol.* 12ᵛ] *answers also became so voluminous [*undel. in error*]'
††12.15 What] 'W' *unreduced in error*
12.15 is] *insrtd. for pencil del.* 'consists of'
12.15-16 but . . . still] *ab. del.* 'only the'

12.16 unanswered.] *period insrtd. bef. del.* 'questions.'
12.18 The] *ab. del.* 'No'
12.18-19 philosophy] 'y' *ov.* 'er'
12.19 cannot] *aft. del.* 'can keep'
12.19 details] ('s' *added*); *aft. del.* 'work of'; *bef. del.* 'as'
12.23 wisdom,] *bef. del.* 'collectors of curious problems generally,'
12.23 a] *ab. del.* 'a'
12.24 interest] *final* 's' *added then del.*
12.24 men] *aft. del.* '*men thinking*,'
12.25 beyond] *bef. del.* 'the [*intrl.*]'
12.25 need] *final* 's' *del.*
12.25 no] *ab. del.* 'not'
12.25-26 problem] *final* 's' *del.*
12.26 but rather] *ab. del.* 'so much as'
12.29 western] *aft. del.* 'our'
12.29 earlier] *ab. del.* 'dawn of'
12.29 lasted,] *comma insrtd. bef. del.* '['from about' *del.*] for about,'
12.30 two] *aft. del.* '25'
12.31 Pythagoras,] *ab. del.* 'Anaxag'
12.32 Parmenides] 'n' *ov.* 'd'
12.34 learning] *ab. del.* 'knowledge'
12.34 such . . . ²was] *ab. del.* 'was supposed to be'
12.34 at] *intrl.*
12.35 their] *alt. fr.* 'the'
12.35 great] *bef. del.* 'sch'
12.36 enlarged] *ab. del.* 'increased'
12.36 its] *insrtd. for del.* 'the'
12.36 application] *aft. del.* 'its'
12.36 turn to] *ab. del.* 'open the index of'
13.1 from] *aft. del.* 'and the relations'
13.2 way.] *period insrtd. for del. comma*
13.2 **The relations**] ('T' *ov.* 't'); *aft. del.* 'and about'; *bef. del.* 'of all these things with each other.'
13.3 the creator] *ab. del.* 'God'
13.3 his creatures,] *ab. del.* 'man,'
13.4 of . . . body,] *intrl.*
13.5 come] *aft. del. doubtful* 'ab'
13.5 up] *ab. del.* 'in'
13.5 theology] *aft. del.* 'completely detailed,'
13.5 a psychology, a] ¹'a' *insrtd.*; ²'a' *intrl.*
13.6 duties and] *intrl.*
13.6 morals] *bef. del.* '[', and' *del.*] and duties'

13.6 physics] *aft. del.* 'in the general principles of physics and of ['the connexion' *del.*] logic the universal principles of'

13.7 logic] *aft. del.* 'of'

13.7 their] *alt. fr.* 'the'

13.8 of] *intrl.*

13.9 resources] *opp.* WJ *mrgn.* 'Insert p. 14½'

13.10-20,37-39 It . . . detail.] *bef. circled heading* 'Insert in p. 14'

13.11-12 different . . . . He] ('to' *ab. del.* 'to'; 'are' *bef. del.* 'most'); *ab. del.* 'peculiar. Everything was duly'

13.12 everything,] *intrl.*

13.14 and changes] *intrl.*

13.15-16 taught. Matter] *period insrtd. aft. del. comma;* 'M' *ov.* 'm'

13.16 was] *ab. del.* 'being'

††13.16 quantitative⌃] *intrl.*

††13.16 passive ['principle,' *del.*] element,] *intrl.*

13.17 qualitative, unifying,] *intrl.; moved fr. orig. intrl. aft.* 'determining,'

13.17 and active] *ab. del.* 'element, matter the'

13.17 principle.] *period insrtd. bef. del.* 'of *quantity [ab. del.* 'extension,'] form that of unity and quality; matter being passive, form ['active.' *del.*] the principle of activity.'

13.18 was] *ab. del.* 'is'

13.18 could] *ab. del.* 'can only'

13.18 act] *bef. del.* 'when'

13.18 only] *intrl.*

13.19 species] *ab. del.* 'kinds'

13.19 was] *ab. del.* 'is'

13.21 men] *aft. del.* 'scholasticism'

††13.22 elaborate a priori] *ab. del.* 'syllogistic'

13.22 treatises] *aft. del.* 'attemp'

13.23 availed not to] *ab. del.* 'could not'

13.24 which . . . sweeping] ('t' *of* 'the' *ov.* 's'); *ab. del.* 'which swept'

13.25 encyclopaedic] 2'c' *ov.* '1'

13.26 Descartes now a days] 'D' *ov.* 'd'; 'a days' *intrl.*

13.27 separated] *aft. del.* 'and'

13.27 from] *aft. del.* 'from matter ['as the the' *del.*] as 'thought' '

13.27-28 as . . . substances,] *ab. del.* 'as *'extension,' [alt. fr.* 'extended']'

13.28 renovated] *aft. del.* 'new version'

13.29 more] *intrl.*

13.30 in our] *ab. del.* 'at the present'

13.30 a] *ab. del.* 'the'

13.30 cosmic] *aft. del.* 'explainer'

13.30 explained] *bef. del.* 'everything'

††13.31-32 "the . . . impact,] ('motion' *bef. del. comma;* 'impact,' *aft. del.* 'motion and'); *ab. del.* 'clear mechanical principles and mathematics and mechanics,'

13.33 apparatus] *ab. del.* 'laws'

13.35 With Locke's] *ab. del.* 'It was not till Locke's time'

††13.35 Human] 'H' *ov.* 'h'

14.1 problem of] *ab. del.* 'questions about'

14.2 subjective] *intrl.*

14.2 and] *aft. del.* '*with Berkeley and Hume, [intrl.]'

14.3 Leibnitz, . . . sage,] 1*comma insrtd.;* 'who . . . sage,' *ab. del.* 'and Wolff on the continent'

14.4 more] *ab. del.* 'older tradition'

14.4 Leibnitz's follower] *intrl.*

14.5 Hume] *aft. del.* 'Berkeley and'

14.7 and] *ab. del.* 'so that'

14.7 the word] *intrl.*

14.7 come to] 'come' *alt. fr.* 'become'; 'to' *intrl.*

14.7 stand for] *intrl. aft. del.* 'more [*ab. del.* 'identified'] and [*insrtd. for del.* 'much'] more *to suggest [*ab. del.* 'with']'

14.8 moral] *bef. del.* '[*on fol.* 15] ['theo' *del.*] | [*fol.* 17] speculations far more than *for [*intrl.*] physical laws or cosmic theories.x |*xOnly a few years ago philosophy was taught in American Colleges under the names of 'mental and moral philosophy,' or 'philosophy of the human mind' exclusively. [*in mrgn.*] [¶] The older tradition is the better'

14.8 physical] *bef. pencil del.* 'and moral'

14.9 Until] 'U' *ov.* 'T'

14.11 mind,'] *comma ov. period*

14.14-15 we . . . into] *intrl.*

14.15 is] *intrl. aft. del.* '*that we live in [*ab. del.* 'that is, [*illeg. letter*] must']'

14.15 as important as] 1'as' *aft. del.* 'be'; 2'as' *aft. del.* 'for *men [*ab. del.* 'us']'

14.15 what . . . anyhow] *intrl. aft. del.*
'*the foundation [*insrtd. for del.* 'conditions'] of the [*ab. del.* 'the principles of
its']'

14.16 abstractly possible.] *alt. fr.* 'abstract
possibility'; *period insrtd. bef. del.* 'and'

14.16 Yet this] ('Y' *triple underl.*); *insrtd.
for del.* 'or the relations of human
knowledge as of worlds anyhow ['and
their' *del.*] the in human intelligence,
for *which [*ab. del.* 'this']'

14.16 has] *aft. del.* 'is by'

14.16-17 treated by many] *ab. del.*
'considered'

14.17 as] *intrl.*

14.17 knowledge] *insrtd.*

14.17-18 of being called] *intrl.*

14.18 Common] ('C' *ov.* 'c'); *aft. del.*
'['Common' *del.*] To'

14.18 feel] *ab. del.* 'the fact as well as'

14.19 Nature . . . momentous] *ab. del.* 'is
the fact? is as important'

††14.19 Kantian] *intrl.*

14.20 Nature] *ab. del.* 'fact anyhow'

14.20 human] *ab. del.* 'their'

14.22 There are] *ab. del.* 'We are coming
back to the wider'

14.22 more] *aft. del.* 'wider tradition'

14.25 thinking] *intrl.*

14.27 man thinks] *alt. fr.* 'man's thinking'

14.27 by] *ab. del.* 'follows'

14.28 He] *ov.* 'It'

14.28 generalizes,] *intrl.*

14.29 and] *insrtd.*

14.29 Philosophy] ('P' *ov.* 'p'); *aft. del.*
'There is no method peculiar to'

††14.29-30 taken as distinct] *ab. del.* 'as
distinguished'

14.33 changes that have] 's' *added*; 'have'
alt. fr. 'has'

14.33 come over] *ab. del.* 'taken place in'

14.33-34 (as . . . believes)] *parens ov.
commas*

14.34 are] *ab. del.* 'is'

14.37 our] *aft. del.* 'of'

15.1 theory on] 'theory' *alt. fr.* 'theories
[*insrtd. for del.* 'thought on']'; 'on'
intrl.

15.1 always] *ab. del.* 'followed three'

15.2 succession.] *period ov. comma bef.*

del. '*having to be first [*ab. del.* 'being
first'] theological *& then [*ab. del.* 'or
[*insrtd. for del.* 'and [*intrl.*] then']']
metaphysical, ['then positive' *del.*]
before it *could [*intrl.*] become [*alt. fr.*
'became'] positive.'

15.2 of [*'our' del.*] theorizing] *intrl.*

15.2-3 phenomena] *ab. del.* 'things'

15.3 them;] (*alt. fr.* 'the'); *bef. del.*
'phenomena;'

15.4 their] *alt. fr.* 'the'

15.4-5 essential . . . is] *ab. del.* 'general
conception of the phenomenon is abstracted, and'

15.5 if it were an] ('were' *ov.* 'was'); *ab.
del.* 'a causal'

15.6 as to their] *ab. del.* 'in general
terms, ['and ultimate' *del.*] that is to
say their 'laws' are formulated, ['their
coexistences' *del.*] our [*doubtful*] order
of'

15.6-7 coexistences] *final* 's' *added*

15.7 successions. Their] ['cessions. ['c' *ov.*
's'] ' *ab. del.* ['cessions [*doubtful final*
's' *added*] *is are [*intrl.*] noted, and';
'T' *ov.* 't'

15.8 explanation] *aft. del.* 'deep [*ab. del.*
'strict']'

15.8 their] *bef. del.* 'existence is looked
for.'

15.8 Thus] *ab. del.* 'In the case of the
planets'

15.9-10 theological, . . . metaphysical,]
commas alt. fr. semicolons

15.11 the] (*ov.* 'all'); *intrl.*

15.12 too . . . definite.] *ab. del.* 'true, in
spite of his making it too definite. ['&'
del.] Primitive theories seem, in the
light of ['sympathetic magic' *del.*]
recent *anthropology [*alt. fr.* 'anthro-
pological'] ['observation' *del.*]'

15.14 special] *intrl.*

15.15 remarkable] *aft. del.* 'only'

15.15 alone,] *ab. caret formed fr. orig.
comma*

15.16 called for it.] *ab. caret formed fr.
orig. period*

15.22 If] *aft. del.* 'The first sciences were
occult sciences'

15.23 should] *alt. fr.* 'could'

15.24 or] *intrl.*

15.24 written.] (*period ov. comma*); *bef. del.* 'and'

15.24 Injuring the substitute,] 'Injuring' *alt. fr.* 'injure'; 'the *substitute, [comma ov. period]*' *ab. del.* 'that.'

15.25 you ... him] ('made' *alt. fr.* 'make'); *ab. del.* 'He would'

15.25 wished] 'ed' *added*

15.26 you sprinkled] 'you' *intrl.*; 'd' *added*

15.26 whistled] 'd' *added*

15.29 poppies] (*alt. fr.* 'poppy'); *bef. del.* 'seeds'

15.29 troubles] 'tr' *ov.* 'dr'

15.31 various] *aft. del.* 'man'

15.33 'Sympathetic'] *aft. del.* 'This'

15.33-34 [''**sympathetic**''*del.*] theorizing ['z' *ov.* 'y'] *ab. del.* '[*on fol.* 20] The beginning of science was witchcraft; *and [intrl.; undel. in error]* all the 'mancies & 'mantics, the omens and auguries, ['also' *del.*] come in here. *This [undel. in error bel. del.* 'There'] | [*fol.* 22] type of theorizing'

15.35 good] *aft. del.* 'very'

15.35 practical] *intrl.*

15.37 all] *bef. del.* 'the'

15.38 will] *aft. del.* 'gets realized.ˣ'

16.3 basis] *alt. fr.* 'base'

16.5 in] *aft. del.* 'in'

16.6 their] *aft. del.* '**what** happened'

16.6 Some ... cold.] *intrl.*

16.7 'violent.'] *period insrtd. bef. del.* 'for Aristotle.'

16.7 The] *ab. del.* 'Plan'

16.9 greater quantity] *ab. del.* 'larger amount'

16.9 embodied in] *ab. del.* 'in'

16.10 winter] *bef. del.* 'be'

16.11 Precious or] *aft. del.* 'The value of *Min [doubtful]*'; *bef. del.* 'rar [*doubtful*]'

16.12 The](**'T'** *ov.* 't'); *aft. del.* 'The diamond ['makes' *del.*] made [*alt. fr.* 'makes']'

16.12 would] *intrl.*

16.13 ¹the] *aft. del.* 'its'; *bef. del.* 'h[*illeg. letter*]'

††16.13-14 if ... bro't near, etc.ₐ] ('diamond' *aft.* 'if a'; 'etc.' *insrtd.*); *ab.*

del. ', etc. [*comma undel. in error*]'

16.15 ideas] *ab. del.* 'things'

16.17 Not] *aft. del.* 'It'

16.20 picked] *aft. del.* 'noticed and'; *bef. del.* 'to'

16.20 out.] *period insrtd. bef. del.* 'to explain them by'

16.21-22 hardly anyone] *ab. del.* 'few persons'

16.22-23 combinations] *ab. del.* 'glasses'

16.23 not ['yet' *del.*]] *ab. del.* '['by' *del.*] but just'

16.24 ²the ... heat,] *intrl.*

16.25 unknown; the] *semicolon ov. period*; 't' *ov.* 'T'

16.25 inexplicable; there] *semicolon ov. period*; 't' *ov.* 'T'

16.26 gravitation; the] *semicolon ov. period*; 't' *of* 'the' *ov.* 'T'

16.27 planets; alchemy] *semicolon ov. comma aft. doubtful del. period*; 'a' *of* 'alchemy' *ov.* 'A [*ov.* 'a']'

††16.28 imposed on everyone's belief.] *ab. del.* '['had everything' *del.*] reigned over all.'

16.28 only] *intrl.*

16.29 Pascal] *aft. del.* 'Pas'

16.30 telling] *aft. del.* 'successively teaching'

16.31 the] *aft. del.* 'what th'

16.31 lives] (*ov.* 'life'); *bef. del.* 'time'

16.33 who] *ab. del.* 'he'

16.35 F. B. Jevons] *aft. del.* 'E. B. *Tylor: [colon alt. fr. comma]* Primitive culture'

16.36 Bough] 'B' *ov.* 'b'

16.38 W. Whewell's] '**W.**' *intrl.*

17.1 readers] *aft. del.* '['many of us.' *del.*] the'

17.3 The] ('T' *ov.*'t'); *aft. del.* 'But'

17.3 began] *bef. del.* '[*illeg. word*] [*ab. del.* 'all']'

17.3 work of] *ab. del.* 'were'

17.5 said] *alt. fr.* 'says'

17.6-7 in .... But] *ab. del.* '*par excellence.* It was only'

17.7 fertility] *aft. del.* 'extraordinary'

17.7 made] *aft. del.* 'that f'

17.9 with] *aft. del.* 'for'

17.10 mechanics] *aft. del.* '['astrono' *del.*] astr'

17.11 **stem.**] *aft. del.* 'tree.'

17.13 aspects] *aft. del.* " '**laws.**' "; *bef. del.* 'by'

17.14 ferretted out] *ab. del.* 'were struck'

17.15 their] *intrl.*

17.15 would] *aft. del.* 'of these aspects which could be formulated in laws'

17.16 our present] *ab. del.* 'the'

17.17 have . . . the] *ab. del.* 'take their rise in those which *these ['se' *added*] XVIIth *Century [*cap. doubtful*] men [*intrl.; undel. in error*] first [*insrtd.; undel. in error*] laid bare, Galileo's v=t, and s=t² , *Pascal ['**P**' *ov.* 'p']'

17.18-19 which . . . proportionality] *ab. del.* 'Pascal's'

17.20 air-] *ab. del.* '['volu' *del.*] gas'

17.21 the refracted] 'the' *intrl.*

17.21 were . . . discovery.] *intrl.*

17.22 There] *aft. del.* 'It'

17.22 was] *insrtd. for del.* 'is'

17.22 nothing] *aft. del.* 'in this way of looking at nature,'

17.23 new] *intrl.*

17.25 soon] *ab. del.* 'quickly'

17.25 itself] *bef. del.* ', however'

17.27 called] *intrl.*

17.27 within] 'with' *ab. del.* 'to'

17.29 with] *bef. del.* 'metaphysical'

17.33 has] *aft. del.* 'mak'

17.34 proceeds] *aft. del.* 'proceeds the objection to which I *am ['a' *ov.* 'n'] now replying,'

17.35 every] *aft. del.* 'all the questions to which successes of philosophy form sciences which drop'

17.36 found] *ab. del.* 'obtained'

17.37 'science,'] *bef.* '**x**' *indicating abortive fn.*

17.37 residuum] *ab. del.* 'stamp collection'

17.37 problems] *aft. del.* 'questions'

17.38 domain] *ab. del.* 'mother soil'

18.2 been] *bef. del.* 'satisfactorily'

18.2 satisfaction] *aft. del.* 'general'

18.2 all] *ab. del.* 'those'

†18.5-6 probably . . . paragraph] ('probably' *aft. del.* '['form' *del.*] are'); *ab. del.* 'will probably count for no more than an instant'

18.6 great romance of] *ab. del.* 'total history of that'

18.6 history] *aft. del.* 'intelle'

18.7 The] ('T' *ov.* 't'); *aft. del.* 'If we look at'

18.7 extraordinary] *intrl.*

18.8 years] *bef. del.* 'what are we not entitled to hope for from the future.'

18.8 way] *bef. del.* 'to'

18.11 the only possible] *ab. del.* 'a mechanical'

††18.11 must . . . mathematical∧] *intrl. for del.* 'alone *can be [*ab. del.* 'is'] 'scientific','

18.12 inquiry] *aft. del.* 'attempts at ['giving' *del.*] clear'

††18.12 the . . . question∧] ('the' *aft. del.* '['the' *del.*] what is'; 'of' *bef. del. insrtd.* 'of things'); *ab. del.* '['anything' *del.*] spiritual [*comma del.*] side'

18.14 questions] *ab. del.* 'aspects'

18.15 philosophic] *intrl.*

18.15 approach] *ab. del.* 'attack'

18.15 **also**] *intrl.*

18.16 been] *aft. del.* 'already'

18.16 already.] *intrl.*

18.16 some respects, indeed,] *ab. del.* 'one sense'

18.18 astonish['t' *del.*]] *aft. del.* 'have'

18.18-19 could . . . composition] ('revisit' *aft. del.* 'be revived.'); 'could . . . com-' *ab. del.* '. The conser'

18.20 the idea of a] *intrl.*

18.21 seem['ed' *del.*] to them] ('seem' *aft. del.* 'have'); *ab. del.* 'sound familiar.'

18.21 enough–] *bef. del.* 'it would be'

††18.22 microscopes . . . and telefones, the] *ab. del.* 'details and practical applications and'

18.23 the sciences,] *ab. del.* 'Science ['by' *del.*] which these predecessors would'

18.24 opened] 'ed' *added*

18.24 metaphysics] *ab. del.* 'philosophy'

18.25 idealistic] *bef. del.* 'subjective,'

18.25 or] *intrl.*

18.26 time] *ab. del.* 'day'

18.26 it . . . long] *ab. del.* 'demand much explanation.**x**'

18.27 took] *ab. del.* 'could take'

18.29 settle . . . pure] *ab. del.* 'appeal to *a priori*'

18.31 collects,] *comma insrtd. bef. del.* 'facts *and [*intrl.*] '

18.31 classes] *bef. del. comma*

18.32   facts,] *ab. del.* 'them,'

18.35   to be] *aft. del.* 'had'

18.36   using] (*alt. fr.* 'use'); *aft. del.* 'by claiming to'

18.36   hypotheses] 2'e' *ov.* 'i'

18.36-37   seeking] *intrl.*

††18.39   (1890)∧ p. 213.] *opp. circled mrgn.* 'note'; *period insrtd. bef. del.* ') Compare [*paren alt. to doubtful dash*] also Paul Janet ['Cour' *del.*] and W. Jerusalem: Einleitung in d. Philosophie §§ 3, 4, 5.'

19.2   more and more] *intrl.*

19.6   philosophers] *alt. fr.* 'philosophy'

19.6   are] *ab. del.* 'is'

19.7   they] *alt. fr.* **'she'**

19.8   Philosophy . . . case,] *ab. del.* 'Since [*intrl.*] She should'

19.8   sciences,] *comma ov. period*

19.9   and must] *ab. del.* 'She *has to [*ab. del.* 'must'] at *least [*ab. del.* 'any rate']'

19.9   methods.] *period insrtd. bef. del.* '['; and' *del.*] There ['T' *ov.* 't'] is no *visible reason [*tr. to* 'reason visible' *then corrected to orig. reading*]'

19.9   One cannot see] ('O' *triple underl.*); *intrl.*

19.9-10   such a policy] *ab. del.* 'that'

19.10   appear] *ab. del.* 'seem'

19.11   whatever,] *intrl.*

19.11   become] *alt. fr.* 'being'

19.11   hypothetical] *aft. del.* 'empirical and'

19.14   for . . . substitutes] *ab. del.* '& treats of'

19.15   abstractions.] *period insrtd. bef. del.* 'only.'

19.16   almost] *aft. del.* 'have [*intrl.*]'

19.16   without . . . have] *ab. del.* 'invariably have'

19.16   simple] *aft. del.* '&'

19.17   ignoring . . . of] *ab. del.* 'shutting their eyes to'

19.17   fact] *final* 's' *del.*

19.17-18   a sort] *aft. del.* 'an'

19.19   Voltaire] *aft. del.* 'Schopenhauer &'

19.20   **due**] *bef. del.* 'th'

19.21   spoke] *ab. del.* 'dared to ['treat *del.*] speak'

19.23   but] *bef. del.* 'there is'

19.24   keep] *aft. del.* 'permanently [*ab. del.* 'remain in the future']'

19.24-25   permanently. Her] *ab. del.* '. in the future as much as **she** has done it in the past. Her whole'

19.25   manners] 's' *added*

19.26   thin and] *intrl.*

19.28   be] *ab. del.* 'have been'

19.28   and more] *ab. del.* 'successfully'

19.28   securely] *alt. fr.* 'surely'

19.29   get . . . 2as] *ab. del.* 'show themselves *not inferior to [*insrtd. for del.* 'to be in as intimate contact with life as']'

19.30   with . . . life.] *ab. del.* '['in' *del.*] for the closeness of their contact with life.'

19.32   its] *ab. del.* 'the'

19.32   acception, ['of' *del.*] meaning the] *ab. del.* 'sense ['of the word,' *del.*] of the most universal'

19.33   must] *intrl.*

19.33   include] *final* 's' *del.*

19.33   the results of] *intrl.*

††19.35-36   'system . . . knowledge.'] *sg. qts. ov. db. qts.*

19.36   more] *intrl.*

19.37   See] 'S' *ov.* 'C'

19.37   chapter] *bef. del.* 'I,'

††19.37   First] 'F' *ov.* 'f'

20.2   2sense,] *bef. del.* 'and as the metaphysical questions get more set theo'

20.3   more] *bef. del.* 'generally'

20.3   and] *ov.* 'as'

20.3   conditions] *aft. del.* 'methodic ['of' *del.*] al'

20.4   finding] *aft. del.* 'suf'

20.4-5   methodically] *ab. del.* 'clearly'

††21.0   CHAPTER II.] *double underl.*

††21.0   THE PROBLEMS OF METAPHYSICS] *triple underl.*

21.1   term] *ab. del.* 'word'

††21.1-2   To . . . 1the] *ab. del.* 'It treats of a certain class'

21.2   problems] *aft. del.* 'The [*ov.* 'of']'; *bef. del.* 'what'

21.2   getting at] *ab. del.* 'explaining'

21.3   various] *aft. del.* 'that sort of problem—'

21.4-5   and life in general] *intrl.*

21.5   solve;] *semicolon alt. fr. colon*

††21.6 questions, all of them,] *intrl.*

21.6 very] *insrtd.*

21.7 thereof.] *bef. del.* 'From [*ab. del.* 'Along with'] logic it inherits *ques- tions [*ab. del.* 'problems'] about ['truth' *del.*] what truth means and about the right methods for pursuing it.'

21.12 What . . . 'truth'?] *opp. del. mrgn.* '3 [*false start for fol.* 37]'

21.14 it] *bef. del.* 'not'

21.20 are] *ov.* 'ho'

21.21 free] *init. sg. qt. del.*

22.1 God] 'G' *triple underl.*

22.4 or . . . of] *intrl.*

22.4 thing?] *ov.* '?'

22.12 Or] 'O' *ov.* 'o'

22.13 And] *bef. del. comma*

22.15 essential] *ab. del.* 'important'

22.17 What . . . do?] *opp. mrgn.* '?'

22.19 all] *intrl.*

22.20 that] *bef. del.* 'set in'

22.21-22 actual, for most] *comma ov. period;* 'for' *insrtd.; double underl. of* 'm' *del.*

22.23 ¹the] *intrl.*

22.23 cause,] *bef. del.* 'the meaning,'

22.28 or] *ab. del.* 'of'

22.28 'A thing] *ab. del.* 'a statement'

22.28 either] *aft. del.* 'be'

22.28 exist] *intrl. bef. del.* 'B [*ab. del.* 'true']'

††22.29 exist.'] (*period undel. in error*); *intrl. bef. del.* 'B [*ab. del.* 'true']'

22.29 'things] *sg. qt. bef. del.* 'a'; 's' *added*

††22.29-30 after they exist['s' *del.*].∧ (*sg. qt. del. in error*); *ab. del.* 'where it *is.' [*period and sg. qt. insrtd.*] or 'to *act, [*ab. del.* 'operate,'] a thing must first be.'

22.31 completion] *aft. del.* 'anything like a harmonious'

22.31 such] *ab. del.* '['the def' *del.*] no'

22.31 definitions have] 's' *added;* 'have' *alt. fr.* 'has'

22.31 only] *ab. del.* 'any more than a *provisional and [*intrl.*]'

22.31 a] *insrtd.*

†22.32-33 *is . . . separate*] *ab. del.* '['ha *del.*] is done over distinct'

22.33 If] *ab. del.* 'When'

22.33 these] *alt. fr.* 'they [*alt. fr.* 'these']'

22.33 should] *intrl.*

22.33 cleared up] *ab. del.* 'advanced to- wards solution'

22.34 unified] *intrl.*

22.38 result] *aft. del.* 'vanish'

22.38 a] *ab. del.* 'being stated in'

23.1 origin; they either] *semicolon alt. fr. period;* 'they either' *ab. del.* 'things ['t' *ov.* 'T']'

23.1-2 completely] *ab. del.* 'all'

23.2 alternatives] *ab. del.* 'questions [*final* 's' *added*]'

23.2 indeed] *intrl.*

23.2-3 impossible of decision;] *ab. del.* 'insoluble,'

23.4 confront us] *insrtd.*

23.4 legitimately,] *comma ov. period insrtd. bef. del.* '*confront us, [*ab. del.* 'exist, [*comma formed into caret*]']'

23.4 and someone] 'and' *ab. del.* 'and'; 'S [*orig. triple underl. then underlines del.*]' *ov.* 's'

23.4 take charge] *ab. del.* '['be' *del.*] attend'

23.4-5 of them] ('of' *ov.* 'to'); *bef. del. comma*

23.6 the learned] *ab. del.* 'philosophers'

23.7 must, in short,] ¹*comma insrtd. on line;* 'in short,' *intrl.*

23.9 that the world] *ab. del.* 'only three: it'

23.9 have] *intrl.*

23.9 been] *alt. fr.* 'be'

23.10 (*twice*) created] *ab. del.* 'made'

††23.10 power,] *comma ov. period*

†23.10-11 —so . . . three.] *intrl.*

23.11 If] 'f' *ov.* 's'

23.11-12 of the three] *intrl.*

23.12 views] 's' *added*

23.13 thick] *ab. del.* 'midst'

23.14 even] *intrl.*

23.15 that] *intrl.*

23.17 never] *ab.* 'can['not' *del.*]'

23.18 successive] *bef. del.* '['th' *del.*] sys'

23.18-19 made . . . addition] ('the' *bef. del.* 'addition'); *intrl. aft. del.* '*['made by' *del.*] composed [*ab. del.* 'composed of successive addition of parts and yet infinite in']'

23.20 hypotheses,] *comma insrtd.*

23.20 for] *aft. del.* 'proof,'

††23.21-22 may . . . proof.] ('proof.' *insrtd.*); *moved from aft.* 'hypotheses,' [23.20]

23.22 Other] 'O' *ov.* 'o'

23.23 again,] *comma insrtd. aft. del. comma*

23.23 for . . . exist,] (*comma ov. period*); *moved from aft.* 'solution. [*period insrtd. bef. del. comma*]' [23.24]

23.24 The] 'T' *ov.* 't [ov.* 'A']'

23.24 classing] *bef. del. comma*

23.25 ¹the] *ab. del.* 'a'

23.25 problems,] *comma ov. period*

23.25 and both] *ab. del.* 'A serious'

23.25 recognized] *aft. del. doubtful* 'thus [*intrl.*]'

23.25-26 as constituting] *ab. del.* 'as inevitable. [*period alt. to caret*]'

††23.26 a . . . learning.ₐ] ('a serious' *and period insrtd.*); *moved by guideline fr. aft.* 'both' [23.25]

††23.27 ourselves.ˣ] 'ves' *aft. del.* 'f'

23.29 types] 's' *added*

23.32 either] *bef. del.* '**an** aristotelian or'

23.33 rationalist;] *semicolon doubtfully alt. fr. colon*

23.34 between] 'be' *insrtd. aft. del.* 'be-' |

††23.34-35 exists, . . . it,] *moved fr. aft.* 'contrast' [23.34] *to aft.* 'them' [23.35] *and then to aft.* 'philosophers' [23.34]

23.35 were] *aft. del.* 'in the light ['or' *del.*]'; *bef. del.* 'thoroughbred'

23.36 kind] *ab. del.* 'types'

23.38 instead] *aft. del.* 'as'

23.38 Aristotle] 'A' *ov.* 'a'

23.38 as his ['examples' *del.*]] *ab. del.* 'as types of'

23.38 empiricist] *aft. del.* 'the [*intrl.*]'

23.38 example['s' *del.*].] *ab. del.* 'way of looking at things.'

†24.1-3 Rationalists . . . perhaps] (*in mrgn. aft.* '¶' *sign*); *moved first to after* ²'wholes.' [24.5]; *guideline undel. in error when moved to replace del. start of* ¶ '**Probably**'

24.4 most . . . going] (¹'l' *of* 'willingly' *ov.* 't'); *ab. del.* 'by preference'

††24.6 the archrationalistₐ] '['usually conceived as' *del.*] the *archrationalist ['arch' insrtd.*]' *intrl.*

24.7 depended on] *ab. del.* '['convin' *del.*] came together in'

†24.8 Democritus] *bef. del.* ', the *empiricist, [intrl.]*'

††24.8-9 & . . . former] (*period aft.* 'empiricists' *del. in error*); *intrl.*

24.9 cosmos,] *ab. del.* 'of things, by its compo'

24.10 by] *alt. fr.* 'but'

24.11 truth,] *aft. del.* 'reason'; *bef. del.* 'as *a name for [ab. del.* 'formed by'] different men's opinions.'

24.13 Rationalists] *opp. mrgn.* '¶'

24.13 prefer] *ab. del.* 'seek'

24.13 facts from] *ab. del.* '**things out of**'

24.14 explain] *aft. del.* 'build them out of facts.'

†24.14-17 Is . . . theory.] (*qst. mk. aft.* 'life' *ov. comma;* 'Empiricism' *aft. del.* 'Ration'); *insrtd. for del.* 'Rationalists'

24.19 usually] *aft. del.* 'apt'

24.20 Aristotle] *aft. del.* 'The older Greeks,'

24.22 claimed] *aft. del.* 'all aimed at sweeping statements, ['and' *del.*] nobly [*alt. fr.* 'noble'] planned systems,'

24.22 in the] *ab. del.* 'at least truth was *closed*, according to them, and the systems *which [intrl.]* had to *showed* ['ed' *insrtd.*] a'

24.23 of] *ab. caret formed fr. orig. period*

24.23 which] *aft. del.* '['The empiricists on the other hand' *del.*] and in'

24.23 as] *ab. del.* 'according to'

24.23 believed,] *ab. del.* ', the account of'

24.23 eternally] *aft. del.* 'held to be forever closed.'

24.24 temper] *aft. del.* 'dogmatic'

24.25 method] *bef. del.* ', [*insrtd.*] *the method [intrl.]*'

24.26 any] *aft. del.* 'their'

24.27 a] *ab. del.* 'any'

24.28 completeness;] *semicolon alt. fr. period bef. del.* 'They'

24.28-29 fragmentary;] *semicolon alt. fr. period bef. del.* 'They'

24.29 rationalists,] *comma alt. fr. semicolon bef. del.* 'they'

24.29 often] *alt. fr.* 'after'

24.29 treating] 'ing' *added*

24.29 ²the] *alt. fr.* 'they'

24.30 virtue] *bef. del.* 'is'

24.32 less subjective] 'less sub' *ab. del.*
'more ob'

24.32 and] *aft. del.* '*than the rationalists
[*intrl.*]'

24.33 in . . . . Socrates,] *ab. del.*
'. Socrates,'

24.34 F. A. Lange] *aft. del.* 'and Lang'

24.34 Dewey,] *intrl.*

24.35 Bergson] *aft. del.* 'and other con-
tempor'

24.36 we find] *ab. del.* 'there are'

24.36 few] *aft. del.* 'in most'

24.37 typical∧] *comma smudged out*

24.37 fairly] *aft. del.* 'fairly'

24.40 show] *aft. del.* 'consequently lean';
bef. del. 'a [*intrl.*] dec'

25.5 philosophic] *start of letter* 'a' *del.
aft.* 'c'

25.7 or question of] *ab. del.* 'of'

25.8 *The*] *init. sg. qt. del.*; '*T* [*triple
underl.*]' *ov.* 't'

25.8 *Believe*] 'B' *ov.* 'b'; *final comma and
sg. qt. del.*

††25.10 I] *aft. del.* '**II**'

††26.0 CHAPTER] *triple underl.*

††26.0 THE PROBLEM OF BEING.]
triple underl.

26.2 might] *aft. del.* 'we'

26.2 Schopenhauer's] *aft. del.* 'This *is
[*insrtd. for del.* 'seems'] both the simplest and the most utterly metaphysical
of all the problems which were written
down above.'

26.2-3 on this question] ('question' *aft.
del.* 'problem ['it' *del.*]'); *ab. del.* 'this
problem'

26.4 being] *aft. del.* 'h [*insrtd.*]'; *bef. del.*
'living [*intrl.*]'

26.4 existence.] *bef. del.* 'To all inferior
forms of life existence seems so *self-
evident [*hyphen doubtful*] that they
*fail to [*ab. del.* 'don't'] remark it.
Only after the inner *principle [*ab. del.*
'essence'] of being has in its long ascent
come *at last [*intrl.*; *undel. in error*] to
self-recognition in the reason of man,
does it wonder at its own work and begin to ask what then am I? The wonder
is all the more serious in that now for
the first time it ['becomes' *del.*] *reflects upon the general [*ab. del.* 'looks
consciously at the'] fact of death, and

['now' *del.*] is impressed ['more or less'
del.] by the finiteness of all existence
and the vanity of all striving. *. . . [*insrtd.*] With such reflection and such
wonder the ['need of' *del.*] peculiarly
human *need of a metaphysic* arises—
*hence-forward [*hyphen doubtful*] is
man an *animal* *. . . [*insrtd.*; *undel. in
error*] *metaphysicum*.'

26.4 man] *ab. del.* 'he'

26.5 he] *aft. del.* ', ['he' *del.*] it is true,'

26.8 seek] *final* 's' *del.*

26.10 less] *bef. del.* 'there is'

26.11 clearer] *bef. del.* '& cooler'

26.11 becomes] *bef. del.* 'and [*ab. caret
formed fr. orig. comma*] ['the' *del.*]
the more material for thinking he ac-
quires by education,'

26.11 ³the] *alt. fr.* 'he'; *bef. del.* 'grasps'

26.15 ²the] *ab. del.* 'whose'

26.16 of which] *ab. del.* 'is'

26.16 is] *intrl.*

26.16 indeed be] *ab. del.* 'be even'

26.17 existence;] *semicolon alt. fr. colon*

26.17 into] *aft. del.* 'over'

26.19 mislead] *aft. del.* 'have the power
to'

26.19 the immense] *ab. del.* '['the force'
del.] the measureless'

26.19 that . . . and] *ab. del.* 'requisite for
its production and'

26.19-20 preserve] *alt. fr.* 'preservation'

26.20 it] *intrl.*

26.20 own] *ab. del.* 'proper'

26.20 interests.] *final* 's' *added*

26.21 thus] *aft. del.* 'is'

27.1 One] *aft. del.* 'Why just this concrete
universe, instead of the bare nothing
that we so easily imagine in its place—
this is the question'

27.1 oneself] *alt. fr.* 'himself'

27.1 closet] *aft. del.* 'dark'

27.2 ¹one's] *insrtd. for del.* 'his'

27.2 ²of one's] *ab. del.* 'with his'

27.2 in] *insrtd. for del. comma*

27.3 (a thing] *paren ov. comma*; 'a' *aft.
del.* 'his queer nature and mind, and'

††27.3-4 of ones fantastic] *ab. del.* 'with
his queer'

27.4 and] 'n' *ov.* 'l'

27.6 ²that] *intrl.*

27.6, 7 should be,] *intrl.*

27.7   very] *intrl.*

27.7   stares] *alt. fr.* 'states [*doubtfully alt. fr.* 'stares']'

27.8   but] *aft. del.* 'at the fact, but mystery'

27.8   reasoned] *intrl.*

27.9   logical] *intrl.*

27.10   are] 'a' *ov. start of illeg. letter; aft. del.* 'are'

27.11   it an] *ab. del.* 'the'

27.11   answer.] *period insrtd.*

27.11   Those . . . extend] ('ask' *ab. del. doubtful* 'feel'; 'extend' *bef. del.* 'we [*undel. in error*]'); *ab. del.* 'to the problem. of the fact of being. It is held to be an ille-' |

27.11-12   illegitimately] 'ille' *insrtd.*; 'ly' *added; bef. del.* 'extension'

27.12   the whole of] *intrl.*

27.12   being] *bef. del.* 'at large of a re'

27.12   a . . . alternative] *ab. del.* 'a previous'

27.13   were] *aft. del.* 'arise from'

27.14   in . . . or] *intrl.*

27.15   the . . . it] *ab. del.* 'it'

27.18   whatever] *intrl.*

27.18   some] *ab. del.* 'even though it were only time, there have never been wanting'

27.19   have . . . ready] *intrl.*

27.19   the] *ab. del.* '['the paradox of infinite regress. Its history must be complet' *del.*] certain'

27.19   paradox] *final* 'es' *del.*

27.20   they ask:] ('t' *ov.* 'T'; 'ask:' *ab. del.* 'say'); *insrtd.*

27.20-21   they go on,] *intrl.*

27.21   whether] *aft. del.* 'it'

27.21   your] *alt. fr.* 'you'

27.21   imagination] *intrl.*

27.21-22   traverses] *final* 's' *added*

27.22   an identical] *ab. del.* 'the same'

27.23   the amount] *ab. del.* 'it'

27.24   ought] *aft. del.* 'mus'

27.24-25   since . . . ¹its] ('now witness its' *insrtd. for del.* 'count its'); *ab. del.* 'having now an'

27.25   some] *aft. del.* 'it must ['have' *del.*] at'

27.25   past] *intrl.*

27.25   must] *intrl.*

27.25   witnessed its] *ab. del.* 'had a'

27.26   that] *ab. del.* 'it'

27.27-28   don't . . . being.] ('passed into being.' *ab. del.* 'ended.'); *ab. del.* 'see no mediating principle.'

27.29   between a] *ab. del.* 'an infinite'

27.29   which,] *comma insrtd.*

27.29   altho . . . infinite,] *intrl.*

27.30   and an] *ab. del.* 'or an'

27.31   part] *bef. del.* ', [*undel. in error*] not only here, but elsewhere'

27.31   philosophy's] *alt. fr.* 'philosophic'

27.31   history.] *aft. del.* '['reasoning' *del.*] argument.'

27.32   exorcising] *alt. fr.* 'banishing'

27.34   —being] *dash ab. caret formed fr. orig. period;* 'being' *alt. fr.* 'Being'

27.34-35   Others, . . . idea,] *commas insrtd.*

27.34   calling] *alt. fr.* 'called'; *aft. del.* 'have'

27.34   the] *aft. del.* 'nonentity a'

27.35   have . . . on] *ab. del. dash*

27.37   ontological . . . called] ('wonder' *insrtd. for del.* 'state of mind'); *ab. del.* 'question is'

27.37-38   grübelsucht] *aft. del.* 'pathological'

27.38   asking] *insrtd.*

††27.38-39   or ‸why . . . triangle?‸] *ab. del.* 'and not another person?'

28.2   more] *intrl.*

28.9   not] *aft. del.* 'the'

††28.10-11   'The . . . existing,'] *sg. qts. alt. fr. db. qts.*

††28.12   existence.' ˣ] *bef. del.* '[*on fol.* 53] This is the doctrine ['of' *del.*] that in certain *notions [*ab. del.* 'concepts'] essence & existence are one, in other words that the 'nature' of certain things ['is to exist.' *del.*] implies that they shall exist. | [*fol.* 55] The anselmian'

28.12   It] *aft. del.* '[*on fol.* 55] [¶] The "ontological" state of mind is easy | [*fol.* 54] produce in one's self.'

28.14   ²is] *bef.* '*nothing intrinsic, but [*pencil and ink del.*]'

28.15   obstructions] 'o' *ov.* 'a'

28.16   power] *final* 'ful' *del.*

28.16   over . . . have.] (*in ink ov. pencil*); *ab. pencil caret and ink del.* 'the *obstructions. [*final* 's' *added in pencil*]'

28.19   criticized] *ab. del.* 'rejected'

28.19 rejected] *ab. del.* 'criticized'
28.20 What] 'Wh' *ov. pencil* 'If [*doubt-ful*]'
28.22 expressly] *aft. del.* 'defined'
28.22,25 Ens] 'E' *alt. fr.* 'e'
28.22 *perfectissimum*] 2'i' *ov.* 'u'
28.24 ¹Ens] 'E' *alt. fr.* 'e'
28.24 *realissimum*] 'is' *ov.* '*li*'
28.31 in . . . being,] (¹*comma insrtd.*; '*mere* being,' *intrl.*); *insrtd. for del.* '[*on fol.* 52] Hegel for example points out | [*fol.* 57] that *since [*intrl.*] mere [*underline del.*] being [*caret for insertion ov. orig. comma*] being without determinations, is indistinguishable from nothing, being in fact'
28.32 it] *intrl.*
28.33 dimly] *intrl.*
28.33 constitutes] *ab. del.* 'makes a dim logical'
28.33 an] *intrl.*
28.34 use] *aft. del.* 'logical'
28.34 made] *bef. del. comma*
28.34 getting] *ab. del.* 'passing'
††28.38 V.] *aft. del.* 'Book'
29.2 all] *aft. del.* 'everything is'
29.2-3 (as . . . have)] *intrl.*
29.3 construction,] 'construction' *bef.* '*[*('(as it seems to have)' *del.*], [*ab. caret formed fr. orig. comma*]'
29.4 get] *ab. del.* 'have'
29.5 signs] *aft. del.* 'polar'; *bef. del. comma ov. period*
29.5 of] *ov.* 'in'
29.6 not probable] 'not' *ab. del.* 'im'
29.6 the] *insrtd. for del.* 'many'
29.6 reader] *final* 's' *del.*
29.6 satisfied] *aft. del.* 'fully [*intrl.*]'
29.6-7 any of these] *ab. del.* '[*'any of these solutions,' *del.*] either [*ab. del.* 'or'] exorcisms or'
29.7 solutions,] *comma insrtd. bef. del.* 'of [*'this feeble' *del.*] such feeble kind;'
29.7 contemporary] *intrl.*
29.7 philosophers] *bef. del.* 'themselves'
29.8-9 on . . . banished] ('on the' *repeated in error*; 'no one has' *in pencil*; 'intelligibly' *insrtd. for del. insrtd.* 'satisfactorily [*in pencil*]'; 'banished' *alt. fr.* 'banishes'); *ab. del.* 'have added themselves, [*'one by one,' *del.*] and the universe as we know it *may [*intrl.*; *undel.*

in error] have thus evolved. [¶] The reader will however perceive that *neither of these **opinions [*ab. del.* 'views'] really [*pencil del.*] mediates between nonentity and being. Neither *deduced [*alt. fr.* 'deduces'] being from nonentity, or *successfully [*intrl.*] gets rid of'
29.9 *fact.* Whether] *period insrtd. bef. del.* ', which'; 'w' *kept l.c. in error*
29.9-10 Nothing] 'N' *ov.* 'n'
29.10 in] *ab. del.* 'into'
29.11 thereupon] *intrl.*
29.13 in the end] *ab. del.* ', so far as our intellect is concerned,'
29.14 assumed] *aft. del.* 'simply'
29.14 by the philosopher.] *pencil intrl. ab. pencil caret ov. ink period*
29.15 difficulty] *aft. del.* '[*'fact is not to ban' del.*] do'
29.15 quench] *ab. del.* 'banish'
29.15 If . . . rationalist] *ab. del.* 'To beg'
29.15 beg] *bef. del.* 'in the one case'
29.16 of . . . once.] *ab. del.* 'of being,'
29.16 if . . . beg] *ab. del.* 'and in the other case'
29.17 successive] *ab. del.* 'separate'
29.17 you beg ['the' *del.*]] *ab. del.* 'it is'
29.17-18 in each case,] *intrl.*
29.18 the same] *insrtd. for del.* '*just as great a [*ab. del.* 'the same']'
††29.18-19 beggar. whatever . . . leave The] *period undel. in error*; 'whatever . . . leave' *intrl.*; 'T' *unreduced in error*
29.19 ['remains' *del*] untouched, of how] *ab. del.* 'is the same how *the coming of whatever is, whether produced gradually or suddenly, all at once or [*ab. del.* '['can [*ab. del.* 'could']' *del.*] this very world, with all its details of *fact [*insrtd. for del.* 'fact'] can possibly [*intrl.*] be understood as the offspring of nonentity.'] [¶] Empiricism, which ['makes' *del.*] stands by brute facts as its first, and induces principles from them *(while [*paren ov. comma*] rationalism starts with the principles and pretends to *get [*ab. del.* 'deduce'] the facts by *logic) [*paren. ov. comma*] seems here to be triumphant. *What *is [*bel. del.* 'Being'] appears in the'
29.20 ²came it] *intrl.*

29.22 gradually] *intrl.*

29.26 at all costs] *intrl.*

29.27 our] *intrl.*

29.28 must] *aft. del.* 'are'

29.28 surface] *in pencil ab. pencil del.* 'superficial'

†30.3-4 For ... forms] ('fact forms' *insrtd. for del.* 'being is'); *insrtd. for del.* 'the coming of whatever is *came it all at [ab. del.* 'whether it ['have' *del.*] came [*alt. fr.* 'come'] gradually or suddenly, piecemeal or all **at**'] once *or piecemeal, [intrl.; comma doubtful] can be intellectually explained and understood. [¶] What I have called *the [intrl.] empirical [alt. fr.* 'empiricism'] school [*insrtd.*] stands by *'facts' [sg. qts. alt. fr. db. qts.] as its *first, [comma doubtful] and considers that all understanding is *'after the fact.' [sg. qts. alt. fr. db. qts.] What *is*, it says, must simply be taken by us as'

30.4 datum] *aft. del.* 'fact.'

30.5 It] 'I' *ov.* 'i'; *aft. del.* 'Practically [*ab. del.* 'morally'] we can welcome it, hate it, submit to it, or otherwise act upon it; but intellectually we can only describe ['what' *del.*] it. [*period insrtd.*] ['has made itself to be.' *del.*] *Somehow*'

30.5 makes] *alt. fr.* 'made'; *aft. del.* '*has*'

30.5 somehow,] *intrl.*

30.6 business] *bef. del.* 'with it ['is' *del.*] as *the [undel. in error] whole of it'

30.6 (*twice*) with] *ab. del.* 'as to'

††30.6 its *that.*] *bef. del.* '[*del.* 'Our minds *surround ['s' ov.* 'r'] fact [*ab. del.* 'it'] as water surrounds ['marble' *del.*] stone. They can dissolve but *traces, [comma insrtd.] ['of it,' del.] and *they [intrl.] find always a remainder that will not yield. Nothing'] This [*insrtd.*] would be ['more' *del.*] natural if our intellect were a faculty organized in us for handling what it finds, but not coeval with creation & still less prior to it, as has sometimes been claimed.'

††31.0 CHAPTER IV] *triple underl.*

††31.0 PERCEPT AND CONCEPT] *triple underl.*

31.5 which] *aft. del.* 'of them'

31.6 may] *intrl.*

31.6 closed.] *bef. del.* 'But sense and idea are strangely interlaced throughout our knowledge. If we *use [ab. del.* 'speak of'] The ['T' *ov.* 't' *in error*] words 'percept' and 'concept' the reader will probably recognize the sort of contrast that is meant.'

31.7 use] *intrl.*

31.7 in ... of] *ab. del.* 'as designating'

31.7 ²the] *bef. del.* 'contrasted elements of our experience in which the'

53.19 all] *aft. del.* 'wading through'

53.19 person] *ab. del.* 'character'

53.20 substitute] *bef. del.* 'the monstrous abridgment of'

53.20-21 systems] *bef. del.* '['one useful' *del.*] each being a serviceable equivalent for some one ['as' *del.*] aspect of the reality which no one can ex-'

53.22 each] *bef. del.* 'a serviceable'

53.23 full] *aft. del.* 'grasp [*ab. del.* 'reality unattainable by us in full perceptual form.']'

53.23 grasp.[*ˣ del.*]] *opp. mrgn. del.* 'ˣThe concepts of matter, mass, atom, ether, inertia, force, *etc., [intrl.] serve ['a' del.] splendidly ['ly' intrl.] ['purpose in' del.] to [insrtd.] ['the scientific' del.] handle [alt. fr.* 'handling'] ['of' *del.*] nature, *by [intrl.] Yet if we *take [ab. del.* '['own' *del.*] see'] them *as [intrl.] revelations of nature's intimate reality we find ourselves arrested by all the mutual contradictions which Stallo has pointed out in his book 'Concepts & Theories of modern physics,' (1882). These concepts are *artefacts *and probably not [ab. del.* ', not realities.'] mental duplicates of physical realities. Compare Stallo, pp 136-140. Also W. Ostwald: Vorlesungen über Naturphilosophie (1902) pp. 308-311. *See above [*in pencil; undel. in error*]'

53.27 now] *ab. del.* 'therefore'

53.28 were] (*alt. fr.* 'be'); *intrl. aft. del.* 'were [*ab. del.* 'be']'

53.28 full] *intrl.*

53.30 subject-matter] *ab. del.* 'contents'

53.31 in such] *ab. del.* 'in immediate'

53.31 reality] (*final* ''s' *del.*); *aft. del.*
'fulness [*ab. del.* 'the']'

53.31 intimately and] 'ly' *added*; 'and'
ab. del. 'quality'

53.32 **But** ... is] *intrl.*; *bef.* 'Unable ['U'
unreduced in error]'

53.33 experience,] *bef. del.* 'the philosopher'

53.36 the] 'th' *ov. doubtful* 'e'

53.36 'Introduction] (*sg. qt. ov. db. qt.*);
aft. del. 'essay'

54.1 ideal] *ab. del.* 'conceptual'

††54.2 moments.ˣ] *period and* 'ˣ' *for fn.
insrtd. aft. del. comma and bef. horiz.
line and* '*It [*alt. fr.* 'and it']' [54.31]
for start of fn.

54.5 wide] *final* 'r' *del.*

54.7 quality] *ab. del.* 'kind'

54.7 ²deeper] *bef. del.* '& **fuller**'

54.8 only] *aft. del.* '[*on fol.* 52] [*del.*
'['These symbols, though too' *del.*] *He
enlarges his [*del. in pencil*] ['perceptions by' *del.*] *view by conceptual
**substituting [*alt. fr.* 'substitutes']
[*del. in pencil*]'] | [*fol.* 53½] *He thus
**embraces [*del. in ink*] [*pencil*]
commands vicariously innumerable [*ab.
pencil del.* 'for the'] percepts [*alt. fr.*
'perceptions'] that are out of range.
*But [*pencil insrtd.*] the [*alt. in pencil
from* 'These'] *concepts [*alt. fr.* 'conceptual'] ['symbols' *del.*], by which he
does this, [*ab. del.* 'substitutes,'] being
thin extracts from perception, are always insufficient['s' *del.*] ['; yet' *del.*]
representatives thereof, [*del.* '; they are
of two orders, *elements* (like velocity,
position, mass) ['and' *del.*] and *entities*
(like atom, ether, soul, force). In both
cases they form worlds additional to
that immediately felt, though homogeneous and continuous ['with it' *del.*]
with the latter therewith and must
['not' *del.*] never be regarded'] and altho they give *wider [*underline del.*]
information, [*insrtd.*] must never be
*treated, after the **fashion [*ov.* 'as']
of [*intrl.*] rationalism, [*alt. fr.* 'rationalists'] a [*ab. del.* 'regard the'] [*ab. del.*
'regarded,'] as *if they [*intrl.*] gave
[*alt. fr.* 'giving'] *a deeper ['fuller' *del.*]

[*ab. del.* 'deeper [**underline del.**]']
truth. *The [*insrtd.*] deeper ['d' *ov.*
'D'] and fuller *features ['objects' *del.*]
of reality ['are' *del.*] found [*ab. del.*
'type of truth is yielded']'

54.8 in ['our' *del.*]] *ab. del.* 'by the'

54.9 immersion [*doubtful* 'running' *del.*]
of] *ab. del.* 'inseparability *of [*undel.
in error*]'

54.9 in] (*alt. fr.* 'into'); *ab. del.* 'from'

54.10 here ... self,] *insrtd.*

54.10 ²with ... qualities,] *intrl.*

54.11 in] *bef. del.* 'all'

54.11 various] *bef. del.* 'aspects and'

54.11 with cause,] *intrl.*

54.13 the ... of] *ab. caret formed fr.
orig. comma*

54.13 conceptual] *alt. fr.* 'concepts'

54.13 translation,] *intrl.*

††54.14 followed ['scrutinized,' *del.*]
out∧] *ab. del.* 'followed,'

54.14 raise its] *insrtd. for del.* '['oppose
their' *del.*] protest'

54.14 *possumus,*] *comma insrtd. aft. del.
period*

54.15 and ... as] *ab. del.* '[*del.* 'The consequence is that *no [*intrl.; undel. in
error*] philosopher [*alt. fr.* 'philosophers
[*alt. fr.* 'philosophy']'] can['not' *del.*]
['possibly' *del.*] gain *truth's fulness
[*bel. del.* 'the 'truth' (which in']']
['eith' *del.*] accuse [*alt. fr.* 'accusing']
the ['immediately experienced as' *del.*]
world of our immediate experience as
either unintelligible or'

††54.16 SOME COROLLARIES] *red ink
w. red ink db. underline*

††54.17 ['Corollary' *black ink del.*] I.]
*red ink w. red ink db. underline; ov.
pencil* 'Corollaries'

54.17 that] *bef. del.* 'philosophy becomes'

54.18 *confirmed.*] *ab. del.* 'corroborated.'

54.19 fundamental] *aft. del.* 'more'

54.20 human] (*ov.* 'our'); *intrl.*

54.21 experience] *bef. del.* 'in general'

54.21 wholes] ('s' *added*); *aft. del.* 'a'

54.21 our] *ab. del.* 'the'

54.22 change] *alt. fr.* 'changing'

54.23 never] *bef. del.* '['in the' *del.*]
literally recurring twice.'

54.23 return['ing' *del.*]] *bef. del.* 'again'

54.23 brings an] ('brings' *aft. del.* 'gives'); *ab. del.* 'is the indefeasible'

54.24 into] *ab. del.* '['on [*doubtful*]' *del.*] in'

54.24 our] *bef. del.* 'concrete'

54.24 This] ('T' *ov.* 't'); *aft. del.* 'Of'

54.24-25 finds . . . the] *ab. del.* 'the con-'|

54.25 conceptual] 'con' *insrtd.*

54.25 method,] *comma insrtd.*

54.25 for] *insrtd for del.* 'can *not reproduce, [*ab. del.* 'give no account;'] for'

54.25 concepts] *bef. del.* ', being ['extracts from what has been abr' *del.*] only partial *aspects of [*ab. del.* 'abstracts from'] what has been already given,'

54.26 experiences] *ab. del.* 'what has been'

54.27 to divine] *ab. del.* '['can' *del.*] foretells ['s' *added*]'

54.27-28 ready- . . . terms.] ('terms.' *aft. del.* 'par'); *ab. del.* 'terms borrowed from the old.'

54.28 actual] *insrtd. for del.* 'of [*intrl.*] absolute'

54.28 future] *ab. del.* 'new'

54.29 the] *ab. del.* 'in'

54.29 makes it] ('makes' *ov.* 'is'); *intrl. aft. del.* '*found **constitutes [*insrtd. for del.* 'involves'] its [*ab. del.* '*means its [*insrtd. for del.* '*entails ['carries' *del.*] [*ab. del.* 'means its']']']'

54.29 novel] *final* 'ty' *del.*

54.31-36 It . . . men.] *orig. part of text*

54.31 'mystical'] *aft. del.* 'certain'

†54.31 his . . . a] *ab. del.* 'the perceptual grasp of the'

54.32 perceptual] *intrl.*

54.32 open] *ab. del.* 'alloted'

54.32 scientific] *ab. del.* 'normal *or [*intrl.*] practical'

54.34 of . . . knowledge,] *ab. del.* 'is'

54.35 has been neglected] ('neglected' *bef. del.* 'is'); *ab. del.* 'and has usually been neglected'

54.35 both] *intrl.*

54.37 Naturally] ('N' *ov.* 'n'); *aft. del.* 'This'

54.37 this] *intrl.*

54.37 in . . . place] *ab. del.* '['only to the' *del.*] ['in philosop' *del.*] here'

54.38 parts,] *comma ov. period*

54.38 for] *insrtd.*

54.38 there] 't' *ov.* 'T'

54.38 plenty of] *intrl.*

54.39 (animal] *paren ov. comma*

54.39 in] *intrl.*

54.39 which] *bef. del.* 'found [*insrtd. for del.* 'precede [*ab. del.* 'condition']']'

54.39 both] *aft. del.* 'their'

54.39 ²the] *alt. fr.* 'their'

54.40 understanding] *ab. del.* 'knowledge'

54.40 ²parts] *ab. del.* 'same'

55.2 use] *ab. del.* 'apply'

55.2 to] *intrl. bef. del.* '*as makeshifts for [*ab. del.* 'prospectively to']'

55.2 define] *alt. fr.* 'defining'

55.3 can] *intrl.*

55.3 a] *ab. del.* 'the'

55.3 bare] *alt. fr.* 'barest'

55.4 or . . . out] *ab. del.* ', within'

55.4 of] *intrl.*

55.4-5 perception . . . invoked.] *insrtd. for del.* 'all sorts of ['novel' *del. intrl.*] variations *are to [*ab. del.* 'may'] be *expected. [*period insrtd. bef. del.* 'concretely to ['fall.' *del.*] occur.']'

55.6 aspired to] *ab. del.* 'aimed at'

55.7 whole] *aft. del.* 'universe, from'

55.7 kinds,] *ab. del.* 'possibilities, [*alt. fr.* 'possibility']'

55.7 from] 'f' *ov.* 'w'

55.7-8 ²the . . . **possible**,] ('['there being' *del.*] any' *insrtd. for del.* 'any'; 'novelty being possible,' *insrtd. for del.* 'novelty is'); *ab. del.* 'the unforeseenness *can [*ab. del.* 'could'] be excluded in kind— essentially ruled'

55.8 is ruled-] *insrtd.*

55.8-9 in advance.] *ab. caret formed fr. orig. period*

55.9 be] *aft. del.* 'th'

55.9 thus] *bef. del.* 'conceptually *limited and [*insrtd.*]'

55.10 by . . . -fence.] ('by' *ov.* 'in' *aft. del.* 'with'; 'ring-fence' *aft. del.* 'circle.'); *ab. caret formed fr. orig. period*

55.11 alters;] *ab. del.* 'changes through and through;'

55.11 novelties] *intrl.*

55.11 may turn into] *insrtd. for del.*
'turns [*ab. del.* 'makes itself']'

55.12 following] *ab. del.* '['pl' *del.*] experiencing ['its' *del.*]'

55.12 singularities] 'ies' *ov.* 'y'

55.13 Empiricist] ('E' *alt. fr.* 'e'); *aft. del.* 'The'

55.13 philosophy] *alt. fr.* 'philosopher'

55.14 -inclusive vision.] *ab. del.* '-surrounding view.'

55.14-15 narrowness ... experience] ('of' *bef. del.* 'the'); *ab. del.* 'flux of life'

55.15 which it] *ab. del.* ', and'

55.15 useful] *aft. del.* 'them sovereignly'

55.15 but] *intrl.*

55.16 stays] *ab. del.* 're-|['plants itself in the flux' *del.*]mains within the'

55.16 inside the] *insrtd.*

55.16 of life] *intrl.*

55.16 recording] 'cording' *aft. del.* '-[*undel. in error*] receiving'; *ab. del.* 'accepting'

55.17 facts,] *bef. del.* 'as a gift,'

55.17 fulminating] *ab. del.* 'imposing'

55.17 laws,] *bef. del.* 'as a necessity, and'

55.17 and] *insrtd.*

55.18 totality] *ab. del.* 'whole'

55.19 from] *aft. del.* 'from different'

55.19 the] *ab. del.* 'any'

55.19 daily] *intrl. bef. del. intrl.* 'practical'

55.20 practical ... events.] 'practical ... events' *ab. del.* 'daily stream'; *period insrtd.*

55.20-21 Philosophy ... open.] ('the doors and' *ab. del.* 'its doors and its'; 'open.' *bef. del.* 'to what may come.'); *ab. del.* 'of life. The re-'

55.22 In the] *opp. mrgn.* '¶'

55.22 2this] *alt. fr.* 'the'

55.23 shall] *insrtd. bef. del.* '[*del.* 'shall stand midway in the stream of life, passively *acknowleging [ab. del.* 'using [*ab. del.* 'accepting']'] data from sense *experiences ['s' added* ['as irreducible in their entirety' *del.*] as integral parts of reality whi'] insist on ['taking expe' *del.*] the day by day character of reality, which the universal concepts help us'

55.23 is created] *ab. del.* 'forms itself'

55.24 sketch-map] *aft. del.* 'devise'

55.24-25 showing ['giving' *del.*] ... bearings,] *ab. del.* 'orienting us, but never through *reality, [ab. del.* 'life,']'

55.25 fitly supersede] ('supersede' *bef. del.* 'reality, ['it' *del.*] ['daily experience.' *del.*] and'); *ab. del.* 'replace life, and least'

55.25 perception, and that ['the' *del.*]] *ab. del.* '*perception reality, and that least [insrtd.*] of all *Can ['C' ov.* 'c']'

55.26 systems] *final* 's' *added; aft. del.* 'relations which connect'

55.26 should ... all] ('should' *bef. del.* 'can'); *intrl.*

55.26 be] *bef. del. caret*

55.26 as] *aft. del.* 'as the platonizing tradition regards *them, [ab. del.* 'it,']'; *bef. del.* 'an altogether higher'

55.26 realms] 's' *added*

55.27 being] *bef. del. comma*

55.27 is a] *ab. del.* 'is the highest'

55.28-29 assumption] *bef. del.* '['should' *del.*] is altogether false.ˣ'

55.29 is quite] *intrl.*

55.29 mark.] *bef. del.* 'ˣ'

55.30 that essential] *insrtd. for del.* 'its'

55.30 which] *ab. del.* 'as'

55.30 argued for] *ab. del.* 'asserted'

††55.32 II.] *in red ink aft. black ink del.* 'Corollary [*red ink*]'

††55.32 realms] *in black ink ab. black ink del.* 'portions'

†55.32-33 The ... that] *ab. del.* 'This does not mean that'

55.34 not] *ab. del.* 'not'

55.34 ∧eternal∧] (*sg. qts. del.*); *ab. del.* 'way as ['the per' *del.*] ['e' *del.*] '**time-less**''

55.35 to say] *intrl.*

55.36 'logical.'] *period insrtd. bef. del.* 'or rational'

55.37 (1907),] *intrl.*

55.37 his] *bef. del.* 'own'

56.1 way.] *bef. del.* 'They are so, only the eternal way of being is inferior to the temporal way, as lacking many characteris'

56.2 know] *bef. del.* 'of reality'

56.2 which] *ab. del.* 'obtained by'

††56.2 rule: gives:] *first colon undel. in error*; 'gives:' *ab. del.* 'Re'

56.3 is] *ab. del.* 'must be held'

56.3 take] *ab. del.* 'keep'

56.3 in] *aft. del.* '.'ˣ'

56.4 Concepts] ('C' *ov.* 'c'); *aft. del.* 'At this rate'; *bef. del.* '*and the relations between them [intrl.]'

56.4 thus] *intrl.*

56.4 a] *ab. del.* 'a['mo' *del.*]'

56.6 ['real' *del.*] being] *ab. del.* 'reality'

56.7 is . . . ²and] *intrl.*

56.7 many] *bef. del.* 'of the'

56.8 possesses.] *period insrtd. bef. del.* 'and remains so static and schematic.'

56.8 Philosophy] *ab. del.* 'We'

56.8 recognize] *bef. del.* 'thus'

56.9 of reality] *ab. del.* 'or levels of being'

56.9 The] *intrl.*

††56.9 Conceptual] ('C' *unreduced in error*; *alt. fr.* 'Concepts'); *bef. del.* '['offer several' *del.*] yield [*insrtd.*] many [*intrl.*] examples of such realms'

56.10 systems of our] ('our' *aft. del.* 'or systems in the'); *intrl.*

56.10 mathematics] *alt. fr.* 'mathematical'

56.10 aesthetics] *final* 's' *added*

56.10 ethics] (*alt. fr.* 'ethical'); *bef. del.* 'systems [*intrl.*]'

56.10-11 , are . . . some] *ab. del.* 'each ['bound together' *del.*] characterized [*insrtd.*] by bec'

56.11 form] *final* 's' *del.*

56.11 relation] *aft. del.* 's[*and false start of letter*]'

56.12 perceptual] *intrl.*

56.12 ²in . . . them] *ab. del.* '*the [*intrl.*] truths ['there is static' *del.*] *display no [*ab. del.* 'they contain are'] static and record no'

56.12 is] *insrtd.*

56.13 displayed.]˙ *ab. caret formed fr. orig. period*

56.13-14 involves . . . systems,] (*final* 's' *del. fr.* 'ideals'; 'systems,' *bef. del.* 'of truth'); *ab. del.* 'contains the whole of such eternal reality'

56.14 besides.] *aft. del.* 'in addition.'; *bef. black ink del.* '[¶] *III. Conceptual and perceptual reality are homogeneous and consubstantial [in red ink]. I mean

by this that ['the' *del.*] in the handling of our percepts by our concepts, the two coalesce and melt together without difficulty.'

56.15 ideal] *red ink ab. red ink del.* 'conceptual [*red ink*]'

56.16 ²means] *ab. del.* 'is'

56.18 objects] *ab. del.* 'meaning'

56.18 our] *ab. del.* 'the'

††56.19 for . . . Once] 'for *a [*ov.* 'A'] relation,' *intrl.*; 'O' *unreduced in error*

56.19 perceived] *aft. del.* 'form'

56.19-20 obtain,] ('bt' *ov.* 'ly'); *bef. del.* 'between ['inalter' *del.*] unaltering things,'

56.20 must] 'm' *ov.* 'a'

56.20 obtain] *aft. del.* 'always'; *bef. del.* 'there'

56.20 always [*comma del.*],] *underline del. fr.* 'always'; *comma insrtd. aft. del.* '*so long as it obtains [*intrl.*]'

56.20 terms] *ab. del.* 'things'

56.21 persons find] *ab. del.* 'thinkers have found a'

56.22 When] *aft. del.* ' 'White' in the snow and 'white' '

56.22 both] *intrl.*

56.23 'white∧'] *comma del.*

56.23 these thinkers] 'these' *ov.* 'no-[*hyphen doubtful*]' | ; 'thinkers' *ab. del.* |'minalist authors'

56.23 there] (*alt. fr.* 'the'); *bef. del.* 'white'

56.24 be] *aft.* 'be [*undel. in error*] ['numerically' *del.*]'

56.24 predicates] *ab. del.* 'things white'

56.25 ¹colour] *bef. del.* 'is an individual'

56.33 nominalist] *intrl.*

56.36 gives] (*alt. fr.* 'given'); *aft. del.* 'has'

56.36 this] *bef. del.* 'de'

57.2 can] *ab. del.* 'is'

57.2 twice be] *intrl.*

57.3 the] *aft. del.* 'same-ness [*hyphen doubtful*]'

57.3 concept] *ab. del.* 'word'

57.4 Applying] *aft. del.* 'The way to ['get' *del.*] interpret it is to apply the pragmatic rule, applying which we see that the concrete difference'

57.4 that . . . call] *ab. del.* ', as *a [*intrl.*] practical consequence['s' *del.*] of'

57.5   objects] *ab. del.* 'things being'

57.5   we . . . that] ('either' *insrtd.*); *ab. del.* 'a) [*ab. del. comma*] that we can'

57.6   or] *ab. del.* 'and'

57.6   we] *ab. del.* 'the one'

57.6   substitute['d' *del.*]] *aft. del.* 'be'

57.7   the one ['for' *del.*]] *intrl.*

57.7   certain] *ab. del.* 'any'

57.7   operations] ('s' *added*); *bef. del.* '&'

57.11   use] *ab. del.* 'substitute'

57.12   be used] *ab. del.* 'serve'

57.13   to set off] *ab. del.* 'for dark objects'

57.13   equally good] *intrl.*

57.14   of] *ab. del.* 'to show'

57.15   pinkish] *ab. del.* 'clean,'

†57.15-16   yellowish . . . both] ('both' *bef. del.* 'the'); *ab. del.* 'the paper yellowish, and the'

57.16   ['itself' *del.*] and paper] *intrl.*

57.16   differ] *bef. del.* '*in hue [*intrl.*]'

57.17   their] *alt. fr.* 'the'

57.17   own selves] *ab. del.* 'same snow'

57.17   and . . . 'white,'—] *intrl.*

57.18   seems] (*final* 's' *added*); *aft. del.* 'may'

57.18   fault.] *period aft. del. comma*

57.18   This] *ab. del.* 'and oblige us to deny that two 'whites' are the same. The diffi'

57.19   tints] *ab. del.* 'whites'

57.20   seems] *aft. del.* 'is well known to house-painters and'

57.20   the . . . that] ('fact' *aft. del.* 'thing'); *ab. del.* 'what the'

57.21   that] *intrl.*

57.21   our . . . are] ('are' *doubtfully ov.* 'is'); *ab. del.* 'what ['a' *del.*] names ['s' *added*] denote are'

57.22   admit] *ab. del.* 'say [*ab. del.* 'then [*insrtd.*] agree']'

57.22   a concept['s' *del.*]] 'a' *ab. del.* 'a'

57.23   can] *ab. del.* 'or black'

57.23   keep] *ab. del.* 'have'

57.24   would] *bef. del.* 'really'

57.24   know] *ab. del.* 'mean'

57.24   the] *bef. del.* 'different'

57.25   dirt] *aft. del.* 'or'

57.25   impurity] *aft. del.* 'or'

57.25   pigment] *aft. del.* 'dye'

57.26   of] *bef. del.* '*['common' *del.*] specific [*intrl.*]'

57.26   different] *aft. del.* '[*del.* 'which our word shall unchangingly mean.']—'

57.27-28   inalterably signify.] *ab. del.* 'unchangingly mean,'

57.28   The]('T' *ov.* 't'); *aft. del.* 'and'

††57.28   & fixing] *pencil intrl. with pencil caret*

57.28-29   physically] *bef. pencil del.* ', so that no *changing light, etc., can fall upon **it [*intrl.*] and [*alt. fr.* 'it'] modify it [*ab. ink del.* 'adventitious determination of illumination etc., shall adhere to it']'

††57.29   & fix] *pencil intrl. with pencil caret*

57.30   say] *ab. del.* 'call anything'

57.30   identical] *intrl.*

57.31-32   Our *meanings*] ('O' *ov.* 'o'; 's' *added*); *aft. del.* '['It is possible that' *del.*] Physical ['P' *ov.* 'p'] reality, not only in its combinations, but in its very elements may *well [*intrl.*] be inconstant, and ['that' *del.*] the same *fact* *may [*intrl.*] never ['cr' *del.*] ['recur' *del.*] identically recur, ['twice,' *del.*] but'

57.32   intend] *insrtd. for del.* 'wish [*aft. del.* 'so intend it']'

57.34   use of] *intrl.*

57.36   or] *ab. del.* 'and'

57.38   means a] *ab. del.* '['is an ideal' *del.*] a [*intrl.*] standard of'

58.1   in] *intrl.*

58.2   have] *ab. del.* 'abstract it and expressly'

58.2   fixed] 'ed' *added*

58.2   ²it] *ab. del.* 'we'

58.2   be] *ab. del.* '['keep it the s' *del.*] make it mean'

58.3   It] *insrtd. for del.* 'There *shall* be no difference, we decide, and it'

58.3   on the supposition] *ab. del.* 'under ['that condition.' *del.*] the decision'

58.4   so] *ab. del.* 'and'

58.4-5   things . . . sort,] *ab. del.* 'our concepts,'

58.5   things] *aft. del.* 'perceptual ['c' *ov.* 'p']'

58.6   **What** . . . here] (*opp. mrgn.* '¶'); *ab. del.* 'This'; *aft. del.* 'we find *such [*ab. del.* 'that'] classing helpful, there *appears no [*ab. del.* 'is no'] reason *on [*ab. del.* 'in'] the earth or *in the [*intrl.*] heavens why we should not ['treat' *del.*] continue to treat ['the' *del.*] snow, paper, *zinc- [*intrl.*] oxide, wood-ashes, or what not, *as [*alt. fr.* 'is'] ['in the' *del.*] being in respect of *the [*intrl.*] whiteness ['*the same.*' *del.*] which they all ['embody' *del.*] ['exhibit,' *del.*] **embody** *the same.* Neither metaphysic, logic, nor psychology can forbid. *What sense indeed **can [*ab. del.* 'is'] there ***be [*intrl.*] in insisting that ****when [*ov.* 'we'] we expressly mean the same it is not the same that is meant? We make the whiteness, ['and we make it as the same,' *del.*], and it works for us as the same, so it must be really the sa[*false start for* 'm'] [*insrtd.*]'

58.6 platonic] *aft. del.* 'doctrine known as logical reali'

††58.6-7 concepts . . . ∧ and that] 'concepts . . . and' *intrl.*

58.7-8 physical realities] *ab. del.* 'things'

58.8 constituted] ('i' *ov.* 'u'); *aft. del.* 'made'

58.9 the] *aft. del.* 'philosophy'

58.10 usually] *aft. del.* '['generally been held' *del.*] been favor'

58.11 minds.] (*period aft. del. comma*); *bef. del.* 'deeming conc'

58.11 concept-] *aft. del.* 'the'

58.11-12 primordial] *ab. del.* 'primary'

58.12 perceptual] *intrl.*

58.12 ∧things∧] *sg. qts. del.*

58.13 book,] *comma insrtd. bef. del.* 'has'

58.13 which] *insrtd.*

58.13 treats] *alt. fr.* 'treating'

58.13 concrete] *aft. del.* 'things'

58.15 combine] *ab. del.* 'yoke'

58.15 an] *ab. del.* 'an [*ab. del.* 'empiricist']'

††58.15-16 otherwise empiricist.] (*period undel. in error*); *moved from aft.* 'thought.'

58.20 ¹the] *ab. del.* 'our'

58.21 condense] *ab. del.* 'dissolve'

58.21 whenever] 'ever' *intrl.*

58.21-22 service summons] *ab. del.* 'use condenses'

58.22 of] 'o' *ov.* 'i'

58.22 thing] *ab. del.* 'book'

58.22 now] *intrl.*

58.23 and reads,] *intrl.*

58.25 of it] *intrl.*

58.25 'book.'] *bef. del.* 'of it.'

58.25 **universal** and] *ab. del.* '['universal and' *del.*] particular is *literally [*ab. del.* 'really'] immersed in'

58.25-26 particular] *ab. del.* 'universal'

58.26 parts] 's' *added*

††58.26-27 are . . . &] *ab. del.* ', and [*comma doubtful*]'

58.28 no] *ab. del.* 'a'

58.28 can] *final* 't' *del.*

††58.29-30 and indefinitely,] *ab. caret formed fr. orig. comma*

58.30-31 what . . . ¹in] *ab. del.* 'that of'

58.31 those] *bef. del.* 'illusory'

58.32-33 detect the] *ab. del.* 'see where the ['one' *del.*] elements ['s' *added*] are [*intrl.*]'

58.37 Bradley:] *colon ov. semicolon*

58.37 (1876)] *init. paren ov. comma*

58.37 (1883)] *init. paren ov. comma*

58.39 his] *bef. del.* 'Logic'

††59.3 Even so do the] ('do' *intrl.*; *aft. del.* '['The two' *del.*] So'); *aft. del.* '[*on fol.* 65] This interpenetration it is which allows *our describing [*ab. del.* 'of the analysis of'] experience *as formed of [*ab. del.* 'into'] the different sorts of 'concept-stuff' into which we analyse it.ˣ |Cf E. B. Holt: |[*fol.* 66] But after *all [*intrl.*] that [*alt. fr.* 'what'] has preceded, it is needless to say that *such an [*ab. del.* 'the'] analysis ['must' *del.*] always remains ['s' *added*; *ab. del.* 'be'] **inadequate,** and that the various ['kinds of' *del.*] concept-stuffs [*final* 's' *added*] are *derivative [*ab. del.* 'secondary'] logical functions.'

†59.12 see . . . while] *ab. del.* 'think,'

††59.12-13 ³more . . . ∧ the] *insrtd.*

59.13 see] *ab. del.* 'see'

59.14 articulateness] (*alt. fr.* 'articulation'); *aft. del.* 'scope of'

59.24 Readers] *aft. del.* '[*del.* 'Since ['S' *triple underl.*; *ab. del.* 'The secondary character of'] the conceptual systems of reality [*comma del.*] are secondary and relatively imperfect forms of being, we'] Those ['T' *ov.* 't'] **who are con-**

vinced of *that [*ab. del.* 'this'] are permitted to return to'

59.24 who] *bef. del.* '['have' *del.*] are'

59.24 agree that] ('agree' *bef. del.* 'realize ['see' *del.*]'); *ab. del.* 'converted to the view that'

59.25 systems] *bef. del.* 'of'

59.26 are] *insrtd. for del.* '*to be [*ab. del.* 'are']'

59.26 now] *intrl.*

59.27 able] *ab. del.* 'themselves permitted'

59.27 and embrace] *ab. del.* 'with a good conscience to'

59.27 their . . . experience] *ab. del.* 'daily existence'

59.28 hearty . . . that] *ab. del.* 'good conscience as regards its being ['an' *del.*] ['a' *del.*] ['the' *del.*] absolutely real'

59.28 may] *intrl.*

59.29-30 with . . . general,] (*final* 'ly' *del. fr.* 'exclusive'; 'interest in' *ab. del.* 'care for'); *intrl.*

59.31 our] *ab. del.* 'our'

59.31 life.] *period insrtd. bef. del.* 'and sought to supersede them by something ['more' *del.*] universal and ['less' *del.*] non- [*insrtd.*] temporal.'

59.31 on] *ab. del.* 'in'

59.32 exorcised . . . veto,] *intrl.*

59.34 Compare] *bef. del.* 'a paper by'

59.34 Schiller:] *colon insrtd. bef. del.* 'in the Journal of Philosophy'

59.35 act as if] ('act' *bef. del.* 'say that'); *ab. del.* '['any' *del.*] analyse'

59.36 consisted . . . but] *ab. del.* 'into'

†59.36-37 into . . . it.] ('we' *bef. del.* 'can'); *ab. del.* 'that it consists of, and'

59.37 Such] 'S' *ov.* 's'

59.37-38 concept-stuff . . . of] (*hyphen ab. del. hyphen*; 'action and even of' *insrtd. for del.* 'action &'); *ab. del.* 'analyses, tho' never *a full['y' *del.*] [*insrtd.*] equivalent, [*ab. del.* 'theoretically adequate,'] [*del.*] may ['complete enough to ap-'|*del.*] approximate ['ap' *insrtd.*] enough [*intrl.*] for practical purposes ['to to ad to adequacy' *del.*] to be substitutable in our discussions'] may come near enough to *equivalence [*alt. fr.* 'equivalent'] to be substituted

in our'

59.38 discussion,] *comma insrtd. aft. final* 's' *del.*

59.38 if it were] *intrl.*

59.38 But it is] *intrl.*

59.39 needless] 'n' *ov.* 'N'

59.39 what] (*alt. fr.* 'that'); *aft. del.* 'all'

††59.39 it can ever] *ab. del.* 'concept-stuff ever can'

59.39 equivalent,] *comma insrtd.*; *aft. del.* 'theoretic'; *bef. del.* 'of reality—[*dash doubtful*]'

59.40 genesis] *bef. del.* 'it is always a'

60.1 —than] *dash intrl.*

60.1 this] *ab. del.* 'that'

†60.2 several . . . are] *ab. del.* 'very life is'

60.5-6 The . . . which] ('belief in' *ab. del.* 'sense of'; *final* 's' *del. fr.* 'moments'); *ab. del.* 'This reality of those particulars of life where the'

60.6 this world's] *ab. del.* 'our'

60.7 actually] *insrtd.*

60.7 here,] *ab. caret formed fr. orig. comma and bef. del.* 'there [*intrl.*]'

60.7 an] *ab. del.* 'the last'

60.8 seek['s' *del.*] in vain] *ab. del.* 'would exile our mind'

60.8 us,] *bef. del.* 'in vain'

60.8 have] *aft. del.* 'can criticize'

60.9 **state of mind.**] *ab. del.* 'philosophy.'

60.10 still] *intrl. aft. del.* 'now [*intrl.*]'

60.10 charge] *ab. del.* 'accuse [*alt. fr.* 'accusing']'

60.10 with] *ab. del.* 'of'

60.12 'Your] *sg. qt. alt. fr. db. qt.*; 'Your' *alt. fr.* 'Our'

60.12 belief . . . insist,] *ab. del.* 'empiricist philosophy, they say,'

60.13-14 (and . . . horses)] *init. paren aft. del. comma*; *final paren ov. comma*

60.13 omission] *ab. del.* 'instinct like ['t' *del.*] failure'

60.14 abstraction] *aft. del.* 'conception. We have'

60.15 Only by using] ('by' *bef. del.* 'dint of'); *ab. del.* '['We have had to' *del.*] using [*alt. fr.* 'use']'

60.15 have ['we' *del.*] you] *ab. del.* '['to' *del.*] ['and' *del.*] to'

††60.15 establisht] *final* 't' *added*

60.16 vital] *ab. del.* 'primordial'

††60.17 dependent,] *alt. fr.* 'derivative,'

60.17 the ['any' *del.*] character] *ab. del.* 'the attribute'

††60.18 endow ... stand] *ab. del.* 'would [*ab. del.* '['may' *del.*] succeeds [*final* 's' *added*] in'] affix [*alt. fr.* 'affixes [*alt. fr.* 'affixing']'] to the *latter percepts. [*ab. del.* 'latter.'] You [*ab. del.* 'We'] stand'

60.18 -contradicted:] (*colon ov. semicolon*); *bef. del.* '; for ['and' *del.*]'

60.19 appear as] *ab. del.* '['remain' *del.*] are'

60.19 sole] *aft. del.* 'trium'

60.20 you] *ov.* 'we'

60.20 proper] *ab. del.* 'own'

60.20 authority,] *bef. del.* 'and no less'

60.21 instal] *ab. del.* '['make perce' *del.*] put'

60.21 authority] *ab. del.* '*a place [*ab. del.* 'the position'] of *supremacy.' [*period and sg. qt. insrtd. bef. del.* 'a']'

60.23 recollects] *aft. del.* 'distinguishes between the'

60.23 a] *intrl.*

60.24 restore] (*alt. fr.* 'restoring'); *aft. del.* 'end by'

60.24 immediate] *aft. del.* 'perception'

60.25 is] *aft. del.* 'designates'

60.25 new] *intrl.*

60.25 kind of] *intrl.*

60.26 reasoning] *aft. del.* 'rationalistic'

60.28 reasoning,] *bef. del.* '(for concepts can remove concepts)'

60.29 seat] *bef. del.* '*in perceptual experience [*intrl.*]'

60.29 That] *intrl.*

60.30 This] *aft. del.* 'As for the charge that it'

60.30-31 answers] *ab. del.* 'disposes'

60.31 the] *aft. del.* 'of'; *bef. del.* 'hasty'

60.32 the credit of] *intrl.*

60.33 Rationalism] 'R' *ov.* 'r'; *aft. del.* 'It is'

60.34 itself it is that] *ab. del.* 'itself that'

60.34 so fatally] *intrl.*

60.34 by] *bef. del.* 'trying ['vainly' *del.*] ['to vainly' *del.*] to make it *yield [*ab. del.* 'work'] intelligibility, and'

60.35 worked] *ab. del.* 'carried'

60.39 objection] *bef. del.* ', which has hardly had time yet to *be often urged

[*ab. del.* 'appear'] in print'

60.39 in] *aft. del.* 'in'

††61.0 ONE & MANY] *db. underlined; aft. preliminary notes*: '[*fol.* [1]] [*del.* 'Homogeneity of con- & percept. **Reality of** conceptual world.'] Being before being experienced? ['many-in-one constitution of percept' *del.*] Obj. that I am proving *by* concepts *etc. [*insrtd.*] What **conceptualism** does is to try to *exclude* **percepts**— what I do is not to exclude concepts but simply to *include* the other. [*del.* '['How' *del.*] Display the homogeneity and coalescence. Also the insufficiency. A conceptual cock wont crow etc.'] | [*fol.* [2]] [*db. qt. doubtfully del.*] *Truth cannot perish*; for should not only the whole world pass away, but even Truth itself, it would still be *true* that the world & Truth had perished. But nothing can be true without Truth. In no sense then can Truth perish." St. Augustine, Soliloquies. *P. [*doubtful*] Are such figures as geometry demonstrates found in bodies? A. On the contrary, it is incredible how inferior the figures of bodies are seen to be. B. Which then of the two do you consider *the [*intrl.*] true. A. Do not, I beg, consider that I | [*fol.* 3] need to be even questioned on that point. For who so blind of mind that he must not perceive that those things which geometry demonstrates dwell in Truth itself or rather that Truth dwells in them? Embodied figures, while they seem as if tending toward these, and so possess I know not what imitation of Truth, are for that reason false." (*ibid.*)'

61.1 The] ('T' *ov.* 't'); *aft. del.* '['The' *del.*] We have reached a frankly empiricist attitude in claiming that ['full reality' *del.*]'

61.1 1full] *ab. del.* 'a[*illeg. letter*]'

61.1 reality,] (*comma insrtd.*); *aft. del.* 'full'

††61.2 we now believe,] *intrl.*

61.2 only] *intrl.*

61.3 portions] *ab. del.* 'parts'

61.4 parts] *aft. del.* 'the [*intrl.*]'

61.4 such] *ab. del.* 'the'

61.4   seems] *ab. del.* '*is ['be' *del.*]
found [*ab. del.* 'may'] effective against
numerous unifying agencies.'

†61.5   of . . . disconnection.] ('work' *aft.
del.* 'break'); *insrtd. for del.* 'of *ways,
[*comma undel. in error*]'

61.5   The latter] *ab. del.* 'The second'

61.6   contain] *ab. del.* '['quite forget the
first *part [*doubtful*]' *del.*] have'

61.6   the ['an' *del.*] earlier] *ab. del.* 'the
first'

61.7   from] *bef. del.* 'com'

61.8   when] *aft. del.* 'if we'

61.8   use] *aft. del.* 'cut'

61.8   for] *insrtd. for del.* 'to'

61.8-9   cutting up] ('ting' *added*); 'up'
intrl.

61.9   flux] *bef. del.* 'up'

61.9   individualizing] 'ing' *ov.* 'e'

61.9   its members,] *ab. del.* 'its *portions
[*ab. del.* 'fractions,']'

61.10   to] *aft. del.* 'to [*undel. in error*]
ascribe [*ab. del.* 'attribute']'

61.10   treat] *ab. del.* 'these'

61.11   as . . . were] *ab. del.* '['a discontinuity in' *del.*] an existence'

61.11   or · · · remotely,] *intrl.*

61.11   another.] *period ov. comma bef.
del.* 'or related only *any [*intrl.*]
mediately.'

61.12   handle them] *orig.* 'have *to handle
[*insrtd.*] them' *alt. fr.* 'have to *consider
them [*aft. del.* '*to treat of them [*ab.
del.* 'practically to handle']']'; 'have to'
then pencil del.

61.12   look at] *intrl. aft. del.* '*consider
['conceive' *del.*] [*ab. del.* 'consider']'

61.13   if it were] *ab. del.* 'being [*ab. del.*
'a sum']'

61.13   encourages] *in pencil ab. pencil del.*
'is'

††61.14   notion, that] *ab. del.* 'doctrine,
*seeing [*ab. del.* 'taking']'

61.14   are] *alt. fr.* 'as'

61.14   distinct] *in pencil ab. pencil del.*
'fundamental'

61.14   ²that] *in pencil ab. del.* 'regarding'

61.15   is] *ab. del.* 'as'

61.16   This] ('T' *ov.* 't'); *aft. del.* 'Against'

61.16   opposes,] *ab. del.* 'considers an
illusion,'

61.16   contending] *alt. fr.* 'contends'

61.17   that] *ab. del.* 'and'

61.17   derive from it] *ab. del.* 'implicitly
belong *to [*ab. del.* 'in'] it'

61.17   all . . . with] *ab. del.* 'to'

61.18   uncritically accept] *ab. del.*
'naively [*ab. del.* 'practically'] find'

61.19   being] *ab. del.* 'being'

61.19   is] *bef. del.* 'really'

61.20   genuine] *ab. del.* '['unit' *del.*] real'

61.20   constituting] (*alt. fr.* 'constitutes');
ab. del. '['be' *del.*] originating, [*alt. fr.*
'originates'; *comma undel. in error*]'

61.21   '*un*] *aft. del.* 'of [*ab. del.* 'as one']'

61.22   here] *intrl.*

61.23   is] *bef. del.* 'beyond all question'

61.23   dilemmas] *intrl. aft. del.* 'alternatives [*insrtd. bef. del.* 'problems' *ab.
del.* 'alternatives']'

62.1   that] *bef. del. illeg. letter*

62.1   articulated] *aft. del.* 'articulately
extricated and distinctly'

62.1-2   distinctly. Does] *ab. pencil del.*
'distinctly. [*ab. del.* 'as [*ov.* 'as'] a
[*insrtd. for del.* 'the form of the']
question. [*period insrtd.*] ['whether'
del. ab. del. '**does**']']'

62.2   exist['s' *del.*]] *bef. del.* 'in'

62.2   distributively?] *qst. mk. ab. del.
comma*

62.3   anys,] *intrl.*

62.3   eithers?] *qst. mk. ov. comma*

62.3   an] *intrl.*

62.3   whole] *aft. del.* 'the'

62.4   An identical] *aft. del.* '['It' *del.*]
The identically'; *bef. del.* 'amount of'

62.5   ¹or] *ab. del.* 'and'

62.5   ³or] *ab. del.* 'and'

62.6   stands] *aft. del.* 'of *course [*insrtd.*]'

62.8   Please] *insrtd. for del.* 'It should be';
opp. mrgn. '¶'

62.8   note['d' *del.*]] *bef. del.* 'at the
outset'

62.8   at the outset] *intrl.*

62.9   particular] *aft. del.* 'for any'

††62.9   disconnection.] *period insrtd. bef.
del.* 'between things.'

62.10   only] *ab. del.* 'mere'

62.10   negative] (*alt. fr.* **'negativitive'**); *aft.
del.* 'purely'

62.12   disconnection.] *aft. del.* 'real

[*intrl.*] '; *bef. del.* 'among the parts of the universe.'

62.12 The irreducible] *ab. del.* 'An infinitesimal'

62.12 of] *aft. del.* 'of any'

62.12 however] *aft. del.* 'provided'

62.13 from] *bef. del.* '(provided [*paren ov. comma*] it ['were' *del.*] had to be written down as *ultimate) [*paren ov. comma*]'

62.14 ruin] *ab. del.* 'break'

62.14 monistic] *aft. del.* 'claim of'

62.17 we find] *intrl.*

62.18 without number.] *ab. del.* 'are innumerable'

62.19 Morgan's] *ab. del.* 'Rockefeller's'

62.19 King] *alt. fr.* 'his'

62.19 Edward the VIIth's] *intrl.*

62.20 is] *bef. del.* 'probably'

62.20 this book.] *ab. del.* 'my philosophy.'

62.20 all such] *ab. del.* 'some more real'

62.21 some] *ab. del.* 'the [*ab. del.* 'a']'

62.21 absolute] *ab. del.* 'and more real'

62.22 and this union] *ab. del.* 'The connexion *now [*doubtful*] affirmed'

62.23 practical] *ab. del.* 'disconnecti'

62.23 appear∧] *comma del.*

62.26 regards] *bef. del.* **'the'**

62.26 To] *aft. del.* 'Thus'

62.27 wonderful] *in pencil ab. pencil del.* 'illustrious'

62.28 One,] *comma ov. doubtful period; bef. del.* 'anyhow'

62.28 of . . . exact] *ab. del.* 'of the principle ['no account' *del.*] no further'

62.28 ['was' *del.*] is] *ab. del.* 'of it could ['not' *del.*] be'

62.28 Plotinus] *aft. del.* '['Plotinus' *del.*] The great monist'; *bef. del.* 'follows'

62.30 For] *aft. del.* 'None'

62.32 is] *ov.* 'an'

62.33 as] *insrtd. for del. doubtful* 'act'

62.39 C. M.] *intrl.*

††62.39 Ancient] *bef. del.* 'B'

63.1 ²of the] *ab. del.* 'principle of Oneness in Nature being One with the'

63.1 Âtman.] *period insrtd. bef. del.* 'or the principle of Oneness in minds.'

63.2 the holy Krishna,] *insrtd. for del.* 'Krishna, the Holy One,'

63.2 speaking . . . One, ['says' *del.*]] *intrl.*

††63.10 wit['h' *del.*] hold] 'h' *del. in error*

63.15 not only revels] *ab. del.* 'takes pleasure'

63.16 defy] *in pencil ab. pencil del.* 'challenge'

63.17 states] *aft. del.* 'special'

63.18 himself] *aft. del.* 'im'

63.19 an] *ab. del.* 'a [*alt. fr.* 'an'] ['illumina' *del.*] state of'

63.19 adds] *ab. del.* 'says'

63.21 and] *aft. del.* '& being unit'; *bef. del.* 'uniting w'

63.21 in] *ab. del.* 'by'

63.22 ineffable] 'a' *ov.* 'i'

††63.22 act.ˣ] ('ˣ' **undel. in error**); *bef. pencil del.* '['F. B.' *ink del.*] Plotinus: les Ennéades, tr. Bouillier, *vol [*insrtd.*] I. p. 27. | *['The hindoos' *del.*] Other [*ink del.*]'

62.23 One] 'O' *ov.* 'o'

63.24 ineffable kind of] *ab. del.* '*meaning of the [*ab. del.* 'sort of way of getting at the']'

63.24 Oneness] 'ness' *added*

63.26 so] *aft. del.* 'for'

63.26 must] *ab. del.* 'will'

63.27 The] *opp. circled mrgn.* '¶'

††63.27 usual filosofic] *ab. del.* 'other most important ['of the' *del.*]'

63.27 way] *final* 's' *del.*

63.27 deeper] *aft. del.* '['oneness' *del.*] the [*ab. del.* 'a']'

63.27 has] *aft. del.* 'which has'

63.28 substance.] *bef. del.* **'As a** grammatical subject carries all its predicates, so the *presence of a [*insrtd.*] 'substance' is taken to carry all the peculiarities **supposed** [*ab. del.* 'invoked'] to explain *how one and the same phenomenal 'thing' can have a multiplicity of [*ab. del.* 'the way in which ['various' *del.*] so [*ov.* 'a'] great *a [*insrtd.*] variety of'] attributes. [*period insrtd. bef. del.* 'are held together in a phenomenal 'thing.']'

63.28 First . . . notion] ('First' *insrtd.*); *ab. del.* 'The substance notion,'

†63.32-41 Al-Ghazzali . . . 1910.) −] *insrtd.*

63.32 Al-Ghazzali] ('A' *ov.* 'a'); *aft. del.*

'Example: [*colon undel. in error*]'

†63.32-33 philosopher . . . idea:] 'philosopher & mystic' *insrtd. for del.* 'pantheist: [*ab. del.* 'philosopher:']'; 'gives . . . idea:' *orig. aft.* 'pantheist' *and then moved to aft.* 'philosopher' *w. carets ov. each following colon*

63.35 Garden] 'G' *triple underl.*

63.40 in] *intrl.*

63.41 Compare for other] ('C' *triple underl.*); *ab. del.* 'See the'

63.41 quotations,] ('q' *ov.* 'v'); *bef. del.* 'in'

64.1 during . . . ages.] *ab. del.* 'by the peripatetic philosophy.'

64.2 any] *ab. del.* '['Ens' *del.*] a'

64.2 ¹that] *ab. del.* 'so'

64.2 exists] *alt. fr.* 'existing'

64.2 so] *insrtd.*

64.2 further] *intrl.*

†64.4 a . . . was] *ab. del.* 'it was'

††64.7 ¹&] *intrl.*

64.8 types,] (*comma insrtd. bef. del.* 'of substance,'); *ab. del.* 'sorts'

64.8 first] *ab. del.* 'primal'

64.8 second,] *alt. fr.* 'secondary,'

64.8-9 simple and compound,] *intrl.*

64.10 material] *aft. del.* 'etc. The scholastics'

64.10 substances.] *ab. del.* ', etc..'

64.10 on . . . is] *ab. del.* 'was'

64.11 but] (*alt. fr.* 'But'); *aft. del.* 'But he was not the substance'

64.11 secondary ['substance,' *del.*] beings,] *ab. del.* 'finite things,'

64.12 is] *ab. del.* 'was'

64.12 substance,] *comma ov. period aft. del. comma*

64.12 for [*comma del.*] once] *ab. del.* 'Once'

64.12 they] *bef. del.* 'can [*ab. del.* 'were subst']'

††64.13 *per se.*] *period aft. del. semicolon*

††64.13 Thus∧ for] *ab. del.* '*so that [*ab. del.* 'and as ['a' *del.*]']'

64.13 the notion] *aft. del.* 'the universe in its totality remained'

64.14 is] *ab. del.* 'was'

64.14 and] *bef. del.* 'the universe'

64.14-15 the . . . a] *ab. del.* 'remains a'

64.16 scholastic doctrine.] (*period ov. comma*); *ab. del.* 'creationist point of view, and *['made of' *del.*] treated [*ab. del.* 'made'] God [*comma del.*] [*ab. del.* 'the pantheistic notion of God *as [*ab. del.* 'being'] the substance of all things almost popular. He proves'] not *as [*intrl.*] the creator but *as [*intrl.*] the substance of all *other [*insrtd.*] beings. [*ab. del.* 'things.'] In the earlier'; *deletion opp. del. mrgn.* '(causa sui)'

64.16 began] *alt. fr.* 'begins'

64.17 demonstrating] *ab. del.* 'proving ['that there can only be one subs' *del.*] more geometric['a' *del.*] o'

64.17 only] *aft. del.* 'in the nature of things'

64.18 ²that] *intrl.*

64.18 can only] *ab. del.* 'must'

64.19 Consult] *alt. fr.* 'Compare'

64.19 the . . . of] ('word' *aft. del.* 'index of'); *intrl.*

††64.20 A∧ Stöckl] *aft. del.* '(1890), or'

65.1 This] *bef. del.* 'pantheistic'

65.1 brought . . . on] *ab.del.* 'caused'

65.1 Spinosa,] *comma insrtd. bef. del.* 'to be reprobated during his life-time,'

65.1-2 favored] (*alt. fr.* 'favorite'); *aft. del.* 'a [*ab. del.* 'the']'

65.2 by] *ab. del.* 'view among'

65.2 poets] *aft. del.* 'ever'

65.2 The pantheistic] *ab. del.* 'Such a ['vast' *del.*] vague all-inclusive'

65.4 Locke] *aft. del.* '['Loc' *del.*] Hobbes,'

65.4-5 began . . . currency] *intrl.*

65.6 notion] *aft. del.* 'whole'

65.6-7 in . . . of] *ab. del.* 'in'

††65.7 idea.ˣ] *period and* 'ˣ' *insrtd. bef. del.* 'began to gain currency.'

65.8 substances] *final* 's' *added*

65.11 He] (*ov.* 'a'); *aft. del.* '[*del.* 'Berkeley *tried to [*intrl.*] banish['t' *del.*] the idea of material substance from'] He *denied [*ab. del.* 'criticized'] the notion *as [*ab. del.* 'of'] *there being [*insrtd.*] a *['separate' *del.*] identical [*ab. del.* 'personal'] substance in each person, showing that ['the sameness' *del.*] our personal self-sameness [*del.* '['is' *del.*] consists in the functional of *our [*intrl.*] later states of mind remember'] is explicable by the perma-'

65.11 notion] *aft. del.* 'substance'

65.11-12 ['a' *del.*] personal substances] *final* 's' *added*

65.12 principles] 's' *added*

65.13 our ... identity] *ab. del.* 'this *con- [*undel. in error*]'|

65.13 consists] 'con' *insrtd.*

††65.13 he said_∧] *intrl.*

65.14 functional] *aft. del.* 'fact that'

65.16 bodily] *ab. del.* 'material'

65.16 substance.] *bef. del.* 'Matter is *known* only as a group of sensations of sight, touch, etc. [*colon del.*] let ['l' *ov.* 'L'] therefore the word signify only such'

65.17 _∧When I consider,_∧] *db. qts. del.*

65.20 annexed] *ab. del.* 'attached'

65.28 which] *ab. del.* 'of'

65.29-30 They ... aspect] ('aspect' *bef. del.* 'denotation [*ab. del.* 'meaning']'); *ab. del.* 'It has no other function'

65.32 designate] *aft. del.* 'denote'

65.32 held] *ab. del.* '['held' *del.*] associated'

65.32 that] *ab. del.* 'which'

65.33 define what groups] *ab. del.* 'trace the unifying principle ['which' *del.*] that ['effects the' *del.*] holds'

65.34 as] *aft. del.* 'we'

65.35 word['s' *pencil del.*]] *bef. del.* 'we use'

65.35 some] *ab. del.* 'an unknown'

65.35 agency] *alt. fr.* 'agencies'

65.36 Nominalists] ('N' *ov.* 'n'; *final* 's' *added*); *aft. del.* 'The'

65.36 treat] *final* 's [*ov. del.* 'e']' *del.*

65.36 analogy,] *pencil comma ov. period*

65.36 and consider] (*in pencil*); *intrl.*

65.37 grouped] *ab. del.* 'collected'

†65.38-39 must ... fact.] *ab. del.* 'will prove to ['be' *del.*] have the nature of an explanatory fact.'

65.41 xxvii,] *aft. del.* '27,'

66.1 The reader] *bef. del.* 'of ['Berk' *del.*] Locke's and Berkeley's'

66.1 that in these] *ab. del.* 'their'

66.1 criticisms] *moved fr. bef.* 'will' [66.1] *and insrtd. aft. del.* 'the [*insrtd.*] application of'

66.2 is used.] *ov. period*

66.2 in ... experience] *intrl.*

66.2 ²is] *ab. del.* 'does'

66.3 supposed to] *intrl.*

66.3 we] (*ov.* 'a'); *bef. del.* 'man should'

66.3 each] *intrl.*

66.4 we ... our] ('can' *aft. del.* 'cease-lessly' *and bef. del.* 'always'; *final* 's' *del. fr.* 'appropriates'); *ab. del.* 'he re-member['s' *del.*] and identifies himself with his'

†66.7 cling ... together] *ab. del.* 'go permanently'

66.7 a] *ov.* 'c'

66.7 The] *aft. del.* 'These'

66.7 certain] *bef. del.* '*sense*'

66.8 thus] *intrl.*

66.11 ²of ... nor] *ov. pencil* 'Insert quotation from Hume'

66.16 substance ... with] ('agrees' *aft. del.* 'is'); *ab. del.* 'the subject is practi-cally the same as'

††66.16 Hume's,] (*comma undel. in error*); *bef. del.* 'save that where Hume ['calls the' *del.*] leave [*ab. del.* 'speaks of'] the *association [*ab. del.* 'connexion'] of sensational elements as ['an association,' *del.*] a mere fact, Kant considers it'

66.16 in denying all] ('denying' *alt. fr.* 'denies'); *ab. del.* 'in that he assigns no'

66.17 It] *ab. del.* 'He'

66.17 differs] *bef. del.* 'from Hume'

66.17 by] *ab. del.* 'it is by a law-giving category of the *understanding-making [*hyphen doubtful*] permanence'

66.18 ['our' *del.*] shifting] *ab. del.* 'the changing'

66.18 ¹the] *ov.* 'a'

††66.18-19 name_∧ ... them] ('name' *intrl. bef. del.* '[*false start of letter*] ['concept,' *del.*] word'; 'unites' *aft. del.* 'makes'); *ab. del.* 'something, it makes them belong'

66.19 and] *aft. del.* 'and so instead of being *barely [*intrl.*] associated in fact,'

††66.20-22 assent ... word.^x] *insrtd. for del.* '*assent to this. [*insrtd. for del.* 'see how this relieves the matter.' *insrtd. for del.* 'to ['see here anything more than' *del.*] see how ['any ['further in' *del.*] greater intelligib' *del.*] the word substance ['is made any **more**' *del.*]

gets interpreted any better by calling it
a law-giving category.']'] [*del.* ' 'Substance' [*triple underlined init.* 'S' *ov.*
's'] ['is a' *del.*] *covers a [*ab. del.* 'The
word covers a *problem*,']'] Quite [*alt.
fr.* 'just'] as much *when you call it a
'category' as when you call it a bare
**word. [*surrounding sg. qts. del.*;
period undel. in error] [*ab. del.* 'in
Kant's ['as on' *del.*] pages as outside
of them.'] *does substance **covers
[*plural error*] a *problem.* [*insrtd.*]
[*del.* 'In [*insrtd.*] Certain ['C' *unreduced in error*] clusters of perceptual
experience the union seems ['accidental'
del.] inessential (as in the paper,']
While certain clusterings in perceptual
experience seem but loosely connected,
['others' *del.*] (*as [*ab. del.* 'e.g.,'] the
type, paper & binding of this book)
others (as the properties of gold, or of
*a human character [*ab. del.* 'a living
body']) seem to *belong* *together.
[*period insrtd. bef. del.* 'more
intimately.'] To *explain the difference
[*ab. del.* '['treat principle of' *del.*] speak
of sub-'] | ['stan' *del.*] *by saying that
[*intrl.*] 'substances' *are [*ab. del.* 'being'] present in the latter *cases [*final
's' added*] means simply that we postulate *in them some actual cause [*ab.
del.* ', a ['without ['s' *del.*] some' *del.*]
principle['s' *del.*]'] of union ['in them'
del. intrl.] *which our minds fail definitely to supply. [*ab. del.* 'without being
able to supply *them [*ab. del.* 'it'] definitely.'] The word substance *thus [*ab.
del.* 'mak'] marks *an emptiness in
['['our places in' *del.*] experience *and
[*del. in error*]' *del.*] over thought &
desiderates a filling. [*ab. del.* 'an empty
spot and makes a claim.'] *By itself it
[*intrl. to replace del.* 'It [*insrtd. for del.*
'In itself it supplies no explanation and
gives no relief']'] explains nothing &
*the [*ab.* 'its' *undel. in error*] relief
['is only' *del.*] it gives is [*ab. del.* 'the
relief it gives is'] illusory. [*period
insrtd. bef. del.* 'relief.'] We have yet to
find out ['the sort of unity which the'
del.] just what the kind of oneness in
things is, which calling them 'substances'

*is [*insrtd. for del.* 'has been'] supposed to *designate. [*ab. del.* 'cover.']
The humian idea *that the [*insrtd. for
del.* 'that in point of fact *['experi'
del.] ['exper' *del.*] there is no oneness,
[*ab. del.* 'nothing *belong*['s' *del.*] together,']'] **properties** of things never do
belong together, but only *are* together,
fails to *satisfy. [*period insrtd. bef. del.*
'one.ˣ']'

66.20 The . . . qualities] *ab. del.* 'Nature'
66.23-28 Let . . . flux.] *insrtd. for del.*
'What *positive [*undel. in error*; *ab. del.*
'other'] principles of oneness, ['are
there [*qst. mk. del.*]' *del.*] ['can we
find.' *del.*] ['not merely verbal' *del.*]
neither ineffable, nor purely verbal, *or
problematic [*ab. del.* 'and postulatory'],
can we find? What can we find that is *a
[*intrl.*] verifiable *fact [*qst. mk. del.*]?
[*ab. del. period*]'
66.23 now] *intrl.*
66.23 turn . . . upon] *ab. del.* '*abandon
all [*ab. del.* 'leave behind us the']'
66.23 or unintelligible] *ab. del.* 'and *the
[*insrtd.*] merely verbal'
66.23 ways] 's' *added*
66.24 accounting for] *ab. del.* 'affirming'
66.24 whether,] *aft. del.* '['whether' *del.*]
what'; *comma insrtd. bef. del.* 'something **perceptually** verifiable may not
be found.'
66.25 the 'oneness'] *aft. del.*'[*comma del.*]
of [*insrtd. bef. del.* 'the oneness itself
may not'] unity, [*comma del. in error*]'
66.25 merely] ('ly' *added*); *aft. del.* 'be a'
66.25 be a] *ab. del.* 'descriptive'
66.26 'substance,'] *comma ov. period*
††66.27 **connexions** are] 'nexions are'
ab. del. | 'nexions ['of' *del.*] among things'
66.27-28 experiential] *aft. del.* 'fl'
66.28 back] *ab. del.* 'straight back'
66.28 to] *alt. fr.* 'ou'
66.28-29 Suppose] 'S' *triple underl.*
66.29 is] *ab. del.* 'be ['one' *del.*]'
66.29 may] *ab. del.* 'will'
66.30 differences] 's' *added*
†66.31-67.20 Our . . . moving.] *insrtd. for
del.* '[*del.* 'Having traced the *facts
[*ab. del.* 'differences'] or differences,
we may then possibly *inquire into [*ab.
del.* '['proceed to find their cause, but'

del.] ascertain'] the causes thereof, but simply *to proclaim ['affirm' *del.*] [*ab. del.* 'to feel'] the oneness mystically, or to *affirm one [*ab. del.* 'refer things to one'] substance, or *simply [*intrl.*] to flourish the word one doesn't help us a bit.'] [¶] *To this question [*ab. del.* 'Asking what *the world's [*intrl.*] oneness may be *known-as, [*hyphen doubtful*]'] we find various answers. ['['When ['a th' *del.*] ['something i' *del.*] anything is mathematically a unit' *del.*] There is' *del.*] Simple ['S' *ov.* 's'] unity and collective *union, [*ab. del.* 'unity,'] for *example, [*comma ov. period*] *are not the same. [*intrl.*] The world is no simple unity, for it has innumerable *parts.; [*period undel. in error*] *and if it be a collection, [*ab. del.* 'Are'] among the parts of a collection there are innumerable ways of being united. If mechanically united, *when one moves all must move, [*ab. del.* 'you cannot move them separately,'] so it is obvious that *all [*intrl.*] the parts of *our [*ab. del.* 'the'] world are not ['all' *del.*] mechanically united, though a great many of them are.'

66.31 Our] ('O' *ov.* 'o'); *aft. del.* 'Thus [*alt. fr.* 'This'] ['turns' *del.*]'; *opp. mrgn.* '¶'
66.31 thus turns] *intrl.*
66.31 sets] *ab. del.* 'puts'
66.32 inquiry.] *ab. del.* 'tack.'
66.33 shall] *alt. fr.* 'should'
66.33-34 We . . . to] *ab. del.* 'They might'
66.38 P.] *ov.* 'B'
67.1 may] *ab. del.* 'might'
67.1 so] *ab. del.* 'utterly'
67.2 so inert] *aft. del.* 'be'; *bef. del.* 'with reference'
67.2 towards] 'wards' *ab. del.* 'each'
67.2 never] *aft. del.* '['not even to jostle' *del.*] to coexist without'
67.3 actually ['exist' *del.*] be] *ab. del.* 'be'
67.3 so] *ab. del.* 'so fundamentally'
67.4 have . . . of] *ab. del.* 'are precluded from'
67.5 their] *alt. fr.* 'them'
67.5 and] *ab. del.* '['as we read these words' *del.*] so that they form'

††67.6 they form] *insrtd.*
67.8 The] ('T' *ov.* 't'); *aft. del.* 'Any chaos *once abstractly [*ab. del.* 'one' *or* 'once'] conceived, becomes a universe of discourse; and'
67.9 attached by] *ab. del.* 'which'
67.9 writers] *in pencil ab. del.* 'writers attach'
67.9 the] *alt. fr.* 'this'
67.9 fact that any] *ab. del.* 'susceptibility of any'
67.10 may] *ab. del.* 'to'
67.10 'universe'] *bef. pencil del.* 'of discourse'
67.10 named, ['as such,' *del.*]] *ab. del.* 'designated,'
67.12 susceptibility] *aft. del.* 'possibility of'
67.12 being](('ing' *added*); *aft. del.* 'many things to'
67.12 mentally] *intrl.*
67.14 connexions] *aft. del.* 'positive['ly' *del.*] perceivable'
†67.14-15 ['now' *del.*] be . . . fact,] ('concretely or' *insrtd.*); *ab. del.* 'obtain'
67.15 ²the] *ab. del.* 'a'
67.15 designated] *ab. del.* 'conceived'
67.15 our] *aft. del.* 'such?'
67.17 modes] *ab. del.* 'ways'
67.17 union] *insrtd. for del.* 'being united'
67.17 its] *ab. del.* 'the'
††67.17 parts, Some] *comma insrtd. bef. del.* 'of our experienced world.'; 'S' *unreduced in error*
67.18 obtaining] ('ing' *added*); *aft. del.* 'are'
67.20 all seem ['all' *del.*]] *ab. del.* 'are chemically'
67.20 however,] *insrtd.*
67.21 material things] ('things' *aft. del.* 'and not mental'); *ab. del.* 'physical'
67.21 Some] ('S' *ov.* 's'); *aft. del.* 'While'
67.21 again] *intrl.*
67.21 these] *alt. fr.* 'them'
67.21 are united] *ab. del.* 'hold together'
67.22 while] *intrl.*
67.22 are] *ab. del.* 'do'
67.22 the like] *insrtd. for del.* 'what is true of chemical connexion'
67.22 thermic] *aft. del.* 'the various modes of physical connexion,'

396

†67.23 and . . . ¹connexions.] *ab. del.*
'etc.'

†67.23-24 These . . . of] ('These' *alt. fr.*
'there'); *ab. del.* '*Are the connexions
[*ab. del.* 'If the connexions are'] consequences of *an [*insrtd. for del.* 'the
[*ab. del.* 'an'] ']' underlying *absolute
[*intrl.*] Oneness? or are they'

67.24 when we] *ab. del.* 'are'

67.25 apply] *alt. fr.* 'applied'

67.25 ¹it] *intrl.*

67.25 our] *ab. del.* 'the'

67.25 world.] *period alt. fr. qst. mk.*

67.25 We should not] *insrtd. for del.*
'Obviously the latter [*comma del.*]
—we'

67.25 ²it] *ab. del.* 'the world'

67.25 unless] *ab. del.* 'because'

67.26 were] *ab. del.* 'are'

67.26 and other] *ab. del.* 'various'

67.26 it . . . that] *intrl.*

67.27 ought to] *ab. del.* 'must'

67.28 chemically] *aft. del.* 'are'

67.28 one] *aft. del.* 'ano'

67.29 or] *ab. del.* 'are'

67.30 some] *aft. del.* 'the'

67.30 conjoined] 'joined' *ab. del.* |'tinuous'

67.31 line of influence] *ab. del.* 'force'

67.32 travel] *insrtd. for del.* 'get [*ab. del.*
'travel']'

67.32 ¹pole] *ov.* 'one'

67.32 to pole] *ab. del.* 'end of it to the
other'

67.32-33 an interruption.] *ab. del.* 'a
break.'

67.34 from] *ab. del.* 'at'

67.35 thus] *intrl.*

67.36 from . . . view,] *ab. del.* 'here,'

††67.37 moreover,] ('m' *not capitalized
in error*); *ab. del.* 'And'

†67.38 seems . . . are] (¹'e' *of* 'seems' *ov.*
'a'); *ab. del.* 'is primordial, they appear
to be on a par in respect of essentiality.'

67.39 the natural ['our' *del.*]] *ab. del.*
'the'

68.1 meant] *ab. del.* 'wrought'

68.2 One] ('O' *ov.* 'o'); *bef. del.* '[*del.*
'We may mean *for instance [*intrl.*]
that *the whole of it can be taken [*ab.
del.* '['it is our' *del.*] we treat the whole

of it'] as one topic of discourse. We do
this by the'] Whenever ['W' *ov.* 'w'] we
use the word 'universe' we *take it thus,
[*ab. del.* 'do this,'] for [*intrl.*] we mean
that no item of reality shall *escape [*ab.
del.* 'be left out'] from what *our word
covers; [*insrtd. for del.* '*we point to,
[*ab. del.* 'is signified,'] '] but this unity
of abstract reference, altho it has been
made much of by *idealistic writers,
[*ab. del.* 'some rationalists,'] is insignificant in the extreme. It carries no
*further [*alt. fr.* 'other'] sort of connection with it, and would apply as well to
*any [*ab. del.* 'an utter'] chaos as to
our actual world. Both would be
knowable-together in *the [*alt. fr.*
'this'] same barren way.'

68.2 Our] *opp. mrgn. circled* 'no break'

68.2 world,] *aft. del.* 'actual'; *bef. del.*
'contains'

68.3 relate] *aft. del.* '['separate things'
del.] keep things apart as well'

68.3 by] *bef. del.* 'speci'

68.5 ought] *ab. del.* 'is'

68.5 to be called] *intrl.*

68.5 'many'] *aft. del.* 'more'

68.5 this] *intrl.*

68.5 or] *ab. del.* 'and'

68.7 from] *ab. del.* 'of'

68.8 similar.] *ab. del.* 'of the same *kind*.'

68.8 When two] *ab. del.* 'So far as two'

68.9 similar] *ab. del.* 'of the same kind'

68.9 make] *bef. del.* 'logical'

68.9-10 hold good] *ab. del.* 'be true'

68.10 this] *aft. del.* '['this gr' *del.*] the
great amount of generic unity in the
world is inexpressibly precious, as *making [*ab. del.* 'rendering'] the application of logic to it possible'

68.10 things,] *comma insrtd.*

68.10-11 ²so . . . obtains,] *intrl.*

68.12 an] *ab. del.* 'our world is only
partly unified thus, for'

68.12 among things] *intrl.*

68.12 exists] *alt. fr.* 'coexists'

68.12 alongside] 'side' *added*

68.13 ¹of] *ab. del.* 'with'

68.13 likeness of kind] *ab. del.* 'homogeneity'

68.13 discover] *ab. del.* 'find'

68.13 and] *bef. del.* 'under this head ['we must write again' *del.*] we can'

68.13 ['should' *del.*] appears] *ab. del.* 'is thus'

68.14 ['as' *del.*] distinctly . . . ¹as] *insrtd. for del.* 'be called [*ab. del.* 'generically']'

68.14 a One] 'a' *intrl.*; 'O' *ov.* 'o'

68.14 ²as a] *intrl.*

68.14 Many,] ('M' *ov.* 'm'; *comma ov. period*); *aft. del.* '*should be called **a [*undel. in error*] [*ab. del.* 'it is generically']'

68.16 We] 'W' *ov.* 'T'

68.17 mean] *aft. del.* 'say 'world' and'

68.17 at once.] *ab. caret formed fr. orig. period*

68.18 Widely . . . from] *intrl. aft. del.* '*In contrast with [*ab. del.* 'Over against']'

68.18 unification . . . designation,] ('designation' *aft. del.* 'word,'); *ab. del.* 'abstract *knowledge [*ab. del.* 'noetic unity']'

68.19 union] *alt. fr.* 'unity'

68.19 by] *bef. del.* 'the existence of'

68.19 of] *bef. del.* 'the'

68.20 type] *ab. del.* 'kind from whose'

68.21 what] *aft. del.* 'the universe at once'

††68.21 In Such] 'In' *intrl.*; 'S' *unreduced in error*

68.21 absolute] *insrtd.*

68.21 all-knower] *bef. del.* '*believed in [*ab. del.* '['imposit' *del.*] affirmed'] a [*ab. del.* 'as'] logical['ly' *del.*] necessity [*alt. fr.* 'necessary'] *by all [*ab. del.* 'by the school of']'

68.22 believe.] *ab. caret formed fr. orig. period*

68.22 Kant] *aft. del.* 'An [*ab. del.* 'The'] Absolute Mind is supposed to'

68.22 they say,] *ab. del.* 'it is said,'

68.22 replaced . . . of] ('replaced' *aft. del.* 'transformed' *and bef. de.* 'superseded'); *ab. del.* '['turned the' *del.*] made the notion pantheistic'

68.23 by] *ab. del.* 'over into'

68.23-24 am . . . of] *ab. del.* 'have [*ab. del.* 'think']'

68.24 on . . . part] *intrl.*

68.25 resort,] *comma insrtd.*

68.25 we are told,] *intrl.*

68.26 ¹of] *ab. del.* 'for'

68.28 just] *ab. del.* 'as much'

68.29 ¹is] 's' *ov.* 't'

68.29 itself] 'self' *added*

68.30 later] *ab. del.* 'from'

68.30 noetic] *aft. del.* 'absolute [*ab. del.* 'such']'

68.30 as] *aft. del.* 'as'; *bef. del.* 'nothing more than'

68.30-31 unverified] *intrl.*

68.31 noetic] *ab. del.* '['more' *del.*] verified'

68.31 pluralism] *alt. fr.* 'pluralistic'

68.32 seek] *ab. del.* 'get'

†68.33 friends . . . the] *ab. del.* 'acquaintances. The whole'

68.33 might] *ab. del.* 'may'

68.34 yet] *ab. del.* 'but'

68.34 everything] (*alt. fr.* 'all'); *intrl.*

68.35 cognitive] *insrtd.*

68.35 —much] *ab. del.* 'just'

68.39 is . . . different] *ab. del.* 'should be distinguisht'

†69.2-4 universe, . . . others.] *comma ov. period*; 'yet . . . know.' *insrtd.*

69.6 We . . . are] ('We ['W' *ov. start of doubtful* 'M']' *ab. del. insrtd.* 'Men'); *insrtd. for del.* 'People love or hate one another, but love stops where acquaintance stops. Men are'

69.7 organizing] *bef. del.* 'trusts and'

69.8 mercantile,] *intrl.*

69.8 colonial,] *intrl.*

69.9 ever] *final* 'y' *del.*

69.9 reticulations. ['nets.' *del.*]] *ab. del.* 'networks.'

69.11 and] *ab. del.* 'or'

69.11,12 connexions] *intrl.*

69.14 thing,] *comma insrtd.*

69.14 moreover,] *intrl.*

69.15 is] *intrl.*

69.15 connected] *alt. fr.* 'connects'

70.26 soberer] *final* 'er' *added*

70.26 question] *aft. del.* 'whole'

70.26-27 One or the Many] *ab. del.* 'world's oneness or manyness'

70.27 may well] *intrl.*

70.27 cease] *final* 's' *del.*
70.27 appear] *bef. del.* 'very'
70.27 The] *ov.* 'It'
70.27-28 amount . . . is] ('either' *insrtd.*); *ab. del.* 'is'
70.29 and] *aft. del. comma; bef. del.* 'to'
70.29 which] *bef. del.* 'however concise,'
70.29-30 complicated] *aft. del.* 'pretty'
70.30 to be] *ab. del.* 'at'
70.30 concise] *alt. fr.* 'concision'
70.32 dismiss] *ab. del.* 'leave'
††70.32 with these words^x] *ab. del.* 'thus; [*ab. del.* 'here']'
70.34 ¹of] *intrl.*
70.35-71.1 ²the . . . with,] *opp. mrgn.* '¶'
70.37 ¹the] *aft. del.* 'I may refer to'; *bef. del.* 'chapter on'
††70.38 (1907)ᴧ] *insrtd. aft. comma in error*
71.1 for many persons] *intrl.*
71.2 confer] *aft. del.* 'have'; *bef. del.* 'an emotional'
71.3 with] *intrl.*
71.3 an irreducible] *ab. del.* 'a'
71.3-4 is . . . clash['es' *del.*].] *ab. del.* 'undermines.'
71.5 Secondly, a] (*opp. mrgn.* '¶'); *ab. del.* 'a [*ov.* 'A']'
71.5 noetic] *intrl.*
71.7 world's] *bef. del.* 'complete'
71.8 do] *insrtd. for del.* 'bel'
71.8 being] *bef. del.* 'strung along loosely from next to next, as if'
71.9 bare ['words' *del.*] conjunctions] *ab. del.* 'preposition'
71.9 'and.'] *aft. del.* 'the conjunction'
71.9 The notion that] *insrtd.*
71.9 this] 't' *ov.* 'T'
71.10 pluralistic . . . obtain] *ab. del.* 'constitution of things'
†71.11 does make['s' *del.*] . . . non-] *ab.* 'is' *undel. in error*
71.12 a] *ab. del.* 'the'
71.13 thus] *ab. del.* 'thus'
71.13 oneness] *bef. del.* 'in things'
71.14 element.] *ab. del.* 'than *the [*alt. fr.* 'their' manyness *in things. [*ab. caret formed fr. orig. period*]'
71.14 unit,] *comma insrtd. bef. del.* 'of beings'

71.15 each] (*alt. fr.* 'Each'); *aft. del.* 'no part has any independence of the rest.'
71.16 from which] ('which' *alt. fr.* 'when'); *intrl.*
71.16 incipiency] *ab. del.* 'tremor'
71.16 independence anywhere] *ab. del.* 'disunion'
†71.17-20 With . . . whole.] *insrtd. orig. aft.* 'view.' [71.12] *then moved to aft.* 'out.'
†71.17 With . . . believe] '[*del.* 'Logical [*insrtd.*] *['affirms' *del.*] says [*ab. del.* 'gladly have us believe]'] Like [*insrtd. for del.* 'with'] Spinosa, *Monism ['M' triple *underl.*] believes [*ab. del.* 'would'] [*moved fr. aft. del. insrtd.* 'Logical']'
71.18 ²from] *aft. del.* 'it follows'
71.18 the nature] *ab. del.* 'that'
71.19 are] *intrl.*
71.19 to] *intrl.*
71.21 monism claims,] ('monism' *ab. del.* 'it'); *insrtd.*
71.21 take] *ab. del.* 'have'
71.22 irreducible] *intrl.*
71.22 is offered ['itself' *del.*],] ('offered' *alt. fr.* 'offers'); *ab. del.* 'exists,'
71.23 only] *intrl.*
71.23 allowed] *intrl.*
71.24 and] *bef. del.* 'that is what'
71.24 can] *ab. del.* 'should'
71.25 that.] *ab. caret formed fr. orig. period*
71.26 is] *bef. del.* 'what is called'
71.26-27 For . . . thinking,] *ab. del.* 'Absolute idealism conceives that'
71.27 no . . . the] *ab. del.* 'as one'
71.27-28 of one infinitely] *ab. del.* 'for an all-knowing mind.'
71.28-29 that . . . hypothesis] *insrtd.*
71.29 that ['with' *del.*] of] *ab. del.* 'own o'
71.29 finite] *intrl.*
71.29-30 which at every] *ab. del.* 'at any'
71.30 composed of] *ab. del.* ', so that with'
71.31 disjunctions] ¹'n' *insrtd.*
†71.32-33 only . . . witnesses,] ('as' *aft. del.* 'us'; 'their' *insrtd.*); *ab. del.* 'for 'consciousness,' '

71.33 both] *intrl.*

71.33 and monistically] *ab. del.* 'based.'

71.34 We] *ab. del.* 'One'

71.34-35 ²of . . . vision] *ab. del.* 'the promises'

†71.35 underlying . . . among] *ab. del.* 'logically rational interlocking of'

††71.35-36 phenomena.] *ab. del.* 'things. which it *yields. [ab. del.* 'holds out.']'

71.36 shows] *(alt. fr.* 'shown'); *aft. del.* 'has'

71.36 also] *intrl.*

71.37 the . . . of] *insrtd.*

71.37 mysticism] *(alt. fr.* **'mystical')**; *bef. del.* 'insights'

73.6 difficulties] *ab. del.* 'troubles'

73.7 ideas] *aft. del.* 'conceptions in'

73.40 this] *(alt. fr.* 'the'); *aft. del.* 'all'

73.40 James's] *final* 's' *ov. colon*

74.1 sought] *ab. del.* '['treated pluralism and monis' *del.*] tried'

74.1 respective] *intrl.*

74.2 doctrines] *ab. del.* 'views,'

74.2 dogmatically] 'dogma-'| *aft. del.* 'making a'; *bef. del.* | **'tic conclusion** between them:'

74.2 deciding] *ab. del.* 'concluding *as to [insrtd.]'*

74.2-3 the more] *intrl.*

74.3 three] *ab. del.* 'the two'

†74.4-10 1. It . . . indescribable.] *insrtd. for del.* '[¶] 1. It is clearer [¶] It is more 'scientific,' in *that it [intrl.]* clings [*alt. fr.* 'clinging'] closer closer to the concrete facts of perception, and *establishes [ab. del.* **'ascertains']** just what ***clearly** veri['concrete' *del.*] fied [*intrl.*] conjunctive ['rela' *del.*] or disjunctive relations the words 'one' or 'many' ['mean.' *del.*] cover.'

74.4 oneness] *aft. del.* 'in insisting that'; *bef. del.* 'shall be'

74.5 it] *aft. del.* 'only in'

74.5 definitely . . . forms.] ('conjunctive' *intrl.*; 'forms' *bef. del.* '['of' *del.*] ['of *conjunction. [period undel.] del.*] *shall be **named. [ab. del.* 'found.'] [*insrtd.*]'); *intrl. w. caret placed in error aft.* 'the' [74.6]

74.6 With these] *ab. del.* 'for which'

74.6 among] *aft. del.* 'found [*insrtd.*]'

74.7 par.] *period insrtd. bef. del.* 'with the conjunctions.'

74.7 The two] *ab. del.* 'They'

74.7 are] *bef. del.* 'fully'

74.8 more] *aft. del.* 'the'

74.8 and . . . separations,] *ab. del.* '['element' *del.*] and essential element'

74.9 abandon] *ab. del.* 'dive *so deep [intrl.]* beneath *our all [insrtd. for del.* 'positively']'

†74.9-10 and . . . indescribable] ('describable.' *bef. del.* 'at all,'); 'and ['the unity it' *del.*] proclaim['s' *del.*] a unity that is ['not' *del.*] strictly in-'| *ab. del.* 'and ['that' *del.*] suppose a oneness that is either merely verbal, or quite in'

74.11 with] *bef. del.* 'our'

74.11-12 **expressiveness [***alt. fr.* 'expression'] of ['phenomenal' *del.*] life.] *ab. del.* 'appearances.'

74.14 for it] *ab. del.* 'it would'

74.14 triumphs] 's' *added*

†74.14 if . . . morsel] '*as soon as the ['very small' *del.*] minutest [*del. then restored; opp. mrgn. circled* 'stet'] morsel [*ab. del.* 'if even an infinitesimal amount']'

74.15 is . . . to] ('is' *bef. del.* 'be'); *ab. del.* 'were proved to'

74.15 exist.] *bef. del.* '[*del.* '*It consists thus [ab. del.* 'Monism on the other hand *can go [insrtd. for del.* 'is obliged']']'] It is thus compatible with the admission of an *almost infinite [*ab. del.* 'enormous'] amount of ['unity' *del.*] union *among things, while [*ab. del.* 'in the whole'] Monism, ['['on the other' *del.*] per contra,' *del.*] is forced to ['prove that no' *del.*] prove that absolutely no disconnection can be allowed.'

74.16 while] 'w' *ov.* 'h'

74.16 that] *aft.* 'that [*undel. in error*] ['nothing' *del.*]'

74.16 what] *intrl.*

74.17 asserts . . . whatever] *insrtd. for del.* '*contends for [ab. del.* 'stands for can']'

74.17 true—] *dash intrl.*

74.19 , in turn,] *intrl.*

74.19　natural] *aft. del.* 'more'
74.19　affinity] *ab. del.* 'combination'
74.20　a . . . religious] *ab. del.* 'pantheistic religious'
74.20　value] *aft. del.* '['value of the concep' *del.*] or mystical'
74.21　a unitary] *aft. del.* '['one' *del.*] ['an indivi' *del.*] ['a unit of fact: but' *del.*] one integral fact.'
74.22　towards] *ab. del.* 'in'
74.23　feel] *ab. del.* '*have felt [*ab. del.* 'have formulated']'
74.24　essential] *aft. del.* 'great pr'
74.24　practical] *ab. del.* 'practical'
74.24　which it] *ab. del.* '['will' *del.*] which ['the truth of pluralism' *del.*] it'
74.24　involves] 's' *ov.* 'd'
74.25　indicate ['give' *del.*]] *ab. del.* 'cover'
74.25, 27　The] *ab. del.* 'If'
74.25　monistic] *alt. fr.* 'monism'
74.25　principle . . . that] *ab. del.* 'be true,'
74.26　is] *ab. del.* 'exists'
74.26　way] *ab. del.* 'sense'
74.27　else] *aft. del.* 'that'
74.27　that is.] *ab. caret formed fr. orig. period*
74.27　pluralistic] *alt. fr.* 'pluralism'
74.27-28　principle . . . things] ('on' *aft. del.* 'allows'; 'some' *aft. del.* 'anything'); *ab. del.* 'be true, any part of things may'
74.28　being] 'ing' *added*
74.28　operations] ('s' *added*); *aft. del.* 'any'
74.29　engaged.] *period insrtd. bef. del.* '—may be absent in principle at any rate, for'
74.30　absent,] *comma insrtd.*
†74.30　from . . . things,] *intrl.; moved fr. aft.* 'are'
74.30　and] *alt. fr.* 'in'
74.30-31　—these] *ab. del.* 'are'
74.31　of course are] *insrtd.*
74.31　a . . . philosophy] *intrl.*
74.32　settle] (*final* 'd' *del.*); *aft. del.* 'be'
74.32　by] *alt. fr.* 'be'
74.32　past,] *ab. del.* 'future is in many ways perceptually absent from'
74.32　and] *aft. del.* 'for example.'
74.33　are] *insrtd.*
74.33　one] 'o' *ov.* 'a'

74.34　in ['for' *del.*] imagination] ('imagination' *alt. fr.* 'imaginatively'); *ab. del.* 'noetically ['be' *del.*]'
74.34　are] *insrtd. for del.* '*may be [*ab. del.* 'are']'
74.35　time-content] *aft. del.* 'future be'
74.36　part∧] (*comma del.*); *intrl.*
74.36　least∧] (*comma del.*); *ab. del.* 'any rate,'
74.36　added] *aft. del.* 's['o' *doubtful*]'
74.37　being] (*alt. fr.* 'been'); *aft. del.* 'having'
74.37　virtually one] *ab. del.* 'implicitly [*ab. del.* 'necessarily given']'
74.38　really] *aft. del.* '['onto' *del.*] entitatively or ontologically,'; *bef. del.* 'as well as apparently (or ontologically)'
74.38　phenomenally] *aft. del.* '['noetically exp' *del.*] ['no[*start of doubtful* 't' *or* 'e']' *del.*] noetically (or'; *bef. del. closing paren*
74.38　may] *aft. del.* 'th [*doubtful*]'
74.39　called] *ab. del.* 'accounted'
74.39　an] *alt. fr.* 'a'
74.39　absolute] *ab. del.* 'genuine'
74.40　Towards this] ('t' *ov.* 'T'); '¶ Towards' *insrtd. for del.* 'In'
74.40　issue,] *ab. del.* 'question,'
74.40　novelty] *aft. del.* 'apparent'
74.40-75.1　that appears,] *ab. del.* '*comes to light [*ab. del.* 'contained in the']'; *bef. pencil del.* '*in the [*insrtd.*] perceptual flux'
75.2　may be] *ab. del.* 'are'
75.3　doctrine] *aft. del.* 'indeterminism of the will'
75.4　novelties] *alt. fr.* 'novelty'
75.4　can occur['s' *del.*]] 'can' *intrl.*
75.5　already] *intrl.*
75.6　We . . . to] *insrtd. for del.* 'Determinism denies ['the' *doubtfully del.*] free-will; and monism is incompatible with the admission of any sort of chance. We are led thus to [*del.* 'a discussion of free-will and of the admissibility of *chance, [*comma ov. period*] ['These are' *del.*] ['as universal determinism,' *del.*] as a consequence']'
75.6　manner] *ab. del.* 'form'
75.7　Is] *aft. del.* '['is it' *del.*] Does it result'

75.7 consequence] *ab. del.* 'result'

†75.8-9 is . . . it] ('goes,' *bef.* 'and'; 'what' *ov.* 'is it' *and bef. del.* 'is'; 'is it' *bef. del.* 'an'); *ab. del.* 'does it bring its own'

75.9-10 in . . . ['reality' *del.*] word?] *ab. del.* 'contribution to the world?'

†75.11-16 We . . . follows.] *insrtd. for del.* 'But the *problem [*ab. del.* 'question'] of new being *or chance-being [*intrl.*] merges *into [*insrtd. for del.* 'in'] that ['question' *del.*] of being in general, ['or anyhow,' *del.*] and ['with' *del. ab del.* 'of'] the [*alt. fr.* 'that'] more [*intrl.*] general problem ['['our next chapter' *del.*] we [*insrtd. for del.* 'we']' *del.*] must *be handled. [*ab. del.* '['treat in' *del.*] ['deal' *del.*] touch on first.'] | *Insert loose sheets 47-**59 ['9' *ov.* '8'] [*circled*]'

75.11 We] *opp. mrgn.* '¶'

75.12 We . . . that] ('W' *triple underl.*); *insrtd.*

75.12 being] 'b' *ov.* 'B'

75.12 datum or] *intrl.*

75.13 begged] *bef. del.* ', we *there [*intrl.*] agreed,'

75.13-14 left . . . must] *insrtd. for del.* 'must [*ab. del.* 'shall'] he'

75.16 defend] *ab. del.* 'expound'

75.16 chapter] *aft. del.* 'next'

76.1 The] *aft. del.* '**We** go back now to the question with which Chapter III left off.'

76.1 have] *bef. del.* 'just'

76.2 is,] *comma insrtd.*

76.2 it . . . recollected,] ('be' *bef. del.* 'noted,'); *intrl.*

76.2 impotence.] *period insrtd. bef. del. semicolon*

76.2 It] 'I' *alt. fr.* 'i'; *aft. del.* 'and'

76.3-4 it . . . us] *ab. del.* 'we find it'

76.4 that] *aft. del.* 'confronting us,'

76.4 feel our powerlessness] *ab. del.* '['become so acutely' *del.*] grow conscious of it'

76.5 followed ['more' *del.*]] *ab. del.* 'treated'

76.5 empiricist['s' *del.*]] *alt. fr.* 'empirically'; *aft. del.* 'matter *as [*intrl.*]'

76.5 method, considering] *ab. del.* 'instead of starting with'

76.6 imagining] *ab. del.* 'putting'

76.7 the] *aft. del.* 'we might have more success'

76.7 subject] *insrtd. for del.* 'explanation [*ab. del.* 'matter']'

76.7 defy us] *ab. del.* 'seem'

76.7-8 We are thus] *ab. del.* 'unintelligible. This'

76.8 brought] *alt. fr.* 'brings us'

76.9 perceptible] *alt. fr.* 'perceptual'; *aft. del.* 'small amo'

76.9 come] *bef. del.* 'into'

76.10 hold] *insrtd. for del.* 'believe [*ab. del.* 'consider']'

76.10 to . . . and] ('to be' *ov.* 'as'); *intrl.*

76.11 Being] 'B' *ov.* 'b'

76.11 shall] *ab. del.* 'can'

76.11 rather] *intrl.*

76.12 that] *aft. del.* '['of there being' *del.*] their'; *bef. del.* 'absolute'

76.12 originality] *bef. pencil del.* 'and novelty'

76.12 itself] *alt. in pencil fr.* 'themselves'

76.13 reality?] *aft. del.* 'our world?'

76.14 concrete perceptual] *ab. del.* 'the whole phenomenal surface of'

76.15-16 'The . . . different.'] *ab. del.* 'Every new'

76.16 every] *aft. del.* 'and'

76.16-17 one . . . presents] (*bef. del.* 'a content whi'); *ab. del.* '**new moment** brings an individual'

76.17 a] *insrtd.*

76.17 in its ['full' *del.*] individuality] *intrl.*; *orig. intrl. w. caret aft.* 'content' [76.17]

76.18 will] *aft. del.* 'in all probability'

76.18 Of] 'O' *ov.* 'o'; *intrl.*

76.18 no] 'n' *ov.* 'N'; *bef. del.* 'two'

76.18 bit['s' *del.*] of] *bef. del.* '**perceptual**'

76.18-19 was . . . framed.] *ab. del.* 'have [*insrtd.*] ever repeated themselves exactly.'

76.19 writes] *ab. del.* 'says Pro'

76.20 love] *aft. del.* 'carelessness,'

††76.20-21 & . . . care,] *intrl.*

76.21 instead] *alt. fr.* 'in their stead'

76.22 often] *ab. del.* 'sometimes'

76.23 which] *bef. del.* 'every hour'

76.23   hour by hour] *intrl.*
77.1   its] *insrtd. for del.* 'its severer'
77.1   untiringly] *aft. del.* 'piles ceaseless'
77.2   remake an Aristotle] ('an' *intrl.*); *ab. del.* 'again form Newton'
77.2   ²an] *intrl.*
77.3   (*twice*) a] *intrl.*
77.3-4   Can . . . again] ('our' *aft. del.* 'the'; 'ever' *del. then restored; del.* 'once more' *ab.* 'again [*del. then restored*]'); *opp. mrgn. circled* 'stet'
77.4   ferns,] *intrl.*
77.5   the same] *ab. del.* 'those'
77.5   crawl] *aft. del.* 'roam'
††77.5-6   & wallow] *intrl.*
77.6   did] *bef. del.* 'bef'
77.7   moves on] *ab. del.* 'passes'
77.7   an . . . tread,] *ab. del.* '['indefati' *del.*] untiring steps,'
77.8   strikes] *ab. del.* 'passes'
77.8   an . . . hour.] *ab. del.* 'over the same dial.'
77.10   can never] *alt. fr.* 'cannot'
77.10   reversed.] *aft. del.* 'undone.'
77.11   The] *alt. fr.* 'This'
77.11   everlasting . . . being] ('coming' *ab. del.* 'irruption'; 'concrete' *intrl.*); *ab. del.* 'desire of'
77.11-12   obvious['ly' *del.*]] *bef. del.* 'true'
77.12   rationalizing] *aft. del.* 'human *in [doubtful]*'
77.12   ever] *intrl.*
77.13   but] *aft. del.* 'save'
77.14   treats] *ab. del.* 'abandons'
77.14   flux] *insrtd. for del.* 'world'
77.15   unceasing] *bef. del.* 'm [*doubtful*]'
77.15-16   mixture, of] ('ture' *aft. del.* 'ture'); *bef. del.* '['elements that' *del.*] unchanging'
77.16   elements] *underline del.*
77.17   only] *intrl.*
77.17   for] *intrl.*
77.18   once] *ab. del. insrtd.* 'which'
††77.18   graspt . . . there] *insrtd. for del.* '['is able to see them ['b[*illeg.*]' *del.*] swarming beneath' *del.*] once attains ['to' *del.*] that [*alt. fr.* 'the'] *['conviction,' *del.*] persuasion, [*ab. del.* 'vision,'] ['of them,' *del.*] there'
77.20   ^science,^] *sg. qts. del.; bef. del.*

'to-day'
77.20   signifies] *ab. del.* 'is'
77.20   only] *bef. del.* 'that of'
77.21   the primal] *ab. del.* 'an original'
77.21   parting] *aft. del.* 'coming'
77.21   meeting . . . us] ('us' *in pencil*); *ab. del.* '[*on fol.* 63] meeting *so as to take on [*ab. del.* 'in'] infinitely diversified *shapes in [*ab. del.* 'forms in'] | [*fol.* 65] the eyes of'
77.22   spectators] *bef. pencil del.* 'like ourselves'
77.22   the] *insrtd.*
77.22   configurations] *in pencil ab. pencil del.* '['collections' *del.*] shapes [*period del.*] to'
77.23   name['s' *del.*]] *aft. del.* 'give the'
77.23   as] *ab. del.* 'of'
77.24-26   —On . . . 22-30.] *under mrgn.* 'Note continued'
77.26   N. Y., 1903,] *intrl.*
77.28   first] *aft. del.* 'fo'
77.28   370] '3' *ov.* '4'
77.29   may] 'ay' *ov.* 'i'
77.31   explanation] *bef. del.* ', the peripatatics or scholastics, continuing the Aristotelian tradition,'
77.31   day,] *comma alt. fr. period*
77.31   for . . . defend] ('some' *aft. del.* 'when'; 'chemists' *bef. del.* 'are'; 'still defend' *ab. del.* 'renewing'); *ab. del.* '"Energetic," in the person of Ostwald & Duhem'
††77.32   which . . . long_^] ('the' *ov.* 'Des'); *ab. del. comma*
77.33   our] *ab. del.* 'that we have the'
77.33   ¹that] *aft. del.* 'that H² & O persist unchanged in 'water,' or'
77.35   assumes] *aft. del.* 'that'
77.36-43   for . . . . —Also] *insrtd.*
77.37   but now manifest['ed' *del.*]] *ab. del.* 'and have assumed'
77.38   feel] *ab. del.* 'notice'
77.41   nonsense."] *period alt. fr. colon; db. qt. added*
78.1   physical] *aft. del.* 'the [*intrl.*]'
78.1   Nature] *ab. del.* 'Science'
78.1   few of us] *ab. del.* 'few['f' *ov.* 'F'] men'
78.2   postulate] *aft. del.* 'doubt the'
78.2   notion] *ab. del.* 'concepts'

78.3 mixture] *bef. del.* 'explains so much, and'

78.3-6 adopt . . . sense] ('attributes' *bel. del.* 'qualities'; 'uniform' *aft. del.* 'absolutely'; 'mathematical sense.' *insrtd. for del.* 'sense.'); *ab. del.* 'are *more than [*ab. del.* 'content'] content to believe in the *inalterability [*alt. fr.* 'inalterable'] ['['of' *del.*] both of' *del.*] of real being and in the ['absolute' *del.*] uniformity of law'

78.8 surface] *aft. del.* 'apparent'

78.8 perceptual] *ab. del.* '['the' *del.*] apparent'

78.8 variety.] *in pencil ab. pencil del.* 'facts.'

78.8 when we come] *aft. del.* 'only'; *bef. del.* 'to living creatures, and especially'

78.9 changes.] *period insrtd. bef. del.* 'so'

78.9 It . . . that] *intrl.*

78.9-10 ²our . . . only] 'our ['o' *ov.* 'O'] *own subjective experiences [*insrtd. for del.* 'feelings'] are *'really' only [*insrtd. bef. del.* 'hard to conceive as so many']'

78.10 arrangements] *init.* 're' *del.*

78.11 beings of a] *ab. del.* '['psychic in their inner nature.' *del.*] fundamentally'

78.11 kind.] *ab. del.* 'entities. [*ab. del.* 'facts.']'

78.12 indeed] *intrl.*

78.13 but] *bef. del.* 'how'

78.14 ¹is] *aft. del.* '*is*'

78.14 Psychologically] 'P' *alt. fr.* 'p'

††78.15 Our experiences [*comma del.*]] ('O' *unreduced in error*); *moved fr. aft.* 'felt?' [78.14]

78.15 reduction, and] *comma ov. period*; 'and' *insrtd.*

78.15 ²our] 'o' *ov.* 'O'; *bef. del.* 'concrete'

78.16 taken simply] *ab. del.* 'are,'

78.16 remain] *intrl.*

78.17 order] *bef. del. period*

78.17 the signals] *ab. del.* 'the determine [*doubtfully alt. fr.* 'determining'] conditions'

78.18 of] *insrtd. for del.* 'of'

78.18 ¹the] *alt. fr.* 'their'

†78.18-20 Biography . . . biographies,] *insrtd. for del.* 'The perceptual flux, in short, is *the [*ab. del.* 'an'] authentic *stuff [*ab. del.* 'factor part'] of each of our biografies; and biografy or life *is

the only ['full' *del.*] immediate form in which ['whatever' *del.*] [*ab. del.* 'is the *full [*ab. del.* 'full'] concrete ['centre of' *del.*] central backbone of'] all ['the' *del.*] experience ['that' *del.*] actually *comes [*ab. del.* 'is'] —*all that [*insrtd. for del.* 'what [*ab. del.* 'whatever ['is' *del.*] more *there is [*intrl.*] is but conceptual building out']'] is is actually given—whatever *else [*ab. del.* 'more'] may be believed in, *consists of [*ab. del.* 'is but'] *['abstract' *del.*] secondary [*intrl.*] conceptual *additions ['to' *del.*] ['of abstractions to' *del.*] [*ab. del.* 'building out round'] to [*intrl.*] this perceptual core.'

78.18 concrete] *aft. del.* 'immediate [*intrl.*]'

78.19 given; the] *semicolon alt. fr. period*; 't' *ov.* 'T'

78.19 ²the] *intrl.*

78.19 authentic] *in pencil ab. pencil del.* 'authentic constituent'

††78.19-20 of . . . biografies∧] *moved by guideline to bef.* 'the' [¹78.19] *but then guideline pencil del.*

††78.20 biografies∧] *bef. del.* '; *and [*undel. in error*] whatever else *we [*ab. del.* 'may be'] believe['d' *del.*] in consists *only [*ab. del.* 'but'] of secondary conceptual additions to this perceptual core.'

78.20 and . . . perfect] *pencil insrtd. for pencil del.* 'and [*insrtd.*] biografically ['b' *ov.* 'B'] we ['lif' *ink del.*] live *in [*undel. in error; ab. ink del.* 'ever on the edge of growing novelty.'] a perfect'

78.20 effervescence] *ab. del.* 'cataract'

78.20 novelty] *alt. fr.* 'novelties'

78.21 all the time.] *intrl. in pencil w. pencil caret ov. ink period*

78.21-22 inventions, enterprises,] *ab. del.* 'buildings,'

78.22 burst] *aft. del.* 'break'

78.23 ['attribute' *del.*] resolve] *ab. del.* 'analyze'

78.23 into] *ab. del.* 'in'

78.23 they] *alt. fr.* 'the'; *bef. del.* 'abstract [*intrl.*]'

78.23-24 belong . . . kinds,] *ab. del.* 'kinds of things they are are old,'

78.24 no one] *ab. del.* 'each'

78.24 them] *bef. del.* 'as'

78.24 full] *ab. del.* 'concrete'

78.25 ¹ever] *alt. fr.* 'never'

78.25 or] *ab. del.* 'and never'

78.25 ever come] *ab. del.* 'be here'

78.25 Men of] *insrtd. for del.* 'The irresistible impression yielded to by scientific men of'

78.26 forget] *aft. del.* '['turn' *del.*] become untechnical,'

78.26 theoretic] *in pencil ab. pencil del.* 'technical [*alt. in ink fr.* 'technicalities,']'

78.26 abstractions,] *intrl.*

78.27 else,] *ab. del.* 'else,'

78.27 ³as] *ab. del.* 'as'

78.28 naively] *bef. del.* 'as anyone *that the world is really growing, [*pencil del.*]'

78.28 even now] *intrl.*

78.28 is] *ab. del.* 'is *still [*intrl.*] in the'

78.28 they] *aft. del.* 'their own *personal [*intrl.*] decisions are determinants'

78.29 'original∧] *sg. qt. del.; intrl.*

78.29 help ... future] ('determine what' *insrtd. for del.* 'create whatever'); *ab. del.* '*contributing to the [*ab. del.* 'are helping to determine what *novelty [*alt. fr.* 'novelties'] that [*intrl.*]'

78.30 become.] *alt. fr.* 'be.'

78.31 I have] *opp. mrgn. pencil* '¶'

78.31 live or] *insrtd.*

78.31 order] *intrl.*

78.32 view.] *period aft. del. comma formed fr. period*

78.32 Conception] *opp. pencil del. insrtd. passage brought by guideline to bef.* 'Conception' *reading* '['So much for the *problematic alternative. [*undel. in error; ab. del.* 'general problematic situation.]' *del.*] In ['closing in upon the question so as to' *del.*] working ['ing' *added*] out *my [*ab. del.* 'our'] own conclusions, I shall ['divide' *del.*] treat of the perceptual view and the conceptual view in two distinct chapters and sum up in a third.'

78.32 Conception knows] *insrtd. for del.* '*Conceptually we know [*insrtd. for pencil del.* '*The ['T' *ov.* 't'] one [*ab.*

ink *del.* 'Perception is'] dynamic, dramatic, and full of **novelty**, *the other [*ab. ink del.* 'while ['perception' *del.*] conception is'] static, and *ever seeking to [*ab. ink del.* '*one of [*intrl.*] its ['s' *added*] ['has' *del.*] chief explanatory interests is *ever **trying [*alt. fr.* 'try'] to [*undel. in error*] ['a passion for' *del.*] [*ab. ink del.* 'to']'] explain['ing' *added then ink del.*] novelty away. (*begin ink del.*)[*del.* 'We can ['expl' *del.*] explain *logically [*init.* 'l' *in pencil ov. doubtful* 'L'] only by deducing the ident'] **Logically we can or intellectually we have**']'

78.34 if the] *ab. del.* 'in [*ov.* 'a'] a'

78.34 is to be ['made' *del.*]] *intrl.*

78.34 rationalized] *ab. del.* '['account' *del.*] intelligible no'

78.34 no] *insrtd.*

78.35 really ['be.' *del.*] come.] *ab. del.* 'ever appear.'

78.35 traits] *ab. del.* 'points'

78.35 that] *alt. fr.* 'the'

78.36 conceptualism] *ab. del.* '*conceptual translation [*ab. del.* '['intellectu' *del.*] the intellectualistic method']'

78.36-37 conceptualism] *ab. del.* '['neither' *del.*] it'

78.37 change] *bef. del.* 'an'

78.37 translate] *aft. del.* 'give *us [*intrl.*] no conceptual equivalent for them, and is forced, against the irresistible *sense [*ab. del.* 'impression'] of life within us,'

79.1-2 forced∧ ... us∧] *commas del.*

79.1 to] *insrtd.*

79.1 contradict] *ab. del.* 'against'

79.1 indestructible] *ab. del.* '**authentic**'

79.2 us∧] *comma del.*

79.2 by] *insrtd. for del.* 'to'

79.2 denying] 'ing' *added*

79.2 grows] 's' *added; aft. del.* 'can'

79.3-18 It ... Infinite.] *pencil insrtd. by pencil and ink guideline for del.* '*No originality, ['for it,' *pencil del. insrtd.*] save in the aboriginal; [*intrl.*] Time *for it [*insrtd.*] is unreal; ['for absolute idealism,' *del.*] God is *eternally the same, [*ab. del.* 'immutable,'] for rationalistic philosophy *stagnates; [*intrl.*] and in all monistic systems the *whole [*intrl.*] world of *mutation [*ab. del.* 'change and happening'] is *only [*doubtful* 'are' *del.*] a [*ab. del.* '['a mirage' *del.*] relative'] mirage. [¶] Suppose *now that [*intrl.*] we assume, without further argument at this point, that ['the verdict of' *del.*] perception *may be [*ab. del.* 'is'] truthful [*caret del.*] in its essence at least; that, even though we may be mistaken as to ['the' *del.*] when and where they come, *authentic ['real genuine' *del.*] [*ab. del.* 'real'] novelties do come into being, and that ['being genuinely' *del.*] (*begin indep. del.*) *reality **does [*pencil insrtd.*] literally ***alters ['s' *undel. in error*] [*ab. del.* 'therefore genuinely changes'] and grow['s' *del.*] in certain spots. This is the pluralist-empiricist view, adopting the perceptual data un-transmuted, and *so [*intrl.*] uncompromisingly expressed that one may say [*del. intrl.* 'as probably to'] that it *will [*intrl.*] scandalize['d' *del.*] ['the' *del.*] the ordinarily soi-disant empiricist as much as it (*end indep. del.*) *Parts [*ab. del.* 'The details'] of the future *will then be genuinely [*ab. del.* 'are in short'] absent *from [*insrtd. for del.* 'through and through from'] the present, ['absent' *del.*] not absent merely ['as to the perceptual' *del.*] in [*intrl.*] fact, *while ['but but' *del.*] fully **represented [*insrtd. for del.* 'anticipated'] in their [*ab. del.* 'of them, and present in their'] posse and *by [*ab. del.* 'as to'] their necessitating *cause, [*còmma insrtd.*] [*del.* '(['this is' *del. intrl.*] as the monistic tradition) ['claimed),' *del.*]'] but absent *utterly, [*ab. del.* 'in every way,'] so that [*del.* 'so far as any *hold of [*ab. del.* 'power over'] them ['is' *del.*] the present *has [*ab. del.* 'goes,']'] they are pure-chance additions to ['what' *del.*] the world, ['contains,' *del.*] *so far as any hold of them goes which the present may **exert. [*ab. del.* 'possess.'] [*intrl.*] This is the pluralist-empiricist view, so uncompromisingly exprest that *it shocks the usual [*ab. del.* 'one may say that the

ordinary'] empiricist teaching [*del.* 'goes against ['it' *del.*] almost as much as *it contradicts all [*intrl.; undel. in error*] rationalist tradition']'
[*begin pencil inscription*]
79.3   It] *aft. ink del.* ink note 'the one obliged to deny what the other affirms'
79.3   to . . . student] *intrl.*
79.5   history] *aft. del. intrl. illeg. word*
79.6   seems . . . continuity;] *['raises the question of' *del.*] seems to ['break upon' *del.*] violate [*ab. del.* 'connects with ['dis' *del.*]'] continuity;'
†79.7 seems . . . gradation;] *ab. del.* 'connects itself with infinity;'
79.7   connects] *intrl. bef. smudged poss.* '*insist on having [*intrl.*]'
79.8   general—] *dash intrl.*
79.9   It] *aft. del.* 'Certain'
79.9   to pass] *ab. del.* 'about'
79.10 been . . . necessitate] *ab. del.* '['led to the admission' *del.*] seemed to some thinkers'
79.11 along] *ink intrl.*
79.11 this its] '*this [*ov. pencil* 'the'] its [*ink*]' *ab. ink del.* 'the finite constitution its'
79.12 or, . . . words,] *commas ink insrtd.*
79.14 Thus] *doubtfully alt. fr.* 'This'
79.14 we find the] *intrl.*
79.14 already] *ab. del.* 'thus'
79.15-16 at . . . ¹of] *intrl.*
79.17 first.] *aft. del.* ', before'
79.18 Infinite.] *bel. is pencil note marked off by pencil line* '**Begin** this new chapter at the other end of the book, p. 70ᵃ'
80.1   The] *aft. del.* '[¶] The alternative that confronts us is that between ['two ways' *del.*] conceiving the *novelty [*alt. fr.* 'novelties'] ['that come' *del.*] as continuously or as discontinuously added. Let *me [*alt. fr.* 'my'] call the discontinuous addition tychistic, and the continuous addition synech'; *bef. pencil del.* 'great [*in pencil ab. pencil del.* 'first']'
†80.1 which . . . of] *ab. del.* '['whether' *del.*] whether it is more rational to assume that a *dis m [*doubtful*]'
80.2   continuous] 't' *ov.* 'd'

80.2   that of] *ab. del.* 'a'

80.2-3   to . . . exists.] *in pencil ab. pencil del.* 'of the novelty [*ink del.* 'admitted' *ab. ink del.* 'supposed'] postulation. Discontinuous addition goes with what I shall call a *tychistic*, continuous addition with what I shall call a *synechistic* pattern of the universe.ˣ | *ˣ*Tychistic from τύχη, meaning chance; synechistic from συνεχὴς, connected. I take these names from C. S. Peirce [*blue pencil del.*]'

80.4-81.9   On . . . divisibility] *substituted for del.* '[¶] ['With' *del.*] The ['T' *ov.* 't'] notions [*ab. del.* 'assumption'] of continuity *and [*ab. del.* 'that'] of infinity *are [*ov.* 'is'] inseparable. If space *& [*ab. caret formed fr. orig. comma*] time *for example [*ab. del.* ', matter,* change, are not *['disc' *del.*] built up [*ab. del.* 'composed'] of ultimate units, ['each being in' *del.*] each inseparable, but'] have a continuous constitution, that means that any part of them, ['which' *del.*] however small, which you *suppose [*ab. del.* 'may take, is'] may be *mentally [*ab. del.* 'ideally'] halved or otherwise divided, and the ['same' *del.*] process repeated on the subdivisions, endlessly. [*del.* '['Otherwise' *del.*] ['The form of extension for' *del.*] If you have any *time [*ab. del.* 'space'] at all, for instance, *its ['s' *added*] ['must have an' *del.*] later bound must be distinct from its earlier one, and ['another bound can' *del.*] it must have a later and an earlier *half, [*comma ov. period*] ['If these' *del.*] and you can insert *an ideal [*undel. in error; ab. del.* 'a'] bound between them.'] For if time, for example, could become so *minutely subdivided that its **last [*intrl.*] parts should fail *** each of them [*intrl.*] to show ['each' *del.*] [*ab. del.* 'small as not to have'] a later & an earlier *half, *the [*ab. del.* 'its bounds would not be separate,'] later and earlier *bounds of these parts [*intrl.*] would coalesce, or in other words *they [*ab. del.* 'it'] would cease to have *duration. [*period ov. comma*]

But [*ab. del.* 'and one'] it is impossible to see how ['out of' *del.*] durationless units can by any amount of addition form duration. The same is true of *extension. [*period ab. del. comma*] [*del.* 'change *& [*doubtful*] motion, etc. We *must [*ab. del.* 'have'] therefore to deny discrete composition']'

80.4   the] *bef. del.* 'tychistic'

80.4   of discontinuity,] ('discontinuity' *alt. fr.* 'discontinuous'); *intrl.*

80.5   either] 'i' *ov.* 'a'

†80.5   nothing . . . certain] *ab. del.* 'those'

80.6   'at] (*sg. qt. added*); *aft. del.* '[', or nothing.' *del.*] all'

80.6   a stroke.] *ab. del.* 'once or nothing.'

80.6   Every] ('E' *alt. fr.* 'e'); *aft. del.* '[*del.* 'The composition of the universe on this view would be'] Numerically considered,'

80.6   feature] *ab. del.* 'part'

80.7   numerical] *intrl.*

80.8   atoms,] *comma insrtd.*

†80.8   not . . . atoms,] *intrl.*

80.10   any . . . of] *ab. del.* '['time' *del.*] the'

80.10   time, space, change,] *final* 's' *del. fr. each*

80.11   we] *aft. del.* '['we saw' *del.*] ['would' *del.*] exist would'

80.13   is] *aft. del.* 'of'

80.14   We] *bef. del.* 'are'

80.14   perceive] *ab. del.* 'aware of'

80.14   something] *aft. del.* 'of [*undel. in error*] a sensible amount'; *bef. del.* 'as [*doubtful*] sensible'

80.17-18   content or] ('content' *pencil intrl. bef. pencil del.* 'space'); *intrl.*

80.19   Intellectually] ('I' *ov.* 'i'); *aft. del.* 'Reflectively and'

80.19   and on reflection] *intrl.*

80.20   immediately] *intrl.*

80.20   they] *aft. del.* 'it is totally'

80.21   come] *ab. del.* 'are given'

80.22   If,] (*comma insrtd.*); *opp. mrgn.* '¶'

80.22   however,] *intrl.*

80.22-23   ¹as . . . data,] *ab. del.* 'conceptually [*ab. del.* 'abstractly']'

81.1   drops or] *intrl.*

81.1   themselves] *aft. del.* 'not'; *bef. del.* 'extend [*doubtful*]'

81.2   inconceivable] *ab. del.* 'impossible'
81.2   adding] *ab. del.* 'summing'
81.3   together] *ab. caret formed fr. orig. comma*
81.3   times . . . spaces] *final* 's' *added to each*
81.3   accrue.] *ab. del.* 'result.'
81.5   temporal] *aft. del.* 'drop of'
81.6   spatial] *aft. del.* 'tempor'
81.6   halves] *alt. fr.* 'half'
81.7   on] *in pencil ab. pencil del.* 'on'
81.8   that] *aft. del.* 'of'
81.9   of] *bef. del.* 'its in an'
†81.10   some . . . with] ('some' *bef. del.* 'tracts'); *ab. del.* 'finite parts of our experience and'
81.11   expansibility] *alt. fr.* 'susceptibility'
81.11   of others] ('s' *added*); *aft. del.* 'to addition'; *bef. del.* 'facts'
81.11   has] *insrtd. for del.* '[*del.* 'involves paradoxes and apparent contradictions which ['have long been' *del.*] have long figured among philosophy's dialectic'] been'
81.12   problems.] *ab. del.* 'difficulties.'
81.13   me] *ab. del.* 'us'
81.15   'How] ('H' *ov.* 'h'); *aft. del.* 'of the *infinite, [comma alt. fr. semicolon]*'
81.17   make] *aft. del.* 'ask 'how'
81.17   When] 'W' *triple underl.*
81.18   such] *ab. del.* 'that'
81.19   with] *bef. del.* 'Zenos'
81.19   against] *ab. del.* 'about'
81.22   points] *bef. del.* 'possessed of magnitude,'
81.23   were meant] *ab. del.* 'tended'
81.23   really] *ab. del.* 'exist, but'
81.24   truly] *intrl.*
81.25   If] *aft. del.* 'His'
81.25   a] *alt. fr.* 'an'
81.25   flying] *intrl.*
81.27   rests,] *comma ov. period*
81.27   for it] *ab. del.* 'It'
81.27   any] *ab. del.* 'the'
81.28   cannot . . . as] *ab. del.* '['must be some' *del.*] cannot be'
81.29   discretely constituted.] *ab. del.* 'compounded.'
81.30   Still] *opp. mrgn.* '¶'
81.31   Suppose] *aft. del.* 'Let'

81.31   tortoise,] *bef. del.* 'and *let [ab. del.* 'give'] the tortoise ['an inch of' *del.*] have an inch head start. Zeno assuming'
81.31   move] *ab. del.* 'go'
81.33   inch,] *bef. del.* 'the torto'
81.33   advanced to] *ab. del.* 'caught up with'
81.35   While] ('W' *triple underl.*); *ab. del.* 'By the time'
81.36   H.] *intrl.*
81.36-37   difficulties] *alt. fr.* 'difficulty'
81.37   consciousness] *aft. del.* 'reference to'
81.38   J. Burnet['t' *del.*]] 'J.' *intrl.*
81.38-39   Pythagoreans)] *paren ov. comma*
81.40   XX] *aft. del.* 'vol'
82.1   inch,] *comma ov. period*
82.1   successive] *intrl.*
82.1   points] *bef. del.* 'success'
82.2   series] *bef. del.* ', of which the limit is the distance'
82.3   Achilles.] *period alt. fr. semicolon bef. del.* 'as follows:—'
82.6-9   Zeno . . . gets] *insrtd. for del.* '['but by no' *del.*] But if space be infinitely divisible (and Zeno assumes that it is so) this series is interminable. *['As often as' *del.*] Each time that [*ab. del.* 'Whenever [*ab. del.* 'Always while'] ']Achilles *['has' *del.*] gets [*alt. fr.* 'got'] [*ab. del.* 'is getting'] '
82.7   occupied] *bef. del.* 'in succession'
82.9-10   it . . . that] *intrl.*
82.10   has already] *ab. del.* 'is'
82.10   moved] *alt. fr.* 'moving'
82.10   a . . . and] *ab. del.* 'his *own [intrl.]* next point, and they never reach'
82.11   ¹the] *alt. fr.* 'their'
82.11   interval . . . points] ('the' *alt. fr.* 'them'); *ab. del.* 'distance'
82.11   it] *aft. del.* 'they'
82.12   the] *alt. fr.* 'they'
82.12   two . . . should] *ab. del.* 'should *ever [insrtd.]* '
82.12-13   any one] *ab. del.* 'the ['las' *del.*] ['som' *del.*] same'
82.13   moment] *ab. del.* 'time'
82.13   Achilles] 'A' *ov.* 'a'
82.13-14   tortoise,] *bef. del.* 'at all,'

82.14   his] *aft. del.* 'he's the tort'
82.14   were] *ab. del.* 'is'
82.16   simply] *aft. del.* 'cannot'
†82.17-18   ['traverse' *del.*] exhaust, . . .
  them,] ('the' *aft. del.* 'and exhaust';
  'them,' *insrtd. for del.* 'it,'); *ab. del.*
  'occupy successively (be the time
  required long or short)'
82.18   which] *aft. del. comma; bef. del.*
  'series [*intrl.*]'
82.18   their] *ab. del.* 'its'
†82.19   ¹to . . . end.] *ab. del.* 'to be
  ['endless.' *del.*] ['interminable.' *del.*]
  endless.'
82.20   Zeno's] *aft. del.* '['The' *del.*]
  Achilles'; *opp. mrgn.* '¶'
82.20   were] *aft. del.* 'tend thus to prove
  that neither space, time, nor ['moth'
  del.] motion can be treated as ['a' *del.*]
  sums [*final* 's' *added*] of points, that
  the *minima sensibilia of [*ab. del.*
  'perceptual units in'] which ['our perception gets them are not the real' *del.*]
  they consist *for [*ab. del.* 'according
  to'] our perception, are not the real
  'being" of them, and finally that real
  being'
82.20   the 'Eleatic'] ('E' *alt. fr.* 'e'); *aft.
  del.* 'his monistic'
82.21   The] ('T' *ov.* 't'); *aft. del.* 'Neither
  space, time, motion, nor changing being
  can be treated as sums of points;'
82.22   space . . . change] *ab. del.* 'they'
82.23   subdivide . . . *infinitum.*] *ab. del.*
  '[*del.* 'lead to interminable processes
  of'] decompose. [*alt. fr.* 'decomposi-
  tion.'] Our perception, being of a
  'many,' is thus false. Real being is continuous, is one. Points *or numbers
  [*intrl.*] cannot *successfully [*intrl.*]
  sum themselves into a continuum, and'
82.24   The] 'T' *ov.* 't'
82.25   hopeless] *intrl.*
82.26   Our own ['contemporary' *del.*]]
  ('O' *triple underl.*); *ab. del.* 'The'; *opp.
  mrgn.* '¶'
82.26   meanwhile] *ab. del.* 'at last'
82.26   what] *aft. del.* 'what to them is an
  adequate point'
82.28   speak again] *ab. del.* 'treat'
82.28-29   return] *ab. del.* 'revert'

82.30   upon] *aft. del.* 'of'
82.31   infinite,] *comma ov. period*
82.31   which . . . section] *ab. del.* 'This
  was Kant's chapter on'
82.31   'Antinomies'] *aft. del.* 'And'
82.33   Kant's] (''s' *added*); *aft. del.* 'What'
82.33   views need] *ab. del.* 'says requires'
†82.33-34   points . . . or] *ab. del.* 'words
  [*ab. del.* 'points'] of explanation. 1.
  That *real or [*ab. del.* 'whatever has']';
  '1. . . . or' *opp. mrgn.* '¶'
82.34   must be] *bef. del.* 'in all respects'
82.35-83.1   dim as to] *ab. del.* 'uncertain'
82.36   This] *ab. del.* 'Which'
82.36   that] *alt. fr.* 'the'
82.36   common . . . of] *ab. del.* 'usual way
  of refuting'
82.36   which] *ab. del.* '**by**'
82.37   **charges**] *alt. fr.* 'charging'
82.37   it] *ab. del.* 'him'
82.37   trying to prove] *insrtd. for del.*
  'saying [*insrtd. for del.* 'needi ['i' *ov.*
  's'; *insrtd. for del.* 'meaning' *ab. del.*
  'maintaining']']'
82.37   overtake] (*alt. fr.* 'overtaking'); *aft.
  del.* 'avert'
82.37   Achilles] *ab. del.* 'he'
82.38   time.] *bef. del.* 'What he *would
  [*intrl.*] require['s' *del.*] is to terminate
  an infinite *number [*ab. del.* 'series']
  of steps in any time'
83.1   see] *underline del.*
83.1   doubtful] *bef. del.* 'as to'
83.2   believe] *underline del.*
83.2   regarding them;] *ab. caret formed
  fr. orig. semicolon*
83.2-3   subjective] *aft. del.* 'vague'
83.3   by] *intrl.*
83.3   exist in] *ab. del.* '*form a [*ab. del.*
  'exist *objectively [*intrl.*] in']'
83.4   number∧] 's' *del.*
83.4   our] *alt. fr.* 'your'
83.4   we] *aft. del.* 'and'
83.5   feel certain,] *ab. del.* 'never doubt
  it,'
83.6   *countable*] *alt. fr.* '*enumerable*'
83.6   to] *intrl.*
83.6   group] *ab. del.* 'sum'
83.7   some] *ab. del.* 'must *make up [*ab.
  del.* '['form' *del.*] be in form'] a'
83.7   must] 'm' *ov. period*

83.8   can never] *alt. fr.* 'cannot'
83.8   completely] *alt. fr.* 'completed by'
83.9   words] *bef. del.* '3'
83.11   anything] *aft. del.* 'a reality is to exist object'
83.11   'given'] *aft. del.* 'really'
83.15   equally] *intrl.*
83.15   past] *aft. del.* '['pa' *del.*] the'
83.18   But [*insrtd.*] the] 't' *of* 'the' *ov.* 'T'
83.18   these] *aft. del.* 'all'; *bef. del.* 'three'
83.18   defy] *aft. del.* 'form'
83.18   ²the] 't' *ov.* 'T'
†83.19-31 |*finitum* ... philosophy] *substituted for del.* '*finitum*, [*comma ov. period*] *['previous' del.*] ['previous ['p' *ov.* 'P']' *del.*] and [*ab. del.* 'Past'] times and causes form an infinitely regressive *series; [*semicolon alt. fr. colon*] ['What becomes here of' *del.*] ['But the axiom that *all [*intrl.*] reality is determinate requires that' *del.*] ['and infinite series' *del.*] ['and' *del.*] *Of [*ov.* 'in'] an [*intrl.*] infinite series [*del.* '['are never 'given' but in indefinite amount' *del.*] you can always add *more [*ab. del.* 'other'] terms to those that are actually 'given,' so that the['ir' *del.*] numerical value of such'] the numerical value is always *indefinite, [*comma ov. period*] [*comma del.*] while [*insrtd. for del.* '*Such ['S' *triple underl.*] a series [*ab. del.* 'and'] can never be 'completed by successive addition,' ['and' *del.*] in other words ['can' *del.*] ['so that between' *del.*] the reality or givenness ['of the supposed fact' *del.*] in point of fact of the supposed 'conditions,' and their infinity in point of form, seem to contradict one another.'] What ['W' *unreduced in error*] is *real [*ab. del.* 'actual'] or given must be numerically *fixed: [*insrtd. for del.* 'definite; what is infinite must be indefinite.'] so that the *infinite [*ab. del.* 'conditions'] form of the conditions *we are considering [*ab. del.* 'supposed here'] would seem to be ['rationally' *del. intrl.*] incompatible with ['the fact of' *del.*] their *existing in fact, [*ab. del.* '*having actually **to [*intrl.*] exist, [*insrtd. for del.* 'existence.']'] *for then they would have to

be in fixed amount. [*insrtd. for del.* 'if they do exist in fact, terms ['which' *del.*] would demand['s' *del.*] ['fully' *del. intrl.*] determinate [*alt. fr.* 'determination']'] [¶] Kant ['calls' *del.*] gives the name of 'antinomies' to *this [*alt. fr.* 'these'] *kind of [*intrl.*] incompatibility; [*alt. fr.* 'incompatibilities of reason;'] and his way of extrication from *it [*insrtd. for del.* 'them'] is one of the most original strokes in his philosophy.'
83.20   series] *aft. del.* 'regressive'
83.22   value,] ('v' *ov. comma*); *insrtd.*
83.22   for] *ab. del.* 'its numerical'
83.22   is] *insrtd. for del.* 'being [*insrtd. for del. doubtful* 'is']'
83.22   whereas] *ab. del.* 'while that of'
83.23   'whole] *aft. del.* 'the [*alt. fr.* 'they'; *del. in error*] are *'all' [*intrl.*] really 'given' conditions to ['be fixed.' *del.*] form a fixed numerical amount.'
83.24   really] *intrl.*
††83.24   exist in] *ab. del.* 'form a'
83.26   Of] 'O' *triple underl.*
83.26   postulate,] *ab. del.* 'axiom,'
83.28   The] ('T' *ov.* 't'); *aft. del.* 'To'
83.29   numerical] *aft. del.* 'deter'
83.29   was ascribed] ('ascribed' *ab. del.* 'called'); *aft. del.* ', [*comma del. in error*] ['Kant gave the name of 'antinomy' of' *del.*] was traced through'
83.30   puzzle] *aft. del.* 'dialectic'
83.31   one] *ov. doubtful* 'an'
83.31   prettiest] *aft. del.* 'most'
83.32   exist] *aft. del.* 'poss [*insrtd.*]'
83.32   it ... that] *intrl.*
83.33   exist] *bef. del.* ', he says,'
83.33   *sich,] comma ov. period*
83.33   but] *ab. del.* 'They *can [*intrl.*] exist'
83.33   Indefiniteness] ('I' *ov.* 'i'); *aft. del.* 'Between *a merely phenomenal [*ab. del.* 'exist their'] existence in that shape *and [*undel. in error*] their'
83.34   amount] *aft. del.* '['an' *del.*] given [*ab. del.* 'numerical']'
83.34   is] *ab. del.* 'there is'
83.34   not] 't' *added*
83.34   incompatible] *alt. fr.* 'incompatibility'

†83.34 with . . . existence,] *ab. caret formed fr. orig. period*

83.35 whether . . . conditioning,] *intrl.*

83.36 form] *aft. del.* 'or'

83.36 of them] *ab. del.* 'in which they appear ['means only that' *del.*] is only *the susceptibility [*ab. del.* 'their potentiality'] of *further [*insrtd.*] subdivision or prolongation [*period del.*] which they present. [*del.* 'It isn't given as a fact, but only as a'] This suscepti-bility ['is only a' *del.*]'

83.36 we] *insrtd. for del.* 'we'

83.38 go on] *bel. mrgn.* 'Note'

83.39 acts of] *intrl.*

83.40 falls into] *ab. del.* 'consists of'

83.41 Kant] *aft. del.* '['T' *del.*] Kant uses'

83.42 only] *aft. del.* 'on'

83.42 (or . . . task),] *ab. caret formed fr. orig. comma*

††83.43 *gegeben,] comma ov. period; bef. del.* '[*del.* ', and this pun is one of the best things in his book.'] or existent in determinate amount. It must be confest that Kant['s' *del.*] ['escape from his' *del.*] showed a successful way of over-coming the antinomies of'

84.1-2 Such . . . it.] *insrtd.; opp. mrgn.* '¶'

84.2 a bad ['an' *del.*] ambiguity] *ab. del.* 'a fallacy'

84.2 the] *ab. del.* 'Kant's'

84.3 'absolute] *aft. del.* ' 'whole sum,' of conditions being given, *or [*undel. in error*] of the'

84.3 totality] 'l' *ov.* 't'

84.3 2the] *alt. fr.* 'their'

84.3 synthesis∧'] *comma del.; sg. qt. insrtd. bef. sg. qt. del. in error*

84.3-4 3of . . . that] *ab. del.* '*['the' *del.*] of the conditions, the words suggest [*ab. del.* 'we are inclined to think *of [*ab. del.* 'that']']'

††84.4-5 of . . . exist.] ('them' *alt. fr.* 'the' *bef. del.* 'conditions'); *ab. del.* 'of them must be meant.'

84.5 When . . . that] *insrtd. for del.* 'They must all'

84.5 'the] 't' *ov.* 'T'

84.6 sum] *intrl.*

84.6 it] *insrtd.*

84.7 all that the] *intrl.*

84.8 that] *bef. del.* 'be they or be they not a whole,'

84.9 demand] *aft. del.* 'requirement'

84.9 that] *ab. del.* '['consistent with' *del.*] ['compatible' *del.*] which we have a right to'

84.10 series.] *bef. del.* '[*del.* 'A number of *antinomies [2'n' *ov.* 'm'] thus fall away of themselves.'] All the antinomies relating to stationary or past conditions thus fall away of themselves. 'No part of space, however remote, must be lacking, [*sg. qt. del.*] if *this [*underline del.*] present part of space is real,' prejudices nothing as to the quantum. The same number of'

84.11 (*twice*) either] *intrl.*

84.12 'all,'] *aft. del.* 'an'

84.12 'each'] *aft. del.* 'a late'

84.12 'any.'] *period aft. del. comma*

84.13 what] *aft. del.* 'finite'

84.13 'all] *insrtd. for del.* '['in no case will any term' *del.*] ['both cases will' *del.*] 'all'

84.13 that] *alt. fr.* 'there'

84.13 will] *intrl.*

84.14 both times. But] *ab. caret formed fr. orig. period*

84.14 things] 't' *ov.* 'T'

84.14 appear under] ('appear' *ab. del.* 'we represent'); *ab. del.* 'take'

84.15 endless] *aft. del.* 'infinite'

84.15 can] *bef. del.* ', however only'

84.15 only] *intrl.*

†84.15-16 if . . . out.] ('if' *bef. del.* 'un-less'; 'wish' *ab. del.* 'are willing'; 'none' *ov.* 'some'); *intrl.*

84.16 When we] *insrtd. for del.* 'If we make a remark about [' 'any' of them' *del.*] 'any' one, or 'every' one of them, we mean ['to' *del.*] that no one should be lacking.'

84.17 fulfilled,] *ab. del.* 'given,'

84.17 impeccable] *ab. del.* 'irrefutable'

84.18 ground,] (*comma ov. period*); *bef. del.* 'If we say that 'all' must be given, meaning that'

84.18 should] *intrl.*

84.18 endless] *ab. del.* 'infinite'

84.19 we] *ab. del.* 'you can'

84.20 But] *aft. del.* 'Those [*alt. fr.* 'Those

[*alt. fr.* 'That'] '] ones ['s' *added*] your formula ['intended to' *del.*] covers ['s' *added*] by anticipation; and in the case of space, of past times, *& causes, [*intrl.*] and of the composition of'

84.20 imagine] *aft. del.* 'because of'

84.20-21 'all' to signify] *ab. del.* 'that this *involves [*ab. del.* 'means']'

84.22 not] *aft. del.* 'not only'

84.23 situation] *aft. del.* 'case, but we'

84.24 may] *intrl.*

84.24-25 to . . . again,] *moved fr. aft.* 'idealism. [*alt. fr.* 'ideal-|ism']' [84.25]; 'again,' *orig. bef. del. insrtd.* 'The antinomy is not *really [*intrl.*] as bad as ['it' *del.*] in ['appeared to' *del.*] Kant's eyes it appeared.'

††84.25 Kants] (*apostrophe omitted in error*); *intrl.*

84.26 works] *ab. del.* 'philosophy'

84.26 Renouvier,] *bef. del.* 'who regarded himself'

84.26 strongest] *ab. del.* 'most mas-|*sive [*undel. in error*]'

84.28 again] *ab. del.* 'also [*intrl.*]'

84.30 and] *aft. del.* 'and ['adopting the' *del.*] ['believing that' *del.*] he concluded that realities must'

††84.32-35 Such . . . ¹that] ('S' *unreduced in error*); *insrtd. for del.* '[*del.* 'the number of *such [*ab. del.* 'every'] realities [*alt. fr.* 'reality'] ['in all its types' *del.*] must be ['in' *del.*] finite in amount—a finite number of'] *as present beings, [*intrl.*] past ['causes of' *del.*] events and *causes, [*insrtd.*] ['and' *del. insrtd.*] ['of' *del.*] parts of matter, *steps of change, ['&' *del.*] [*ab. del.* '['of' *del.*] present *beings [*ab. del.* 'things'], and *steps of change [*ab. del.* 'the like,']'] must *needs [*intrl.*] exist in limited amount.['ˣ'*del.*] [*del.* '*Change | [*fn.*] ˣEmpty space & time Renouvier allowed to keep their infinite form, because, *unlike [*alt. fr.* 'like'] *the beings that appear in them, they ['thought them to be' *del.*] were, according['to him, only [*ab. del.* 'Kant, he regarded them not as existing *in se*, but as'] formal [*alt. fr.* 'forms'] *conditions of our sensibility. [*ab. del.* 'of our

['phenomenal' *del.*] representation only'] | must proceed by definite finite steps, for *to suppose its [*insrtd. for del.* 'its'] continuity would involve the completion of infinity. This made of him a radical pluralist. Better, he said, admit ['abrupt beginnings of' *del.*] that']'

84.33 parts of matter,] *moved fr. aft.* 'causes,' [84.33]

84.36 absolute numbers,] ('absolute' *ab. del.* 'positive'); *insrtd.*

†84.37 intellectually . . . ¹to] ('seem,' *aft. del.* 'be,'); *insrtd. for del.* '*in-[*undel. in error*]| tellectually ['incomprehensible,' *del.*] ['unmediated' *del.*] opake to us, [*ab. del.* 'unmediated ['by' *del.*] to our intelligence, than try ['to mediate one fact with another by a continuity' *del.*] to ['comprehend' *del.*] make the ultimate manyness more comprehensible by assuming a continuity that']'

84.38 rationalize] *ab. del.* 'remedy'

84.38-39 working- . . . conditions] *ab. del.* '['invoking a' *del.*] ['mediating' *del.*] the mediation of a continuity'

84.39 would] *intrl.*

84.39 involve] *final* 's' *del.*

84.39 self-] *intrl.*

85.4 gifts, ['and' *del.*]] *ab. del.* 'and'

85.4-5 and . . . faith.] *intrl.*

85.5 overlapped] *aft. del.* 'did not'

85.5 short;] *semicolon alt. fr. colon*

85.6 must] *aft. del. doubtful* 'bes'; *bef. del.* 'be begged, not'

85.6 end] *ab. del.* 'last resort'

85.6 piecemeal,] *ab. caret formed fr. orig. comma*

85.6 everlastingly] *ab. del.* 'in every case'

85.7 empiricist,] *ab. del.* 'perceptual,'

85.8 rationalist] *insrtd. for del.* 'conceptual'

85.9 our] *aft. del.* '['o[*start of doubtful* 'u'] *del.*] the'

85.9 ¹I] *insrtd. for del.* 'The present writer'

85.9 think] *final* 's' *del.*

85.9 I find['s' *del.*]] 'I' *intrl.*

85.11 philosophic] *underline del.*

85.11 **characters,**] *comma insrtd. bef. del.* 'on record;'

85.12 ¹the] *aft. del.* 'his'

85.12 decisive . . . made] *ab. del.* 'vital effect made'

85.12-13 masterly] *bef. del.* 'and pertinacious'

85.13 the] *ab. del.* 'my native'

85.14 under . . . up.] ('under' *intrl.*); *insrtd. for del.* '*was native to me, [*ab. del.* 'and']'

85.14 The] 'T' *ov.* 't'

85.15 volume ['indeed' *del.*]] *ab. del.* 'book'

85.15 This] *aft. del.* 'For this *reason I have [*ab. del.* 'service I am endlessly'] gratefully ['ly' *added*] ['and *have accordingly [*ab. del.* 'have']' *del.*] dedicated *the [*alt. fr.* 'this'] volume to Renouvier's memory.'

85.16 thankful] *alt. fr.* 'grateful'

††85.16 my text-book] *ab. del.* 'the volume'

85.19 always] *intrl.*

85.20 infer['ences' *del.*]] *aft. del.* 'draw'; *bef. del.* '['from' *del.*] to'

85.20 from] *bef. del.* 'formal or'

85.20 Real [*insrtd.*] novelty [*alt. fr.* 'Novelties']] *aft. del.* 'The question'

85.21 would be a] *ab. del.* 'are'

85.21 matter] *final* 's' *del.*

85.21 would . . . *idealistic [*alt. fr.* 'non-realistic']] *ab. del.* 'is the idealistic'

85.22 but] *insrtd. for del.* 'but they are [*doubtful* 'ducuc' *del.*] deduced from necessities of thought ['obtaining' *del.*] by comparing the abstract'

85.23 from] *aft. del.* '*out of [*ab. del.* 'by merely comparing'] the abstract ideas of'

85.23 purely] *insrtd.*

85.23 impossibility of an] ('of' *ab. del.* 'that'); *ab. del.* 'contradictoriness of'

85.23 number of] *intrl.*

85.24 getting] *ab. del.* 'should be'

85.24 truth; but] *semicolon ov. period*; 'b' *ov.* 'B'

††85.25 fair cut,ˣ] *ab. del.* 'sound one,'

85.25 possibility] *ab. del.* 'doubt'

85.26 scrutinize] *ab. del.* 'close in upon'

85.26 with] *aft. del.* 'even more closely'

85.26 care.] *bef. del.* 'ˣ' *for fn.*

85.27 in the class] *ab. del.* 'we must dis-tinguish between two classes'

85.27-86.1 infinitely] 'ly' *added*

85.28 works] *aft. del.* 'list of'; *bef. del.* 'is'

85.28 make] *alt. fr.* 'made'

85.29 tour,] *insrtd. for del.* '4,'

85.29 six] *ab. del.* '6'

85.30 latest] *aft. del.* 'latest wor[*start of poss.* 'k']'

85.30 opinions [*comma del.*]] *ab. del.* 'views,'

85.32 (entitled] *paren ov. del. paren*

††85.32-33 an autobiografic] *alt. fr.* 'a biografical'

85.33 his] *ab. del.* 'the relati'

††85.33 Derniers] 'D' *ov.* 'd'

85.34 is] *ab. del.* '['show' *del.*] ['are' *del.*] ['show us a man' *del.*] are'

85.35 coming as if] ('coming' *aft.* 'is [*undel. in error*]'); *ab. del.* '*and sounds [*ab. del.* 'as if coming']'

85.36 ourselves conclude] *ab. del.* 'agree'

85.37 conceptual] *aft. del.* 'logical'

85.38 concluding that] *ab. del.* 'rejecting'

85.38 the] *intrl.*

85.39 of [*insrtd.*] change] *aft. del.* '(namely that'; *bef. del.* 'is infinitely constituted)'

85.39 any other] 'any' *insrtd. for del. init.* 'an' *of* 'other'

85.40 shall] 's' *ov.* 'a'

85.40 simply] *aft. del.* 's[*start of poss.* 't']'

86.1 conditioned] *intrl.*

86.1 we] *aft. del.* 'those in which'

86.3 Things] ('T' *ov.* 't'); *aft. del.* 'The'

86.3 conceived] *ab. del.* 'of which is de-fined'

86.3 time,] *comma ov. period*

86.3-4 existing beings.] *insrtd.*

86.6 In] *ab. del.* 'Of'

86.6-7 objection . . . real] *ab. del.* 'rational repugnance between'

86.7 a . . . copiousness] *ab. del.* 'an infi-nite constitution'

86.8 its] *ab. del.* 'the'

86.8 description.] *period insrtd. bef. del.* 'of its form.'

86.8-9 consider . . . assume] *intrl. bef. del.* 'believe [*ab. del.* '['ask' *del.*] con-ceive']'; *caret placed orig. in error bef.* 'we'

86.9 them] ('m' *added*); *bef. del.* 'stars'

86.10 term] *ab. del.* 'number'

86.11 numbers] *aft. del.* 'growing'

86.11 growing endlessly [*comma del.*]]
intrl.

86.12 exceed] *ab. del.* 'exhaust'

86.12 there] *ab. del.* 'ready'

86.13 own] *intrl.*

86.13 waiting] *aft. del.* 'a-'; *bef. del.* 'it
[*intrl.*]'

86.14 to be numbered,] *ab. del.* 'its application,'

86.15 used.] *ab. caret formed fr. orig.
period*

86.16 need] *ab. del.* 'ought to'

86.16 One *cannot ['t' *added*]] 'One can'
ab. del. 'There is ['no l' *del.*] surely'

86.16-17 well see how] *ab. del.* 'logically
['ly' *added*] ['co' *del.*] *['reason why'
del.] conceive that [*ab. del.* 'incompatibility between']'

86.17 should oblige['s' *del.*]] *ab. del.*
'['and' *del.*] should ['necessitate' *del.*]
require'

86.17 whole] *intrl.*

86.18 'star['s' *del.*]'] *aft. del.* 'of'

86.18 require it to] *ab. del.* 'to'

86.19 number.] *period insrtd. bef. del.*
'at all.'

86.20 component] *aft. del.* 'subdivisions
of space, and'

86.20 matter,] *bef. del.* 'to'

86.21 such] *ab. del.* 'the'

86.21 piecemeal,] *bef. del.* 'as 'any' or
'each,''

86.24 talking] *aft. del.* 'thinking and'

86.25 out of which] *ab. del.* 'which
*creates [*insrtd.*] ['gives' *del.*]'

86.26 difficulties] *alt. fr.* 'difficulty'

86.26 emerge.] *aft. del.* 'emerges.'

86.26 condition] *final* 's' *del.*

86.27 there,∧] *sg. or db. qt. del.*

86.27 for] ('f' *ov.* 'F'); *aft. del.* 'and thus
we surreptitiously *foist ['foreign' *del.*]
[*ab. del.* '**bring in**'] the wholly new and
foreign notion of a *bound* ['. Other'
del.] into a situation of which the only
essential feature is that no ['one' *del.*]
condition should be ['lacking' *del.*] absent. The presence of each is *indispensable. [*period doubtful*]'

86.28 means] *ab. del.* 'can'

86.28 that] *ab. del.* 'mean'

86.29 [*sg. qt. del.*] 'not . . . absent.'] 'absent.' *aft. del. init. sg. qt.*

86.29 in . . . people,] (*bef. del.* 'take it,
use it,'); *ab. del.* 'as *I have just quoted
it, [*ab. del.* 'currently applied to *these
[*alt. fr.* 'the'] questions, [*ab. del.* '['situ-
ati' *del.*] composition of reality,']']'

86.30 bounded] 'ed' *ov. period*

86.30 total.] *insrtd.*

86.31 similar] *ab. del.* 'psychological'

86.31 asked] *bef. del.* ', can ['a' *del.*]
standing conditions not eventually be
overtaken by *an ['n' *added*] ['growing' *del.*] endlessly growing series?''

86.32 student] *ab. del.* 'reader'

86.32 men!] *bef. del. insrtd.* 'E. g.
Renouvier et Prat: la nouvelle mona-
dologie, p.'

86.33 an 'amount.'] *ab. del.* 'a sum. *All*
of it has been, then.'

86.33 this] *alt. fr.* 'the'

86.33 2amount] *bef. del.* 'of it'

86.35 result.] *ab. del.* '['result' *del.*]
count.'

86.36 a like] *ab. del.* 'an'

86.36 must] *bef. del.* 'thus'

86.37 its] (*alt. fr.* 'is'); *ab. del.* 'the'

86.37 here] *intrl.*

86.40 ending] 'ing' *added*

86.40 series] *aft. del.* 'beginningless'

86.41 tracts] *aft. del.* ' real'

86.42 the abstract] *ab. del.* 'the abstract
series of'

86.42 regression] 'sion' *aft. del.* |'sion'

87.1-2 ∧can . . . bulk'?∧] *sg. qts. del.*

87.1 'growing] *aft. del.* 's[*start of poss.*
't']'

87.1 fail] *bef. del.* 'eventually'

87.2 Any standing] *ab. del.* 'This again
foists in the closed-collective form.'

87.2 existence] ('e' *ov.* 'E'); *bef. del.*
'**therfore**'

†87.2-3 must . . .-series,] *insrtd.*

87.3-4 numerical] *intrl.*

87.4 determination['s' *del.*].] *bef. period
undel. in error*

87.4 foists] *aft. del.* '['foists in, in the
word' *del.*] assumes, *in the words [*ab.
del.* 'that'] 'standing bulk''

87.5-6 in . . . but] *insrtd. for del.* 'is'

87.6 and to call] *insrtd. for del.*
'*[*doubtful* '&' *del.*] and [*intrl.*] to
treat'

87.6 these] *alt. fr.* 'the'

87.6 eaches] *bef. del.* 'as'

87.7 beg] *ab. del.* '[*start of doubtful
letter*] beg *the **finitest [*alt. fr.*
'finite'] answer [*ab. del.* 'the whole
question'] beforehand *or* assume'

87.7 at issue.] *insrtd. for del.* 'in dispute.
In spite of logic, however, it has to be
confest that the natural man feels a
great repugnance to admitting that
standing things can form an endless
series *of [*ab. del.* 'in'] themselves.
['The axiom of determinate existence
seems to' *del.*] Such a series is for us
['a' *del.*] variable [*illeg. word*] indefinite, and'

†87.8-10 But . . . that] *insrtd. for del.*
'Again, [*opp. mrgn. undel.* '¶']'

87.8 But] *opp. mrgn.* '¶'

87.8 real] *alt. fr.* 'really'

87.8 reason . . . to] *ab. del.* 'effective
objection to the'

87.9 is] *ab. del. comma*

87.9 reason] *aft. del.* 'objection that'

87.9 speak] *aft. del.* 'call it'

87.9 it as] *intrl.*

87.10 ¹ever] *insrtd. for del.* 'more, more,'

††87.10 ¹more,] *(comma undel. in error);
bef. del.* 'of [*intrl.*]'

87.10 ²ever more] *intrl.*

87.11 ever more ['or' *del.*]] *ab. del.* 'and'

87.11 need is] *ab. del.* 'is [*ab. del.* 'is [*ab.
del.* 'would be'] the use, or the significance, of'] the need of all that?'

87.12 ¹there,] *alt. fr.* 'the'

87.12 what] *insrtd.*

87.12 is there, for] *ab. del.* 'of'

87.12 Not] ('N' *ov.* 'n'); *aft. del.* 'It is'

87.12-13 of anything] *insrtd.*

87.13 absolutely] *intrl.*

†87.14 for ['with' *del.*] . . . them.] *ab.
del.* 'to befriend themselves to our
mentality'

87.14-15 with . . . other] *ab. del.* 'gladly
on Kant's idealism, or'

87.15 ²of] (*alt. fr.* 'on'); *bef. del.* 'a'

87.16 static] *aft. del.* '['stat' *del.*] the'

87.16 growing] *aft. del.* 'the'

87.16 forms] 's' *added*

87.18 dialectic] *aft. del.* 'objection'

87.19 a] *ab. del.* 'an endless'

87.19 must needs] *ab. del.* 'has to'

87.21 which we] *intrl.*

87.21 conceive] *final* 'd' *del.*

87.22 continuously] *underline del.*

87.22 must be] *ab. del.* 'is'

††87.24 addition, or] *intrl.*

87.25-26 ['count' *del.*] touch ['attain'
del.] . . . . *process.*] (*period insrtd. bef.
del.* 'of enumeration.'); *ab. del.* 'enumerate a sum total. ['The type of' *del.*]
Achilles ['occupying in' *del.*] ['success'
del.] occupancy in'

87.26 That] *insrtd. for del. insrtd.* 'For'

87.26 Achilles] 'A' *ov.* 's'

87.27 should] ('sh' *ov.* 'to'); *intrl.*

87.27 occupy] *final* 'ing' *del.*

87.27 continuous] *intrl.*

87.28 ['inad' *del.*] inadmissible] *ab. del.*
'impossible'

87.28 that he should] *ab. del.* 'for
Achilles to'

87.29 'infinite,'] 'e' *added*

87.30-31 and the] 'and' *intrl.;* 'the' *alt.
fr.* 'The'

87.31 it is that] ('t' *of* 'it' *ov.* 's'); *insrtd.*

87.31 An] ('A' *ov.* 'a'); *aft. del.* 'For'

87.32-33 offers . . . for] *ab. del.* 'yields
none of it, for'

87.34 The] *aft. del.* 'Let the reader not
fail to observe that in working the distributive point of view as I have worked
it in this discussion,'

87.34 note] *aft. del.* 'observe'

87.34 am . . . on] *ab. del.* 'am [*undel. in
error*] holding to the legitimacy of'

87.35 or piecemeal] *intrl.*

87.35 The] *aft. del.* 'It will appear more
and more clearly as *the book [*ab. del.*
'we'] proceeds ['s' *added*] that the distributive way is the [*doubtful* 'm' *del.*]
way in which'

87.35 is . . . with ['the' *del.*]] *ab. del.*
'point of view is'

87.36 pluralistic,] *comma insrtd. bef. del.*
'point ['p' *ov. doubtful* 'v'] of view,'

87.36 with] *intrl.*

87.36 conception.] *ab. del.* 'point of
view.'

87.37   clearly~] *comma del.*
††87.37   piecemeal existence is] *ab. del.*
'the ['two' *del.*] point['s' *del.*] of view
['are' *del.*]'
††87.38   of] *ov. comma*
††87.38   complete collectibility,] *insrtd.*
87.38   some] *aft. del.* 'a p'
87.38   facts,] *ab. del.* 'parts of the world'
87.39   form] 'f' *ov.* 'v'
87.39   (even ... number)] *parens over commas*
87.39-40   need ['do' *del.*] ... any] *ab. del.* 'can in no'
87.40   experience] *ab. del.* 'realize'
87.40   get experienced] *ab. del.* 'be realized'
87.41   members of an all.] *ab. del.* 'effectively [*intrl.*] making *up [*intrl.*] an all.'
88.1   each successive] (1'c' *of* 'successive' *ov. orig. sg. qt. bef.* 'more'); *ab. del.* 'the'
88.1   'more'] *init. sg. qt. intrl.*
88.2   thought of as] *bel. del.* 'conceived as'
†88.2-4 1as ... infinity] ('as' *repeated in error*); *insrtd. for del.* 'previous, as already having been paid in, and *not [*insrtd. for del.* 'doesn't'] *as something [*ab. del.* 'for'] the paying in of which ['our end' *del.*] will **keep the [*intrl.*] end of the process ***continually [*ab. del.* 'must keep'] waiting. [*insrtd. for del.* '*as something that forever [*intrl.*] keeps ['s' *added*] our [*ab. del.* 'the forward'] end of the process waiting.'] [*del.* 'In [' 'progressions' on the contrary' *del.*] the words of Kant's pun, the infinite *amount [*ab. del.* 'process'] is *gegeben*, not *aufgegeben*, ['any more than' *del.*] just'] ['Just as' *del.*] The infinity *is [*ab. del.* 'belongs'] in short'
††88.2   paid in~] *ab. del.* ', as previous,'
88.3   having] *aft. del.* 'yet to be'
88.3   paid] *intrl.*
88.3   before] *bef. del.* 'we reach'
88.4   our] *ab. del.* 'the'
88.4   here is] *intrl.*
88.4   of] *ov.* 'to'
88.7   on the contrary,] *intrl.*
††88.7   it is a *task*;—] *intrl.*
88.7   for] *ov.* 'to'

88.8   philosophic] *intrl.*
88.8   any] *ab. del.* 'the agent'
88.8   who might] *ab. del.* 'traversing the *process. [*period doubtful*]*'
88.8   try] *final* 'ing' *del.*
†88.9   physically ... performance.] *ab. del.* 'to complete the process.'
88.9-10   is ... $1$to] *intrl.*
88.10   find] *final* 's' *del.*
88.10   remainder,] *bef. del.* 'undone,'
88.10-11   yet to be paid,] *ab. del.* 'due,'
88.11   due] *intrl.*
88.13   *Infinitum*] *aft. del.* 'This impossibility of'
†88.14   quantum ... is] *ab. del.* 'process is expressly'
88.15   infinite.] *bef. del.* '['in act' *del.*] It would seem'
88.16   be to] *insrtd.*
88.16   give up] *ab. del.* 'change'
88.16   that] *alt. fr.* 'the'
88.16   real] *ab. del.* 'our [*intrl.*]'
88.17   being] *intrl.*
88.17 2as] *insrtd. for del.* 'as ['composed' *del.*] sums of steps'
88.18   finite ... steps,] *insrtd. for del.* 'successive ['units' *del.*] steps *of change [*intrl.*] that are *discrete and finite, [*ab. del.* 'discrete,']'
88.19   a cask] *ab. del.* 'a leaking ['reservoir' *del.*] barrel [*ab. del.* 'tank']'
88.19   is filled, when] *ab. del.* 'may be emptied, a'
88.19   drops] 's' *added*
†88.19   fall ... once~] '*falls ['s' *undel. in error ov.* 'ing'] into it successively, [*ab. del.* 'at once,']'
88.20   or] *intrl.*
88.23   qualifying it so as] 'qualifying [*alt. fr.* 'qualifi-'|]' *aft. del.* 'with a slight'; 'it so as' *ab. del.* |'cation'
88.23   fit] *aft. del.* 'make it'
88.23 2it] *intrl.*
88.25   in mathematics] *moved fr. bef.* 'has' [88.25] ; *orig.* 'in' *bef.* 'mathematics' *del.*
88.26   quashed] *ab. del.* 'got rid of all'
88.26   whom] ('m' *added*); *bef. del.* 'is troubled by'
88.27   in ... bothers] *intrl.*
††88.27   very naif] *ab. del.* 'naif and *old-

fashioned [*hyphen doubtful*]'
††88.28   Naif ... mathematics,] *intrl.*
88.28   must,] *bef. del.* 'still [*ab. del.*
'therefore,']'
88.29   add] *ab. del.* 'say'
88.29   rebuttal ['comment' *del.*] of] *ab.
del.* 'answer to'
†88.29-31   criticisms ... mystification.]
insrtd. for del. '[*on fol.* 70aa] ['challenges.' *del.*] criticisms. The only application of the new infinite that ['we here are' *del. intrl.*] concerned ['ed' *ov.* 's'] us ['here' *del. intrl.*] with, [*intrl.; undel. in error*] is to the field of continuous quantity. What may be called the Zenonian tradition['has' *del.*] in mathematics has admitted that ['unitary' *del.*] *quanta* like *an inch [*ab. del.* 'a cubic yard'] of space, *a step [*ab. del.* 'an ['n' *added*] ['certain' *del.*] amount'] of change, *an [*ab. del.* 'a certain'] intensity, or speed, *felt [*ab. del.* 'taken'] perceptually or *given [*ab. del.* 'taken'] 'at a stroke,' *can [*ab. del.* 'could'] not be *['adequately' *del.*] ['actually' *del.*] translated ['into' *del.*] *in actu* into [*ab. del.* 'exhaustively translated into'] numbers, because *of the [*intrl.*] *inner character of continuity in these *quanta*, [*insrtd. for del.* 'an *ideal [*ab. del.* 'infinite'] number of points, steps, degrees, or what not, which they seem to imply, and because of ['the inexpansibility' *del.*] continuity [*ab. del.* 'infinity'] of the['ir' *del.*] *ideal structure [*ab. del.* 'composition'] ['of' *del. intrl.*]']' and of the [*del.* 'non-existence of an *infinith* number. 'Intuition' *does here [*ab. del.* 'has [*ab. del.* 'was supposed'] to do'] at once what enumeration *cannot [*ab. del.* 'could not be'] compass. But if the *progressive [*undel. in error ab. del.* 'additive'] enumeration doesn't ['have to' *del.*] proceed beyond a fixed point, we may ['get more and more points' *del.*] touch an infinith ['term' *del.*] point, ['supposed ['ass' *del.*] [*del. fol.* 70bb] discreteness,' *del.*] supposed irremediable, of the *num- | [*del. in error*]'] ber-series. But

['Bolzan' *del.*] the mathematicians [*comma del.*] ['Bolzano,' *del.*] Dedekind, Cantor and others, ['had' *del.*] have at last been able to *construct and define concept- | **tually ['t' *in error*] [*ab. del.* 'define intercalary numbers between all possible serial numbers so as to make'] a genuine 'number-continuum.' We can ['dicho' *del.*] halve *a unit [*ab. del.* 'an inch'], and halve its *halves, ['l' *insrtd.*] and halve again *ad infinitum.* But between *the sections ['fractions' *del.*] ['fractionally numbered' *del.*] numbered thus, [*ab. del.* '['these fractions the' *del.*] points thus created there remains'] room *is left [*intrl.*] for infinite *others ['s' *ab. del.* 's'] ['points' *del.*] created by using 3 as a divisor, for infinite others made by using 5, 7, etc, *etc, [*comma ov. period*] ['till' *del.*] until all possible rational fractions *shall have been made use of. [*ab. del.* 'are included.'] Still the *unit [*ab. del.* 'inch'] is not exhaustively *filled up [*ab. del.* 'covered'] by the numbers thus interpolated, for it has been shown ['by Dedekind' *del.*] that [*intrl.*] *between* any two of these 'rationally' numbered *divisions in it, ['however close neighbors,' *del.*] [*ab. del.* 'fractions, of the original *quantum ['n' *intrl.*],'] there is room for *still [*ov.* 'an'] *another ['new' *del.*] division, numberable **as [*ab. del.* 'by'] an [*ab. del.* 'irrational fractional number, of the'] 'irrational' *fraction. [*ab. del.* 'order. The place of'] These *latter [*intrl.*] numbers, if I understand the *argument [*ab. del.* 'demonstration'] *(which [*paren ov. comma*] is too technical for reproduction *here) [*paren ov. comma*] are *defined* as *being [*intrl.*] intermediary in magnitude between any number on one side and any number on the other side [*del. fol.* 70bb *verso, notes in pencil:* 'Russell, 306 | Class vs. collection | *references! [*in ink*] Continuity defd, 193 | arithmetization | Dedekind's continuum 278-9, 280 | the mass of unanalyzed prejudice which Kantians call intuition, 260 |

compare 287'] [*del. fol.* 70ᶜᶜ] of them. They are created by this definition, *which simultaneously creates the place [*ab. del.* 'and obviously there is room'] for them. They being *inserted, [*insrtd. for del.* 'added,'] however, it seems agreed that there is no room ['for any other sort of subdiv' *del.*] left in the unit for any other sort of *section. [*ab. del.* 'subdivision.'] These [*alt. fr.* 'That'] ways [*ab. del.* 'way'] of *sub-dividing, [*comma insrtd.*] *taken to-gether, [*intrl.*] have [*ov.* 'has'] ex-hausted the material. [¶] If [*aft. del.* 'The'; *opp. mrgn.* '¶'] the unit be not the *bare abstract [*ab. del.* '['num[*poss. start of* 'b']' *del.*] bare'] number 1, but *something [*ab. del.* 'a'] concrete, [*comma insrtd.*] ['unit' *del.*] like ['an in' *del.*] one inch of space, *then ['n' added] *the sections signify [*ab. del.* 'subdivisions become'] 'points,' and the inch is *thought [*ab. del.* 'con-ceived'] of as a 'point-continuum' of which each point without exception can be *numbered by ['with' *del.*] some one [*ab. del.* '['put into' *del.*] a 'one-to-one relation,' or numbered, by one ['of the' *del.*]'] number['s' *del.*] of the number-continuum. The inch here is *represented as wholly [*ab. del.* 'wholly filled ['with points' *del.*] up with and'] made of *points. [*period insrtd.*] The [*aft. del. dash*; 'T' *ov.* 't'] points *ex-press it adequately, its [*ab. del.* 'are *its ['t' *ov.* 's'] equivalent. ['The' *del.*] Its'] infinity is exhausted. [¶] In a general way *the [*alt. fr.* 'this'] *number-con-tinuum is [*ab. del.* 'is'] supposed to show that *intellection [*alt. fr.* 'con-ception'] is a *full [*intrl.*] match for intuition, and that [*del.* '['the od in a' *del.*] we ought no longer to complain of *them [*doubtful*]'] we *must stop [*ab. del.* 'can no longer'] accusing [*alt. fr.* 'accuse'] ['translations of percep-tion into' *del.*] conception *of [*ab. del.* ', as being'] substituting [*alt. fr.* 'substitutions'] the discrete for the continuous, and of ['being [*fol.* 70ᵇᵇ] an inadequate translation of' *del.*]

translating [*intrl.*] perception inade-quately. [¶] The student will notice, however, two things:—[¶] 1ˢᵗ, that the number or point continuum is the con-ception of something static. The unit is given all at once, whether to ['defini-tion' *del.*] intuition,'

88.30 repeated] *intrl.*

88.30 novices,] *comma insrtd. bef. del.* 'in the field,'

88.32 'number-continuum'] *aft. del.* 'point-'; *bef. del.* 'form parts of a general attempt'

88.32 outgrowths] *ab. del.* 'incidents'

88.33 to accomplish] *ab. del.* 'at th'

88.33-34 'arithmetization'] *sg. qts. ov. db. qts.*

88.34 (ἀριθμὸς . . . number)] *intrl.*

88.35 grades of] *intrl.*

88.35 intensity] *alt. fr.* 'intensities'

88.36 until recently] *ab. del.* 'always'

88.36 immediate] *intrl.*

88.36-37 [' 'intuition,' or' *del.*] percep-tive] *ab. del.* 'our intuitive'

88.37 or 'intuition';] *ab. caret formed fr. orig. comma*

88.38 now] *intrl.*

88.38 getting a] *aft. del.* 'making'; *bef. del.* 'full'

88.39 created by] *ab. del.* 'defined by their indefinite'

88.40 indefinitely.] *insrtd.*

89.1 on.] *period insrtd. bef. del.* 'indefi-nitely'

89.4 divisions] *ab. del.* 'fractions'

89.5 shown] *ab. del.* 'proved'

89.5 cuts] *aft. del.* 'irrational'

89.6 and . . . these] *ab. del.* 'until [*ab. del.* 'so that']'

89.7 gets] *ab. del.* 'is'

89.7 filled *full*,] *ab. del.* '*filled* with cuts, and its continuous'

89.7 now being] *ab. del.* 'is'

†89.8 and . . . infinite.] *intrl.*

89.9 formulaᵥ] *comma del.*

89.10 alone] *intrl.*

89.11 original] *intrl.*

89.14 as] *bef. del.* ''almost'

††89.15 ²The] *aft. del.* 'The notion of 'the new infinite,' or rather of 'transfi-nite numbers,' results *(if [*paren ov.*

comma] I understand it rightly) from
the notion of 'class' being substituted
for that of 'quantity' in *our [*ab. del.*
'the'] operations of measuring. A quantity is a definite whole; a 'class' ['taken
in logical extension,' *del.*] may be defined by enumerating all its individuals,
in which case it ['is' *del.*] also *is [*intrl.*]
a definite whole; but it may *again [*ab.
del.* 'also'] be defined by a general concept, ['under which' *del.*] such that if
*that concept [*ab. del.* ''any' individual
it'] be predicable of 'any' individual
*thing, [*intrl.*] that *thing [*ab. del.*
'individual'] belongs to the *class,
[*comma ov. period*] the number
of which thus remains *indefinite.ˣ
['ˣ' *insrtd.*] | *ˣTo [*insrtd.*] Stu-
dents ['S' *unreduced in error*] of logic
['will recognize['s' *del.*]' *del.*] the difference ['as the' *del.*] will be familiar
as that between *the [*insrtd.*] denotation and the connotation, [', or the extensive and' *del.*] of general terms, or
*between [*intrl.*] their use in extension
and in intension, or comprehension. |
The class of numbers, taken ordinally
in due succession, as 1, 2, 3, 4, . . . , is
defined by enumerating, and is endless,
because by the *ever recurrent [*intrl.*]
law of its formation, *1 [*ab. del.* 'one
more'] can always be added. But any
*standing [*intrl.*] multitude of things
['of a *class [*ab. del.* 'kind']' *del.*] can
be measured against this *growing [*ab.
caret formed fr. orig. comma*] number
series, by pairing its terms, one to one,
with the successive numbers, *or [*ab.
del. paren*] in other words by counting *them.[*period aft. del. paren*] [¶]
Now the standing multitude 'transfinite
[*closing sg. qt. del.*] number' is created
by *a class concept. [*ab. del.* 'an arbitrary definition.'] It is an ens rationis,
like the 'infinite distance' at which parallel lines would meet (if they *did *meet)
[*paren ov. comma*]; and *the question
[*insrtd.*] whether *actual [*ab. del.*
'real'] entities of any sort exist ['or'
del.] or ['that' *del.*] not in that number,
is not prejudged by the *definition.

[*period ov. comma bef. del.* 'which is
simply that of the class of numbers that
cannot be produced by successive addition of one as the']'
89.16   only] *bef. del.* 'the use of'
89.16   infinity] (*alt. fr.* 'infinite'); *aft. del.*
    'the'
89.16-17   indefinitely . . . number-] *ab.
    del.* '['entire' *del.*] number'
89.17   in] *aft. del.* 'with an'
89.18   component] *aft. del.* 'seri'
89.18   'even'] *aft. del.* '['even' *del.*] the'
††89.21   collectively *taken ['t' *ov. poss.
    caret*],] *intrl.*
89.22   in the] *ab. del.* 'or numerically
    'equivalent' to the whole in the str'
89.24   so] *aft. del.* 'and the series com-
    pared will *['have' *del.*] exhibit a thor-
    oughgoing [*ab. del.* '['suffice' *del.*]
    ['m[*illeg. letters*]' *del.*] for each
    other's'] correspondance ['ance' *intrl.*]
    ['numerically' *del.*] with each other.'
89.24   prove to be] *ab. del.* 'are'
89.26   are] *ab. del.* 'seem [*ab. del.* 'are']'
89.27   numbers] *aft. del.* 'who'
89.28   appear to be] *ab. del.* 'seem to be'
89.28   ◬equally copious◬] *sg. qts. del.*
89.29   The terms of] *intrl.*
89.29   each] 'e' *ov.* 'E'
89.29   partial series] *ab. del.* '['forms a
    class' *del.*] forms a series *whose terms
    [*ab. del.* 'that']'
89.29   numbered] *aft. del.* 'successively
    [*intrl.*]'
89.30   using the] *bel. del.* '['the use of the'
    del.*] ['whole numb' *del.*] series of'
89.30   in succession.] *ab. del.* '. [*insrtd.*]
    ['; and' *del.*]'
89.34   ['form a' *del.*] be . . . than] *ab.
    del.* 'be fewer ['that the' *del.*] than'
89.34   that] *alt. fr.* 'the'
89.34   series] *ab. del.* 'sum'
89.34   odd and even] (*opp. mrgn. circled*
    'tr'); *orig.* 'even and odd'
89.36   result,] *ab. del.* 'were ['long judged
    absurd, and re' *del.*] long treated as a
    reductio ad absurdum of the notion
    that'
89.37   from] *aft. del.* 'result'
89.37   infinity of the] *intrl.*
89.37   is of] *ab. del.* 'belongs to'

89.38 variety] *bef. del.* 'of infinites'

††89.38 p. 70ᵂ).] *period ov. comma*

89.38 They] *insrtd. for del.* 'They [*ab. del.* 'and']'

89.40 287] *aft. del.* 'compare *also [*intrl.*] p.'

†90.1 [*doubtful* 'in' *del.*] such . . . infinity] *ab. del.* 'such infinity exists'

90.2 standing] *bef. del.* 'form.'

††90.2 form.ˣ] 'ˣ' *insrtd.*

90.3 But contemporary] (*opp. mrgn.* '¶'); *alt. fr.* 'contemporary ['c' *ab. del.* 'c' *ov.* 'C']'

90.4 Instead] *aft. del.* '['Instead' *del.*] They have'

90.4 treating such] *ab. del.* 'using the'

90.4 properties] *aft. del.* 'definitions of the'

90.5 *reductiones*] ('*nes*' *added*); *aft. del.* 'a'

90.5 turned] *ab. del.* 'used'

90.6 into] *ab. del.* 'as'

90.6 definition [*comma del.*]] *aft. del.* '['definition' *del.*] class'

90.6 classes] *aft. del.* 'things, [*comma ov. period*] and they have'

90.7 now . . . infinite] ('in' *added to* |'finite'); *insrtd. for del.* 'in-'|; *bef. del.* 'if it contains a par'

90.7 if] *ab. del.* '**When**'

90.7 numerically] ('ly' *added*); *aft. del.* 'number'

90.8 If] *ab. del.* '**When**'

90.8 dissimilar,] *ab. del.* 'less than itself'

90.11 certain concepts] *ab. del.* 'a class, of tra'

90.11 called] *bef. del.* 'that of'

90.11 are] *alt. fr.* 'is'

††90.12 definition.] *period ab. del. period aft. del. comma*

††90.12 They are to] *ab. del.* 'as'

90.12 belong] *final* 'ing' *del.*

90.13 not] *aft. del.* 'as not being formed'

90.13 formed] *bef. del.* 'by the law of growth of the natural number-series,'

90.13 *ad infinitum*,] *ab. del.* 'but rather like the *['ordinal' *del.*] natural [*ab. del.* 'natural'] number series,'

90.14 be postulated] *ab. del.* 'come [*ab. del.* 'be postulated outright as existing']'

90.14 as coming] *ab. del.* '(in the world of pure mathematics) as coming'

††90.15 addition.ˣ] *period and* 'ˣ' *insrtd. bef. del.* '—not after any one of them, for there is no last one, but after *them ['m' *added*] ['class of them' *del.*] as a *class, [*comma ov. period*]ˣ or generally.'

90.16 lowest] *aft. del.* 'f'

90.16 It] ('I' *ov.* 'i'); *aft. del.* 'An example of'

90.17 for instance,] *intrl.*

90.17 point] *ab. del.* 'position'

90.18 overtakes] *alt. fr.* 'overtakes' *to* 'would overtake' *to* 'overtakes' *to* 'would overtake' *to* 'overtakes'

90.18 tortoise—] *dash ab. caret formed fr. orig. comma*

90.18 does overtake] 'does' *ab. del.* 'could'; 's' *added to* 'overtake', *then del.*

90.18 him?—] ('?—' *intrl.*); *bef. del.* 'at all'

90.18 exhausting all] ('exhausting' *alt. fr.* 'occupying'); *ab. del.* 'enumerating'

90.19 intervening . . . ['in' *del.*] successively. [*alt. fr.* 'succession.']] *ab. del.* 'series of successive positions requisite'

90.21 would be] *ab. del.* 'would be'

90.21 meet] *aft. del.* 'would'

90.22 whole] (*bef. del. intrl.* 'first ['whole' *del.*]'); *intrl.*

††90.22-23 numbers . . . one,] *ab. del.* '['infin' *del.*] growing numbers,'

90.23 other∧] *comma del.*

90.23 it] *intrl.*

90.24 passing us] *ab. del.* 'getting'

90.25 The] *opp. mrgn.* '¶'

90.25 pass] *ab. del.* 'get'

90.25 its help] *insrtd. for del.* 'it'

90.25-26 number of the] *intrl.*

90.26 ¹continuum] *intrl.*

90.27 making] *ab. del.* 'actual process'

90.28 is] *insrtd. for del.* 'is endless forms'

90.28 an] 'n' *added*

90.28 infinitely] *intrl.*

90.28 process;] *ab. del.* 'infinite,'

90.29 paired] *intrl.*

90.29 to] *ab. del.* 'by'

90.29 the terms] *aft. del.* 'the [*intrl.*]'; *bef. del.* 'of two series should'

90.30 for] 'f' *ov.* 'b'

90.30　(or] *paren ov. comma*

90.31　vastly] *bef. del.* 'differ'

90.32　need only] *ab. del.* 'only have to'

90.32　steps . . . or] *ab. del.* 'steps in one
series longer than'

90.33　numerically ['ly' *added*] similar['ity'
del.]] ('numeri-'|*ab. del.* 'numeri-'|);
bef. del. 'with greatly unequal'

90.34　Moreover] *aft. del.* 'The moment a'

††90.36　ˣThe] ('T' *ov.* 't'); *aft. del.*
'Conceptually'

90.36　come] *final* 's' *del.*

†90.37-38　provided . . . one] ('*eaches* or
anys,' *ab. del.* 'piecemeal, [*comma alt.
fr. colon*]'); *insrtd. for del.* 'even though
there be no one number that comes immediately before it. *Any* number in the
class, be there a last one or ['not' *del.*]
not, will precede the whole transfinite
class [*period del.*] provided we ['do
not' *del. insrtd.*] take the class ['do'
del.] ['piecemeal and not' *del.*] in logical 'extension.' *Any* ['number' *del.*]'

90.38　them] ('m' *added*); *bef. del.* 'class'

90.39　one] *aft. del.* 'number in the'

90.39　²tho] *ab. del.* 'if'

91.1　transfinite] *aft. del.* 'nu'

91.2-3　assimilated to] *insrtd. for del.*
'converted | [*horiz. line del. ab. del.*
'ˣTho any *amount of* [*intrl.*]
subdivision reached is finite,'] |into'

††91.4　equated with] *ab. del.* 'converted
into'

††91.5　Thus] *aft. del.* '['with the additional advantage that since' *del.*] ['The'
del.] Since ['both' *del.*] the growing
*numbers [*intrl.*] and the standing
number are *both [*intrl.*] of the
infinite *class; [*semicolon ov. colon*]
and *since [*intrl.*] any portion of the
growing series is enveloped by *(or
[*paren ov. comma*] is a constituent
part of) the standing ['ω' *del.*] *omega*;
it follows ['that' *del.*] from the *new
[*intrl.*] definition of infi-|['nity (above,
p.　) that' *del.*] ['nite classes, that'
del.] nite classes (above, p.　) that
omega and the ['number of' *del.*] points
in ['a line or of' *del.*] an inch or *the
possible [*intrl.*] fractions between 0
and 1 are numerically similar or equiva-

lent, and can be substituted for each
other. We'

91.5　do we] *intrl.*

91.5　indefinite] *ab. del.* 'interminable'

91.6　which] *aft. del.* 'by'

91.8　infinite] *aft. del.* 'new [*intrl.*]'

91.8　number] *ab. del.* 'moreover'

††91.12　contempt-|tuous] (2't' *in error*);
ab. del. 'supercilious'

†91.12-13　enthusiasts . . . treat] *ab. del.*
'novelty-mongers speak of'

91.13　still] *aft. del.* 'are [*intrl.*]'; *bef. del.*
'['hug th' *del.*] believe that *the [*ab.
del.* 'a'] whole is greater than the'

†91.14-15　Because . . . some] *insrtd. for
del.* 'It all ['reverts to the' *del.*] depends,
as we saw (p.　), on whether [*del.*
'we take *the [*ab. del.* 'a'] collective
or *the [*ab. del.* 'a'] distributive, the
'intensional' or the 'extensional' ['view'
del.] point of view.'] we take a class to
mean *all* its members or to mean *each*,
or *any*, of its members. It is in the latter
*sense [*ab. del.* 'case'] that ['the number of' *del.*] the ['number of' *del.*]
points in *an [*insrtd. for del.* '*a continuous [*ab. del.* 'an']'] inch ['of space'
del.] are infinitely numerous. *One [*ab.
del.* 'One'] by one, they *are similar to
['those in omega.' *del.*] [*ab. del.* '['are'
del.] ['are a match for omegas.' *del.*]
can be paired with'] omega's constitu-
ents. But ['that an' *del.*] for all that the
inch is ['less than a foot; and for the
inch to' *del.*] greater [¹'e' *ov.* 'a'] than
['its *half [*alt. fr.* 'halves'] or quarter['s' *del.*]' *del.*] its halves or quarters,
though its number be the same as theirs.
Because *any [*ab. del.* 'the'] point['s'
del.] in *an imaginary inch [*ab. del.* 'an
['n' *added*] half'] is [*ov. hyphen*]
['inch or a quarter-inch' *del.*] *conceivable as holding [*ab. del.* 'can be put
into'] a *one- [*hyphen ab. del.* 'to']
one relation with those in [*del.* 'to
[*ab. del.* 'a']'] some'

91.16-17　of . . . that] *ab. del.* 'is held to
mean that for all purposes, *even for
[*intrl.*] physical *purposes[*ab. del.*
'ones'] included, a half'

91.18　quarter-] *aft. del.* 'and'

91.18 and inches] *intrl.*

†91.19-20 things . . . neglect.] (*comma ov. period in* 'anyhow,'; 'facts' *ab. del.* 'things'; 'practically neglect.' *insrtd. for del.* 'neglect.'); *insrtd. for del.* 'with inches. ['The' *del.*] To traverse a full inch and get beyond it is a physical achievement. So ['is the' *del.*] it is to traverse any remainder of the inch, however small, after *any ['of it' *del.*] previous part of it [*ab. del.* 'the first part'] has been traversed. But'

†91.20-36 expounders . . . nu-||] *substituted for del.* '*exposers of [*insrtd. for del.* '*exploders of [*bel. del.* 'critics of']'] Zeno's famous ['arguments,' *del.*] 'sophisms,' but they seem to me *now [*intrl.*] to *say [*ab. del.* 'think'] that because three-quarters of an inch are ['numerically' *del.*] similar in *the [*ab. del.* 'po'] number of points they contain, to ['a' *del.*] full *inches, ['es,' *ov. comma*] therefore ['the' *del.*] remainders ['s' *added*] may be neglected, ['and any' *del.*] and Achilles and the tortoise treated as reaching the same spot. [¶] Mr. Bertrand Russell['s' *del.*] [*del.* 'exposure of the 'fallacy' *of the Achilles, [*intrl.*] [*del.* 'consists, as I see it, in the following steps: [¶] 1. The *inch of [*intrl.*] head-start given by Achilles to the tortoise obliges him to traverse the whole path of the tortoise, plus one inch, if he is to catch up with the reptile. [¶] 2.—'] amounts, [*undel. in error ab. del.* 'consists,'] as I apprehend it, *to [*insrtd.*] ['in'. *del.*] resolving the race between the hero and'] the reptile into *the two [*ab. del.* 'a'] series of *points [*ab. del.* 'positions, equally numerous,'] occupied by *the ['runners' *del.*] respective runners [*ab. del.* 'each'] at corresponding instants of time. [*del.* 'As Achilles has to *traverse what the [*ab. del.* 'run the'] tortoise's *traverses [*ab. del.* 'distance'] *plus* the head-start ['he has' *del.*] given, [*comma insrtd.*] ['him,' *del.*] ['the ordin' *del.*] ['common sense' *del.*] the tortoise's ['distance' *del.*] path, ['wh Ac' *del.*] if Achilles catches up, will be a part only of the path of Achilles, *something like this [*ab. del.* ', common sense']'] The tortoise owing to his head-start, ['has to' *del.*] traverses ['s' *added*] only a part of the path traversed *which [*ab. del.* 'by'] Achilles ['A' *ov.* 'a'; *period del.*] *has to traverse and since [*ab. del.* 'But'] both paths are continua, and *are to [*insrtd. for del.* 'can be ade'] consist of *nothing but [*ab. del.* 'infinite'] points. [*period ov. comma*] Common sense, ['(according to Mr. Russell' *del.*] (still [*paren ov. comma*] believing that that 'the whole is greater than the part['s' *del.*]') cannot see how ['the' *del.*] two *such [*ab. del.* 'continua can have the same'] unequal continua can furnish the *same [*ab. del.* 'equivalent'] number of points, [*comma insrtd.*] ['required,' *del.*] and treats the *notion of the point- [*ab. del.* '['notion of' *del.*] idea of'] continuum [*alt. fr.* 'continuous'] ['division of the ['lin' *del.*] paths' *del.*] as self-contradictory or paradoxical. ['It forgets that' *del.*] The ['T' *ov.* 't'] points *meanwhile, *being [*ab. del.* 'are'] *infinite* ['and that infinite classes' *del.*] have the same number ['as their parts' *del.*] in both cases, so no paradox is involved. [¶] The common sense of the matter hinges, to my mind, not on the number of ['points, but' *del.*] points in the larger path (*begin fresh start for material following lines 16-17,* 'exposure of the 'fallacy' of the Achilles') ['amounts,' *del. ab. del.* 'consists'] as I apprehend *him, conceives the **modern [*intrl.*] Zenonian to argue somewhat as follows. [*ab. del.* 'it, *to [*ov.* 'is'; *undel. in error*] something like this.'] The tortoise, owing to his head-start, traverses only a part of the path which Achilles has to traverse in the race. Both paths are continua, and (according to the point-continuum *theory) [*paren ov. comma*] are *exhaustively described as [*ab. del.* 'resolvable into the'] two ['in points' *del. intrl.*] series of *space- [*intrl.*] points occupied by the respective runners at *corresponding points [*ab. del.* 'succes-

sive instants'] of time. [*del.* 'These points form correlated pairs, and are equally numerous therefore. But to suppose the'] The paths *are to consist of [*ab. del.* 'mean'] nothing but these points. Yet if one path *be [*insrtd. for del.* 'is'] equal to the other *plus* a remainder, *and if [*ab. del.* 'no one who ['believes' *del.*] still believes that'] the *whole [*ab. del.* 'part'] is *necessarily greater [*insrtd. for del.* 'less'] than the *part, [*ab. del.* 'whole, can believe that *they ['y' *added*] ['paths' *del.*] are point by point the same. Common sense ['finds' *del.*] therefore ['that' *del.*] agrees with Zeno that'] there must be more points in Achilles' path than in the reptile's, and the ['notion of the parallel series is' *del.*] ['notion of' *del.*] description of the race as consisting of two similar point-series will not work. [¶] The remedy, for Mr. Russell, lies in remembering that the points are infinitely nu-' |

91.21 'sophism∧'] *comma del.*
91.21 what] *aft. del.* 'they seem to me'
91.22 virtually] *alt. fr.* 'practically'
91.22 be] *aft. del.* 'amount to ['this' *del.*] nothing less than this'
91.25 ['is' *del.*] lay ['in' *del.*] only] *ab. del.* 'consisted'
91.25 the paths] *aft. del.* 'two *unequal [*intrl.*] static quanta—'; *bef. del.* ', namely,'
†91.26-27 measured . . . to] *ab. del.* '*['taken & measured' *del.*] treated [*ab. del.* '—taken after the race is *done— [*dash ab. del. comma; undel. in error*]'] '
91.27 points] *aft. del.* 'points'
91.27 coincident with ['the same' *del.*]] *ab. del.* 'correlated ['with' *del.*] pair wise'
††91.28 upon a scale] *intrl.*
†91.28-29 -measure . . . themselves] *ab. del.* '-limits without being'
91.29-30 But . . . for] *intrl.*
91.30 owing] 'o' *ov.* 'O'
91.30 -start,] *bef. del.* 'the path of Achilles has *the [*ab. del.* '['the' *del.*] a'] greater *length, [*comma ov. period*] ['*, and [*insrtd.*] if ['i' *ov.* 'I'] so,' *del.*]

and if the ['lanes' *del.*] paths are only points,'
91.31 if] *bef. del.* 'the'
91.32 measurement,] *ab. del.* 'comparison, can the'
91.33 time?] *bef. del.* 'x|xMr. Russell's own *paraphrase of the Achilles argument is too long & technical [*ab. del.* 'statement is too intricate'] for reproduction in a book like the present one, so I have to paraphrase it in turn. I hope that no essential injustice has been done.'
91.36 infinite] *final 's' del.*
91.36 multitudes] *intrl.*
91.37 to say] *ab. del.* '['parts are' *del.*] ['that the' *del.*] the *belief [*ab. del.* 'notion']'
91.37 whole] *ab. del.* 'part'
91.37 greater] *ab. del.* 'less'
91.37 part] *ab. del.* 'whole'
†92.11-93.3 It . . . case.] *substituted for del.* 'It seems to me that the question hinges not *so much [*intrl.*] on the [*del.* '*logical question of [*ab. del.* 'numbers of points'] the 'class' to which the ['various' *del.*] two specimens of [*doubtful* 'lar' *del.*] longer and the short bit of space continuum belong to be *predicable [*alt. fr.* 'predicated'] of the shorter and the longer path. To **s*'] number of *the [*intrl.*] points into which *a [*ab. del.* 'the'] longer and *a [*intrl.*] shorter paths can be *resolved, [*comma insrtd.*] ['analytically,' *del.*] as on [*del.* 'the physical question of ['how to ['annihilate' *del.*] traverse' *del.*] ['how to get to a limit' *del.*] how to touch a *goal [*ab. del.* 'limit'] when something always intervenes. There is no need of bringing in two runners. Achilles'] or the tortoise alone, ['will do;' *del.*] or *even [*intrl.*] the flight of empty time, *will ['do' *del.*] [*insrtd. for del.* 'is sufficient to'] show the difficulty. ['The' *del.*] A half second & a whole second may be "gleichmachtig" *or not, [*ab. del.* 'numerically,'] *if time be [*insrtd. for del.* 'can be reached if'] infinite in composition, *but one doesn't understand how either [*moved by guideline fr. aft. del.* 'numerically'] can *elapse.*

['Russell takes the paths as static quanta' *del.*] ['*If* the limit can be reached the long' *del.*] Russell assumes the *paths [*ab. del.* 'quanta'] which he compares to be already *traversed. [*ab. del.* 'given.'] They are static *quanta [*ab. del.* 'things'] of which the larger has the *['same number as the less. But the paths |Russell' *del.*] [*opp. mrgn. circled* 'no break'] compares the paths of the two runners *statically, [*comma insrtd.*] *or after the fact. [*intrl.*] They are *quanta* of which ['if' *del.*] the *longer, [*alt. fr.* 'larger'] *if it [*intrl.*] exists, ['it' *del.*] will *show [*ab. del.* 'have'] the same number as the shorter; but this *static number is irrelevant [*ab. del.* 'is irrelevant'] to the real question, which is whether either quantum, *if *its* ['s' *added*] *infinite points [*ab. del.* '['has to be traversed' *del.*] parts'] *have to be *traversed [*ab. del.* 'counted'] *in succession,* ['can' *del.*] (as they must be ['counted' *del.*] by the *runners) [*paren ov. comma*] can be *traversed [*ab. del.* 'counted'] to an end. Two runners are not required to show the difficulty— either *alone, [*intrl.*] ['will do, alone' *del.*] or even the flight of empty *time, [*comma ov. period*] *will do. [*intrl.*] How can *the first second, if all its [*ab. del.* 'it, if its infinite'] points must be *enumerated,* possibly be understood to elapse? ['One hardly knows whether to call the difficulty logical or physical. In either case' *del.*] The law of formation of a growing infinite, *which is by enumeration,* forbids its ever coming to an end. [*del.* 'Russell ['turns his back on *the [*insrtd.*] process['es' *del.*], and assumes the finished' *del.*] ignores the ['formations' *del.*] manner of formation and takes the result as given by some other law.'] Of course the same thing can be *produced [*ab. del.* 'given'] in various ways, and ['th' *del.*] a limit ['reach' *del.*] unattainable by *the [*ab. del.* 'one'] process of *enumeration [*ab. del.* 'addition,'] may be got, ['by 'creation' all at once,' *del.*] as the number ω

of any point continuum is *got, [*intrl.*] by a single *act of [*ab. del.* 'effort at'] 'definition' on the part of the mind. 'The definition of whole and part *without enumeration* is the key to the whole mystery' of the infinite, in Mr. Russell's ['own' *del.*] words. But *surely [*ab. del.* 'Achill'] physical processes of change are processes of enumeration; so they must take place by *finite ['f' *ov.* 'd'] steps, or not complete themselves at all.'

92.12 ['problem,' *del.*] difficulty,] *ab. del.* 'question, *the [*poss.* 'He'] question, [*intrl.*]'

92.12-13 exclusively,] *insrtd.*

92.13 which] *aft. del.* 'into'

92.13 is . . . he] *ab. del.* '['he' *del.*] ['R *del.*] he translates *exclusively [*intrl.*] the facts by'

92.15 only] *aft. del.* '*problem ['difficulty' *del.*] [*ab. del.* 'problem is']'

†92.15 problem . . . of] ('is' *intrl.*); *ab. del.* 'that of measu'

92.16 real] *intrl.*

92.20 an] *aft. del.* 'an [*ab. del.* 'a permanently recurrent obstacle']'

92.20 needing] *intrl.*

92.20 keeps] *intrl.*

92.21 reproducing . . . in] *orig.* 'reproduces itself and blocks' *ab. del.* '['po' *del.*] pops up in y'

92.22 manners.] *insrtd. for del.* 'ways.'

92.22-25 This . . . with] *insrtd. for del.* 'God, [*comma insrtd.*] *we think, [*intrl.*] *['can' *del.*] produced ['d' *added*] any quantity of [*ab. del.* 'produces a cubic yard of'] space, *['enveloping' *del.*] with [*ab. del.* 'with']'

92.23 2letter] 1't' *ov.* 'e'

92.23 printed] *bef. del.* 'for the reader'

92.25 already∧] *comma del.*

92.26 now] *aft. del.* '—however made!'

92.27 may ['similarly' *del.*] conceivably] *ab. del.* 'might'

92.28 was] *ab. del.* 'is'

92.28 by] *bef. del.* 'Prof. Cantor *in [*ab. del.* 'by'] a single effort of conception.'

92.29 in] *insrtd. for del.* 'on the part of'

92.30 whoso] *aft. del.* 'Achilles and the

tortoise, traversing'

92.30　*traverses*] *bef. del.* 'a [*undel. in error*] path'

92.31　act.] *ab. del.* 'process.'

92.31-32　order of] *intrl.*

92.32　necessarily] *ab. del.* 'to be'

92.32　end] *bef. del.* 'simply [*intrl.*]'

92.33　reached,] *comma ov. period*

†92.33-34　for . . . neglect.] *insrtd.*

92.34　cannot] *alt. fr.* 'can't'

92.34　'Enumeration'] ('E' *ov.* 'e'); *aft. del.* 'The process of'

92.34-35　['one' *del.*] sole possible] *ab. del.* 'essential thing in'

†92.37-40　Mr. . . . done.] *insrtd.*

92.37　¹of . . . remedy] *moved by guideline fr. orig. position aft. del.* 'Both' *and bef.* '['remedy' *del.*] Mr.'

92.37-38　technical] *aft. del.* 'long and'

92.38　verbatim] *aft. del.* 'li'

92.38　As] ('A' *ov.* 'a'); *aft. del.* 'So,'

93.1　as he does,] *intrl.*

93.2　deliberately] *intrl.*

93.4　After ['all' *del.*] . . . I ['have to' *del.*]] *ab. del.* '['The result' *del.*] I'

93.5　need] *ab. del.* 'can'

93.5　block] *aft. del.* 'be understood to'

93.5　empiricist ['conception' *del.*] opinion] *ab. del.* 'pluralist conclusion[*doubtful* 's' *del.*] ['to' *del.*]'

93.6　reached provisionally] *ab. del.* 'came to'

††93.6　though they ['are' *del.*] be] *intrl.*

93.7　¹the] *aft. del.* 'where'; *bef. del.* ''totality' of the'

93.7　of which] *ab. del.* 'is repre-'

93.7　²the] *ab. del.* 'a'

93.7　sort,] *ab. del.* 'order,'

93.8　apply] *bef. del.* 'to cases'

93.9　all] *ab. del.* 'all'

93.9　supposedly] *ab. del.* 'real change and growth of'

93.10　The . . . fulfilled] *ab. del.* 'Such changes are accomplished'

93.11　endless['ly' *del.*],] *comma insrtd. bef. del.* 'convergent,'

93.13　stomach] *aft. del.* 'pocket'

93.13　therefore] *aft. del.* 'or suppose'

93.15　perceptible] *ab. del.* 'finite'

93.15　steps] *ab. del.* 'atoms'

93.16　coming] *aft. del.* 'created once for all, and'

93.16-94.1　when . . . coming] ('when . . . come,' *insrtd.*); *ab. del.* 'or'

†93.17　The . . . 361.−] *ab. mrgn. insert* 'Note continued on p. 70ss'

93.17　Mr. Russell] *opp. mrgn.* 'note continued from p. 70qq'

93.18　counterpart] *ab. del.* 'pendant'

93.18　(according to Sterne)] *parens ov. commas*

93.20　²that] *alt. fr.* 'the same'

93.20　life] *aft. del.* 'whole'

93.20　But Mr.] *ab. del.* 'Mr.'

93.22　written] *aft. del.* 'be'

93.22　remain] *aft. del.* 'left unfinisht.'

93.23　²the] *insrtd. for del.* '*his own [*ab. del.* 'a phys'] making *the [*ab. del.* 'a']'

93.24　which . . . saying:] *ab. del.* ',−namely that exprest in his own *words:−[*dash doubtful*]'

††93.24　'if T. S.] *aft. undel. in error* 'If ['*Γ*' *ov.* 'i'] T. S.'; *opp. mrgn.* 'Note continued from p. 70ss'

93.25　of] *bef. del.* 'change ['someth' *del.*] an analogous physical h'

93.25　a] *ab. del.* 'some'

93.26　absurd] *ab. del.* 'impossible'

93.26　'live] *aft. del.* 'life'

93.27　outliving] *insrtd. for del.* 'living down'

93.27-28　wearying' . . . task [*sg. qt. del.*].] 'ing'' *added to* 'weary [*sg. qt. del.*]'; 'of his impossible' *insrtd. for del.* 'of his'

93.29　shyness] *ab. del.* 'trepidation'

93.30　from] *bef. del.* '['Mr Bertrand Russell, in particular because his reasonings are too intric' *del.*] Bertrand Russell and his'

93.30　dim] *ab. del.* 'poor [*intrl.*]'

93.31　['intricate and' *del.*] technical] *ab. del.* 'intricately exprest'

93.31　to] *aft. del.* '['to q' *del.*] incorporate the det'

93.31　cite] *ab. del.* 'follow the'

93.33　consult] *intrl. bef. del.* 'follow [*ab. del.* 'use']'

93.33　Baldwin's . . . 'continuity';] *insrtd.*

93.33　tables of] *ab. del.* 'index and'

93.33-34 contents] *bef. del.* 'and index'
93.34 ²of] *aft. del.* '*and ['or' *del.*]
[*ab. del.* 'and'] that contents'
93.35 his] *ab. del.* 'that *of [*pencil del. in
error*] the'
93.35 *Principes*] '*e*' *ov.* '*le*'
††93.35 *Mathématiques.*] *period insrtd.*
bef. del. 'of the same author.'
†93.38 C. . . . ²as] *insrtd.*
93.40 more] *ab. del.* 'a'
93.40 discussions] *ab. del.* 'introduction'
93.41 Supplementary] *aft. del.*
'Appendix;'
93.41 29,] *comma insrtd. bef. del. semicolon*
93.41-42 and . . . 390;] *insrtd. opp.
mrgn.* 'continued on p. 70ᵗᵗ'
††93.43 LEIGHTON:] *bel. horiz. line and
heading* 'Note continued from p. 70ʳʳ'
93.43 finally the] *ab. del.* 'the contents'
93.43 tables] '*s*' *added*
93.44 with] *aft. del.* 'on 'Science.''
93.45 liveliest] *ab. del.* 'most persuasive'
93.45 attack] *ab. del.* 'statement'
93.45 upon] *ab. del.* 'of the [**'Zenonian**
position' *del.*] argument against an'
93.45 infinites] '*s*' *added*
93.46 that] *intrl.*
94.2 concrete experience['*s*' *del.*]] 'concrete' *ab. del.* 'our perceptual'
94.2-3 changes . . . stays] *final* '*s*' *added
to each*
†94.2 sensible . . . or] ('sensible' *ab. del.*
'['small' *del.*] ['perceptible' *del.*]
given'); *ab. del.* 'a much-at-once, or not
at all,'
94.3 The] *aft. del.* 'They are in short discontinuous in the mathematical sense,'
94.4 act] *aft. del.* 'abstract'
94.5 given] *intrl. aft.* 'given [*ab. del.*
'supposed']'
††94.5-6 The . . . treatment,] ('*s*' *added
to* 'facts'; 'do' *alt. fr.* 'does'; 'the sub-'|
insrtd. for del. '['the conceptual' *del.*]
our sub-' |; 'treatment' *aft. del.* 'subdivi-
sion'); *ab. del.* 'material given lends itself to the conceptual manipulation,'
94.6 believe] *aft. del.* 'suppose that'
94.6-8 that . . . existence.] ('brought
['about.' *del.*] into existence.' *ab. del.*
'made.'); *ab. del.* 'them [*ab. del.* 'it'] to

have made *themselves [*ab. del.* 'itself']
in that self contradictory way.'
94.9 The] *opp. mrgn.* '¶'
94.10 more] *intrl.*
94.10 our] *ab. del.* 'the'
94.10-11 transformation] *ab. del.*
'manipulation'
94.11 makes] *ab. del.* 'leaves'
94.11 less comprehensible] *alt. fr.* 'more
incomprehensible'
94.11-12 than ever.] *ab. del.* 'than it was
before.'
94.12 immediately . . . quantities] *intrl.*;
orig. caret aft. 'itself' [94.13] *undel. in
error*
94.13 indeed . . . which] *ab. del.* 'be what'
††94.14-15 be . . . summation] ('summation' *ab. del.* 'addition'); *ab. del.*
'result from successive synthesis'
94.15 chain] *ab. del.* 'series'
94.15-16 no one] *alt. fr.* 'none'
94.16 amount whatever] *ab. del.* '['ab'
del.] of the amount'
94.17 expected to result,] ('expected' *bef.
del.* 'destined'; 'result,' *ab. del.* 'come,');
ab. del. '['to be produced,' *del.*] thus
to be made,'
94.18-20 The . . . success.] (*insrtd. orig.
aft.* 'absurd.' [94.22], *then guideline
del.*); *insrtd.*
94.18-19 substitution of] *intrl.*
94.19 for] *ab. del.* 'of'
94.19 intuition] (*alt. fr.* 'intuitive'); *bef.
del.* 'data'
94.19-20 thus . . . taken] *ab. del.* 'may
be a useful device for certain practical
purposes of *calculation, [*ab. del.* 'formulation,'] but'
94.20 description] *ab. del.* 'theory'
94.20 to] *aft. del.* 'it ['has' *del.*] ['conspicuously *fails. [*period insrtd. bef.
del. poss.* 'or' *or* '&'] *del.*] seems'
†94.21 opaquely . . . perception] *ab. del.*
'fact *as simply [*intrl.*] unmediated,''
††94.22 concept . . . absurd.['ˣ' *del.*]]
bel. del. 'notion contradictory.ˣ'
94.23 ¹the] *bef. del.* 'mathematical infin'
94.23-24 interpretation] *ab. del.* '['in-'|
del.] latest explanation'
94.24 new] *aft. del.* 'theory of'
94.24 infinity.] *ab. del.* 'that word.'

94.24   We] *aft. del.* '[*del.* 'We find ourselves remanded to the ['mas' *del.*]
['idea that' *del.*] notion of real changes
taking place by steps that are discrete']
We *conclude that the notion that
reality [*ab. del.* 'find it more acceptable
*to imagine [*ab. del.* 'to suppose'] that
real *for [*insrtd.*]'] changes ['s' *ov.
del. comma*] ['to [*intrl.*] take [*alt. fr.*
'taking'] place' *del.*] by steps finite in
number and discrete is ['the' *del.*] more
acceptable to the imag'; *bef. del.* 'for
our part'

††94.25   -continuum,] (*comma insrtd.
and undel. in error*); *bef. del.* '[*del.*
'*is obnoxious to [*ab. del.* 'illustrates
beautifully'] the charge I made against
the ['conceptualist method,' *del.*]
intellectualistic method (above, p.   ),
of translating ['the' *del.*] living facts
into terms'] tho it seems in a way to
*elude['d' *del.*] [*ab. del.* 'have met']
my charge of turning the flowing into
the discrete (above, p.   ), yet'

††94.26   ¹the ... (above∧ [*opening paren
del.*] p.   ).] *ab. del.* '['the moving
into' *del.*] it into the *static. [*period
doubtful*]'

94.26   buds] *aft. del.* 'finite'

94.27   ¹of ... being,] ('primal' *bef. del.*
'data of'); *ab. del.* 'which *empiricism
[*ab. del.* 'pluralism'] leaves ['unal' *del.*]
['ar' *del.*] unsubdivided,'

94.28   ²of] *intrl.*

94.29   the] *ab. del.* 'the new infinite'

94.29   have got rid.] *insrtd. for del.* 'have
*abolished. [*ab. del.* 'eliminated.']'

††94.30   'Weierstrass] *sg. ov. db. qt.*

94.30   he] *aft. del.* 'by'

94.37   so called,] *ab. del.* 'in'

94.38   an] *aft. del.* 'identified with'

94.39   ²and] *ab. del.* 'agrees with'

94.39   agree] *intrl.*

94.39   perceptual] *ab. del.* 'our perceptual
*categories, [*comma doubtful*] for the
one only'

94.40   (*twice*) a pure] *ab. del.* 'only'

95.1   that] *ab. del.* 'that'

95.2   ['to' *del.*] remains ... acceptable]
ab. del. 'is more permissible'

95.2,3   our] *ab. del.* 'the'

95.3   as before;] *ab. caret formed fr. orig.
semicolon*

95.4   barren] *aft. del.* '['some' *del.*] rather'

95.4   we] *ab. del.* 'we return to'

95.5   laid it down.] *ab. del.* 'left it.'

95.7   now] *ab. del.* 'hence forward [*ab.
del.* 'now [*ab. del.* '['hen' *del.*] now']']'

95.8   continu-|] *bef. del.* |'ity is that
property'

95.8   two] *bef. del.* 'terms or'

95.9   directly ... to] *ab. del.* 'quite different from'

95.9   more] *intrl.*

95.10   or ... that] *ab. del.* 'description
[*ab. del.* 'definition'] which ['asserts
that' *del.*] requires that the *idea,
which calls [*ab. del.* 'parts of']'

95.10   is] *intrl.*

95.10-11   when ... immediate] 'when ...
appear' *ab. del.* 'should be im-' |; 'as im'
insrtd.

95.12   the] *bef. del.* 'more empirical or
physical conception.'

95.14   philosophy∧] *comma del.*

††96.0   SECOND ... EFFECT.] *db. underlined*

96.2   bits] *bef. del.* 'that come'

96.2   come] *bef. del.* 'thu'

96.2-3   Remember] *aft. del.* 'If'

††96.3-4   *überhaupt* ... large∧] *intrl.*

96.4   found to be] *ab. del.* ' saw was'

96.4   undeduceable. For] *period ov.
comma*; 'For [*ov.* 'from']' *aft. del.* 'and'

96.4   our] *ab. del.* 'the'

96.4   *intellect*['ual' *del.*]] *bef. del.* 'point
of view'

96.4-5   it remains] *intrl.*

96.5   quantum] (*alt. fr.* 'quantity'); *ab. del.*
'matter of fact'

96.6   May] *ab. del.* 'Can'

96.6   ¹bit] *aft. del.* 'pieceme'

96.6   itself?] *qst. mk. ov. comma*

96.10   With these questions] *intrl.*

96.11   ¹face] *aft. del.* 'here'

96.11   again.] *ab. period undel. in error*

96.13   ['is' *del.*] has been taken] *ab. del.*
'has usually been understood'

96.13   mean] *ab. del.* 'require'

96.13   the] *alt. fr.* 'they'

96.13   in] *aft. del.* 'is'

96.14   exists] *ab. del.* 'contained'

96.15 in] *aft. del.* 'pl'

96.16 review] *ab. del.* 'pass'

96.16 facts] *aft. del.* 'principle of *causality. [period insrtd.] ['in' del.] I take it first in'

96.16 in] *aft. del.* 'first'; *bef. del.* 'the more con'

96.17 form.] *bef. circled note* 'Turn to page 71 at other end of book'

96.18 ¹The] *aft. del.* ¦'stacle to pluralism has always been what is known in philosophy as 'the principle of causality.' Before *proceeding farther [*ab. del.* 'closing in upon our pluralistic inquiry,'] it will be well to *study [*ab. del.* 'treat'] that subject in a ['chapter by itself.' *del.*] *ways of perceiving change, that few philosophers treat it as ['more than' *del.*] absolutely true. Yet, even when treated as **merely ['m' *ov.* 'a'] a descriptive expedient, its prestige injures other philosophy, and the actual situation among thinkers ['must be regarded' *del.*] is [*ov.* 'as'] ['most' *del.*] confused and unsatisfactory. [*moved by guideline to missing passage on* verso *of stub betw. fols.* 69 *and* 71] *Chapter ['C' *ov.* 'c'] VI ¦**Second **Sub-problem:** [*pencil; pencil db.* underl.] [*pencil and ink del.*] ¦*['Concerning' *del.*] Causation: [*db.* underl.] *I. The conceptual view. [*insrtd.; triple underl.*]'

96.18 inquiry into] *ab. del.* 'analysis of'

96.18 made] *ab. del.* 'given'

96.19 he . . . furnished] *ab. del.* 'is *answered [*ab. del.* 'given']'

96.19 principles:] (*colon ov. comma*); *aft. del.* 'causes,'

†96.20 when . . . a] (*comma aft.* 'brass' *undel in error*); *ab. del.* 'bronze of the'

96.21;97.1 (*first*) when] *intrl.*

96.21 makes] *ab. del.* 'of'

††96.22 or . . . metaphysics,] *intrl.*

96.22 gives] 's' *aft. del.* 's'

96.23 views.] *bef. del.* 'x'

97.1 makes] *ab. del.* ', of'

97.1 child);] *semicolon ov. colon*

97.2 one ['takes' *del.*] 'exercises'] 'o' *ov.* 'w'; *final* 's' *of* 'exercises' *ov. sg. qt.*

97.2 Christian] ('C' *ov.* 'c'); *aft. del.* 'Sc'

97.2 adopted] *aft. del.* 'elaborated the Aristo'

97.4 immediately] *intrl.*

97.5 that] *ab. del.* '['it alone.' *del.*] efficient cause'

97.6 An] *ab. del.* 'The'

97.6 cause] *bef. del.* 'of *an [*ab. del.* 'a given'] effect'

97.6 scholastically] *intrl.*

97.6 that] *bef. del.* 'on [*intrl.*]'

97.6 produces] *aft. del.* '[*del.* 'involves ['the' *del.*] in itself'] the existence of something ['else' *del.*] depends [*intrl.*] in such wise that it'

97.7 something else] *ab. del.* 'this other'

97.8 the] *aft. del.* 'a [*ab. del.* 'the'] common-sen'

97.8 sense;] *semicolon ov. colon*

97.9 grown quite] *ab. del.* 'made very'

97.9 Passing over] *ab. del.* 'Without touching on'

97.9-10 many classes] *ab. del.* 'various ['k' *del.*] species'

97.10 specifies] *aft. del.* 'enumerates, I class:'

97.11 three important] *ab. del.* 'the more important'

97.13 1.] *bef. del.* 'The'

††97.13 come into being] *ab. del.* 'be [*ab. del.* 'come']'

97.14 if . . . be] *insrtd. for del.* 'if'

97.15 without a cause] *underline del.*

97.17 is] *aft. del.* 'has been'

97.19 proportionate] *alt. fr.* 'proportional [*alt. fr.* 'proportionate']'

97.22 been] *bef. del.* 'contained'

97.23 that . . . effect,] *ab. del.* 'literally,'

97.23 one] *aft. del.* 'the *effect [*ab. del.* 'cause is *lik [*doubtful*]'] copies the cause'

97.24 cause] *aft. del.* 'eff'

97.24-25 somehow involves] *ab. del.* 'has the power *over [*ab. del.* 'of'] that ['effect' *del.*] to [*ab. del.* 'over']'

97.25 resembling it,] *ab. del.* 'literally containing the effect,'

97.26 statue] *bef. del.* 'is [*doubtful*] eminently'

97.26 possesses not] *ab. del.* 'doesn't'

97.26 its ['statuesque' *del.*]] *ab. del.*

'possess ['its' *del.*]'

97.28 overcomes] ('s' *added*); *aft. del.*
'can ['caus' *del.*]'

97.28 lion's [' 's' *added*] ... by]
'strength by' *ab. del.* 'by his'

97.29 principle] *ab. del.* 'conception
[*ab. del.* 'principle']'

97.29 which] *bef. del.* '['the las' *del.*]
['all the' *del.*] both causal pr'

97.30 flows] *aft. del.* 'logically'

97.32 which] *bef. del.* '['the con-' | *del.*]
phenomena ['p' *ov. poss. start of* 't']
of'

97.33 contains] *ab. del.* 'are'

97.33 or] *bef. del.* 'mor'

97.33 with extreme] *ab. del.* 'more'

97.33 concision] *alt. fr.* 'concisely'

97.34 ¹moment] *aft. del.* 'prior'

97.34 in its totality] *ab. del.* 'is the'

97.34 causes] (*final* 's' *added*); *bef. del.*
'of'

97.34 next] *bef. del.* 'subsequent'

†97.35-36 Read ... iii.] *insrtd.*

97.35 concise] *ab. del.* 'convenient'

97.35 in] *bef. del.* 'by'

††97.36 General] *aft. del.* 'in his'

97.36 Book] 'B' *ov. poss.* 'ch'

97.36 I] *aft. del.* 'x'

97.36 from my text] *intrl.*

97.37 causal] *aft. del.* 'conceptual'

97.38 ¹causes] *final* 's' *added*

97.38 produce] *ab. del.* 'always has'

97.38 ²effects] 's' *added*

97.38 'causes] (*final* 's' *added*); *aft. del.*
' 'a'

97.39 act only when] *ab. del.* 'must be'

97.39 present';] ';' *insrtd. bef. del.* 'to its
effect'

97.40 conditioning] *alt. fr.* 'conditions'

97.41 indispensable] *ab. del.* 'necessary'

97.41 ∧causes∧] *sg. qts. del.*

98.1 But if] *ab. del.* 'So far [*poss.* 'as' *del.*
intrl.] ['then' *del.*] as'

98.1 firm] *intrl.*

98.2 it ... that] *intrl.*

98.3 original] *ab. del.* 'novel'

98.3 ¹that] *insrtd.*

98.3 the] *bef. del.* 'perceptual [*intrl.*]
appearance['s' *del.*] of'

98.3-4 ²that ... illusion] ('lives' *ab. del.*

'world'); *ab. del.* 'must be ['reckoned'
del.]'

98.5 ascribable] *alt. fr.* 'ascribed'

98.5 the ... the [*ab. del.* 'our']] *ab. del.*
'['our taking too' *del.*] superficiality of
['the' *del.*]'

98.6 respected] *ab. del.* '*clung to [*ab.
del.* 'compromised with']'

98.6 in this case] *ab. del.* 'took refuge'

98.7 frank] *ab. del.* 'unnaturalness of *a
[*insrtd.*] ['such a' *del.*]'

98.7 by] *bef. del.* 'introducing [*intrl.*]'

98.7 modo.'] *period insrtd. bef. del.* 'into
its proposition.'

98.8 also to] *ab. del.* 'to be'

98.8-9 ['also' *del.*] *aliquo modo*,] *ab.
del.* 'indefinitely'

98.9 But] *bef. del.* 'the general con'

98.9,10 have] *intrl.*

98.10 as] *aft. del.* 'by'

98.11 A] (*ov.* 'a'); *aft. del.* '['Conce' *del.*]
As conceived,'

98.13-14 already ['already' *del.*] ... the]
ab. del. 'being the'

98.14 itself?] *ab. del.* 'disguise? ['The
effect is' *del.*] Causation *thus [*insrtd.*]
changes from *a [*ab. del.* 'something']
concretely ['ly' *added*] *experienced
thought [*ab. del.* 'and physical *or psychological [*intrl.*] *into an [*ab. del.*
'into something'] abstractly ['ly' *added*]
['and' *del.*] logical relation']—the cause
become a logical ground and the effect
a logical consequence. Identity is the
only ['logical' *del.*] basis of logical sequence, so the ['final shape' *del.*] ['cop'
del.] conceptual philosophy of causation has led directly to the'

98.14 cause] *aft. del.* 'the'

98.15 perceptual] *aft. del.* 'ap'

98.16 concretely experienced] *ab. del.*
'['physical into an' *del.*] purely logical
conception, the ['cause' *del.*] effect'

98.16-17 between differents] *intrl.*

98.17 between similars] *intrl.*

98.17 of] *intrl.*

98.18 reason,] *ab. del.* 'ground,'

98.19-20 logical ... same,] ('follows'
insrtd. for del. 'goes'); *ab. del.* 'identity
[*ab. del.* '*we can [*intrl. bef. del.*

'identity'] '] is the only *reason [*ab. del.*
'basis'] for *logical['ly' *del.*] ['deducing' *del.*] consequence['s' *del.*; *word
undel.*] [*ab. del.* '['logical derivation'
del.] rational deduction,']'

98.20   older] ('er' *added*); *aft. del.* 'only'
98.20   vaguer] *intrl.*
98.20   developes] ('s' *ov.* 'd'); *aft. del.*
'has'
98.21   sharp] *intrl.*
98.21   dogma] *ab. del.* 'doctrine'
98.21   **cause**] *aft. del.* 'the'
98.22   one . . . being] *ab. del.* 'the same
*fact, [*ab. del.* 'thing,']'
98.22   ¹the] *ab. del.* 'two'
98.23   no . . . novelty] *aft. del.* 'there can
be'; *bef. del.* '['under the sun.' *del.*] can
possibly'
98.24   overthrow] *aft. del.* 'complete [*ab.
del.* 'monistic'] monistic'
98.25   ['here' *del.*] in this field.] *ab. del.*
'in the causal field.'
98.25   theory] *ab. del.* 'doctrine'
98.27   the] *aft. del.* 'were *two [*alt. fr.*
'to'] at'
98.27, 28 purely] *intrl.*
98.28   absolutely] *ab. del.* 'too ['heto'
del.] unlike'
98.28   dissimilar.] *period insrtd. bef. del.*
'in nature for the interaction be'
98.28-29 If . . . such] ('any' *ab. del. comma*); *ab. del.* 'any'
98.29   as . . . perceive] *intrl.*
98.31   is . . . ¹the] *ab. del.* 'makes [*ab. del.*
'amounts to calling'] it ['the' *del.*] to be'
98.32   neither is] *intrl.*
98.32   case] *bef. del.* 'is not'
98.33   fragmentary] *ab. del.* 'salient'
98.33-34 name. . . . fragment,] *period ov.
comma*; 'It . . . fragment,' *intrl.*
98.34   along ['its' *del.*] with] *intrl.*
98.34   its] *ab. del.* 'its'
98.34   concomitants—] (*dash insrtd. for
del. comma*); *bef. del.* '*as well, [*intrl.*]'
98.34   it is] *intrl.*
98.36   expresses] 'es' *added*
98.38   [i.e. the amount]] *intrl.*
98.41   even] *aft. del.* 'to'
99.1   ceased to be] *ab. del.* 'to be intellig'
99.1   'rational['ly' *del.*].'] *sg. qts. and
period insrtd. bef. del.* '*is [*doubtful*]

acceptable. [*ab. del.* 'understood.']'
99.2   **the great**] *ab. del.* 'a'
99.2   absurdities∧ —he] 'absurdities [*semicolon del.*] —he' *alt. fr.* 'absurdity. He'
99.3   Descartes' disciples] *intrl.*
††99.4   Geulinx,] *bef. del.* '['disciples of
Descartes,' *del.*] ['invoked *him [*insrtd.
for del.* 'God'] as the immediate cause
of' *del.*] denying the'
††99.4-5   the . . . *pschophysical ['y'
omitted in error] interaction [*comma
del.*] altogether. [*period ov. comma*]]
ab. del. 'the agency of secondary cause
['and' *del.*] ['They' *del. intrl.*] and
[*insrtd.*] considered'
99.5   according to them, ['was' *del.*]] *ab.
del.* 'to be the'
99.5-6   immediately] 'ly' *added*
99.6   caused] *insrtd. for del.* 'produced
[*ab. del.* 'causal [*ab. del.* 'causal']
agent of']'
99.6   ¹in] *aft. del.* 'either'
99.6   ¹our] *intrl.*
99.6   mind] *bef. del.* 'or body,'
99.7   those] *aft. del.* 'of'
99.7   events] *aft. del.* 'the'
99.7   appear] *ab. del.* 'seem'
99.9-10   took . . . our] ('the next' *ab. del.*
'another'; 'forward in' *aft. del.* '['still—'
del.] towards' *and bef. del.* 'the'; ²'the'
insrtd. for del. 'of the'); *ab. del.* 'went
farther in the ['way of' *del.*] abolition
[*alt. fr.* 'abolishing'] of [*undel. in error;
intrl.*] the truth of ['our' *del.*] causal'
99.10   freed] *ab. del.* 'economized God's
work, *and [*ab. del.* 'by'] dispensed
[*alt. fr.* 'dispensing']'
99.10   God] *ov.* 'him'
99.10   the duty of] *intrl.*
99.11   hourly] *intrl.*
99.11   by] *insrtd. aft. del.* 'from moment
to moment and'
99.11   supposing] 'ing' *ov.* 'ed'
99.11   decreed] *ab. del.* '['instituted all'
del.] ['tr [*ov.* 'f'] ' *del.*] ['pre esta-' |
del.] established [|'esta' *insrtd.*] all the'
99.12   in] *bef. del.* 'all'
99.12   several] *intrl.*
99.12-13   coincide] *ab. del.* 'synchroni-
cally harmonize'
99.13   after] *aft. del.* 'much'

99.14   clocks] *aft. del.* 'two'

†99.15   'pre-established . . . called,] ('harmony'' *bef. del.* 'as my'); *ab. del.* ', the [*comma undel. in error*] reader will observe,'

99.16   of . . . given,] ('immediately' *aft. del.* 'given'); *ab. del.* 'gets completed,'

99.16   its never failing] *ab. del.* 'the usual'

99.17   negating both] *ab. del.* 'destroying *both [undel. in error*] the [*insrtd.*]'

99.17   and] *bef. del.* 'the [*intrl.*]'

99.17-18   is . . . dramatic] ('is' *aft. del.* '['found' *del.*] ['in perception,' *del.*] there, [*doubtful*]'); *ab. del.* '. For the dramatic'

99.18   bare] *intrl.*

99.19   terms] *aft. del.* 'discrete'

99.19   causally] *ab. del.* 'independently discrete series—dynamically'

99.20   is set up.] *insrtd. aft. del.* ', is [*comma intended to be smudged out*] substituted. But the notion *is [*ab. del.* 'is'] set up. The *notion is [*ab. del.* 'substitute is conceptually'] as [*intrl.*] monistic and fatalistic *as the rationalist heart [*ab. del.* '['to the' *del.*] as anyone'] can desire, and *of course [*ab. del.* 'of course ['real novelty is' *del.*] it rules real novelty out'] there can be no real novelty if Leibnitz's'

99.20   of anything,] *intrl.*

99.21   The] *aft. del.* 'Cause means creation, not procession.'

99.21   theory] *intrl. bef. del.* 'conception [*ab. del.* 'notion']'

99.22   impossible] *ab. del.* 'absolutely excluded from the world'

99.23   made [*alt. fr. doubtful* 'make'] the] *insrtd. for del.* '*contributed the [*ab. del.* 'was the author of the']'; *opp. circled mrgn.* '¶'

99.23   step in discrediting ['the' *del.*]] *ab. del.* 'criticism of perceptual'

99.24   chapters] *aft. del.* 'chapters on such'

99.26   a positive] *ab. del.* 'the 'efficiency' of a cause by the conceptual method and failed to find any *distinct [*ab. del.* 'positive']'

99.26   ¹of] *aft. del.* 'in *one's [*insrtd. for del.* 'the'] mind'

99.26   'efficacy'] (*ov.* 'efficiency'); *bef.*

del. 'of a cause,'

99.26-27   causes . . . ¹to] *ab. del.* 'it'

99.27   exert] *final* 's' *del.*

99.27   He . . . neither] ('n' *ov.* 'N'); 'He shows that' *intrl. aft. del.* '['In' *del.*] ['He followed the conceptual method' *del.*] We can abstract and isolate no such ['relation' *del.*] dynamic relation between causes.'

99.29   effects.] *aft. del.* 'their [*ab. del.* 'what we call']'

99.29   This] *aft. del.* 'As the concept ['is' *del.*] of energy is isolated, and'

††99.33   'We] *aft. del.* 'Hume's conclusion was'

99.36   effect. . . .] *last 3 dots intrl.*

†99.40-100.3   "Nothing . . . united."] *insrtd.*

100.4   The] *insrtd. for del.* 'The'; *opp. mrgn.* '¶'

100.4   of a connexion,] *ab. del.* 'Hume then'

100.5   is] *aft. del.* 'the [*intrl.*]'

100.5   but] *bef. del.* 'a mental'

100.5   misinterpretation] *ab. del.* '['b' *del.*] habit'

100.6   custom.] *ab. del.* 'consequ secution.'

100.6   the] *ov.* 'a'

100.14   ¶Nothing] *aft. del.* '¶ [*undel. in mrgn.*] ['**Nothing**' *del.*] Hume's famous criticism, the reader will have observed, is an *fresh [*undel. in error ab. del.* 'exquisite'] example of the breakdown of conceptual translations. Causation, perceptually *or concretely [*intrl.*] taken is given in ['the way in' *del.*] the way in which'

100.14   could] *ab. del.* 'can'

100.15   of] *insrtd. for del.* 'which [*ab. del.* 'of which']'

100.15   philosophy . . . ['facts' *del.*] events] ('made' *alt. fr.* 'makes'); *ab. del.* 'works [*intrl. aft. del.* 'mind [*ab. del.* 'opinion']'] is composed. Facts'

100.15-16   neighbors . . . if] *ab. del.* '**successors** [*insrtd. for del.* '['contiguous and' *del.*] ['coexistent and successive' *del.*] neighbors ['like the ['bone['s' *del.*]' *del.*] dice in a box.' *del.*] with'] like'

100.16 were] *intrl.*
100.16 might] *ab. del.* 'mind'
100.17 have] *intrl.*
100.17 real] *ab. del.* 'absolute'
100.17 novelties] *alt. fr.* 'novelty'
100.19 half-hearted] *ab. del.* 'flagrant example'
100.19 ²the] *aft. del.* 'the'
100.19 lot] *ab. del.* 'class'
100.20 insists] *intrl. aft. del.* '*stoutly offer [*ab. del.* 'holds']'
100.20 the] *insrtd. for del.* '['nature's sequences,' *del.*] nature's'
100.20-21 which we experience,] *intrl.*
100.22-23 flower out of] *ab. del.* '*come into [*ab. del.* 'be added to the world']'
100.24 recognize] *ab. del.* 'find'
100.24 pages] *ab. del.* 'criticism of causation'
100.25 which] *bef. del.* 'the'
100.25 translations ['substitutes' *del.*] always] *insrtd. for del.* 'method is *forced to [*intrl.*]'
††100.25 matreat['s' *del.*]] ('l' *omitted in error*); *bef. del.* 'perceptual'
100.26-27 (as . . . later)] *parens ov. commas*
100.27 names the manner] *ab. del.* 'presents itself in the way'
100.27 some ['of our' *del.*]] *ab. del.* 'one whole'
100.27, 28 fields] 's' *added*
100.28 introduce['s' *del.*] other] 'other' *alt. fr.* 'another'
100.28 but] *intrl.*
100.28 forms] *aft. del.* 'many'
100.29 appears] *ab. del.* '['seems immediately to be continuous.' *del.*] comes'
100.29 flow] *alt. fr.* 'flux'
100.29 Our] *alt. fr.* 'All our'
100.30 other] *ab. del.* 'such'
100.31 successfully] ('ly' *added*); *aft. del.* 'far discrimination has been carried out'
100.31 we can] *intrl.*
100.31 discriminate] *alt. fr.* 'discrimination'
100.31 within the flow.] *ab. del.* 'handles been.'
100.32 ['rule' *del.*] conceptualist rule is] *ab. del.* '['basis of' *del.*] conviction of intellectualism is'

100.32 that] *aft. del. intrl. illeg. letters*
100.32 separate] *intrl.*
100.33 ought . . . fact] *ab. del.* 'is a thing, that the [*del.* 'a concept, [*del. intrl. illeg. letter*] that the ['thing th' *del.*]'] fact the concept stands for is as distinct from other facts as | as the concept is from other concepts. ['an insu-'| *del.*] a fact'
100.33 separate;] *ab. del.* 'insulable as the name is;'
100.34 such fact] ('such' *alt. fr.* 'separate'); *ab. del.* 'insulated 'impression''
100.35 By] *ab. del.* 'At [*aft. del.* 'A']'
100.35 rule] *alt. fr.* 'rate'
100.36 human speech] *ab. del.* 'any language'
100.36 meaningless—] *dash ov. period*
100.36 in,] *ab. del.* 'In,'
100.37 but] *aft. del.* 'nevertheless'
100.37 if,] *ab. del.* 'how,'
100.37 are] *ab. del.* 'must be'
100.38 neither the] *ab. del.* 'the immed'
100.38 fact nor] *ab. del.* 'our experience and'
100.38 are] *ab. del.* '['do not' *del.*] come'
100.39 separable] *alt. fr.* 'separate'
100.39 are] *aft. del.* 'do.'
100.39 original] *ab. del.* 'immediate presen'
100.39 fact comes] *alt. fr.* 'they come'
100.40 *durcheinander*, holding] *ab. del.* 'much-at-once, in which *with [*ab. del.* 'both']'
100.40 ¹as] *aft. del.* 'and rel'
101.1 in . . . or] *insrtd. for del.* 'are ['diffused into' *del.*] ['interpenetration.' *del.*] interlocked and'
101.1 cemented.] *ab. del.* 'locked together *in it. [*ab. caret formed fr. orig. period*]'
101.2 in the muchness,] *insrtd. for del.* '*the total [*intrl.*] of the ['hole' *del.*] complex *successively, [*ab. caret formed fr. orig. comma*]'
101.2 a man by] *ab. del.* 'by'
101.3 tube may] *ab. del.* 'small hole *in a screen [*intrl.*] ['one can' *del.*]'
101.3 limit] *final* 's' *del.*
101.4 But] *insrtd. for del.* '['Ou' *del.*] our

[*ab. del.* 'the'] '

101.4 is] *aft. del.* '['breaks' *del.*] no more breaks the'

101.5 Concepts] ('C' *ov.* 'c'); *aft. del.* 'Our ['abstract' *del.*]'

101.5 notes,['ˣ' *del.*]] (*comma ov. period*); *aft. del.* 'not parts, they are ['what *in [doubtful]' del.*] our'; *bef. del.* '['or view' *del.*] our'

††101.6 taken on reality,ˣ] *ab. del.* 'of reality—'

101.6 pieces . . . house.] ('of' *bef. del.* 'components of'); *ab. del.* 'natural['ly' *del.*] [*ab. del.* 'originally'] constituent fractions of reality,'

101.7 Causal] *alt. fr.* 'Causation'

††101.7 activity, in short ∧] *insrtd.*

101.7 play . . . growing] *ab. del.* '['then' *del.*] be an element in *flowing [*ab. del.* 'making']'

101.8 substantive] *ab. del.* 'separate'

101.8 should stand['s' *del.*] . . . itself.] *ab. del.* 'can be insulated.'

101.9 assumption] *alt. fr.* 'postulation'

101.9 any . . . be] *ab. del.* 'all real elements are'

101.10 his] *bef. del.* 'view that'

101.10 no] *ab. del.* 'all'

101.10 relation] *final* 's' *del.*

101.10 can be] ('can' *ov.* 'is'); *ab. del.* 'are un'

101.10 real] *bef. del. sg. qt.*

††101.10 'All] *sg. ov. poss. db. qt.*

††101.11 he writes∧] *intrl.*

†101.13-14 Nothing . . . else.] *insrtd.*

101.15 the] *ab. del.* 'the *conceptu['alist' doubtful]'

101.15 method] *ab. del.* 'philosophy ['lay' *del.*] triumph over life, and'

101.16 espoused] *ab. del.* 'welcomed'

101.17 opinion] *ab. del.* 'view of'

101.17 is] *ab. del.* 'was'

101.18 unwilling simply] *insrtd. for del.* '['dissatisfied with' *del.*] ['Humes ['notio' *del.*] acceptance' *del.*] unwilling'

101.18 as] *insrtd. for del.* '*['tout' *del.*] ['naively' *del.*] as simply as [*ab. del.* 'without relief, as']'

101.19 invoked] *ab. del.* 'invented an'

101.20 its ['s' *added*] bits] 'bits' *intrl.*

101.20 by] *aft. del.* 'again'; *bef. del.* 'its'

101.21 ['quotes' *del.*] inscribes] *ab. del.* '['wrote the' *del.*] cited'

101.22 for] *aft. del.* 'as'

101.24 is] *bef. del.* 'one of'

101.24 part] *final* 's' *del.*

101.25 and] *aft. del.* 'and'

101.25 its] *ab. del.* 'his exact'

101.25 catch.] *ab. del.* 'discern.'

101.26 his text,] *ab. del.* 'it, after taking considerable pains,'

101.26 just] *aft. del.* 'practically'

101.27 cancel] *ab. del.* '['deny that any 'power'' *del.*] dispense with'

101.28 ¹that] *ab. del.* '['of eff' *del.*] ['that the' *del.*] previous pheno']

101.28 ['any' *del.*] phenomena ['a' *ov.* 'on'] . . . that a] ('or that a' *insrtd. for del.* 'in the'); *ab. del.* 'causal has 'efficacy' or exerts 'Zwang' in any'

†101.29 would . . . effect.] ('causal' *not corrected to* 'cause' *bef. del.* 'connexion'; *period insrtd. bef. del. doubtful comma*); *intrl.*

101.29 In] 'I' *ov.* 'i'

101.30 Kant] *aft. del.* 'they both deny'

101.30 contradicts] *ab. del.* 'denies'

101.30 does,] *ov. comma*

101.30 like] *aft. del.* 'makes tran'

101.31 mere time-] *ab. del.* 'habitual'

101.31 only] *bef. del.* 'he makes the succession more 'objective' than Hume does by'

101.33 Kant['s' *del.*]] *bef. del.* 'says it'

101.34 law] *ab. del.* ''rule''

101.34 our] *aft. del.* '['the' *del.*] our *Verstand* imposes on'

101.34-35 |ceives . . . -causal] *bel. del. horiz. line then placed aft.* 'rule.ˣ' [101.36]

101.37 These] *alt. fr.* 'This'

101.37 are] *ab. del.* 'is'

††101.38 Entited] ('E' *ov.* 'e'; 'l' *omitted in error*); *ab. del.* 'Called'

101.40 a] *intrl.*

101.40 inconstruable by me.] *alt. fr.* 'incomprehensible.'

102.1 account] *bef. del.* 'of causality'

102.1 if] *bef. del.* '['making ['the' *del.*] causality intellig' *del.*] ['it made ['the' *del.*] causal relation' *del.*] as und'

102.2 supposed to] *insrtd.*

102.2 set] *final* 's' *del.*

102.2 to sensation] *intrl.*

102.2 things] *aft. del.* '['th' *del.*] causality any'; *bef. del.* 'what happens'

102.3 any] *insrtd. bef. del.* 'causation any'

102.3 rule] *ab. del.* 'law'

102.4 non-rationality] 'non-' *ab. del.* 'ir'

102.4 leaves] *aft. del.* 'has ['proved' *del.*] made it w'

102.5 removes dynamic] *ab. del.* 'denies ['*live* causation, and' *del.*] perceptual'

102.5 substitutes] *aft. del.* 'the conceptual sequence'

102.6 for] *ab. del.* 'of'

102.6 It] *aft. del.* 'Later conceptual criticism, building on the logic of the physical sciences,'

102.6 yields] *ab. del.* 'serves only ['for **external**' *del.*] the purpose of'

102.7 assimilates all] *ab. del.* 'applies to'

102.7 to those] *intrl.*

102.7 discover] *ab. del.* 'know'

102.8 ascertained.] *period aft. del. comma*

102.9 Our . . . bare] ('in' *aft. del.* 'are' *and bef. del.* 'largl'); *ab. del.* 'Science *consists largely of [ab. del.* 'is full of ['such' *del.*] ['laws' *del.*] ['merely' *del.*] descriptions. ['ons' *ov. doubtful* 've'] The'] of [*repeated in error*] mere'; *opp. mrgn.* '¶'

102.10 Yellowness] *aft. del.* 'Wh'

102.10 malleability] *ab. del.* 'ductility'

102.11 redness] ('r' *ov.* 'R'); *bef. del.* 'follows boiling in'

102.11 lobsters,] *comma ov. semicolon bef. del.* 'and if on'

102.11 ²in] *aft. del.* 'succeeds'

102.12 to him who] *ab. del.* 'if we'

102.12 asks] 's' *added*

102.12 Why] 'W' *ov.* 'w' *triple underl.*

102.12-13 only replies:] *ab. del.* 'has to say'

102.13 laws] *aft. del.* 'generalized descriptions'

102.13 are . . . and] *insrtd. for del.* 'tell us what to expect always, and there is a sect'

102.14 writers on science] *ab. del.* '['scientific logicians' *del.*] **think this humian** or Kantian position'

102.14 all . . . demand.] *ab. del.* 'is [*del. in error*] *enough to [ab. del.* 'as much as we should'] ask.'

102.14-15 To explain,] 'To' *intrl.*; 'explain,' *alt. fr.* 'Explanation,'

102.15 way] *aft. del.* 'positivistic'

102.15 called positivistic,] *ab. del.* ', can never mean more than that ['a wider law' *del.*] ['a wi' *del.*] a narrower'

102.16 to] *ab. del.* 'the'

102.16 substitute] (*alt. fr.* 'substitution'); *bef. del.* 'of a'

102.16 ¹or] *aft. del.* 'fo'

102.16 for] ('f' *ov.* 'b'); *bef. del.* 'a'

102.17 ²laws] *aft. del.* 'laws express widest'

102.17 at their widest] *ab. del.* 'can'

102.18 ¹the] *ab. del.* 'a'

102.18 ²the] *intrl.*

102.18 air['s' *del.*]] *bef. del.* 'weight'

102.19 keeps] *ab. del.* 'keeps'

102.19 it] *bef. del.* 'aga'

102.19 Why] *aft. del.* 'But'

102.21 such] *aft. del.* 'and in the end'

102.21 being . . . ['very' *del.*] more] *ab. del.* '['must' *del.*] ['is but an in' *del.*] is ['but' *del.*] a more'

102.22 sort of] *intrl.*

102.22 Laws, [*comma insrtd.*] . . . view, [*semicolon del.*]] 'according . . . view,' *moved fr. bef.* 'they' [102.22]

102.23 don't] *ab. del.* 'do fail'

††102.23 connect them._] *ab. del.* '['to' *del.*] explain their *con [*intrl.*]'

102.24-25 _inductive_ . . . _deductive_] *sg. qts. del.*

102.25 interpretation] *ab. del.* 'way'

102.25 If] *aft. del.* 'The antecedent member of the sequent pair'

102.26 a succession] *ab. del.* 'the sequent pair'

102.27 the 'tie' in] *insrtd. aft. del.* 'we should ['see into the ['nee' *del.*]' *del.*] feel the *rationality ['ity' *added*] ['necessity' *del.*] of'

102.27-28 particular . . . us] ('be unmistakeable' *ab. del.* 'sauter aux yeux ['it.' *del.*]'); *ab. del.* '['succession' *del.*] particular sequence. *It would be a *denknothwendigkeit.* ['But necessity of thought' *del.*] But necessities ['proceed' *del.*] [*ab. del.* 'But the only ['dedu' *del.*] logical deduction proceed['s' *del.*]']'

102.29 follows_] *comma del.*

102.29 we] *bef. del.* 'have the'
102.30 popular . . . view,] *ab. del.* '['popular d' *del.*] dynamic view of common sense,'
102.30 any] *ab. del.* 'the'
102.30 would] *ab. del.* 'would [*intrl.*] suffice['s' *del.*] for'
102.30 exhibit['ing'' *del.*]] *bef. del.* 'causality'
102.30 even] *ab. del.* 'even'
102.32 of . . . what] *ab. del.* 'seem to'
102.32 Be] *aft. del.* 'He simply cannot run them backwards as he does his ideas,'
102.33 turn] *ab. del.* 'run'
102.34 *sequences . . . in*] *ab. del.* 'cases to *follow [insrtd. for del.* 'succeed'] in'
102.34 which] *ab. del.* 'as'
102.34-35 sequence ['showed' *del.*] observed?] *ab. del.* 'case?'
102.35 do this] *ab. del. comma*
102.36 that . . . ['a' *del.*] causal, ['one,' *del.*]] *ab. del.* 'as to a certain sequence being causal,'
102.37 *of*] *aft. del.* 'follow his judgments, be this'
102.37 judgments,] *comma ov. period*
102.37 latter] *intrl.*
102.38 would] *ab. del.* 'does'
102.38 *flounders,*] *comma alt. fr. semicolon*
102.39 truthful] *ab. del.* 'intelligible'
102.39 ['sh' *del.*] can . . . has] *ab. del.* 'can he be taken to have'
102.39 'refuted Hume.'] *sg. qts. alt. fr. db. qts.*
102.40 For] *ab. del.* '**As**'
102.40 consult] *ab. del.* '['cons' *del.*] compare Mil'
103.1 phase] *ab. del.* 'fruit'
103.1 at . . . the] *ab. del.* 'only the'
103.2 *aequat*] **1**'a' *ov.* 'e'
103.3 illustrated] *aft. del.* 'specified at l'
103.4 worked] *ab. del.* 'carried'
103.5 with the] *ab. del.* 'into'
103.5-6 of . . . conscious] ('perceptually' *ab. del.* 'immediately'); *ab. del.* 'due to our ['sensi' *del.*] fallacious *sense [alt. fr.* 'sensibility'] organs [*intrl.*]'
103.8 effect] *aft. del.* 'find a rest for their foot.ˣ'
103.12 classic] *aft. del.* 'great'

103.12 ²the . . . of] *intrl.*
103.12 pluralism's] ''s' *added ov. comma*
103.12-13 additive world.] *ab. del.* 'with its belief in chance and novelty.'
103.13 The . . . a ['vague' *del.*]] ('The' *insrtd. bef. del.* 'Ka'; 'principle of causality' *ab. del.* 'principle is ['a' *del.*]'; 'begins' *alt. fr.* 'beginning'; 'as' *insrtd. for del.* '*by being [insrtd. for del.* 'is a']'); *ab. del.* 'Scholastic['ism' *del.*] starts with a principle'
103.14 and] *ov.* 'are'
103.15 it says,] *intrl.*
103.15 'in some way'] *ab. del.* ''in some way' own it already.'
103.16 insulated,] *bef. del.* '['as power, first denied as' *del.*] ['the notion developes' *del.*] the activity *perceived in [*insrtd. for del.* 'element of'; *undel. in error*] the ['situation' *del.*] **se**quence gets converted into a static logical relation'
103.17 ['is' *del.*] erelong gets] *ab. del.* 'has to be'
103.17 suppressed,] *bef. del.* 'with hardly an apology,'
103.18 vague['ly' *del.*]] *aft. del.* '['sta' *del.*] rel'
103.18 latency, ['*aliquo modo*,' *del.*] . . . *modo*] *ab. del.* '['presence ['of the effect' *del.*] in the' *del.*] implication of the effect'
103.19 cite] *ab. del.* 'take'
103.19 mode] *aft. del.* 'st [*ab. del.* '**K**antian [*ab. del.* ''critical'']']'
103.21 all] *bef. del.* 'the'
103.24 on] *bef. del.* '['the' *del.*] reality'
††103.24 V] *aft. del. poss. start of* '5'
103.25 conception of] *ab. del.* 'theory *that [ab. del.* '['that' *del.*] tha'] ['of' *del.*] the ['ultra- [*intrl.*] 'scientific' ideal of causation ['is' *del.*] is that' *del.*]'
103.25 effect.] *period insrtd. bef. del.* '*is that [ab. del.* 'are but'] the successive state of one thing.'
103.26 causal] *insrtd.*
103.26 indeed] *intrl.*
103.26 by] *aft. del.* 'in this way'
103.27 cause;] *semicolon alt. fr. colon and insrtd. bef. del. comma bef. del. semicolon*

103.27 remainder] *ab. del.* 're [*insrtd. for del.* 'others']'

103.27 for comfort] *intrl.*

103.28 *aliquo*] *aft. del.* 'scholastic'

103.28 Such] *insrtd. aft. del.* '['So far as this method *succeeds*, however, it' *del.*] The *final [*ab. del.* 'complete'] success, *if it came, [*intrl.*] of such'

103.28-29 nature,] *bef. del.* '*in the degree in which it succeeded [*intrl.*]'

103.29 of course relegate] ('of' *doubtfully insrtd.*); *ab. del.* '['cause' *del.*] relegate ['all' *del.*]'

103.29 activity] *aft. del.* 'an'

103.29 limbo] *ab. del.* 'status'

103.30 ¹as . . . its] *ab. del.* 'and *as [*insrtd.*]'

103.30 cancel living] *insrtd. for del.* '*['drive out' *del.*] cancel['led' *del.*] [*ab. del.* 'would triumph over living']'

103.30-31 is . . . sincere,] *ab. del.* '*violates our instinct, [*ab. del.* 'is so hard, ['to' *del.*]']'

103.31 in following] *alt. fr.* 'to follow'

103.31 and ['many' *del.*] of the [*poss. start of* 'w' *del.*]] *ab. del.* 'that ma'

103.32 think . . . some] *ab. del.* 'defend this view ['are' *intrl.*] usually give up the'; *caret and guideline placed in error bef.* 'who' [103.32]

103.32 willingly] ('ly' *added*); *bef. del.* 'to'

103.33 all such] *ab. del.* 'the'

103.33 explanation] *ab. del.* 'scheme'

103.33 more or less] *intrl.*

103.33 that] *aft. del.* 'only a sort of ['scheme' *del.*] logical scheme ['for short hand, ['are' *del. intrl.*] or scheme' *del.*] for hanging facts whose terms'

103.33,34 identical] *intrl.*

103.33 and] *aft. del.* 'are'

103.34 pegs in a conceptual] *ab. del.* 'a logical short ar'

103.35 for] *aft. del.* 'of conceptual *pegs [*insrtd. for del.* 'hooks']'

103.35 in . . . relations,'] *ab. del.* 'in an econ'

103.35 predict] *aft. del.* 'get about in an a'

103.35 facts] *ab. del.* 'things'

103.35 'elegant' or] *ab. del.* 'an'

103.36 ways] 's' *added*

103.36 universe] *ab. del.* 'scheme'

103.37 insisted on;] *ab. del.* 'advocated;'

103.37-38 Almost . . . metaphysically.] *intrl.*

103.38 for] *ab. del.* 'to hear'

103.39 discussion] *intrl.*

103.39 of . . . may] *ab. del.* 'may'

103.40 (1879)] *aft. del. opening paren*

††103.41 wissenschaftlichen] 'enschaftlichen' *ov. poss. period*

103.42 iv.] *period aft. del. comma and bef. del.* 'For the best general'

104.1 about] *ab. del.* 'which ['it' *del.*] is on its way'

104.1 be] *intrl.*

104.1 produced,] 'd,' *added*

††104.1 de-| [*undel. in error*] developed] *ab. del.* 'sharpened'

104.2 ['the' *del.*] ['an absolutely' *del.*] a] *ab. del.* '['the' *del.*] the'

104.2 relation] *aft. del.* '*['logical' *del.*] logical [*intrl.*]'; *bef. del.* '—of [*dash intrl.*] a [*poss.* 'an'] *sharp logical [*ab. del.* 'logic['al' *del.*]'] identity between two concepts—that of ['logical' *del.*] ground and sequence, which *in [*ov.* 'is'] its turn is sharpened into *of [*undel. in error*] ['a sharp' *del.*] ['are' *del.*] a conceived [*ab. del.* 'the'] identity ['of [*insrtd. for del.* 'between [*insrtd. for del.* 'of']'] the concepts' *del.*] ['of the successive' *del.*] *of the [*intrl.*] two *percepts [*ab. del.* 'phenomena'] between [*ab. del.* 'in'] which the causal ['a' *del.*] tie was originally found.'

104.2 two] *aft. del.* 'the'

104.2 which] *aft. del.* 'into'

104.5 'enlightened] *intrl.*

104.7 The] *alt. fr.* 'And the'

104.7 easier] 'ier' *ab. del.* 'y'

104.7-8 believe] *ab. del.* 'understand,'

104.8 not . . . believe] ('believe' *insrtd.*); *ab. del.* 'harder ['er' *added*] to ['make an object of' *del.*]'

104.8 metaphysically] ('ly' *added*); *bef. del.* 'belief'

104.8-9 violates . . . strongly.] *ab. del.* 'demands too much sacrifice of *instinct. [*ab. del.* 'perceptual reality.']'

104.9 make] *intrl.*

104.10 interdependencies] 'inter' *intrl.*

104.10   ²of] *insrtd.*

104.11   ¹*a*] *aft. del.* 'as'

104.12   value] *aft. del.* 'mag [*doubtful*]'

104.12   an] ('a' *ov.* 'o' *or* 'i'); *aft. del.* 'a'

104.16   listing] *aft. del.* 'writing'

104.18   in short∧] (*comma omitted in error*); *intrl.*

104.18   phenomena,] *ab. del.* 'the system,'

104.19-20   have . . . in] *ab. del.* 'are *recognized. [ab. del.* 'mentioned.'] Elegance and prediction are the only *ends reached [ab. del.* 'purposes ['s' *added*] ['soul' *del.*] served'] by'

104.20   world of] *ab. del.* 'rarified'

104.20   the] *insrtd. for del.* 'our common'

104.21   so . . . be] *intrl.*

104.22   (so . . . Bradley)] *parens ov. commas*

104.23   ballet] *aft. del.* 'ballet'

104.24   omit] *bef. del.* 'from the text'

104.24   about] *bef. del.* 'the principle'

104.24-25   Popular . . . that] ('often' *insrtd.*); *ab. del.* 'Many persons talk as if'

104.25   has ['s' *ov.* 'd'] demonstrated] *bef. del.* 'the existence of'

104.26   which] *aft. del.* 'invariable'

104.26   connect [*ab. del.* 'identify'] with] *bef. del.* 'felt [*intrl.*]'

104.26   ²with] *bef. del.* 'conceived [*intrl.*]'

104.27   this] (*alt. fr.* 'the'); *bef. del.* 'doctrine of'

104.27   not] *bef. del.* 'an active'

104.28   for . . . ['all these' *del.*] immediate] *insrtd. for del.* 'for'

104.29   ¹reality] *alt. fr.* 'realities'

104.29   when . . . in] *insrtd. for del.* '*that can [insrtd. for del.* '*when they are once her [ab. del.* 'when measured in certain']']'

104.29   its] *aft. del.* 'us to'; *bef. del.* 'write their ['changes so ['as' *del.*] ['functional' *del.*]' *del.*]'

104.29   changes] 's' *added*

104.29-30   to be written] *insrtd.*

104.30   get] *bef. del.* 'always a'

104.30   an] ('n' *added*); *bef. del.* 'metaphysical or ['ontog' *del.*] ['ontogig' *del.*]'

104.30-31   magnificently ['ly' *added*] economic] 'economic' *intrl.*

104.31   keeping . . . ¹of] *ab. del.* 'sticking to'

104.31   functional . . . the] *intrl.*

104.32   phenomena.] *period insrtd. bef. del.* '& ['their' *del.*] avoiding al'

††104.32   *non fingo*] *ab. del.* 'non dynamic 'law' in contrast with'

104.32   since] *aft. del.* 'its affinities leaves'

104.32   ∧it] (*sg. qt. del.*); *bef. del.* 'comes'

104.33   reality] *aft. del.* 'phen'

104.33   our] *ab. del.* 'the'

104.34   W.] *aft. del.* 'J'

††105.1   Most persons,] ('M' *ov.* 'm'; *comma undel. in error*); *aft. del.* 'In'

105.1   remain quite incredulous] ('remain' *ab. del.* 'are'); *intrl.*

105.1   are told] *ab. del.* 'hear'

105.2   the rational . . . has] *ab. del.* '['the' *del.*] Kauselprinzip ['denies' *del.*] ended ['ed' *ab. del.* 's'] by ['denying the existence' *del.*] suppressing the belief in'

105.2-3   our . . . in] ('belief' *aft. del.* 'acceptance of'); *ab. del.* 'the *naif* belief of men in ['work,' *del.*] activity, and that *in [intrl.*]'

105.3   as] *alt. fr.* 'is'

105.3   something] *intrl.*

105.3   our . . . that] ('naive' *insrtd.*); *ab. del.* 'that new'

105.3-4   genuinely] 'ly' *added*

105.4   new fact] *ab. del.* 'alterations of reality'

105.4   created] *insrtd. for del.* '*brought about [ab. del.* 'produced']'

105.4   done.] *period insrtd. bef. del.* '['on *its [ab. del.* 'their'] behalf,' *del.*] are quite incredulous.'

105.5   snaps] *aft. del.* 'dismisses [*ab. del.* 'rejects'] the causal philosophy *at once. [*ab. del.* 'out of hand.'] The present writer also believes'

105.6   'critical'] *aft. del.* 'causal'

105.6   The] ('T' *ov.* 't [*ov.* 'T']'); *aft. del.* 'For [*insrtd.*]'

105.6   has just called] *ab. del.* '['sees the' *del.*] thinks that'

105.7   an] *aft. del.* 'is'

105.7   abstraction] *aft. del. doubtful* 'a'

105.7   'functional ∧laws'] *sg. qt. del. and insrtd. bef.* 'functional'

105.8 ¹are] *bef. del.* 'so'

105.8 ²are] *aft. del.* 'certainly'; *bef. del.* 'certainly'

105.9 is commonly] *ab. del.* 'we instinctively'

105.9 supposed] 'd' *ov. period*

105.9 We] *aft. del.* '*We ['W' *triple underl.*] often see [*ab. del.* '['Just as' *del.*] We ['W' *ov.* 'w'] assume'] trains *as [*ab. del.* 'to be'] moving when they are standing still at stations; *we ['I' *del.*] [*ab. del.* 'we'] feel [*del.* 'my ['m' *ov.* 'a'; *ital. doubtful*] 'will' ['to c' *del.*] as moving my'] as if my writing hand were now moved by my 'will,' whereas, as Hume showed, there are innumerable as'

105.10 we] *intrl.*

105.10 **ignore**] *bef. del.* 'entirely'

105.10 brain-cells] *ab. del.* 'cortical centre'

105.11 that will] *ab. del.* 'it'

105.11 arouse] *aft. del.* 'cause'

105.11 cause] *ab. del.* 'ring'

105.11 bell-] *hyphen insrtd. bef. del.* 'to'

105.12 close] 'l' *ov.* 'o'

105.12 contact] *bef. del.* ', when we push the button,'

105.13 a . . . star's] *ab. del.* 'the its star's ['s' *added*] is the'

105.13 cause] *aft. del.* 'immediate'

105.13 now] *insrtd.*

105.14 it,] *ab. del.* 'the star,'

105.14 causes,] ('s,' *added*); *aft. del.* 'closer [*ab. del.* 'immediate'] '; *bef. del.* 'of our seeing and'

†105.15-16 We . . . harm.] *insrtd.*

105.15 ['catching' *del.*] 'cold'] *ab. del.* '['cold' *del.*] catarrh'

105.16 could] 'c' *ov.* 'w'

105.16 do] *insrtd. bef. del.* 'have *done [*ab. del.* 'had']'

105.16 harm] *aft. del.* 'such effect'

105.18 *close*] 'l' *ov.* 'o'

105.18 In] *ab. del.* '['All over nature' *del.*] Throughout'

105.18 nature's] ' 's' *added*

105.18 **numerous**] *ab. del.* 'so many intermediate *po[*doubtful*]'

105.19 hidden,] *comma insrtd. bef. del.* 'from us'

105.19 seldom] *insrtd. for* 'seldom [*bel. del.* 'never.']'

105.19 which] *ab. del.* 'what'

105.20 Often *the ['t' *ov.* 'T']] 'Often' *intrl.*

105.20 name] *ab. del.* 'assume often'

105.22 frequently then most] *ab. del.* 'often more'

105.22 when] *aft. del.* 'than'

105.22-23 assume ['consider' *del.*] . . . be ['asking' *del.*]] *ab. del.* 'say they are'

105.23 upon.] *ab. del.* 'on.'

106.1 This] *alt. fr.* 'The'

106.1 vast amount ['omnipresence' *del.*]] *ab. del.* 'immense abundance'

106.1 perceptions [*alt. fr.* 'affirmations'] of] *ab. del.* 'predications of'

106.2 encourages] *ab. del.* 'strongly reinforces'

106.2 conceptualist] 'ist' *intrl.*

106.2 A] (*ov.* 'a'); *aft. del.* 'It is but'

106.2-3 farther . . . suppose] ('begin to' *insrtd.*); *ab. del.* 'to say that the whole notion of'

106.3-4 anywhere . . . blunder,] *ab. del.* 'is an error,'

106.4 consecutions] 'cu' *ov.* 'qu'

106.4-5 can be] *ab. del.* 'are'

106.5 quite] *intrl.*

106.5 uncalled for] *alt. fr.* 'unnecessary'

106.6 Other] ('O' *ov.* 'o'); *aft. del.* 'In'

106.6 expose us] *ab. del.* 'are subject'

106.6 to] *bef. del.* 'abundant'

106.6 that] *intrl.*

106.7 moving] *aft. del.* 'as if'

106.8 falsely] *intrl.*

106.8 ourselves] *bef. del.* ', when giddy,'

106.9 such . . . to] *insrtd. for del.* '*['that' *del.*] such a reason [*ab. del.* '['for' *del.*] such ['a' *del.*] reasons [*final* 's' *added*]']'

106.9 deny] *final* 'ing' *del.*

106.9 that] *ab. del.* 'that'

106.10 anywhere] *ab. del.* '['anywhere to occur.' *del.*] to'

106.10 ¹exists] *final* 's' *added*

106.10 ²exists] *bef. del.* ', we know'

106.10 problem] *aft. del.* 'only'

106.11 place] *ab. del.* 'localize'

106.13 the . . . by] *pencil intrl.*

106.14 we locate] *moved by pencil guideline fr. aft.* 'and' [106.13] *to aft. del.*

'there experienced,'

106.14   various other] *ab. del.* 'other'

106.15   typical] *aft. del.* 'original *and [*undel. in error*]*'

106.17   what] *intrl.*

106.17   is that a] *ab. del.* 'a'

106.18-19   developes gradually] *ab. del.* 'continues without interruption'

106.19-20   appears] *in pencil ab. pencil del.* 'figures'

106.21   still]*intrl.*

106.21   now] *intrl.*

106.21   write,] *comma insrtd. bef. del.* 'these words'

106.22   ¹I] *bef. del.* 'seem half to'

106.23   prefigure,] *ab. del.* 'perceive beforehand,'

106.23   when] *aft. del.* '['shall' *del.*] must'

106.23   shall have] *intrl.*

106.23   satisfactorily] *orig.* 'satisfactorily.'; *period del. when moved fr. bef.* 'The' [106.24]

106.24   complete] *ab. del.* 'clothe'

106.24   what . . . be.] *in pencil bel. pencil del.* 'them,'

106.25   which] *ab. del.* 'and'

106.25   that] *intrl.*

106.25   actuates] *ab. del.* 'moves'

106.26   either ['of an' *del.*]] *intrl.*

106.26-27   resistance or of effort.] *ab. del.* 'the resistance.'

106.28   instigates] *ab. del.* 'produces'

106.28-29   new instalment] *in pencil ab. pencil del.* 'increment'

106.29   my] *insrtd. for del.* '*['the' *del.*] the [*ab. del.* 'my']'

106.29   more or less] *ab. del.* '['exertion' *del.*] the'

106.31   or] *aft. del.* 'of'

106.31   less] *ab. del.* 'but slightly'

106.32   the . . . only] *in pencil ab. pencil del.* 'it'

106.32   it] *in pencil ab. pencil del.* 'the resistance'

106.32-33   in . . . may] ('in . . . kind,' *in pencil*); *ab. del.* 'it may make ne'

106.34   ²I . . . aim.] ('I have' *in pencil bef. del.* '*brought out what I aim at, [*in pencil*]'); *ab. pencil del.* 'the result *is straightened out. [*in pencil aft. pencil*

del. 'comes satisfactorily.']'

106.35   in] *intrl.*

106.35-36   continuously . . . series] ('ly' *added to* 'continuous'; 'experiential' *alt. fr.* 'experience'; 'series' *in pencil*); *ab. del.* 'perceptual succession is'

106.36   is found] *intrl.*

106.38   What] *aft. del.* 'The experiencer of such a situation'

106.38   is] *ab. del.* 'is [*ab. del.* 'are']'

†107.20   way . . . our] *ab. del.* 'continuing of the'

107.20   'fields'] *aft. del.* '**perceptual**'

107.21   in] *aft. del.* 'is evidently'

107.21   orthodox] *aft. del.* 'common-sense'

107.23-32   It . . . and] ('It' *aft. del.* 'Final and efficient cause combine in these personal activities. The result pursued is the final'); *substituted for del.* 'There is *indeed [*intrl.*] a continuity, but it doesn't exist in the shape of a ['such' *del. intrl.*] separate conjunctive thing called 'power,' sticking out by itself between the fields, ['and joining them together, as' *del.*] (where [*intrl.*] Hume supposed it ['must. It consists' *del.*] but couldn't find *it) [*paren ov. period*] *and joining them together. [*intrl.*] It consists rather in that total ['interpenetration ['of' *del.*] and belonging together of the fields' *del.*] interfusion of the fields which ['I s' *del.*] was spoken of earlier (p.) as *that [*ab. del.* 'the'] characteristic *differentia [*alt. fr.* 'difference'] of the perceptual flux which the *discontinuous [*intrl.*; alt. fr.* 'discontinues'] conceptual translation fails forever to embody. In ['the' *del.*] cases *like our example [*intrl.*] I [*undel. in error*] ['speak' *del.*] now write about' *del.*] the cause doesn't contain the effect literally. The ['effect often surprises us, even wh' *del.*] words I write often surprise me *when they come, [*in pencil ab. del.* 'by their fitness as well as'] yet I *know [*ab. del.* 'adopt'] them as effects of my ['writing' *del.*] scriptorial efficacy. The 'containing' means only that *inner [*intrl.*] continuity between adjacent parts of the perceptual flux which *I pointed to [*ab.

del. 'was dwelt on'] (on pp. 000, above) as ['its characteristic' *del.*] the feature which *distinguishes ['es' *ab. del.* 't'] it from ['any' *del.*] ['the' *del.*] any conceptual series. They telescope and interfuse their contents, ['you' *del.*] it is impossible to find they belong together'

107.23   ²it] *aft. del.* 'and pursuing'

107.23   the end ['of pursuit.' *del.*] pursued.] *ab. del.* 'the final cause of the activity.'

107.24   of that end] *ab. del.* 'of it'

107.24   see] *aft. del.* 'have to'

107.24   ³the] *alt. fr.* 'these'

107.24-25   total fact of] *intrl.*

107.25   activity] *alt. fr.* 'activities'

107.26   oftenest] *ab. del.* 'only'

107.26   only,] *intrl.*

107.26   seldom] *final* 'es' *del.*

107.26   explicitly] *ab. del.* 'literally'

107.27   sets] *aft. del.* 'instigates'

107.27   literally.] *ab. caret formed fr. orig. period*

107.28   defined] *aft. del.* 'only generally'; *bef. del.* 'usually'

107.29   in wait.] *ab. caret formed fr. orig. period*

107.32-33   'fill . . . and] *ab. del.* 'are satisfactory equivalents which'

107.33   them,] *ab. caret formed fr. orig. comma*

107.33   exact shape] *ab. del.* 'literal body'

107.34   outside] *aft. del.* 'o[*poss. start of* 't']'

107.34   explicit] *ab. del.* 'articulated'

107.35   general] *intrl.*

107.36   men] *ab. del.* 'mankind'

107.36   here] *alt. fr.* 'there'

107.36   broad] *ab. del.* 'generalized'

107.37   man's] *ab. del.* 'human'

107.37   desires] *final* 's' *added*

107.37   If not] *aft. del.* 'I'; *bef. del.* 'an' *or* 'un'

107.38   causes] *final* 's' *added*

107.38   John] *intrl.*

107.39   calls] *ab. del.* 'means by'

107.39   causes‸] *comma del.*

107.40   could] *alt. fr.* 'would'

107.40   Human] *aft. del.* 'We come'

108.2   find ['see,' *del.*],] *ab. del.* 'come,';

comma insrtd.

108.2   something] (| 'some' *insrtd.*); *aft. del.* 'upon some' |

108.3   ²a] *insrtd. for del.* 'there is a continual'

108.3   thought] ¹'t' *ov.* 'T'

108.4   from] *aft. del.* 'from the vague to the definite,'

108.5   things,] (*comma ov. period*); *aft. del.* 'actual'

108.5   is . . . on.] ('everywhere' *insrtd.*); *insrtd.*

108.5   Since] 'S' *pencil triple underl.*

108.5   each phase] *ab. del.* 'every step'

108.6   novelties turn] *alt. fr.* 'novelty turns'

108.9   in these] *ab. del.* 'through our'

108.9   of ours?] *ab. del. qst. mk.*

108.10   aught] *ab. del.* 'anything'

108.10   in kind] *intrl.*

108.14   analogies] 'ies' *ab. del.* 'y'

108.15   I say ['a' *del.*]] *insrtd. for del.* 'A'; *opp. mrgn.* '¶'

108.15   be] *aft. del.* '(*or [ab. del.* 'our'] 'conation,' to use Stout's term)'; *bef. del.* 'an'

108.16   ['as a' *del.*] causal] *ab. del.* 'creative'

108.16   only] *intrl.*

108.16   we] *ab. del.* 'the causes'

108.17   acquainted] *aft. del.* 'known to us'

108.17   creative] *intrl.*

108.17-18   desire . . . but] *ab. del.* 'it certainly is not'

108.18   even there.] *ab. del.* 'to *use ['u' *ov.* 'a'] Mr. Venn's expression again.'

108.18   The] *bef. del.* 'closest effects of our mental activity'

108.18   world] *aft. del.* 'material'

108.19   ['mind' *del.*] desires] *ab. del.* 'mental activity'

108.19   lie] *final* 's' *del.*

108.19   is,] *comma insrtd. bef. del.* 'the'

108.19   the . . . physiologists,] *ab. del.* 'all [*ab. del.* 'the *unchallenged [*ab. del.* 'unamim']'] ['voice of' *del.*] physiological authority,'

108.20   they act] *ab. del.* 'our mind act['s' *del.*]'

108.20   their] *ab. del.* 'its im'

108.21   neural] *aft. del.* '['ne' *del.*] other'

108.21 instrumental] *aft. del.* 'remoter'

108.22 that last] *alt. in pencil fr.* 'the'

108.22 they] 'y' *added*

108.22 consciously] *ab. del.* 'mind'

108.23 brought] *aft. del.* 'produced.'

108.23 Our] *aft. del.* 'The continuity of cause and effect which our perceptual experience embodies thus appears impeached'

108.23 was] *bef. pencil del.* 'thus [*insrtd.*]'

108.24 is] *bef. del.* '*really n [*intrl.*] '

108.25 in] *intrl.*

108.25 was . . . appear.] *in pencil ab. pencil and ink del.* 'showed. The real ['lik [*doubtful*]' *del.*] links of causation *separate [*ab. del.* 'disrupt'] the perceptual termini completely.'

108.26-27 what . . . ¹is] ('we' *insrtd. aft. del.* '['the our our naively genuin' *del.*] termini *which [*intrl.*; *pencil del.*] '; *final* 'd' *del. fr.* 'assumed'; 'be' *bef. del.* 'such'); *ab. del.* 'our perceptual termini are'

108.27 by] *bef. del.* 'real'

108.29 logical] *intrl.*

108.29 conclusion] *alt. fr.* 'consequence'

108.30 were] *ab. del.* 'be'

108.30 our] *aft. del.* 'the immediate *consciousness [*alt. fr.* 'consequence'] of'

108.31 should be] *ab. del.* 'are'

108.31 if we] *pencil insrtd. for pencil del.* 'in'

108.31 supposed] 'ed' *in pencil ov.* 'ing'

108.32 the ['real' *del.*] . . . is ['just' *del.*]] *ab. del.* 'it *is [*ab. del.* 'is'] authentically'

108.32 there.] (*alt. fr.* 'where [*alt. fr.* 'here']'); *bef. del.* '*to our percep [*insrtd.*]'

108.32 we ['should' *pencil del.*] seem] *ab. del.* 'our life would'

108.33 start] *ab. del.* 'would *seem to [*intrl.*] begin'

108.33 It] *aft. del.* 'We [*ab. del.* 'It'] should [*alt. fr.* 'would'] *be as a baby born [*ab. del.* 'as if we *came ['into' *del.*] to *birth ['i' *ov.* 'eg'] [*ab. del.* 'were born']'] at a kinetoscope-show and there *made [*ab. del.* 'became'] acquainted with *aspects [*ab. del.* 'innumerable kinds'] of reality, light,

darkness, ['mo' *del.*] the nature of movement in *the [*ab. del.* 'in a very'] compl'

108.34-35 his . . . ¹of] ('his' *aft. del.* 'became made got made'); *ab. del.* 'got acquainted there both'

108.35 that . . . place.] *ab. del.* 'in the completest way. He ['would' *del.*] regarded the movements as really taking place. The *true [*ab. del.* 'movement's'] *nature *of movement would be [*ab. del.* 'would be'] real, but ['for' *del. in error ab. del.* '['an' *del.*] re [*intrl.*]'] *['a' *del.*] genuine ['occur' *del.*] ['for' *del.*] instances of such [*ab. del.* 'illusion in that place, and all real'] movement ['would' *del.*] he would have to look ['elsewhere.' *del.*] outside the show.'

108.35 The] *bef. del.* 'true'

108.36 indeed] *intrl.*

108.36 but] *bef. del.* 'for'

108.36 real] *insrtd. in pencil*

108.37 will-acts] *ab. del.* 'conations'

108.38 reveal] *ab. del.* 'yield'

108.38 just] *intrl. in pencil*

109.1 are] *bef. del.* 'exactly'

[*begin pencil*]

109.2 leaves off comparing] *ab. del.* 'steps out of'

109.2 with] *in ink ab. ink del.* 'analysis and'

109.3 experience . . . into] *in ink ab. ink del.* 'discipline into the realm of'

109.4 facts.] 's.' *added in ink*

109.4 has] *ab. del.* 'having'

109.4-5 causal agency,] *ab. del.* 'something *fit [*intrl.*] to be called causation,'

109.5 but it] *ab. del.* 'the question'

109.6 whether] *aft. del.* 'or'

109.6 aught] *ab. del.* 'anything'

109.6 finally] *intrl.*

109.7 with] *intrl.*

109.7 we are led] *ab. del.* 'inquiry *leads [*ab. del.* 'takes'] us'

109.8 into] *ab. del.* 'to study'

109.8 since] *ab. del.* 'since'

109.8 such a] *ab. del.* 'a hard &'

109.9 topic,] *ab. del.* 'subject,'

109.9 interrupt] *ab. del.* 'close'

109.10 when] *bef. del.* 'we pass'

109.11 problem] *ab. del.* 'subject'

109.12 Our] *aft. del.* 'The upshot'

109.12 therefore] *intrl.*

109.12 only] *intrl.*

109.13 ['for [*ov. illeg. word*]' *del.*] for]
intrl.

109.13 conceptual] *final* 'ly' *del.*

109.13 purposes,] *ab. caret formed fr.
orig. comma*

109.13 separable] *aft. del.* 'separate link'

109.14 has failed] *alt. fr.* 'fails,'

109.14 historically,] *intrl.*

109.14 ²has . . . efficient] *insrtd. for del.*
'*led [*alt. fr.* 'leads'] to the denial of
treatment [*ab. del.* '*results in making
[*ab. del.* '['results in the' *del.*] makes']
intellectualist philosophers deny of
efficient']'

109.14-15 causation,] *comma insrtd. in
ink*

109.15 and . . . ¹of] *in ink ab. ink and
pencil del.* 'altogether, [*comma ov.
period*] and substitutes ['the n' *del.*]
for it the merely descriptive *notion
[*ab. del.* 'category'] of uniform *as
something for which [*insrtd. for del.*
'as a['n' *del.*] ['inadmissible' *del. ab.
del.* 'nonintelligible'] category *for
[*ab. del.* 'to'] which']'

109.15 bare] *final* 'ly' *del.*

109.15 ²of] *bef. ink del.* 'a'

109.16 among] *in ink ab. ink del.* 'of'

109.16 events.] *period insrtd. in ink bef.
ink del.* 'must in any case be substituted'

109.16 Thus [*alt. fr.* 'This'] has] 'has' *ab.
del.* 'denial [*intrl.*] is but one ['more'
del.] of the ways in which'

109.17 once . . . butcher] ('once' *insrtd.
bef. del.* '*has found [*ab. del.* 'finds']';
'had' *ov. doubtful* 'needs'); *intrl.*

109.17-18 in . . . it] *intrl.*

109.18 'comprehensible.'] *init.* 'in' *del.
and sg. qts. insrtd.*

109.18 Meanwhile the concrete] *ab. del.*
'['¹If we turn to' *del.*] For [*ov.* 'the']
immediate'

109.18-19 taken . . . offers] (*comma aft.*
'comes' *in ink*); *ab. del.* 'we find'

109.19 own] *intrl. bef. del.* 'personal [*ab.
del.* 'own']'

109.19 perfectly] *ab. del.* 'absolutely'

109.20 'transitive'] *ab. del.* 'cause-part of
the phenomenon'

109.20 ∧causation∧] *sg. qts. del.*

109.21 them∧] *comma del.*

109.21 piece of fact] *ab. del.* 'element'

109.22,23 a] *ab. del.* 'the'

109.22 subsequent] 'sub' *insrtd.*

109.23-24 field . . . ¹of] ('new being of'
in ink); *ab. del.* 'one ['because' *del.*]
because it is the nature of the one to
introduce the other, and the ['causality
or ['ge' *or* 'ga' *del.*] agency' *del.*]
sense of causality or agency pervades
the whole as *yielding [*ab. del.* 'realiz-
ing']'

109.24 called] ('ed' *ov.* 's'); *aft. del.*
'which the other'

109.24 feeling] *ab. del.* 'sense'

109.25 -at-work flavors] *ab. del.* 'or
agency *inhabits [*ab. del.* 'pervades']'

109.25 concrete sequence] *ab. del.*
'process'

109.27 these] *alt. fr.* 'this'

109.27 experiences] *intrl.*

109.27 actual] *intrl.*

109.28 cases] *aft. del.* 'physical'

††109.28-29 outside . . . case [*final* 's'
omitted in error] also,] *intrl.*

109.29 an] *final* 'd' *del.*

109.29 experiential] *ab. del.* 'mental'

109.29 nature. In] *period insrtd. bef. del.*
'or'; 'I' *ov.* 'i'

109.31 that] *bef. del.* 'brain-events are
'closer' to'

109.32 appear to be] *ab. del.* 'present
themselves as'

109.33 directly] *intrl.*

109.33 lead] *ab. del.* 'have led'

109.33 interrupt] *ab. del.* 'postpone the
rest of'

109.33 here provisionally.] *ab. del.* 'of
causation.'

109.34 are in] *ab. del.* 'are'

109.34 as] *ab. del.* 'as [*ov.* 'the']'

109.34,35 than] *bef. del.* 'the'

109.35 chain of causes] *ab. del.* 'causal
series'

109.36 hold] *final* 's' *del.*

††109.36-37 extreme['s' *del.*], terms,]
¹*comma ov. period undel. in error*;

'terms,' *ab. del.* 'This consideration'

109.37 causal] *intrl.*

109.37 span] *bef. del.* 'causality'

109.38 falsehood ['with' *del.*]] *ab. del.* 'illusion'

109.38 which] *bef. del.* 'criticism of'

109.39 criticism finds in] *ab. del.* 'criticism of ['cons' *del.*] perceptual'

109.39 consciousness] *aft. del.* 'activity'; *bef. del.* 'produces.'

110.1 up . . . point,] *in ink ab. ink del.* 'so far,'

110.2 ¹the] *ab. del.* 'conceptual and'

110.2 perceptual] *bef. del.* 'treatment.'

110.3 philosopher] *ab. del.* 'one except Bergson'

110.3 admitted that] *ab. del.* 'thought of taking immediate'

110.3 can] *ab. del.* ', untranslated, as'

110.3 give [*alt. fr.* 'giving'] us] *bef. del.* 'us'

110.3 relations₍] *comma del.*

110.3-4 immediately.] *ab. caret formed fr. orig. period*

110.6 elaborate work the] *ab. del.* 'masterly work'

110.7 conscious['ness' *del.*]] *bef. del.* 'of'

††110.9 (vol₍ i, p. 180).] *ab. del. period and db. qt.*

110.10 discrete] *aft. del.* 'sep'

110.10 manner ['in' *del.*]] *ab. del.* 'way in which'

110.11 [why] *bkt. alt. fr. paren*

110.11 no] *bef. circled note* 'transfer from p *96, [comma in ink] bottom. [insrtd. in ink]*'

†110.11-17 scientific . . . 375).] (*on fol.* 95ᵛ; *in ink*); *aft. del.* '['It is useful' *del.*] Like all ['concep' *del.*] abstract conceptual schemes, it serves a purpose [*com-*

ma del.] . It secures predictability, & from the point of view of intellectual esthetics it is matchlessly elegant and economical. But it violates life too much to have establisht itself in secure possession, even in the minds of those who use it. Probably few persons would accept 'whole-heartedly' the truth of *words as radical as [intrl.] Mr S. H. *Hodgson's. [period insrtd.] ['words' del.] : **Causality *per se* is a conception [pencil del.]* belonging to the common sense form of experience, and has no'; *opp. mrgn. pencil note* 'transfer to p 111'

110.12 on] *aft. del.* 'into'

110.15 conditions] *bef. del.* 'an'

110.15 phenomenal] *intrl.*

††110.17 vol] *aft. pencil del.* 'The Metaphysic of Experience,'

††110.17 374-8).] *bef. del.* 'A1'

110.17 author] *aft. del.* 'treatment'; *bef. del.* 'most'

110.19 Ward] *final* ''s' *del.*

110.19 his] *aft. del.* 'th'

110.19 words] *aft. del.* 'index'

110.20 Index).] *period insrtd. bef. del.* 'especially'

††110.21 I.] *in ink bef. ink del.* '6 [*ink*]'

110.22 Some] *aft. del.* 'B. [period doubtful]'

110.22 do] *intrl.*

110.22 an ideal] 'n' *added*; '['positive' *del.*] ideal' *intrl.*

110.22 genuine] *ab. del.* 'real'

110.23 least . . . ones,] *ab. del.* 'of activity in detail'

110.24 activity] *ab. del.* 'it'

110.24-25 ['bel' *del.*] imagine,] *ab. del.* 'suppose,'

110.25 occupy] *ab. del.* 'hold'

DELETED VERSOS FOR *SOME PROBLEMS OF PHILOSOPHY* MANUSCRIPT

[*del. fol.* 2ᵛ: *unidentified*] '['our' *del.*] instrumentality, noetic relations. ['Without the' *del.*] The prior causal tendencies, altho'

[*del. fol.* 16ᵛ: *revision of top of fol.* 17, *then replaced by fol.* 16; *corresponds to text* 14.8-14.24; *L. L. Brown typewriter paper*] 'speculations [*ab. del.* 'theory'] far more than ['cosmic speculation' *del.*] physical laws or cosmic theories. [¶] The older tradition is the better as well as the *completer. [*period undel in error*] *one. To know [*intrl.*] the ['t' *ov.* 'T'] actual *peculiarities [*ab. del.* 'structure'] of the world that is must surely be as important *for us [*ab. del.* 'to know'] as *to know the ['general' *del.*] principles of its **abstract [*insrtd.*] possibility, or [*intrl.*] ['or the' *del. intrl.*] the conditions of our knowing *a world anyhow. [*ab. del.* 'it. [*period bef. del. period*]'] Common men feel this; *so [*ab. del.* 'and'] philosophy, to keep their respect, must *not lose [*ab. del.* 'still keep in'] touch [*insrtd. for del.* 'close contact'] with *objective [*ab. del.* 'the general'] cosmic problems. ['In' *del.*] Paulsen's Introduction to philosophy contains pages to this effect so excellent that I refer my readers to them.[x]|[x] F. Paulsen, op. cit., pp. 19-44 of the American translation.'

[*del. fols.* 50[v]-52[v], 57[v]: *described in* Appendix I]

[*undel. fol.* 54[v]: *trial for fol.* 54; *corresponds to text* 28.12; *L. L. Brown typewriter paper*] 'to understand, even if in strict logic it lacks coerciveness. It is a prejudice'

[*undel. fol.* 56[v]: *trial for fol.* 56; *corresponds to text* 28.29-31; *L. L. Brown typewriter paper*] '[¶] To *the ['t' *ov.* 'T'] same Hegel is due another attempt to mediate logically between nonentity & being. Since 'being,' in the abstract, *mere* being, means'

[*del. fol.* 58[v]: *cont. of orig. lost fol.* 51; *relates to text on fol.* 55(54)(28.24-25) *and fol.* 53 (28.3-8); *L. L. Brown typewriter paper*] 'ens perfectissimum (or *realissimum*) is thus the *ens necessarium*, and, *it once there [*intrl.*] the minor forms of being *can [*intrl.*] come ['by way of creatio' *del.*] from it as *their [*ab. del.* 'a'] creative principle. Empiricists since 'evolutionism' became prevalent, seem to have adopted the exactly contrary position. According to ['every' *del.*] evolutionism all things whatever began imperceptibly, as alterations of something else that was previous. ['Their 'nasce' *del.*] They existed first of all in a state of 'nascency.''

[*del. fol.* 59[v]: *trial for fol.* 58(54); *corresponds to text* 29.8-9; *L. L. Brown typewriter paper*] 'whole agreed that neither of these opinions really deduces being from nonentity or successfully banishes the mystery of fact. Whether the'

[*del. fol.* 60[v]: *probably intended for insertion on fol.* 61 *somewhere aft. text at* 76.7-9] 'The problem is a complicated one and had better be treated in two chapters.'

[*del. fol.* 69[v]: *brought by guideline to del. addition on upper half of fol.* 71; *refers to beginning of* Chapter VII *found turned end for end in notebook*] 'Rest of chapter to be found at *other ['o' *ov.* 'ei'] end of book, p. 70[a]'

TMs DELETED VERSOS

[TMs[1b] *undel. fol.* 25½[v]: *typed; trial for fol.* 25½ (*not renumbered*); *corresponds to text* 43.32-33] 'More beautifully still does Emerson write; 'Each man sees over his own experience a certain stain of error, whilst that of other men looks fair & ideal.'

[TMs[1a] *undel. fol.* 52[v]: WJ *ink inscription; unidentified*] 'No candid person can deny that when concepts once are formed the relations between them'

Alterations in the Manuscript

[TMs^1a *undel. fol.* 74^v (*orig.* 28^v), TMs^1b *fol.* 28^v (*not renumbered*): *typed; trial for bot. of fol.* 73(27) *and top of fol.* 74(28) (TMs^1b *not renumbered*); *corresponds to text* 44.11-15] 'The senses according to this opinion ['are' *del.*] ['organ' *typed-del.*] are an unfortunate secondary complication which stands in the way of knowledge in the only worthy sense and on which philosophers may safely turn their backs'

[TMs^1a *del. fol.* 81^cv, *numbered* 81^c: WJ *ink inscription; trial for fol.* 81^c; *corresponds to text* 47.30 ff.] 'change would bring him. It *may replace['s' *del.*] [*ab. del.* 'designates'] the change, but doesn't copy it. I think that ['Prof. Hib' *del.*] Mr. Hibben's other claims for *concepts ['s' *ov.* 'ion'], that *they [*ab. del.* 'it'] can exhaustively describe ['the' *del.*] individual cases, and that they express a synthesis of opposed elements, ['can' *del.*] are *also rebutted by distinguishing [*ab. del.* 'disarmed of their force, when one holds fast to the difference'] between their designative ['or denotative,' *del.*] and their substantive function. They *de-| [*added*] ['can lead us' *del.*] note complexities and name syntheses'

[TMs^1a *undel. fol.* 122^bv: WJ *pencil inscription written vertically across the page as a note, perhaps making reference to fn.* 6 *at* 34.26 *and to fn.* 1 *at* 62.39] 'Unity Cf. Plato & Plotinus in Bakewell'

Word-Division

The following is a list of actual or possible hyphenated compounds divided at the end of the line in the manuscript copy-text, and at the end of the line in TMs[1] for Chapter IV where the manuscript does not exist and thus TMs[1] is the copy-text. In a sense, then, the hyphenation or non-hyphenation of possible compounds in the present list is in the nature of editorial emendation. Coincidentally, all the forms noted here are hyphenated forms in the present edition. One special case, noted by an asterisk, is an emendation to a hyphenated form where the hyphen is doubtful in the manuscript.

10.16	text-books	65.12	self-sameness
26.15	non-existence	71.11	non-rational
33.23	common-sense	87.3	number-series
34.15	so-called	89.22	-to-one
46.2	self-sufficing	*97.11	sub-principles
51.8	manyness-in-	98.20	causation-philosophy
51.20	light-heartedly	107.38	all-sufficient
64.15	-point-of-	109.8	mind-brain

The following is a list of words divided at the end of lines in the present edition but which represents authentic hyphenated compounds as found within the lines of the copy-text, whether manuscript or TMs[1]. Except for this list, all other hyphenations at the ends of lines in the present edition are the modern printer's and are not hyphenated forms in the copy-text. Two special cases marked by asterisks indicate missing hyphens in the manuscript which were added in hand by James to TMs[1a] and are adopted as emendations in this edition.

18.24	lecture-|room	72.9	all-|knowing
24.30	self-|interest	*91.24	Achilles-|puzzle
27.32	Non-|being	91.28	time-|measure
36.5	grass-|blade	91.31	time-|points
39.1	Class-|names	*92.7	time-|instant
48.13	birth-|place	103.6	by-|product
57.17	no-|difference	108.24	cause-|and-
60.10	self-|stultification	109.31	brain-|events
63.1	*Bhagavad-|gita*	112.10	good-|will
70.14	small-|change		

Special Case:

The following are actual or possible hyphenated compounds broken at the end of the line in our edition and in the Appendix "Faith and the Right to Believe" where TMs[1b] is the copy-text.

112.37 faith-\|tendencies (*i.e.*, faith-tendencies)
113.18 good-\|will (*i.e.*, good-will)

Index
Key to the Pagination of Editions

This index is a name and subject index for the text of *Some Problems of Philosophy* and Appendix I.

It is an index of names only for the "Notes," "A Note on the Editorial Method," "The Text of *Some Problems of Philosophy*," and Appendix III. Names of persons, localities, and institutions and titles of books, articles, lectures, and periodicals, where discussed, are indexed. Such items are not indexed where no information about them is provided, if they are only part of an identification of a discussed item, or are used merely to indicate the location of such an item.

References to William James and incidental references to *Some Problems of Philosophy* are not indexed. Also not indexed is Professor Hare's Introduction.

Index

449

Index

Index

Key to the Pagination of Editions

The plates of the Longmans, Green first edition of *Some Problems of Philosophy* have been reprinted a number of times, but always with the same numbering regardless of the date. Since the original edition has been widely used in scholarly reference, a key is here provided by which the pagination of the original Longmans, Green printing can be readily equated with the text in the present ACLS edition. In the list that follows, the first number refers to the page of the May 1911 original edition and its printings of different date. The number to the right after the colon represents the page(s) of the present edition on which the corresponding text will be found.

3:9	45:29	87:49	129:68
4:9-10	46:29-30	88:49-50	130:68-69
5:10	47:31	89:50	131:69
6:10-11	48:31-32	90:50-51	132:69-70
7:11	49:32	91:51	133:70
8:11	50:32-33	92:51-52	134:70
9:11-12	51:33	93:52	135:70-71
10:12	52:33-34	94:52-53	136:71
11:12-13	53:34	95:53	137:71-72
12:13	54:34-35	96:53-54	138:72
13:13-14	55:35	97:54	139:72
14:14	56:35-36	98:54	140:72-73
15:14	57:36	99:54-55	141:73
16:14-15	58:36	100:55	142:73-74
17:15	59:36-37	101:55-56	143:74
18:15-16	60:37	102:56	144:74
19:16	61:37-38	103:56-57	145:74-75
20:16-17	62:38	104:57	146:75
21:17	63:38-39	105:57	147:76
22:17	64:39	106:57-58	148:76-77
23:17-18	65:39-40	107:58	149:77
24:18	66:40	108:58-59	150:77-78
25:18-19	67:40	109:59	151:78
26:19	68:40-41	110:59-60	152:78-79
27:19-20	69:41	111:60	153:79
28:20	70:41-42	112:60	154:80
29:21	71:42	113:61	155:80-81
30:21-22	72:42-43	114:61-62	156:81
31:22	73:43	115:62	157:81-82
32:22-23	74:43-44	116:62-63	158:82
33:23	75:44	117:63	159:82
34:23	76:44	118:63	160:82-83
35:24	77:44-45	119:64	161:83
36:24	78:45	120:64-65	162:83-84
37:24-25	79:45-46	121:65	163:84
38:26	80:46	122:65	164:84-85
39:26-27	81:46-47	123:65-66	165:85
40:27	82:47	124:66	166:85
41:27-28	83:47-48	125:66-67	167:85-86
42:28	84:48	126:67	168:86
43:28	85:48-49	127:67-68	169:86-87
44:28-29	86:49	128:68	170:87